WESTERN CIVILIZATION VOLUME I

Sixth Edition

The Earliest Civilizations Through the Reformation

Editor

William Hughes
Essex Community College

William Hughes is a professor of history at Essex Community College in Baltimore County, Maryland. He received his A.B. from Franklin and Marshall College and his M.A. from the Pennsylvania State University. He continued graduate studies at the American University and the Pennsylvania State University. Professor Hughes is interested in cultural history, particularly the role of film and television in shaping and recording history. He researched this subject as a Younger Humanist Fellow of the National Endowment for the Humanities, and he was a participant in the Image as Artifact project of the American Historical Association. He is author of the chapter on film as evidence in *The Historian and Film* (Cambridge University Press) and has written articles, essays, and reviews for *The Journal of American History, The New Republic, The Nation, Film and History, American Film,* and *The Dictionary of American Biography*. Professor Hughes also serves as an associate editor for *American National Biography*, a twenty-volume reference work to be issued by Oxford University Press.

Cover illustration by Mike Eagle

The Annual Editions Series

Annual Editions is a series of over fifty volumes designed to provide the reader with convenient, low-cost access to a wide range of current, carefully selected articles from some of the most important magazines, newspapers, and journals published today. Annual Editions are updated on an annual basis through a continuous monitoring of over 200 periodical sources. All Annual Editions have a number of features designed to make them particularly useful, including topic guides, annotated tables of contents, unit overviews, and indexes. For the teacher using Annual Editions in the classroom, an Instructor's Resource Guide with test questions is available for each volume.

VOLUMES AVAILABLE

Library of Congress Cataloging in Publication Data
Main entry under title: Annual editions: Western civilization, vol. I: The Earliest Civilizations through the Reformation.
    1. Civilization—Addresses, essays, lectures—Periodicals. 2. World history—Addresses, essays, lectures—Periodicals. Title: Western civilization, vol. I: The Earliest Civilizations through the Reformation.
901.9′05   82-645823   ISBN 1-56134-033-2

Sixth Edition

Manufactured by The Banta Company, Harrisonburg, Virginia 22801

To The Reader

In publishing ANNUAL EDITIONS we recognize the enormous role played by the magazines, newspapers, and journals of the *public press* in providing current, first-rate educational information in a broad spectrum of interest areas. Within the articles, the best scientists, practitioners, researchers, and commentators draw issues into new perspective as accepted theories and viewpoints are called into account by new events, recent discoveries change old facts, and fresh debate breaks out over important controversies.

Many of the articles resulting from this enormous editorial effort are appropriate for students, researchers, and professionals seeking accurate, current material to help bridge the gap between principles and theories and the real world. These articles, however, become more useful for study when those of lasting value are carefully *collected, organized, indexed,* and *reproduced* in a *low-cost format*, which provides easy and permanent access when the material is needed. That is the role played by *Annual Editions*. Under the direction of each volume's *Editor*, who is an expert in the subject area, and with the guidance of an *Advisory Board*, we seek each year to provide in each *ANNUAL EDITION* a current, well-balanced, carefully selected collection of the best of the public press for your study and enjoyment. We think you'll find this volume useful, and we hope you'll take a moment to let us know what you think.

What exactly are we attempting to do when we set out to study Western civilization? The traditional course in Western civilization is a chronological survey of sequential stages in the development of European institutions and ideas, with a cursory look at Near Eastern antecedents and a side glance at the Americas and other places where westernization has occurred. So we move from the Greeks to the Romans to the medieval period and on to the modern era, itemizing the distinctive characteristics of each stage, as well as each period's relation to preceding and succeeding developments. Of course, in a survey so broad (usually moving from Adam to the Atom in two brief semesters) a certain superficiality seems inevitable. Key events whiz by as if viewed in a cyclorama; often there is little opportunity to absorb and digest the complex ideas that have shaped our culture. It is tempting to excuse these shortcomings as unavoidable. But to present a course on Western civilization that leaves students with only a jumble of events, names, dates, and places is to miss a marvelous opportunity. For the great promise of such a broad course of study is that by examining the great turning points or shifts in the evolution of our culture we can understand the dynamics of continuity and change over time. At best, the course can provide a coherent view of our traditions and offer the opportunity for reflection about everything from the forms of authority to the nature of humankind to the meaning of progress.

One way to bring coherence to the study of our civilization is to focus on what is distinctly "Western" about Western civilization. Much has been written about the subject. Vera M. Dean, for example, has argued, "There is no real difference between West and non-West except that created by the West's chronologically earlier acquisition of technology." She concludes that industrialization will shortly obliterate all differences between East and West.

Not all Western observers are so monolithic in their views. Arnold Toynbee, Herbert Muller, and F.S.C. Northrop, to mention just a few, have written with pride of the unique qualities of the West, while urging our civilization to learn from the East.

What about the Eastern perspective? The West, writes Zen philosopher D. T. Suzuki, is "analytical, discriminative, differential, individualistic, intellectual, objective, scientific, generalizing, conceptual, schematic, impersonal, legalistic, organizing, powerwielding, self-assertive, disposed to impose its will upon others." The East is "synthetic, totalizing, integrative, non-discriminative, deductive, non-systematic, intuitive, subjective, spiritually individualistic, and socially group-minded."

As students become attuned to the distinctive traits of the West, they develop a sense of the dynamism of history—the interplay of the forces of continuity and change. They begin to understand how ideas relate to social structures and social forces. They come to appreciate the nature and significance of conceptual innovation and recognize the way values infuse inquiry. More specifically, they develop an understanding of the evolution of Western ideas about nature, humankind, authority, and the gods—in other words, they learn *how* the West became distinctly Western.

Of course, the articles collected in this volume cannot deal with all of these matters, but by providing an alternative to the synthetic summaries of most textbooks, they can help students acquire a fuller understanding of the dynamics of Western civilization and a clear sense of its unique components. This book is like our history—unfinished, always in process. It will be revised biennially. Comments and criticisms are welcome from all who use this book. To that end a postpaid article rating form has been included at the end of the book. Do you know of any articles that would improve the next edition? With your assistance, this anthology will continue to improve.

William Hughes

Editor

Contents

Unit 1

The Earliest Civilizations

Six articles discuss some of the dynamics of early civilizations. The topics include the development of social organization, the early Mediterranean world, and early civilization's relationship with the environment.

Unit 2

Greece and Rome: The Classical Tradition

Twelve articles focus on Greek and Roman societies. The role of religion and sport, the role of women, and the impact of philosophy and exploration on the development of Hellenic society are discussed.

The concepts in bold italics are developed in the article. For further expansion please refer to the Topic Guide and the Index.

Unit 3

The Judeo-Christian Heritage

Five articles examine the impact that Jesus, Paul, politics, and clashing cultures had on the Judeo-Christian heritage.

The concepts in bold italics are developed in the article. For further expansion please refer to the Topic Guide and the Index.

Unit 4

Moslems and Byzantines

Five selections discuss the effects of Greek Hellenic and Christian cultures on the development of the Moslem and Byzantine worlds.

Unit 5

The Medieval Period

Eleven selections examine the medieval world. The topics include knighthood, trade exploration, education, and culture.

The concepts in bold italics are developed in the article. For further expansion please refer to the Topic Guide and the Index.

Unit 6

Renaissance and Reformation

Nine articles discuss the importance of trade and commerce on the development of the modern state, the role of art in Renaissance culture, and the emergence of religion.

The concepts in bold italics are developed in the article. For further expansion please refer to the Topic Guide and the Index.

Topic Guide

This topic guide suggests how the selections in this book relate to topics of traditional concern to students and professionals involved with the study of Western civilization. It can be very useful in locating articles that relate to each other for reading and research. The guide is arranged alphabetically according to topic. Articles may, of course, treat topics that do not appear in the topic guide. In turn, entries in the topic guide do not necessarily constitute a comprehensive listing of all the contents of each selection.

TOPIC AREA	TREATED IN:	TOPIC AREA	TREATED IN:
Agriculture	36. Medieval Mill	Economics	29. Viking Saga 40. How Jacques Coeur Made His Fortune
Art and Architecture	39. How a Mysterious Disease Laid Low Europe's Masses 41. Our Man from Arezzo	Empires	17. Up Against the Wall 37. Images of Ireland 44. Portugal's Impact on Africa 45. Death March of Hernando de Soto
Christianity	19. Jews and Christians in a Roman World 20. Who Wrote the Dead Sea Scrolls? 21. Who Was Jesus? 22. Last Days of Jesus 23. Heaven 30. Baptism of Kiev 31. Crusade by Children 38. Jan Hus—Heretic or Patriot? 46. Luther: Giant of His Time and Ours 47. Explaining John Calvin 48. That Others Might Read	Evolution	1. Cosmic Calendar
		Exploration	29. Viking Saga
		Greek Society	7. Olympics B.C. 11. Love and Death in Ancient Greece
		Islam	26. The World of Islam 27. Muslim Women and Fundamentalism 28. Master-Chronologers of Islam
City-States	4. Civilization and Its Discontents 9. Two Thousand Years' War	Jews/Judaism	19. Jews and Christians in a Roman World 20. Who Wrote the Dead Sea Scrolls? 21. Who Was Jesus?
Commerce	29. Viking Saga 40. How Jacques Coeur Made His Fortune	Justice	11. Love and Death in Ancient Greece
Crime	11. Love and Death in Ancient Greece	Medieval Society	32. When Knighthood Was in Flower 31. Crusade by Children
Culture	1. Cosmic Calendar 5. Egypt and the Mediterranean World 7. Olympics B.C. 8. Herodotus—Roving Reporter 13. Bibliotheca Alexandrina 19. Jews and Christians in a Roman World 24. Byzantium: The Emperor's New Clothes 28. Master-Chronologers of Islam 30. Baptism of Kiev 32. When Knighthood Was in Flower 41. Our Man from Arezzo 48. That Others Might Read	Modern Society	40. How Jacques Coeur Made His Fortune
		Moslems	26. World of Islam 27. Muslim Women and Fundamentalism 28. Master-Chronologers of Islam
		Nation-States	3. Where Nations Began 4. Civilization and Its Discontents
Ecology	6. Early Civilizations and Natural Environment	Philosophy	42. Machiavelli

TOPIC AREA	TREATED IN:	TOPIC AREA	TREATED IN:
Politics	3. Where Nations Began 4. Civilization and Its Discontents 9. Two Thousand Years' War 10. A Patriot for Whom? 15. Emperor Who Never Was 16. Nero, Unmaligned 18. Murderous Games 22. Last Days of Jesus 25. Byzantine Secrets of Procopius 42. Machiavelli	**Social Organization**	3. Where Nations Began 4. Civilization and Its Discontents
		Sports/Games	7. Olympics B.C. 18. Murderous Games
Religion	7. Olympics B.C. 19. Jews and Christians in a Roman World 21. Who Was Jesus? 22. Last Days of Jesus 23. Heaven 26. World of Islam 38. Jan Hus—Heretic or Patriot? 46. Luther: Giant of His Time and Ours 47. Explaining John Calvin 48. That Others Might Read	**Technology**	2. How Man Invented Cities 36. Medieval Mill
		Trade	29. Viking Saga 40. How Jacques Coeur Made His Fortune
		Vikings	29. Viking Saga
		War	9. Two Thousand Years' War 17. Up Against the Wall 18. Murderous Games 34. Cid of History 35. Horsemen of Cruel Cunning 37. Images of Ireland
Renaissance	41. Our Man from Arezzo 42. Machiavelli 43. Women of the Renaissance	**Women**	11. Love and Death in Ancient Greece 27. Muslim Women and Fundamentalism 32. When Knighthood Was in Flower 33. Margery Kempe and the Meaning of Madness 43. Women of the Renaissance
Roman Society	14. Ancient Roman Life 18. Murderous Games		

The Earliest Civilizations

Civilization is a relatively recent phenomenon in the human experience, as Carl Sagan demonstrates in "The Cosmic Calendar." But what exactly is civilization? How did it begin? How do civilized people differ from those who are not civilized? How is civilization transmitted?

Civilization, in its contemporary meaning, denotes a condition of human society marked by an advanced stage of artistic and technological development and by corresponding social and political complexity. Thus, civilized societies have developed formal institutions for commerce, government, education, and religion—activities that are carried out informally by pre-civilized societies. In addition, civilized people make much more extensive use of symbols. The greater complexity of civilized life requires a greater degree of specialization.

Symbolization, specialization, and organization enable civilized societies to extend greater control over their environments. Because they are less dependent than pre-civilized societies upon a simple adaptation to a particular habitat, civilized societies are more dynamic. Indeed, civilization institutionalizes change.

In sum, civilization provides us with a wider range of concepts, techniques, and options to shape our collective destinies. Or, as popular historian Sprague de Camp puts it, civilized men "are organized in larger masses and possess technical skills beyond those of uncivilized men."

In the West, the necessary preconditions for civilization first emerged in the great river valleys of Mesopotamia and Egypt with the development of irrigation techniques, new staple crops, the introduction of the plow, the invention of the wheel, more widespread use of beasts of burden, improved sailing vessels, and copper metallurgy. These developments revolutionized society. Population increased and became more concentrated and more complex. The emergence of cities ("the urban revolution") marked the beginning of civilization.

Civilization combines complex social, economic, and political structures with a corresponding network of ideas and values. The Sumerians organized themselves in city-states headed by kings who acted in the name of the local patron deity. The Egyptians developed a more centralized and authoritarian system. Aspects of the earliest state structures are explored in "Where Nations Began" and "Civilization and Its Discontents." These early civilizations allowed for very little individualism or freedom of expression. As historian Nels M. Bailkey notes, "Their thought remained closely tied to religion and found expression predominantly in religious forms." Elaborate myths recounted the deeds of heroes, defined relations between mankind and the gods, and generally justified the prevailing order of things. Thus, myths reveal something of the relationship between values and the social order in ancient civilizations.

We are inclined nowadays to make much of the limitations of such systems of thought and authority. Yet the record of the Mesopotamians and Egyptians demonstrates, from the very beginning, civilization's potential for innovation and collective accomplishment. They developed writing and mathematics, monumental architecture, law, astronomy, art, and literature rich with diversity and imagination, and a sense of righteousness and justice. In addition, they made heroic efforts to bring nature under human control, an enterprise described in "Early Civilizations and the Natural Environment."

For a time the great river valleys remained islands of civilization in a sea of barbarism. The spread of civilization to rain-watered lands required that outlying areas find the means to produce a food surplus and develop the social mechanisms for transferring the surplus from farmers to specialists. The first condition was met by the diffusion of plow agriculture, the second by culture contacts that came about through conquest, trade, and migration. Along these lines, "Egypt and the Mediterranean World" explores cultural contacts between the Nile and the Aegean.

Several satellite civilizations evolved into great empires, which further enhanced cultural exchange between diverse and dispersed societies. The problem of governing scattered and often hostile subjects required that conquerors create new patterns of authority. The establishment of empires like those of the Assyrians and Persians were not mere acts of conquest; they were innovations in government and administration.

Looking Ahead: Challenge Questions

Relatively speaking, how recent a development is civilization?

What price has mankind paid for civilization?

What would account for the development of the earliest states?

What were the ecological consequences of the earliest civilizations?

Describe the nature of the contacts between Egypt and other Mediterranean cultures.

THE COSMIC CALENDAR

Carl Sagan

How a Pulitzer Prize-winning scientist-author visualizes cosmic history—from the Big Bang creation of the universe up to present-day time on Earth. His "calendar" may stagger your imagination.

The world is very old, and human beings are very young. Significant events in our personal lives are measured in years or less; our lifetimes, in decades; our family genealogies, in centuries; and all of recorded history, in millennia. But we have been preceded by an awesome vista of time, extending for prodigious periods into the past, about which we know little—both because there are no written records and because we have real difficulty in grasping the immensity of the intervals involved.

Yet we are able to date events in the remote past. Geological stratification and radioactive dating provide information on archaeological, paleontological, and geological events; and astrophysical theory provides data on the ages of planetary surfaces, stars, and the Milky Way galaxy, as well as an estimate of the time that has elapsed since that extraordinary event called the Big Bang—an explosion that involved all of the matter and energy in the present universe. The Big Bang may be the beginning of the universe, or it may be a discontinuity in which information about the earlier history of the universe was destroyed. But it is certainly the earliest event about which we have any record.

The most instructive way I know to express this cosmic chronology is to imagine the 15-billion-year lifetime of the universe (or at least its present incarnation since the Big Bang) compressed into the span of a single year. Then every billion years of Earth

PRE-DECEMBER DATES	
January 1	Big Bang
May 1	Origin of the Milky Way galaxy
September 9	Origin of the solar system
September 14	Formation of the Earth
September 25	Origin of life on Earth
October 2	Formation of the oldest rocks known on Earth
October 9	Date of oldest fossils (bacteria and blue-green algae)
November 1	Invention of sex (by microorganisms)
November 12	Oldest fossil photosynthetic plants
November 15	Eucaryptes (first cells with nuclei) flourish

history would correspond to about 24 days of our cosmic year, and 1 second of that year to 475 real revolutions of the Earth about the sun. I present the cosmic chronology in three forms: a list of some representative pre-December dates; a calendar for the month of December; and a closer look at the late evening of New Year's Eve. On this scale, the events of our history books—even books that make significant efforts to deprovincialize the present—are so compressed that it is necessary to give a second-by-second recounting of the last seconds of the cosmic year. Even then, we find events listed as contemporary that we have been taught to consider as widely separated in time. In the history of life, an equally rich tapestry must have been woven in other periods—for example, between 10:02 and 10:03 on the morning of April 6th or September 16th. But we have detailed records only for the very end of the cosmic year.

The chronology corresponds to the best evidence now available. But some of it is rather shaky. No one would be astounded if, for example, it turns out that plants colonized the land in the Ordovician rather than the Silurian period; or that segmented worms appeared earlier in the Precambrian period than indicated. Also, in the chronology of the last 10 seconds of the cosmic year, it was obviously impossible for me to include all

DECEMBER

SUNDAY	MONDAY	TUESDAY	WEDNESDAY	THURSDAY	FRIDAY	SATURDAY
	1 Significant oxygen atmosphere begins to develop on Earth.	**2**	**3**	**4**	**5** Extensive vulcanism and channel formation on Mars.	**6**
7	**8**	**9**	**10**	**11**	**12**	**13**
14	**15**	**16** First worms.	**17** Precambrian ends. Paleozoic era and Cambrian period begin. Invertebrates flourish.	**18** First oceanic plankton. Trilobites flourish.	**19** Ordovician period. First fish, first vertebrates.	**20** Silurian period. First vascular plants. Plants begin colonization of land.
21 Devonian period begins. First insects. Animals begin colonization of land.	**22** First amphibians. First winged insects.	**23** Carboniferous period. First trees. First reptiles.	**24** Permian period begins. First dinosaurs.	**25** Paleozoic era ends. Mesozoic era begins.	**26** Triassic period. First mammals.	**27** Jurassic period. First birds.
28 Cretaceous period. First flowers. Dinosaurs become extinct.	**29** Mesozoic era ends. Cenozoic era and Tertiary period begin. First cetaceans. First primates.	**30** Early evolution of frontal lobes in the brains of primates. First hominids. Giant mammals flourish.	**31** End of the Pliocene period. Quaternary (Pleistocene and Holocene) period. First humans.			

significant events; I hope I may be excused for not having explicitly mentioned advances in art, music, and literature, or the historically significant American, French, Russian, and Chinese revolutions.

The construction of such tables and calendars is inevitably humbling. It is disconcerting to find that in such a cosmic year the Earth does not condense out of interstellar matter until early September; dinosaurs emerge on Christmas Eve; flowers arise on December 28th; and men and women originate at 10:30 p.m. on New Year's Eve. All of recorded history occupies the last 10 seconds of December 31; and the time from the waning of the Middle Ages to the present occupies little more than 1 second. But because I have arranged it that way, the first cosmic year has just ended. And despite the insignificance of the instant we have so far occupied in cosmic time, it is clear that what happens on and near Earth at the beginning of the second cosmic year will depend very much on the scientific wisdom and the distinctly human sensitivity of mankind.

DECEMBER 31

1:30 p.m.	Origin of *Proconsul* and *Ramapithecus*, probable ancestors of apes and men
10:30 p.m.	First humans
11:00 p.m.	Widespread use of stone tools
11:46 p.m.	Domestication of fire by Peking man
11:56 p.m.	Beginning of most recent glacial period
11:58 p.m.	Seafarers settle Australia
11:59 p.m.	Extensive cave painting in Europe
11:59:20 p.m.	Invention of agriculture
11:59:35 p.m.	Neolithic civilization; first cities
11:59:50 p.m.	First dynasties in Sumer, Ebla, and Egypt; development of astronomy
11:59:51 p.m.	Invention of the alphabet; Akkadian Empire
11:59:52 p.m.	Hammurabic legal codes in Babylon; Middle Kingdom in Egypt
11:59:53 p.m.	Bronze metallurgy; Mycenaean culture; Trojan War; Olmec culture; invention of the compass
11:59:54 p.m.	Iron metallurgy; First Assyrian Empire; Kingdom of Israel; founding of Carthage by Phoenicia
11:59:55 p.m.	Asokan India; Ch'in Dynasty China; Periclean Athens; birth of Buddha
11:59:56 p.m.	Euclidean geometry; Archimedean physics; Ptolemaic astronomy; Roman Empire; birth of Christ
11:59:57 p.m.	Zero and decimals invented in Indian arithmetic; Rome falls; Moslem conquests
11:59:58 p.m.	Mayan civilization; Sung Dynasty China; Byzantine empire; Mongol invasion; Crusades
11:59:59 p.m.	Renaissance in Europe; voyages of discovery from Europe and from Ming Dynasty China; emergence of the experimental method in science
Now: The first second of New Year's Day	Widespread development of science and technology; emergence of a global culture; acquisition of the means for self-destruction of the human species; first steps in spacecraft planetary exploration and the search for extraterrestrial intelligence

How Man Invented Cities

John Pfeiffer

The most striking mark of man's genius as a species, as the most adaptable of animals, has been his ability to live in cities. From the perspective of all we know about human evolution, nothing could be more unnatural. For over fifteen million years, from the period when members of the family of man first appeared on earth until relatively recent times, our ancestors were nomadic, small-group, wide-open-spaces creatures. They lived on the move among other moving animals in isolated little bands of a few families, roaming across wildernesses that extended like oceans to the horizon and beyond.

Considering that heritage, the wonder is not that man has trouble getting along in cities but that he can do it at all—that he can learn to live in the same place year round, enclosed in sharp-cornered and brightly-lit rectangular spaces, among noises, most of which are made by machines, within shouting distance of hundreds of other people, most of them strangers. Furthermore, such conditions arose so swiftly, practically overnight on the evolutionary time scale, that he has hardly had a

chance to get used to them. The transition from a world without cities to our present situation took a mere five or six millenniums.

It is precisely because we are so close to our origins that what happened in prehistory bears directly on current problems. In fact, the expectation is that new studies of pre-cities and early cities will contribute as significantly to an understanding of today's urban complexes as studies of infancy and early childhood have to an understanding of adolescence. Cities are signs, symptoms if you will, of an accelerating and intensive phase of human evolution, a process that we are only beginning to investigate scientifically.

The first stages of the process may be traced back some fifteen thousand years to a rather less hectic era. Homo sapiens, that new breed of restless and intelligent primate, had reached a high point in his career as a hunter-gatherer subsisting predominantly on wild plants and animals. He had developed special tools, special tactics and strategies, for dealing with a wide variety of environments, from savannas and semideserts to tundras and tropical rain forests and

mountain regions. Having learned to exploit practically every type of environment, he seemed at last to have found his natural place in the scheme of things—as a hunter living in balance with other species, and with all the world as his hunting ground.

But forces were already at work that would bring an end to this state of equilibrium and ultimately give rise to cities and the state of continuing instability that we are trying to cope with today. New theories, a harder look at the old theories, and an even harder look at our own tendencies to think small have radically changed our ideas about what happened and why.

We used to believe, in effect, that people abandoned hunting and gathering as soon as a reasonable alternative became available to them. It was hardly a safe or reliable way of life. Our ancestors faced sudden death and injury from predators and from prey that fought back, disease from exposure to the elements and from always being on the move, and hunger because the chances were excellent of coming back empty-

From *Horizon*, Vol. XIV, No. 4, Autumn 1972. Copyright © 1987 by John Pfeiffer.

1. THE EARLIEST CIVILIZATIONS

handed from the hunt. Survival was a full-time struggle. Leisure came only after the invention of agriculture, which brought food surpluses, rising populations, and cities. Such was the accepted picture.

The fact of the matter, supported by studies of living hunter-gatherers as well as by the archaeological record, is that the traditional view is largely melodrama and science fiction. Our preagricultural ancestors were quite healthy, quite safe, and regularly obtained all the food they needed. And they did it with time to burn. As a rule, the job of collecting food, animal and vegetable, required no more than a three-hour day, or a twenty-one-hour week. During that time, collectors brought in enough food for the entire group, which included an appreciable proportion (perhaps 30 per cent or more) of dependents, old persons and children who did little or no work. Leisure is basically a phenomenon of hunting-gathering times, and people have been trying to recover it ever since.

Another assumption ripe for discarding is that civilization first arose in the valleys of the Tigris, Euphrates, and Nile rivers and spread from there to the rest of the world. Accumulating evidence fails to support this notion that civilization is an exclusive product of these regions. To be sure, agriculture and cities may have appeared first in the Near East, but there are powerful arguments for completely independent origins in at least two other widely separated regions, Mesoamerica and Southeast Asia.

In all cases, circumstances forced hunter-gatherers to evolve new ways of surviving. With the decline of the ancient life style, nomadism, problems began piling up. If only people had kept on moving about like sane and respectable primates, life would be a great deal simpler. Instead, they settled down in increasing numbers over wider areas, and society started changing with a vengeance. Although the causes of this settling down remain a mystery, the fact of independent origins calls for an explanation based on worldwide developments.

An important factor, emphasized recently by Lewis Binford of the University of New Mexico, may have been the melting of mile-high glaciers, which was well under way fifteen thousand years ago, and which released enough water to raise the world's oceans 250 to 500 feet, to flood previously exposed coastal plains, and to create shallow bays and estuaries and marshlands. Vast numbers of fish and wild fowl made use of the new environments, and the extra resources permitted people to obtain food without migrating seasonally. In other words, people expended less energy, and life became that much easier, in the beginning anyway.

Yet this sensible and seemingly innocent change was to get mankind into all sorts of difficulties. According to a recent theory, it triggered a chain of events that made cities possible if not inevitable. Apparently, keeping on the move had always served as a natural birth-control mechanism, in part, perhaps, by causing a relatively high incidence of miscarriages. But the population brakes were off as soon as people began settling down.

One clue to what may have happened is provided by contemporary studies of a number of primitive tribes, such as the Bushmen of Africa's Kalahari Desert. Women living in nomadic bands, bands that pick up and move half a dozen or more times a year, have an average of one baby every four years or so, as compared with one baby every two and a half years for Bushman women living in settled communities an increase of five to eight babies per mother during a twenty-year reproductive period.

The archaeological record suggests that in some places at least, a comparable phenomenon accompanied the melting of glaciers during the last ice age. People settled down and multiplied in the Les Eyzies region of southern France, one of the richest and most-studied centers of prehistory. Great limestone cliffs dominate the countryside, and at the foot of the cliffs are natural shelters, caves and rocky overhangs where people built fires, made tools out of flint and bone and ivory, and planned the next day's hunt. On special occasions artists equipped with torches went deep into certain caves like Lascaux and covered the walls with magnificent images of the animals they hunted.

In some places the cliffs and the shelters extend for hundreds of yards; in other places there are good living sites close to one another on the opposite slopes of river valleys. People in the Les Eyzies region were living not in isolated bands but in full-fledged communities, and populations seem to have been on the rise. During the period from seven thousand to twelve thousand years ago, the total number of sites doubled, and an appreciable proportion of them probably represent year-round settlements located in small river valleys. An analysis of excavated animal remains reveals an increasing dietary reliance on migratory birds and fish (chiefly salmon).

People were also settling down at about the same time in the Near East for example, not far from the Mediterranean shoreline of Israel and on the border between the coastal plain and the hills to the east. Ofer Bar-Yosef, of the Institute of Archaeology of Hebrew University in Jerusalem, points out that since they were able to exploit both these areas, they did not have to wander widely in search of food. There were herds of deer and gazelle, wild boar, fish and wild fowl, wild cereals and other plants, and limestone caves and shelters like those in the Les Eyzies region. Somewhat later, however, a new land-use pattern emerged. Coastal villages continued to flourish, but in addition to them, new sites began appearing further inland — and in areas that were drier and less abundant.

Only under special pressure will men abandon a good thing, and in this case it was very likely the pressure of rising populations. The evidence suggests that the best coastal lands were supporting about all the hunter-gatherers they could support; and as living space decreased there was a "budding off," an overflow of surplus population into the second-best back country where game was scarcer. These people depended more and more on plants, particularly on wild cereals, as indicated by the larger numbers of flint sickle blades, mortars and pestles, and storage pits found at their sites (and also by an increased wear and pitting of teeth, presumably caused by chewing more coarse and gritty plant foods).

Another sign of the times was the appearance of stone buildings, often with impressively high and massive walls. The structures served a number of purposes. For one thing, they included storage bins where surplus grain could be kept in reserve for bad times, when there was a shortage of game and wild plants. They also imply danger abroad in the countryside, new kinds of violence, and a mounting need for defenses to protect stored goods from the raids of people who had not settled down.

Above all, the walls convey a feeling of increasing permanence, an increasing commitment to places. Although man was still mainly a hunter-gatherer living on wild species, some of the old options no longer existed for him. In the beginning, settling down may have involved a measure of choice, but now man was no longer quite so free to change locales when the land became less fruitful. Even in those days frontiers were vanishing. Man's problem was to develop new options, new ways of working the land more intensively so that it would provide the food that migration had always provided in more mobile times.

The all-important transition to agriculture came in small steps, establishing itself almost before anyone realized what was going on. Settlers in marginal lands took early measures to get more food out of less abundant environments—roughing up the soil a bit with scraping or digging sticks, sowing wheat and barley seeds, weeding, and generally doing their best to promote growth. To start with at least, it was simply a matter of supplementing regular diets of wild foods with some domesticated species, animals as well as plants, and people probably regarded themselves as hunter-gatherers working hard to maintain their way of life rather than as the revolutionaries they were. They were trying to preserve the old self-sufficiency, but it was a losing effort.

The wilderness way of life became more and more remote, more and more nearly irretrievable. Practically every advance in the technology of agriculture committed people to an increasing dependence on domesticated species and on the activities of other people living nearby. Kent Flannery of the University of Michigan emphasizes this point in a study of one part of Greater Mesopotamia, prehistoric Iran, during the period between twelve thousand and six thousand years ago. For the hunter-gatherer, an estimated one-third of the country's total land area was good territory, consisting of grassy plains and high mountain valleys where wild species were abundant; the rest of the land was desert and semidesert.

The coming of agriculture meant that people used a smaller proportion of the countryside. Early farming took advantage of naturally distributed water; the best terrain for that, namely terrain with a high water table and marshy areas, amounted to about a tenth of the land area. But only a tenth of that tenth was suitable for the next major development, irrigation. Meanwhile, food yields were soaring spectacularly, and so was the population of Iran, which increased more than fiftyfold; in other words, fifty times the original population was being supported by food produced on one-hundredth of the land.

A detailed picture of the steps involved in this massing of people is coming from studies of one part of southwest Iran, an 880-square-mile region between the Zagros Mountains and the Iraqi border. The Susiana Plain is mostly flat, sandy semidesert, the only notable features being man-made mounds that loom on the horizon like islands, places where people built in successively high levels on the ruins of their ancestors. During the past decade or so, hundreds of mounds have been mapped and dated (mainly through pottery styles) by Robert Adams of the University of Chicago, Jean Perrot of the French Archaeological Mission in Iran, and Henry Wright and Gregory Johnson of the University of Michigan. Their work provides a general idea of when the mounds were occupied, how they varied in size at different periods and how a city may be born.

Imagine a time-lapse motion picture of the early settling of the Susiana Plain, starting about 6500 B.C., each minute of film representing a century. At first the plain is empty, as it has been since the beginning of time. Then the pioneers arrive; half a dozen families move in and build a cluster of mud-brick homes near a river. Soon another cluster appears and another, until, after about five minutes (it is now 6000 B.C.), there are ten settlements, each covering an area of 1 to 3 hectares (1 hectare = 2.47 acres). Five minutes more (5500 B.C.) and we see the start of irrigation, on a small scale, as people dig little ditches to carry water from rivers and tributaries to lands along the banks. Crop yields increase and so do populations, and there are now thirty settlements, all about the same size as the original ten.

This is but a prelude to the main event. Things become really complicated during the next fifteen minutes or so (5500 to 4000 B.C.). Irrigation systems, constructed and maintained by family groups of varying sizes, become more complex. The number of settlements shows a modest increase, from thirty to forty, but a more significant change takes place—the appearance of a hierarchy. Instead of settlements all about the same size, there are now levels of settlements and a kind of ranking: one town (7 hectares), ten large villages (3 to 4 hectares), and twenty-nine smaller villages of less than 3 hectares. During this period large residential and ceremonial structures appear at Susa, a town on the western edge of the Susiana Plain.

Strange happenings can be observed not long after the middle of this period (about 4600 B.C.). For reasons unknown, the number of settlements decreases rapidly. It is not known whether the population of the area decreased simultaneously. Time passes, and the number of settlements increases to about the same level as before, but great changes have occurred. Three cities have appeared with monumental public buildings, elaborate residential architecture, large workshops, major storage and market facilities, and certainly with administrators and bureaucrats. The settlement hierarchy is more complex, and settlements are no longer located to take advantage solely of good agricultural opportunities. Their location is also influenced by the cities and the services and opportunities available there. By the end of our hypothetical time-lapse film, by the early part of the third millennium B.C., the largest settlement of all is the city of Susa, which covers some thirty hectares and will cover up to a square kilometer (100 hectares) of territory before it collapses in historical times.

All Mesopotamia underwent major transformations during this period. Another city was taking shape 150 miles northwest of Susa in the heartland of Sumer. Within a millennium the site of Uruk near the Euphrates River grew from village dimensions to a city enclosing within its defense walls more than thirty thousand people, four hundred hectares, and at the center a temple built on top of a huge brick platform. Archaeological surveys reveal that this period also saw a massive immigration into the region from places and for reasons as yet undetermined, resulting in a tenfold increase in settlements and in the formation of several new cities.

Similar surveys, requiring months and thousands of miles of walking, are completed or under way in many parts of the world. Little more than a millennium after the establishment of Uruk and Susa, cities began making an independent appearance in northern China not far from the conflux of the Wei and Yellow rivers, in an area that also saw the beginnings of agriculture. Still later, and also independently as far as we can tell, intensive settlement and land use developed in the New World.

The valley of Oaxaca in Mexico, where Flannery and his associates are working currently, provides another example of a city in the process of being formed. Around 500 B.C., or perhaps a bit earlier, buildings were erected for the first time on the tops of hills. Some of the hills were small, no more than twenty-five or thirty feet high, and the buildings were correspondingly small; they overlooked a few terraces and a river and probably a hamlet or two. Larger structures appeared on higher hills overlooking many villages. About 400 B.C. the most elaborate set-

tlement began to appear on the highest land, 1,500-foot Monte Albán, with a panoramic view of the valley's three arms; and within two centuries it had developed into an urban center including hundreds of terraces, an irrigation system, a great plaza, ceremonial buildings and residences, and an astronomical observatory.

At about the same time, the New World's largest city, Teotihuacán, was evolving some 225 miles to the northwest in the central highlands of Mexico. Starting as a scattering of villages and hamlets, it covered nearly eight square miles at its height (around A.D. 100 to 200) and probably contained some 125,000 people. Archaeologists are now reconstructing the life and times of this great urban center. William Sanders of Pennsylvania State University is concentrating on an analysis of settlement patterns in the area, while Rene Millon of the University of Rochester and his associates have prepared detailed section-by-section maps of the city as a step toward further extensive excavations. Set in a narrow valley among mountains and with its own man-made mountains, the Pyramid of the Sun and the Pyramid of the Moon, the city flourished on a grand scale. It housed local dignitaries and priests, delegations from other parts of Mesoamerica, and workshop neighborhoods where specialists in the manufacture of textiles, pottery, obsidian blades, and other products lived together in early-style apartments.

The biggest center in what is now the United States probably reached its peak about a millennium after Teotihuacán. But it has not been reconstructed, and archaeologists are just beginning to appreciate the scale of what happened there. Known as Cahokia and located east of the Mississippi near St. Louis, it consists of a cluster of some 125 mounds (including a central mound 100 feet high and covering 15 acres) as well as a line of mounds extending six miles to the west.

So surveys and excavations continue, furnishing the sort of data needed to disprove or prove our theories. Emerging patterns involving the specific locations of different kinds of communities and of buildings and other artifacts within communities can yield information about the

forces that shaped and are still shaping cities and the behavior of people in cities. But one trend stands out above all others: the world was becoming more and more stratified. Every development seemed to favor social distinctions, social classes and elites, and to work against the old hunter-gatherer ways.

Among hunter-gatherers all people are equal. Individuals are recognized as exceptional hunters, healers, or storytellers, and they all have the chance to shine upon appropriate occasions. But it would be unthinkable for one of them, for any one man, to take over as full-time leader. That ethic passed when the nomadic life passed. In fact, a literal explosion of differences accompanied the coming of communities where people lived close together in permanent dwellings and under conditions where moving away was not easy.

The change is reflected clearly in observed changes of settlement patterns. Hierarchies of settlements imply hierarchies of people. Emerging social levels are indicated by the appearance of villages and towns and cities where only villages had existed before, by different levels of complexity culminating in such centers as Susa and Monte Albán and Cahokia. Circumstances practically drove people to establish class societies. In Mesopotamia, for instance, increasingly sophisticated agricultural systems and intensive concentrations of populations brought about enormous and irreversible changes within a short period. People were clamped in a demographic vise, more and more of them living and depending on less and less land an ideal setting for the rapid rise of status differences.

Large-scale irrigation was a highly effective centralizing force, calling for new duties and new regularities and new levels of discipline. People still depended on the seasons; but in addition, canals had to be dug and maintained, and periodic cleaning was required to prevent the artificial waterways from filling up with silt and assorted litter. Workers had to be brought together, assigned tasks, and fed, which meant schedules and storehouses and rationing stations and mass-produced pottery to serve as food containers. It took time to organize such activities efficiently. There were undoubtedly many false starts, many attempts by local people to work things out among themselves and their neighbors at a community or village level. Many small centers, budding institutions, were undoubtedly formed and many collapsed, and we may yet detect traces of them in future excavations and analyses of settlement patterns.

The ultimate outcome was inevitable. Survival demanded organization on a regional rather than a local basis. It also demanded high-level administrators and managers, and most of them had to be educated people, mainly because of the need to prepare detailed records of supplies and transactions. Record-keeping has a long prehistory, perhaps dating back to certain abstract designs engraved on cave walls and bone twenty-five thousand or more years ago. But in Mesopotamia after 4000 B.C. there was a spurt in the art of inventing and utilizing special marks and symbols.

The trend is shown in the stamp and cylinder seals used by officials to place their "signatures" on clay tags and tablets, man's first documents. At first the designs on the stamp seals were uncomplicated, consisting for the most part of single animals or simple geometric motifs. Later, however, there were bigger stamp seals with more elaborate scenes depicting several objects or people or animals. Finally the cylinder seals appeared, which could be rolled to repeat a complex design. These seals indicate the existence of more and more different signatures and more and more officials and record keepers. Similar trends are evident in potters' marks and other symbols. All these developments precede pictographic writing, which appears around 3200 B.C.

Wherever record keepers and populations were on the rise, in the Near East or Mexico or China, we can be reasonably sure that the need for a police force or the prehistoric equivalent thereof was on the increase, too. Conflict, including everything from fisticuffs to homicide, increases sharply with group size, and people have

known this for a long time. The Bushmen have a strong feeling about avoiding crowds: "We like to get together, but we fear fights." They are most comfortable in bands of about twenty-five persons and when they have to assemble in larger groups which happens for a total of only a few months a year, mainly to conduct initiations, arrange marriages, and be near the few permanent water holes during dry seasons they form separate small groups of about twenty-five, as if they were still living on their own.

Incidentally, twenty-five has been called a "magic number," because it hints at what may be a universal law of group behavior. There have been many counts of hunter-gatherer bands, not only in the Kalahari Desert, but also in such diverse places as the forests of Thailand, the Canadian Northwest, and northern India. Although individual bands may vary from fifteen to seventy-five members, the tendency is to cluster around twenty-five, and in all cases a major reason for keeping groups small is the desire to avoid violence. In other words, the association between large groups and conflict has deep roots and very likely presented law-and-order problems during the early days of cities and pre-cities, as it has ever since.

Along with managers and record keepers and keepers of the peace, there were also specialists in trade. A number of factors besides population growth and intensive land use were involved in the origin of cities, and local and long-distance trade was among the most important. Prehistoric centers in the process of becoming urban were almost always trade centers. They typically occupied favored places, strategic points in developing trade networks, along major waterways and caravan routes or close to supplies of critical raw materials.

Archaeologists are making a renewed attempt to learn more about such developments. Wright's current work in southwest Iran, for example, includes preliminary studies to detect and measure changes in the flow of trade. One site about sixty-five miles from Susa lies close to tar pits, which in prehistoric times served as a source of natural asphalt for fastening stone

blades to handles and waterproofing baskets and roofs. By saving all the waste bits of this important raw material preserved in different excavated levels, Wright was able to estimate fluctuations in its production over a period of time. In one level, for example, he found that the amounts of asphalt produced increased far beyond local requirements; in fact, a quantitative analysis indicates that asphalt exports doubled at this time. The material was probably being traded for such things as high-quality flint obtained from quarries more than one hundred miles away, since counts of material recovered at the site indicate that imports of the flint doubled during the same period.

In other words, the site was taking its place in an expanding trade network, and similar evidence from other sites can be used to indicate the extent and structure of that network. Then the problem will be to find out what other things were happening at the same time, such as significant changes in cylinder-seal designs and in agricultural and religious practices. This is the sort of evidence that may be expected to spell out just how the evolution of trade was related to the evolution of cities.

Another central problem is gaining a fresh understanding of the role of religion. Something connected with enormous concentrations of people, with population pressures and tensions of many kinds that started building up five thousand or more years ago, transformed religion from a matter of simple rituals carried out at village shrines to the great systems of temples and priesthoods invariably associated with early cities. Sacred as well as profane institutions arose to keep society from splitting apart.

Strong divisive tendencies had to be counteracted, and the reason may involve yet another magic number, another intriguing regularity that has been observed in hunter-gatherer societies in different parts of the world. The average size of a tribe, defined as a group of bands all speaking the same dialect, turns out to be about five hundred persons, a figure that depends to some extent on the limits of human memory. A tribe is a community of people who can identify closely with one another and engage in repeated face-to-face encounters and recognitions; and it happens that five hundred may represent about the number of persons a hunter-gatherer can remember well enough to approach on what would amount to a first-name basis in our society. Beyond that number the level of familiarity declines, and there is an increasing tendency to regard individuals as "they" rather than "we," which is when trouble usually starts. (Architects recommend that an elementary school should not exceed five hundred pupils if the principal is to maintain personal contact with all of them, and the headmaster of one prominent prep school recently used this argument to keep his student body at or below the five-hundred mark.)

Religion of the sort that evolved with the first cities may have helped to "beat" the magic number five hundred. Certainly there was an urgent need to establish feelings of solidarity among many thousands of persons rather than a few hundred. Creating allegiances wider than those provided by direct kinship and person-to-person ties became a most important problem, a task for full-time professionals. In this connection Paul Wheatley of the University of Chicago suggests that "specialized priests were among the first persons to be released from the daily round of subsistence labor." Their role was partly to exhort other workers concerned with the building of monuments and temples, workers who probably exerted greater efforts in the belief that they were doing it not for mere men but for the glory of individuals highborn and close to the gods.

The city evolved to meet the needs of societies under pressure. People were being swept up in a process that had been set in motion by their own activities and that they could never have predicted, for the simple reason that they had no insight into what they were doing in the first place. For example, they did not know, and had no way of knowing, that settling down could lead to population explosions.

There is nothing strange about this state of affairs, to be sure. It is the essence of the human condition and involves us just as intensely today. Then as now, people responded by the sheer instinct of survival to forces that they understood vaguely at best—and worked together as well as they could to organize themselves, to preserve order in the face of accelerating change and complexity and the threat of chaos. They could never know that they were creating what we, its beneficiaries and its victims, call civilization.

Where Nations Began

Excavations on the Nile suggest how a powerful elite welded prehistoric villages into the world's first nation-state.

Michael Allen Hoffman

Michael Allen Hoffman, an archeologist at the University of South Carolina's Earth Sciences and Resources Institute, returned to Egypt in January 1983 for his seventh season. He is the author of Egypt Before the Pharaohs.

He was called Catfish, or Narmer in the language of the ancient Egyptians, and in his day, 5,100 years ago, he was probably the most politically powerful man in the world. For it was he who founded humanity's first nation-state, a political empire far bigger and more complex than any city-state. Known by the legendary name of Menes in later times, Narmer was Egypt's first pharaoh, founder of the First Dynasty and first ruler of a new form of political organization that would last nearly 3,000 years. In 1898 English archeologists found a large, carved slate palette, inscribed with Narmer's name and carved on both sides with scenes of the king vanquishing his foes in battle. On one side Narmer wears the white crown of Upper Egypt while on the other he sports the red crown of Lower Egypt. Together the crowns symbolize the monarchy's early role as unifier of all Egypt.

The unification of separate regions under a single ruler was a catalytic event, climaxing nearly a thousand years of Predynastic development and triggering a flowering of art and architecture, of writing and religion that has seldom, if ever, been matched.

The achievements of ancient Egypt, however, could hardly have arisen *de novo,* nor could they have been the work of one man. Cultures and new forms of social organization don't just happen; they grow out of what came before. The question that fascinates me, as an archeologist specializing in Egypt, is the origin of the political structure we call the nation-state. What was happening in Predynastic Egypt that made it possible for Narmer to take the decisive step, portrayed so graphically on his palette, of unifying the disparate entities in Upper and Lower Egypt? How, in other words, did our species make the first transition from scattered, politically independent towns and chiefdoms into a unified nation administered by a central government?

After several seasons of digging in the ruins of an ancient Egyptian town called Hierakonpolis, I believe our research team is close to an answer. Two things led us to Hierakonpolis: previous discoveries, including the Narmer palette, and ancient Egyptian legends. The English archeologists, Quibell and Green, had found, in addition to the palette, a giant decorated macehead belonging to a predecessor of Narmer by the name of Scorpion and an even earlier painted tomb, probably of a local Predynastic king. Also, a whole succession of expeditions had shown that the early historic town of Hierakonpolis—or Nekhen, as the ancient Egyptians called it—was surrounded by the largest Predynastic settlement complex in all of Egypt. The final link to the site's importance came from Egyptian legends that traced the ancestry of the pharaohs to the "Divine Souls of Nekhen" and to the "Followers of Horus," the falcon-headed god. Hierakonpolis, which means City of the Falcon, is the name the Greeks later applied to Nekhen.

Though many of the settlements and tombs we excavated at Hierakonpolis had long since been rifled, enough scraps of evidence remained for us to piece together the story of what was happening in the Nile Valley in the centuries just preceeding Narmer's rise.

The process appears to have begun at Hierakonpolis about 3800 B.C., 700 years before Narmer was born. In those days, according to staff archeological surveyor Fred Harlan of Washington University in St. Louis and geologist-chemist Hany Hamroush of Cairo University and the University of Virginia, Hierakonpolis was situated on a protected embayment of the Nile floodplain. There it enjoyed light seasonal rainfall and easy access to the river, the fertile floodplain, and the wooded grasslands that covered what is now the barren Western Desert.

Two centers of settlement dominated the landscape from 3800 B.C. to 3500 B.C. Each included zones for habitation, industry, and trash disposal. Around these were smaller farming hamlets, herders' camps, cemeteries, and other holy places. Dwellings ranged from small, circular huts in seasonal camps to more substantial, rectangular houses of mudbrick and wattle-and-daub in the towns. The wattle-and-daub houses, in which mud was plastered over a wovenwood and reed framework, often had floors dug below ground level.

Houses were sometimes bunched closely together and sometimes surrounded by spacious, fenced enclosures. These dwellings and the different, often specialized objects found in them, reflect underlying economic and social differences in the community that allowed the eventual emergence of a politically powerful elite.

The area covered by the housing sites—some 100 acres—suggests that during this period, called the Amratian, or Naqada I, the regional population of Hierakonpolis had soared from perhaps several hundred people to several thousand—between 2,300 and 10,500. Such large populations were necessary for state development.

Although the evidence from settlements suggested that Amratian society was big enough and complex enough to support elite groups, clear proof of their existence eluded us until we began digging in a cemetery on the banks of a dry stream bed, or wadi, called Abu Suffian. Carter Lupton of the Milwaukee Public Museum and Barbara Adams of the Petrie Museum, University College, London, cleared some sand-filled graves and came upon the largest Amratian tombs ever found.

The large tombs were arranged in curving rows and confined to one area apparently reserved for the elite members of the society. Although hardly spectacular by later Egyptian standards, the tombs were impressive for their time, consisting of rectangular holes cut into the hard wadi terrace. One grave, for example, was more than eight feet long, five feet wide, and almost six feet deep. It had been looted in ancient times but still contained several beautiful black-topped clay jars of the type called Plum Red Ware, well known from other Amratian and Gerzean sites. We also found the remains of baskets, braided leather rope, painted reed arrow shafts, flint arrowheads, grass matting, and even pieces of a wooden bier.

In the neighboring tomb we found painted scraps of a paper-like material from a plant related to papyrus. This, along with some complex graffiti scratched onto some of the pots, suggests that the origins of Egyptian writing may be much older than previously suspected. Clearly we were dealing with the remains of a people more advanced than Egyptologists used to think.

Finally, under a heap of broken furniture and small bones, we found a beautiful, disc-shaped macehead made of polished green and white porphyry, a key piece of evidence for the development of a political elite. Maceheads have long been recognized as symbols of political authority. Unfinished examples have been found in our village sites, showing they were produced locally. This one must have been a forerunner of the much larger limestone macehead found at Hierakonpolis 85 years ago. This pear-shaped macehead showed Narmer's predecessor, Scorpion.

Our porphyry macehead, predating Scorpion by about 500 years, tells us that the process of political centralization was already well underway at Hierakonpolis. Whoever wielded that macehead was hardly a pharaoh, but he was clearly someone with considerable wealth and political power. As such, he is one of the earliest candidates for the "Divine Souls of Nekhen," the semi-mythical rulers of Hierakonpolis in the remote times before Narmer.

Several other Amratian sites have produced maceheads, suggesting they too had chiefs. Still Hierakonpolis must have had some advantage that allowed its leaders ultimately to prevail. How could it afford the biggest tombs in the first place, and how was it able to prosper and grow through the succeeding centuries? One factor was the large population. Another was its ideal environment. Our excavations point to one other outstanding advantage at Hierakonpolis. In Amratian times it appears to have been the center of a huge pottery industry, one that would have given its proprietors enormous economic power. Even today an estimated 50 million pieces of broken bowls, jars, and other vessels litter the desert, and we have identified and mapped at least 15 Amratian pottery kilns in the area. The largest were massive, industrial-scale installations covering more than 1,200 square yards.

The pottery barons profited from the belief in an afterlife.

Around each ruined kiln were scraps of pottery representing one of two distinctive types—a coarse, Straw-tempered Ware and a fine, untempered Plum Red Ware. Most of the coarse pots were used for everyday household or industrial purposes, but the finer pots were usually used as grave offerings.

All the kilns used to make the high-quality Red Ware were situated high in desert cliffs, in natural wind tunnels overlooking the elite Amratian tombs. There the prevailing breezes could fan the hotter flames needed to fire the better pots. In studying vessels fired at these kilns, student Jeremy Geller found that each kiln specialized in certain types and quantities of pots. Together all the kilns appeared to be part of one well-organized industrial complex. The volume of production appears to have been far greater than needed to meet the local demand. Most likely, pottery, along with other locally made prestige goods such as maceheads and beads, was not only supplied for the elaborate burials in local cemeteries but also traded up and down the Nile.

Here was the key to the power of Hierakonpolis. By providing prized offerings for the deceased, the pottery barons encouraged and profited from the pervasive Egyptian belief that the dead could take their wealth with them into an afterlife. By successfully managing the production, transport, and exchange of their goods, the local "big men" gained leadership experience, acquired clients, and forged useful trading contacts with other population centers.

Eventually, however, their flourishing industrial center collapsed. Just after 3500 B.C. the fragile desert-savannah ecosystem suddenly became more arid, and the far desert settlements, along with their pottery kilns, were abandoned as people moved into more thickly settled villages along the wetter Nile floodplain. This traditionally marks the end of the Amratian period of the Egyptian Predynastic era and the beginning of what is called the Gerzean, or, as some authorities prefer, Naqada II, which lasted from about 3500 B.C. until the century preceding the founding of the nation-state and the First Dynasty in 3100 B.C.

The cause of the ecological shift is not known for certain, but the pottery industry may have been a major factor. Botanist Nabil El Hadidi, keeper of the Herbarium at Cairo University, in studying the ashes at the kilns, has identified large amounts of burned acacia and tamarisk wood. These were the principal trees in the savannah ecosystem, and it looks as if the forests along the wadi were cut down to feed the kiln fires. Zoologist John McArdle of the Humane Society of America points also to the hundreds of sheep and goat bones found in Amratian settlements as evidence of heavy grazing. Finally, indirect evidence suggests the local rains ended about this time.

The collapse of the pottery industry and the migration of the population closer to the Nile Valley must have presented the pottery barons of Hierakonpolis with both a problem and an opportunity. Either they reinvested their wealthy or they lost it. Studies elsewhere suggest the situation was typical of many societies on the threshold of statehood. In some cases they returned to more egalitarian ways, but at Hierakonpolis the elite tightened its grip by aggressively reinvesting the "capital" it held in the form of valuable objects and real estate. As the new villages grew, the elite class used its wealth to build town walls, temples, palaces, and bigger tombs and to help develop and support the irrigation canals that some prehistorians believe originated at this time. Irrigation rendered the Nile floodplain more attractive because it led to bigger and more reliable harvests, but it also encouraged more centralized water management and greater reliance on stored grain surpluses. With each step more power was concentrated in the hands of the elite class and its leaders.

Signs of wealth, power, contacts with Eastern civilizations, and armed conflict all increase in the archeological record of the late Gerzean period. In the iconography of the time one finds symbols such as crowns that are later associated with the kingship. Regional kingdoms were appearing throughout the Nile valley from northern Sudan to the apex of the delta near modern Cairo at sites such as Abydos, Naqada, Qustul, and, of course, Hierakonpolis.

Sometime around 3200 B.C., Predynastic society achieved critical mass and regional power struggles became a way of life. For a century battles flared, and pieces of territory shifted from one local king to another, each trying to establish a permanent hold on adjacent kingdoms. Among the contesting kings, it was Narmer who succeeded, extending his conquests and the process of political unification to the entire Egyptian Nile valley.

During these troubled times, the ambitious rulers of Hierakonpolis—the predecessors of Scorpion and Narmer—returned to the long abandoned desert cemetery of their Amratian ancestors. As if to recall their links with the past, they built their tombs near those of their pottery baron predecessors.

Their new cemetery formed an idealized map—a model in miniature—of the new state, spelling out the ideal relationships among a divine king, the geographical regions of Upper and Lower Egypt, the diverse provinces or "nomes" that had been absorbed by political alliance or military conquest, and a multitude of regional gods.

Tombs in the cemetery appear to have been arranged to symbolize the unification of northern and southern Egypt. The idea that Egypt was actually two regions that became one remained prominent throughout Dynastic times. In fact, the ancient Egyptians called their country Tawy, the "Two Lands." They are usually referred to as Upper Egypt—the land upstream on the Nile, toward

1. THE EARLIEST CIVILIZATIONS

Sudan—and Lower Egypt—the land downstream, toward the Mediterranean. Because the Nile flows northward, Upper Egypt is south of Lower Egypt. These same orientations were symbolized in the desert cemetery, where the Wadi Abu Suffian represented the Nile.

The tombs occupied by the Protodynastic rulers of Hierakonpolis were built of mudbricks, in the style of Lower Egypt (at that time probably not the Delta, but simply a kingdom downstream from Hierakonpolis) and, accordingly, are situated in the lower, or downstream, part of the cemetery. They were built in groups of threes, fours, and fives, suggesting that rulers were buried with close members of their families or courts. In size and splendor, these tombs exceed those of the preceeding Gerzean period like the Painted Tomb. One was a chamber about 16 feet long and eight feet wide with a central, L-shaped burial pit. It has given us our first glimpse of the paraphernalia of a prehistoric court.

The most surprising find was a fragmented wooden bed. No longer the simple bier of the earlier tombs, this was a finely carved and joined work of art. Two legs, carved from sycamore wood to resemble a bull's legs, are the direct ancestors of the furniture found in Tutankhamon's tomb.

The largest mudbrick tomb in the cemetery (number 1 in our site numbering system) stands on the downstream, or Lower Egyptian, border of the site. It is about 21 feet long and 11½ feet wide. Its style, location, pottery, and one radiocarbon date indicate that it was probably the last tomb built before Narmer and may well have belonged to his ancestor Scorpion.

Careful excavation of this and other tombs, using trowels and brushes instead of the more common mattocks and picks, has allowed us to solve one of the mysteries of Egyptian archeology. Although everyone knows that great monumental buildings covered the tombs of later pharaohs, until our work in the Hierakonpolis cemetery there was no clear evidence of anything over the graves of Predynastic rulers.

Now we have found the remains of extensive wooden structures that once capped the tombs. The evidence survives in the form of circular, brown discolorations in the soil around the borders of tomb pits. They are rotted posts—postmolds in archeological jargon—and they clearly outline ancient buildings and their fenced enclosures. In plan these closely resemble temples and palaces depicted on stone cylinder seals and ivory and wooden labels of this period from Hierakonpolis and Abydos.

In its heyday the cemetery was a veritable city of the dead—a necropolis—with wooden and reed shrines or model palaces surrounded by low reed fences. Some of these same structures and architectural motifs were imitated 500 years later in stone when King Djoser built Egypt's first pyramid at Saqqara, near modern Cairo. For example, stone chapels at Saqqara were built to look as though they were made of bundled reeds with wooden picket fences along the base of their walls,

apparently honoring a tradition established at the Hierakonpolis cemetery.

Our desert necropolis, like the Saqqara complex, seems to have been deliberately planned. There is a posthole cut into the rock atop a cliff overlooking Tomb 1, the possible Scorpion tomb. We had no idea what its function might have been until a staff architect suggested it provided an excellent view of our excavations at Tomb 1. After clearing the remains of the wooden structure and fence over the tomb, we discovered a row of postmolds marking the centerline of the wooden structure. They were perfectly in line with the posthole atop the cliff. In ancient times the hole must have held a post used by a surveyor to align the tomb. We now believe that much of the necropolis was similarly surveyed.

Tomb 1's mudbrick lining represented the architecture of Lower Egypt but at the opposite end of the cemetery—upstream with respect to the wadi—is a stone tomb, in the architectural style of Upper Egypt during the Protodynastic period between 3200 and 3100 B.C. It is a long, narrow trench with an L-shaped hole in the middle of the floor. From one side a burial chamber reaches under the rock.

The political implications are obvious—the joining of Upper and Lower Egypt in one royal cemetery just at the time Egypt was undergoing the struggles that would lead to her unification under Narmer and his successors.

One curious feature of the cemetery is an animal precinct surrounding the stone tomb at the Upper Egyptian end. It was a veritable zoo that included the remains of elephant, hippopotamus, crocodile, and baboon in addition to the more prosaic cattle, sheep, goat, and dogs. These burials must have had religious significance and at least some animals were mummified. Bits of resin and molded dung still cling to some of the bones. In one animal tomb were three cattle—a bull, a cow, and a calf. We believe the three represent one of the "family triads" common in ancient Egyptian religion.

The animal tombs seem to be another way of mixing religion with politics as only the ancient Egyptians could do—symbolically involving the various gods and provinces in the new royal mortuary cult. It is already known that the Egyptians of this period used various animals as godlike symbols of the different provinces, or "nomes," of Egypt. Some of the nome symbols can be seen on the Narmer palette, displayed atop standards. But animal gods could possess other attributes. For example, in keeping with the symbolic directional orientation of the necropolis, the easternmost animal tomb contained the remains of six baboons, animals the ancient Egyptians associated with the rising sun.

If our interpretation is correct, Narmer's forefathers, the descendents of the pottery barons, combined symbols of all the key elements of the new nation-state in the cemetery at Hierakonpolis. There they devised an extraordinary royal death cult that would define the political order of pharaonic Egypt for thousands of years to come. The cemetery on the banks of Wadi Abu Suffian lies at the wellsprings of that cult. It immediately became the prototype for the royal necropolis of the First Dynasty at Abydos and of its successors for the next 2,500 years.

The desert graveyard played a critical role in developing the symbols and relationships that gave the Egyptian state its distinctive style: extreme centralization under a divine king, the use of a royal mortuary cult and cemetery as symbols of national social integration, the division of the state into the ritualized geographic halves of Upper and Lower Egypt, and the practice of incorporating the gods and peoples of earlier political units into the new state through a complex but pragmatic religious-familial hierarchy. These principles could be readily accepted because throughout Predynastic times an active trade along the Nile diffused and homogenized everything from material goods such as pottery to religious beliefs and political ideology. The Predynastic merchants who controlled that trade had begun to unify Egypt culturally long before their descendents did it politically.

In contrast to other early states in the Middle East and Southwest Asia, Egyptian symbols of political integration were less deeply rooted in great walled towns than in royal cemeteries and temple complexes. By developing a concept of political authority not tied to any particular city or town, Egypt (like China 1,500 years later) anticipated the great, centralized "super urban" states of the modern world rather than the overgrown city-states of Mesopotamia, Greece, or Rome.

Through a combination of favorable climate and environment, mercantile acumen, a dense population and archeological imponderables like individual genius and the lust for power, the wealthy elite of Hierakonpolis evolved from successful pottery merchants to divine kings like Narmer who established the world's first and most enduring nation-state.

Civilization and Its Discontents

Why did the world's first civilization cut a swath across the Near East?

BRUCE BOWER

Investigators from the German Archaeological Institute in Cairo, Egypt, make an annual slog through the Nile Delta to the waterlogged site of Buto, the legendary ancient capital of Lower Egypt. Strategically located near the Mediterranean Sea, Buto was a major port during the 4th millennium B.C.—a poorly understood period of Egyptian history preceding the emergence of the pharaohs around 3100 B.C.

During four field seasons that began in 1983, the German researchers repeatedly drilled through the mud, sand and water-saturated soil covering Buto until they reached pottery fragments and other ancient debris. Since 1987, the investigators have siphoned off groundwater at

Limestone cylinder seal from southern Mesopotamia (top), circa 3500 to 3100 B.C., and a modern clay impression taken from the ancient seal.

Courtesy, Metropolitan Museum of Art, Gift of Martin & Sarah Cherkasky, 1983

the spot with diesel-driven pumps and then carefully dug into Buto's muddy remains. Their dirty work is yielding important evidence not only about Lower Egypt's early days but also about the world's first civilization, which began developing in Mesopotamia around 5,400 years ago.

"We've found the first archaeological evidence of cultural unification in Egypt at the end of the 4th millennium B.C., before the first dynasty of pharaohs appeared," says project director Thomas von der Way. Excavations show that during the final stages of the predynastic era at Buto, local methods of pottery and stone-blade production were replaced by more advanced techniques that originated in Upper Egypt, which lay farther to the south. Apparently, Upper Egyptian invaders had conquered this prominent city and port, von der Way says.

Some of the Upper-Egyptian-style pottery is poorly made and probably represents the handiwork of Buto residents who were allowed to stay on and adapt to

the new regime, he maintains. Those individuals were most likely commoners, von der Way says, adding, "Buto's ruling class and its followers might in fact have been wiped out."

Even more intriguing is evidence of close contact between Buto's Egyptian residents and the Sumerians of southern Mesopotamia (now southern Iraq), who fashioned the world's first full-fledged civilization and state institutions during the last half of the 4th millennium B.C. Not only does pottery at Buto display Mesopotamian features, but clay nails uncovered at the delta site are nearly identical to those used to decorate temples at sites such as Uruk — the largest Sumerian settlement and the world's first city. In Mesopotamia, workers inserted the nails into temple walls and painted their heads to form mosaics. The researchers also found a clay cone at Buto that closely resembles clay decorations placed in wall niches inside Mesopotamian temples.

Scientists have long argued over ancient Egypt's relationship to early Mesopotamia. Much of the debate centers on Mesopotamian-style artifacts, such as cylinder seals and flint knife handles, found in 4th-millennium-B.C. graves situated on slopes above the Nile Valley near Buto. Traders who regularly traveled through Mesopotamia and Syria may have brought those artifacts to Egypt, says David O'Connor of the University of Pennsylvania in Philadelphia.

At Buto, however, Egyptians may have copied temple decorations shown to them by Sumerians more than 5,000 years ago, suggesting "direct and complex influences at work" between the two societies, O'Connor observes.

"It's not possible to trade architecture," von der Way asserts. "Direct personal contact between people from Lower Egypt and Mesopotamia led to the adoption of foreign architecture at Buto."

Buto fuels the growing recognition among archaeologists that early Mesopotamian civilization experienced an unprecedented expansion between 3400 and 3100 B.C. The expansion occurred during the latter part of a phase called the Uruk period (named after the major city of the time), which began around 3600 B.C. Excavations conducted over the past 15 years indicate that southern Mesopotamian city-states, each consisting of one or two cities serving as political hubs and providing goods and services to thousands of people living in nearby farming villages, established outposts in neighboring territories lying within modern-day Iraq, Iran, Syria and Turkey. Even artifacts recovered at sites in the Transcaucasus of the Soviet Union show signs of Sumerian influence.

Such discoveries leave investigators pondering what made the Sumerians such hard-chargers in a world largely made up of subsistence farmers.

Many subscribe to the view of Robert McCormick Adams of the Smithsonian Institution in Washington, D.C., who calls the Uruk expansion "the first urban revolution." Adams says the economic demands of burgeoning Mesopotamian cities led to a great transregional civilization in the Near East.

Others, such as Henry T. Wright of the University of Michigan in Ann Arbor, contend the term "urban revolution" masks the fundamental significance of the Uruk expansion — the introduction, for the first time anywhere, of political states with a hierarchy of social classes and bureaucratic institutions that served powerful kings.

"Whatever the case, it was a revolutionary time, a moment of extraordinary innovations in art, technology and social systems," Adams says. For instance, in the late 4th millennium B.C., Mesopotamia witnessed the emergence of mass-produced pottery, sculpture as an art form and the harnessing of skilled craftsmen and pools of laborers by an administrative class to produce monumental buildings. The world's earliest clay tablets, portraying simple labels and lists of goods with pictographic symbols, also appeared, foreshadowing the birth of fully expressive writing around 3000 B.C.

The Mesopotamian revolution paved the way for modern societies and political states, Wright observes. "A number of competing formulations of what was driving the Uruk expansion have been proposed and must be tested with new archaeological studies," he says.

Map shows modern-day Baghdad and several 4th-millennium B.C. Uruk sites in Mesopotamia and nearby regions.

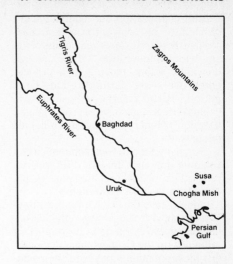

Perhaps the most controversial of these theories, proposed by Guillermo Algaze of the University of Chicago's Oriental Institute, holds that advanced societies in southern Mesopotamia were forced to expand northward, beginning around 5,400 years ago, to obtain scarce resources desired by powerful administrators and social elites.

These northern regions held items crucial to the growth of the incipient civilization, including slaves, timber, silver, gold, copper, limestone, lead and bitumen (an asphalt used as a cement and mortar), Algaze argues in the December 1989 CURRENT ANTHROPOLOGY. To guarantee a reliable flow of imports, Sumerian settlers colonized the plains of southwestern Iran and established outposts at key points along trade routes traversing northern Mesopotamia, he suggests.

Excavations at a number of ancient villages in southwestern Iran indicate the area was "part and parcel of the Mesopotamian world" by the end of the Uruk period, Algaze notes. Cultural remains, such as ceramic pottery, record-keeping tablets, engraved depictions of religious offerings and architectural styles, are strikingly similar at sites in the Iranian plains and southern Mesopotamia, he says. Apparently, Sumerians colonized "a fertile and productive area that was only lightly settled and could surely mount only minimal resistance."

Uruk-period cities and smaller settlements also popped up farther to the north, especially where east-west trade routes intersected with the Tigris and Euphrates rivers, Algaze argues. A good example is the Uruk city of Habuba Kabira, which lies along the upper Euphrates in what is now Syria. Habuba Kabira once encompassed at least 450 acres, according to estimates based on Algaze's assessment of the site. Cultural remains in its metropolitan core and in clusters of sites outside its huge defensive wall are identical to those found in southern Mesopotamia. With its neatly planned residential, industrial and administrative quarters, Habuba Kabira was well situated to control the flow of trade goods through the region, Algaze says.

Although Sumerians produced surplus grain, leather products, dried fish, dates and textiles for export, they most likely took more from colonized areas and northern traders than they gave in return, Algaze maintains. The influx of imports, he says, added new layers of complexity to Mesopotamia's urban centers as fresh legions of administrators scurried to coordinate distribution of the bounty.

Sumerian city-states, of which there were at least five, almost certainly engaged in fierce competition and warfare for imported goods, Algaze says. Cylinder seals from various southern Mesopotamian sites, depicting military scenes and the taking of prisoners, reflect these rivalries.

Cylinder seals are engraved stone cylinders that were used to roll an impression onto clay seals for documents and bales of commodities. A variety of scenes, often including domestic animals, grain, deities and temples, are found on the seals.

Algaze's assertion that the Uruk expansion was primarily fueled by an urgent need for resources available only in foreign lands is receiving much attention, and a good deal of criticism, in the archaeological community.

Piotr Steinkeller of Harvard University contends that, contrary to Algaze's argument, southern Mesopotamians did not need to establish such a far-flung network of settlements to obtain such resources, which were available in the foothills of the nearby Zagros mountains. The Uruk expansion was purely a commercial venture aimed at making a profit, Steinkeller asserted at December's annual meeting of the American Institute of Archaeology in Boston.

"The Sumerians wanted to become middlemen in international trade networks and reap big profits," he says. "They weren't forced to expand because of internal growth."

In Steinkeller's scenario, Uruk migrants did not colonize new territories. Instead, they forged intricate trade agreements with foreign communities to divvy up local and imported goods.

Both colonization and commerce are difficult to pin down through archaeological research, observes Adams of the Smithsonian Institution. "There's no evidence for goods moving in a private-enterprise sense during the Late Uruk period," Adams asserts. At most, he says, valuable items may have been exchanged between distant royal palaces or religious temples.

"Today we tend to treat economics as a separate domain," he says. "But in Uruk times, the economy probably wasn't separated from politics and religion."

Indeed, says Carl C. Lamberg-Karlovsky of Harvard University, religious beliefs may have exerted an important influence on the Uruk expansion. Southern Mesopotamians believed their temple gods owned the land and humans were its stewards. Thus, Uruk city-states may have pursued a type of "manifest destiny," he suggests, claiming nearby lands in the name of their deities.

Harvey Weiss of Yale University downplays religious factors. He contends that the emergence of social classes — particularly elite groups seeking exotic items to signify their elevated status — may lie at the heart of the Uruk expansion.

Weiss says archaeologists lack substantial evidence for extensive imports during the Uruk period, with the exception of copper and the semiprecious stone lapis lazuli.

"It's a good bet the Sumerians were acquiring foreign materials that weren't necessary for their survival," he says. "Newly emerging social elites defined what types of exotica were imported."

However, he adds, it is far from clear what types of social classes characterized Sumerian civilization and why they emerged at that time.

Knowledge about Sumerian settlements built before 3400 B.C. is similarly scant, observes Wright of the University of Michigan. "The Uruk expansion must have started earlier and been more complex than Algaze assumes," he argues.

While Algaze proposes that long-distance trade resulted in the explosive growth of Sumerian city-states, Wright argues just the opposite. As he sees it, competitive city-states attempted to control ever-larger territories, and trade was an outgrowth of their political jousting.

In a fundamental challenge to this already-diverse collection of views, Gregory A. Johnson of the City University of New York, Hunter College, questions the whole notion of a strong, expanding Sumerian civilization in Uruk times. Instead, he contends, the period was one of political collapse and fragmentation.

Johnson says the Sumerian colonists described by Algaze were most likely a group of refugees, initially consisting of administrative elites who had been defeated in the political power struggles that flared up in budding city-states.

"Why were Uruk outposts established in distant areas fully equipped with household utensils, administrative paraphernalia, husbands, wives, children, sundry relatives, animals, architects, artisans — all the comforts of home? Perhaps things at home were not that comfortable," he suggests.

If, as Algaze argues, traders founded communities such as Habuba Kabira, they could easily have adapted to local ways of life without taking with them everything but the kitchen hearth, Johnson points out. Refugees, however, are more likely to recreate the lives they were forced to leave behind.

And masses of Mesopotamians indeed left their lives behind. Populations declined sharply in many southern Mesopotamian cities and their surrounding villages at the end of the 4th millennium B.C. Surveys conducted by Johnson and others indicate the abandonment of nearly 450 acres of occupied areas representing as many as 60,000 people.

The populations of inhabited areas of seven major Sumerian cities dropped by an average of 51 percent in the last few centuries of the Uruk period, Johnson notes. Only at the city of Uruk have archaeologists documented significant expansion during that time.

Moreover, widespread abandonment of settlements on Iran's Susiana plain created an uninhabited, 9-mile-wide "buffer zone" between two large Late Uruk communities known as Susa and Chogha Mish. What once had been a single state in its formative stages was thus sliced in half, Johnson says. The buffer zone probably became the site of intense warfare between administrative elites from the two sides, who wrestled for control of rural labor and agriculture on the plain. Some Sumerian cylinder seals portray political conflicts of this type rather than economic rivalries, he asserts. Susa gained the upper hand and remained an urban center into the 3rd millennium B.C., while Chogha Mish became a ghost town.

Johnson says competing political factions undoubtedly plagued other nascent states, creating a reservoir of disgruntled Sumerians with plenty of incentive to haul their belongings to distant greener pastures.

Further archaeological work, particularly in areas remote from the intensively surveyed river sites, may clarify some of the controversy surrounding the rise and rapid fall of the world's first civilization. But a consensus will be difficult to dig out of the ground.

"Quite frankly, no one has come up with a good explanation for the Uruk expansion," concedes Weiss. "It remains a great mystery."

Egypt and the Mediterranean world

GABALLA ALY GABALLA

GABALLA ALY GABALLA, *of Egypt, is Professor of Egyptology at Cairo University. He was formerly visiting Professor at the Mohamed V University (Morocco), at the University of Central Florida (USA), and at the University of Kuwait. He is the author of two books published in English,* Narrative in Egyptian Art, *(1976) and* The Memphite Tomb—Chapel of Mose *(1977), and of many articles.*

HISTORIC Egypt emerged as a unified country, with its own system of writing, towards the end of the fourth millennium BC. It rapidly became the seat of a brilliant civilization in which flourished philosophy and literature, architecture and art, science and medicine, administration and social organization. From ancient times, thanks to the country's situation on the Mediterranean coast, the Egyptians made increasingly numerous contacts with Europe. The contribution made by Egypt to Western culture enriched civilization as a whole.

Around the same time, the Minoan civilization (named after Minos, the legendary king), came into being on the shores of the Aegean, centred on the island of Crete.

Although the Mediterranean was no obstacle between Egypt and the Aegean, contacts between Egyptian and Aegean traders and emissaries were made first of all in the Phoenician coastal ports, Byblos in particular. Egyptian trading vessels no doubt set sail from these ports to Crete, and called at Cyprus, Rhodes, Karpathos and Kasos before returning directly to Egypt (some 270 nautical miles from Crete), carried along by the north winds that blow in summer. The voyage then took three days and two nights.

There is no lack of archaeological evidence for relations between the two peoples. Many Egyptian cylindrical stone jars have been found in Crete and eventually the Cretans

adopted the Egyptian technique of manufacturing these jars. On the island of Kithira, an alabaster vase has been found bearing the name of an Egyptian king of the Fifth Dynasty (c. 2465-2323 BC). From the twenty-second century BC, Egyptian writings began to mention Kaftiou, an Egyptian adaptation of the Semitic name for Crete, Caphtor, which also appears in the Bible.

At the beginning of the second millennium BC, there was a thriving trade between Middle Kingdom Egyptians and Cretans of the period known as Middle Minoan. Many Egyptian objects from that era, including everyday utensils, scarabs used as seals and a diorite statuette, have been found in Crete, while Minoan pottery in the Kamares style, and silver vases showing an Aegean influence, have been discovered in a temple near Luxor.

Around 1500 BC, Egypt cast off the yoke of the Hyksos[1] and emerged from its traditional isolationism to become an international power, strengthened by a series of military victories. Phoenicia and Syria fell under its sway, and the Egyptian fleet controlled the Phoenician ports, probably extending its influence as far as Cyprus. This Egyptian presence created a new situation in the eastern Mediterranean basin. The Aegeans of the Late Minoan period and the Mycenaeans of Hellas[2] had thereafter to deal directly with the Egyptians if their merchant ships were to have access to the traditional markets of Palestine and Syria. In all probability, the Cretans and the Mycenaeans came to an agreement with the powerful Pharaoh Tuthmosis III (c. 1479-1425 BC). The tomb of his vizier Rekhmire, at the necropolis of Thebes, depicts Cretan emissaries bearing tribute from their island. The Egyptian inscription describes the scene: "The arrival of the princes from Kaftiou and the islands in the midst of the sea, submissive and with bowed heads before the might of

His Majesty Tuthmosis III". There is every reason to believe that these "islands in the midst of the sea" were those of the eastern Mediterranean and the city of Mycenae in the Peloponnese.

Brown-skinned Aegeans, wearing brightly coloured loincloths and with thick manes of hair hanging to their shoulders or worn in one or more plaits bound around their foreheads, became a familiar sight to the Egyptians as they threaded through the streets of Thebes to bear their gifts, called "tribute" by the Egyptians, to Pharaoh: large, ornate goblets with handles shaped like animals, or elongated vases with small handles, decorated with floral motifs or horizontal polychrome lines.

Towards the middle of the fifteenth century BC, the Cretan civilization foundered, probably as a result of internal power struggles. Small wonder, then, that the name of Kaftiou should have disappeared from Egyptian sources after the end of that century. However the expression "islands in the midst of the sea" continues to occur frequently in these writings, before disappearing, in its turn, in the twelfth century BC, when successive waves of the barbarians known to the Egyptians as the "sea peoples" were surging into the Peloponnese peninsula and wreaking havoc. These hordes crossed Anatolia (where they annihilated the Hittites) and Greece, and advanced on Egypt overland across Syria and by sea via the Mediterranean islands. But they were repelled by such powerful Pharaohs as Ramesses II, Merneptah and Ramesses III, who saved Egypt from destruction on a massive scale.

The Greek presence in Egypt made itself felt in the early seventh century BC through mercenaries serving in the Egyptian armies and merchants who set up trading posts in various towns of the Delta. Greek philosophers, historians and geographers followed them, dazzled by Egyptian civilization with its gigantic monuments, its beliefs and its wealth of knowledge.

The Greek astronomer, philosopher and mathematician, Thales of Miletus, is said to have brought back the 365-day solar calendar from Egypt at the end of the seventh century BC. The Athenian statesman Solon (c. 640-560 BC) visited Egypt at the time when, according to Herodotus, the Sixteenth-Dynasty king Amasis II promulgated a law under which each Egyptian was obliged to make an annual declaration of income and return it to the governor of the province. Any person guilty of illicit gains was condemned to death. Solon had an identical law adopted in Athens. Another Greek historian, Diodorus of Sicily, recounts that Lycurgus (legendary king of Sparta) drew inspiration from Egyptian legislation, as did Plato.

Egypt's influence on early Greek art is evident, too. The *kouros* figure of a young man, characteristic of archaic statuary, has an Egyptian air about it. The tall, slim youth stands with his left leg forward, his arms held straight by his sides and his hands clenched. This type of statue not only imitates the attitudes of Egyptian figures, but also abides by the traditional rules governing Egyptian art, in particular the "rule of proportion" that its creators had been applying for over 2,000 years. The human body was originally divided into 18 equal squares, and into 21 from the Saite[3] period (seventh century BC), when the unit of measurement of length, the cubit, was modified. Diodorus of Sicily relates that in the sixth century BC Telekles and Theodorus, two famous Greek sculptors, drew on that tradition for a statue of Apollo by dividing the body into 21 $\frac{1}{4}$ squares.

Over the centuries, the Greeks became increasingly involved in the history of Egypt. In 332 BC, the country was conquered by Alexander the Great, and a Macedonian Dynasty was founded which governed the country for some three centuries. Egypt became part of the Hellenistic world encompassing the eastern basin of the Mediterranean. Alexandria, the new Egyptian capital founded by the Greeks, brought fresh prestige to Hellenism through its writers, geographers, historians, architects and astronomers.

When the Roman general Marcus Antonius, ally of Cleopatra VII, lost the battle of Actium in 31 BC, Egypt became a Roman province. As the granary of Rome it helped to supply the Roman army during its major conquests.

As regards religion, the cult of Isis and Osiris (Serapis, in its Ptolemaic form), and of their son Horus-Harpocrates, was widely adopted in the Graeco-Roman world. The legend of Osiris, based on belief in the afterlife of the soul in a better world, has strong popular appeal, since it promises salvation to all, a concept lacking in the official worship of the Greek and Roman divinities. To the Greeks, Isis was the incarnation of destiny, since she succeeded in freeing herself from the control of the gods and thereby acquired absolute power. The Isis cult in Rome competed with the Roman religion and emperor-worship. Moreover, the Osirian triad foreshadowed the Christian trinity. Before the advent of Christianity, Isis-worship in Europe became as prevalent as the later cult of the Virgin Mary.

The world also owes the invention of the calendar and the alphabet to the ancient Egyptians.

Like other peoples, the Egyptians first devised a dating system which divided time into lunar years of 354 days. But before long they realized that it was not sufficiently accurate and was unsuited to the organization of their complex bureaucratic system, so it fell into disuse except for the celebration of certain religious events. Around 3000 BC they invented a solar calendar of 365 days divided into twelve months of thirty days each, to which at the end of the year were added five extra, or "epagomenal", days. The Egyptians knew that their year was six hours shorter than the solar year (365 $\frac{1}{4}$ days), but for a long time they did nothing to remedy this discrepancy. Only under Greek rule did they begin to add one day to the official year every four years, to bring it into alignment with the solar year. That calendar was adopted by Julius Caesar and imposed in Rome from 45 BC. The Julian calendar was used in Europe and the West until, at the end of the sixteenth century, it was refined by Pope Gregory XIII and, as the Gregorian calendar, became known throughout the world.

Towards the end of the fourth millennium BC, the Egyptians invented a system of writing which used hieroglyphic signs, i.e. pictures, rather than letters. These pictures were chosen, not for their meaning, but for the sounds that they represented.

It is true that the modern European alphabet is derived from the Graeco-Roman alphabet, which is directly based on the Phoenician alphabet. But what system of writing influenced the Phoenicians? The oldest Semitic texts known to us date back to the fifteenth century BC. They were discovered in the Sinai desert, and contain Semitic terms transcribed with signs that resemble hieroglyphs. It is very likely that this Semitic writing was based on hieroglyphs, using a system of pictured sounds, and that it developed over several centuries into the Phoenician alphabet, in which each sound is represented by a single letter. It seems probable, therefore, that the alphabet, one of the greatest achievements of the human mind, is of Egyptian origin.

---

1. Asiatic invaders of northern Egypt who ruled as the Fifteenth Dynasty (c. 1640-1532 BC).
2. Greeks of the classical period called their country Hellas and themselves Hellenes.
3. Named after the Twenty-Sixth Dynasty (664-525 BC) capital city, Saïs, in the Nile Delta. *Editor.*

Early Civilizations
and the Natural Environment

J. Donald Hughes

J. Donald Hughes holds the Ph.D. in history from Boston University and has taught ancient history at the University of Denver since 1967.

Cities, temples, palaces, and tombs of once-flourishing societies now lie in ruins throughout the Middle East. Here people first developed high civilizations, and here, in a particularly telling way, the surviving evidence shows that the course of history is not always that of upward human progress. The rise of civilizations depended upon the increasing ability of people to use and control their natural environment, and the downfall of these same civilizations was due to their failure to maintain a harmonious balance with nature. They suffered a true ecological disaster: not simply a change in climate—for people have weathered climatic changes before and prospered—but a disaster of their own making. This chapter will examine the successes and failures of the Mesopotamians and Egyptians in their relationships to the ecosystems in which they lived.

Mesopotamia, the broad plain of the Euphrates and Tigris rivers, borders the Mediterranean Basin on the east, and at one point north of Antioch in modern Turkey, the Euphrates comes within 90 miles of the Mediterranean coast. But the climate of Mesopotamia is very dry, with an annual rainfall of only six to eight inches. Summer temperatures of 120 degrees in the shade are not uncommon, and 137 degrees has been recorded. Most life in Mesopotamia is dependent on the water brought down from the mountains by the two rivers. The twin rivers begin in the snows of the Armenian mountains, which reach an elevation of almost seventeen thousand feet at Mount Ararat, and flow down into the head of the Persian Gulf, a distance of 1150 miles for the Tigris and 1780 miles for the more circuitous Euphrates. A major tributary stream, the Karun, flows down from the Persian mountains. The plain is an alluvial deposit of sand and silt brought down by the rivers in past geological times, and the process is still going on. This undoubted fact once caused historians to believe that at the time of the earliest civilizations in Mesopotamia, the Persian Gulf extended much further northwest, providing Sumerian cities with a seacoast, and many maps in ancient history textbooks show it that way. But careful

studies by geologists in the area have shown that in spite of the sediment still being brought down by the rivers, the land area in the delta region has not increased, because lower Mesopotamia has been undergoing periods of geological subsidence.[1] The coastline today, with minor variations, is in about the same position as it was 5,000 years ago.

The world's first cities, which arose in Mesopotamia and nearby, were made possible by a changed relationship between human beings and the environment, based on a new agriculture using two important inventions: systematic irrigation and the plow. The fertile, sandy, easily turned Mesopotamian soil made the plow useful. The rivers provided the essential water, but with a flow so undependable that control by major irrigation works was demanded. The new agriculture enabled a much larger human population to live in a given area, and an increasing portion of the population, freed from the need to work the soil, could take up specialized occupations.

The earliest cities seem to have shared some of the problems which have become so annoying in their modern counterparts. Babylon, in its day the largest city of the area, had a city wall ten miles long, and even including its suburbs was consequently only of moderate size by modern standards. The evidence of narrow streets and small rooms in houses huddled within the compass of defensible walls tells us that crowding in ancient cities was extreme. Garbage accumulated in the houses, where the dirt floors were continually being raised by the debris, and human wastes were rarely carried further than the nearest street. The water supply, from wells, rivers, and canals, was likely to be polluted. Life expectancy was short, due in part to the high infant mortality. Flies, rodents, and cockroaches were constant pests. Even air pollution was not absent. In addition to dust and offensive odors, the atmosphere filled with smoke on calm days. Even today, in large preindustrial cities such as Calcutta the smoke of thousands of individual cooking fires, in addition to other human activities, produces a definite pall of smoke and dust which seldom dissipates for long. Under these unhealthy conditions, the death rate must have been high in Mesopotamian cities.

As an alluvial land, the Mesopotamian plain had no stone or

From chapter 4, *Ecology in Ancient Civilizations*, by J. Donald Hughes, pp. 29-42, published by University of New Mexico Press, 1975. Copyright © 1975 by J. Donald Hughes. Reprinted by permission of the author.

deposits of metallic ore, and these had to be brought in from the mountains or imported from other countries. While this encouraged the early development of trade, it also meant that the inhabitants had to use the native materials, swamp reeds and clay, for ordinary construction. They built mighty works of baked and unbaked clay bricks—temples, shrines raised on lofty ziggurats, palaces, and walled cities—but the system of canals and other irrigation works is their most remarkable achievement. Incidentally, it is interesting to note that petroleum, the most important natural resource of modern Iraq, did not escape their notice. They used the oil which oozed forth in some places as fuel for their lamps and bitumen for waterproofing their boats.

The attitude of the peoples of Mesopotamia toward nature, from early Sumerian writings down through the Akkadian and Assyrian literatures, is marked by a strong feeling of battle. Nature herself was represented in Mesopotamian mythology as monstrous chaos, and it was only by the constant labors of people and their patron gods that chaos could be overcome and order established. Mesopotamian gods, though they retained their earlier character as nature deities to some extent, were primarily figures which sanctioned order, guarded the cities, upheld government and society, and encouraged the construction of works which would reproduce on earth the regularity of heaven. The order of heaven was quite apparent to the Mesopotamians, who developed both astrology and astronomy to a high degree and noticed that the motions of the moon and sun, stars and planets are constant and predictable. The labors of the Mesopotamian hero-god Enlil, or Marduk, in slaying the primeval monster of chaos, Tiamat, and creating the world out of her sundered body, reflected the labors of the Mesopotamians themselves, who built islands in the swamps, raised their cities above the flood plains, and irrigated desert stretches with an orderly series of well-maintained canals. They planned their cities so that the major streets of Babylon, for example, crossed each other at right angles in a regular grid pattern, and they laid out their canals in the same way wherever possible. Left to itself, Mesopotamia would have remained a land at the mercy of the capricious river and the merciless sun, in a precarious, shifting balance between tangled marsh and parched desert. But careful works of irrigation conquered sections of that land and won rich sustenance from its basic fertility. Thus a Mesopotamian king could list the construction of a new canal, along with the defeat of his enemies in battle, as the major events of a year of his reign.

Mesopotamians had a well-developed sense of the distinction between the tame and the wild, between civilization and wilderness. The proper effort of mankind toward wild things, they believed, is to domesticate them. They did this with such native animals as the donkey and the water buffalo, in addition to keeping the cows, pigs, sheep, and goats already known to their ancestors. They learned the uses of the palm tree and planted it widely. Animals which could not be truly domesticated were hunted—some, like the lion, to extinction. In the Epic of Gilgamesh, Enkidu was presented as a man of the wild, a friend and protector of beasts. But when he had been tamed by womanly wiles, his former animal friends feared and fled from him. One of the great feats of Gilgamesh and his now-tamed

companion was the slaying of Humbaba, the wild protector of the cedar forests in the west, and the seal set upon the defeat of Humbaba was the subjugation of the wilderness; the trees were felled for human use. This ancient legend described an actual ecological event; the cedars of Lebanon, after centuries of exploitation and export to all the surrounding lands, were completely destroyed except for a few small groves, leaving their mountain slopes open to severe erosion.

The Mesopotamians also displayed curiosity toward and interest in the natural environment. They compiled many lists, which survive on clay tablets, of animals, plants, and minerals. These might be regarded as a step toward genuine scientific classification. However, the lists always classify natural things on the basis of the uses to which they were put by man. Mesopotamian thought was intensely practical and anthropocentric. This principle was illustrated in a Sumerian legend which told how the god Ninurta fought a war in which some stones helped him and others opposed him. Ninurta rewarded the former by making them jewels and semiprecious stones, while the latter he punished by making them into paving stones and thresholds, trodden under foot by people.

The Mesopotamian fondness for building high ziggurats and towers has been seen as a compensation for the flatness of the land by people who had moved in from hilly regions and longed for the forests and mountains of their former homes. This motive might have been felt by the first generation or two of invaders in the country, who came from the mountains, and the persistence of the same forms among their descendants could be explained by the almost universal conservatism of religious architecture. The mountainlike appearance of ziggurats and palaces in Mesopotamia was undoubtedly emphasized by the trees, shrubs, and vines which were planted on them. Archaeologists have noticed that ziggurats were provided with interior channels to drain the water which seeped down from the carefully watered plants on top. So striking were they in appearance that they were among the wonders of the ancient world, the Hanging Gardens of Babylon. Kings enjoyed collecting plants and animals from distant parts of the world to add interest to their gardens, which became botanical and zoological parks as a result. Some things discovered in this way may well have been adapted to agriculture; perhaps the grapevine and olive tree first came to Mesopotamia as gifts of specimens to a royal garden. Domestication seems to have been a key idea in royal collecting. One king had a pet lion who was supposed to have fought beside him in battle against his enemies.

The cities of Mesopotamia have been desolate mounds for a score of centuries, and only a poor remnant of the "Fertile Crescent," that green, cultivated area which once arched across the Middle East from Sumeria to Palestine, is visible in photographs taken from space today. This disaster is due not simply to changing climate or the devastating influences of war, though both of these have had important effects. It is a true ecological disaster, due partly to the difficulty of maintaining the canals and keeping them free of silt, but more importantly to the accumulation of salt in the soil. Irrigation water, carried over large areas, was allowed to evaporate with insufficient drainage, and over the centuries in this land of low humidity and scanty rain, the salts carried in by the water concentrated. Such areas had to be abandoned, while new sections were brought under irrigation and cultivation until they in turn suffered the same salinization. A similar process occurs in many places where deserts have been irrigated, as in the Imperial Valley of California today, where the best efforts of modern technology have barely been able to combat it. Salt would not have accumulated in well-drained soil, but in Mesopotamia the problem of drainage was especially difficult. Silt and mud carried by the rivers and canals settled out rapidly, so that constant dredging was necessary to keep the canals flowing. Excavated mud piled up along the sides of the canals to a height of thirty feet or more, serving as a barrier to drainage. Eventually the river level was raised well above the surrounding country. The natural remedy to this, flooding and a major shift in the course of the rivers, was catastrophic whenever it happened.

It is significant that the first urban societies were also the first societies to abandon a religious attitude of oneness with nature and to adopt one of separation. The dominant myth and reality in Mesopotamia was the conquest of chaotic nature by divine-human order. Such societies, it must be noted, were ultimately unsuccessful in maintaining a balance with their natural environment.

Far to the east of Mesopotamia, but in contact with it, another civilization flourished in the Indus River Valley. It is mentioned here because many scholars say that it fell because of mistreatment of its fragile semidesert environment. While Mesopotamian cities were built largely of sun-dried clay bricks, the Indus Valley cities used baked bricks almost exclusively, and great quantities of wood were required to fire them. This, combined with other uses of wood, produced widespread deforestation, while grazing of cattle, goats, and sheep further reduced the vegetative cover. The results included desiccation, flooding, and erosion. Some authors also theorize that the dust blown from the dried, denuded land produced a permanent layer of dusty haze in the atmosphere over the Indus Valley, which actually altered the climate by causing a temperature gradient that shifted the monsoon rains to the east, out of the area, and also caused premature seeding of the clouds which did develop in the area, further reducing the rainfall. Other scholars postulate a series of disastrous floods, which could also have been caused by deforestation.

The attitude of the Indus Valley people toward nature is virtually unknown. They did represent animals on their stamp seals, but their language has not yet been deciphered. Whatever their attitude, their practices may have made them a prime early example of the principle that human societies which fail to live in harmony with the natural environment eventually disappear or change beyond recognition.

Without the Nile River, Egypt would be part of the Sahara Desert. The facts of Egypt's climate speak for themselves. The average annual rainfall at Cairo is one inch, and southward in Upper Egypt there may be one shower every two or three years. The average temperatures are typical of the desert belt; in the valley they vary from about 50 degrees to 110 degrees on the average, while on the adjoining desert the range is even more extreme, varying from below freezing to above 120 degrees.

The Nile is the world's longest river. Rising in the mountains of Ethiopia and the lakes of East Africa, it flows northward through the swamps of the southern Sudan and then begins its course as an exotic river in the desert. Its total length is thirty-five hundred miles. Spring and summer rains on the headwaters of the Blue Nile and its tributaries, which always occurred at the same time of the year, reaching their height in September, fed the annual floods of the Nile, which brought both moisture and new alluvial soil to the fields of Egypt and were one of the major environmental influences in that country. During flood stage, the Nile usually carred fifty times as much water as at its lowest stage.

The contrast between the land watered by the Nile and the desert which borders it is abrupt and extreme. The ancient Egyptians recognized this, dividing the earth into two parts, the fertile black land of Egypt and the dry red land of the hostile desert. The black land, in turn, had two major divisions, the long, narrow strip of Upper Egypt, from one to thirteen miles wide, often guarded by high cliffs, and the broad delta of Lower Egypt, containing two-thirds of the arable land of the country.

In very ancient times, much of the black land was covered by marshes which supported an amazing variety of plant and animal life, including millions of water birds in the Biblical "land of whirring wings."[2] The Egyptian crocodile and hippopotamus are only the best known of the vast assemblage of wild animals. The marshes also provided the papyrus reed, subject to many uses, including the manufacture of paper.

The agricultural civilization of Egypt depended on harnessing the Nile's annual flood and distributing its waters and its fertile load of silt through the fields by a series of canals and basins with the use of the shadoof, a simple water-lifting machine consisting of a bucket with an arm and counterweight attached. The Nile's flood was regular and predictable, although its height varied from year to year, a very low Nile producing drought and famine and a very high Nile devastating the works of man and even eroding the soil. Still, most years brought a moderate, useful flood.

Egyptian attitudes toward nature reflect the dependable periodicity of their natural environment. Their gods were deities of nature, intimately sharing the characteristics of the animals and plants which were their attributes. Ra, the sun god, was worshiped beyond the others. His movements were regular, and all nature responded to them. When he rose, day came and life flourished, and when he set, the Egyptians associated the failing light with death, but a new dawn inevitably followed. The Egyptians calculated the solar year of 365 days, and noticed that the Nile's flood depended on the sun's cycle. Another major god, Osiris, represented the dying and rising vegetation, intimately associated with the Nile and the sun. All Egyptian gods represented aspects of the natural world, and most of them were conceived as friendly to mankind.

In the temples and sacred precincts, the Egyptians protected animals and plants which embodied the presence of gods, and often gave them divine honors. For example, crocodiles sacred to the god Sebak were kept in the lake at Shedet, fed with offerings, and even decorated with jewelry. Other animals were generally venerated throughout Egypt, such as the cat of Bubastis and the ibis of Thoth.

1. THE EARLIEST CIVILIZATIONS

To the Egyptians, all nature was animate and filled with gods. In the paintings, sculpture, and objects of daily life made by them, an artistic joy in nature can be sensed. Their hieroglyphics include many animals, birds, and plants, often represented with great attention to natural detail. Columns bore capitals representing the lotus and papyrus plants. Egyptian poems enumerate and glorify the appearance and workings of the natural world.

> All beasts are content with their pasturage;
> Trees and plants are flourishing.
> The birds which fly from their nests,
> Their wings are stretched out in praise to thy
>   spirit.[3]

This poem comes from the time of Ikhnaton the montheist, when art and literature emphasized the natural, but the Amarna period (named after Ikhnaton's residence city) in this respect simply reasserted a tendency which was present in Egypt from the earliest surviving evidence.

Thus it is not surprising to discover that well-to-do Egyptians loved gardens, that they planned them carefully with symmetrical beds of flowers and shallow pools of water, and that they collected vegetables, herbs, vines, and fruit and shade trees to plant in them.

Practical knowledge of the workings of those parts of the environment directly useful to them the Egyptians had in abundance, and with it they maintained a flourishing agriculture throughout their history, except for the worst periods of invasion and internal unrest. Then the canals might go unrepaired and the desert and swamp readvance at the expense of the cultivated fields.

Egyptian science is known from treatises on mathematics, astronomy, and medicine. The medical writings include some directions regarding the use of plants and drugs in treating ailments.

The history of the Egyptian environment in antiquity is marked by a great reduction in the numbers and abundance of wildlife. This was primarily due to the conversion of marshes into fields, but partially also due to hunting. Egyptians from the pharaoh on down hunted water birds and animals in the remaining wetlands, and pursued lions, wild cattle, deer, and antelope in the nearby desert. Today even once-abundant species are seldom seen.

As Egypt was never forested, most wood had to be imported from Lebanon or the Upper Nile. The chief material for major construction, stone, was abundant in Egypt and widely quarried. Copper and tin were mined in Sinai and other desert margins or imported from abroad.

The regularity of the Nile saved Egypt from some of the problems of Mesopotamia. The floods provided annual drainage, and salinization was not widespread in Egypt. In fact, Egypt continued to produce food surpluses throughout the ancient period and was a major exporter of grain to Greece and Rome.

All told, the unique environment of Egypt tended to shelter it from some of the bad effects of ecological change felt elsewhere in the ancient world, and helped to ensure its long continuity as a relatively conservative civilization.

The Persians had a unique view of the natural world which gives them an important place in any consideration of ecology in ancient times. Their empire eventually stretched from India to Egypt and Greece, altering and influencing much of the Mediterranean Basin. The eastern neighbors of Mesopotamia, the Persians inhabited an arid, mountainous region where agriculture required extensive irrigation. For this purpose, the Persians developed underground channels, called *qanats*, through which water could flow from the aquifers without too much loss by evaporation. Cities had developed in this area before the arrival of the Persians themselves, and besides settled irrigation agriculture, many of the inhabitants practiced seminomadic herding of cattle.

The Persian religion, based upon an Indo-European pantheon of nature deities, developed a strong sense of reverence for the elements of the natural world. Earth, water, and especially fire were regarded as sacred in themselves, and much of Persian religion was concerned with the need to keep them free from ritual pollution. The Persians had many rules concerning cleanliness, and those who broke them could be severely punished. Water was to be kept in a state of pristine purity, whether it was flowing or standing in a lake or well. Sewage of any sort, whether urine or excrement, or even hair or fingernail parings, was not permitted to enter water, although water might itself be used as an agent of purification. The worst sort of pollution in Persian eyes resulted from contact with dead bodies of human beings or animals, and anyone seeing one of these in the water was duty bound to remove it and perform the necessary purifications. The earth was also sacred, and burial of dead bodies was considered the worst possible violation of the will of the gods. Since fire, an object of great veneration, could not be polluted either, bodies were simply exposed in rocky places or in special towers to be eaten by "unclean" animals such as wolves and vultures.

Along with the elements, the Persians worshiped sacred plants, animals, and stars. Certain human activities, such as agriculture, were regarded as acts of reverence to the earth which made the earth happy and fruitful. Domestic animals were given reverent care.

When the prophet Zoroaster reformed the Persian religion, he left intact the basic reverence for nature and the ritual maintenance of purity associated with it. He emphasized the dualism of Persian thought, however, including a certain ambivalence toward nature. While the elements are pure and must remain uncorrupted, the creatures of the earth are divided into two classes, good and evil. Ranged on the side of Ahura Mazda, the god of light and goodness, according to Zoroastrian thought, were all the good creatures, such as dogs, cattle, trees, and the sun itself, whose very rays helped to purify. On the other side, with Ahriman, the evil prince of darkness, were noxious creatures like wolves, snakes, demons of disease, and flies. Killing such creatures was regarded as an act of merit, so that condemned criminals were sometimes given the task of killing a certain number of them as a means of expiating their guilt.

In the Persian view, then, people were regarded as responsible for their actions in regard to the natural environment. They were seen as coworkers of the good Creator, charged with maintaining the purity and fruitfulness of the earth in defiance of the attempts of the forces of evil to pollute and destroy the earth and its good creatures.

It could be expected that people who observed the Persian religious rules would be healthier and cleaner than their neighbors in the ancient world, and this may have been the case. It would be nice to add that the Persian attitude of human responsibility toward the natural environment retarded the deterioration of the Persian landscape, but this does not seem to be true. The hillsides of Persia, like those of Lebanon, were deforested and subjected to erosion. Persian fields, like those of Mesopotamia, suffered salinization. Wildlife was gradually eradicated. Some of these results may be put down to the attitude of warfare toward the "evil" part of nature, and the belief that agriculture is invariably good. But more than this, the Persians illustrate a general principle of human ecology, that is, that a good attitude toward nature is not enough. Combined with a good attitude must be accurate knowledge of the workings of nature and the ability to control and direct human impact upon nature in channels which will help, rather than hinder, the balance of nature. The Persians' considerable experience with the natural environment is reflected in many of their wise rules. But they had no science worthy of the name, and their level of technology and social control, while high enough to be one of the wonders of the ancient world, was insufficient to put into effect the limited ecological insights which were contained in their religion.

Greece and Rome: The Classical Tradition

For the West civilization began in Mesopotamia, but it was in Greece that civilization became distinctly Western. The Greek ideas of order, proportion, harmony, balance, and structure—so pervasive in classical thought and art—inspired Western culture for centuries, even into the modern era. Their humanism, which made man "the measure of all things," not only liberated Greek citizens from the despotic collectivism of the Near East, but also encouraged them, and us, to attain new levels of creativity and excellence. Judith Swaddling explores the Greeks' commitment to excellence in "Olympics B.C." Though the Greeks did not entirely escape from the ancient traditions of miracle, mystery, and authority, they nevertheless elevated reason and science to new levels of importance in human affairs, and they invented history as we know it (see Carmine Ampolo's article on Herodotus). It was their unique social-political system, the polis, that provided scope and incentive for the great achievements of Greek culture. Although the civil order rested on slavery, and excluded women from the political process, each polis was an experiment in local self-government.

Yet for all its greatness and originality classical Greek civilization flowered only briefly. The weaknesses of the polis system surfaced in the Peloponnesian Wars. Walter Karp compares this conflict to America's cold war with the Soviet Union in "The Two Thousand Years' War," while Paul Cartledge in "A Patriot for Whom?" examines the meaning of patriotism during the conflict between Athens and Sparta. During and after the war the polis ceased to fulfill the lives of its citizens as it had in the past. The Greeks' confidence was shaken by events.

But it was not the war alone that undermined the civic order. The Greek way of life depended upon unique and transitory circumstances—trust, smallness, simplicity, and a willingness to subordinate private interests to public concerns. The postwar period saw the spread of disruptive forms of individualism and the privatization of life. Above all, as H. D. F. Kitto has forcefully argued, the polis ideal, with its emphasis on public participation and the wholeness of life, eschewed specialization. "If one man in his time is to play all the parts," Kitto writes, "these parts must not be too difficult for the ordinary man to learn. And this is where the polis broke down. Occidental man, beginning with the Greeks, has never been able to leave things alone. He must inquire, improve, progress; and Progress broke the polis."

Eventually, Alexander's conquests and the geographical unity of the Mediterranean enabled the non-Greek world to share Greek civilization. Indeed, a distinctive stage of Western civilization, the Hellenistic age, emerged from the fusion of Greek and Oriental elements. "Bibliotheca Alexandrina" describes this facet of Hellenistic civilization. But, as Peter Green's "Greek Gifts?" indicates, some scholars question whether most Greeks respected or understood subject peoples and their cultures. At best the Hellenistic period was a time when new cities were built on the Greek model, a time of intellectual ferment and cultural exchange, travel and exploration, scholarship and research. At worst it was an era of amoral opportunism in politics and derivative styles in the arts.

Later, the Greek ideal survived Rome's domination of the Mediterranean. "Conquered Greece took her savage conqueror, and introduced the arts into rustic Latium," as a Latin poet put it. Modern scholars continue that theme, depicting Roman culture as nothing more than the practical application of Greek ideals to Roman life. Yet the Romans were not merely soulless imitators of the Greeks. They were creative borrowers (from the Etruscans, as well as from the Greeks). Furthermore, they invented a marvelous system of imperial government and a unique conception of law. Their social order is described by John Woodford in "Ancient Roman Life"; their political order is illumined by Karen Huber's article on Caesar and Lionel Casson's piece on Nero; and their empire is addressed by William S. Hanson and Lesley Macinnes' essay on Hadrian's Wall and beyond. The Romans bequeathed their language and disseminated Greek thought and values to Europe. Greek culture provided the basis for the cultural unity of the Mediterranean, and the Romans provided the political unity. Between them they forged and preserved the standards and assumptions upon which our tradition of civilization is built—the classical ideal.

Looking Ahead: Challenge Questions

How do the modern Olympic Games differ from the Greek original?

What restrictions did Greek women have to contend with?

What were the strengths and weaknesses of the histories by Herodotus?

What analogies are there between the Peloponnesian War and America's rivalry with Russia?

Describe living conditions in ancient Rome.

Explain the political functions of Roman gladiatorial contests.

How has Nero been misjudged by history?

What determine the outer limits of the Roman empire in Britain?

Olympics B.C.

Far more than a love of sport spurred the ancient athletes

Judith Swaddling

Judith Swaddling is a curator in the Department of Greek and Roman Antiquities, British Museum.

The 1988 Olympics will again provoke comparison between the simplicity and idealism of the original Olympics and the lavish, high-security spectacle of the modern games. But even before the influence of the Romans, with their love of grandiose public entertainment, the ancient Greek contests were a big event, drawing tens of thousands of spectators and turning top athletes into living legends. Moreover, in addition to the meets at Olympia, held every four years, Greek sports fans flocked to three other festivals: the Pythian games at Delphi, the Isthmian games at Corinth, and the Nemean games. Together with the Olympics, these formed the *periodos*, or "circuit," arranged so that there was one major sports event every year. Other Greek localities sponsored smaller meets, and by Roman times hundreds of sports festivals throughout the classical world had been granted "Olympic" status, their events and programs modeled closely on the original.

At the circuit festivals, the only prizes were symbolic honors, crowns of olive at Olympia, laurel at Delphi, fresh parsley and later pine at Corinth, and dried parsley at Nemea. The victors' home states, however, provided ample cash rewards, along with such civic honors as free board and lodging and theater seats, not to mention, by the third and second centuries B.C., extravagant homecomings and celebratory processions.

Sometimes, states would erect statues of their victors where they won or in their home towns. This was no mean reward, for a life-size statue in bronze or marble by the average craftsman could cost the equivalent of ten years' wages. One man, Dikon, had fifteen statues, equal to his number of Olympic wins. Famous poets, most notably Pindar, the great Greek lyricist, were paid large sums to write verses in the victors' honor. Wins were recorded

with pride on the athletes' epitaphs and in stone inscriptions that hailed them as benefactors of the state. The names of the winners in the Olympic footrace were even used as a dating system made up of four-year periods (Olympiads), by tradition going back to 776 B.C.

The main reason athletes were so honored was that these games were bound up with religion. The circuit games were held at the chief religious sanctuaries of Greece, where each was performed in honor of a god: Zeus at Olympia and Nemea, Apollo at Delphi, and Poseidon at Corinth. The Greeks believed athletes received their prowess from the gods, and therefore it was to the gods that athletes prayed for victory and gave gifts, both to curry favor and in thanks. As early as the fourth century B.C., however, the inscriptions on the stone bases of the victors' statues tell us that the athletes themselves and their city-states were receiving primary recognition.

States would sometimes pay for an athlete's training, and there are even instances of top athletes being "bought" by city-states that hoped to benefit from athletic or equestrian triumphs. The wealthy Greek colonies of southern Italy and Sicily had a very strong penchant for sports, in which they invested heavily, particularly by recruiting athletes from other cities. In the early fifth century B.C., Astylos of Croton (in southern Italy), victor in the long-distance race and in the race in armor, mysteriously changed his national allegiance to Syracuse (in Sicily) between one Olympics and the next, while in the fourth century, a Syracusan tyrant tried to bribe the father of a winner in the boys' boxing contest to have the boy proclaimed a Syracusan. Similarly, the city of Ephesus in Asia Minor succeeded in acquiring a Cretan long-distance runner after his second Olympic victory.

The national sanctuaries were cultural and religious centers that provided arenas not only for sporting events but also for music, dance, drama, and public debate.

In the fifth century B.C. the sports complex at Olympia included both indoor and outdoor facilities for field and track events, a swimming pool, a bathhouse, accommodations for athletes, a stadium, and a racecourse. On the other hand, because of the vast crowds, accommodations for spectators were makeshift; the majority slept in tents or under the open sky. When Plato attended the Olympic games he shared a tent with strangers, who did not realize who he was until he later entertained them at Athens.

Olympia was crammed with temples and altars to the gods and treasury buildings where city-states and colonies could display their wealth. To impress visitors, states erected monuments to their deities, athletes, statesmen, heroes, and military triumphs. There were also some monuments reflecting unsportsmanlike behavior. Right from the beginning, only victory in the games counted (the word *athlete* literally meant "prize seeker"); simple participation and effort were insignificant. On some occasions a state had to foot the bill when its overeager contestants were fined for breaking the rules; the proceeds were used to pay for bronze statues of Zeus set up at Olympia, so that the transgressions would be a permanent warning to potential offenders. The Athenians were required to set up six statues after the Athenian Kallipos bribed his opponents in the pentathlon.

The ancient world was full of internal strife, so a truce from hostilities was instituted to safeguard competitors and spectators traveling to and from the Olympic games. This "sacred truce"—one existed for the Nemean games as well—eventually lasted as long as three months to protect participants coming from as far afield as southern Spain and the eastern coast of the Black Sea. As a result of the truce, countries openly at war could compete against one another with no apparent intention of resolving their more fundamental differences.

With permission from *Natural History,* Vol. 97, No. 8, August 1988, pp. 8, 10. Copyright the American Museum of Natural History, 1988.

The original function of physical education in ancient Greece, as training for warfare, was apparent in events such as the race in armor. The pyrrhic, or war, dance was also staged at some festivals. This is one reason that women rarely participated in sports, except in Sparta, where their physical toughness was believed to enable them to produce fine warrior sons. In Sparta, physical education was specially designed to promote endurance, and Sparta's athletes achieved a substantial number of Olympic victories in track and combat events.

Although the Eleans, in whose territory the sanctuary of Olympia was situated, were of minor political significance, they inevitably became embroiled in hostilities as a result of their role in the festival. This was particularly so when, siding with the Athenians during the Peloponnesian War, they banned the Spartans several times from competing in the games or worshiping at the Temple of Zeus. On one such occasion, a Spartan named Lichas wanted to enter his horse in the chariot race, and so he registered his chariot in the name of the Theban people. His team won, and he decked the charioteer with the victory ribbons, without waiting for them to be presented by the judges. When the judges discovered that Lichas was a Spartan, they had him publicly whipped as a punishment. In retaliation, the Spartans invaded Olympia.

Whereas in Sparta tough physical training was part of the regimen forced on all boys from the age of seven, in Athens it was part of general education at schools, which were probably nearly all privately run for the sons of the well-to-do. For the rest of the populace, sports were a leisure activity in which both the rich and the poor participated.

Nearly all Greek towns had a gymnasium, a kind of clubhouse with accommodations for various sporting activities, where professional trainers could be hired for instruction, massage, and dietary advice. There were also *palaistrai*, facilities often amounting to little more than open sports grounds, which even villages usually possessed. Watching men and boys train and compete against one another was a popular pastime: artists and sculptors found many of their models this way and used wrestling, in particular, as a means of depicting mythical battles between gods and heroes. At the sporting grounds, too, older men readily chose lovers from among the young boys. Athletes themselves had sexual favorites: in the entrance

tunnel to the stadium at Nemea, where the competitors waited to be summoned for their events, one of them scrawled "Akrotatos is beautiful"; another athlete added words to the effect, "Well, his father thinks so, anyway."

Gymnasiums and sports meets were also natural locations for discussing current affairs. Athletes occasionally served as political envoys or took up politics after their retirement. Such was the case of Theogenes of Thasos, a boxer and wrestler who ventured into public affairs after a stunning sports career spanning more than twenty years, with twenty-three victories in the circuit games and more than a thousand at lesser festivals. Unfortunately, his successes, if not the rigors of his sport, seem to have gone to his head, for he also began to proclaim himself the son of the superman Herakles.

While the expense of maintaining horses and equipping a team meant that only the wealthy could compete in chariot races, a young athlete from the lower classes could probably work his way up to the top in other athletic events. The first known Olympic victor, Koroibos, is recorded as a cook, while other early victors included a cowherd and a goatherd. There were no regulations prohibiting professional athletes from competing at the ancient games, as there are now; a successful athlete could have probably earned his living simply by traveling around from one athletic meet to another. While cash prizes were not given at the Olympics themselves, elsewhere a single sprint race could earn the winner a prize large enough to buy a luxury house. Celebrity sports-

men were occasionally paid huge fees by entrepreneurs to appear at local festivals: in one case as much as five talents, the equivalent of nearly sixty pounds of silver.

At the Panathenaic festival in Athens, held every four years in honor of Athena, patron goddess of the city, vast quantities of olive oil were presented as prizes. The olive oil was contained in amphorae decorated with the goddess Athena on one side, and the contest for which the prize was won on the other. The oil was used for lighting, heating, and cooking and for cleansing and lubricating the body. The vessels, with or without oil, were occasionally sold, often to buyers in Italy. Athletes were apparently allowed to export vessels without paying the usual duty. Each vessel was worth a minimum of twelve days' wages, and the biggest prize, for the sprint, was one hundred amphorae.

In addition to material rewards, ancient athletes enjoyed the adulation of the crowds, which at times was oddly expressed. The Rhodians had the restrained habit of applauding a performance by smacking their lips, while the people of Tarsus used a strange kind of snort. But a scene with spectators of a kind more familiar to us is described by the orator Dio Chrysostom, writing in the first century A.D. and speaking of athletic festivals at Alexandria:

When they enter the stadium, they behave as if under the influence of drugs; they forget everything they have ever learned, and say and do the first thing that comes into their heads.... Who could describe the yelling and uproar, the frenzy, the change of color and look on [their] faces, not to mention the foul language.

Discus thrower, on a silver coin from the island of Kos, early fifth century B.C.

Herodotus

Roving reporter of the Ancient World

CARMINE AMPOLO

Carmine Ampolo, of Italy, teaches Greek history at the University of Pisa. He has carried out research on the origins of ancient Rome, on Greek politics and society, and on the relationship between myth and history. Among his published works are La citta antica *(1980; "The Ancient City") and, with M. Manfredini,* Le vite di Teseo et di Romolo *(1988; "The Lives of Theseus and Romulus").*

'HERODOTUS of Halicarnassus, his *Researches* are here set down to preserve the memory of the past by putting on record the astonishing achievements both of our own and of other peoples... that the great deeds of men may not be forgotten... whether Greeks or foreigners: and especially, the causes of the war between them."*

In this introduction to his *Histories,* Herodotus (c. 490-425 BC) provides us with perhaps the earliest definition of the historian's aims and concerns. Some sixty years earlier, his precursor Hecataeus of Miletus, who had sought to inquire rationally into the mythical legends of the Greeks, explained his intentions in the following terms: "Thus speaks Hecataeus of Miletus: I write these things inasmuch as I consider them to be truthful; in fact, the legends of the Greeks are numerous and, to my mind, ridiculous." In this tetchy assertion of the author's role we can already see the two requirements of historiography in the Hellenic world: it must be written and it must be truthful.

With Herodotus the tone changes. He does not seek to give his own personal interpretation of what he relates, and usually he compares the different versions of stories he has collected. He

* Quotations from *Herodotus: The Histories,* translated by Aubrey de Sélincourt, Penguin Classics, 1954.

wants to talk about his researches, tell of his inquiries. History as he understands it is at once the gathering of information and the recounting of a story. He thus inaugurated the two main trends in Greek historiography for centuries to come. Sometimes one would be given prominence, sometimes the other, but the prime imperative was always truthfulness, even in the case of historians who attached very great importance to narrative.

The art of storytelling

When Herodotus describes his work as an "exposition of his researches, the narration of an inquiry", these ambivalent terms must be taken to mean both the oral transmission of a story and its written formulation. The blending of oral and written styles in the *Histories* can be explained by the fact that Herodotus would give public readings of the various stories *(logoi)* making up his work. This is confirmed by the allusions in the text to audience reaction, and by the circular structure of the writing.

This practice had a marked effect on the composition of the work, which may seem to be something of a patchwork, with its countless digressions that sometimes fit into one another like Chinese boxes or Russian dolls. More a painter than a sculptor, Herodotus excels in the art of storytelling and possesses the gift of enthralling his audience, whether listener or reader, by his descriptions of a detail, an episode or an individual.

He often tells a story which he has heard at second or third hand. For example, after describing the victory of the Athenians over the Persians at Marathon, he tells what happened to the

Athenian soldier Epizelos, who lost his sight while fighting in the battle, though nothing had hit him: "I am told that in speaking about what happened to him he used to say that he fancied he was opposed by a man of great stature in heavy armour, whose beard overshadowed his shield; but the phantom passed him by, and killed the man at his side." It would be a mistake to see this as Herodotus directly reporting what he has heard, but rather as an example of the mirror play that is a common feature of the *Histories:* Epizelos tells his story, others repeat it, Herodotus hears it and tells it in his turn.

This is not simply a taste for the fantastic or the marvellous, for which Herodotus is so often criticized, but a delight in intriguing and surprising his audience. He is able to arouse people's curiosity because his own is so great. He is interested in all kinds of out-of-the-way details, the customs of each people and all the wonders of the world, whether events, inventions or monuments like the pyramids of Egypt, the labyrinth above Lake Moeris and the walls of Babylon. In his quest for knowledge, Herodotus would travel and make inquiries of those who might have information about the countries visited—scholars, priests or people whose names are not recorded: "I learn by inquiry."

The reason for this passion for research emerges clearly in the introduction to the *Histories:* it is the historian's task to combat time, to preserve what he considers to be memorable. In the Greek cities and sanctuaries there were already "memorizers" *(mnemones)* responsible for recollecting and recording divine and human occurrences. But the historian's concerns are much loftier than the purely administrative, legal and religious functions of the *mnemones.* All the illustrious deeds and labours *(erga)* that he relates must retain their *kleos,* their aura of glory, their renown. In some ways Herodotus seems to carry on where the epic poets left off. They recounted the deeds of heroes, the historian recounts the deeds of men.

The insatiable curiosity shown by Herodotus in his investigations and travels considerably broadened the scope of written history, which ceased to consist solely of myths, genealogical lists and ethno-historical material relating to particular peoples or communities. Although he wanted to preserve as much as possible, he had to select which of the facts to save. For the historian who takes as his subject "great and marvellous actions", not everything is memorable.

Herodotus was aware of the amount of space given in his *Histories* to the long parentheses of the storyteller. On one occasion he even confesses: "I need not apologize for the digression—it has been my plan throughout this work." To understand this attitude, we should not use modern criteria nor even refer to later Greek authors whose works, which were designed exclusively to be read, seem to be better constructed. In a work addressed primarily to listeners and only subsequently to readers, not only the form but the choice of material were determined by the exigencies of spoken communication. It is not enough for details to be historically revealing or admirable; they must also be entertaining and, whether glorious or despicable, arouse the curiosity of the narrator and strike a chord in the minds of his audience.

An investigator at work

What was Herodotus' raw material? Much of the *Histories* records the history and customs of peoples incorporated in the Persian empire (or those of peoples like the Scythians which were unsuccessfully fought by the empire) as well as facts about the Greek cities in the sixth and fifth centuries BC. The culmination is confrontation between the Greeks and the Persians, which accounts for less than half the work.

Herodotus does not speak of a single people, nor even of a single Greek city, nor of Greece in its entirety. He erects no barriers, shows no scorn. He does not really differentiate between the Greeks and other peoples, the "Barbarians". Born at a time which, under the influence of the Sophists, saw the development of cultural relativism, and originating from a region at the meeting-point of East and West, he showed curiosity, consideration and even respect for other cultures.

He nevertheless viewed them through Greek eyes. In keeping with a typically Hellenic way of seeing the foreigner as a reversed image of oneself, he depicted the behaviour of other peoples as the antithesis of that of the Greeks. Among the "strange practices" of the Egyptians, for example, he mentions that "women attend market and are employed in trade, while men stay at home and do the weaving.... Men in Egypt carry loads on their heads, women on their shoulders...." His enumeration of their differences ends as follows: "In writing or calculating, instead of going, like the Greeks, from left to right, the Egyptians go from right to left—and obstinately maintain that theirs is the dexterous method, ours being left-handed and awkward."

This comparative method can be seen as a way of classifying and hence of understanding. But Herodotus also observes similarities, which he scrupulously notes, as in the case of the Spartans. Customs on the death of a king, he reports, "are the same in Sparta as in Asia", and "the Spartans resemble the Egyptians in that they make certain callings hereditary: town-criers (heralds), flute-players and cooks are all, respectively, sons of fathers who followed the same profession."

Although he does not go as far as Thucydides in saying that the Greeks lived formerly in the same way as the Barbarians today, and although he maintains a distance between the two worlds, he does not regard them as two monolithic blocks, one of which is in certain respects inferior to the other or culturally backward. Different though they may be, he acknowledges the many qualities of the Barbarians, considering, for example, that the Greek gods have Egyptian origins, that Egyptian civilization is older than that of the Greeks, and that the Persians have numerous virtues.

The *Histories* end with a revealing anecdote. To convince his people not to attempt to settle in more fertile lands, the Persian King Cyrus the Great declares to his troops that "soft countries breed soft men", pointing out that the Greeks have preferred to keep their freedom on a harsh land rather than to be slaves cultivating fertile plains for others. It is thus a Persian sovereign who enunciates a truth applying chiefly to the Greeks. Herodotus also sets among the Persians

a discussion on the best form of government—democracy, oligarchy or monarchy. They are foreigners, enemies, but not completely different. They could even, in theory at least, be like the Greeks, in the same way that the Greeks in some respects resemble them.

Herodotus does not try to describe a series of mythical or historical events since their origins or even from one of the traditional milestones in Greek history, as other historians were to do after him. His field of study—the Median wars and the events that led up to them—covers a fairly recent period. That which is remote in time is left to poets and genealogists. He displays the same attitude towards Egypt, distinguishing what he has witnessed personally from the information he has collected from the Egyptians. If he consults Persian, Phoenician or Egyptian scholars about mythical episodes, such as the abduction of Helen and the Trojan War, it is mainly in order to retrace and understand the causes of the Median wars.

In choosing as his area of investigation recent history of which he could have direct knowledge, Herodotus had a decisive influence on the development of historiography. Thucydides, half a generation younger, would go even further than his great predecessor, directing his gaze to current events.

THE TWO THOUSAND YEARS' WAR

Walter Karp

AROUND THE TIME Republicans were vowing to "roll back Communism," a wise old college professor of mine suggested that his Humanities 1 class might get more out of Thucydides if it compared the Peloponnesian War to the ongoing struggle between America and Russia, then only recently named the Cold War. This, he assured us (quite needlessly), would not do violence to the great Athenian historian, since Thucydides himself believed that "human nature being what it is, events now past will recur in similar or analogous forms." Of the profundity of that remark Humanities 1 had not the slightest inkling. Nonetheless, analogies fell at our feet like ripe apples.

The combatants we identified readily. Authoritarian Sparta, ruling over a mass of terrified helots, was plainly the Soviet Union. Democratic Athens was America, of course. There were even neat correspondences between the two sets of foes. Sparta, as Thucydides tells us, was an insulated, agricultural, and sluggish state, rather like Russia. Athens, like America, was commercial, fast-moving, and far-ranging. "They are never at home," complained a Corinthian envoy to the Spartans, "and you are never away from it." In Athens and America, commerce and democracy seemed, 2,300 years apart, to have nurtured the very same kind of citizen. "I doubt if the world can produce a man," said great Pericles, "who, where he has only himself to depend upon, is equal to so many emergencies and graced by so happy a versatility as the Athenian." What the Athenians possessed, concluded Humanities 1, was Yankee ingenuity.

More striking than the analogies between past and present combatants were the resemblances between the two conflicts. In neither struggle do the enemies fight alone. Like America and the Soviet Union, Athens and Sparta are leaders of great confederations of inferior and subordinate allies. Similarly, they represent hostile political principles, Athens championing democracy, Sparta a traditional oligarchy. In the Peloponnesian War, as in the Cold War, the enemies are "ideological" foes. And neither is physically capable of winning. Sparta, with its invincible infantry, is so superior by land that Athens avoids pitched battles at all costs. Athens is so superior by sea that Spartan ships flee her peerless navy on sight. As a result, the Peloponnesian War, like the Cold War, is fought indirectly, peripherally, and spasmodically.

That was about as far as Humanities 1 got in its hunt for analogies between the ancient struggle for supremacy in Hellas and the ongoing struggle for supremacy in the modern world. Youth and ignorance doubtless limited our inquiry, but a greater handicap was the fact that the Peloponnesian War lasted twenty-seven years while the Cold War had not yet survived six.

THAT WAS NEARLY three decades ago, decades in which the struggle for supremacy between America and Russia did not cease for a single day. When I decided to reread Thucydides, the struggle was about to enter a new and more vigorous phase, under a newly elected president and a political faction that Thucydides would have unhesitatingly described as the war party. Two things struck me as I read: that the Cold War, now so long protracted, had come to resemble the Peloponnesian War more than ever and that in this resemblance lay a wholly unexpected vindication of political history, created by Thucydides, despised by the modern *eruditi*, and barely kept alive today by Grub Street hacks and doting amateurs.

The grounds for vindication are clear enough. Ancient Hellas and the modern world have nothing in common technologically, economically, or socially, none of those "factors" so dear to the hearts of the modern historian. If the ancient war and the modern war bear strong and essential resemblances, only political causes could have produced them; precisely those political causes that Thucydides' titanic genius found operating in the Peloponnesian War.

"Of the gods we believe, and of men we know," an Athenian envoy tells an ally of Sparta's, "that by a necessary law of their nature they rule wherever they can." Our nature as *political* beings is what Thucydides describes. Nothing compels men to enter the bright, dangerous arena of political action, but what lures them there—love of fame, power, glory, fortune, distinction—makes it fairly certain, a "law," that they will strive to rule over others. According to Pericles, Athenians, out of a love of splendid deeds and for the glory of their city, "forced every sea and land to be the highway of [their] daring." In doing so they also forged

2. GREECE AND ROME

a far-flung empire, which they had to struggle continuously to maintain; for if men strive for dominion, others strive to resist it. "You risk so much to retain your empire," the Athenian envoy is told, "and your subjects so much to get rid of it."

In the striving to gain dominion and in the inevitable struggle to maintain it, men produce one thing with certainty—they "make" history. Such was Thucydides' great discovery. History is the story woven by men's deeds, and the political nature of man provides a completely intelligible account of the story. That is why the great Athenian dared to predict that the tragic events of the Peloponnesian War would one day recur in similar forms.

CONSIDER THE ORIGINS of the Peloponnesian War. Thucydides describes the petty squabbles that poison relations between certain allies of mighty Sparta and those of upstart Athens. The squabbles set in motion the great train of events, but, like Soviet–American squabbles over the Yalta accords, they are not, says Thucydides, the "real cause" of the war. "The growth of the power of Athens and the alarm which this inspired in Lacedaemon [Sparta] made war inevitable."

In 432 B.C. the Hellenic world reached a political condition that the modern world was to duplicate in 1945 A.D.— and with much the same result. Two superpowers, Athens and Sparta, have so completely absorbed all the available power in Hellas that any further gain by one appears a menacing loss to the other. Under such conditions no real peace is possible. Of course if men and states accepted the diminution of their power there would have been no Peloponnesian War (and precious little human history), but that is just what men and states do not accept.

War with Sparta is unavoidable, Pericles tells the Athenian assembly (it is pondering whether to accede to a Spartan fiat), because "we must attempt to hand down our power to our posterity unimpaired." Moral scruple has nothing to do with it. The Athenian empire "is, to speak somewhat plainly, a tyranny," says Pericles, referring to Athens' crushing subjugation of her nominal allies. "To take it [the empire] perhaps was wrong, but to let it

go is unsafe." With respect to its unwilling allies, Athens resembles the Soviet Union and, like it, must expend a great deal of her strength keeping her "allies" down.

Because such tyranny is inherently unstable, Pericles urges his countrymen to fight a strategically defensive war and seek no "fresh conquests" in the course of it. The result of the Periclean policy reveals the extraordinary, history-making dynamism released by merely trying to hang on to one's own. Framed by a statesman of the highest genius, the policy scores a brilliant success and then leads Athens to its ultimate ruin.

To the astonishment of the Hellenic world, the newfangled Athenian navy, as Pericles foresaw, proves tactically superior to Sparta's great infantry, which the Athenians, safely walled up in their city, can avoid with impunity. Facing a foe so swift, so daring, so immune to injury, Sparta, after seven years of war, becomes deeply unnerved. "Being new to the experience of adversity," observes Thucydides, "they had lost all confidence in themselves."

Buoyed up by their unexpected triumphs over the traditional leader of Hellas, however, the Athenians fall prey to the fateful temptation inherent in all political action—rashness. Success "made them confuse their strength with their hopes," says Thucydides, providing, at least, a definition of political rashness that cannot be improved upon. After a Spartan garrison surrenders without a fight, something unprecedented in Spartan history, the Athenians are ripe for any daring folly; just as President Truman, blinded by General MacArthur's sweeping victory at Inchon, rashly attempted to conquer North Korea; and just as President Kennedy, puffed up by his Cuban missile triumph, was ripe for the Vietnam war—a confusion of strength and hope that drained the country of both.

The Peloponnesian War, like the Cold War, brings civil war and revolution in its wake. The political causes are the same in both cases. When states are at peace, hostile factions and classes within countries are willing to rub along together. But when the great powers are desperately competing for allies, domestic rivals are no longer willing to preserve internal peace. Popular leaders can call on the opposing power to put their domestic enemies to

the sword; oligarchic factions, to set their own cities aflame.

Love of dominion, the desire for "the first place in the city" (never far from the surface in peacetime), convulses all Hellas in wartime. Men betray their own cities without scruple and cheer foreigners for killing their own countrymen. Political exiles, aided by foreign powers, wage ceaseless war against their own cities. The Peloponnesian War, which spawns a half dozen analogues of the Bay of Pigs and of Moscow-trained revolutionary brigades, blights the integrity of the city-state, just as the Cold War now erodes the integrity of the nation-state.

ATHENS IS by no means immune to the war's corrupting effects on domestic politics. At one point Athenians undergo a spasm of political paranoia that duplicates with remarkable fidelity the American McCarthy era. The causes here, too, are the same, as the sequence of events clearly shows. Shortly after the Spartan garrison's stunning surrender, Sparta humbly sues for peace, and the Athenians, a little out of breath themselves, reluctantly and ruefully accept. Thucydides regards the peace, which lasts six years, as a mere incident in a continuous war. It was, says Thucydides, "an unstable armistice [that] did not prevent either party doing the other the most effectual injury."

The chief reason for the instability is the emergence in Athens of a self-serving war party. Ten years have passed since the outbreak of war. Great Pericles is dead; new men have arisen with ambitions of their own, Pericles' own ward Alcibiades among them. The Periclean policy of deadlock, based on the determination to preserve past glories, does not content them. They want to win fresh glory for themselves, and with it, says Thucydides, "the undisturbed direction of the people." Their real complaint about the peace with Sparta is that it is an unambitious use of Athenian power (which is exactly what the American foes of détente believe).

Confusing strength with hope, the leaders of the war party think Athens can do far more than merely hold Sparta at bay; it can destroy Spartan pretensions forever. Like the Republicans of 1951–52, the war party will accept, in effect, "no substitute for victory." Like millions of Americans in 1951–52, the Athenian people, "persuaded that nothing could withstand them," find deadlock exasperating. Why must irresistible Athens suffer the endless tensions of the unstable armistice? Is it possible that there are oligarchy-loving pro-Spartans in their midst?

A shocking act of impiety, analogous to the Alger Hiss trial, turns baseless suspicion into angry conviction: "oligarchical and monarchical" Athenians are conspiring to subvert the democratic constitution. The enraged citizenry demands arrests; blatant perjurers supply the evidence; nonconformists, including Alcibiades, fall prey to the mania. At the war's outset Pericles had proudly noted the extraordinary personal freedom enjoyed by Athenians, who "do not feel called upon to be angry with our neighbor for doing what he likes." Now those

who live differently from their neighbors fall under suspicion of treason. A war begun to safeguard the power of a democracy profoundly corrupts democracy.

Firmly in control of a rapidly degenerating polity, the war party launches its grandiose plan to tilt the balance of power once and for all against the Spartans. Beyond the little world of Hellas, across the Ionian Sea, lie the broad island of Sicily and a dozen Greek colonial city-states. The Athenians, as Thucydides icily remarks, do not even know Sicily's size; they are ignorantly contemptuous of the island's colonial "rabble." Nonetheless, the self-vaunting, overconfident Athenians intend to conquer it and use that huge accession of imperial power to throw down Sparta itself. When an opponent of the enterprise warns Athenians of the enormous costs and hazards of a war so far from home, enthusiasm for the expedition grows even warmer.

In the seventeenth year of the Peloponnesian War, "by far the most

costly and splendid Hellenic force that had ever been sent out by a single city" sets sail for faraway Sicily. Vietnam is but a pale analogy to what fortune inflicts on the great armada. Thucydides' account of its hideous, heartbreaking fate—how its leaders blundered, how its strength drained away, how its dauntless Athenian oarsmen, the backbone of the democracy, lost their nerve and their courage—is one of the great feats of historical writing. On the hostile shores of a distant island, before the walls of an underestimated enemy, the power of Athens crumbles away forever.

Since the Cold War continues with no end in sight, its story remains incomplete. Still, it seems fairly certain even now that the same principle that makes the Peloponnesian War intelligible, 2,300 years after its end, will make the Cold War intelligible to posterity: "Of the gods we believe, and of men we know, that by a necessary law of their nature they rule wherever they can."

A Patriot for whom?

Rebel without a cause?
Paul Cartledge probes
whether the chequered
career of one of fifth-
century Athens' most
famous sons reveals more
about conflicting codes of
loyalty than just the
machinations of a
turncoat.

ALCIBIADES OF ATHENS

IN THE *POETICS* ARISTOTLE TRIED to distil the quintessence of poetry and history:

> Poetry is something more philosophical and worthy of serious attention than history. For while poetry is concerned with universal truths, history treats of particular facts ... what, say, Alcibiades did, or what happened to him.

Readers of *History Today* ought not, perhaps, to be bowled over by this *parti pris*. But the quotation does incontrovertibly show that Alcibiades, thanks above all to Thucydides, was one of the most famous characters of Classical Greece. Or rather one of the most notorious, as a brief life may suggest.

He was born in about 451 BC at the very apex of the Athenian aristocratic élite. Yet he was born into the most radical democracy the world had yet – or maybe has ever – known. As we shall see, this contradiction or tension between aristocracy and democracy, and their respective codes, lies at the heart of Alcibiades' apparently shameless betrayal of his *patris* ('fatherland', whence ultimately our 'patriotism').

Following his father's death in battle in 447 he was brought up in the household of his guardian and cousin, Pericles, then at the height of his influence over the fortunes of Athens' democratic political system at home and empire overseas. In 432 Alcibiades saw his first military service, in northern Greece. Here Athens was suppressing a major revolt within her Aegean maritime empire that preluded the outbreak of the Great Peloponnesian War in 431. This war was begun by Sparta and her allies ostensibly to liberate Athens' subject-allies from Athenian imperial tyranny; in reality (so Thucydides persuasively argued) Sparta felt that her precarious domestic security was being intolerably jeopardised by the seemingly inexorable growth of Athenian power.

In 424 Alcibiades participated – as a cavalryman, since he belonged to the very few richest Athenians – in a campaign designed to give Athens a stranglehold on central Greece. The campaign was a failure and so corroborated the views of those like Nikias who began to advocate peace with Sparta. But it also reportedly gave Alcibiades his chance to repay in kind his former teacher Socrates for

having saved his life in 432.

By 422 Alcibiades had contracted a lucrative marriage to the daughter of possibly the richest Athenian of all. But before he could capitalise on his wealth and connections by being elected to Athens' highest office, the Generalship, peace was indeed made with Sparta in 421. The Peace of Nikias, however, proved to be a phoney peace, and Alcibiades was prominent among those would-be demagogues (in its original sense of 'leaders of the People') who were happy to keep it that way. Between 420 and 416 he combined lavish expenditure on public and private projects with risky but on balance successful diplomacy that skilfully exploited his personal connections with high-ranking politicians in Sparta and Argos. He thereby raised himself in popular esteem onto a level at least equal to that of the comparably rich and ambitious but more cautious and unoriginal Nikias. Indeed, the rivalry and parity between these two became such that early in 416 recourse was had to the procedure of ostracism.

The main aim of this device, which had served its turn a dozen times in

From *History Today*, October 1987, pp. 15-21. Reproduced by kind permission of History Today, Ltd., 83-84 Berwick Street, London W1V 3PJ, England.

the seventy years since its first operation, was to prevent the sparks generated by rival popular leaders with crucially opposed policies from igniting into civil war. At least 6,000 citizens (perhaps 20 per cent of the citizen body in 416) had to vote, and the 'candidate' with the most votes cast against him was forced into a sort of honourable exile for ten years. The air was then cleared, and the programme of the victor implemented the more harmoniously. In 416, however, the two prime 'candidates' colluded, and a third, less prominent politician received his marching orders. Its purpose thwarted, ostracism was reasonably enough never employed again. But in 415 the flawed legacy of the cynical manoeuvre of Alcibiades and Nikias became painfully apparent.

In an atmosphere inimical to calm deliberation the Athenians voted for a vast naval expedition to conquer Sicily or at any rate its most powerful Greek city, Syracuse. Even Alcibiades, though he favoured expansionist imperialism in the west as a means of turning the cold war against Sparta into a hot one, had not recommended so large an enterprise. And he was less than entirely thrilled by the appointment of Nikias, who opposed the expedition on principle, as one of his fellow commanders-in-chief. To cap it all, an unholy combination of Alcibiades' political enemies – rival demagogues, ideological anti-democrats, pragmatic opponents of the Sicilian (ad)venture – secured his recall to face a grave charge of impiety shortly after the armada had left Peiraeus.

An earlier attempt to stop the expedition by means of the sacrilegious and inauspicious mutilation of Herms (ithyphallic pillars representing Hermes, the god of travel and fertility amongst much else) had not succeeded. But in the climate of superstitious terror whipped up thereby it not unnaturally proved possible to persuade the Assembly to recall Alcibiades for trial on a charge of profaning the Mysteries of Eleusis by mimicking their awesome rituals in private houses without proper priestly supervision. In due course some fifty people, including Alcibiades and his paternal uncle, Axiokhos, were convicted of either mutilating the Hermes or profaning the Mysteries and condemned to

death or exile. Their extensive property was confiscated and sold at public auction, and in 414 details of this sale of the century were laboriously inscribed on stone for public display in the approved democratic manner.

By then, though, Alcibiades was far from home both spiritually and geographically. He was ensconced in, of all places, Sparta, where chameleon-like he had adapted himself to such properly Spartan austerities as a pallet of river-reeds in place of his accustomed soft-furnished bed. For in 415, while being officially escorted back to Athens from Sicily, Alcibiades and his entourage had jumped ship in southern Italy and made their way to the seat of Athens' principal enemy who had accorded them an honorific reception. In short, Alcibiades had defected.

If we are to believe Thucydides, it was the advice Alcibiades gave his Spartan hosts that helped transform the course of the Peloponnesian War. Athens' total defeat at Syracuse in 413 followed shortly on the Spartan occupation of a fort well within Athens' borders and in easy striking distance of the city itself. Soon after that Sparta made her first serious venture into the formerly Athenian waters of the Aegean which promoted defections by some of Athens' most important allies.

By late 412, however, Alcibiades had thoroughly alienated one of the two Spartan kings and, more to the point, exhausted his obvious credit and utility as a defector. Caught between Spartan and Athenian hostility he therefore emulated another wily and foresighted Athenian popular leader of an earlier generation, Themistocles, and decamped to Tissaphernes, the Persian *generalissimo* in the west. For Persia was no less anxious than Sparta to exploit Athens' temporary naval weakness, and at the very least Alcibiades could present himself as a valuable source of information on both Athens and Sparta.

Unlike Themistocles, though, Alcibiades seems always to have intended to use his turn to Persia as a way of achieving his recall, with honour, to his native city. For he bent his considerable charm and diplomatic adroitness towards persuading Tissaphernes to abandon Sparta in favour of Athens, so that he might be

hailed home as a reward for securing sorely needed Persian financial aid. But Tissaphernes was not to be persuaded. His aim was that Sparta and Athens should conduct a war of mutual attrition to Persia's and his benefit. Moreover, at Athens in 411 bitter and bloody civil strife culminated in the replacement of democracy by a regime of narrow oligarchy. So Alcibiades, seeing that the oligarchy was dominated by enemies of his and offered no hope of recall, presented himself instead to the staunchly democratic fleet based on Samos as the indispensable middleman between them and Tissaphernes' moneybags. Remarkably, the ploy succeeded, despite both Alcibiades' lack of ideological commitment to democracy and his failure to deliver the Persian goods, not to mention the distrust of him engendered by his proneness to defection.

So it was that Alcibiades, who had helped Athens lose part of her empire, yet found himself a rôle among the leaders of the Samos-based democracy-in-exile. At least he performed the unambiguously patriotic act of dissuading the fleet from sailing from Samos to overthrow the oligarchy, since that would have lost them the rest of the empire and so cost them the Peloponnesian War. In any case, the extreme oligarchy was replaced after only a few months by a more moderate oligarchic regime that Thucydides hailed as the best, ideologically and practically speaking, form of government Athens enjoyed in his lifetime; and this regime formally invited Alcibiades to return home.

But it was not long before full, radical democracy was restored at Athens in 410, and Alcibiades preferred to build up a healthy credit balance of goodwill and obligation at Athens as well as Samos before venturing to set foot again on native soil. Between 410 and 408 he had at least a hand in such successes as the Battle of Kyzikos, which even stirred the Spartans to sue for peace, and the recovery of Byzantium, crucially situated to control the passage of merchantmen bringing vital South Russian wheat to overpopulated Athens. Early in 407 Athens at last gave Alcibiades the signals he had been waiting for by cancelling the conviction of 415 and electing him General.

Greek cavalrymen (from a sixth-century vase) — members of an elite officer-class whose loyalty to each other sometimes transcended that to their polis.

Thus in summer 407 Alcibiades returned to his *patris* and to a hero's welcome after an absence of eight years. Ever the able propagandist, he led that year's procession of initiates to Eleusis to celebrate the Mysteries and, for the first time since the occupation of Dekeleia in 413, he conducted it by land along the Sacred Way under the noses almost of the Spartan garrison. With their morale high the Athenians appointed Alcibiades their Supreme Commander. No doubt this was a pragmatic measure, but it was also a symbolic honour not accorded even to Pericles.

By now, though, Athenian public funds were desperately straitened, whereas the finances of Sparta had recently received a sudden boost, thanks to the accord between the Spartan admiral Lysander and Cyrus, the young Persian prince who had displaced Tissaphernes as supreme Persian commander in the Aegean sphere. On one of his inevitable fund-raising side-trips Alcibiades rashly entrusted the Athenian fleet to a personal friend, a skilled steersman rather than experienced commander, who against advice engaged with Lysander at Notion and lost. Alcibiades prudently decided not to return to the fleet, let alone Athens, and so anticipated the inevitable sen-

tence of death or exile dealt out to those whom the Athenian people deemed to have deceived or otherwise failed them. Instead, he retired for the rest of the war to a sort of barony he had carved out in advance in the Thracian Chersonese (Gallipoli peninsula).

In the spring of 404 Athens eventually capitulated through starvation to the blockade of Lysander, who utilised Sparta's (and Persia's) military victory to instal the kind of oligarchic puppet regime at Athens that he favoured as the instrument for Sparta's assumption of all Athens' former Aegean-wide empire. These 'Thirty Tyrants' — a sobriquet they richly merited for their savagely brutal as well as unconstitutionally dictatorial rule — placed Alcibiades high on their death-list, not so much for his political opinions as for his potential leadership of a democratic resistance abroad. Lysander was easily convinced that Alcibiades was best done away with, and the assassination was performed on Persian orders in Phrygia.

* * * * *

Modern discussion of Alcibiades' career normally follows the lead of Thucydides by trying to assess his part in Athens' catastrophic defeat in the Peloponnesian War. But the rôle in

history of individuals, no matter how heroic or charismatic, is always problematic, and the question of his patriotism or lack of it is not less intriguing, much more topical and above all potentially soluble on the evidence we have. What must be determined, therefore, is what it might have meant for a Greek of the fifth century BC, specifically an Athenian Greek, to be or be thought to be 'patriotic', and how the behaviour of Alcibiades fits into any pattern of patriotic (or otherwise) activity and mentality that we may be able to discern or create.

The first point to establish is a negative one. The locus and focus of patriotic feeling in Classical Greece was not and could not have been the nation-state that we in the twentieth century have come to know and love-hate. For there was no Greek nation. Or rather, such 'national', that is panhellenic, consciousness as did undoubtedly exist did not contain a properly political, state-oriented component or at any rate not one strong enough to result in a stable, panhellenic federation of states. A famous passage of Herodotus is decisive on this score, alike because of its rarity and its content. When in 480/79 the Spartans feared the Athenians might go over to the Persians, the Athenians – according to Herodotus – haughtily reassured them that they could not possibly do so: not just for selfish reasons, but on account of (literally) 'the Greek thing' or (to paraphrase) the fact of being Greek. This was constituted, they said, by common language, blood-relationship, common religious and other social mores. To be traitors to 'the Greek thing', they added, would not be well.

The context in which this passage is set, the massive Persian invasion of Greece, was of course unique in Greek history, and Herodotus may fairly be suspected of giving a persuasive definition of a concept that for most Greeks most of the time was at most latent. But it does at least show that the notion of treachery to some panhellenic entity beyond and above their immediate political horizons was conceivable in the lifetime of Alcibiades, since he was in his early twenties when Herodotus was putting the finishing touches to his history in the bitter knowledge that

Athens and Sparta were then, again, at war. However, as that Peloponnesian War classically illustrated, inchoate panhellenic consciousness was not proof against other, narrower loyalties. For in place of the nation or its political embodiment, the nation-state, the Classical Greeks typically situated feelings that we might want to label patriotic within the smaller, intensely localised frame of the *polis*.

The nature of the Classical *polis* was the subject of Aristotle's 'Matters relating to the *Polis*' or *Politics*. Like Herodotus, Aristotle was guilty of some persuasive definition, most famously his usually misunderstood contention that mankind was designed by its nature to achieve its proper end and realise the good life only within the *polis* state-form. But he was also enough of an empirical investigator and impartial analyst to discern that the essence of the *polis* resided in the notion of *politeia* – that is, citizenship construed full-bloodedly as eligibility to participate equally in the holding of political office and the making of judicial and other public decisions. Since *politeia* was regarded as the very life and soul of a Classical Greek community, the citizens of a *polis* were indeed political animals in both our and Aristotle's very different senses.

It seems to have been the Spartans who first articulated the idea of the *polis* as the be-all and end-all of a man's (not woman's – the *polis* has aptly been called a men's club) social existence. But, as in most other respects, here too the Spartans represented the extreme version of a generally accepted Greek view of life. Loyalty to one's *polis*, in other words, was supposed to be total and unconditional, subsuming and if necessary overriding the affective and instrumental ties woven by family, schooling, friendship, religious association or whatever. As Sophocles' Kreon put it, when Alcibiades was about ten, 'he who counts another greater friend/than his own fatherland, him I put nowhere' (*Antigone* lines 182-3).

Perhaps the most famous and unquestionably the most immediately relevant instance of this *polis*-patriotism in deed was the refusal of Socrates to evade, by flight into exile, the sentence of death for impiety imposed on him in 399 by an Athenian People's Court that duly incarnated the lawful sovereignty of the Athenian democracy. Why, then, did Socrates' most famous pupil not see things in the same way in 415? Why did Alcibiades not merely not return to stand trial at Athens but actually seek and receive political asylum from Athens' deadliest enemies, to whom he gave both advice and practical service that damaged his *patris*? Was he acting out of purely selfish, opportunistic motives, or from a peculiar sort of inverted patriotism, or in accordance with an alternative and diametrically opposed politico-moral code to that sponsored officially by the *polis*? Evidence and arguments can be brought in support of all three of these. But, as I shall hope to show, it is the third explanation that best accounts for his seemingly egregious conduct.

Without doubt Alcibiades was both egoistic and egotistic. But these were not simply contingent traits of his personal character. They were also a faithful reflection of the structure of Athenian society and politics. Classical Athens was for most purposes what Peter Laslett has called a 'face-to-face' society; it was also an extraordinarily competitive society. High politics in such an environment was a zero-sum game, defeat in which meant not merely the loss of a deposit but the loss of one's life, whether literally or, in the shape of exile tantamount to civic death, figuratively. Naturally enough, therefore, 'issues were very readily translated into terms of "face"' (as Dover puts it), as on at least two important occasions in Alcibiades' career.

The first was in the late 420s. Alcibiades had gone out of his way to look after the interests of some 120 Spartan prisoners of war whom the Athenians were holding as hostages. Nevertheless, the Spartans had preferred to negotiate peace terms through Nikias and another Athenian politician rather than himself – and that despite his family's long-standing personal connections with Sparta (of

A city siege — from the Xanthos 'Monument of the Nereids', c.400 BC.

Warriors running with shields (c.500 BC); the fractured nature of Greek city-state society meant that not only was warfare endemic but also internal strife, and 'foreign intervention' to support one warring ideological faction against another was commonplace.

ALCIBIADES: KEY DATES	
c.451	Born to Kleinias and Deinomakhe
432	First military service
431	Outbreak of Peloponnesian War
424	Fights at Delion
c.422	Marriage to Hipparete
421	Peace of Nikias
420	Elected General for first time
418	Battle of Mantineia
416	Ostracism of Hyperbolos Chariot-victory at Olympic Games
415	Appointed to joint command of Sicilian Expedition, recalled to face impiety charge, defects to Sparta
413	Athens defeated in Sicily, Sparta occupies Dekeleia
412	Defects from Sparta to Persia
411	Oligarchic counter-revolutions at Athens: A. appointed general by democracy-in-exile
410	Battle of Kyzikos, restoration of democracy at Athens
410-08	Commands fleets in approaches to Black Sea
407	Elected General by restored democracy, returns to Athens, appointed Supreme Commander, leads celebration of Eleusinian Mysteries
406	Battle of Notion, second (and final) exile
404	Athens loses Peloponnesian War, imposition of oligarchic junta by Sparta, assassination of A. in Phrygia

which more anon). Alcibiades therefore felt justified, and perhaps moved, to foul up the uneasy Athens-Sparta *détente* of 421 by any means available.

In that case, however, the policy which Alcibiades helped persuade the Athenians to adopt towards Sparta can certainly not be labelled unpatriotic and might even be considered to have furthered Athens' best interests abroad. Not so, of course, his behaviour in 415. True, 'face' was again involved, but the actions he took in response were quite clearly treasonous, both on the ancient definition of *prodosia* ('betrayal') and any modern definition of patriotism. So loss of face is hardly a sufficient explanation.

Could it be, then, that (as Hatzfeld believed) his flight to Sparta and the advice he gave his state's enemies

represented an inversion of patriotism, that is the venting of feelings of frustrated love for the *patris* that had rejected him by harming it as much as he could, combined perhaps with the pragmatic notion that the Athenians might be induced to cut their losses and recall him? No doubt personal psychology and cultural conditioning had something to do with it. It has recently been said of the conductor Wilhelm Furtwängler, who in 1934 was suddenly stripped of all his high honours and positions, that he was too profoundly German in his innermost being to contemplate a life outside Germany, and the same might be suggested, *mutatis mutandis*, of Alcibiades. Again, however, such a hypothesis seems to me to lack adequate explanatory force; and it has to be said that if Alcibiades did wishfully think the Athenians would move

quickly to recall him from Sparta he was being uncharacteristically unrealistic.

It is time therefore to consider how Thucydides represented Alcibiades' own perception of his behaviour. For Thucydides was a fellow-Athenian, fellow-aristocrat and fellow-exile, who could consult Alcibiades in person as an equal and whose mentality and ideology were not perhaps very distant from his. And in accordance with his usual historiographical practice, when he wanted to dramatise and bring out the underlying essentials of a critical situation, Thucydides wrote an apologetic speech purporting to represent what Alcibiades said before the Spartan assembly in 415.

Three passages in this speech bear most relevantly on our topic. First, and most celebrated, Alcibiades' own definition of *polis*-patriotism, what he calls *to philopoli* or 'the *polis*-loving thing':

> The Athens I love is not the one which is wronging me now but that one in which I used to have secure enjoyment of my rights as a citizen. The state that I am attacking does not seem to me to be mine any longer; it is rather that I am trying to recover a state that has ceased to be mine.

On one level this is a piece of self-serving sophistry, just the sort of thing a man educated in the super-subtle, immoral rhetoric castigated by Aristophanes as typically Socratic would say. But it is not simply sophistical. For what Alcibiades is claiming is the right to define and identify the state of Athens in terms of his own political evaluation.

This passage derives its full flavour and significance from an earlier, almost throw-away remark, that democracy in the eyes of prudent men like himself – and his oligarchically minded Spartan audience – was 'an acknowledged madness'. For Alcibiades, despite or because of his upbringing within Pericles' household, was not ideologically a radical democrat; and to men like him democracy was not government of the people by the people for the people, but mob-rule, the dictatorship of the proletariat – that is, the dictation of policy by the ignorant and poor mass of Athenian citizens to their rich and aristocratic superiors. Hence it could seem to him perfectly reasonable not to feel obligated, politically or morally, to respond to his recall by the Athenian democratic state.

This attitude was not idiosyncratic, let alone unique to Alcibiades. On the contrary, it was precisely this essentially class-based political morality, which arose out of the constant struggle between rich and poor citizens for control of their *polis*, that explains the otherwise puzzlingly frequent and widespread occurrence of betrayals of their state to a foreign power by either oligarchs or democrats. It was, they reckoned, better to have power within their own *polis*, even at the cost of subjection to a foreign state, than to be enslaved to their class enemies among their fellow-citizens.

Both oligarchs and democrats, then, might regularly feel no compunction about 'treason'. There was, though, a further institutional reason why aristocrats like Alcibiades, who were usually oligarchic in outlook, were particularly prone to be actively involved in betraying their states. This reason is implicit in my third passage from Alcibiades' speech at Sparta, where he refers to his family connections with the *polis* in which he now found himself a refugee.

His ancestors, he says, used to hold the hereditary post of *proxenos*, official diplomatic representative, of Sparta's and Spartans' interests at Athens. Classical Greek states did not maintain permanent ambassadorial missions to other states but instead appointed leading citizens of states with which they had regular dealings to the honorific post of *proxenos*. Naturally the men so appointed were ones who already had strong personal links with the state in question, specifically those who had contracted or inherited a bond of *xenia*, ritualised guest-friendship, with a leading citizen of the appointing state. Hence the term *proxenia*, substitute *xenia*, since the *proxenos* represented the interests not just of his own particular guest-friends but of all the citizens of the state which appointed him.

Xenia as an institution was characteristically aristocratic and had developed across the Greek world before the *polis* and its community ethic had arisen. Yet it was not abandoned when the *polis* officially assumed all interstate responsibilities, since it was a valuable channel of contact and communication between states that were all too often in conflict. At the same time, however, its preservation involved the continuous risk that a private tie of *xenia* might contradict the needs and interests of the *polis* to which the guest-friends belonged, most conspicuously in time of war. For the sacred power of the bond of *xenia* was so great that aristocratic guest-friends by no means always found the civic ideology of the *polis* compelling. It is within that institutional framework that Alcibiades' behaviour *vis-à-vis* Athens and Sparta in 415 can at last be most satisfactorily explained.

For it was through a tie of *xenia* that the originally Spartan name Alcibiades had been introduced into the Athenian aristocracy about a century before the birth of our Alcibiades; and this hereditary personal tie was still actively operating in the late fifth century between Alcibiades of Athens and Endios son of Alcibiades of Sparta, a leading aristocrat. Thus although Endios in 420 (when he was a member of an abortive Spartan embassy to Athens) and Alcibiades in 415 could rightly be held to be acting contrary to the officially designated interests of their respective states, on

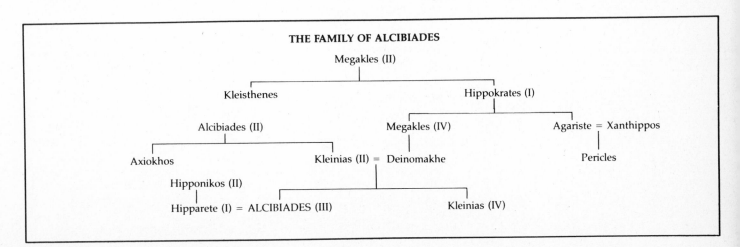

THE FAMILY OF ALCIBIADES

Megakles (II)

Kleisthenes — Hippokrates (I)

Alcibiades (II) — Megakles (IV) — Agariste = Xanthippos

Axiokhos — Kleinias (II) = Deinomakhe — Pericles

Hipponikos (II)

Hipparete (I) = ALCIBIADES (III) — Kleinias (IV)

both occasions they were also fulfilling what they took to be the prior and overriding personal obligations of the aristocratic, pre-political code of *xenia*. The contrast between the behaviour of Alcibiades and that of Pericles, who in 431 went out of his way publicly to neutralise in advance any possible adverse effects of his *xenia* with the Spartan king Arkhidamos, could not be more palpable or revealing.

For whom, then, was Alcibiades a patriot? For himself partly, since that was the law of the intensely competitive political jungle in which would-be Athenian demagogues operated. For his *patris*, Athens, in the weak sense that other things being equal Alcibiades wished to be top dog in Athens rather than any other state. But against that must be set the essential point that patriotism – in the sense of disinterested and unconditional love of his *polis* – was neither affectively nor instrumentally the mainspring of Alcibiades' political career. The *polis* of Athens was not an abstraction like our 'state' or 'country', but concretely the rule of the poor majority of Athenian citizens over (as Alcibiades saw it) their social and intellectual betters. He could never have been brought to endorse the dictum uttered by the quintessential democratic patriot Demosthenes: 'The most valuable thing in man's life is supporting the policy of the many and having the same friends and enemies as one's *patris'*.

FOR FURTHER READING:
J. Hatzfeld, *Alcibiade. Étude sur l'histoire d'Athènes à la fin du Ve siècle* (Paris, 1940); P.J. Rhodes, 'What Alcibiades did or what happened to him' (Durham Inaugural Lecture, 1985); H.D. Westlake, *Individuals in Thucydides* (Cambridge University Press, 1968); C.W. Macleod, *Collected Essays* (Oxford University Press, 1983); D.M. MacDowell, *The Law in Classical Athens* (London 1978); K.J. Dover, *Greek Popular Morality* (Blackwell, 1974); N.M. Pusey, *Harvard Studies in Classical Philology* vol. 51 (1940); G. Herman, *Ritualised friendship and the Greek City* (Cambridge University Press, 1987); M.I. Finley, *The Use and Abuse of History* (London, 1986); F.W. Walbank, *Selected Papers* (Cambridge University Press, 1985).

Love and Death in Ancient Greece

Catching him in the act, an obscure citizen of Athens slew his wife's lover. But was it a crime of passion—or premeditated murder?

Kenneth Cavander

Euphiletos was tired. He had been out in the country all day attending to business, and now he was home trying to get some sleep, and the baby was crying. His house was on two floors; the baby slept with a maid on the first floor; above, there was a combined living-dining-sleeping area for him and his wife. Euphiletos told his wife to go downstairs and nurse the baby. She protested that she wanted to be with him; she'd missed him while he was in the country—or did he just want to get rid of her so that he could make a pass at the maid, as he had the time he got drunk? Euphiletos laughed at that and at last his wife agreed to go downstairs and hush the child, but she insisted on locking the door to their room. Euphiletos turned over and went back to sleep. It never occurred to him to ask why his wife had gone through the charade of keeping him away from the maid, or why she had spent the rest of the night downstairs. But a few days later something happened that made him ask these questions, and by the end of the month a man was dead, killed in full view of a crowd of neighbors and friends.

This drama took place nearly two thousand five hundred years ago in ancient Athens. The characters were none of the brilliant and celebrated figures of the times—Socrates, Plato, Euripides, Aristophanes, Alcibiades—but members of the Athenian lower-middle class, obscure people who receded into the shadows of history. Their story is a soap opera compared to the grander tragedies being played out at the festivals of Dionysos in the theatre cut into the slopes of the Acropolis.

By a quirk of fate and an accident of politics the speech written for the murder trial that climaxes this story was the work of a man named Lysias. As a boy, Lysias sat in the company of Plato and Socrates, who often visited his father's house. As an adult, he was active in politics, and when a coup by the opposition party sent his family into exile, his property was confiscated and he narrowly escaped with his life. But a countercoup soon allowed him to return to Athens, and Lysias, now without a livelihood, had to find a profession.

He found one in the Athenian legal system. Athenian law was complex and attorneys were unknown; every citizen had to prosecute or defend himself in person. As a result, a class of professional legal advisers emerged that made a living supplying litigants with cogent, legally sound briefs. In time, Lysias became one of the most sought-after of these speech writers and several examples of his elegant and literate Greek style have been preserved, including the speech written for the defendant in this case.

Euphiletos, like many Athenians of modest means, lived in a small house in the city and commuted to the country to attend to his farm or market garden. He cannot have been well-off, for his house had the minimum number of slaves—one. Even a sausage seller or baker had at least one slave. Euphiletos had recently married and he was a trusting husband, so he said, giving his wife anything she asked for, never questioning her movements, trying to please her in every possible way. The most exciting event in the marriage was the birth of their child, whom his wife nursed herself. But the most significant event was the death of his mother: the whole family attended the funeral and, although Euphiletos did not know it at the time, his marriage was laid to rest that day along with his mother.

After the birth of their child Euphiletos and his wife had rearranged their living quarters. It was too dangerous to carry the baby up and down the steep ladder to the upper floor every time the child needed to be washed or changed, so the family was split up. Euphiletos and his wife moved into the upper part of the house, while the baby, with the slave girl to look after it, stayed downstairs.

The arrangement worked well, and Euphiletos's wife often went down in the middle of the night to be with the baby when it was cranky. But on the evening of the day Euphiletos came back tired from the country, two things in addition to the little drama of the locked door struck him as unusual. One was his wife's makeup: it was only a month since her brother had died—yet he noticed that she had put powder on her face. And there were noises in the night that sounded like a hinge creaking. When his wife awakened him by unlocking the bedroom door the next morning, Euphiletos asked her about these sounds. She said she had gone next door to a neighbor's house to borrow some oil for the baby's night light, which had gone out. As for the makeup, when Euphiletos thought about it he remembered his wife saying how much she had missed him and how

"Love and Death in Ancient Greece," by Kenneth Cavander, *Horizon*, Spring 1974.

47

reluctantly she had left him to go down and take care of the baby. Reassured, he dismissed the whole episode from his mind and thought no more about it—until something happened to shatter this comforting domestic picture and rearrange all the pieces of the puzzle in quite a different way.

One morning, a few days later, Euphiletos was leaving his house when he was stopped in the street by an old woman. She apologized for taking his time. "I'm not trying to make trouble," she said, "but we have an enemy in common." The old woman was a slave. Her mistress, she said, had been having an affair, but her lover had grown tired of her and left her for another woman. The other woman was Euphiletos's wife.

"The man is called Eratosthenes," said the old slave. "Ask your maid about him. He's seduced several women. He's got it down to a fine art."

In the midst of his shock and anger Euphiletos revealed a streak of something methodical, almost detached, in his character. Instead of going straight to his wife or her lover, he proceeded like an accountant investigating an error in the books.

He retraced his steps to his house and ordered the maidservant to come with him to the market. His wife would see nothing unusual in this, for respectable married women did not go out shopping in fifth-century Athens. That was left to the men and the slaves. Halfway to the market Euphiletos turned aside and marched the girl to the house of a friend, where he confronted her with the old woman's story. The girl denied it. Euphiletos threatened to beat her. She told him to go ahead and do what he liked. He talked of prison. She still denied it. Then Euphiletos mentioned Eratosthenes' name, and she broke down. In return for a promise that she would not be harmed, she told Euphiletos everything.

Her story was bizarre as well as comic and macabre. It began at the funeral of Euphiletos's mother. Eratosthenes had seen Euphiletos's wife among the mourners and had taken a fancy to her. He got in touch with the maid and persuaded her to act as go-between. Whether it was a difficult or an easy seduction we don't know; but, as the old woman had said, Eratosthenes was a practiced hand.

This love affair, first planned at a funeral and then set in motion by proxy, was carried on mostly at Euphiletos's house when he was away in the country. On one occasion his wife may have contrived to meet her lover away from the house, for she had gone with Eratosthenes' mother to the festival of the Thesmophoria, one of several festivals celebrated in honor of feminine deities. During these festivals a woman could leave the seclusion of her own house without arousing suspicious comment.

The slave girl also told Euphiletos that on the night he came back tired from the country, her mistress had told her to pinch the baby to make it cry, which gave her an excuse to go downstairs. His wife's parade of jealousy, Euphiletos now realized, was an act, designed to provide her with a reason to lock the door on him. So while he was a temporary prisoner in his own bedroom, his wife was downstairs in the nursery with her lover, and the maid was keeping the baby quiet somewhere else.

In a crisis, a person will often revert to archetypal behavior. For the Greeks of the fifth century B.C. the Homeric poems provided a mythological blueprint for almost any life situation, and it is interesting to see how Euphiletos's next move re-created a scene out of the legends. In *The Odyssey* Homer tells the story of what happened when Hephaistos, the god of fire, found out that his wife, Aphrodite, had been sleeping with the war god, Ares. Hephaistos decided not to face Aphrodite with her infidelity; instead, he wove a magical net that was sprung by the two lovers when they climbed into bed together. Then, as they lay there trapped, Hephaistos invited the other Olympians to come and view the guilty pair, "and the unquenchable laughter of the gods rose into the sky." In his own mundane way, but without the magic net, Euphiletos would follow the example of Hephaistos. He made his slave promise to keep everything she had told him a secret; then, pretending to his wife that he suspected nothing, he went about his business as usual and waited for a chance to spring his trap.

The part of cuckold is a mortifying one to play, and it was particularly so in ancient Athens where the relative status of men and women was so unequal. A freeborn Athenian woman was free in little more than name. She could not vote, make contracts, or conduct any business involving more than a certain sum of money; legally she was little more than a medium for the transmission of property from grandfather to grandchildren through the dowry she brought with her to her husband. Her husband, of course, was invariably chosen for her by her father or by the nearest male relative if her father was dead. Almost the only thing she could call her own was her reputation, which depended on good behavior, an unassertive demeanor, a life spent dutifully spinning, weaving, dyeing clothes, cooking, bearing and raising children, and, above all, on not interfering in the serious business of life as conducted by the men. In a famous speech in praise of the Athenian men who died during the Peloponnesian War, Pericles makes only one reference to women: according to Thucydides, who reports the speech in his history of the war, Pericles said that women should never give rise to any comment by a man, favorable or unfavorable. In the tragic dramas, moreover, women who offer their opinions unasked or who go about alone in public usually feel they have to apologize for behaving in such a brazen and immodest way.

Such was the official status of women. Unofficially, the women of ancient Athens found ways, as their sisters have done in every age and culture, to undermine the barriers of male prejudice. In Euripides' play *Iphigeneia at Aulis* (written within a year or two of Euphiletos's marriage), Agamemnon tries to assert his authority over his wife, Clytemnestra, in order to get her out of the way while he sacrifices his own daughter, Iphigeneia, to Artemis. Clytemnestra, with a show of wifely stubbornness that surely came out of the playwright's contemporary observation, refuses to be dismissed and finally cuts the conversation short by sending her husband about his business. In another play by Euripides, *Hippolytos,* there are some lines that might have been written specifically for Euphiletos himself to speak. Hippolytos, told that his stepmother, Phaidra, is in love with him, remarks scathingly: "I would have no servants near a woman, just beasts with teeth and no voice, [for] servants are the agents in the world outside for the wickedness women do."

Drink and sex are the traditional outlets for the oppressed. The comedies of Aristophanes are studded with snide references to the excessive drinking habits of women. According to Aristophanes, festivals such as the Thesmophoria were excuses for massive alcoholic sprees. More likely, these mystery cults were the safety valve for pent-up emotions, a chance to transcend the cruelly narrow boundaries imposed on women by their roles in a rigidly male society.

As for sex, women were the weaker vessel when it came to this human urge. In *Lysistrata* Aristophanes has the women wondering whether they can hold out long enough to bring the men to their knees. And in the legends that canonized popular wisdom on the subject there is a story about Zeus and Hera squabbling over who gets the greater pleasure out of sex—the man or the woman. When they finally appeal to Teiresias, the blind seer and prophet, who, as part man and part woman, ought to be able to settle the question for them, he duly reports that in the sexual act the woman, in fact, gets nine-tenths of the pleasure, and the man only one-tenth.

These scraps of myth and folklore, however, filtered through male fantasy as they are, reveal a sense of unease about women. In the Orestes myth, for instance, it is Clytemnestra who takes over the reins of government in the absence of Agamemnon, then murders him when he returns; and it is her daughter Electra who pushes a faltering Orestes into taking revenge for the slain king. A whole army of formidable heroines—Electra, Clytemnestra, Antigone, Hecuba, Andromache, Medea—marches through the pages of Greek drama. The Fates, the Muses, and the Furies are all women. None of these female figures is anything like the meek and passive drudge that the Greek woman of the fifth century was expected to be.

But were they real types, these mythological heroines, or were they phantom projections of male fears and desires, mother imagoes, castration anxieties dressed up as gods, embodiments of the part of a man he most wants to repress—his own irrational and emotional side, his moon-bound, lunatic aspects—thrust onto women because he dare not admit them in himself?

It is possible. Every mythologized figure embodies inner and outer worlds. We see what we wish to see, and the picture we perceive turns into a mirror. Were there actual women in Athens capable of organizing a fully functioning communistic state and pushing it through the assembly, like the Praxagora of Aristophanes' play *Ekklesiazousai?* Were there Electras and Clytemnestras and Medeas? If there were, they never reached the pages of the history books. We hear of Aspasia, Pericles' "companion" (the Greek word is *hetaira,* meaning "woman friend"), for whom he divorced his legal wife. But Aspasia was a member of the demimonde of "liberated" women who lived outside the social order, not necessarily slaves, but not full citizens either. They were often prostitutes, but some of them were cultured and educated, better traveled and more interesting to Athenian men than their own wives. Custom permitted one or more relationships with *hetairai* outside the marriage, but a *hetaira* had no legal claim on a man, and he could sell her or dispose of her any time he liked. Meanwhile, for the trueborn Athenian woman who wanted a more varied life than the one prescribed by convention, what was there? Gossip with the neighbors. The bottle. A festival now and then. A clandestine love affair.

Four or five days passed while Euphiletos brooded over the wrong done to him. Suppose a child was born from this liaison: who could tell whether it was his or Eratosthenes'? All kinds of complications might follow. But whatever he was feeling, Euphiletos managed to hide it from his wife. She never suspected that he knew anything at all.

Euphiletos had a good friend named Sostratos. Less than a week after his interview with the maid Euphiletos met Sostratos coming home from the country, and since it was late Euphiletos invited his friend to his house for supper. This casual meeting was to become important later at the trial. The two men went upstairs, ate and drank well, and had a pleasant evening together. By custom Euphiletos's wife was not present. After Sostratos had gone home Euphiletos went to sleep.

Some time in the middle of the night there was a knock on his door. It was the maid. Eratosthenes had arrived.

Leaving the maid to keep watch, Euphiletos slipped out a back way and went around the neighborhood waking up his friends. Some of them were out of town, but he managed to collect a small group who went to a nearby store and bought torches. Then they all trooped off to Euphiletos's house where they stood outside in the street holding the lighted torches while Euphiletos tapped on the door. Quietly the maid let him into the courtyard. He pushed past her into the room where his wife was supposed to be asleep with the baby. A few of Euphiletos's friends managed to crowd in behind him.

For a split second the scene must have been like a tableau out of Homer: Eratosthenes naked in bed, Euphiletos's wife in his arms, the two lovers trapped in the light of torches held by the neighbors.

Then Eratosthenes, still naked, sprang up. Euphiletos shouted at him, "What are you doing in my house?" and knocked him off the bed, pulled his wrists behind his back, and tied them.

Eratosthenes offered to pay Euphiletos any sum he named. Euphiletos had a choice: he could accept the bribe, or he could take a form of revenge allowed by law—brutalizing and humiliating Eratosthenes by such methods as the insertion of tough thistles up his rectum. There was also a third option open to him under the circumstances: since he had caught Eratosthenes in the act, and there were witnesses present, Euphiletos could kill him.

Euphiletos interrupted the other man's pleas. "I won't kill you," he said, and then, in the kind of logical twist the Greeks loved, he added, "but the law will."

And in the name of the law he killed Eratosthenes.

Athenian homicide law required the dead man's family, not the state, to bring charges of murder. Eratosthenes' family undertook the task, and approximately three months later Euphiletos found himself facing a jury of fifty-one Athenians in the court known as the Delphinion, located in the southeast corner of Athens, where cases of justifiable homicide were tried. Eratosthenes' family charged Euphiletos with premeditated murder on the grounds that he had sent his maid to lure Eratosthenes to the house; they may also have tried to prove that Eratosthenes was dragged into the building by force, or took refuge at the hearth before he was killed. In the speech he writes for Euphiletos, Lysias sets out to rebut all these charges.

Lysias puts into Euphiletos's mouth some ingenious legal arguments. The law (of which a copy is read to the court) says that a seducer caught in the act may be killed. "If you make it a crime to kill a seducer in this way," he argues, "you will have a situation in which a thief, caught burglarizing your house, will pretend that he is an adulterer in order to get away with a lesser crime." Lysias also refers the jury to the law on rape. Rape carries a lower penalty than seduction. Why? Because, theorizes Lysias, the rapist simply takes the woman's body, while the seducer steals her soul.

Nevertheless, in spite of Lysias's able and sophisticated defense, there is a flaw in Euphiletos's argument. His defense rests on the assumption that his action was unpremeditated, committed in the heat of the moment, under the shock and stress of finding his wife in bed with another man. That is surely the intent of the law, and Euphiletos goes to great lengths to prove he had not planned the encounter. He cites the dinner invitation to Sostratos, which, he says, is not the behavior of a man planning murder. But the rest of his story contradicts this. The signals by which the maid warned him that Eratosthenes had arrived and by which he let her know

that he was waiting at the front door; the rounding up of friends to act as witnesses; the presence of the murder weapon on his person—all point to prior preparation. Euphiletos may prove to the jury's satisfaction that he did not lure Eratosthenes deliberately to his house that night, but he fails to prove that he was taken totally by surprise or that he tried to do anything to stop the affair before it reached that point. His action looks suspiciously like cold-blooded revenge executed under color of a law that forgives even violent crimes if they are committed in the heat of passion.

Neither the speech for the prosecution nor the testimony of witnesses has survived, so we do not know if the wife or the maid gave evidence. Though women were not allowed to appear as witnesses in court cases, the rules for murder trials may have been different. A slave could not testify at all, but a deposition could have been taken from her under torture and read to the court. On the other hand, Euphiletos may have wanted to avoid bringing the women into it: after all, they had been in league against him throughout the whole unhappy affair.

There is something touching in the alliance between the slave, an object without rights or status, and the wife, legally a free citizen but in reality a kind of slave too. The maidservant probably accepted a bribe from Eratosthenes, but all the same she had a moment of heroism when, threatened with a beating and prison, she refused to incriminate her mistress. Afterward, when she became Euphiletos's accomplice, there is an eerie reversal of the situation: the slave admits her master to the house in the same stealthy way that she had opened the door for her mistress's lover a few minutes earlier. But still, there was a moment when Euphiletos was the outsider, barred from his own house and his wife's arms, with only his rage and his group of male friends for company.

Finally there is the wife herself, the center of the drama and its most shadowy character. Apart from his grudging admission that she was thrifty and capable and a good housekeeper, Euphiletos tells us little about her. From what we know of Athenian marriage customs, we can guess that she was probably married at fourteen or fifteen to a virtual stranger and expected to keep house for this man who spent much of his time away from home on business. Was she satisfied with the trinkets that Euphiletos says he let her buy, and with all of the household duties and her young baby?

A small fragment survives from a lost play by Aristophanes in which a character says, "A woman needs a lover the way a dinner needs dessert." Euphiletos's wife was no Lysistrata, able to express her frustration and rebellion in some dramatic act of revolutionary will, but she did find a way to rebel all the same. It cost her dear. By Athenian law, if a man discovered that his wife had been raped or seduced, he was expected to divorce her. And from what we know of Euphiletos's character, we can be sure that he obeyed the law.

Eponymous hero; Alexander the Great's thirteen spectacular years of conquest 336-323 BC left cities bearing his name throughout the East – this sandstone head comes from the Egyptian Alexandria.

GREEK GIFTS?

Lesser breeds without the law? In a revealing new study of the Hellenistic world in the three centuries after Alexander carved out an empire in the East, **Peter Green** argues that condescension and cultural arrogance rather than a mission to civilise marked Greek reaction to the population they ruled over.

Peter Green is the Dougherty Centennial Professor of Classics in the University of Texas at Austin, and the author of Alexander to Actium: The Historical Evolution of the Hellenistic Age *published by the University of California Press and Thames and Hudson.*

Hellenisation, that primarily eastward diffusion of Greek language and culture, has been defined – ever since the German historian and nationalist J.G. Droysen proclaimed it in his *Geschichte der Diadochen* (1836) – as the essence of Hellenistic civilisation, the banner carried by Alexander the Great and his successors. Yet as a phenomenon it calls for very careful scrutiny. Its civilising and mission-

ary aspects have been greatly exaggerated, not least by modern historians anxious to find some moral justification for aggressive imperialism. So has its universality. This trend has been matched by a persistent tendency to underplay both lure of conquest and commercial profits (which, with land-hunger, provided the main driving-force behind this Greek diaspora), as well as the stubborn refusal of allegedly inferior races to embrace the benefits of Greek enlightenment thus rudely thrust upon them.

Analysis of the evidence is revealing. The Greeks had long assumed in themselves, partly on environmental grounds, a cultural and ethnic superior-

ity over all alien societies. This superiority even extended, in the visual arts, to idealising themselves (perfect bodies, nobly straight noses) while portraying outsiders with a realism often not far this side of caricature. Yet they never evinced any noticeable urge to convert or enlighten the 'barbarians', whom no less an intellectual than Aristotle regarded as slaves by nature, to be treated 'like animals or plants'. In classical drama, for example, Aristophanes' *Acharnians* (425) or *Thesmophoriazusae* (410), and Euripides' *Orestes* (408), the jabbering foreigner had always been good for a laugh. No one ever thought of *educating* him. Curiosity about the rest of the world undoub-

From *History Today*, June 1990, pp. 27-34. Reproduced by kind permission of History Today, Ltd., 83-84 Berwick Street, London W1V 3PJ, England.

51

tedly existed, but was not, perhaps mercifully, accompanied by any desire to improve it.

Thus the dissemination of Hellenism, when it came, was incidental rather than conscious or deliberate. Further, those Macedonian soldiers and Greek businessmen who, in the wake of Alexander's conquests, exploited the indigenous populations of Ptolemaic Egypt or the Seleucid East could not, by any stretch of the imagination, be regarded as a cultural élite, much less as cultural missionaries. The stupid, bombastic, drunken, cowardly *miles gloriosus* who appears in literature from Menander's day onwards, with his toadying servant and chestfuls of Persian plunder, had all too real a basis in fact. Such men, like their counterparts in any age, were massively indifferent to the language and civilisation of any country they happened to be occupying, an attitude which their victims, for the most part, reciprocated.

Any Egyptian who wanted to get anywhere under the Ptolemies had to speak, and preferably also write, *koinē* Greek, that vernacular Attic which, from the fourth century BC on, became the *lingua franca* of the Mediterranean world. We have a letter of complaint (c.256/5) to an official from his (probably Egyptian) servant about the contemptuous ill-treatment he has received 'because I am a barbarian', and petitioning for regular pay in future 'so that I don't starve because I can't speak Greek'. Similarly an Egyptian priest is resentful of a Greek settler who 'despises me because I am an Egyptian'. Though later a certain degree of low-level acculturation took place, in the fourth and third centuries imperial racism was rampant among the Greeks and Macedonians of Alexandria, and never really died out. No Macedonian of note before Cleopatra VII, and very few Greeks, ever bothered to learn Egyptian.

Borrowings and adaptations, then, we would expect to find in those areas which, first, required no linguistic skill, and, second, were commonly accessible without conscious intellectual effort: that is, the visual arts, architecture, and music. Apart from music, for which there is only the sketchiest of literary evidence (suggesting possible Oriental influence on Greek modes and instruments rather than vice versa), this is precisely the case. Yet even in the area of art and architecture what is often pointed to as evidence for cultural dissemination is, in the sense proposed, nothing of the sort. I am thinking particularly of the export of Greek building styles, pottery, statuary, mosaics, gymnasia, temples, theatres, and the rest of the civic impedimenta essential for any self-respecting *polis*, into regions as far afield as, say, Bactria. Ai Khanum on the Oxus is a good case in point. Like all Alexander's foundations, it was settled exclusively by Macedonian and Greek colonists.

Thus what we find in such cases, far from any real diffusion, is an alien enclave, an artificial island of Greek social and cultural amenities almost totally isolated from the indigenous population which it dominated. That much-touted respect for exotic 'alien wisdom' occasionally found in Greek literature – for example, Herodotus' astonishment, later shared by Plato and Aristotle, at the hoary, unchanging, Egyptian priestly tradition – depended in the main on unfamiliarity (because of the language barrier) with the actual literature in which such supposed wisdom was enshrined. Nor do we find any substantial evidence, in Ptolemaic Egypt, the Seleucid East, or India, for local interest in Greek literature or Greek ideas – the Hellenised Egyptian was not required to read, much less to enjoy, Greek poetry or philosophy, any more than his masters knew, or cared about, the age-old literary heritage of Egypt – but rather a great deal that suggests implacable hostility, with a religious and ideological no less than an ethnic basis.

Local acclimatisation tended, inevitably, to be restricted to two well-defined categories. On the one hand we find those still-independent rulers who 'went Greek' for their social and political advancement. Scions of Anatolian royal families (Ariarathes V of Cappadocia or Nicomedes IV of Bithynia) were sent west for their education, normally to sit at the feet of fashionable philosophers in Athens, as Indian princes under the Raj went through the privileged rigours of Harrow and Sandhurst. On the other, there were the intelligent and ambitious collaborators who set out to make a career in the administrative system of the occupying power: a tiny cadre – in the Seleucid empire, it has been calculated, not more than 2.5 per cent of the official class, and even that only after two generations – but of considerable significance. These were the men who became interpreters, scribes, tax-collectors, accountants, or other categories at sub-executive level in the bureaucracy. The whole Ptolemaic administration, for example – still, ironically, in essence Pharaonic – functioned at middle level through a corps of more or less bilingual native officials: competition for such posts, as in the earlier Pharaonic period, was intense.

Such men had an outside chance of clawing their way up the ladder of advancement to a position of real power as senior administrators or military (including police) officers. By so doing they committed themselves to the foreign regime they served in a social no less than a professional sense. Like Indians under the British Crown angling for the *entrée* to European club membership, they developed the taste for exercising naked, for worshipping strange gods, for patronising the theatre: they also courted municipal kudos by the lavish generosity of their benefactions. The prime motive in such cases was, clearly, social and professional ambition, even if a little genuine acculturation took place at the same time. Against this must be set that deep resentment and hostility felt by most of their fellow-countrymen towards an occupying power (not to mention the angry contempt, mixed with jealousy, that they themselves would attract), and, on the Graeco-Macedonian side, a powerful distaste for those who in any sense 'went native'.

When all these factors are taken into account, a radically modified picture of Hellenisation emerges. It is restricted, for the most part, to some curious instances of architectural and sculptural hybridisation; some limited social assimilations among non-Greek rulers and in the administrative sector of the major (particularly the Ptolemaic) kingdoms; a few religious syncretisations that transmuted their borrowings out of all recognition (Isis and Sarapis); and the establishment of the Attic *koinē* as a useful international language, primarily for administrative and commercial purposes, but also, later, for religious propaganda. The impact of the Greek and Macedonian colonists was, first and foremost, economic and demographic. It is hard to trace any conscious diffusion of Greek intellectual ideas in the Hellenistic East with any real confidence, and of genuine literary interpenetration between Greek and other cultures there is vir-

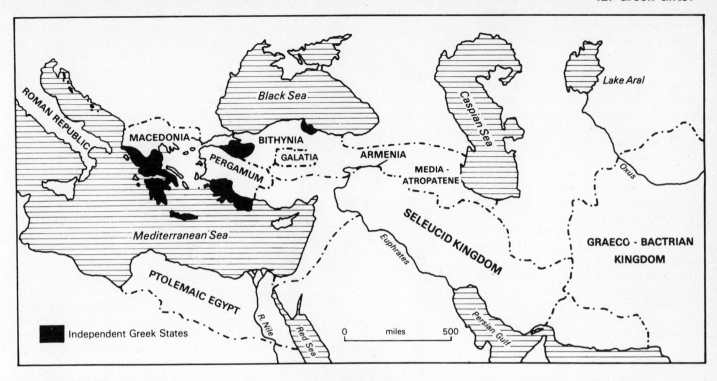

The Hellenistic world c.240 BC, showing how Alexander's great empire had been split into a number of successor kingdoms.

tually no trace. For one thing, literary translations – as opposed to those of medical, mathematical, astronomical, or similar practical treatises – seem to have been non-existent, a sure sign of aesthetic indifference. Thus whatever the Greeks and, *a fortiori*, the Macedonians were up to (over and above financial exploitation) in the kingdoms ruled by Alexander's heirs, spreading cultural light formed a very small part of it. Itinerant sophists might peddle the latest philosophical clichés of Academy or Stoa at street corners, while the local-boy-made-good, with his Greek-style education, would have a small stock of well-worn quotations from Homer, Euripides or Menander at his disposal. It does not add up to very much. To what extent the locals would ever patronise a Greek theatre (for example, that of Ai Khanum in Bactria), and what they absorbed, or even understood, if they did, remain highly problematical questions.

The failure of Hellenism to catch on among the indigenous inhabitants of the Ptolemaic and Seleucid kingdoms thus has nothing to do with its intrinsic intellectual or cultural merits as a system of ideas, a creative matrix, a way of life. It failed for several good and compelling reasons wholly unrelated to the

criteria by which we would assess it: the bitter resentment of defeat, that found expression in passionate ethnocentrism; a theocratic temper that subordinated arts and sciences alike to the requirements of religion, and was chary of translating religious texts; a language barrier that no one cared to break except for the immediate requirements of commerce and administration. This general rejection throws into prominent relief the two striking exceptions for which we have evidence, and in both cases, as is at once apparent, special circumstances apply.

The first concerns the large and influential community of Jews in Alexandria, perhaps originating as prisoners of war settled there by Ptolemy I Soter. This community, though ethnically debarred by its own religious laws from inter-marriage, contained a high proportion of intellectuals, and, equally important, became bilingual in Greek. To a surprising extent, the external aspects of synagogue ritual were adapted to Greek custom. Even more important was the production, begun under Ptolemy II Philadelphos, but not completed until the second century, of the Septuagint, the Greek version of the Hebrew Bible. It is noteworthy that the

prime motive for translation in this case was the increasing inability of the Greek-speaking Alexandrian Jews to understand either Hebrew or Aramaic. As a result, a considerable body of Helleno-Judaic literature passed into circulation.

Yet, once again, despite favourable conditions for direct mutual influence – they were all living in the same city, must often have passed one another in the street – the evidence reveals an almost total lack of contact, certainly in the third century BC and arguably for much longer, between this Jewish-Alexandrian literary movement and the contemporary tradition of Callimachus, Theocritus, Apollonius Rhodius and their successors. The *cognoscenti* of the Alexandria Museum reveal no interest in, or knowledge of, the prophetic mode of discourse so characteristic of Jewish thought, while the dominant influence on Jewish-Alexandrian literature is not Homer, much less Callimachus or Menander, but the Septuagint. The form and substance of those works that survive remain Jewish, prophetic, religious-inspired throughout. The nearest we come to classical influence are a couple of dull attempts at Jewish epic, and an extraordinary fragment of tragedy, in flat iambic trimeters, entitled *Exodus* and covering most of the life of Moses. This could hardly be described as an impressive cross-cultural record.

The one shining exception to all these predictable, if depressing, conclusions is, of course, provided by the greatest, and most historically significant, cultural confrontation of them all: that between Greece and Rome. Though the lack of a home-grown intellectual tradition has probably been exaggerated, Horace's familiar picture of 'captive Greece captivating her savage conqueror, and bringing the arts to rustic Latium' remains true enough in essence. The Roman attitude to Hellenism was highly ambivalent. On the one hand they swallowed Greek culture whole (a feast that gave the more old-fashioned among them severe indigestion), imitated Greek literature, rehashed Greek philosophy in ponderous, awkwardly abstract Latin, sedulously pastiched Greek art. On the other, perhaps not least because, as R.E. Smith once wrote, they 'had eaten of the apple of knowledge and knew themselves to be culturally naked' – a situation always liable to arouse resentment – they despised and mistrusted the Greeks themselves as slippery, unreliable, unwarlike, covetous mountebanks, confidence-tricksters with no moral principles and a quicksilver gift of the gab. Paradoxically, it was (as Horace notes) on the one occasion when the Greeks came as a defeated nation rather than as conquerors that their culture had most influence.

No accident, either, that it was the Romans – the most enthusiastic promoters of Hellenising standards, perhaps because they were so morbidly conscious of being cultural *parvenus* themselves – who were seriously worried about the real or fancied decline of those standards. Livy reports the consul Cn. Manlius as claiming that the latter-day Macedonians of Alexandria or Babylon had 'degenerated into Syrians and Parthians and Egyptians'. Juvenal in his notorious anti-Greek tirade makes precisely the same point. What proportion of the dregs washed across from Orontes to Tiber, he asks rhetorically, is really Greek anyway? In they all swarm, with their unintelligible native lingo and disgusting habits and weird musical instruments and gaudy prostitutes, to corrupt decent Romans. Long before the end of the first century AD Rome had taken over the Greek

In transit; this statue of Maitreya, the future Buddha, from first-century AD Grandhara, shows trappings of Greek influence.

xenophobic attitude to *barbaroi*, and was applying it, with gusto, to the Greeks themselves.

This ingrained sense of superiority – whether masquerading as pan-hellenism to sanction the rape of the East, or, later, helping to keep Ptolemies and, to a lesser degree, Seleucids in cultural isolation, century after century, from the peoples they ruled and exploited – is an extraordinarily constant factor in the history of the Hellenistic era. The Macedonians in particular began with a total indifference to, and contempt for, the cultures on which they imposed their rule. Yet in the interests of profit

and efficiency they were more than willing to take over, virtually unchanged, not only existing modes of production, serf-labour, and land tenure (particularly throughout Asia), but also the various administrative systems, some more familiar than others, that they found *in situ*. Hence the indispensable corps of interpreters.

Alexandria was held – a nice distinction – to be *by* Egypt, but not *of* it. Alexander's attempts at racial fusion (whatever their motive) were abandoned immediately after his death. Seleucus, alone of his marshals, remained faithful to the 'Persian' (actually Bactrian) wife wished on him by Alexander at the time of the Susa mass-marriages. In all instances what the Successors set up were enclaves of Graeco-Macedonian culture in an alien world, government ghettos for a ruling élite. When we come to assess the ubiquitous Greek temples, Greek theatres, Greek gymnasia, Greek mosaics, and Greek-language inscriptions scattered throughout the Seleucid East, we should never forget that it was for the Hellenised Macedonian ruling minority and its Greek supporters, professional or commercial, that such home-from-home luxuries – not to mention the *polis* that housed them – were, in the first instance, provided.

In Egypt, for example, and probably elsewhere, the gymnasium resembled an exclusive club: entry was highly selective, by a scrutiny (*eiskrisis*) designed to keep out undesirables (that is, non-Greeks) and to foster Hellenism. There was a waiting-list, and children from suitable families were put down on it from a tender age. Only by the very end of the Ptolemaic period were wealthy local citizens sometimes admitted. Far from promoting Hellenisation, the gymnasium seems rather to have encouraged xenophobia and separatism. Again, the parallel of British India springs to mind, where the acceptance of English as a lingua franca, and the appetite of a minority of educated Indians for such plums of power as they could grab within the system as it stood (along with the social *mores* of club or cantonment) in no way mitigated the deep-abiding resentment of British rule, much less made any inroads against India's own ancient cultural and religious traditions.

If it had not been for the Romans, whose strong obsession with Greek culture formed part of the overall impe-

The temple of Apollo at Didyma – part of the network of Greek settlements along the coast of Asia Minor.

rial legacy that Rome dis-seminated throughout her far-flung provinces, the impact of Hellenism might well have been less fundamental, less widespread, and less enduring. Where Greek rulers lacked the authority of Rome to maintain and perpetuate their institutions, their impact tended to be minimal. As we have seen, the customary method of diffusion was by way of imposed rule, military settlements, commercial exploitation, by men who brought their own language and culture with them, and enforced their authority by means of a mercenary army. Exploitation exacerbated poverty, so that resistance was often felt at all social levels, with an abused peasantry rallying behind a dispossessed aristocracy or priesthood. The conquerors' artificial islands of culture were no more assimilable at first than a wrongly matched heart transplant.

The Ptolemies never cared about Egyptian civilisation, even when they went through the mummery of a pharaonic coronation (placating the powerful priesthood was another matter); the Egyptians still rebelled against them whenever they could. The extent and intensity of Iranian resistance – passive, militant, messianic or proselytic – to Alexander's conquest and occupation can be gauged from the considerable body of surviving literature (mostly prophetic and oracular) attacking it. Alexander is the 'Evil Invader'; above all, like the Ptolemies in Egypt, he is presented as a blasphemous disrupter of sacred tradition, while both he and his conquistadors figure as 'the demons with dishevelled hair of the race of wrath'. This was not the kind of atmosphere, to put it mildly, that encouraged acculturation across formidable religious and linguistic barriers. It could, indeed, be argued, with only minimal hyperbole, that the whole concept of Hellenisation as a beneficial spreading of light among the grateful heathen was a self-serving myth, propagated by power-hungry imperialists. Such a notion formed a useful reinforcement to panhellenism, and was later popularised by Plutarch. Bullying people for their own good has a long and depressing history.

Those who wore Greek dress (and removed it in the gymnasium), who aped Greek accents, attended Greek plays, and dropped their pinch of incense on Greek altars, had good and sufficient reasons for their behaviour, into which aesthetic or moral considerations seldom entered. Genuine cultural conversions did undoubtedly take place, but they seem to have been very much in the minority. What we find instead, more often than not, is a steely determination to get on in the world: the eagerness of some locals to assume Greek names should not necessarily be attributed to philhellenism. We know of no case where a Greek work was translated into an oriental language:

hostility will have been at least as strong a reason for this as ignorance or mere indifference. The few intellectuals who did take the trouble to investigate Greek culture tended to borrow its style (as Ezekial from Euripides) or scholarly techniques and methodology (as Jewish historians from the Museum of Alexandria) or formal logic (as the Pharisees from the Stoa or Academy), husking out the theoretical insights and discarding the substance as irrelevant.

While all three Successor dynasties patronised scholarship and the arts for reasons of prestige, such activities remained exclusively a court function, pursued by Greeks for the benefit of Greeks. There is no hint of fusion or collaboration with the local culture. This omission is particularly striking in the case of Ptolemaic Egypt, since the (unwilling) host nation had a long and distinguished cultural history of its own. Prosopographical research shows something over two hundred literary figures in Ptolemaic Egypt: all are foreigners. Even in medicine and science, where we would expect a higher proportion of native practitioners, out of more than a hundred known names only about a dozen are Egyptian (though it is of course true, and too seldom stressed, that an unknown proportion of these Greek names may in fact conceal Egyptian owners).

These statistics, fragmentary and uncertain though they are, nevertheless still tell their own story. The arrogance and xenophobia of Greek culture, at home or abroad, remains a constant factor. Not surprisingly, then, such assimilation as did take place (for example, among the urban poor of Alexandria in the second to first centuries BC) worked best at a low social level unaffected by intellectual prejudice: and on such occasions it was the Greeks who tended to pick up local habits rather than *vice versa*. The only cases of scholarly acculturation we know about are the compilations of Manetho on Egypt and Berossos on Babylonia, Greek-language digests of local science or history made by compliant bilingual priests for their new overlords. Neither in Egypt, Iran, nor India did Greek culture arguably leave any substantial trace – certainly not in the literature.

Perhaps the most extraordinary example of Greek enclave culture – finally, in this case, absorbed by something larger than itself – is that of the isolated

Greek kingdoms in Bactria and India. For over two centuries, beginning with the renegade Seleucid satrap Diodotus about 250 BC, a series of more than forty Graeco-Macedonian kings ruled in the east, from Bactria to the Punjab. There are a few scattered literary references, but most of the story has been pieced together from these rulers' self-promoting and highly idiosyncratic coinage. Alexander had settled thousands of Greek colonists and time-expired Macedonian veterans and mercenaries in these frontier provinces, where they formed a handy buffer against the constant threat of invasion by northern nomads. Many of them (like white settlers in Rhodesia) gladly chose these fertile uplands rather than the unpredictable future of a retirement in Greece. When Diodotus broke away from the Seleucid empire, the large number of Greeks and Macedonians in Bactria gave his rule powerful support, and created an ethnic enclave of a most unusual sort: at once passionately Hellenic and cut off *in toto* from its Greek roots.

The inscrutable East; the Greek rulers of the enclave at Bactria, though their coin portraits are classical – such as the fine profile above of Antimachus I (190-180 BC) – gradually embraced Indian ways, as in the case of Menander (155-130), a convert to Buddhism.

Antiochus IV (175-163 BC), the Seleucid king whose intolerance of Judaism provoked the national revolt of the Maccabees.

The recently excavated city of Ai Khanum, on the northern Afghan frontier with Soviet Russia, offers a marvellous example of persistent Hellenism in isolation. The Greek theatre, the great palatial complex with its peristyle courtyard, the funerary cult-shrine (*herōon*) the lush Corinthian capitals of the hypostyle hall, a sophisticated sundial, fragments of what appears to be a post-Aristotelian philosophical treatise, the pottery, the bronze and terracotta figurines, perhaps above all the Delphic maxims inscribed, in Greek, on a base in the *herōon* (copied at Delphi, to be set up and paid for by a loyal globetrotting citizen), all reflect the inhabitants' determination to create a Hellenic oasis in this remote Bactrian wilderness beside the River Oxus. The gymnasium or palaestra covered an area of nearly a hundred square yards. There was a beautiful public fountain with carved gargoyles and waterspouts in the form of lions' and dolphins' heads.

Yet isolation exacted its price, and in more than one way. The large pebble-mosaic in the palace bathing-quarters is not only poor provincial work, but also, in its ignorance of cubes (*tesserae*) and the subtle modulations they made possible, over a century out of date. The mosaicists who went East clearly handed down their skills without any fresh infusion of outside talent. They will not have been the only ones to do so. Rootlessness also, in this special case, produced an unusual, but predictable, susceptibility to the *genius loci*. Just as a surprising number of Englishmen, despite their own caste system and xenophobic assumptions, were fatally seduced by the lure of Eastern mysticism, so the Indo-Greeks, in a very similar situation, capitulated to some highly un-Greek local influences before they were done. Indian legends and Indian scripts invaded their coinage. Greek sculpture adapted itself to the lotus position, and – after a gap of four centuries – came up with a new and more enduring version of the mysterious 'archaic smile'.

For more than a hundred and fifty years these Graeco-Macedonian dynasts ruled in Bactria and western India, independent monarchs still long after Greece and Macedonia themselves had succumbed to the power of Rome. Yet Menander (ruled c.

Copycats; the Romans absorbed Hellenistic culture voraciously into their empire – this mosaic from Pompeii of actors performing a scene from a Greek comedy is a copy of an original 3rd-century BC painting from Pergamum. Their enthusiasm for the Greeks themselves – or at least their Hellenistic descendents – was considerably more muted.

155-130) was the only one of them to survive in Indian literature, under the name of Milinda – and not on account of his royal achievements, but because he was a convert to Buddhism (traditionally because of discussions with the Buddhist priest Nagasena). He may have set Pallas Athena on the reverse of his coins, but he also employed the Dharma-Chakra (Wheel of Law) symbol, and was associated with the building of stupas and the original iconography of the Buddha image. The ghost of Apollo still lurked behind the Buddha's features, but it was a losing battle. Far more important than Menander's prowess as a warrior was his status as a sage and thinker, who had embraced Eastern ways: when he died, he was revered as a saint, and his ashes were divided between the chief cities of his kingdom. Whatever impressed Menander's Indian subjects, it was not his superior Greek culture.

FOR FURTHER READING:
S.K. Eddy, *The King is Dead: studies in the Near Eastern Resistance to Hellenism 334-31 BC* (University of Nebraska-Lincoln Press, 1961); A. Momigliano, *Alien wisdom: The Limits of Hellenisation* (Cambridge University Press, 1975); M. Avi-Yonah, *Hellenism and the East: Contacts and Interrelations from Alexander to the Roman Conquest* (Bell & Howell (UMI), 1978); J.W. Sedlar, *India and the Greek world: A Study in the Transmission of Culture* (Rowman, 1980); Amélie Kuhrt and Susan Sherwin-White (eds.), *Hellenism in the East: The Interaction of Greek and non-Greek civilizations from Syria to Central Asia after Alexander* (University of California Press, 1987).

Bibliotheca Alexandrina

LOTFALLAH SOLIMAN

LOTFALLAH SOLIMAN, Egyptian writer and journalist, is currently preparing a study on the history of Palestine.

ALEXANDER the Great is said to have been welcomed in Egypt as a liberator. He showed great respect for the people's customs and beliefs, and as a professed defender of religion, won the support of the priests. He openly consulted the Egyptian oracles, particularly that of Amon, to which he journeyed with great ceremony. Moreover, he very quickly understood the central role which Egypt could play in the expansion of world trade, and he lost no time in lending his support to it.

One of the most far-reaching decisions that Alexander made in this connection was to found the city of Alexandria. Legend has it that he chose the location himself—a small Mediterranean port whose site had attracted him, as the shelter of the offshore island of Pharos formed two natural harbours, ideal as a Greek naval base. Legend also relates that Alexander personally traced out the boundaries of the new city, construction of which began in 332 BC to the design of the Rhodian architect Dinocrates.

Thanks to its favourable geographical situation and its shrewdly designed port, Alexandria became one of the most renowned commercial and maritime crossroads of Antiquity. Until it was conquered by the Arabs in 641 AD,

the city played a major role in Egypt's history.

When Alexandria was first built its population included, in addition to the indigenous Egyptians, the Macedonian guard, a colony of Greek immigrants and a Jewish minority. The city grew rapidly, and during the rule of King Ptolemy I Soter* it welcomed many scholars and artists, who enjoyed royal protection and patronage. The king closely followed the spirit of the policies instituted by Alexander. Respectful of the local civic and political institutions, creeds and religions, he created a climate of tolerance and security in Egypt that was exceptionally favourable to cultural development. Thanks to him, Alexandria began to approach its founder's dream of an ideal capital city, an illustrious centre of intellectual and artistic influence.

Ptolemy I ordered the construction of the famous Pharos lighthouse, one of the seven wonders of the ancient world, and during his reign plans were laid for the most celebrated public library of Antiquity, the Library of Alexandria. His son, Ptolemy II Philadelphus (308-246 BC), brought the library project to fruition. At the same time, he

made Alexandria the world's leading commercial centre. Greeks, Romans, Ethiopians and Jews came to this cosmopolitan city to conduct their business among copyists, clerks, librarians, interpreters, ambassadors, court officials and public administrators. A patron of the arts and of literature, Ptolemy II surrounded himself with eminent scholars and poets, including Callimachus (died 240 BC), whose name would come to be associated with the expansion of the great Library.

The first known library is thought to have been built at Memphis, where visitors were welcomed by the words "Medicines for the Soul". However, when Ptolemy I decided to create a library in Alexandria, he chose to model it on that of Aristotle in Athens. He may have even acquired the books from Aristotle's library, one of the richest collections of Antiquity.

Right from the start attempts were made to obtain copies of all the works of Greek literature for the Alexandrian Library. This objective was soon achieved, however, and copies of all works of good quality in other languages were sought. Finally, complete universality became the goal, and the Library tried to obtain copies of all existing manuscripts.

Acquiring these copies became one of

---

* Ptolemy Soter ("the Saviour"), Macedonian general of Alexander the Great, became ruler of Egypt (323-285 BC) on Alexander's death. *Editor.*

the main tasks of the librarians, who arranged for all known works to be sent on loan from Athens in return for a deposit, and to be borrowed long enough to make one, or sometimes several copies. Manuscripts found on ships moored in the harbour were also temporarily "confiscated" and copied.

Thanks to this gigantic effort to collect and conserve writings from all over the world, the Library of Alexandria became the first truly universal library in history and attracted the most eminent philosophers, scholars and researchers of their day. The exact number of papyrus scrolls which made up the collection is not known. Estimates vary between 400,000 and 700,000, as one scroll could contain several works, just as a single work could cover several scrolls.

The Library did not confine itself to collecting manuscripts written in their original languages; it also embarked on a massive translation programme. For example, seventy-two Jewish scholars were given the task of translating the Old Testament into Greek, and translations of Babylonian and Buddhist manuscripts were commissioned.

It was also the first library in history to establish a set of rules for the classification and inventory of its collection. The monumental catalogue was compiled by Callimachus, who perfected a method of retrieving each work, together with a synopsis or even a critical appraisal. These listings, known as the "Pinakes", from the Greek word for "tablets", have unfortunately been lost. Records of them from the ancient world are sufficiently abundant, however, to give an idea of the enormity of the task.

The Library of Alexandria formed part of a larger complex, the Mouseion ("Museum", or temple of the Muses), a research institute which opened its doors to the arts and the sciences, with an astronomical observatory, a zoological and botanical garden, and meeting rooms.

Thus some of the greatest scholars and creative artists lived in or visited Alexandria, delving into the Library's priceless treasures to help them in their work and their discoveries. An intellectual and cultural movement grew up around them, embracing all fields of knowledge and creativity.

Among these men were Herophilus (c. 340-300 BC), who established the rules of anatomy and physiology; Euclid (330-280 BC), the inventor of geometry; Eratosthenes (284-192 BC), who calculated the circumference of the Earth; Aristarchus (215-143 BC) and Dionysius Thrax (170-90 BC), who systematized the grammar of classical Greek; Hero (fl. 62 AD), who wrote several books on geometry and mechanics and invented the dioptre, a surveying instrument; and Claudius Ptolemaeus (90-168 AD), founder of cartography and developer of astronomy. Thus the Library played a vital role in the development of Graeco-Roman culture.

Nothing remains today of this monument to human genius. It is thought that the main part of the collection was destroyed in a fire which ravaged the port when Julius Caesar took Alexandria in 48 BC. Mark Antony made amends for the damage to a certain extent when he gave Cleopatra the rich collection of the library at Pergamum (Asia Minor). This library, carefully built up by Eumenes II, the king of Pergamum, is thought to have possessed some 200,000 works written, for the first time, on parchment.

Other catastrophes were to follow, as if to emphasize the great fragility of works of the mind. The Library and the Museum of Alexandria may have been destroyed in the civil war which tore Egypt apart in the third century AD.

But Alexander's dream was not in vain. The Government of Egypt and the University of Alexandria, in collaboration with Unesco and the United Nations Development Programme (UNDP), have initiated a project to revive the famous Library. It is intended to endow the new Library with modern facilities which should enable it, at the dawn of the third millennium, again to fulfil its ancient role. But this time it will be linked by computer with archives and documentation centres all over the world. While recapturing the spirit of the original, the new Library of Alexandria will, at last, be indestructible.

ANCIENT ROMAN LIFE

John Woodford

Life in the Early Roman Empire (roughly the first two centuries A.D.) was indeed nasty, brutish and short, according to Bruce W. Frier, professor of classical studies, whose article on the demography of that era will be published in the forthcoming edition of *The Cambridge Ancient History*.

"We look at this ancient civilization as a wellspring of Western civilization, for we find a similarity of values between ancient authors and ourselves," Frier notes. "And we also acknowledge its organizational and administrative achievements. But despite these facts, when we examine something like life expectancy at birth — one of the fundamental measures of human welfare — we may conclude that in certain important respects, the Roman Empire's achievements were nil."

But Frier adds that in these respects, the Empire did not differ from contemporaneous societies. The picture of mortality, fertility and migration in the Early Roman Empire "generally corresponds," he says, "to what we'd expect of a pre-industrial society with limited medical development."

His and other scholars' "informed conjectures" about the far-flung empire that stretched from Egypt to Britain rest upon such scanty reliable data as tax documents, skeletal evidence and cemetery inscriptions, explains Frier, whose specialty is Roman law and social history.

Despite the lack of detailed local records like those that exist for the Middle Ages and Renaissance, it is probable that life expectancy for newborn females was around 25 years and 23 years for males, Frier reports. On the average, a year-old child would survive only to age 35, a 10-year-old to 46, and a 20-year-old to 50. A 40-year-old was likely to reach 60 — but only one newborn in eight could expect to reach 40.

The odds against living that faced any newborn can be expressed another way: Of a cohort of 1,000 newborn girls, fewer than half would live past 15; and of a similar cohort of boys, fewer than half would live much past 5.

These estimates are based on evidence that is somewhat skewed, Frier adds, "because the data tend to over-represent upper-class persons and families; for the population as a whole, life expectancy at birth was probably lower than these estimates put it."

Exploring why life was so short in the Early Roman Empire also reveals its nasty and brutish aspects.

The very high annual death rate of 40 to 44 per thousand resulted to a great extent from the population's virtual defenselessness against typhus, typhoid, Malta fever, malaria, tuberculosis, pneumonia, childhood diarrhea and other ailments.

Poor nutrition — brought on by very low wages and by an inability to transport food overland from thriving areas to the famine-stricken in nearby cities — was probably a greater factor in the high death rate than was poor medical care. The latter, according to Frier, "probably had no effect on mortality one way or the other."

"The population also suffered a very high violence rate, and a high level of death by accident," he continues. "One reads on epitaphs, for example, of a man of 22 from Ephesus who died of a

Filth, plagues and infanticide could make it nasty and short

hemorrhage after drinking a massive dose of wine. Or of a 35-year-old African who died after being 'deceived by a bull,' as his widow put it." Surprisingly, violent deaths did not, in the main, result from military activity, which was extremely low. Less than half of a percent of the empire's population was in the army (about 350,000 men.)

Sanitation practices took their toll, too, especially the dumping of a million cubic meters of human waste into the Tiber River each year. "That gives one pause," Frier comments, "when one reads of people bathing in the Tiber River. In fact, during the later years of this period, the physician Galen warned against eating fish caught in the Tiber."

At about this same time (A.D. 164), when the population of the Empire had presumably reached 60 million (a fifth of the world's total), Roman diplomatic and trading missions contacted China's Han Empire and also the Kushana Empire on the Indian subcontinent.

Roman traders may have imported more than silk and other luxuries upon their return. "Many scholars think smallpox, measles and the other plagues that afflicted the Later Roman Empire for several centuries were introduced into the Mediterranean by these contacts with Asia," Frier reports.

Whatever its cause, when Avidius Cassius and his army returned from Parthia (present-day Iran) in A.D. 165, the first smallpox pandemic struck, exacerbating the problem of everyday pestilence. "The plague rose and fell across the entire empire for 25 years," Frier says. "By 190, the city of Rome, which had a population of 700,000 to a million, was losing 2,000 residents a day to smallpox."

From the birth of Jesus to this time, the Empire's population had grown from 45 million to 60 million, but the scourge reduced it by 5 million over the next three decades.

Countervailing these overwhelming agents of disease and death, however, was the fertility of the Empire's adults.

"For any population to endure over a long period," Frier notes, "each generation of women must reproduce itself, which means that, on the average, each woman who reaches menarche must have a daughter who does so."

It appears that the average woman in the Early Roman Empire, bore five to six children if she reached menopause, or 2.5 to 3 daughters per woman, a very high reproduction rate by modern standards.

Unwanted daughters were far more often the victims of infanticide and exposure than were sons, who tended to be accepted if they weren't unhealthy or deformed. Neither of these family-planning practices was considered immoral; they weren't outlawed until the late Empire.

Various methods of contraception and abortion also were practiced. Some were likely to have been effective, others were dangerous, but most were folk-magical practices with no effect — like the effort of teen-age girls to induce a miscarriage by tying wool around their ankles.

"The 'advantage' of infanticide and exposure to the Romans," Frier says, "was that it gave parents control in determining whether they would rear a male or female child in instances where a female child was unwanted. However, Jews, and the Christians who followed Jewish law, did not practice direct forms of contraception or abortion, but unlike most Romans, they did know about, and practice, *coitus interruptus*."

Taken as a whole, the several family-planning practices may have resulted in a population of 107 men for every 100 women.

"We read many complaints from men about their difficulty in finding marriageable women," Frier says. "This disproportion also shows up in the high number of girls who married early and in the many men who married women of lower status. According to evidence on inscriptions, 30 percent of the females were married by age 13, and 50 percent by 15. Men tended to be 10 years older than their first wives, many of whom were prepubescent. Records indicate that 95 percent of women of marriageable age were married or had been married. Celibacy was rare; Rome had no spinster class."

These estimates reflect statistics about women from well-off families that prized legal marriages and who were important enough to reach the tallies of census-takers and other data-keepers. Many imperial residents, however, were barred from legal marriage: slaves, soldiers and sailors during the entire 20 years of their tour of duty and others. In addition, some Romans, such as freed slaves, were restricted in their marriage opportunities.

Men and women in these non-marriageable categories often entered into a relationship of concubinage, the Roman version of significant otherhood. The children of these unions were illegitimate.

Although the lack of data on illegitimate births is a problem for historical demographers, Frier says that there was probably no great difference in mores, fertility rates or other mating indices between persons living in concubinage versus those who were married.

"The Romans were relentlessly monogamous," he reports. "A married man was unlikely to have a concubine. But men and women who lived in concubinage weren't seen as 'living in sin.' Divorce was unregulated and could be initiated by a woman as well as a man, but it was uncommon, nonetheless, except among the upper classes. A man with a concubine seems to have been no more likely to leave his mate than was a married man. On the whole, the image of Roman life as riotous is false. Stable domestic life was the norm."

From a demographic standpoint, Frier concludes, the Early Roman Empire's mortality and fertility rates may have influenced its population growth far less than did the migration that gradually shifted the center of gravity of its population from east to west.

"The scope and direction of this migration was made possible by Rome's political unification of the Mediterranean," Frier says, "and it was undoubtedly the most important and enduring demographic achievement of the Empire."

Even if a larger population gave no other edge to the Western Empire than greater numbers to survive the decimating plagues, that advantage alone was profound, Frier says. In fact, however, the population shift had a qualitative significance as well.

"The Empire had few formal barriers to movement within its borders," Frier points out. "As a result, many Easterners from the commercial and intellectual classes — Greeks, Syrians, Jews and others — headed westward to Italy, Spain and Gaul in hope of gain. They spread Eastern religions, including Christianity, which we can trace in the New Testament as Paul visits Jewish merchant communities on his way to Rome."

Slavery and slave migrations also greatly affected the Empire's growth and development. The chief suppliers of these "involuntary immigrants," who made up 10 to 15 percent of the Empire's population, were slave traders; next came the military.

Demographers theorize, Frier says, that the growth rate of the West Empire's population over its Eastern half "may have been accomplished entirely through migration."

During the first two centuries A.D., the Western portion of the Empire gradually assumed a population density comparable to that of the East. Regions like modern Spain, France and Britain, thinly populated by local tribes at the time of the Roman conquest, began to emerge as important centers of urban life and culture. Not even the great plague of 165 undid this fundamental change.

There is no doubt, Frier sums up, that the plague "ushered in or immensely complicated a host of social and economic problems, to cope with which a new imperial dynasty was ultimately required."

The Emperor Who Never Was

Caesar conquered Gaul, but awaiting him was the treacherous Brutus.

Karen C. Huber

Stretching green and fertile toward the south and west, buttressed by purplish mountains on the east, the rolling hill country of central France is both beautiful and strategic. It traditionally has been the home of well-to-do farmers and vintners. Merchants for ages have made it their convenient corridor to places throughout western Europe. So have armies. Thus, central France has seen its share of invaders—at times, simply ragged bands in search of something to eat; at others, far stronger, more determined visitors.

Among the latter, Julius Caesar and his legions are probably the most famous. For eight years they labored to bring this rich territory under Roman control. As a byproduct of their efforts, the language and civilization of Europe's largest nation were converted to a Latin cast. For Caesar personally, there was also a crucial byproduct. His victory in the Gallic War was the catalyst which thrust him, the son of a moribund patrician family, from relative obscurity to the full light of notoriety. Gaul was both the making of Julius Caesar, and his eventual undoing.

The man himself is one of those controversial geniuses who so confound historians. Some see him as the consummate gentleman, generous to friend and foe alike; others as the far-sighted statesman, rescuing Rome from tyrannous factions. Still others say that the only tyranny was Caesar himself. Ancient sources are little help, for they present the same schizophrenic contradictions. In half the authors, he is the white-robed Father of His Country. In the other half, he is a black-hearted villain. The truth probably lies somewhere in the middle.

This enigma was born on the 12th day of July, 100 BC. Like all Romans, he took three names "Gaius," commonest of Latin appellations, was his personal name. He was further designated by a "Julius" (the family at large) and a "Caesar" (the branch thereof). The Julians, though aristocratic in origin, were comparatively impoverished and had political ties with the anti-aristocratic People's Party. Both circumstances followed and fashioned Caesar throughout his lifetime. His poverty made him ambitious and his plebian connections made him enemies.

However anomalous their politics and finances, the Julians endowed their young heir with the standard accouterments of the Roman noble: a dynastic marriage, political ambitions and an education stressing rhetoric and oratory, disciplines at which he excelled. He was always a master in the art of swaying masses to his way of thinking—and that, perhaps as much as his courage or uncanny battle skills, kept the legions steadfastly by his side.

These legions, as it happened, materialized only when Caesar was middle-aged. As a young man, he experienced incidental military action in the east, winning himself a civic crown, the bronze oak-leaf cluster awarded when one Roman saved another during combat. Soon back in Rome, he lived a gypsy existence—traveling to foreign universities, hiding in central Italy when a hostile politico seized Rome's helm, returning to the city when a friend rotated into office, finagling for money, and—because he had remarkable charm—making contacts with influential people.

His climb to power began in Spain. He was sent there in 61 BC as quaestor, the post in which political-military (the two were inextricably entwined for ancient Romans) novices learned the ropes. He left two years later, more experienced militarily and richer financially. He had collected a fortune large enough to unburden himself of some rather onerous debts and was now free to maneuver politically.

Politics was a discipline at which he excelled. By 59 BC he had moved center stage in Rome's power play. Through alliances with Pompey and Crassus, the city's strongmen, he obtained an annually renewable proconsulship in Gaul, giving him almost plenary powers. His mettle was tested there immediately, for the Helvetii were also on the move. Pushed by famine and bellicosè German neighbors, the tribes that inhabited what is now called Switzerland were poised on the edge of Roman territory. Rome, which 50 years before had been seriously threatened by similar wanderings, was not disposed to sit idle. To Caesar fell the duty of representing the Roman interest.

With decisiveness and cunning, he ordered his legionaries to build a 19-mile earthen wall, stretching from Geneva to the Jura Mountains. Then he dawdled at negotiation and rushed five legions, some 17,000 men, from Italy to support the solitary legion then stationed in Gaul. When the Helvetii became suspicious and attempted to break out of their geographical corral, Caesar cut their grain supply and ambushed their rear guard. Trapped and hungry, the Helvetii surrendered and were chaperoned back to their mountainous homeland. Such was the opening of the Gallic War.

Gallia Transalpina, as the Romans termed it, was a sprawling expanse that incorporated France, Belgium, Holland, Switzerland, and Germany west of the Rhine. Numerous Celtic tribes, distant relatives of the Scots and Irish, lived there in varying degrees of amity. As a people, they

Karen C. Huber. Reprinted from *Military History*, December 1987, pp. 8, 69-74. Reprinted with permission.

were proud, high-spirited, impetuous, and occasionally given to appalling acts of barbarism.

Throughout the Greco-Roman world, the Gauls were best known for their belligerent streak. Armed with longswords and stout wooden shields, they would unexpectedly rush over an enemy emplacement with the force of a windstorm, counting on the surprise and the impact of the initial onslaught to carry the day.

To do battle with such people, Caesar brought with him a methodical military machine, disciplined to a razor's edge and tightly organized. As *imperator* (a general who has won a victory), Caesar personally planned strategy and executed battle plans, aided by a staff of *legati*. Theoretically, the *legati* were appointed by the Roman Senate, but Caesar handpicked his own. In times of grave danger, he wanted to rely on trusted men to lead a beleaguered legion to safety. As for the ordinary soldiers, they were fanatically devoted to Caesar—he could count on them regularly to perform superhuman feats. Caesar by his constancy had earned that devotion. Although he was a stern disciplinarian (liars or thieves were subjected to the *fustuarium*, public beating to death without compunction), he was also generous in praise and largesse, magnanimous in victory, imperturbable in the few setbacks that came his way, and as unsparing of himself as of his men. During the heat of battle, he plunged into the fray wearing a red cloak.

After his encounter with the Helvetii, Caesar set about the conquest of Gaul in earnest. He spent a year contending with Germans from beyond the Rhine and with Belgic Gauls, a people whom he thought the bravest of all. He explored Britain. He built a small navy to fight off the maritime Gauls and their leather-masted ships along the littoral of Brittany. By 53 BC, he had opened the region's eastern borders, heartland and Atlantic coast to Roman settlement.

It had all been easy and swift. But the climax of the Gallic War, in which Roman domination would be confirmed or denied, was about to begin. Caesar was soon to meet his worthiest, most dangerous foe.

The *imperator* had spent the winter of 53 BC as he spent all winters—ensconced in northern Italy to better gauge the complex political plottings back in Rome. But there were plots in Gaul as well. A deep resentment was

stirring among the people, and the chiefs were restive, waiting for an auspicious moment to throw off the Roman yoke. The Gauls had their own communications network—they knew that Rome recently had been wracked with riot and unrest. Caesar, as much a political as military creature, might well be so entangled that he must remain in northern Italy. Emboldened by this possibility, the insurgents massacred a Roman settlement at Orléans and elected themselves a commander.

There is a statue of Vercingetorix in France today. Tall and handsome, heavily muscled, purposefully grasping the Gallic longsword, he looks every inch a leader. His bold even desperate behavior in the rebellion deserves such a heroic representation.

Though lord of only the Arverni, he was able to attract the loyalties of all the tribes as no one before—not an easy task, given the fierce independence and rivalries of the clans. This ability was critical. Caesar's policy had been to divide and conquer the isolated tribes. Now he must subdue something like a nation.

Vercingetorix first called for volunteers to man a cavalry strike deep within Roman territory. Soon a large force was ravaging Provence. The Gauls penetrated far enough to frighten Narbo, an important city on the Mediterranean.

The *imperator* sped to Narbo with a relief force and repelled the Gallic horse. Then, with a small company of men, he quietly crossed the Cevennes Mountains, beating his way through six feet of midwinter snow. Such unceremonious journeying was necessary. So dangerous was the situation in Gaul that he could not call his northern legions south to aid Narbo, nor could he travel to join them openly.

His swiftness, as so often in his career, paid off. He appeared suddenly in the central hill country, home to the Arverni, and laid waste to the farms and cities, forcing Vercingetorix to return and rescue his own people. Caesar then reached two of his legions in mid-Gaul—with them, he captured three rebel strongholds and marched on Avaricum, the most heavily fortified town of the region. Within a month, the city fell. Of its 40,000 defenders, 800 escaped.

Gergovia was Vercingetorix's capital, strongly protected behind the so-called *murus gallicus*, or Gallic wall, boxes of timber filled with rubble and

faced with stone. After the defeat at Avaricum, Vercingetorix and his loyalists had withdrawn to this citadel. When the legions arrived, the Gauls launched a barrage of missiles (the Romans replied with their catapults) and waited for Caesar to make a mistake. Eventually, and uncharacteristically, he did. He left camp to negotiate with wavering allies. During his absence, Gergovia's defenders mounted a deadly assault. The Roman counterattack was poorly executed and went awry, costing many casualties. Only Caesar's quick return saved his camp from capture.

For the first time, Caesar found himself in serious straits. The rebellion was reaching flood stage while he sat mired at Gergovia. He thus chose what was, under the circumstances, the lesser of several evils. He abandoned the siege and marched his troops to safer territory.

For Vercingetorix's forces, Caesar's retreat was cause for celebration. So was the knowledge that the legions were dangerously scattered and their supplies running short. Wooed by such glad tidings, all but three Gallic tribes rallied to Vercingetorix's side. Together, they sent another large cavalry raid into Provence. Then, before the Romans could mount a counteroffensive, they retired to Alesia, which means "rocky hill" in the ancient Celtic tongue. There, some hundred miles southeast of modern Paris, Vercingetorix and 95,000 warriors prepared to stand fast.

This time, Caesar left nothing to chance—the science of archaeology has since confirmed the awesome scope of his siegeworks. A 12-mile chain of camps and forts circled the city. Between Caesar's *castra* and Alesia's walls, there were a ditch, two trenches, and a massive earth revetment. The ditch reached 20 feet across, with sheer walls dropping for eight feet. The trenches, slightly smaller at 15 feet wide, were filled with water from a river diverted for that purpose. The palisade was 12 feet high and bristled with iron prongs. In the noman's land between ditch and palisade, Caesar's legionaries sowed *liliae* and *stimuli*—"lilies" and "stings." The lilies were sharpened and firehardened stakes hidden in small ditches and covered over with brush, the ancient equivalent of a tank trap. The stings were foot-long stakes embedded with iron barbs. To the rear of the camp, there were parallel fortifications.

Inside Alesia, the defenders easily grasped the purpose of these constructions. Vercingetorix sent out cavalry, but their do-or-die assault, designed to bring down the iron ring before it choked off all help, was soundly repulsed. He then sent envoys under the cover of night to beg assistance from all confederate tribes. The response was six weeks in coming but it was formidable. A quarter of a million infantrymen and 8,000 horsemen, representing 42 tribes, encircled the Romans from the outside.

It was now late September and the battle for Alesia began in earnest. The noncombatants of the city, those "who were useless for war, either from age or health," were expelled by Vercingetorix, lest they hinder the warriors or fall prey to starvation and cannibalism. Caught between the city and army camp, they pleaded with Caesar to make them Roman slaves. But he, short on supplies and fearing deception, declined. The noncombatant refugees were left to starve beneath the walls of the city.

For Caesar and his 50,000 legionaries, it was imperative to break Alesia soon, caught as they were between two large forces with winter approaching. Opportunity came shortly. Though courageous, the Gauls were badly organized and deployed. Three of their assaults were turned back easily. Vercingetorix then made a last wild attack on the siegeworks. It was a herculean effort. Caesar himself reported: "in every place, there was fighting at this particular time. Every possibility was attempted. Whichever spot seemed in danger, to that place the battle shifted."

The onslaught momentarily overcame Roman forces. As they buckled, Caesar himself pushed forward and rallied the men. Then, at the critical moment, Germanic cavalry, which he had held in reserve, burst out of the forest to the rear of the Gauls, hemmed them in and slaughtered them.

On the next day, Vercingetorix, alone and in full military panoply, rode down the hill to Caesar's camp. Then he dismounted and sat at Caesar's feet. Gaul (30 battles fought, 800 towns captured, and by Caesar's estimate more than a million persons killed) was now, for all intents and purposes, Roman.

Rome had not universally applauded his extraordinary exploits beyond the Alps. He had been the junior member of the coalition which set the cadence to which Roman politics marched, and junior members of any organization are expected to climb only so far. On the day Vercingetorix adorned his horse and rode down the hill in defeat, Caesar's band of envious and influential enemies in Rome were working for his elimination.

Their chance came two years after the capitulation of Vercingetorix. Caesar had remained in Gaul to quell sporadic outbreaks and to stabilize the region as a Roman province. All the while his Roman enemies cajoled the Senate. The Gallic War, they whispered, was complete. Caesar's command should be revoked. Finally, on January 1, 49 BC, the Senate acted, prodded by Pompey the Great, a masterful general in his own right and Caesar's former patron. Caesar was issued orders which offered no compromise—he must disband his army immediately and return to Rome as a private citizen.

Caesar had no alternative except to resist. Had he acquiesced, he would, at best, have been forced to sacrifice any further ambitions. At worst, he might well have expected an assassin's blade in the dead of night.

And so, with the speed which had rescued him so often before, he took matters in his own hands. He gave the main body of his Gallic legions marching orders to prepare quickly and meet him in Italy. In the meantime, Caesar himself led a small force to the Rubicon River, near present-day Ravenna. At this river, which divided Gaul from Italy, he agonized over a decision which would have resounding consequences. If he and his troops crossed, they would make civil war inevitable. Caesar famously did decide to cross the Rubicon.

As he rapidly approached Rome, his enemies dispersed to buy time and ready themselves. Pompey withdrew his men to the heel of the peninsula and ferried his way across the Adriatic to Greece. For three years Caesar and his lieutenants (most notably Mark Antony) attempted to ferret out the Pompeians. Murderous encounters stained the soil of Spain, North Africa, Greece, southern France, and northern Turkey. At last, on August 9, 48 BC, Caesar lured his great opponent to combat at Pharsalus in east-central Greece. It was a convulsive struggle between two bands of well-trained Roman veterans, each commanded by a brilliant leader. In the end, the greater experience of Caesar's troops carried the day.

The world was now Caesar's. He made brief forays to Egypt (where he dallied with the charming and duplicitous Cleopatra) and to the Near East (where the defeat of an oriental despot prompted his famous aphorism, "I came, I saw, I conquered"). Then he turned to Rome, there to be voted monarchial powers and to embark on a campaign of civic improvement and political renovation.

But Caesar had made a deadly miscalculation. After Pompey's death, he had chosen to forgive his former enemies, wishing for reconciliation and healing. It was an illusory hope. Many of his enemies' families—in particular, that of "the lean and hungry" Cassius Longinus—had feuded with the Julians for generations, a tradition which bred little gratitude and large animosity. These patricians would not tolerate the diminution of their powers at the hands of a hereditary enemy.

Their success is well-known, thanks largely to Shakespeare's famous play. On March 15, 44 BC, the day on which the Senate was to discuss granting Caesar the title of king, the *imperator* was surrounded and stabbed to death. Accounts of his last moments have him saying different farewells. One historian reported that he shouted, "Vile Casca, what does this mean?" Another says that Caesar gasped, "*Et tu Brute*"—"And you, Brutus"—to the man he had befriended and who was, according to rumor, his son from an early love affair.

Whatever his last words. Caesar had his own revenge on his assassins. His vigorous career had made it virtually inevitable that Rome would change from government by oligarchy to rule by an individual. It was part of Caesar's continuing legacy that his heir effected that very transition. For, waiting quietly in the shadows of obscurity on those fateful Ides of March, was a youngster named Gaius Julius Octavianus, the future Emperor Augustus, Caesar's grandnephew and adopted son. The need to avenge Caesar's murder galvanized Octavian into embarking on his own civil wars and achieving victories which eventually made him undisputed ruler of the Roman world. Every Roman emperor thereafter, whether related to the great Gaius Julius Caesar or not, took as his title the name "Caesar," meaning king and military leader. Thus did Rome pay eternal tribute to her most famous son, the Emperor who never was.

NERO, Unmaligned

Remembered for his excesses and little else, the eccentric emperor was a discriminating patron of the arts, a keen judge of men, and—while Rome burned—an energetic fire fighter

LIONEL CASSON

Gnaeus Domitius Ahenobarbus was a human beast. He once slaughtered a servant merely for refusing to drink as much as he was told. Driving on the Appian Way, he deliberately whipped up his horses to run over a child. When someone criticized him in the Forum, he gouged out the man's eyes on the spot. In A.D. 37 he was brought before the emperor Tiberius on charges of treason, adultery, and incest; only Tiberius's unexpected death saved him. About the one respectable thing he did was to marry a princess of the royal blood, Agrippina, a great-granddaughter of Augustus himself. He had one child by her, a boy whom they named Lucius Domitius; history knows him as the emperor Nero.

Nero's mother was a match for his father in cruelty, but in her it was disciplined by a calculating intelligence and cloaked by ostentatious deportment as a proper Roman matron. Her husband died in A.D. 40. Agrippina played her cards with such consummate skill that within nine years she had become the fourth wife of the emperor Claudius, despite his sworn resolve never to marry again (he had executed his third for publicly cuckolding him). A few months after the wedding Agrippina talked her new husband into adopting Nero, even though he had a son and two daughters of his own by previous marriages. In the ensuing years she manipulated the emperor into giving Nero all the outward

marks of preference, and in 53 she engineered the boy's marriage to Octavia, one of Claudius's daughters. Then, in 54, when her husband dropped dead— she had fed him a dish of poisonous mushrooms, so the rumors said—she got the troops of the palace guard to acclaim Nero as the successor.

And so a sixteen-year-old youth suddenly found himself heading an empire whose lands stretched from Gibraltar to the Syrian desert, from Britain to the Sahara, and whose subjects ran the gamut from primitive tribesmen to the highly civilized inhabitants of the ancient centers of Greece and the Near East. He was an absolute autocrat. His power rested, in the first place, on an army whose loyalty his predecessors had carefully secured, and, in the second, on the good will of Rome's multitudinous subjects to whom his predecessors had promised and furnished decent government. However, he was obliged to make it look as if he were but a partner in power, as if he shared the rule with the members of Rome's aristocracy who sat in the traditional governing body, the senate. This was a bit of theatre which, though it fooled nobody, for form's sake had to be maintained. Augustus, the founder of the Roman Empire, had devised the arrangement, and the elderly Tiberius and Claudius had kept it up, though with nowhere near his success, since they lacked his gift for public relations. In between was the brief reign of the young whippersnapper Caligula, who was clear-eyed enough to see that a Roman emperor was little short of a god on earth but not clear-headed enough to

realize he dare not act like one; he treated the senate with contempt—and was assassinated within four years.

However, Nero was no Caligula. What is more, he had some of the best brains in the nation at his side to guide him during his apprenticeship. Since the age of eleven he had been the pupil of Seneca, the philosopher and moralist; Seneca was now promoted from tutor to confidential assistant in the administration of the empire. One of Agrippina's adroit moves in paving the way for her son's elevation to the purple had been to get in her own man, Sextus Afranius Burrus, as head of the palace guard; he was made a high-level administrator and turned out to be a particularly able one. And then, at least in the beginning, there was Agrippina herself, the canniest politician in Rome, to keep the boy from any missteps.

The first five years or so of Nero's reign were, by all accounts, an unqualified success. His enemies—practically everything we hear about Nero comes in one way or another from his enemies— claimed that it was his advisers who were responsible for the operation of the government, and that the young emperor frittered away his time in frivolities and degeneracy. No doubt Seneca and Burrus did a great deal, but in many a key area Nero made his own contribution. He had a vast charm and an inborn sense of courtesy, gifts that helped him maintain harmonious relations with the stiff-necked senate, eternally resentful of their loss of power. He had a knack for selecting competent subordinates, and this resulted in the choice of a fine ad-

"Nero, Unmaligned," by Lionel Casson, *Horizon*, Autumn 1976. Reprinted with the permission of the author.

ministrator for the city of Rome. His keen intelligence produced reforms in the law and the system of taxation (although a visionary proposal of his to abolish all indirect taxes and customs within the empire proved too heady for Rome's commercial interests).

Even in the quicksands of foreign policy he did well. He had inherited two troubling areas, Britain and the Near East, and he handled both with outstanding success, in good part because of the way he had of picking the right men for his jobs. Rome had invaded Britain in A.D. 43, during the reign of Claudius. A program of pacification followed, and this seemed to be going ahead without snags. Then, in 61, a revolt headed by a redoubtable native queen, Boudicca, exploded, the Roman forces that rushed to stop her were cut to pieces, her men massacred tens of thousands of Romans and other settlers, and the whole Roman position on the island hung by a thread. Nero's military appointee, however, kept his nerve and managed to save the day. At just the right moment Nero replaced him with a man whose talents lay in administration rather than leading troops, and Britain gave the emperors no further trouble for more than three centuries.

Beyond Rome's eastern border lay the only nation strong enough to be a political rival to Rome, Parthia. A century earlier Rome had tried war—and left the field licking her wounds. Augustus, astute and practical, settled for diplomacy, and that worked well enough for a time. However, when Nero ascended the throne, it had lost its effect; that year the Parthians invaded Armenia, which Rome up to then had carefully maintained as a buffer state. Nero's solution was to appoint as commander in chief of the forces in the area a certain Gnaeus Domitius Corbulo and leave it to him to rectify matters. Corbulo, a martinet of the old school, drilled and drilled his men into Rome's best fighting force, and by the year 60 he had the Parthians out and Armenia back in the hands of a local king.

No doubt about it, the young ruler was bright and able. Yet certain things about him gave people pause—his artis-

tic and cultural interests, for example. Nero was a passionate devotee of literature and music: he composed verse, acted parts from Greek tragedy, and assiduously listened to the lyre-playing of the greatest virtuoso of the day. These were not qualities one looked for in a Roman, least of all a Roman chief of state. Even worse, Nero was distressingly cavalier about doing what was expected of an emperor, such as maintaining a grave demeanor, taking an interest in army matters, and watching gladiators spill each other's blood.

And there were disturbing indications that he was, after all, the son of his father. With a gang of kindred spirits, he used to roam the streets at night incognito, having a wild time housebreaking, looting, raping, and mugging passersby. During one of these escapades his career was all but cut short when he barely missed being clobbered to death by a resolute husband who stood his ground to defend his wife.

It was Nero's relations with his mother that revealed once and for all the Mr. Hyde that this charming, youthful Jekyll had within him. Agrippina, having won a crown for her son, settled down to enjoy pulling the strings from behind the throne. Nero quickly discovered how strong-willed a partner in power his mother could be, and equally quickly decided that there was no reason he had to put up with her. He neatly cut her out of all official business and removed one of her most useful tools, the minister of finance (replacing him with a man so able that four subsequent emperors retained him in office—yet another instance of his gift for picking subordinates). And when Octavia, the dutiful princess to whom Agrippina had married Nero, turned out to be unable to handle the imperial sexual appetite, he took on as mistress one of his servants, a freed slave, thus thumbing his nose at his mother and court propriety. Agrippina flew into a rage and let it be known that she was thinking of taking up the cause of her stepson, whose claims to the succession were as good as Nero's, maybe better. This was a serious blunder. In 55 the emperor eliminated this rival—the story given out was that the

boy had died of an epileptic fit—stripped Agrippina of her bodyguard, and moved her out of the palace.

For three years she managed to steer clear of danger, until Nero met Poppaea, the *femme fatale* of the day. The new inamorata was no mere slave: she belonged to one of Rome's best and most wealthy families, and being Nero's mistress was not enough for her. But Nero was still married to Octavia, and Agrippina, though she willy-nilly had to stomach her son's liaisons, would under no circumstances swallow a divorce. In 59 Nero settled matters by committing his second bloody crime: he killed his mother. The murder, of course, had to look like an act of god, and the scheme he thought up reveals yet another facet of the man, his fascination with mechanical devices. He concerted with the admiral of the fleet to design a collapsible boat. While his mother was staying at her seaside villa on the Bay of Naples, he invited her to dinner at his own villa nearby and then sent her home in the death trap. The boat collapsed on schedule but, by a freak, Agrippina escaped and made it safely to shore. So Nero perforce sent assassins; the story goes that, as one raised his sword for the *coup de grâce*, she pointed to her womb and cried, "Strike here!"

Nero had consulted with Burrus and Seneca about the murder. If not before, certainly by this time they must have realized they had a tiger by the tail. Somehow they managed to hold their charge in check for another two years, largely by encouraging his artistic interests and his appetite for grandiose public works. His passion for taking the stage to declaim or sing was stronger than ever, and he indulged it by giving ever more elaborate private performances; a special "emperor's claque" of five thousand young men carefully drilled in the art of rhythmic handclapping guaranteed adequate applause. He instituted a festival, to be held every four years, that featured Greek events—contests in singing, dancing, and recitation, rather than gladiatorial fights, chariot races, and other typical Roman fare. He started the first of his great construction projects (and the only one he was ever to complete), a public gymnasium and bath in Rome not far from where the Pantheon stands. The building was vast and sumptuous, the forerunner of the celebrated edifices that Caracalla and Diocletian were to put up. "What was worse than Nero?" quipped the Roman wit Martial a half century later, "what better than his baths?"

Then, in 62, Burrus died, Seneca was allowed to resign his office and go into retirement, and Nero, just twenty-five, was on his own. In the first eight years of his reign he had committed but two murders, one a political execution and the other very likely inspired by tortured psychological drives. This year he added three more. Two of his victims were senators who had fallen under suspicion, the third was his unhappy wife. He had already divorced Octavia on the grounds of sterility and twelve days later had married Poppaea. Octavia was banished to a remote island, but somehow banishment was not enough for him, so the wretched woman was beheaded.

• • •

The year 64 was climactic. Nero's handling of its events graphically reveals the extraordinary mix of traits in his make-up his sure hand in directing the affairs of his realm, his yearning to be recognized as a concert star, his feeling for art, his technological bent, and his brutal cruelty. The whole empire was at peace except for the old sore spot, Armenia. Two years earlier the country had slipped back into Parthian hands. Corbulo once again rescued it, and Nero then elected to try Augustus's method, diplomacy. He negotiated an agreement whereby the Parthians would put their man, Tiridates, on the Armenian throne but Nero would hand over the crown and scepter at Rome in other words, give Parthia control of Armenia but make it look like Rome's free gift. When Tiridates arrived in Rome, Nero, with his flair for public relations and his taste for the theatrical, built up the ceremony into a stupendous spectacle. Backbiters griped at the fortune he spent on it; they had no way of knowing that the peace the money helped to buy was destined to last half a century.

While waiting for Tiridates to arrive,

Nero finally satisfied a wish dear to his stage-struck heart—he made his public debut as a concert performer. Too nervous to open in Rome, he went to Naples; after all, the population there, being largely of Greek origin, could be counted on to appreciate the finer things more than a Rome audience with its taste for gladiators and chariot racing. We may be sure he was a *succès fou*.

And then came the event that was to make the name of Nero a household word. On the night of July 18, fire broke out in part of the Circus Maximus. For six days it raged unabated until a firebreak, by heroic efforts, was finally opened and the conflagration checked. Then it flared up again, though less intensely, in other parts of the city for three days more. By the time it was all over, only four of Rome's fourteen districts were intact; three had been wiped out, and seven nearly so.

Nero had been at his seaside villa at Anzio, some thirty miles away, when the fire started. He raced back to town and swung into action: he welcomed the homeless into his own gardens and all public buildings still standing, ordered additional emergency housing to be hastily erected, rushed in food from the waterfront and neighboring towns, and drastically cut the price of grain. His enemies rewarded him by putting about the story that, inspired by the spectacle, he had gone into his private theatre and sung "The Burning of Troy." In fact, he had been directing the fire fighting in his palace, which was near where the flames had first broken out, so careless of his own security that he came within a hair of being assassinated.

Once the crisis was over, Nero planned the resurrection of the city in a way that only one with a talent for technology could have devised. The ravaged areas were to be rebuilt with regular rows of streets and wide avenues, in place of the old narrow, crooked alleys, and with houses of a uniform height. The houses were to have adjoining yards in the back and continuous arcades along the front; the yards guaranteed light and air and served as a firebreak, and the arcades would be a blessing in the summer heat and the winter rains.

He enacted ordinances requiring that a certain portion of every house be made of stone, with no wooden timbers or beams, that no house was to share a wall with its neighbor, and that the stone come from two specified quarries in the hills about Rome which furnished a particularly fire-resistant variety.

The populace, filled with helpless rage at the calamity, was ready to believe ugly rumors, assiduously spread by the many who had no love for Nero, that the emperor himself had started the blaze. Nero's defense was to supply a scapegoat. He picked out a small religious sect so un-Roman in its make-up and practices that the whole city, nobles as well as plebeians, viewed it with instinctive mistrust. Members of this sect were rounded up and given the full dose of Nero's cruelty: turning over his gardens for the spectacle, he had some torn to pieces by dogs, others made into human torches. It was Christianity's baptism of fire as a persecuted religion.

The devastation of Rome had included Nero's own palace. Its replacement, he decided, would be a totally new kind of imperial residence, a luxurious country home complete with farmland, woodland, flocks, game, and gardens, all in the very heart of the city. To accommodate all this he confiscated a vast piece of Rome's choicest real estate. The southern half of the Forum supplied one part of the grounds, the place where the Colosseum stands today was marked off for an ornamental pond, and the hill to the east of the Colosseum was cleared to take the main building, the Domus Aurea, or Golden House. After Nero's death, the emperor Trajan razed the structure and had a public bath put up on the site. Parts of the Golden House were incorporated in the foundations, and, by this quirk of fate, escaped total annihilation. These surviving remains lay hidden right till the end of the fifteenth century. Their sudden discovery brought a stream of artists and notables burrowing underground to visit them. Raphael sent a young assistant; he returned with sketches of the wall paintings he had seen, and Raphael was so impressed he included a number of motifs from them in his decorations for the Vatican loggias. The discoveries later inspired a school of painting.

Today art historians recognize that Nero's palace was strikingly avant-garde, that its murals represented a distinct new direction in painting and its architecture a veritable revolution. Its use of concrete rather than squared stone, its octagonal rooms and domed ceilings to provide novel interior spaces, and its other innovations made it a pioneer building, and prototype of such glories of Roman architecture as the Pantheon and Hadrian's vast villa at Tivoli. Quite possibly the radical departures were inspired by the art-minded emperor himself; at the very least he gets the credit for giving them his enthusiastic approval. There is no question that he had a hand in the ingenious mechanical gadgets the new palace boasted: overhead pipes in the dining rooms that sprayed perfume and overhead panels that opened to shower down flowers, a ceiling in the main banqueting hall that revolved in imitation of the heavens.

Rome's rank and file had nothing against Nero: his victims never came from their number, he was careful to see that their rations of bread and circuses were as regular as ever, and his cultural antics rather amused them. But the powerful aristocracy, the members of the senate, were not amused: on top of having to rubber-stamp whatever the young tyrant set his heart on, on top of having to pretend wild enthusiasm at his endless musicales, they now had to watch what they considered a pretentious and costly folly take over the very heart of their city. So, in the year 65, the eleventh year of Nero's reign, when the empire was still enjoying peace and a new Rome was rising from the ashes of the old, a powerful group formed a conspiracy to assassinate Nero. Its leader, a senator named Gaius Calpurnius Piso, was better known for degeneracy than political idealism, and most of the members were equally unsavory. The day before the murder was to take place, a freed slave got wind of the plot, and the affair was nipped in the bud.

The reaction was predictable: Nero became a killer for fair. Of the forty-odd people implicated in the attempt, sixteen who were undeniably guilty lost their lives (most were allowed to kill themselves), and a large number, including no doubt some who were innocent, were exiled and degraded. But it did not stop there: for the Roman aristocracy sudden accusation, conviction, and death became from that time on a routine part of daily life. Among the many who in these days received the order to do away with themselves was Petronius, Nero's "arbiter of taste" and the author of the unique and brilliant *Satyricon*; he went to his death in the elegant and unhurried style that had marked his life. Even old Seneca fell into disfavor and had to commit suicide.

With hate hanging heavy all about him, Nero serenely continued to pursue the passion of his life, his career as a concert artist. By now the Greek festival he had inaugurated was due again, and this time he did not hesitate to appear on the public stage in Rome. The senate, we are told, voted to award the prizes to him in advance, hoping to avoid the scandal of having the emperor appear in his own capital in a line-up of professional singers and actors, but Nero would have none of it. He insisted not only on being a contestant but on behaving exactly like the other competitors: he remained standing throughout, never let mucus from the nose or spittle from the mouth be visible, awaited the judges' decision on bended knee. We are further told that to ensure a full house spies informed on any who stayed away, and that spectators went home with their hands bruised from compulsory clapping.

All this acclaim still left Nero unsatisfied. He must needs reap laurels in the land of discriminating audiences—Greece. So, in September of 66, leaving the government in the hands of low-level subordinates, he set sail. The Greeks obligingly lumped together in 67 their four great festivals—the Olympian, Pythian, Isthmian, and Nemean games—which normally fall in different years, so he could attain what only the most renowned virtuosos had attained, victory in all four. He was applauded so wildly, carried off such a plethora of prizes, that, in an access of fellow feeling, he announced to the Greeks his decision to return to them their ancient freedom. It was a grand gesture which helped the Greek ego enormously, relieved them of the taxes they paid to Rome, and cost Nero very little, since the take from so poor a country was minimal. Also on behalf of his beloved Greeks, he launched the most ambitious public works project of his career, a canal through the Isthmus of Corinth, to spare ships the long and sometimes dangerous trip around the Peloponnese. At least three great rulers before him, including Julius Caesar, had gotten matters as far as the drawing board; Nero actually got the work under way, personally carrying off the first basketful of earth. Like his other brainstorms, it was dropped when he died, but the little that was completed shows his customary technological expertise: the French engineers who tackled the canal again in 1881 followed the course he had mapped out and even used some of the cuttings his men had made.

By now danger signals were flying all over the empire. In Palestine there had erupted the bitter revolt that was to end with the razing of Jerusalem and the destruction of Solomon's temple. Another uprising was brewing in Gaul. And from Rome came frantic reports of unrest and cabals. Finally Nero tore himself away and early in 68 returned to the capital.

By March the revolt in Gaul was in the open, and Galba, the governor of Spain, had joined the dissidents. Though the trouble in Gaul was soon snuffed out, leaving mainly Galba to worry about, it was clear that something had happened to Nero. His cause was far from lost; all he had to do was issue appropriate orders, as he had so successfully done for years. But instead of taking action he talked, and so wildly or so grandiosely or so irrelevantly that he seemed mad. One day, for example, when the situation in Gaul was at its most critical, he convened a meeting of his key advisers and spent most of the time demonstrating a new type of water organ he planned to install in theatres.

In June the commanders of the palace guard, a pair of opportunists who figured it was time to desert a sinking ship, talked their men into switching allegiance to Galba, and the curtain was rung down on Nero's career. The senate scrambled to declare Galba emperor and Nero a public enemy. Only his freed slaves showed any loyalty. He fled to the house of one of them and there committed suicide. It is reported that during his last hours he ordered a grave to be prepared and then kept crying out, "To die! An artist like me!"

. . .

Christians, the victims of Nero's most hideous act, have made his name anathema. Yet, in a sense, they only picked up where the Romans themselves had left off: the two Roman authors who are the only sources we have for the facts of Nero's life had already destroyed his reputation. The first, Tacitus, wrote about half a century after Nero died. A staunch member of the senatorial class, he purports to write history, but deliberately slants it to tell a tale of moral degradation: the decline that began with the subtle scheming of Augustus, was hastened by the hypocrisy of Tiberius, and reached its nadir with the mad and sinister antics of Nero. The second, Suetonius, who composed a short biography of Nero a few years later, gives us in effect a condensed version of Tacitus's account decked out with every lurid detail he could dig up. To judge Nero dispassionately is about as easy as judging Judas Iscariot.

As a leader of the state he deserves high marks, certainly for the first ten years of his fourteen on the throne. The bureaucracy of the empire functioned as efficiently and fairly as it ever had. The watchword of his reign was peace, and by and large he achieved it; his settlement of the Parthian problem, lasting as it did a full fifty years, was a masterstroke. He squandered money on spectacle and display, on public works that were often more showy than essential, but he avoided that most expensive luxury of all, wars of conquest. He was a murderer—but though he killed the innocent, he did not kill many; he was no Ivan the Terrible.

What made the opposition to Nero so intense was not his cruelty but his ever-burgeoning megalomania and the way it drove him to demean his high office. When he merely played at being a performing artist, he could be indulged, and, in any event, the spectacle was contained within the palace grounds. When he took himself seriously and paraded his talents publicly, he was not only being a fool but disgracing the office he held and by implication all who were associated with him in it, that is to say, the entire membership of the senate.

As for Nero's subjects in general, in their thinking the peace he maintained counted far more than the state of Rome's majesty. Indeed, among the masses of Greek-speaking peoples of the empire, his manifest partiality for all things Greek was a distinct asset. They mourned with true feeling when he died. Many even refused to believe he was dead. During the next half century at least two imposters arose who claimed to be Nero, and both immediately gained a following.

Nero may have gone awry about his talents as a performer, but that was the only lapse of his critical sense. No other Roman emperor was a man of arts and letters in the way he was. He was a poet, and his verse, as we can tell from the few surviving samples, was not at all bad. His artistic taste is reflected in the coins struck during his reign; aesthetically they are the finest ever to come out of a Roman mint. Where art was concerned he had, too, the admirable quality of being receptive to new currents—witness the avant-garde architecture of the Golden House and the novel paintings decorating its walls. He even managed to make a contribution in the world of music and song, though for the benefit of Rome's Tin Pan Alley rather than her concert halls: Suetonius reports that he used to act out "comic ditties about the leaders of the revolts [i.e., in Gaul and Spain], which . . . have become popular favorites."

And then there is that dimension that is uniquely his: no other Roman emperor, in fact no other Greek or Roman writer or thinker we know of, possessed his avid interest in matters scientific and technological. The fiendish contraption for killing his mother is of a piece with the gadgetry in his new palace, with the down-to-earth specifics in his plans for a fireproof Rome, with the new type of water organ he was puttering over while the world was collapsing about him. He tackled the greatest public works project of ancient times, the Corinth canal; he did not complete it, but for other than technological reasons. He was responsible for a scientific voyage of exploration to the reaches of the upper Nile (his men came back with an exact measurement for the distance between Aswan on the First Cataract and Meroë just north of Khartoum). In Greece he took time off from his artistic endeavors to try to sound the bottom of a lake that, tradition had it, was bottomless. And what ruler or savant is there from any age who has earned renown in pharmacy? "A brimming tablespoon . . . of Nero's marvelous 'Quick Acting,'" states the author of a fourth-century treatise on medicines, "taken before meals . . . settles the stomach marvelously."

Nero deserves a better grade than history has assigned him. He was at times a monster, at times a fool, and he ended up a hopeless megalomaniac; but he was also a statesman, connoisseur, poet, songwriter and musician, mechanic, engineer, pharmacist—the closest equivalent to a "Renaissance man" to come out of the ancient world.

Up Against the Wall

Adept as they were at governing indigenous peoples, the Romans failed to subdue the tribes of northern Britain

William S. Hanson and Lesley Macinnes

William S. Hanson, a lecturer in archeology at the University of Glasgow and president of the Council for Scottish Archeology, is currently working on publishing the results of the excavation of a complete first-century A.D. Roman fort at Elginhaugh, near Edinburgh. Coauthor Lesley Macinnes, who is Hanson's wife, wrote her doctoral dissertation on later prehistoric settlement patterns in Scotland. She is employed by the government archeological service as an inspector of ancient monuments in Wales and Scotland.

Of all the Britons by far the most civilized are the inhabitants of Kent, a purely maritime region, whose way of life is little different from that of the Gauls. Most of those inhabiting the interior do not grow corn, but live instead on milk and meat and clothe themselves in skins. All the Britons dye themselves with woad, which produces a blue color, and as a result their appearance in battle is all the more daunting.
Julius Caesar

By the time of contact with Rome, the people of Britain were Celts, a name first coined by the Greeks in the sixth century B.C. in reference to tribes that occupied lands in northern and western Europe. Although linked by a common language and culture, these tribes never achieved political unity and became a single nation. How and when Celts came to Britain is uncertain, but close cross-channel links between Britain and Gaul (roughly what is now France and Belgium) are attested from as early as the second century B.C. According to Caesar, one king, Diviciacus, even ruled over territory on both sides of the channel for a time.

The term *Britain* derives from Pritani, a pre-Roman Celtic name that meant figured or tattooed people. This name was probably applied by the Gauls and was not one the inhabitants used for themselves.

Roman sources suggest that native society in Britain was in the main tribal, consisting of a number of different, culturally homogeneous groups, each with its own territory. The names of some of the tribes are recorded in historical accounts of Roman campaigns, but most are known from the geography of Ptolemy, written in the second century A.D. and probably based on original military maps. Ptolemy's map of Britain lists the names of many tribes, but gives their locations imprecisely.

The Romans were best informed about the tribes of southern England; both economic and political contacts between southern England and Rome prior to the invasion of A.D. 43 are well documented. The British tribal aristocracy filled their graves with wine amphorae and other high-quality Roman goods. In one case this included a silver medallion depicting the head of the emperor Augustus, presumably some form of diplomatic gift. Various Roman authors refer to political refugees from Britain appearing in Rome, including Adminius, one of the sons of the great king Cunobelinus (Shakespeare's Cymbeline). Such contacts probably played a major part in the speed with which southern England was brought under Roman control.

Roman descriptions of the northern people are rare. The most populous tribe in the north were the Brigantes, whose territory, centered on Yorkshire, spread across the whole of northern England and possibly into southern Scotland. They had early dealings with Rome and may have been more politically developed than the tribes farther north. Shortly after the invasion of A.D. 43, their queen, Cartimandua, made a political alliance with Rome whereby she insured that peace would be maintained on the northern frontier in return for Roman support for her faction

and access to Roman goods. The collapse of that relationship in A.D. 69, brought about by a clash of political factions within the Brigantes, precipitated a new phase of Roman expansion in the north. When constructed, Hadrian's Wall cut through the Brigantes' territory.

The only other northern tribe that figures prominently in the Roman sources were the Caledonii of northern Scotland (hence the term Caledonian as a modern alternative for Scotsman). They engineered the main opposition to the Roman conquest of the north, and their leader Calgacus led the native forces assembled against the Roman general Agricola at Mons Graupius in A.D. 83. This decisive battle marked the end of native resistance in the north for at least a generation.

Tacitus, remarking in the first century A.D. about the possible ethnic origins of the Caledonii, draws attention to their reddish hair and large limbs. Two Greek writers, commenting on the campaigns of Severus in the early third century A.D., provide more detail about northern tribes. Herodian reports that they

are unfamiliar with the use of clothing, but decorate their waists and necks with iron, valuing this metal as an ornament and as a symbol of wealth in the way that other barbarians value gold. They tattoo their bodies with various patterns and with pictures of all kinds of animals. This is why they do not wear clothes, so as not to cover up the pictures on their bodies.

Although much of this account is exaggerated, there are elements of truth in it—the Celtic custom was to fight naked, a custom that must have been repeatedly related by the troops that fought these tribes and one that is confirmed by contemporary Roman depictions on military inscriptions.

Dio paints a similar picture of a primitive society, although much of the account cannot be substantiated:

They inhabit wild and waterless mountains and lonely swampy plains, without walls, cities, or cultivated land. They live by pasturing flocks, hunting, and off certain fruits; for although the stocks of fish are limitless and immense they leave them untouched. They live in tents, unclothed and unshod, sharing their women and bringing up their children together. Their government is for the most part democratic, and because their especial pleasure is plundering, they choose the bravest men to be their rulers. They fight both in chariots with small, quick horses, and on foot, when they run very fast and also stand their ground with great determination. Their arms are a shield, and a short spear with a bronze apple on the end of the shaft, which they can shake and make a din with to dismay the enemy, and they also have daggers.

Unfortunately there are no contemporary accounts by the barbarians to balance these descriptions. All the evidence favors Rome, not merely because it was the more powerful society but because it was literate. A similar bias exists in archeology since Roman sites are both easier to locate and—because of the many mass-produced goods left by that consumer-oriented society—more readily dated. In recent years, however, more attention has been paid to the indigenous populations.

Although it is difficult to equate archeological sites directly with particular named tribes, considerable regional diversity is evident. In southern Scotland and northern England settlements tended to be quite small; most, such as Doubstead in northern Northumberland, enclosed no more than an acre. Here a rectangular, single-ditched enclosure of just over half an acre contained at least two circular timber-built houses fronted by a cobbled yard. Large quantities of coarse domestic pottery were recovered by the excavator, George Jobey, along with some more unusual items, including a ring, bracelet, and brooch, all of bronze, and fragments of glass bangles. These finds date to the first or second century A.D.

Some settlements, occupying hilltops and surrounded by deep ditches and large earthen banks, show a particular concern for defense. These hill forts were gradually superseded, however (often on the same site, such as at Edin's Hall), by less defensive, ditched or banked enclosures. Scholars have long believed that the Romans enforced this abandonment of hilltop fortifications, but there is growing evidence that this change occurred before the Roman conquest. Both types of settlements contained circular houses of timber

or stone, some of elaborate architecture, with external entrance passageways, internal paved areas, and walls capable of supporting an upper story.

A distinctive feature of southern and western Scotland are the houses built on man-made islands known as crannogs, such as that at Milton Loch, excavated by C. M. Piggott. Here large logs had been laid in the mud, side by side, to make a circular platform some forty feet in diameter. On this was placed a floor of split logs. Surrounding the platform were rings of upright piles, to support the walls of a house and perhaps an external walkway.

Large settlements are rare and accordingly distinctive. Two hill forts at Traprain Law and Eildon Hill North probably represent the tribal capitals of the Votadini and Selgovae, respectively. Each was some forty acres in extent, suggesting a population of considerable size. More than 300 house platforms are still visible within the ramparts at Eildon Hill. The capital of Queen Cartimandua of the Brigantes at Stanwick in Yorkshire was even larger. A massive stone rampart and rock-cut ditch enclosed some 730 acres of the valley floor, including grazing land and areas of habitation. In the limited sample of the interior that has been excavated, large, well-built, circular stone-walled houses have been revealed and great quantities of Roman pottery recovered, including imported tablewares and wine amphorae. The presence of Roman roofing tiles points to the adoption of Roman building techniques.

In the lowlands of northeastern Scotland there were no such large centers and fewer enclosed settlements. Dispersed groups of circular timber houses were the norm, often associated with extensive field systems and underground storage passages, generally called souterrains. These consist of curving passageways some fifty feet long and up to thirteen feet wide, lined with dry-stone walling. They were usually sunk to a depth of about six feet and had steep, narrow entrances, sometimes within a house.

In the mountainous terrain of the northwest the pattern is different again. Stone was the main building material, and settlements were small and defensive in character. The most distinctive buildings were the brochs, such as that at Dun Carloway on the island of Lewis, which are unique to the area. These structures are circular, hollow-walled, dry-stone towers some fifty feet in diameter, which may have reached as much as fifty feet high. Access to upper stories was by means of stairs and passageways within the walls. The ground floor, sometimes partitioned with upright stone slabs, contained stone water tanks and a central hearth.

Although Dio suggests that the native people were pastoralists and hunters, they were farmers as well. Eastern Scotland in particular includes some of the best farmland in northern Britain. Pollen analysis, evidence of prehistoric field divisions, grinding stones, and carbonized cereals, particularly barley, all confirm that the terrain was already extensively farmed.

The lack of intermediate-size settlements seems to indicate a fairly simple twofold hierarchical social structure consisting of a small warrior aristocracy and the population it controlled. Occasional preservation of highly decorated metalwork, such as the massive bronze armbands and snake bracelets unique to northern Scotland, illustrates the wealth of some elements of the population and their concern for personal adornment. Much of this metalwork relates to warfare—swords, chariot and horse fittings, and even a bronze war trumpet in the shape of a boar's head—lending weight to the assessment of one Greek writer of the first century A.D. that the Celts in general were "war-mad."

Perhaps inevitably, the primary interaction between Rome and the northern population was military. The most famous battle of all was that of Mons Graupius, an unidentified mountain in the eastern Scottish highlands. According to Tacitus, who is generally regarded as a reliable source, more than 30,000 native warriors faced Agricola there, of whom one-third lost their lives. The warriors, united under Caledonian leadership, came from all the tribes of the north. Slightly more than a century later all these northern tribes had been subsumed into two groups, the Caledonii and the Maeatae. Less than a hundred years after that, they had coalesced further into a single nation, the Picts (Latin Picti, or "painted people").

After Mons Graupius, major encounters were rare. Indeed, Severus found difficulty in persuading the Caledonii to face him in open conflict. They preferred less direct methods, taking advantage of the mountainous terrain to employ guerrilla tactics. Even when Rome was no longer actively campaigning, armed resistance continued to flare up. Nor was it limited to the tribes beyond the frontier. There is some evidence that the Brigantes, whose territory lay mostly to the south of Hadrian's Wall, rose in revolt in about A.D. 155. Tribes to the north of the wall caused

Native Peoples of Great Britain at the Time of Hadrian, ca. A.D. 126

the campaigns of Severus at the beginning of the third century do we see any lengthy period without unrest on the frontier.

"The Romans rule the most important part of Britain—more than half—and have no need of the rest; in fact that part which they have brings little by way of return." So wrote Appian in the preface to his mid–second century A.D. history of the Roman Wars. This judgment, whether accurate or not, illustrates Rome's attitude toward her provinces. They were there for the benefit of Rome: to be conquered, occupied, exploited, abandoned, or reconquered at her convenience. So it was with northern Britain. Over the centuries there were several Roman attempts to conquer Scotland, and as a result native contact with Rome varied in nature and intensity. The peoples of southern Scotland experienced Roman military occupation on several occasions; those in the far north and west may have rarely, if at all, encountered a Roman army on campaign. Of all the frontiers that Rome established in northern Britain at different times, Hadrian's Wall was by far the most enduring, but even during its use it did not always represent the limit of direct Roman control, let alone Roman influence. This extended considerably farther north, as reflected in the location of the so-called outpost forts beyond the wall.

Nor were all the northern tribes implacably hostile to Rome. Two tribes in Scotland may have established friendly relations with Rome at an early stage, perhaps even acquiring client status; even when the frontier was moved northward, Roman troops do not seem to have occupied large parts of the territories of either the Votadini or the Venicones, located to the south and north of the Firth of Forth.

In general, Rome preferred to deal with the native elite of conquered territories and use the preexisting social structure to control the area. Thus the capital of the Votadini played an important role in contact with Rome. This would have been necessary for the collection of taxes. Whether the Votadini continued to pay tribute to Rome when the frontier was withdrawn to the south of their territory is difficult to judge; however, during the latter part of the second century A.D. Roman outpost forts continued to extend as far north as Newstead.

How taxes were paid, we are unsure, since there is no evidence that the tribes of northern Britain used coins for daily exchange purposes. Possibly the taxes were paid in kind, for the demands of the Roman army were considerable, including

problems not long after. A religious dedication by a legionary commander, found at the western end of the wall, gives thanks for "the fortunate outcome of an action conducted beyond the wall," while another commemorates the "rout of a mighty host of barbarians." In about 180

the tribes of the north swept down and overran the eastern end of the wall, destroying several Roman forts in the process. Although peace was soon restored, in order to maintain it Rome was soon obliged to buy off at least one of the northern tribes, the Maeatae. Not until after food for the troops and horses and leather for all manner of equipment, including boots, clothing, saddles, and even tents. Wherever possible these needs were met locally. These requirements need not have put any major strain on the indigenous economy: the pollen record from northern England indicates that sometime before the Roman invasion, there was an increase in the levels of cultivation, a process that seems to have continued.

Individual tribesmen may have realized that Rome had new opportunities to offer. Able-bodied men from newly conquered tribes were recruited into the Roman army and posted abroad: units of Britons are known to have served on the German frontier from the mid–second century or earlier. Some northern tribesmen apparently moved south into Roman territory. In the early third century, one Lossio Veda refers to himself as a "Caledo" on a religious dedication set up in Colchester, in southeast England, making him the earliest attested emigrant from Scotland.

One apparent effect of the Roman conquest was an increase in population, reflected in the size and number of settlements. This occurred on both sides of Hadrian's Wall, but more so to the south, perhaps as a result of the greater security and economic stimulus provided by continuous Roman occupation. Despite this trend, the northerly regions seem to lack villa-style farms, the typical country residences of the wealthy romanized natives in the south of England. The vast majority of the fifty or so examples of villas that archeologists have found in northern England lie well to the south of Hadrian's Wall, mainly in southeastern Yorkshire, in the territory of the Parisi.

Some settlements were established as a direct result of the Roman occupation, growing up outside forts to house the sol-diers' wives and families (even though, until the reforms of the early third century, troops were not legally entitled to marry). Some soldiers took local women as wives; eventually most of the soldiers themselves were recruited locally. These settlements, particularly along Hadrian's Wall, gradually grew to become the markets for the local area. Although most do not seem to have long outlasted the eventual departure of the Roman army, two, Corbridge and Carlisle, became towns in their own right.

This contrasts sharply with the situation to the north of Hadrian's Wall, where no urban development is discernible. In northern Scotland, Roman impact was virtually nonexistent, although some Roman goods, mainly pottery, brooches, and glassware, did find their way to settlement sites. Even in southern Scotland, the occupation was never sufficiently long-term for substantial settlements to become established outside the forts. And while the native population of southern Scotland was able to trade or exchange goods with the Roman troops, the types of sites where these goods are found suggests that it was only the elite within native society who had ready access to this market. For example, large quantities of Roman material, including coins, brooches, pottery, glassware, and various bronze objects, have been recovered from the hilltop capital of the Votadini at Traprain Law. This site is also exceptional for it continued to receive Roman material until the fifth century, probably in the form of diplomatic gifts, confirming the favored status of the Votadini (although the presence of fine late-Roman silverware cut up for melting down into bullion might be more indicative of booty from raiding).

If we are to believe the Roman historian Tacitus, the effect of the Roman occupation was devastating: "They create a desolation and call it peace." But this was said largely for rhetorical effect and is not borne out by archeology. Although the conquest of new territory and its security depended on her army, if Rome was to continue to expand her empire, she had to persuade the peoples on both sides of the frontier of the benefits of Roman rule.

To appreciate what Rome had to offer, particularly the different social and economic values of urban life, the native peoples themselves had to be sufficiently advanced along the road to nationhood. The Brigantes of northern England apparently were at this stage of development and therefore open to the process of romanization. The majority of the tribes of Scotland perhaps were not, and although some in the south might have been favorably inclined toward Rome, those in the north were openly hostile. Even though Rome always had the military power to defeat any native aggressor, the sheer persistence of the northern tribes enabled them to retain their independence. The strength of the Picts was what effectively blocked the northern expansion of the Anglo-Saxons in the late seventh century A.D. But eventually they too fell victim to invaders, not from the south but from the west. By the middle of the ninth century A.D., they had succumbed to the power of the Scots.

For additional reading the authors recommend *Agricola and the Conquest of the North,* by William S. Hanson (London: Batsford, 1987); *Barbarians and Romans in North-west Europe,* edited by J. C. Barrett, A. P. Fitzpatrick, and L. Macinnes (Oxford: British Archaeological Reports, 1989); and *Scotland: Archaeology and Early History,* by A. Ritchie and G. Ritchie (London: Thames and Hudson, 1981).

MURDEROUS GAMES

Gladiatorial shows in Ancient Rome turned war into a game, preserved an atmosphere of violence in time of peace, and functioned as a political theatre which allowed confrontation between rulers and ruled.

Bronze sculpture
of a retiarius – a
fighter with a trident.

Keith Hopkins

ROME WAS A WARRIOR STATE. AFTER the defeat of Carthage in 201 BC, Rome embarked on two centuries of almost continuous imperial expansion. By the end of this period, Rome controlled the whole of the Mediterranean basin and much of north-western Europe. The population of her empire, at between 50 and 60 million people, constituted perhaps one-fifth or one-sixth of the world's then population. Victorious conquest had been bought at a huge price, measured in human suffering, carnage, and money. The costs were borne by tens of thousands of conquered peoples, who paid taxes to the Roman state, by slaves captured in war and transported to Italy, and by Roman soldiers who served long years fighting overseas.

The discipline of the Roman army was notorious. Decimation is one index of its severity. If an army unit was judged disobedient or cowardly in battle, one soldier in ten was selected by lot and cudgelled to death by his former comrades. It should be stressed that decimation was not just a myth told to terrify fresh recruits; it actually happened in the period of imperial expansion, and frequently enough not to arouse particular comment. Roman soldiers killed each other for their common good.

When Romans were so unmerciful to each other, what mercy could prisoners of war expect? Small wonder then that they were sometimes forced to fight in gladiatorial contests, or were thrown to wild beasts for popular entertainment. Public executions helped inculcate valour and fear in the men, women and children left at home. Children learnt the lesson of what happened to soldiers who were defeated. Public executions were rituals which helped maintain an atmosphere of violence, even in times of peace. Bloodshed and slaughter joined military glory and conquest as central elements in Roman culture.

With the accession of the first emperor Augustus (31 BC – AD 14), the Roman state embarked on a period of long-term peace *(pax romana)*. For more than two centuries, thanks to its effective defence by frontier armies, the inner core of the Roman empire was virtually insulated from the direct experience of war. Then in memory of their warrior traditions, the Romans set up artificial battlefields in cities and towns for public amusement. The custom spread from Italy to the provinces.

Nowadays, we admire the Colosseum in Rome and other great Roman amphitheatres such as those at Verona, Arles, Nîmes and El Djem as architectural monuments. We choose to forget, I suspect, that this was where Romans regularly organised fights to the death between hundreds of gladiators, the mass execution of unarmed criminals, and the indiscriminate slaughter of domestic and wild animals.

The enormous size of the amphitheatres indicates how popular

From *History Today*, June 1983, pp. 16-22. Reproduced by kind permission of History Today, Ltd., 83-84 Berwick Street, London W1V 3PJ England.

these exhibitions were. The Colosseum was dedicated in AD 80 with 100 days of games. One day 3,000 men fought; on another 9,000 animals were killed. It seated 50,000 people. It is still one of Rome's most impressive buildings, a magnificent feat of engineering and design. In ancient times, amphitheatres must have towered over cities, much as cathedrals towered over medieval towns. Public killings of men and animals were a Roman rite, with overtones of religious sacrifice, legitimated by the myth that gladiatorial shows inspired the populace with 'a glory in wounds and a contempt of death'.

Philosophers, and later Christians, disapproved strongly. To little effect; gladiatorial games persisted at least until the early fifth century AD, wild-beast killings until the sixth century. St Augustine in his *Confessions* tells the story of a Christian who was reluctantly forced along to the amphitheatre by a party of friends; at first, he kept his eyes shut, but when he heard the crowd roar, he opened them, and became converted by the sight of blood into an eager devotee of gladiatorial shows. Even the biting criticism quoted below reveals a certain excitement beneath its moral outrage.

Seneca, Roman senator and philosopher, tells of a visit he once paid to the arena. He arrived in the middle of the day, during the mass execution of criminals, staged as an entertainment in the interval between the wild-beast show in the morning and the gladiatorial show of the afternoon:

All the previous fighting had been merciful by comparison. Now finesse is set aside, and we have pure unadulterated murder. The combatants have no protective covering; their entire bodies are exposed to the blows. No blow falls in vain. This is what lots of people prefer to the regular contests, and even to those which are put on by popular request. And it is obvious why. There is no helmet, no shield to repel the blade. Why have armour? Why bother with skill? All that just delays death.

In the morning, men are thrown to lions and bears. At mid-day they are thrown to the spectators themselves. No sooner has a man killed, than they shout for him to kill another, or to be killed. The final victor is kept for some other slaughter. In the end, every fighter dies. And all this goes on while the arena is half empty.

You may object that the victims committed robbery or were murderers. So what? Even if they deserved to suffer, what's

your compulsion to watch their sufferings? 'Kill him', they shout, 'Beat him, burn him'. Why is he too timid to fight? Why is he so frightened to kill? Why so reluctant to die? They have to whip him to make him accept his wounds.

Much of our evidence suggests that gladiatorial contests were, by origin, closely connected with funerals. 'Once upon a time', wrote the Christian critic Tertullian at the end of the second century AD, 'men believed that the souls of the dead were propitiated by human blood, and so at funerals they sacrificed prisoners of war or slaves of poor quality bought for the purpose'. The first recorded gladiatorial show took place in 264 BC: it was presented by two nobles in honour of their dead father; only three pairs of gladiators took part. Over the next two centuries, the scale and frequency of gladiatorial shows increased steadily. In 65 BC, for example, Julius Cæsar gave elaborate funeral games for his father involving 640 gladiators and condemned criminals who were forced to fight with wild beasts. At his next games in 46 BC, in memory of his dead daughter and, let it be said, in celebration of his recent triumphs in Gaul and Egypt, Cæsar presented not only the customary fights between individual gladiators, but also fights between whole detachments of infantry and between squadrons of cavalry, some mounted on horses, others on elephants. Large-scale gladiatorial shows had arrived. Some of the contestants were professional gladiators, others prisoners of war, and others criminals condemned to death.

Up to this time, gladiatorial shows had always been put on by individual aristocrats at their own initiative and expense, in honour of dead relatives. The religious component in gladiatorial ceremonies continued to be important. For example, attendants in the arena were dressed up as gods. Slaves who tested whether fallen gladiators were really dead or just pretending, by applying a red-hot cauterising iron, were dressed as the god Mercury. Those who dragged away the dead bodies were dressed as Pluto, the god of the underworld. During the persecutions of Christians, the victims were sometimes led around the arena in a procession dressed up as priests and priestesses of pagan cults, before being stripped naked and thrown to the wild beasts. The welter of blood in gladiatorial and wild-beast shows, the

squeals and smell of the human victims and of slaughtered animals are completely alien to us and almost unimaginable. For some Romans they must have been reminiscent of battlefields, and, more immediately for everyone, associated with religious sacrifice. At one remove, Romans, even at the height of their civilisation, performed human sacrifice, purportedly in commemoration of their dead.

By the end of the last century BC, the religious and commemorative elements in gladiatorial shows were eclipsed by the political and the spectacular. Gladiatorial shows were public performances held mostly, before the amphitheatre was built, in the ritual and social centre of the city, the Forum. Public participation, attracted by the splendour of the show and by distributions of meat, and by betting, magnified the respect paid to the dead and the honour of the whole family. Aristocratic funerals in the Republic (before 31 BC) were political acts. And funeral games had political implications, because of their popularity with citizen electors. Indeed, the growth in the splendour of gladiatorial shows was largely fuelled by competition between ambitious aristocrats, who wished to please, excite and increase the number of their supporters.

In 42 BC, for the first time, gladiatorial fights were substituted for chariot-races in official games. After that in the city of Rome, regular gladiatorial shows, like theatrical shows and chariot-races, were given by officers of state, as part of their official careers, as an official obligation and as a tax on status. The Emperor Augustus, as part of a general policy of limiting aristocrats' opportunities to court favour with the Roman populace, severely restricted the number of regular gladiatorial shows to two each year. He also restricted their splendour and size. Each official was forbidden to spend more on them than his colleagues, and an upper limit was fixed at 120 gladiators a show.

These regulations were gradually evaded. The pressure for evasion was simply that, even under the emperors, aristocrats were still competing with each other, in prestige and political success. The splendour of a senator's public exhibition could make or break his social and political reputation. One aristocrat, Symmachus, wrote to a friend: 'I must now outdo the reputation earned by my own shows; our family's

The handle of a knife with the figure of a gladiator carved in ivory.

Graffiti of gladiators from the walls of Pompeii, showing their 'show-biz' appeal.

recent generosity during my consulship and the official games given for my son allow us to present nothing mediocre'. So he set about enlisting the help of various powerful friends in the provinces. In the end, he managed to procure antelopes, gazelles, leopards, lions, bears, bear-cubs, and even some crocodiles, which only just survived to the beginning of the games, because for the previous fifty days they had refused to eat. Moreover, twenty-nine Saxon

prisoners of war strangled each other in their cells on the night before their final scheduled appearance. Symmachus was heart-broken. Like every donor of the games, he knew that his political standing was at stake. Every presentation was in Goffman's strikingly apposite phrase 'a status bloodbath'.

The most spectacular gladiatorial shows were given by the emperors themselves at Rome. For example, the Emperor Trajan, to celebrate his conquest of Dacia (roughly modern Roumania), gave games in AD 108-9 lasting 123 days in which 9,138 gladiators fought and eleven thousand animals were slain. The Emperor Claudius in AD 52 presided in full military regalia over a battle on a lake near Rome between two naval squadrons, manned for the occasion by 19,000 forced combatants. The palace guard, stationed behind stout barricades, which also prevented the combatants from escaping, bombarded the ships with missiles from catapults. After a faltering start, because the men refused to fight, the battle according to Tacitus 'was fought with the spirit of free men, although between criminals. After much bloodshed, those who survived were spared extermination'.

The quality of Roman justice was often tempered by the need to satisfy the demand for the condemned. Christians, burnt to death as scapegoats after the great fire at Rome in AD 64, were not alone in being sacrificed for public entertainment. Slaves and bystanders, even the spectators themselves, ran the risk of becoming victims of emperors' truculent whims. The Emperor Claudius, for example, dissatisfied with how the stage machinery worked, ordered the stage mechanics responsible to fight in the arena. One day when there was a shortage of condemned criminals, the Emperor Caligula commanded that a whole section of the crowd be seized and thrown to the wild beasts instead. Isolated incidents, but enough to intensify the excitement of those who attended. Imperial legitimacy was reinforced by terror.

As for animals, their sheer variety symbolised the extent of Roman power and left vivid traces in Roman art. In 169 BC, sixty-three African lions and leopards, forty bears and several elephants were hunted down in a single show. New species were gradually introduced to Roman spectators (tigers, crocodiles, giraffes, lynxes, rhinoceros, ostriches, hippopotami) and killed for

their pleasure. Not for Romans the tame viewing of caged animals in a zoo. Wild beasts were set to tear criminals to pieces as public lesson in pain and death. Sometimes, elaborate sets and theatrical backdrops were prepared in which, as a climax, a criminal was devoured limb by limb. Such spectacular punishments, common enough in pre-industrial states, helped reconstitute sovereign power. The deviant criminal was punished; law and order were re-established.

The labour and organisation required to capture so many animals and to deliver them alive to Rome must have been enormous. Even if wild animals were more plentiful then than now, single shows with one hundred, four hundred or six hundred lions, plus other animals, seem amazing. By contrast, after Roman times, no hippopotamus was seen in Europe until one was brought to London by steamship in 1850. It took a whole regiment of Egyptian soldiers to capture it, and involved a five month journey to bring it from the White Nile to Cairo. And yet the Emperor Commodus, a dead-shot with spear and bow, himself killed five hippos, two elephants, a rhinoceros and a giraffe, in one show lasting two days. On another occasion he killed 100 lions and bears in a single morning show, from safe walkways specially constructed across the arena. It was, a contemporary remarked, 'a better demonstration of accuracy than of courage'. The slaughter of exotic animals in the emperor's presence, and exceptionally by the emperor himself or by his palace guards, was a spectacular dramatisation of the emperor's formidable power: immediate, bloody and symbolic.

Gladiatorial shows also provided an arena for popular participation in politics. Cicero explicitly recognised this towards the end of the Republic: 'the judgement and wishes of the Roman people about public affairs can be most clearly expressed in three places: public assemblies, elections, and at plays or gladiatorial shows'. He challenged a political opponent: 'Give yourself to the people. Entrust yourself to the Games. Are you terrified of not being applauded?' His comments underline the fact that the crowd had the important option of giving or of witolding applause, of hissing or of being silent.

Under the emperors, as citizens' rights to engage in politics diminished, gladiatorial shows and games provided repeated opportunities for the dramatic confrontation of rulers and ruled. Rome was unique among large historical empires in allowing, indeed in expecting, these regular meetings between emperors and the massed populace of the capital, collected together in a single crowd. To be sure, emperors could mostly stage-manage their own appearance and reception. They gave extravagant shows. They threw gifts to the crowd – small marked wooden balls (called *missilia*) which could be exchanged for various luxuries. They occasionally planted their own claques in the crowd.

Mostly, emperors received standing ovations and ritual acclamations. The Games at Rome provided a stage for the emperor to display his majesty – luxurious ostentation in procession, accessibility to humble petitioners, generosity to the crowd, human involvement in the contests themselves, graciousness or arrogance towards the assembled aristocrats, clemency or cruelty to the vanquished. When a gladiator fell, the crowd would shout for mercy or dispatch. The emperor might be swayed by their shouts or gestures, but he alone, the final arbiter, decided who was to live or die. When the emperor entered the amphitheatre, or decided the fate of a fallen gladiator by the movement of his thumb, at that moment he had 50,000 courtiers. He knew that he was *Cæsar Imperator*, Foremost of Men.

Things did not always go the way the emperor wanted. Sometimes, the crowd objected, for example to the high price of wheat, or demanded the execution of an unpopular official or a reduction in taxes. Caligula once reacted angrily and sent soldiers into the crowd with orders to execute summarily anyone seen shouting. Understandably, the crowd grew silent, though sullen. But the emperor's increased unpopularity encouraged his assassins to act. Dio, senator and historian, was present at another popular demonstration in the Circus in AD 195. He was amazed that the huge crowd (the Circus held up to 200,000 people) strung out along the track, shouted for an end to civil war 'like a well-trained choir'.

Dio also recounted how with his own eyes he saw the Emperor Commodus cut off the head of an ostrich as a sacrifice in the arena then walk towards the congregated senators whom he hated, with the sacrificial knife in one hand and the severed head of the bird in the other,

(Above) Clay lamp showing gladiators' weapons. (Right) A clay pot depicting gladiators fighting.

clearly indicating, so Dio thought, that it was the senators' necks which he really wanted. Years later, Dio recalled how he had kept himself from laughing (out of anxiety, presumably) by chewing desperately on a laurel leaf which he plucked from the garland on his head.

Consider how the spectators in the amphitheatre sat: the emperor in his gilded box, surrounded by his family; senators and knights each had special seats and came properly dressed in their distinctive purple-bordered togas. Soldiers were separated from civilians. Even ordinary citizens had to wear the heavy white woollen toga, the formal dress of a Roman citizen, and sandals, if they wanted to sit in the bottom two main tiers of seats. Married men sat separately from bachelors, boys sat in a separate block, with their teachers in the next block. Women, and the very poorest men dressed in the drab grey cloth associated with mourning, could sit or stand only in the top tier of the amphitheatre. Priests and Vestal Virgins (honorary men) had reserved seats at the front. The correct dress and segregation of ranks underlined the formal ritual elements in the occasion, just as the steeply banked seats reflected the steep stratification of Roman society. It mattered where you sat, and where you were seen to be sitting.

Gladiatorial shows were political theatre. The dramatic performance took place, not only in the arena, but between different sections of the audience. Their interaction should be included in any thorough account of the Roman constitution. The amphitheatre was the

Roman crowd's parliament. Games are usually omitted from political histories, simply because in our own society, mass spectator sports count as leisure. But the Romans themselves realised that metropolitan control involved 'bread and circuses'. 'The Roman people', wrote Marcus Aurelius' tutor Fronto, 'is held together by two forces: wheat doles and public shows'.

Enthusiastic interest in gladiatorial shows occasionally spilled over into a desire to perform in the arena. Two emperors were not content to be spectators-in-chief. They wanted to be prize performers as well. Nero's histrionic ambitions and success as musician and actor were notorious. He also prided himself on his abilities as a charioteer. Commodus performed as a gladiator in the amphitheatre, though admittedly only in preliminary bouts with blunted weapons. He won all his fights and charged the imperial treasury a million sesterces for each appearance (enough to feed a thousand families for a year). Eventually, he was assassinated when he was planning to be inaugurated as consul (in AD 193), dressed as a gladiator.

Commodus' gladiatorial exploits were an idiosyncratic expression of a culture obsessed with fighting, bloodshed, ostentation and competition. But at least seven other emperors practised as gladiators, and fought in gladiatorial contests. And so did Roman senators and knights. Attempts were made to stop them by law; but the laws were evaded.

Roman writers tried to explain away these senators' and knights' outrageous

Fresco showing riots between men of
Pompeii and Nuceria in and around the
amphitheatre in AD 59.

behaviour by calling them morally degenerate, forced into the arena by wicked emperors or their own profligacy. This explanation is clearly inadequate, even though it is difficult to find one which is much better. A significant part of the Roman aristocracy, even under the emperors, was still dedicated to military prowess: all generals were senators; all senior officers were senators or knights. Combat in the arena gave aristocrats a chance to display their fighting skill and courage. In spite of the opprobrium and at the risk of death, it was their last chance to play soldiers in front of a large audience.

Gladiators were glamour figures, culture heroes. The probable life-span of each gladiator was short. Each successive victory brought further risk of defeat and death. But for the moment, we are more concerned with image than with reality. Modern pop-stars and athletes have only a short exposure to full-glare publicity. Most of them fade rapidly from being household names

into obscurity, fossilised in the memory of each generation of adolescent enthusiasts. The transience of the fame of each does not diminish their collective importance.

So too with Roman gladiators. Their portraits were often painted. Whole walls in public porticos were sometimes covered with life-size portraits of all the gladiators in a particular show. The actual events were magnified beforehand by expectation and afterwards by memory. Street advertisements stimulated excitement and anticipation. Hundreds of Roman artefacts – sculptures, figurines, lamps, glasses – picture gladiatorial fights and wild-beast shows. In conversation and in daily life, chariot-races and gladiatorial fights were all the rage. 'When you enter the lecture halls', wrote Tacitus, 'what else do you hear the young men talking about?' Even a baby's nursing bottle, made of clay and found at Pompeii, was stamped with the figure of a gladiator. It symbolised the

hope that the baby would imbibe a gladiator's strength and courage.

The victorious gladiator, or at least his image, was sexually attractive. Graffiti from the plastered walls of Pompeii carry the message:

Celadus [a stage name, meaning Crowd's Roar], thrice victor and thrice crowned, the young girls' heart-throb, and Crescens the Netter of young girls by night.

The ephemera of AD 79 have been preserved by volcanic ash. Even the defeated gladiator had something sexually portentous about him. It was customary, so it is reported, for a new Roman bride to have her hair parted with a spear, at best one which had been dipped in the body of a defeated and killed gladiator.

The Latin word for sword – *gladius* – was vulgarly used to mean penis. Several artefacts also suggest this association. A small bronze figurine from Pompeii depicts a cruel-looking gladiator fighting off with his sword a dog-like wild-beast which grows out of his erect and elongated penis. Five bells hang down from various parts of his body and a hook is attached to the gladiator's head, so that the whole ensemble could hang as a bell in a doorway. Interpretation must be speculative. But this evidence suggests that there was a close link, in some Roman minds, between gladiatorial fighting and sexuality. And it seems as though gladiatoral bravery for some Roman men represented an attractive yet dangerous, almost threatening, macho masculinity.

Gladiators attracted women, even though most of them were slaves. Even if they were free or noble by origin, they were in some sense contaminated by their close contact with death. Like suicides, gladiators were in some places excluded from normal burial grounds. Perhaps their dangerous ambiguity was part of their sexual attraction. They were, according to the Christian Tertullian, both loved and despised: 'men give them their souls, women their bodies too'. Gladiators were 'both glorified and degraded'.

In a vicious satire, the poet Juvenal ridiculed a senator's wife, Eppia, who had eloped to Egypt with her favourite swordsman:

Gladiator's dress helmet found at Herculaneum.

pared. One would have imagined that these were the pirates. The trumpets sounded their foreboding notes; stretchers for the dead were brought on, a funeral parade before death. Everywhere I could see wounds, groans, blood, danger . . .

He went on to describe his thoughts, his memories in the moments when he faced death, before he was dramatically and conveniently rescued by a friend. That was fiction. In real life gladiators died.

Why did Romans popularise fights to the death between armed gladiators? Why did they encourage the public slaughter of unarmed criminals? What was it which transformed men who were timid and peaceable enough in private, as Tertullian put it, and made them shout gleefully for the merciless destruction of their fellow men? Part of the answer may lie in the simple development of a tradition, which fed on itself and its own success. Men liked blood

Bronze tintinnabulum of a gladiator from Pompeii.

What was the youthful charm that so fired Eppia? What hooked her? What did she see in him to make her put up with being called 'The Gladiator's Moll'? Her poppet, her Sergius, was no chicken, with a dud arm that prompted hope of early retirement. Besides, his face looked a proper mess, helmet scarred, a great wart on his nose, an unpleasant discharge always trickling from one eye. But he was a Gladiator. That word makes the whole breed seem handsome, and made her prefer him to her children and country, her sister and husband. Steel is what they fall in love with.

Satire certainly, and exaggerated, but pointless unless it was also based to some extent in reality. Modern excavators, working in the armoury of the gladiatorial barracks in Pompeii found eighteen skeletons in two rooms, presumably of gladiators caught there in an ash storm; they included only one woman, who was wearing rich gold jewellery, and a necklace set with emeralds. Occasionally, women's attachment to gladiatorial combat went further. They fought in the arena themselves. In the storeroom of the British Museum, for example, there is a small stone relief, depicting two

female gladiators, one with breast bare, called Amazon and Achillia. Some of these female gladiators were free women of high status.

Behind the brave façade and the hope of glory, there lurked the fear of death. 'Those about to die salute you, Emperor'. Only one account survives of what it was like from the gladiator's point of view. It is from a rhetorical exercise. The story is told by a rich young man who had been captured by pirates and was then sold on as a slave to a gladiatorial trainer:

And so the day arrived. Already the populace had gathered for the spectacle of our punishment, and the bodies of those about to die had their own death-parade across the arena. The presenter of the shows, who hoped to gain favour with our blood, took his seat . . . Although no one knew my birth, my fortune, my family, one fact made some people pity me; I seemed unfairly matched. I was destined to be a certain victim in the sand . . . All around I could hear the instruments of death: a sword being sharpened, iron plates being heated in a fire [to stop fighters retreating and to prove that they were not faking death], birch-rods and whips were pre-

Terracotta relief of a gladiatorial circus.

and cried out for more. Part of the answer may also lie in the social psychology of the crowd, which relieved individuals of responsbility for their actions, and in the psychological mechanisms by which some spectators identified more easily with the victory of the aggressor than with the sufferings of the vanquished. Slavery and the steep stratification of society must also have contributed. Slaves were at the mercy of their owners. Those who were destroyed for public edification and entertainment were considered worthless, as non-persons; or, like Christian martyrs, they were considered social outcasts, and tortured as one Christian martyr put it 'as if we no longer existed'. The brutalisation of the spectators fed on the dehumanisation of the victims.

Rome was a cruel society. Brutality was built into its culture in private life, as well as in public shows. The tone was set by military discipline and by slavery. The state had no legal monopoly of capital punishment until the second century AD. Before then, a master could crucify his slaves publicly if he wished. Seneca recorded from his own observations the various ways in which crucifixions were carried out, in order to increase pain. At private dinner-parties, rich Romans regularly presented two or three pairs of gladiators: 'when they have finished dining and are filled with drink', wrote a critic in the time of Augustus, 'they call in the gladiators. As soon as one has his throat cut, the diners applaud with delight'. It is worth stressing that we are dealing here not with individual sadistic psycho-pathology, but with a deep cultural difference. Roman commitment to cruelty presents us with a cultural gap which it is difficult to cross.

Popular gladiatorial shows were a by-product of war, discipline and death. For centuries, Rome had been devoted to war and to the mass participation of citizens in battle. They won their huge empire by discipline and control. Public executions were a gruesome reminder to non-combatants, citizens, subjects and slaves, that vengeance would be exacted if they rebelled or betrayed their country. The arena provided a living enactment of the hell portrayed by Christian preachers. Public punishment ritually re-established the moral and political order. The power of the state was dramatically reconfirmed.

When long-term peace came to the heartlands of the empire, after 31 BC, militaristic traditions were preserved at Rome in the domesticated battlefield of the amphitheatre. War had been converted into a game, a drama repeatedly replayed, of cruelty, violence, blood and death. But order still needed to be preserved. The fear of death still had to be assuaged by ritual. In a city as large as Rome, with a population of close on a million by the end of the last century BC, without an adequate police force, disorder always threatened.

Gladiatorial shows and public executions reaffirmed the moral order, by the sacrifice of human victims – slaves, gladiators, condemned criminals or impious Christians. Enthusiastic participation, by spectators rich and poor, raised and then released collective tensions, in a society which traditionally idealised impassivity. Gladiatorial shows provided a psychic and political safety valve for the metropolitan population. Politically, emperors risked occasional conflict, but the populace could usually be diverted or fobbed off. The crowd lacked the coherence of a rebellious political ideology. By and large, it found its satisfaction in cheering its support of established order. At the psychological level, gladiatorial shows provided a stage for shared violence and tragedy. Each show reassured spectators that they had yet again survived disaster. Whatever happened in the arena, the spectators were on the winning side. 'They found comfort for death' wrote Tertullian with typical insight, 'in murder'.

FOR FURTHER READING:

An expanded version of this article with references appears in K. Hopkins, *Death and renewal, Sociological Studies in Roman History*, Volume 2 (Cambridge University Press, May 1983, £19.50). The most extensive review of the evidence on gladiatorial games is by L. Friedlaender, *Roman Life and Manners, Volume 2 with references in Volume 4* (London, 1913). A more accessible and readable account is given by M. Grant, *Gladiators*, (Weidenfeld and Nicolson, 1976). On the methods used here, see C. Geertz, *The Interpretation of Cultures* (Weidenfeld and Nicolson, 1973).

The Judeo-Christian Heritage

Western civilization took root in the Graeco-Roman world but, notwithstanding all we owe to the classical idea, we are no less indebted to the Judeo-Christian tradition. If we derive humanism and materialism, philosophy and science, from the former, we derive our God and our forms of worship from the latter. Of course, it is difficult (and perhaps misguided) to separate these traditions, for the Judeo-Christian heritage comes to us through a Hellenistic filter. "Jews and Christians in a Roman World" explores this angle.

On the political surface the history of the Jews seems similar to that of other small kingdoms of the Near East, caught as they were between such powerful neighbors as the Babylonians, Assyrians, and Persians. Yet of all the peoples of that time and place, only the Jews have had a lasting influence. What appears to differentiate the Jews from all the rest, writes Crane Brinton, is "the will to persist, to be themselves, to be a people." The appearance of Israel on the map of the modern world 2,000 years after the Romans destroyed the Jewish client-state is a testimonial to the spirit described by Brinton.

The legacy of the Jews is a great one. It includes the rich literacy traditions found in their sacred texts. Among the significant writings left by the ancient Jews are the Dead Sea scrolls, which are re-examined here in the essay by Norman Golb. In addition to such materials, the Jews have bequeathed to Western civilization their unique view of history, which is at once linear and, based as it is on the Covenant idea, miraculous—God intervenes in history to punish his Chosen People; a messianic impulse that inspired Christianity and other cults; the elemental morality of the Ten Commandments and the moral wisdom of the prophets; and monotheism, the worship of their unique God, Yahweh.

A brief comparison of Yahweh and the Greek god Zeus illustrates the originality of the Jewish conception. Both gods began as warrior deities of tribal cultures. But, as Zeus evolved, he was concerned chiefly with Olympian rather than human affairs. Yahweh, on the other hand, was more purposeful and had few interests except his people. And unlike Zeus, who was in and of the universe, Yahweh was the creator of the universe. As Herbert Muller writes of Yahweh, "Once he had been endowed with benevolent purposes, and taught to concern himself with all mankind, he could become, as he did, the God of Judaism, Christianity, and Muhammadanism."

Certainly Christianity bears the stamp of Judaism. After all, Christ himself was a Jew. To his early followers, all of them Jews, he satisfied the powerful messianic impulse latent in Judaism. The New Testament recounts the growth and spread of Christianity from an obscure Jewish sect in Palestine to a new religion with wide appeal in the Roman world. Yet the central figure in this great drama remains shrouded in mystery, for there is a dearth of firsthand materials. The Gospels, our greatest and most reliable source, contain wide gaps in their account of the life of Jesus. Nevertheless, they remain a profound record of early Christian faith. "Who Was Jesus?" and "The Last Days of Jesus" confront some of the problems we face in our quest for the historical Jesus.

As it split away from Judaism, Christianity took on new dimensions: the promise of private salvation by sacramental means. From the start, its theology reflected the teachings of St. Paul, who was instrumental in spreading the faith to the Gentiles. Then, as it took hold in the Mediterranean, Christianity absorbed various Hellenistic elements. Among those trained in Greek learning, Stoicism and Platonism prepared the way for an amalgamation of classical philosophy and Christianity. The personal God of the Jews and Christians increasingly became the abstract god of the Greek philosophers. Biblical texts were given symbolic meanings that might have confounded an earlier, simpler generation of Christians. Perhaps it was Christianity's combination of simple faith and abstract theology that explains its broad appeal in the later Roman world. Certainly its teachings about the afterlife, spelled out in "Heaven" illustrate this point.

Looking Ahead: Challenge Questions

Describe the relationship that existed among Jews, Christians, and pagans during the Roman era.

Who wrote the Dead Sea scrolls? What light, if any, do these documents shed on early Christianity?

How do we know what we think we know about the life of Jesus? Why is the quest for the historical Jesus so controversial?

Describe Christian views of heaven. How and why have they changed over the years? How do they differ from the views of other major religions?

JEWS *and* CHRISTIANS *in a* ROMAN WORLD

Eric M. Meyers
and
L. Michael White

New evidence strongly suggests

that both in Roman Palestine and

throughout the Diaspora,

Judaism, Christianity, and

paganism thrived side by side.

MORE THAN A CENTURY AGO, ARCHAEOLOGISTS BEGAN TO rediscover the ancient world of the Mediterranean: the world of Homer and the Bible. Much of the early fieldwork in the classical world arose from a romantic quest to bring ancient literature to life. One thinks instinctively of Schliemann at Troy, a shovel in one hand and a copy of Homer in the other. In the Holy Land, the first biblical archaeologists were theologians and ministers who sought to identify and explore cities of the biblical world and to authenticate biblical stories and traditions; thus they arrived with preconceived ideas drawn from biblical texts and other literary sources. Because many were Old Testament scholars, New Testament archaeology in the Holy Land took a back seat. Outside the Holy Land, it remained for years in the shadow of classical archaeology.

Since World War II, and especially since the discovery of the Dead Sea scrolls in 1947, archaeology has been more attentive to the world of the New Testament. But the new archaeological knowledge has only slowly begun to have an impact because New Testament scholars have been slow to take archaeology seriously. Some scholars think archaeology is of peripheral concern to early Christian studies, concluding debatably that the "earthly" dimension of early Christianity is irrelevant. New Testament archaeology is also given low priority in Jewish studies, which traditionally have placed far greater emphasis on sacred texts. Many believe New Testament archaeology to be of limited value in the study of ancient Palestine, erroneously assuming that the archaeological time frame is restricted to only two generations, from the time of Jesus to the destruction of Jerusalem in the year 70. In fact, one cannot understand the development of either Judaism or Christianity without looking at the historical context over centuries, beginning with the introduction of Greek culture into the ancient Near East.

THE HOMELAND

SCHOLARLY UNDERSTANDING OF JUDAISM AND CHRISTIANity in the Roman province of Palestine during the early Common Era (abbreviated C.E. and chronologically the same as A.D.) has long been burdened by some dubious suppositions. One is the belief that after the First Jewish

 From *Archaeology*, March/April 1989, pp. 26-33.

Revolt against Rome in 66–70 C.E., the new Jewish-Christian community fled the Holy Land. Certainly there was significant emigration to other Mediterranean lands, but in light of archaeological evidence from the first two or three centuries C.E., a growing number of scholars have found the idea of wholesale Jewish-Christian migration untenable.

Actually, the first followers of Jesus were basically indistinguishable from their fellow Jews. Although they believed Jesus was the Messiah and professed a radical love ethic that had few parallels in Judaism—for example, love for one's enemies—the first Jewish-Christians observed most of the Jewish laws and revered the Temple in Jerusalem. They apparently got along well with their fellow Jews, contrary to the impression created in the Gospels and other New Testament writings, where the Pharisees, the "mainstream" religious party of ancient Judaism, are presented in a negative light. The new Christians, in fact, were at odds mostly with the Sadducees, who were much more rigid in their religious outlook than the Pharisees, and far fewer in number. When the Apostles were persecuted by the Sadducean high priest, it was the Pharisee Rabbi Gamaliel who intervened to save them (Acts 5:17–42); when Paul was called before the Sanhedrin (the High Council) in Jerusalem, he obtained his release by appealing to the Pharisees (Acts 22:30–23:10); and according to the Jewish historian Josephus, when Jesus' brother James was put to death by order of the Sadducean high priest in 62 C.E., the Pharisees appealed to the king to depose the high priest. Jesus' natural constituency was the Pharisees, whose doctrine of love for one's fellow humans must surely have been the foundation for Jesus' ethical teaching.

The belief that all or most of the Jewish-Christians left Palestine after the First Revolt stems partly from the lack of clear material traces of the Christian community in the Holy Land from about 70 to 270 C.E. Early Christianity, however, vigorously sought to win converts both among gentiles and in the many Jewish communities throughout the Mediterranean. It is exceedingly hard to imagine these efforts bypassing the large Jewish community in Palestine.

Moreover, Jews from Jerusalem and the surrounding area fled in large numbers to Galilee after the revolt was crushed. Would the first Jewish-Christians have ignored Galilee, where Jesus spent his childhood and where he conducted his ministry? Later generations of Christians certainly did not, as evidenced by the numerous churches they built in Galilee. The presence of important Christian centers of worship makes it difficult to imagine a great Christian "repopulation" of Palestine between the third and fifth centuries. Rather, it seems there was a large community of Jewish-Christians in Palestine from the first century onward, a community later augmented by pilgrims in the age of Constantine.

Jerusalem is central in the study of early Christianity.

It is there that the new religion received its most compelling moments of inspiration in the death and burial of Jesus; and it is from there that its followers took their message to the other cities and towns of the land. As long as the Temple stood, the first Christians continued to worship there and in private household meetings. With the destruction of the Temple, however, both Jews and Christians had to establish new patterns of worship. Thus the local synagogue, which was both a meeting place and a center of worship, became the focus of spiritual life for Jew and Jewish-Christian after 70 C.E.

Recent synagogue excavations have revealed that Jewish life enjoyed remarkable vitality in Palestine during the Roman period, and in some localities into the Byzantine period and beyond. In the pre-Constantinian era, the synagogue was quite possibly where Jewish-Christians worshiped as well. Although the archaeological record shows very little definitive evidence of Christianity until the end of the third century, the textual record is quite clear. In a reference that may go back to 100 or 120 C.E., the Jerusalem Talmud implies that Christians are a sect of *minim,* or heretics. Irenaeus, the first Christian theologian to systematize doctrine, speaks of Ebionites, who read only the Gospel of Matthew, reject Paul, and follow the Torah and the Jewish way of life. Epiphanius, another early Christian writer, speaks of Nazarenes, or Elkasaites, as Christians who insist on the validity of the Torah and laws of purity.

Whether one looks at early Christianity or rabbinic Judaism in Roman Palestine, it is clear that this was a period of great cultural and religious pluralism. One finds this pluralism in the Lower Galilee, at Sepphoris, and at the great site of Capernaum on the northwestern shore of the Sea of Galilee. The octagonal Church of St. Peter in Capernaum is built over what some excavators believe is a Jewish-Christian "house-church" dating back to about the third century. The excavators have also found evidence of a first-century house below this church edifice that may have been Peter's residence. It is clear that by the fourth century, Christians venerated the site by erecting churches there. Next to these Christian structures are Jewish buildings, including a reconstructed synagogue. Archaeologists once thought the synagogue was from the first century C.E., the very building in which Jesus would have walked. Today there is universal agreement that it is a later structure, dating to the fourth or fifth century, that survived for hundreds of years into the early medieval period. Excavators have recently claimed finding another synagogue, from the first century, beneath this fourth- or fifth-century synagogue. If they are right, then in Capernaum a Jewish synagogue and a Jewish-Christian church existed side by side from the end of the first century on. The grander structures above both the early synagogue and the house of Peter in Capernaum suggest that Jewish and Christian communities lived in harmony until the seventh century. The continuous Christian presence for six centuries also casts serious doubts on the idea that the early Christians fled Palestine after 70 C.E. Evidence like that found in Capernaum is plentiful in the Beth Shean Valley and in the Golan Heights, although the evidence there begins later, toward the end of the Roman period and into the Byzantine period.

In the middle of the fourth century, pluralism began to suffer as the Roman period in Palestine came to an end and the Byzantine period began. The transition from Roman to Byzantine culture as revealed by the archaeological and textual records was dramatic and coincides with either the so-called Gallus Revolt against Roman occupation in 352 or the great earthquake of 363. In the case of the revolt, the Byzantine emperor might have taken the opportunity to place the unruly province under his direct rule. In the case of the earthquake, the damage to Roman buildings would have presented the opportunity for a Byzantine architectural and cultural style to emerge as cities were rebuilt.

In either case, the revolt and the aftermath of the earthquake mark the beginning of a difficult period for Jews, in which they had little choice but to adjust to Christian rule. The Palestine of the Roman period, when Jewish sages spoke in Greek and when Rabbi Judah the Prince reputedly numbered the Roman emperor among his friends, became a land undergoing thorough and vigorous Christianization after the conversion of Constantine. Money poured into Palestine, and much of it went into building churches.

Nevertheless, archaeological evidence prompts us to exercise caution. Pockets of Judaism and Christianity remained in close contact during the Byzantine period. They may well have continued the harmonious relations established during the period of pluralism, even as

SURPRISE FINDINGS FROM EARLY SYNAGOGUES

THE SYNAGOGUE PROVIDES A rare opportunity to study the Jewish people—and Jewish-Christians—as they forged a new religious way in Roman Palestine after the fall of Jerusalem. Even within a given region, we find a great variety of architectural forms and artistic motifs adorning the walls and halls of ancient synagogues. This great divergence of synagogue types suggests great variety within Talmudic Judaism, even though the members of different congregations belonged to a common culture.

Such diversity resulted in part from the catastrophe of 70 C.E., after which many sectarian groups were forced to fend for themselves in a new and often alien environment. Some groups settled in towns, others in urban centers; their choices reflected their understanding of how hospitable a setting their beliefs would find in either the sophisticated cities or the agrarian towns.

Synagogue excavations also attest to the primacy of Scripture in Jewish worship and provide a clearer view of the place held by the *bema*, or raised prayer platform, and the Ark of the Law. The Ark is the fixed repository for the biblical scrolls, which were stored in a central place in the synagogue by the third century C.E. Until recently, the dominant view was that the Ark remained portable throughout most of antiquity.

Some synagogue mosaics even suggest that Jewish art played an integral part in the composition of new poetry recited in the synagogue. In late Roman synagogue mosaics, themes based on the zodiac begin to appear. These mosaics are followed in the textual record by poems that name the actual constellations of the zodiac. The setting for reciting such poems, or *piyyutim*, was undoubtedly the synagogue, where the intelligentsia would have gathered and included the poems in their worship.

Finally, survey and excavation of numerous synagogue sites in the Golan Heights have revealed an astonishingly lively and vigorous Jewish community in Palestine in late Roman, Byzantine, and early Islamic times. The supposed eclipse of Jewish life at the hands of early Christendom—especially after the conversion of Constantine and, later, the establishment of Christianity as the state religion in 383 C.E.—needs to be reexamined. In fact, one of the surprises of recent synagogue studies is the generally high level of Jewish culture in Palestine at the end of the Roman period (third and fourth centuries C.E.) and the continued though sporadic flourishing of synagogue sites in the Byzantine period (from the middle of the third century to 614 C.E., the year of the Persian conquest of Palestine). All the evidence points to a picture of a Judaism in Palestine that was very much alive until the dawn of the medieval period.

The work of archaeologists should not be used to prove New Testament stories about Paul. The remains of his day are simply too hard to find.

Christianity became the dominant religion.

THE DIASPORA

ARCHAEOLOGY HAS ALSO ENRICHED OUR UNDERSTANDING of the New Testament world outside Palestine. It is significant to both Jewish and Christian history that the bulk of the New Testament is set outside the Jewish homeland. Jews and Christians alike called their communities outside Palestine the Diaspora, or "dispersion."

While the religious heritage of the New Testament may be Hebrew, its language is Greek. Its cultural heritage is not that of the ancient Near East but that of Greece and Rome. The world of the New Testament was fluid and pluralistic, with an extensive transportation network crisscrossing the Mediterranean. Christians and Jews traveled the highways and seaways, carrying their religion with them. This mobility is vividly reflected in the extensive journeys of Paul.

The New Testament record of Paul's travels provided early investigators with both an itinerary for their archaeological work as well as a "case" to be proved. From the 1880s to the 1920s, for example, the eminent Sir William Ramsay sought to corroborate the account given in the Acts of the Apostles of Paul's activities on his way to Rome, in Ephesus, Athens, Corinth, and Philippi. Shaping Ramsay's approach were attractive images of Paul, such as the one in chapter 17 of Acts, where he is depicted preaching to the philosophers on the Areopagus, or Mars Hill, below the entrance to the Acropolis. The story in Acts, and later Christian legends attributed to Paul's followers, are the only evidence we have for this. Paul left no footprints on the Areopagus for archaeologists to follow. It is also interesting that Paul, in his own letters, never once mentioned his activities or this episode in Athens. Still, this remains a popular tourist spot, and the legacy of early archaeologists like Ramsay lives on.

All over the eastern Mediterranean, tourists play out variations on this theme with local guides. (Though Paul was a tireless traveler, if he had visited every one of these places, he might have died of old age before he got to Rome.) Often the difficulties arise when local legends, which seem to grow like stratigraphic layers, become attached to a site. A prime example of this occurs at Paul's *bema* at Corinth.

Excavations at Corinth have revealed a fifth-century Christian church erected over what appears to be a bema, or speaking platform. The obvious assumption was that this was the site of Paul's defense before the Roman governor Gallio in Acts 18:12 ("But when Gallio was proconsul of Achaia, the Jews made a united attack upon Paul and brought him before their tribunal"). Indeed, the story is given further credence by the discovery of an inscription from Delphi that bears the name of Gallio as well as his title. This inscription has been very important in dating Paul's stay in Corinth to around the years 51 and 52 C.E. But it is most difficult to place Paul's trial on this particular bema, since the South Stoa of Corinth, where the bema is found, was expanded and rebuilt during the next two centuries. Other evidence found at Corinth does little to clear matters up. A pavement bearing the name of Erastus, the city treasurer named in Romans 16:23, identifies him as an *aedile,* a minor administrative official, not as treasurer ("Erastus, the city treasurer, and our brother Quartus greet you"). Is this a tangible record of a follower of Paul at Corinth? One cannot be sure. As at the Areopagus, the best advice may be *caveat* pilgrim.

Similar problems arise in trying to place Paul or John in Ephesus, since Byzantine and medieval accounts have been overlayed on the biblical stories. Current excavations at Ephesus have revealed an elaborate Roman city of the second to sixth centuries C.E., but evidence of the first-century city remains sparse. Extensive excavations at Philippi, in Macedonia, have uncovered a second-century forum and main roadway, but most of the remains come from churches and basilicas dating from the fourth to the seventh centuries. Once again, the remains of Paul's day are difficult to identify.

In some cases, the connection of a site with Paul is demonstrably wrong. For example, Christian pilgrimage and devotion in Philippi helped to equate a Hellenistic pagan crypt with Paul's "prison," as described in chapter 16 of Acts. In the late fifth century, a basilica was built around this site. In short, the work of archaeologists should not be used to prove such New Testament stories. Instead, archaeological work should be used more as a "backdrop" for the discussion of Paul's letters to Christian congregations living in these cities of the Roman world. The focus of archaeology should be placing the Christians and Jews in a cultural context.

More recent archaeological perspectives shed light on the development of Jewish and Christian institutions of the New Testament world. Originally, "church" (the Greek *ekklesia*) and "synagogue" (the Greek *synagoge*) were synonymous terms for assembly or congregation. Especially in the earliest days of the Diaspora, Christian groups, including gentile converts, were considered to be following a form of Jewish practice. Only in the second century would the terms "church" and "synagogue" begin to become specific to Christians and Jews. In fact, distinct architectural differences between them did not begin until the fourth century. In other words, if we were following Paul through Ephesus or Corinth, we would not be able to distinguish Christian or Jewish meeting places from the exteriors of the buildings.

Most of the congregations founded by Paul met in the houses of individual members. Significantly, Diaspora Jewish groups would have met in houses, too; but over time, more formal synagogue buildings appeared. If anything, house-synagogues were in use earlier in the Diaspora than in Palestine (as early as the first century B.C.E.). Of the six early Diaspora synagogues known from excavations—at Delos, Priene, Ostia, Dura-Europos, Stobi, and Sardis—five were originally houses that were renovated and adapted to special religious use. The earliest of these, from Delos, dates to the very beginning of the Common Era, or even slightly earlier.

There is evidence that Jews and Christians worshiped as neighbors in the Diaspora, as in Roman Palestine. One of the most impressive discoveries in this regard comes from Dura-Europos, a Roman garrison on the

PALESTINE'S SOPHISTICATED CITIES

IN RECENT DECADES, A NUMBER of important cities besides Jerusalem have undergone major excavation, yielding evidence of a sophisticated life-style in Palestine. These were Roman cities, built for the administrative infrastructure of imperial rule, but they also became conduits through which Greco-Roman culture was introduced into Palestine.

These cities dominated Palestine, except for the Upper Galilee and Golan regions in the North, but the level of sophistication dropped steeply when one moved away from these urban cores. In the surrounding areas, the older agrarian life-style was still very much dominant, and it was town more than city that ultimately encompassed most of Jewish, and Jewish-Christian, life in Palestine.

Nonetheless, there were some Hellenized centers of Jewish life, mostly along the major roadways, the Lower Galilee, the Rift Valley, and the coastal plain. The primary language here was Greek, and the surrounding Jewish population used Greek for trade and day-to-day discourse. In time, Greek eclipsed Hebrew as the common language, and many of Israel's most important sages buried their loved ones, or were themselves buried, in containers or sarcoph-

agi that bore Greek epigraphs or Greco-Roman decorations. In striking contrast, virtually no Greek is found in the Upper Galilee or the Golan.

Such tombs are exceptionally instructive. For example, the Jewish catacombs of the sages in Beth Shearim, excavated in the late 1920s, attest to the high level of Greek spoken by the sages. They attest as well to the fact that the sages were comfortable with a style of decoration in their tombs that was thought by contemporary scholars to be incompatible with Jewish sensibilities and law, and with the proscription against representational and figural art contained in the Second Commandment. With the discovery in 1987 of the extraordinary Dionysos mosaic at Sepphoris, the heartland of the Jewish sages, an exciting new perspective was provided on the Hellenization of Roman Palestine.

It is not yet clear who commissioned the colorful mosaic stone carpet, found near both the Roman theater and Jewish buildings and homes, but the ramifications of the discovery are most significant. The mosaic dates to about 200 C.E., the time of Rabbi Judah the Prince, who was both a leader in the compilation of the Mishnah (Jewish traditional doctrine) and

reputedly a close friend of the Roman emperor Caracalla. The central panel of the carpet shows Herakles/Dionysos in a drinking contest. The 15 panels that surround this scene depict the life and times of Dionysos, god of wine, the afterlife, revelry, fertility, and theater. What is so amazing is that they are all labeled in Greek, either to clarify the contents for those who didn't know Greek mythology—a gap in knowledge probably not uncommon in these eastern provinces—or to jog the memory of those who ate in the hall in which the stone carpet was located.

The implications of this discovery are many, but the three most important may be summarized as follows: the extent of Hellenization in Palestine by the third century C.E. is greater than was previously believed; Jews were more accepting of great pagan centers than was previously believed, and had more access to them; Jewish familiarity with Hellenistic culture in urban centers such as Sepphoris was a positive force affecting Jewish creativity. It hardly seems coincidental that the Mishnah was codified and published at Sepphoris during the very same period when a highly visible Hellenistic culture and presence flourished in Palestine.

Euphrates River in what is now Iraq, dating to before 256 C.E. On one street was a house that had been renovated, in three stages, into a sanctuary of Mithras, a Persian god whose cult spread thoughout the Roman empire from the second half of the first century C.E. onward. Farther down the same street, another house had been converted, in two stages, into a synagogue. Its assembly hall contained one of the earliest datable Torah niches, and on its walls were elaborate frescoes depicting stories from the Hebrew Scriptures. Farther down the same street was a house that was renovated to become a Christian church, with a small assembly hall and a room set aside for baptism. The baptistry room in particular has attracted considerable attention, since it contains

comes hundreds of years later with the renovation of a public hall, part of the bath-gymnasium complex, to serve as a synagogue. Thus we know that Jews and Christians were both in Sardis for a long time, but apparently with no distinctions by which we can recognize their daily activities. The synagogue was in use from the third century to the sixth century, and its size and opulence attest to the vitality of Jewish life in Sardis. The synagogue was renovated by Jews at least twice after its initial adaptation, and these renovations were extensive and costly. Moreover, its inscriptions give evidence of the social standing and connections of the Jewish community: a total of 12 known donors to the renovations are titled "citizen" or "city councillor," and in

The evidence suggests that Jews and Christians were able to live in much closer harmony with one another than has often been assumed.

some of the earliest clearly datable Christian art, including representations of Jesus in scenes from the Gospels.

More evidence of religious pluralism in the Diaspora can be seen in Rome. Excavations beneath several basilicas, such as those of St. Clement and SS. John and Paul, reveal earlier buildings—houses or apartment complexes—that were being renovated for religious use as early as the first century. The house-church of St. Clement, for example, is generally identified with the first-century levels below St. Clement's Basilica. Interestingly, the second-century house adjacent to the house-church of St. Clement was used as a Mithraic cult sanctuary. Seven such Mithraic halls are known from Rome, and another 14 from the nearby port of Ostia. In addition, inscriptions from Jewish catacombs suggest at least 11 synagogues existed in Rome during imperial times.

The complex society that sustained such pluralism is now the focus of much research. A new group of biblical archaeologists, using what they refer to as a "social history" approach, are attempting to bring biblical texts and archaeological evidence into a more cohesive historical framework. The basis of their work is the use of archaeological evidence not merely as proof or illustration but as a key to the historical and social context of religion. In the Hellenized Roman cities of Palestine, such as Sepphoris, and in major urban centers of the Diaspora, such as Corinth, the activities of Jews and Christians must be seen as part of a complex culture and viewed over several centuries of development.

For example, textual evidence shows the existence of a Jewish community at Sardis in Roman Lydia (western Turkey) since the time of Julius Caesar; however, the first significant archaeological evidence of its activities

some cases both. Other notables, including several Roman bureaucrats, are also named in the roster of donors. Here the archaeological record yields a picture of a Jewish community, over several centuries, that was politically favored and socially "at home" in the civic life of Sardis. To understand the life of the Jews of Sardis, however, one must place them not only in the context of their city but also ask how their local conditions compare to other Jewish groups from the Diaspora.

This same social history approach may be applied to Christian groups as well. At stake are a number of traditional assumptions about Judaism and Christianity in relation to their social and religious environment. It would seem that Jews and Christians were able to live in much closer harmony both with one another and with their pagan neighbors than has often been assumed. To an outsider, both church and synagogue might have resembled foreign social clubs or household cults.

The mobility within the Diaspora produced cultural as well as theological diversity, even within the Jewish and Christian traditions. We should not assume that the Diaspora synagogue communities conformed to Talmudic Judaism. A good case in point is seen in recent archaeological evidence, especially from inscriptions, for active participation and even leadership by women in Diaspora synagogues—something also seen in the homeland. This could eventually shed light on the significant role of women in Paul's churches. To date, however, the main information comes from the New Testament writings, which give evidence of women as house-church patrons, as in Romans 16:2–5.

There are numerous ways in which Jews and Christians of the Diaspora were influenced by their cultural

3. JUDEO-CHRISTIAN HERITAGE

environment. Especially noteworthy are conventions of letter writing drawn from the analysis of papyri, which can enhance our understanding of the letters of Paul. Likewise, conventions of building or donation inscriptions offer a means of understanding many synagogue inscriptions, such as those at Sardis. Still more common are Jewish and Christian burial inscriptions. Both in burial inscriptions and in funerary art one finds that the earliest Jews and Christians, when one can distinguish them at all, regularly used motifs and language common in the larger pagan environment.

Thus there is a wide array of new and old archaeological data available for students of Judaeo-Christian antiquity. Whether it comes from East or West, whether it is inscribed with letters or decorated with figural art, it constitutes the most significant body of evidence for reconstructing the cultural context in which Jews and early Christians lived.

Of all the human sciences, archaeology is best equipped to deal with such complex matters. When strongly tied to the literary and historical disciplines, it becomes the most reliable tool for reconstructing the ancient societies in which Judaism and Christianity, orphaned from Jerusalem, found new homes.

WHO WROTE THE DEAD SEA SCROLLS?

A New Answer Suggests a Vital Link Between Judaism and Christianity

NORMAN GOLB

Norman Golb, professor of Hebrew and Judaeo-Arabic studies at the University of Chicago, and a member of the Société de l'Histoire de France, has written widely on historical themes and is well known for his manuscript discoveries. A student of the Qumran scrolls for more than thirty years (his doctoral dissertation at Johns Hopkins dealt with the subject), he regularly leads graduate seminars on the texts at Chicago's Oriental Institute. Recently he was awarded an honorary doctorate in history by the University of Rouen, in France.

FORTY YEARS AGO THIS SPRING, on a desert cliff near the western shore of the Dead Sea, two bedouin shepherd boys ventured into a cave and, quite by accident, made one of the most important archaeological finds of the century. Hidden deep within the recess were seven parchment scrolls containing texts that had not been read since the first millennium. Over the next nine years, hundreds of such scrolls—some in small fragments, others fully intact, many surrounded by the remains of linen packets or pottery jars—would be discovered in this and other caves near the ancient settlement called Khirbet Qumran. The findings would include a broad array of biblical and nonbiblical Hebrew writings and one scroll written on copper. But no one could have foreseen all this at the time. The chance recovery of such a wealth of cultural history from a single cave in the Palestinian wilderness seemed a miracle.

When opened in Jerusalem, the parchment rolls were found to include two copies of the Book of Isaiah, as well as a number of previously unknown writings. One text, the so-called Genesis Apocryphon, or Abraham Romance, was an embellished version of events described in the Book of Genesis. Another, the War Scroll, contained visionary descriptions of an apocalyptic battle to take place between "sons of light" and "sons of darkness" at the end of days—a theme that pervades the Apocrypha, Jewish writings that appeared in Palestine during the centuries between the Old and New Testaments. A third text, often called the Hodayot, contained hymns in the style of the Book of Psalms. There was also a fragmentary text interpreting the Book of Habakkuk (Habakkuk was an Old Testament prophet) as a prediction of events of the interpreter's own time and the impending future, as well as a scroll describing the initiation ceremonies and ritual practices of an unnamed religious brotherhood.

The latter work, the Manual of Discipline, was particularly intriguing, for it strayed radically from what was thought to be mainstream Jewish thinking of the time, and even foreshadowed Christian doctrines later espoused in passages of the New Testament. Unlike the Hebrew Bible and known writings of the Apocrypha, the Manual of Discipline declared personal wealth spiritually defiling. It placed great emphasis on ritual purity—but, in a notable departure from the Bible, dismissed ceremonial bathing as worthless unless accompanied by a similar cleansing of mind and spirit. The manual also described regular communal study sessions in which members of a hierarchical holy order were to explore the "secrets" and hidden meanings of scripture—a concept that stands in stark contrast to the type of personal wisdom extolled in the Book of Proverbs and the apocryphal Ecclesiasticus.

As investigators at the Hebrew University and at the American School of Oriental Research (both in Jerusalem) studied the seven newly discovered scrolls, they became convinced that the Manual of Discipline—and hence the other texts as well—must have been written by the Essenes, a small, four-thousand-member Jewish sect said to have inhabited parts of Palestine around the time of Christ. According to the contemporary Jewish writers Philo of Alexandria and Flavius Josephus, the Essenes had eschewed personal wealth, espoused ritual purity, and, like the sect described in the text, held communal study sessions to probe the secrets of the Torah. Moreover, Pliny the Elder, in his *Natural History,* had placed Essenes on the western shore of the Dead Sea, stating that "below" their settlement was the town of En-gedi, which is in fact only twenty miles south of the caves where the scrolls were found.

These coincidences were so striking that, by the mid-fifties, virtually every scholar studying the scrolls believed they were the work of Essene monks who had lived at Qumran. Further, it became widely accepted that, because some of the texts found at Qumran contain ideas that appear later, in the New Testament, the Essenic sect must have had a formative influence on Christianity. The American literary critic Edmund Wilson embraced the theory of Essenic authorship in his popular 1955 book, *The Scrolls from the Dead Sea,* and it has enjoyed virtually universal acceptance ever since. Today, encyclopedias, museum catalogues, textbooks, and even scholarly jour-

This article is reprinted from *The Sciences* and is from the May/June 1987 issue, pp. 40-49. Individual subscriptions are $18.00 per year. Write to The Sciences, 2 East 63rd Street, New York, NY 10020 or call 1-800-THE-NYAS.

nals and doctoral dissertations all propagate the theory of Essene authorship. Readers of the current *Encyclopaedia Britannica* learn that the scrolls were "all part of a library belonging to a Jewish religious sect (Essenes) that flourished at Qumrān from the mid-2nd century BC to AD 68." And visitors to the Treasures of the Holy Land exhibition that opened at New York's Metropolitan Museum of Art last year, and is now at the Los Angeles County Museum of Art, read in the exhibition catalogue that Qumran was "the center of the Jewish sect that had owned and used the scrolls." Those who see the scrolls displayed at the Israel Museum, in Jerusalem, are told the same story.

What they are not told is that the Qumran–Essene theory, however widely accepted, is at odds with almost every shred of evidence that has surfaced during the past thirty-five years. In fact, the evidence makes demonstrably clear that the Dead Sea Scrolls originated not with an obscure monastic sect but with Palestinian Jews. And if the theory that Essene monks wrote the scrolls is dubious, so are the larger, historical beliefs it has inspired. That early Christian doctrines drew from the same sources as Essenism is now a tenet of conventional wisdom. "Such concepts in the New Testament as predestination, election, contradistinction of flesh and spirit, and the dualism of light and darkness and of truth and falsehood...are related to the theology of the Dead Sea sect," the Treasures of the Holy Land catalogue declares, expressing a view repeated endlessly over the past forty years with varying nuance. But what analysis of the scrolls actually reveals is that Judaism as a whole, not just one obscure sect, was the salient influence on the new religion.

THERE WERE SIGNS almost from the outset that something was not quite right with the theory of Essenic authorship. The Essenes, as described by Pliny the Elder, were insular, peace-loving, celibate monks; their order "has no women," he wrote, "and has renounced all sexual desire." Yet when archaeologists excavated a portion of the cemeteries at Khirbet Qumran, they found the graves of women as well as of men. Moreover, the doctrine of unqualified sexual abstinence—which, according to Josephus, Philo, and Pliny, was a primary tenet of the Essene creed—could be found neither in the Manual of Discipline nor in any of the other original seven scrolls.

Rather than reconsider the fledgling theory, however, the authorities of the day—such eminent archaeologists and Hebrew scholars as Eleazar Sukenik and his son, Yigael Yadin, of Israel; André Dupont-Sommer and Father Roland de Vaux, of France; and many others in England, Germany, and the United States—clung to it, citing a statement by Josephus, in his *Jewish War,* to the effect that although most of the Essenes were celibate, some were not. The Qumran area, the experts argued, must have had its share of noncelibate Essenes. It is possible, the Hebrew and Bible scholar Frank Moore Cross, of Harvard, wrote in *The Ancient Library of Qumran and Modern Biblical Studies,* "that the older celibate community later became mixed, or we may suppose that within the environs of the desert of Qumrân was an order of married Essenes alongside a larger celibate community."

This explanation, unfortunately, does more to damage the Qumran–Essene theory than to defend it, for the theory is based on Pliny's statement that there was a group of *celibate* Essenes living above En-gedi. Moreover, the theory holds that Qumran was not just a remote Essene settlement but the nerve center of the Essene movement—the "laura," or "motherhouse," where many of its doctrines had been formulated and its books written. How could it be claimed that members of this very center did not practice celibacy, one of the sect's most conspicuous doctrines?

A more serious difficulty arose when the Qumran settlement was excavated, during the early 1950s. Pliny had described the Essenic monks as having "only palm trees for company," implying that they had lived a rudimentary existence. Yet the ruins that archaeologists uncovered were far from rudimentary. The excavations showed a well-developed settlement, with cisterns, pools, and reservoirs for water storage, and a complex of stone buildings that had included a dining hall and kitchen, stables, a pottery, and a tower adjoined by a building whose identity remains uncertain. To account for these troublesome findings, some archaeologists—Father de Vaux, for example, in his book *Archaeology and the Dead Sea Scrolls,* and Cross, in his *Ancient Library of Qumran*—proposed that the Essenes must have lived in caves on the escarpment above the settlement or in nearby huts, and that the settlement buildings themselves served only as administrative headquarters. (The Treasures of the Holy Land catalogue treats this speculation as fact, explaining that the monks "lived in the neighboring caves...and most probably in tents and huts, of which nothing has remained.")

There *was* evidence of temporary habitation in some of the caves, but it is hard to believe that the Qumran settlement was a mere commons for cave-dwelling monks. Besides being too elaborate, Khirbet Qumran bears too many marks of a military fortress. Not only did excavations reveal fortifications and a siege wall, but the presence of large supplies of food and water, and of many signs of battle, indicated that the settlement had housed a troop of Jewish soldiers, who fought a protracted battle with the Romans around the time Jerusalem was overrun, in 70 A.D. Evidence of this fierce siege includes smashed walls, the remnants of a great fire, and a large number of arrowheads. The approximate date of the battle, and identity of the besiegers, was provided by dated Roman coins found amid the rubble.

Josephus did refer in *The Jewish War* to an Essene named John who had taken part in the war against the Romans. But Philo characterized the Essenes as the most peaceful of men, saying, "You would not find among them ...anyone pursuing a war-involved project." And there is no written record that the Essenes defended a fortress or fought in pitched battles against Roman troops.

HAD THESE INCONSISTENCIES been broached early on, the notion that Essene monks wrote the Dead Sea Scrolls might never have taken hold. But by the time Qumran was fully excavated, in 1956, the theory had taken on a life of its own. Scrolls were by then being discovered in ever greater numbers in other caves on the escarpment. And archaeologists working at the site, rather than considering new explanations, began to look for evidence that would connect the scrolls to the settlement.

When, for example, three plaster-covered tables and two small inkwells were found amid the ruined stone buildings at Qumran, the room containing them was identified as a scriptorium, where, it was claimed, scribes had produced the manuscripts hidden in the caves. The room had constituted the second floor of the unidentified building near the watchtower. Apparently at the time of the Roman attack, the second story had been destroyed, and its contents had fallen through to the floor below. Because those contents included the tables and inkwells, archaeologists inferred the existence of a scriptorium. When word of the impending Roman attack reached Qumran, Father de Vaux and others theorized, the Essenes must have hastily gathered up the manuscripts being produced in this room, carried them to the caves above the settlement, and hidden them there in specially made pottery containers or in linen packets.

This assertion has at least two obvious problems. First, as numerous researchers have pointed out, ancient depictions of scribes do not show them sitting at tables while engaged in their art but rather seated on benches with their work propped up on their knees. Second, and more important: given that a large amount of rubble had formed a protective covering over the site until its excavation, the supposed scriptorium should have contained many inkwells—not just two—as well as other scribal tools, including reed pens, rolls of blank parchment, and instruments for indenting rules in it. But no scribal tools were found amid the debris, and not a single scrap of parchment

All of this would suggest that the room served not as a scriptorium but as a chamber where several men held meetings, perhaps for civic or military purposes, and where some small amount of official (documentary, as opposed to literary) writing may have been done. To suggest that a military fortress contained such a room requires no elaboration or special pleading; the room was, after all, located near the watchtower, in the center of the complex of stone buildings. By contrast, the assumption that a chamber containing two inkwells and three tables was used by pious Essene scribes for the wholesale copying of literary manuscripts has never been convincingly documented. Despite the lack of evidence, however, the ruined chamber is still labeled Scriptorium by the conservators of the Qumran site. And other authorities (including the authors of the Treasures of the Holy Land catalogue), while making no mention of the scriptorium theory, continue to assert that "the copying of sacred books" was among the activities carried out at Qumran.

One detail that seemed, despite the weakness of the scriptorium theory, to bolster the claim that the manuscripts were created at Qumran is that pottery fragments found near the scrolls in the caves were similar to shards excavated at the settlement. To the excavators of the site, this finding, and the fact that the pottery shards were roughly the same age as the manuscripts, favored the view that jars and manuscripts alike had originated at Qumran and that the scrolls had been placed in the jars before they were hidden. This line of reasoning was proposed by Father de Vaux, in *Archaeology and the Dead Sea Scrolls*, and remains an article of faith among scroll scholars today.

It is entirely possible, of course, that the jars found in the caves were made at Qumran, but that possibility hardly establishes that the scrolls were. In fact, the military character of the settlement, and the lack of evidence that the scrolls were produced there, weigh heavily against such an assumption. Leaving aside for now the question of where the scrolls did originate, we can say that the excavation of Khirbet Qumran, far from confirming the theory of Essenic authorship, raised serious questions about it. And as the theory began to show weaknesses, its burden grew heavier, for more and more scrolls were being discovered in the caves.

By THE SPRING OF 1956, a total of eleven caves, spread over a distance of about two miles along the escarpment extending north from the Qumran settlement, had been found to contain manuscripts. And a Jerusalem-based team of scholars, headed by Father de Vaux and the British archaeologist G. Lankester Harding, continued to study them. Some scrolls were found intact, others in thousands of fragments. This made an exact count impossible, but it was clear that the fragments came from at least five hundred manuscripts and perhaps as many as eight hundred. The painstaking work of reassembling, editing, and publishing these texts—still far from finished—was divided among the eight members of the team, each taking responsibility for a number of fragments.

It was soon apparent that the scrolls embraced a wide variety of literary themes and genres. The texts were found to include hymns and liturgical compositions, commentaries on biblical books, and previously unknown apocryphal writings, including the Book of Mysteries and the Sayings of Moses. There were wisdom texts, messianic speculations, even horoscopes—in short, every type of literature one would expect to find among the Palestinian Jews of the first century A.D., and much more that was totally unexpected. Few of these new texts espoused the doctrines associated with Essenism, and many in fact contradicted the doctrines emphasized by Philo and Josephus. One such text—a fragment once evidently appended to the Manual of Discipline—defined an appropriate age for the beginning of sexual activity, and another, the so-called Psalms Scroll of Cave Eleven, expressed views that have been characterized as Hellenistic or even anti-Essenic.

The Qumran–Essene theory, which was first proposed as an explanation for just seven scrolls, could not convincingly account for such an astoundingly large and heterogeneous body of literature. Still, its founders and their disciples stood by it; rather than concede that such diverse texts might have been written by diverse authors—and not by a small, isolated group of monks—they expanded their characterization of Essenism. The French scholar André Dupont-Sommer argued in his 1959 book, *The Essene Writings from Qumran*, that the Essenes must have been numerous and widely dispersed, and that the sect's beliefs must have taken different forms over a long period of evolution. And even though both Josephus and Philo had stated that there were only four thousand Essenes in Palestine in the first century A.D.—and despite the lack of proof that the settlement at Qumran was an Essene monastery—virtually no one dissented from that view. Instead, the Essenes were designated a large and important group, and Qumran came to be seen as a major center of Hebrew literary production.

This facile pan-Essenism was no panacea, though, for it was not only the number and diversity of texts that strained the theory but also their *scribal character.* It does not normally occur to archaeologists, when unearthing ancient texts, to ask whether they are authors' originals or scribal copies, or to consider whether they are of a documentary or a literary character. Likewise, a Bible scholar has no particular reason to wonder whether a particular parchment manuscript was written in the hand of a prophet or in that of a scribe; he is interested primarily in content and has no hope of ever seeing the original. Manuscript specialists are quick to raise these questions, but the team assembled in Jerusalem included no scholar whose field was Hebrew manuscript studies. As a result, these distinctions—crucial ones, as it turns out—were missed.

AUTHORS' ORIGINALS (sometimes called autographs) are usually rugged specimens, full of insertions and deletions, whereas scribal copies are characterized by careful margins, graceful calligraphy, and few marks of interference. If, as the theory holds, the Qumran settlement was the motherhouse of Essenism; and if the monks at Qumran were not mere copyists but creative thinkers whose writings inspired people throughout Palestine; and if they had hastily hidden their work in caves as the Roman army approached, then surely the surviving manuscripts would show signs of work in progress. Yet, of the hundreds of scrolls recovered from the Qumran caves and subsequently published, only one was an author's original. The rest were finished scribal copies of previously written texts.

That there were five hundred to eight hundred extremely diverse texts in the Qumran caves, and that these included only one autograph, clearly suggest that the scrolls derived not from an authors' workshop (such as the scriptorium the Qumran settlement is said to have contained) but from one or more large *libraries.* Apparently in response to this problem, some scholars have recently suggested that the monks at Qumran must have had such a library in addition to the alleged scriptorium. And since no evidence of a library has ever been found at Khirbet Qumran, they assert that the library, like the Essenes themselves, must have been based outside the settlement —in the caves where the scrolls were found. This view was reported as fact by *The Jerusalem Post Magazine* in June of 1985, in an article describing scholarly speculation about a group of scroll fragments found in Cave Four in 1952. "Cave Four had been the sect's library," the article declares, "unlike the other caves where scrolls had been hurriedly hidden."

This hypothesis seems to account neatly for the lack of original manuscripts among the texts found in the caves; libraries, after all, are normally devoted to finished works, not rough drafts. But it is hard to imagine that such a small, isolated desert community would contain so extensive a library. And it is harder still to believe that the purported Essenes of Qumran, while maintaining a complex of fine stone buildings, would have climbed into cliffside caverns to engage in reading and scholarship. That such a notion could be seriously proposed only demonstrates what a small corner proponents of the original theory have painted themselves into. Forced to concede that the purported scriptorium should have contained original texts as well as copies, they propose the existence of a library. And faced with the troubling fact that the Qumran settlement contained no library, they now place the library in a cave.

Even if the library-in-a-cave hypothesis made sense, however, it would not exonerate the larger theory. The next question would be: Why, if the Qumran site was such an important religious center, did its occupants produce and save only *literary* texts? The study of other ancient settlements along the Dead Sea leaves no doubt that the Jews of Roman times preserved other kinds of documents. In 1952, when archaeologists excavated the caves in Wadi Murabba'at, a gorge just eleven miles south of Qumran, they discovered not only letters dating to 132 A.D.—written in the hands of senders and containing many precise geographical and personal names—but a wealth of equally specific legal documents. If Qumran was the administrative center of a large religious sect, one would expect to find the same sort of correspondence and archival records along with the sect's literary scrolls.

In the absence of any such documents, we can only assume that the imputed Essenes of Qumran kept archival records strictly segregated from literary ones and that the ravages of time were highly selective; or that the Essenes, unlike their immediate neighbors, attached no importance to civil, personal, or administrative documents; or that something else prompted them to store hundreds of literary texts but not a single page of correspondence. Proponents of the Qumran–Essene hypothesis have yet to address any of these problems; so far, they have simply ignored them.

THESE GRAVE and numerous contradictions would seem to render the Qumran–Essene theory worthless. Yet scroll scholars continue not only to skirt serious questions about the theory but to ignore two discoveries that point directly to an alternative explanation. The first of these involves the artifact known as the Copper Scroll.

In 1952, when the Copper Scroll was unearthed in two pieces from Cave Three, it was so brittle that it could not be safely opened. But the investigators could see from the images that appeared in reverse on the scroll's outer surface that it contained descriptions of precious objects buried in various hiding places. Within four years, the scroll had been sawed into narrow strips at a laboratory in Manchester, England, and deciphered. But long before the text was made public, those in charge issued a statement to the world press casting doubt on its historical veracity. The scroll did contain inventories of buried treasures, the experts said, but the treasures were purely fictional. "It is difficult to understand why the Essenes of Qumran were so concerned with these stories of hidden treasure," the statement reads, "and especially why they saw fit to engrave them on copper, which at that time was a costly metal. . . . At all events this guide to hidden treasure is the most ancient document of its kind to have been found, and is of interest to the historian of folk-lore."

But when the text of the Copper Scroll was finally published in the early sixties, it appeared to be anything but folkloric. In fact, unlike the vast majority of scrolls found near Qumran, this one seemed to provide explicit clues about its own and the other scrolls' origins. The Copper Scroll had been executed not in a scribe's elegant book hand but in the relatively crude and haphazard style of lettering associated with documentary autographs. As for content, it was a terse, straightforward enumeration of various prized artifacts—*including written documents*—that had been sequestered at burial sites throughout the Judean wilderness.

The Copper Scroll even included a statement to the effect that "the duplicate of this writing" could be found "in a pit... to the north of Kohlat." This locality can no longer be identified, nor do we know which of the place-names in the Copper Scroll designated the Qumran site. But many of the hiding places described in the text are, like Qumran, located in the wadis, or dry desert river-beds, that extend eastward and southward from Jerusalem. The text describes caches hidden near Jericho, for example—where books were indeed discovered during the third and ninth centuries (in the latter case, ironically, by Jews who were alerted by shepherds).

The use of so many place-names, the character of the handwriting, the manner of enumeration, and the reference to another copy of the same work—together with the fact that the entire text was inscribed on copper rather than parchment—all point to the scroll's authentic historical quality. It should finally have served as the point of departure for a new hypothesis concerning the origin of the Qumran texts. What it describes, after all, is not the hiding of scrolls in a single group of caves (as the Qumran–Essene theory requires) but the widespread sequestration of books and valuable artifacts at sites scattered throughout the Judean wilderness—in a pattern radiating not from Qumran but from Jerusalem. That the scroll was officially dismissed as folklore—and that the dismissal came several years before its complete text had been published and thus long before conclusions about its significance were warranted—can be explained only as an attempt to protect the original theory from an obvious and devastating challenge.

THE OTHER DISCOVERY affecting the Qumran–Essene theory also occurred in the early sixties, and it served to confirm the statements contained in the Copper Scroll. In two seasons of excavation at Masada, a Herodian fortress located thirty miles down the Dead Sea coast from Qumran, archaeologists located the site at which the Jews of Palestine made their last stand against the Romans after the fall of Jerusalem, in 70 A.D. At that site, fragments of fourteen more scrolls, containing an assortment of biblical and apocryphal texts, were discovered. These scrolls were similar in age and scribal character to those at Qumran; among them, in fact, were fragments of a work represented in the Qumran finds—a liturgical text called the Songs of the Sabbath Sacrifices. When archaeologists found fragments of this poetic work at Qumran, they attributed it (like all the other texts) to the ostensible Essene monks. But the disposition of the fragments at Masada suggests quite a different origin.

No one has ever proposed that the scrolls found at Masada were written there; from their position in the ruins, it appears that they had been in the possession of the defenders of the site, who had fled there during the Roman invasion of 70 A.D. (The defenders occupied only one section of the settlement, and it was in that section, amid remnants of the siege, that all the scrolls were found.) Insofar as many of those defenders were refugees from Jerusalem, it would have been logical to infer that the scrolls were brought to Masada by such refugees, along with other items they managed to salvage when fleeing the capital. Jerusalem was, after all, the greatest metropolis of the Palestinian Jews and, until the Roman siege, the teeming center of their thought and culture. When the walls were finally breached, the line of flight moved southeastward, toward Masada.

The Qumran–Essene theorists have never refuted this fact. Yet they have insisted that the Songs of the Sabbath Sacrifices, because it is also represented among the Qumran texts, was brought to Masada not by refugees from Jerusalem but by Essenes from Qumran. When the archaeologist Yigael Yadin advanced this hypothesis, in 1966, in *Masada: Herod's Fortress and the Zealots' Last Stand*, he bypassed the question of where the other thirteen scrolls might have come from—and proponents of the hypothesis have remained silent on that question ever since. In current books and articles, the Songs scroll is treated as if it had been found in pristine isolation—as if its similarity to a text found at Qumran were the only clue to its origin.

One reason for this narrow focus on one out of fourteen scrolls may be that the mere mention of Jerusalem could have placed the whole Qumran–Essene theory in danger. If one concedes that thirteen of the scrolls emanated from Jerusalem, it becomes difficult to argue that the fourteenth had a unique origin. And if all the Masada scrolls originated in Jerusalem, might not the Qumran scrolls have originated there, too? The Masada scrolls are no different in scribal character from those found in the Qumran caves; the handwriting styles are similar and all are of the same general age. Is it not therefore conceivable that the scrolls discovered at Qumran—in caves a dozen miles downhill from Jerusalem—were also carried into the wilderness by inhabitants of the capital before and during the siege?

THIS IS EXACTLY what the Copper Scroll intimates, and what the totality of evidence now clearly shows. The manuscript finds at Qumran and Masada, as others of earlier centuries, testify that inhabitants of Jerusalem undertook a massive concealment of scrolls at Qumran and elsewhere between 68 and 70 A.D., before or during the siege on Jerusalem, and that a small number of scrolls was carried to Masada by refugees fleeing the Roman invaders. This explanation not only accounts for all of the available evidence but is free of the strange anomalies that plague the Qumran–Essene theory. It avoids the tortured assumption that marrying and celibate Essene monks lived together in caves. It requires no Essenic warriors; no dubious chamber where monkish scribes produced great numbers of Hebrew scrolls; no insistence that the one Qumran scroll bearing the hallmarks of an autograph is a whimsical fantasy; no determined silence concerning the origin of thirteen of the Masada scrolls. And it is compatible with the absence of autograph texts among the scrolls found in the Qumran caves.

According to this new theory, the Qumran fortress was only a fortress, the chamber with two inkwells nothing more than an office or meeting room, and the Copper Scroll written on durable copper for good reason. And the hundreds of texts found at Qumran depict not conflicts or developments within a single exotic sect but the surprising breadth of Jewish literary culture during the centuries between the Old and New Testaments. That many of the ideas contained in the scrolls seem uncharacteristic of early Judaism reflects only our lack of familiarity with certain strains in prerabbinic thought. Splinter groups or individuals were responsible for some of the writings found at Qumran, but their ideas only add to the richness of the literary remains that were, by good fortune, preserved there.

The idea that the Essenic sect had a major influence on early Christianity—and, by implication, that mainstream Judaism did not—has no doubt affected the way people in many countries think about the relationship between the two faiths. A Catholic or a Presbyterian, thumbing through the catalogue of the Treasures of the Holy Land exhibition, might have felt a certain kinship with the obscure sect that supposedly created the texts at Qumran. But if, as the evidence now compellingly suggests, the Christian ideas attributed to the Essenes—among others, predestination and election, and the dualities of flesh and spirit, darkness and light, falsehood and truth—evolved out of Judaism as a whole, then that sense of theological kinship should extend a good deal further. Judaism and Christianity cease to be distant theological cousins and become much closer relatives.

Had the Masada manuscripts and the Copper Scroll been discovered before the other texts, interpretation would surely have proceeded along these lines. But by the time those discoveries were made, scholarly opinion had ossified, and no amount of evidence now seems sufficient to reform it. To date, no adherent of the Qumran–Essene theory—archaeologist, Bible scholar, or historian—has offered a point-by-point response to this critique. Meanwhile, doctoral theses, books, and articles continue to treat the Qumran–Essene theory as fact while failing to address the crucial questions raised by the new configuration of evidence. May we not hope that in this, the fortieth anniversary year of the first discoveries, the reassessment will begin?

WHO WAS JESUS?

As Christians round the world gather to celebrate the birth of Jesus, once again they recite the story of a child born to a virgin. The details are familiar yet fabulous: harkening angels, adoring shepherds, a mysterious star. But is the story true? To the literal-minded, the infancy narratives of Matthew and Luke are the opening chapters in the official biography of Jesus. To scholars of the New Testament, however, they are not history at all but something infinitely more important: symbol-laden stories created to dramatize a deeper mystery—that the Jesus who was born 2,000 years ago was truly Christ, the Lord.

Since the nineteenth century, scholars have sought to isolate "the historical Jesus" from "the Christ of faith" proclaimed in the Gospels. But today, most Biblical scholars no longer make such a facile distinction. For one thing, there are no firsthand written accounts of Jesus' life from which a verbal or visual portrait could be fashioned. For another, while there were eyewitnesses to his public ministry, it is highly unlikely that any of them can be identified with the authors of the four Gospels, which were written 40 to 60 years after his death. Thus scholars agree that the real Jesus can no more be separated from the theology of the Gospel writers than the real Socrates can be separated from the dialogues of Plato.

ORAL TRADITIONS: In their quest for the real Jesus, scholars today emphasize the creative role of the four evangelists. Each of the four Gospels, they say, presents a different portrait of Jesus fashioned to meet the needs of the community for which it was written and to rebut views of Jesus with which they disagreed. By using the modern tools of historical criticism, linguistics and literary analysis, Biblical scholars try to distinguish the layers of oral traditions embedded within each Gospel and to confront the essential mind-set—if not the actual words—of Jesus. "Primarily, the Gospels tell us how each evangelist conceived of and presented Jesus to a Christian community in the last third of the first century," says Father Raymond Brown, a leading expert on the Gospel of John and a professor at New York's Union Theological Seminary. "The Gospels offer only limited means for reconstructing the ministry and message of the historical Jesus."

Despite these limitations, New Testament scholars today know more about the Gospels themselves and the milieu in which they were formed than any previous generation of Biblical researchers. In the past decade alone, translations of several ancient texts from the period 200 B.C. to A.D. 200 have vastly enriched the Biblical trove. One is the Temple Scroll, longest of the Dead Sea Scrolls, which indicates that Jesus' strictures against divorce and other of his teachings were very similar to those held by the ascetic Essene sect at Qumran. Another is the recently translated Nag Hammadi codices, which contain gospels composed by second-century Gnostic rivals of orthodox Christians. And next year, Duke University professor James H. Charlesworth will publish the most complete edition of the Pseudepigrapha, a collection of some 53 texts by Jewish and early Christian scribes, many of which were regarded as sacred books by the Jews of Jesus' time.

MEANING OF TEXTS: In the effort to master all this new material, the burden of Biblical scholarship has shifted from Europe to the U.S. The 3,000 North American members of the Society of Biblical Literature now represent the largest group of Scripture scholars in the world, and their annual production of commentary and criticism outweighs that of all European countries combined. Moreover, modern Biblical research is thoroughly ecumenical; Roman Catholics teach the Bible at Protestant divinity schools, and Protestants publish books for use by Catholic schools and parish study groups. Equally important, first-rate Scriptural scholars now occupy chairs of religious studies at secular universities. This trend, together with a new wave of popular handbooks on Biblical criticism, has made access to the Gospels available to millions of Americans, including those who prefer to discover Jesus without joining a church.

Most New Testament scholarship purposely focuses on what the texts meant to first-century Christians, but some of its implications call into question the authority sometimes claimed by Christian churches today. Roman Catholic analysts, for example, agree that the papacy in its developed form cannot be read back into the New Testament and that the words of Matthew's Gospel, "Thou art Peter and upon this rock I will build my church," were not necessarily uttered by Jesus during his ministry. Protestants, on the other hand, can find little support for the claim that Scripture alone is the basis for Christian authority; on the contrary, modern scholarship demonstrates not only that the church existed before the Gospels were written but also that the church shaped the New Testament writings. "It is much more difficult now for Protestants to speak naïvely about Biblical faith or Biblical religion," says professor Donald Juel of Northwestern Lutheran Theological Seminary in St. Paul, Minn. "The diversity of Scripture is a fact and it is something to which Christian tradition must now speak."

The Christians most threatened by contemporary scholarship are those conservative evangelicals who insist that every statement in the Bible—whether historical, scientific or religious—is literally true. Scholars who accept any form of modern Biblical research are under attack in several Protestant denominations, including the nation's largest—the Southern Baptist Convention. The issue of Biblical inerrancy has already created a schism in the Lutheran Church-Missouri Synod and now, with the editorial blessing of Christianity Today magazine, influential fundamentalists are pressing a new battle for the Bible at the risk of splitting the already wobbly evangelical movement. In Rome, meanwhile, the Vatican began a formal inquiry last week against Dutch Catholic theologian Edward Schillebeeckx on the widely disputed ground that his recent book, "Jesus: An Experiment in Christology," uses modern Biblical criticism to deny the divinity of Christ.

Virtually all Biblical scholars would vigorously deny that their work undercuts the central message of the Christian faith: that God was incarnate in human form and that He died and rose again from the dead to redeem mankind from sin. To call into question some of the historical assertions in the four Gospels is not to dispute their spiritual truth. "The truth of the Gospels is not simply historical and anyone who tries to identify their truth with historicity is misunderstanding them completely," says Jesuit Joseph Fitzmyer, a top Scripture scholar at the Catholic University of America. The problem, Fitzmyer complains, is that "in Scripture matters, education today is so retrograde that one cannot even pose a critical question without shocking people."

FOUR SHADOWY FIGURES: What is known about the historical Jesus is that he was born in the last years of Herod the Great and died during the reign of Tiberius Caesar when Pontius Pilate was Procurator of Judea. He was an itinerant rabbi—his thinking was close to the liberal school of Pharisees—who ate with sinners and publicans, was regarded by some as a prophet and religious visionary, aroused the antagonism of influential Jewish leaders, violated at least some Sabbath laws, entered Jerusalem during the Passover celebration, was interrogated by the Sanhedrin, tried before a Roman court and crucified as a common criminal.

Aside from this bare outline, not much is certain. The four Gospels contain individual sayings and stories based on memories of Jesus' earthly ministry, which were transmitted—and inevitably stylized in the process—by the oral traditions of the various Christian communities. The four evangelists themselves are extremely

mysterious figures. Although there have been many guesses about their identities, Matthew, Mark, Luke, and John are simply names attributed to shadowy figures who may even have been groups of people, not individual authors. Moreover, no one has yet pinpointed the Christian communities for which the Gospels were written, though several locations have been suggested.* What is known is that because of the Resurrection experience, followers of Jesus began to proclaim him as Christ, the Messiah, who would return shortly to judge the world.

PASSION: Most scholars now believe that the early Christians worked backward in developing their account of Jesus. At first, Christians focused on Jesus as the heavenly Messiah who would return soon in glory as the crucified redeemer who was raised from the dead. Only gradually did they incorporate into their preaching the earthly Jesus who had ministered to the people of Israel. The written Gospels, many scholars argue, also developed in reverse—from the Passion story to the earthly ministry (which is all there is in the earliest Gospel, Mark), to the infancy narratives (added by Matthew and Luke), to the pre-existence of Jesus as the eternal Word of God (unique to the last Gospel, John).

"Unfortunately, the majority of people carry around in their minds a composite picture of Jesus made up of whichever happens to be their favorite Gospel, plus some historical reminiscences about the first century and a whole lot of personal predilections which we all have," says Werner Kelber of Rice University, a specialist on Mark. "People do not take the trouble to read each Gospel separately or to recognize that each author gives us a different portrait of Jesus—and of all the other figures in the Gospel." Here, in brief, are the different slants of the four Gospels:

MARK: In this, the earliest and the shortest of the four, Jesus emerges as the long-awaited Messiah who redeems the world from Satan's grip by his own Passion and death. Mark signals his theological intent at the outset when John the Baptist announces the coming Messiah and is shortly "delivered up" to his enemies. This presages what will happen to Jesus and what Mark himself believes all followers of Christ must expect. "Mark is putting all of the early traditions about Jesus under the interpretive control of the Passion story," says New Testament scholar Paul Achtemeier of Union Theological Seminary in Virginia.

When Jesus begins his ministry, Mark presents him as a stereotypical miracle worker, a stock figure of Hellenic culture familiar to his gentile readers. His miracles

win him little faith: Mark's Gospel is the only one in which those who should best understand him—his family, the scribes and especially his own disciples—all fail to recognize him as the Messiah, or misunderstand his mission. In the same episode in which Peter acknowledges Jesus as Messiah, for example, his Master repudiates him—"Get behind me, Satan"—for failing to accept that "the Son of Man" has not come to rule the world through personal power, but to redeem it by his death. Mark's crucifixion scene is exceedingly lonely. None of the disciples is present. Jesus dies with a cry of ultimate abandonment: "My God, My God, why hast thou forsaken me?" And it is left to a Roman centurion—a pagan who has watched Jesus die—to profess what the disciples could not: "Truly this man was the Son of God." In Mark's original conclusion, the disciples are never informed of the resurrection and thus are never reconciled with Christ.

This conclusion has created a major controversy among New Testament scholars. Some point out that verses later added to Mark by another author or authors do indicate a reconciliation in Galilee between the disciples and the risen Christ. Others believe that Mark's negative assessment of the disciples was intended to shift the focus of Christianity away from the church in Jerusalem, which was identified with the disciples, after that city was destroyed by Roman forces in A.D. 70. But the most radical conclusion is that of Professor Kelber, who believes Mark's disciples were the chief opponents of Jesus, repudiated by him and so not saved. Mark's point, says Kelber, is that readers of his Gospel were to look to the cross for salvation—a Lutheran position—and not rely solely on Jesus' miracles and message. Jesuit scholar John Donahue of Vanderbilt University does not go that far, but he concedes Mark is suggesting that knowledge of the historical Jesus is inadequate for salvation without faith in the crucified Christ.

MATTHEW: Here, Jesus is presented as a royal Messiah, the last King of Israel and the Son of God, sent to teach his people as well as to die for them. He is also a remarkably humble king, as Matthew's story of the Nativity makes clear. Though descended from the royal line of David, Jesus is born not in Jerusalem, but in Bethlehem, where foreign wise men come to worship him. This kingly image rivals that of Jesus as rabbi, which other scholars of Matthew emphasize. "In Matthew, Jesus' followers call him Lord and other royal titles," says New Testament specialist Jack Kingsbury of Union Theological Seminary in Virginia. "Only the Pharisees call him teacher and Judas alone calls him 'Rabbi'."

Matthew's Jesus is particularly antagonistic toward the Jewish establishment; he calls the scribes and Pharisees a "brood of

---

*It has been thought that Mark wrote to a Roman audience; that Matthew and Luke both addressed themselves to people living at Antioch, in Syria, and that John's community was based at Ephesus, in Asia Minor.

vipers." In part, these passages seem to reflect Matthew's efforts to distinguish Christianity from rabbinical Judaism, which the Pharisees were developing in response to the catastrophic destruction of Jerusalem. Matthew's Jesus is presented as a new Moses when he delivers his Sermon on the Mount, one of five teaching discourses in the Gospel. But in Matthew's portrait, Jesus is not just an interpreter of the law; he is the lawgiver and personal fulfillment of Jewish prophecy. Christianity, Matthew wants to make clear, is a natural, long-expected development of Judaism. Time and again, the author follows an episode in Jesus' life with an Old Testament quotation introduced by a formula phrase such as, "This was done to fulfill what the Lord had spoken through the prophet."

Although Matthew incorporates a great deal of Mark's material, he bends it to his own theological purposes. Matthew's miracle stories, for example, are presented as demonstrations of Jesus' mercy and compassion, rather than as illustrations of his power. Where Mark's Jesus rebukes the disciples for failing to understand his power to walk on water, Matthew's Jesus helps the faltering Peter, whose hesitant faith nearly causes the disciple to drown.

LUKE: In this Gospel, Jesus is the innocent savior of the world, full of forgiveness and love, and the text follows the literary conventions of Hellenic culture. Written for a sophisticated gentile audience, Luke's portrait is the first effort to present a biography of Jesus. Gone is Mark's angst-ridden emphasis on the cross; in its place is a peaceful universality. Luke not only relates Jesus to events of Roman, Palestinian and church history, he goes on to trace his genealogy all the way back to Adam. In this way, the evangelist locates the words and deeds of Jesus within a scheme of "salvation history," which describes what God is doing—and will continue to do—for man.

Despite this universal framework, Luke's Jesus is very much concerned with teaching Christians how they should spend their lives from moment to moment. For example, Luke amends The Lord's Prayer so that it asks the Father to "give us each [Matthew says "this"] day our daily bread"; elsewhere, his Jesus reminds Christians that they must bear their burdens "daily." In part, this concern with time reflects the fact that by A.D. 85 or thereabouts, when Luke wrote his Gospel, the Christians were beginning to realize the Second Coming might not be imminent and therefore were more concerned with the here and now. Moreover, says Father Fitzmyer, an international expert on Luke's writings, "Luke is the only evangelist who stresses that Christians have to live ordinary lives, and he has played the Christian message to fit this fact."

But the dominant theme in Luke's verbal portrait is Jesus' ready forgiveness of sinners. They love him and he loves them and other social outcasts. When Jesus works a miracle, the typical response from the crowd in Luke's Gospel is joy, rather than Mark's wonder at his power or Matthew's show of faith. Luke's Jesus is perhaps best understood in his crucifixion scenes, where the innocent savior manages to pray for his executioners: "Father, forgive them, for they know not what they do."

JOHN: There is no need for a nativity scene in John; he simply asserts in his Gospel's famous prologue that Jesus is "the Word of God" made flesh. Thus John's Gospel begins where the others leave off, with the recognition of Jesus as the Son of God. In John, the disciples immediately know who Jesus is.

John's Gospel differs from the three Synoptic Gospels in other ways as well. His Jesus works only seven miracles—none of them exorcisms—preaches no ethical exhortations and issues no apocalyptic warnings about the end of the world. On the contrary, the kingdom of God has already arrived in the person of John's Jesus, who comes "from above" and therefore speaks with God's authority. The implications of this sometimes confuse his entourage. Nicodemus, a secret admirer, does not understand that disciples, too, must be "begotten from above"—a reference to Divine election that modern evangelists still sometimes interpret, instead, as requiring "born again" experiences.

Jesus' ultimate conflict with the Jews in the fourth Gospel reflects antipathies which were aroused when members of John's community were expelled from the synagogue for professing faith in Christ. "The key to current scholarly discussions about John is the extent to which conflicts in his own community are superimposed by the author on the struggles Jesus had in his ministry," observes Father Brown, author of the two-volume Anchor Bible commentary on John's Gospel. Both concerns are reflected in the controversy between John's Jesus and the Jews, who eventually condemn him for making himself equal to God.

Even in his passion and death, John's "Son of God" remains in full control. Unlike the other Gospels, John does not show Jesus suffering on his knees in Gethsemane. Instead, the Roman soldiers fall to their knees when they arrive to arrest him. And on the cross, Jesus is lucid enough to give John, his "beloved disciple," to Mary, a gesture symbolizing that he is leaving behind him a church. Then, satisfied that his work is done, he announces: "It is finished."

MIDDLE-CLASS ETHICS: At the very least, then, Biblical scholarship has shown that the Gospel writers all shaded the stories of Jesus' ministry according to their own

interests and theological concerns. This is also true of the founders of modern Biblical criticism in the nineteenth century. In their various efforts to reconstruct a "naturalistic" life of Christ, they attempted to uncover the human Jesus before Christian doctrine had muddied the view. The result, with varying details, was a Jesus who looked very much like a nineteenth-century teacher of middle-class ethics. In his famous 1906 book, "The Quest of the Historical Jesus," Albert Schweitzer ended the life-of-Jesus movement by astutely observing that nineteenth-century scholars had looked into the well of the Bible and seen their own faces. In his patient dismantling of his predecessors' work, Schweitzer showed that Jesus was an apocalyptic Jew.

PARADOX: The temptation to see Jesus through contemporary eyes will probably never cease. In our own century, German scholar Rudolph Bultmann sought to demythologize the Biblical Jesus and his message by translating the apocalyptic language into such modern, existential categories as angst and authenticity. Today, however, the search for Jesus is guided less by cultural or philosophical presuppositions than by the tentative assumption that scriptural analysis can yield more about him than old-fashioned rationalists ever imagined.

For example, after lengthy study of the miracle stories to determine whether they were purely literary inventions, Prof. Carl Holladay of the Yale Divinity School has concluded that Jesus was indeed a miracle worker and that the miracle stories are authentic. "Superimposing a post-Enlightenment view of such matters on the first century does injustice to what was truly going on," says Holladay. "But scholars must leave it up to believers to evaluate the claim that they were really the work of God."

What's more, most New Testament scholars believe that at least some sayings attributed to Jesus are authentically his, and a national conference is being planned, in which scholars will try to reach a consensus on which passages qualify. Among the likeliest candidates are Luke's version of the Lord's Prayer, several proclamations that "the Kingdom of God is at hand," certain "aphorisms of reversal," such as Mark's "The first shall be last, the last first" and Jesus' familiar Aramaic word for God—"Abba," or Father—which many analysts believe captures the essence of Jesus' consciousness of his relationship to God.

Analysis of Jesus' parables has convinced other scholars that by understanding them as paradoxes readers can gain direct access to the mind of Jesus. This approach is based on the assumption that the deep structures of the human mind are universal, permitting twentieth-century readers to understand a first-century Jesus. For instance, they cite the famous parable of the good Samaritan, in which a Jewish traveler is robbed and left for dead. Both a priest and a Levite pass him by, but a Samaritan—a social and religious outcast—binds up his wounds and lodges him at the Samaritan's own expense. This story can be interpreted as a moral example of the neighborliness expected of Christians—as it often is in sermons—or as an allegory, as Saint Augustine did. But scholars see it as a paradox designed to transmit Jesus' special understanding of what God demands of everyone who would truly do his will.

WARY: "In this parable, Jesus is asking his Jewish audience to think the unthinkable by identifying goodness with the hated Samaritan," says theologian John Dominic Crossan, an expert in parable analysis at DePaul University in Chicago. In response, the listener either rejects the story or questions his deepest values and assumptions about life. When this happens consciousness changes, just as it does when a Buddhist solves a Zen koan. Mark takes this a step further. The crucified Jesus becomes Christ, the Messiah. And so the parable-teller becomes himself a parable told by the early church—the paradox of Christ crucified—which demands a conversion of consciousness.

Biblical scholars insist that better understanding of how the Gospels were written is a boon rather than an obstacle to faith. But defenders of traditional doctrine in all churches are wary of Biblical investigators. Catholic theologian Edward Schillebeeckx, for example, has tentatively argued from scriptural sources that Jesus' identity as Christ was evident even before the Cross—in the rejection he experienced during his life. Last week, during Schillebeeckx's secret hearing in Rome, Vatican inquisitors demanded to know instead whether he really believed that Jesus was divine. "Rome's inquisitorial behavior suggests they do not want Catholic understanding of the Bible enriched by contributions from the church's most gifted intellectuals," says one U.S. scholar.

Southern Baptists, meanwhile, are under increasing attack from Biblical fundamentalists who want to fire any teacher who does not agree that the Bible is literally true. At Baylor University, for instance, Prof. H. Jack Flanders has been criticized by fundamentalists for writing a book that questions the historicity of Adam and Eve and treats the story of Jonah in the whale as a parable. In Dallas, the administration of Dallas Baptist College has instructed all teachers to sign a statement of belief in Biblical inerrancy—a statement that Dr. Wallie Amos Criswell, the influential fundamentalist pastor of the nation's largest Southern Baptist church, wants the faculties of all Texas Baptist schools to affirm.

The fundamentalists' doctrine of inerrancy, says Professor Achtemeier, is rooted in the post-Reformation era, when Protestant scholastics countered the authority asserted by Rome with the authority of the Bible itself. The scholastics also came to regard the Bible as a sourcebook for systematic theology in which the verses were regarded as dogmatic propositions about scientific questions as well. When nineteenth-century scientists challenged the Christian world view, and historians discovered inconsistencies in the Bible, U.S. fundamentalists at Princeton University responded with a theory that fundamentalists still hold today: the Bible, they say, is inerrant in its original "autographs," or manuscripts, and even copies must be regarded as literally true.

TRUTH: To most Biblical scholars today, these demands for inerrancy are beside the point. The point is that the differences, even the contradictions, between the Gospel accounts do not detract at all from the spiritual truths that they contain. "God can reveal himself through inspired fiction, like the story of Jonah, just as well as through inspired history," says Father Brown.

Who was Jesus? Mark's Jesus dies alone, feeling forsaken but true to his Father's will. This Jesus will appeal to Christians who embrace life's tragedies with confidence. Matthew's Jesus dies only to return and promise his guidance to those who follow him. This Jesus will appeal to Christians who find assurance in the church. Luke's Jesus dies forgiving his enemies, knowing his Father awaits his spirit. This Jesus will attract Christians who have learned in life to trust God by imitating his mercy. John's Jesus dies in the confidence that he will return to the Father. This Jesus is for those Christians who have traveled the mystical way. All of these accounts express a truth; none of them is complete. All of these Jesuses are accessible only to those whose faith compels them on the search for "the way, the truth and the light."

KENNETH L. WOODWARD with RACHEL MARK and JERRY BUCKLEY in New York and bureau reports

The Last Days · · · · *of* · · · · Jesus

THE PASSION OF CHRIST. It is an age-old story that divides Western history and forms the foundation of the Christian faith. Over the centuries, arguments have raged, wars have been fought, martyrs have died over the veracity of the New Testament accounts of the last days of Jesus of Nazareth—his death, burial and resurrection.

Yet, for an event so momentous, the crucifixion of Jesus is even today the subject of much historical controversy. Prior to the 18th century, few Christian theologians challenged the historical accuracy of the Passion, as related in the Gospels of Matthew, Mark, Luke and John. But by the 18th century, skeptics and believers alike were examining the Scriptures and other records in a quest for "the historical Jesus." They found disappointingly little to corroborate the Gospel texts, a compendium of oral traditions written 20 to 60 years after the events and sometimes differing on important details of the story.

That has changed dramatically in recent years. Since shortly after the discovery of the Dead Sea Scrolls some 40 years ago, theologians, Bible scholars, archaeologists and cultural anthropologists have refocused their search, hoping to illuminate the theological meaning as well as the historical accuracy of the Gospel accounts of the final events in Jesus' life.

Where has it all led? Some scholars, frustrated in their pursuit of a purely "historical" Jesus, have come to reject the Passion as pure fiction. For others, the account of Jesus' death, burial and resurrection some 2,000 years ago remains a story worthy of faith, its truth protected through the centuries by the very hand of God. Still others have put forth intriguing evidence that the truth lies somewhere in between: That the Gospel narratives are a mix of legend and fact that attempt to describe a historical and mystical human encounter with one who called himself the Son of Man.

The Triumphal Entry

hen they brought the colt to Jesus and threw their garments on it, and He sat on it. And many spread their garments on the road, and others cut down leafy branches *from the trees and spread them on the road. Then those who went before and those who followed cried out, saying: "Hosanna! Blessed is He who comes in the name of the Lord!" . . . And Jesus went into Jerusalem and into the temple . . . and began to drive out those who bought and sold in the temple.*

From the Gospel According to Mark

IT WAS A HERO'S welcome, the early Palestinian equivalent of a ticker-tape parade, that greeted the Galilean preacher and his band of followers as they rode into Jerusalem for the Passover observance. Today, the Palm Sunday story of Jesus' triumphal entry into the City of David is often cited to demonstrate the fickleness of the Jerusalem crowd whose excited shouts of *Hosanna*—loosely translated as "save us"—would soon give way to vengeful cries of "Crucify him!"

Now, however, modern scholars, examining the Scriptures and other more recently discovered documents that relate to first-century Judaism, take a more sympathetic view of the actions of the Jerusalem crowd. They find plenty of reason to suspect widespread confusion about the political and theological importance of Jesus of Nazareth.

It is unlikely, some theologians now believe, that the Palm Sunday event was the spontaneous outpouring of acclaim that tradition has depicted. They note, for instance, that Luke's Gospel suggests Jesus sent messengers ahead to Jerusalem—advance men who presumably spread word of his purported miracles and his rebelliousness. Stories of run-ins with religious leaders in nearby towns would have played well with the common people of Jerusalem, who despised the Romans and were disenchanted with the Temple hierarchy. Even those who did not believe Jesus to be the Messiah, says Donald Senior, a New Testament scholar and president of the Catholic Theological Union of Chicago, "would have been willing to band around someone who was seen as an anti-establishment figure."

Though many of the Palm Sunday revelers no doubt thought they were cheering the Messiah, their understanding of "Messiah" was almost certainly different from that embraced by Christian orthodoxy today. Judaism in Jesus' time was wracked by sectarian rivalry. The Pharisees, a lay reform movement strong in the village synagogues but not in Jerusalem, were at odds with the Sadducees, the priests who dominated the Temple. In the countryside were the Essenes, a radical monastic sect that rejected the Temple establishment, and the insurrectionist Zealots, whose main objective was throwing off Roman rule. Each had different expectations for the Messiah: A military deliverer, a priestly king who would restore Israel's religious fervor, a mystical figure who would usher in a new age.

Whoever they thought Jesus was, it is likely that many in the Jerusalem crowd expected him to march into the city and lead an attack on the Roman garrison. Instead, he attacked the abuses of the Temple court, challenging the very power structure of Jerusalem.

In the traditional story, Jesus often is described as suddenly enraged when he enters the Temple and sees the rampant buying and selling. But some modern commentators contend that his actions were carefully premeditated. A passage in Mark suggests Jesus made a quick visit to the Temple on Sunday, then spent the night in Bethany considering what action he would take. When he returned the next day to drive out the money-changers, it amounted to open defiance of the Temple authorities.

Why did he do it? Some scholars are convinced Jesus was merely purging the Temple of commercial corruption, while others believe he was challenging the Temple establishment itself as a first step toward a new religious order.

Whatever Jesus' motives, experts agree that his actions in the Temple made his execution quite predictable. The Temple was of enormous economic importance to the people of Jerusalem. It was being rebuilt at the time, and many were employed in the rebuilding. It was the religious, social and commercial center of the city. Historians note that the priests earlier had sent an army to destroy the Samaritan temple, because it had been perceived as a threat. "What Jesus did," says Jerome Nerey of the Weston School of Theology in Boston, "was like attacking the Bank of America, and they simply squished him."

THE ARREST AND TRIAL of Jesus have attracted the interest of historians and theologians who, through the centuries, have sought to answer the compelling, central question of the Passion: "Why did Jesus die?" It is a query that traditional Christian dogma answers quite easily: "It was God's will—Jesus died to provide salvation to the world." But for generations, Biblical scholars have looked for a more historical understanding by seeking to unravel the legal and political intricacies of what is without question the world's most celebrated case of capital punishment.

Stripped to the essentials, the charges

The Arrest and Trial

hen, having arrested Him, they led Him and brought Him to the high priest's house. . . . As soon as it was day, the elders of the people came together and led Him into their council, saying, "If you are the Christ, tell us." But he said to them, "If I tell you, you will not believe." . . . Then the whole multitude of them arose and led Him to Pilate. And they began to accuse Him. . . . So Pilate asked Him, saying, "Are you the King of the Jews?" And He answered him and said, "It is as you say." Then Pilate said to the chief priests and crowd, "I find no fault in this man."

From the Gospel According to Luke

against Jesus were blasphemy and sedition. He was accused by religious leaders of claiming to be the Messiah and of threatening the Temple. And he was accused before Pontius Pilate, the Roman procurator, of claiming to be "King of the Jews"—a title that the ancient chronicler Josephus notes was commonly assumed by revolutionaries of that era. It is that charge, scholars believe, that accounts for Jesus' execution at the hands of the Romans. "The Romans," says Donald Senior of the Catholic Theological Union of Chicago, "would hardly become excited about any Jew's claims to be a Son of God or a Messiah, unless those claims implied political power, as Jesus' enemies suggested they did."

The extent to which Jewish authorities contributed to the death of Jesus is a complicated and sensitive issue, given the anti-Semitic theologies that have used the New Testament accounts to promote their legitimacy. In fact, the Gospels suggest that opposition to Jesus among Jewish leaders was by no means unanimous. At least two members of the Jewish high court, or Sanhedrin—Joseph of Arimathea (who buried Jesus) and Nicodemus—are portrayed as sympathizers. Today, theologies that seek to use the Passion narratives to excuse anti-Semitism are universally rejected.

Even so, Jesus did have plenty of enemies among Jewish leaders. He had accused the Pharisees of hypocrisy, challenged the Sadducees' theology and espoused unconventional interpretations of Mosaic law. Most important, his perceived threat to "destroy the Temple . . . and rebuild it in three days" was an affront the priests could not tolerate. They felt little choice but to move against Jesus.

Jesus' seeming indifference to the charges and the manner in which he testified in his own defense are left unexplained in the Gospel accounts. The narratives quote him responding differently when asked if he was the Messiah: "I am," in Mark; "That is what you say," in Matthew; "If I tell you, you will not believe," in Luke. In John's Gospel, Jesus spars verbally with Caiaphas, the high priest, and tells Pilate that his kingdom "is not of this world." While each of the portrayals may accurately reflect aspects of Jesus' character as understood by the Gospel writers, few modern scholars believe any of Jesus' followers were present at the proceedings. Thus, for many historians, Jesus' conduct at the trial remains a mystery.

Pilate, too, may have been long misunderstood. In each of the Gospel accounts, the apparently indecisive and weak-willed Roman procurator declares Jesus innocent, yet ultimately yields to the demands of the priests and the angry crowd to condemn him. But some historians believe Pilate's main concern was to prevent anti-Roman sentiments, which always ran high during Jewish feast days, from exploding in a city crowded with Passover pilgrims. He was justifiably concerned about offending the chief priests and Herod Antipas, the governor of Galilee. Pilate had been reprimanded by the emperor Tiberius for offending the Jewish leaders on two previous occasions. He could not afford another incident.

That, say scholars, is why in Luke's account, a frustrated Pilate sends Jesus to Herod. Rather than an act of indecision or of principled reluctance to condemn an innocent man, suggests Harold Hoehner, professor of New Testament at Dallas Theological Seminary, it was a "diplomatic courtesy" to improve relations with Herod by acknowledging his jurisdiction in Galilean affairs. The strategy worked. Pilate and Herod later became friends. An "incident" had been avoided. Now if the Temple priests wanted Jesus condemned, Pilate would oblige.

JUST 20 YEARS AFTER the trial and crucifixion of Jesus in Jerusalem, the Apostle Paul, a former Pharisee, would write to Christians in Corinth: "Jews demand signs and Greeks seek wisdom, but we preach Christ crucified . . . the power of God and the wisdom of God." In that

The Crucifixion

o he delivered Him to them to be crucified. So they took Jesus and led Him away. And He, bearing His cross, went out to a place called the Place of the Skull . . . where they crucified Him, and two others with Him.

◆ ◆ ◆ ◆ ◆ ◆ ◆ ◆ ◆ **From the Gospel According to John**

relatively short time, the followers of Jesus had come to see his brutal execution on a hill outside of Jerusalem as a source of triumph, and the instrument of his death—the cross—as a symbol of hope.

But on the day of the crucifixion, the cross was an object of suffering and horror. According to the Gospels, Jesus was flogged and beaten and forced to carry a heavy wooden beam through the city to the place of his execution. There he was attached to the cross with iron nails driven through his feet and hands. He died within 6 hours, probably of asphyxiation. A spear was thrust into his side to assure death.

While some of the details may be disputed, the fact that Jesus, a man in his late 20s or early 30s, was executed in Roman-occupied Palestine is one part of the Passion story that modern historians believe is well corroborated by extra-Biblical sources. The Roman historian Tacitus, for example, writing in A.D. 110 of the persecution of Christians under emperor Nero, refers to followers of "Christ, whom the procurator Pontius Pilate had executed in the reign of Tiberius." And the Talmud—a compendium of Jewish law, lore and commentary—depicts Jesus as the illegitimate son of a Roman soldier who was hanged on the eve of Passover because "he seduced Israel, leading her astray."

Yet the mode of Jesus' execution, as graphically described in the Gospels, has long been a subject of historical inquiry and, until recently, some skepticism. During the 19th and early-20th centuries, some scholars questioned the crucifixion story on a number of counts. Some have argued, for instance, that it was more common in first-century Palestine for criminals to be executed by some other means—stoning, burning,

beheading or strangling—and their bodies "hanged on a tree" as a warning to others. Other theologians have added that crucifixion was a Roman mode of execution and was not permitted in Jewish law. Consequently, it is unlikely that the Temple priests would call for Jesus to be crucified, as the Gospels report. Still other scholars have questioned the historicity of such details as the shape of the cross depicted in Christian tradition and the use of nails rather than bindings to attach the victim to the cross.

But archaeological discoveries and textual research in recent years have added considerable weight to the Gospel accounts. Found among the Dead Sea Scrolls, for example, was a Temple document; scholars say the text suggests that the Law of Moses may have been understood in Jesus' time to prescribe crucifixion in certain cases. The German theologian Ernst Bammel has noted that execution by crucifixion had been used in Palestine since the second century B.C.— even by Jewish courts. Because it was a particularly gruesome form of punishment, said Bammel, "it was used especially in political cases such as those branded by the Romans as rebellion."

Striking corroboration of the type of crucifixion that is described in the Gospels was discovered in 1968 at an excavation site near Mount Scopus, just northeast of Jerusalem. Three tombs were found at the site, one of them containing the remains of a man who had been crucified between A.D. 7 and 70. The man's feet had been nailed together at the heels, his forearms had nail wounds and the bones of his lower legs had been broken— wounds that are entirely consistent with the description in John's Gospel of the crucifixion of Jesus and the two thieves.

Another aspect of the crucifixion account that has been challenged is the description of midday darkness over the city as Jesus hung on the cross. Using computer models, astronomers have ruled out a solar eclipse in Palestine at that time. And while they say a lunar eclipse did occur on April 3 in A.D. 33, it could not have been seen in Jerusalem during the daylight hours. However, some scholars speculate that a spring sirocco—a high-altitude, dust-laden wind common to that part of the Middle East—could easily have darkened the midday sky just as the Gospel writers described.

AFTER THE DRAMATIC events at Golgotha, site of the crucifixion, the burial scene depicted in the Gospels seems subdued and anticlimactic. Yet it serves an important function in the Passion story by confirming the somber reality of the crucifixion: That Jesus was indeed dead.

With the confused and frightened disci-

ples in hiding, by most accounts, a member of the Sanhedrin stepped forward to claim the body and give it a hasty but decent burial in a rock tomb. In the days that followed, the tomb would take on great significance as friends and foes of the crucified carpenter were confronted with one of the greatest paradoxes of history.

Although many questions concerning Jesus' fate would echo through the ages, his actual death was never widely disputed. There were many witnesses at Golgotha, including the Roman soldiers specifically charged with overseeing the execution. Additionally, Mark's narrative notes that Pilate personally confirmed Jesus' death. There was no reason to suspect that Jesus had survived the cross. Even later, when "counterpropaganda" challenged the Christian claim of resurrection, notes Reginald H. Fuller, professor emeritus at Virginia Theological

The Burial

ow when evening had come, there came a rich man from Arimathea, named Joseph, who himself had also become a disciple of Jesus. This man went to Pilate and asked for the body of Jesus. . . . And when Joseph had taken the body, he wrapped it in a clean linen cloth and laid it in his new tomb which he had hewn out of the rock; and he rolled a large stone against the door of the tomb and departed.

From the Gospel According to Matthew

Seminary in Alexandria, Va., "it relied on the thesis of the theft of the body, not that Jesus had not died."

Despite general agreement that Jesus did indeed die on the cross, however, some details of the burial accounts are now being challenged by textual critics who see inconsistencies in some traditional interpretations. Why, for example, would Pontius Pilate have given the body of Jesus to a known disciple, as two of the Gospels describe Joseph of Arimathea—or, for that matter, to a member of the Sanhedrin who, according to Luke, had sided with Jesus during the trial? Doing either would have seemed to invite mischief. The narratives make clear that Pilate and the Jerusalem authorities were worried that Jesus' followers might steal the body in order to claim a miracle that would keep the movement alive. Matthew even relates that Pilate posted a guard at the tomb, although some modern scholars believe that that detail may have been added to the narrative later to refute the theft theory.

One current explanation is that Joseph was not a disciple at the time, but became one later. In that case, argues Raymond E. Brown of Union Theological Seminary, Matthew may be understood as mistakenly "reading Joseph's postresurrectional career into the burial account by describing him as a disciple."

Other critics of the text find it implausible that a "good and righteous" Jew like Joseph would willingly handle a corpse, let alone that of a crucified criminal; such an act would have rendered him unclean under Mosaic law. Yet Brown, in a 1988 article on "The Burial of Jesus," suggests that a "pious, law-observant member of the Sanhedrin" would also have been aware of the law's requirement that a body not be left on the cross after sunset, a situation perhaps made even more urgent by the approach of the Sabbath. Burial, says Brown, "was seen as a necessary good that overshadowed the accompanying impurity."

Other evidence favoring Joseph's role in the burial is that he is one of just a handful of lesser characters in the Passion story whose names were remembered through the period of oral tradition. Another is Simon of Cyrene, whom the Gospels describe as having helped Jesus carry the cross and who, tradition says, also became a disciple sometime after the events of Easter.

Others question whether the "borrowed" tomb of Jesus actually belonged to Joseph, as only Matthew states. Some Bible scholars deem it unlikely that a wealthy member of the Sanhedrin would own a tomb so close to a crucifixion site, an area where criminals were buried. Others speculate that Joseph did not own the tomb at the time, but bought it later, after the Easter event would have transformed it into a site of reverence and awe.

IT IS CHRISTIANITY'S most irreducible tenet: On the third day, Jesus arose from the dead. From the very beginning, Christians have proclaimed the bodily resurrection as a validation of all that Jesus taught and all that they believe. It is the foundation upon which all else rests. The Apostle Paul recognized this when he wrote to the Corinthians in A.D. 56 that "if Christ has not been raised, then our preaching is vain [and] your faith is also vain."

Yet despite its centrality, the resurrection has been, for believers and nonbelievers alike, one of the most problematic of Christian doctrines. The Gospel narratives contain no resurrection stories per se, no eyewitness accounts of Jesus rising from the tomb. For modern readers of the Gospels, as for the disciples on the first Easter, the resurrection is largely a deduction drawn from two pieces of data: The discovery of an empty tomb and reports of post-crucifixion appearances by Jesus in Jerusalem and Galilee.

The Resurrection

 ery early in the morning, on the first day of the week, they came to the tomb when the sun had risen. . . . But when they looked up, they saw that the stone had been rolled away. . . . And entering the tomb, they saw a young man clothed in a long white robe sitting on the right side; and they were alarmed. But he said to them, "Do not be alarmed. You seek Jesus of Nazareth, who was crucified. He is risen! He is not here."

◆◆◆◆◆◆◆◆◆◆◆◆◆◆◆◆ **From the Gospel According to Mark**

Although some theologians are troubled by conflicting "testimony" on the details, the weight of evidence presents a strong case that the empty tomb was part of the earliest Gospel tradition. All four narratives relate the early-morning discovery by Mary Magdalene and others. Yet there are discrepancies in the accounts. Were there three women visitors (Mark), two (Matthew) or one (John)? Did they arrive before dawn (Matthew, John) or after (Mark)? Was the stone rolled away after (Matthew) or before they arrived (Mark, Luke, John)? Were angels present (Matthew, Mark and Luke, yes; John, no)? Such textual disagreements are widely viewed as the result of later embellishments of the original story. But few New Testament experts think they obscure the basic fact: It was an empty tomb that was discovered.

Archaeological evidence is sometimes cited as indirectly supporting the notion of an empty tomb. It was customary in Judaism at the time for relatives of the deceased to return to a grave a year later

to put the remains into an ossuary, or bone box, so that at the final resurrection, God would have all the parts needed to reconstruct the body. Hence, the ideas of resurrection and an empty tomb were linked. Any claims that Jesus had been resurrected, says British theologian James D. G. Dunn, "would be unlikely to cut much ice" among Jesus' contemporaries "unless the tomb was empty."

While the Gospels are unclear on the chronology, some theologians point out that by the time some of the disciples received Mary's report, they already had had "sightings" of the resurrected Christ. In all, he appears 10 times to the disciples to reassure them and instruct them to continue his work. But as with the tomb accounts, Bible scholars have found confusion on the details. Matthew and John have Jesus appearing first at the tomb; Mark puts him elsewhere. And while Matthew, Mark and John describe appearances in Galilee, Luke seems to limit Jesus to Jerusalem.

The writers also differ in how they describe the risen Jesus. Luke and John depict him in concrete, physical terms: He eats; he invites a doubting disciple to touch his wounds. Paul's risen Christ, who appears later on the road to Damascus, is more spiritual than physical.

In some circles, the term "resurrection" itself has become a matter of debate. What does the Bible mean when it says God raised Jesus from the dead? Christian tradition says Jesus was physically resurrected, that his dead flesh and bones were miraculously reanimated. But some theologians have sought to reconcile the resurrection with a more rationalist view by describing it as a metaphor appropriated by early Christians who "thought mythically" and for whom a resurrection of their fallen leader had occurred "in their hearts and minds."

Yet even the most skeptical Biblical scholars concede that something extraordinary happened in Jerusalem after Good Friday to account for the radical change in the behavior of the disciples, who at Jesus' arrest had fled to their own homes in fear. Could Jesus' resurrection account for the fact that within a few weeks they were boldly preaching their message to the very people who had sought to crush them?

Along with the many other riddles in the last days of Jesus, it is a question that academic inquiry alone probably never will answer satisfactorily. Ultimately, the events of the "third day" in Jerusalem must remain, as they have for 2,000 years, in the realm of things unprovable—matters, like the very existence of God, to be grasped only by faith.

by Jeffery L. Sheler

HEAVEN

This is the season to search for new meaning in old familiar places

BY KENNETH L. WOODWARD

You are looking for Jesus the Naza-rene, who was crucified. He has risen! He is not here.

—MARK 16:4

As the Gospels tell it, the women and men who stared at Jesus' empty tomb were not inclined to believe the good news. Frightened, scattered, fearful that they had been misled, the apostles themselves were slow to accept the idea of Christ's resurrection from the dead. And yet, just as Easter is the holiest day in the Christian year, so is the Resurrection the deepest wellspring of Christian faith—and hope. If God can raise Jesus to everlasting life, can humankind also expect to dwell with him in heaven?

Easter is the one Sunday in the year when Christians can anticipate a sermon about life after death. But out of principle, many Christian clergy are loath to mention heaven—or, for that matter, hell. For some pastors, it's a question of rhetorical modesty: after centuries of cajoling listeners with overly graphic sermons on the pleasures of heaven and the horrors of hell, preachers today are hesitant to describe places that no one has actually seen. For others it's a matter of intellectual integrity. "The problem is that the [mainstream Protestant] clergy simply don't believe in the afterlife themselves, either the Biblical view or any view," says Douglas Stuart, an evangelical theologian at Gordon-Conwell Theological Seminary in South Hamilton, Mass.

While the pulpit may be full of agnostics, the pews are filled with believers. "The laity wants something more than abstractions," insists conservative Roman Catholic philosopher Peter Kreeft of Boston College, the author of three books on heaven. "They want Mother Teresa in this life and heaven in the next." In fact, public-opinion polls show that most Americans not only believe in God but also anticipate some kind of heaven. According to a recent NEWSWEEK Poll, 94 percent of Americans believe that God exists and 77 percent believe in a heaven. Among these believers, three out of four rate their chances of getting there good or excellent.

What the "other side" looks like, who is there to greet us and what goes on in heaven is everybody's guess. The Bible itself teases us with contradictory images: a wedding feast, a celestial throne room, a majestic city with streets of gold. Believers are free to take their pick or conjure up images of their own. But how we imagine heaven tells us more about who and where we are now than what the afterworld is like.

What do Americans imagine when they think of heaven? According to a recent study, "Heaven, a History,"* two images of paradise have dominated in Western culture: the theocentric and the anthropocentric. One image anticipates meeting "my Maker"; the other expects to meet "my family and friends." Today, says the sociologist Father Andrew Greeley, who has been surveying attitudes toward the hereafter for the last 16 years, Americans look forward to a heaven where they reunite with earthly relations. Meeting God, Greeley reports, takes a distinct back seat to the family reunion because "they've never met God. They don't know what God is like, so it would be hard to imagine what it would be like having God as a neighbor down the street." As for the quality of life in heaven, Greeley finds that most Americans expect a continuation of life on earth, but without the wars, diseases and other inconveniences that cramp their present

*By Colleen McDannell and Bernhard Lang. 410 pages. Yale University Press. $29.95.

pursuit of happiness. That's true, too, for scholarly novelist-priests. Aided by a hypnotist, Greeley discovered that his own submerged image of heaven is an emerald city on a lake which, as he approached it, turned out to be his hometown of Chicago.

Beneath his whimsy, Greeley is delivering a serious message. He says that the principal atheistic architects of the modern mind, chiefly Freud, Marx and Nietzsche, were wrong when they argued that hope in a heaven inhibits us from enjoying or caring about earthly life. On the contrary, his most recent polling data suggests that "those who believe in life after death lead happier lives and trust people more. The people who believe in [heaven] are just as committed to this world as those who don't. Belief in personal survival is not the coward's way out."

Heaven remains open to all speculators. The healthy and wealthy are free to imagine a celestial Caribbean island with an endless blue horizon and a loved one whispering, "It doesn't get better than this." More often heaven is a subject raised at times of crisis. For the aged and the terminally ill, heaven is often a release from what ails them. The Rev. Sam Geli, a Seventh-day Adventist chaplain at Santa Monica Hospital Medical Center, finds that for many pediatric cancer patients, heaven "is a place where they will no longer have to listen to Mom and Dad cry and fight, a place where they won't have to come to the hospital for chemotherapy treatments." For AIDS patients, heaven is freedom from pain. For the elderly, heaven is the ultimate rest. "They're tired," says Geli. "Their greatest fear is that heaven is an asexual place with no husbands or wives. They want to know that they won't be alone." Geli himself thinks of heaven as a place of harmony and worries that he may be right. "Conflict is my life," he admits. "What could a hospital chaplain do in heaven if there's no conflict?"

Visions of Eternity

Most Americans have faith in a heaven, and expect to find their way there. Some hope to meet their Maker, others just their friends and family. Hell is a different matter.

About Heaven:

77% Believe there is a heaven
76% Think they have a good or excellent chance of getting there

About Hell:

58% Believe there is a hell
 6% Think they have a good or excellent chance of getting there

What It Might Be Like in Heaven:

91% Think it will be peaceful
83% Think they will be with God
77% Think they will see people they know
74% Think there will be humor
32% Think they'll be the same age in heaven as when they die on earth

For this NEWSWEEK Poll, The Gallup Organization interviewed a national sample of 750 adults by telephone Dec. 21-22, 1988. The margin of error is plus or minus 4 percent; The NEWSWEEK Poll © 1989 by NEWSWEEK, Inc.

Missing from most contemporary considerations of heaven is the notion of divine justice. Yet such a yearning, initially developed by Zoroastrians in Persia, has long been crucial to the Judeo-Christian tradition. For centuries the ancient Israelites believed that at death everyone descended into Sheol, a kind of shadowy underground parking lot similar to the Greeks' Hades. By the time of the Maccabean revolt against occupying Syrians (164–64 B.C.), the Israelites began to question the justice of a God who demands obedience in life but delivers the wicked and the faithful alike to inert oblivion. The answer that evolved was resurrection: the just, like the prophet Elijah, would be restored to the bosom of the Lord and the wicked would feel the flames of an everlasting Gehenna, or Hell. This view prevailed in rabbinic literature. The Babylonian Talmud (circa A.D. 600) has 300 arguments for the resurrection of the dead.

For Christians, heaven was the final judgment rendered as a reward, God's promise of salvation for those who believe in him. And, woe to those who reject the Savior. Even as the Talmudists fashioned their arguments, Christian preachers amplified the importance of the afterlife with concrete descriptions of the spiritual rewards of heaven—and even more graphic depictions of the agonies of the damned.

In Dante's "Divine Comedy," heaven, hell and purgatory are imagined as actual places, each as much a part of the late-medieval map as Florence itself. For Martin Luther, they became spiritual states corresponding to faith, despair and doubt. With the advent of 18th-century rationalism, all that remained of the afterlife for enlightened thinkers was a distant deity who enforced civic and moral behavior: if reason couldn't make one virtuous, fear of God would. With Marx, the intellectual revolution was complete. Heaven was to be found, if at all, in this life, not the next.

Meantime, observes American church historian Martin Marty, "Hell disappeared. And no one noticed." For liberal Protestants, hell began to fade in the 19th century along with Calvinism's stern and predestining God. In once Puritan New England, the Universalists decided that God is much too good to condemn anyone to hell, while the Unitarians concluded that humanity is much too good for God to punish—if, indeed, there is a God. Today, hell is theology's H-word, a subject too trite for serious scholarship. When he prepared a Harvard lecture on the disappearance of hell, Marty consulted the indices of several scholarly journals, including one dating back to 1889, and failed to find a single entry.

Although the Roman Catholic Church still teaches that eternal damnation is possible, the lurid descriptions of burning flesh which were once part of the retreat master's rhetorical arsenal vanished—like much else—through the open windows of Vatican Council II. Indeed, between 1963 and 1965 the Council fathers produced hundreds of pages of official documents, but they did not mention hell even once. "Heaven and hell is not about ending up in two different places," says moral theologian James Burtchaell of the University of Notre Dame. "It's about ending up in this life, and forever in the next, being two very different kinds of persons. It's about character, not context." In other words, heaven and hell are no longer thought of as different locations, with separate ZIP codes, but radically opposed states of intimacy with and alienation from God. One damns oneself by what one chooses to do or neglects to do and thus remains forever alienated from God—and from those who enjoy his love. "Eternal life doesn't begin with death," Burtchaell insists. "It's already under way."

Even conservative evangelicals are losing their taste for fire and brimstone. At the core of evangelicalism is the belief that one must accept Jesus Christ as personal Lord and Savior or suffer in hell for all eternity. There is no purgatory for minor sinners or limbo for those good souls who never had the Gospel preached to them in this life. But now, says University of Virginia sociologist James Hunter, author of two books on contemporary evangelicalism, "many evangelicals have a difficult time conceiving of people, especially virtuous nonbelievers, going to hell." In one of his studies, for example, Hunter asked evangelical students if they thought Gandhi was in hell. "They recognized that by their own theology Gandhi should be in hell, but the idea made them extremely nervous," Hunter says. "They recognized that to say a good man like Gandhi is in hell is to say that friends of theirs who are not born again will also go to hell, and socially that's a difficult position to maintain." As a result of this social conflict, he concludes that evangelicals are tempering their images of hell: "People say now, 'I think there is a hell but I hope it will be a soul-sleep'."

Fundamentalists, however, have no doubts about hell or heaven—and who is going where. "The thing about heaven that is most precious to me," says Bill Prince, a born-again member of a Southern Baptist church in suburban Atlanta, "is the thought of being in the presence of the Savior and in an environment where everyone there is a believer. Everyone has met the standards of God's entrance requirements, which means that we should all be very much alike."

If hell has, for all its old intents and purposes, disappeared from modern consciousness, can heaven be far behind? Within some liberal religious circles it already has slipped from polite conversation. "There's not much hell and not much heaven either," observes United Church of Christ theologian Max Stackhouse, a professor at Andover-Newton Theological School. "The prevailing opinion is that when you die you're dead but God still cares." Rabbi Terry Bard, director of pastoral services at Boston's Beth Israel Hospital, sums up the views of many Jews: "Dead is dead," he says, and what lives on are the children and a legacy of good works. At

Harvard Divinity School, theologian Gordon Kaufman traces four centuries of decline in the concepts of heaven and hell; what is left is intellectually empty baggage. "It seems to me we've gone through irreversible changes," Kaufman declares. "I don't think there can be any future for heaven and hell."

If liberal Judaism and Christianity is a way of having God without an afterlife, reincarnation is an option for those who want an afterlife without God. The NEWSWEEK Poll shows that 24 percent of Americans believe in reincarnation. For some New Age enthusiasts like actress Shirley MacLaine, much of the fascination with reincarnation lies in checking out one's past lives the way genealogists trace out a family tree. For traditional Buddhists and Hindus, however, reincarnation is not a substitute for Western ideas of immortality but part of a whole process of self-realization leading to release from the cycle of death and rebirth and into nirvana, or pure freedom.

Indeed, religions that were once confined to Asia are now rivals for American allegiance—in part because of the ways they solve the problem of life after death. Among the many varieties of Buddhism, the Tibetan tradition stresses that what happens after death depends on how one progresses spiritually in this life. The karma, or effects of behavior in past lives, determines who or what one will become in the next. According to Lama Wang Chen of Rime Dakshang Tagyu, a Tibetan Buddhist organization in Los Angeles, death brings a three-day suspension of consciousness followed by 49 more days of wandering the universe as a spirit. A common or unenlightened person will then return to the cycle of life as an animal or a slave. The Bodhisattva, or enlightened Buddhist, however, can return as an artist, a teacher, or whatever else he chooses. "The incarnation of Bodhisattva is limitless," says the lama. "And you can never know who's who."

Heaven in Hindu tradition is like an extended vacation, a place where the soul rests, perhaps for thousands of years, between reincarnations. The ambience of heaven varies according to the resident god or goddess, but each is a kind of garden party with flowers, choice foods, music and beautiful women. Hindus also have a variety of spectacular hells, each with its own exquisite torture. "If you failed to feed the hungry while you were living, you might be chained to a rock where birds come to eat your stomach," says Wendy Doniger O'Flaherty, author of "Other People's Myths" and a professor at the University of Chicago. As a punishment for adultery, a sinner may be forced to embrace a beautiful woman whose temperature is white-hot.

Islam is much closer to Christianity in its conception of the afterlife. After death, each individual will be questioned by two angels, Munkar and Nakir, about his faith. The dead remain in their graves until the end of the world, when everyone will assemble before Allah for the final judgment. Each person must then walk the Path, the bridge that stretches over hell; the faithful will complete the journey into paradise while the damned will fall off into the fiery pits of hell. Both heaven and hell have seven grades of pleasure and torment and both are eternal. According to the Koran, the damned will be roasted, boiled and afflicted with pus. The Islamic heaven is like the original Garden of Eden only more crowded. It is also a male-dominated fantasy: the just will enjoy abundant fruits, "sweet potions" and compliant maidens. But the greatest delight, the Prophet Muhammad stressed, is spiritual: seeing the Lord. Compared to that meeting, he taught the people of the desert, all the pleasures of the body [are] "as an ocean surpasses a drop of sweat."

Although the Hebrew Bible does not offer a detailed description of heaven, belief in an afterlife has been central to normative Judaism. The Babylonian Talmud describes a heavenly Yeshiva where the just will have Moses for a teacher. Another image is of a banquet in which the righteous will feed on the Leviathan (sea monster) and a third features a great festival in which the Messiah is lord of the dance. More important than these images, says Jacob Neusner, a Judaism scholar at Brown University, is the conviction that individuals will enjoy a communal life with God in the world to come. This belief, he says, "predominated among Jews until modern times and are still professed by the Orthodox and many Conservative Jews today"—including Neusner himself. On the other hand, hell is no longer a part of the Jewish afterlife. Sin, in the Jewish perspective, is atoned for in this life through repentance and the experience of death itself. "Jews have been through the Holocaust," adds Rabbi Daniel Landes of Temple Beth Jacob in Beverly Hills, Calif. "There's just no need to talk about hell."

The most vividly imagined heaven belongs to the Mormons. Indeed, as the first made-in-America vision of the afterlife, it provides everything that a busy, family-oriented, hellbent-for-progress society could possibly imagine. According to Mormon doctrine, God—who was once a man—is married to a "heavenly mother"; together they procreated "spirit children" who took bodies and inhabited the earth. Like their heavenly parents, Mormons are expected to marry "for time and eternity" in a Mormon temple, the first step (after baptism) toward becoming gods themselves. If they keep the commandments

and ordinances of the church, Mormons can expect to enter a paradise death. This Mormon heaven is much like others, complete with lakes, forests and cities with splendid tall buildings—but it is no place to relax. There Mormons continue to work nonstop for the church, converting deceased nonbelievers and helping to "seal" their non-Mormon predecessors into the body of faithful. The more they do the greater their progress to ultimate exaltation as gods.

There's room for everyone in the Mormon heaven and only a handful of adamant reprobates who refuse conversion are expected to inhabit hell. But only the properly married can progress to full godhead. The wife reaches exaltation by participating in her husband's eternal priesthood. Eventually, everyone receives glorified bodies and the exalted couples spend all of eternity in painless—but presumably pleasurable—procreation. Their spirit children, in turn, take bodies, inhabit other planets and worship their parents as the Heavenly Father and Mother.

Compared to such robust accounts of the afterlife, the studied evasions emanating from most American pulpits leave a real void for laymen seeking some assurance that being human has more than transitory significance. "The idea of life after death is clearly an embarrassment to modern thinking—most major philosophers have ridiculed it—but it is just as clearly the touchstone of all religion," says Neusner. "Religion says that being human has eternal meaning. If religion announces that life is over at the grave, then it is not talking about what people expect religion to discuss."

In rejecting heaven and hell, the rationalistic modern consciousness also rejects the awesome seriousness of moral and immoral behavior. But for those who take God seriously, human freedom means the capacity to make moral decisions which have radical and enduring consequences. Hell, then, is not a place created by a God bent on getting even, but the alienation we choose for ourselves. Heaven, on the other hand, is for lovers—of others and of God. "Thou hast made us for Thyself," wrote Saint Augustine nearly 17 centuries ago, "and our hearts are restless, till rest in Thee." If most Americans imagine heaven as a family reunion, the reason, perhaps, is that that is all we know of love. The hell of thinking about heaven is that we cannot imagine—or trust—a love that surpasses our own understanding.

With MARK STARR *in Boston,* LINDA BUCKLEY *in Los Angeles,* REGINA ELAM *in New York and bureau reports*

Moslems and Byzantines

With the fall of Rome three emergent orders came to dominate the Mediterranean world. In Europe various Germanic kingdoms filled the vacuum left by Rome. In the Balkan peninsula and Asia Minor the eastern remnants of Rome evolved into the Byzantine Empire. The Middle East and North Africa fell to an expanding Arab empire. Each area developed a unique civilization, based in each instance upon a distinctive form of religion—Roman Catholicism in Western Europe, Orthodox Christianity in the Byzantine sphere of influence, and Islam in the Arab world. Each placed its unique stamp upon the classical tradition to which all three fell heir. The articles in this unit, however, concentrate on the Byzantine and Moslem civilizations. The medieval culture of Europe is treated in the next chapter.

Western perceptions of Islam and Arabic civilization have been clouded by ignorance and bias, as "The World of Islam" points out. To European observers during the medieval period, Islam seemed a misguided version of Christianity. In the wake of Arab conquests, Islam increasingly came to represent terror and devastation, a dangerous force loosed upon Christendom. Reacting out of fear and hostility, Christian authors were reluctant to acknowledge the learning and high culture of Arabic civilization.

Moslem commentators could be equally intolerant. Describing Europeans, one of them wrote: "They are most like beasts than like men. . . . Their temperaments are frigid, their humors raw, their bellies gross . . . they lack keenness of understanding . . . and are overcome by ignorance and apathy."

The stereotypes formed in early encounters between Christians and Moslems survived for generations. Centuries of hostility have tended to obscure the degree of cultural exchange between the Arab world and the West. Indeed, as William H. McNeill has observed, Moslems have been written out of European history.

However, the domain of Islam encroached upon Europe at too many points for the two cultures to remain mutually exclusive. In western Europe Islam swept over Spain, crossed the Pyrenees, and penetrated France; in the central Mediterranean it leapt from Tunis to Sicily and then into Italy; in eastern Europe, Islam finally broke through Asia Minor and into the Balkans and the Caucasus. It is useful to recall, too, that early Islam was exposed to Jewish, Christian, and classical influences. History and geography determined that there would be much cross-fertilization between Islam and the West.

Yet there is no denying the originality and brilliance of much of Islamic civilization. For a start, there is Islam itself, unquestionably one of the great religions of mankind. Additional evidence of Arabic creativity can be found in the visual arts, particularly in the design and decoration of the great mosques. The article "The Master-Chronologers of Islam" describes the Arabs' contributions to the philosophy and practice of history.

The medieval West borrowed extensively from the Arabs. The magnificent centers of Islamic culture—Baghdad, Cairo, Cordoba, and Damascus—outshone the cities of Christendom. Islamic scholars surpassed their Christian counterparts in astronomy, mathematics, and medicine—perhaps because the Arab world was more familiar than medieval Europe with the achievements of classical Greece. (European scholars regained access to the Greek heritage at least partially through translations from the Arabic!)

As for the Byzantine Empire, it was for nearly 1,000 years a Christian bulwark against Persians, Arabs, and Turks. But it also made some important cultural contributions. The distinctive icons of Byzantine artists set the pattern for subsequent visualizations of Christ in the West. Byzantine missionaries and statesmen spread Orthodox Christianity, with its unique tradition of Caesaropapism, to Russia. Byzantine scholars and lawmakers preserved much of the classical heritage. Even hostile Islam was subject to a "constant flow of ideas" from the Byzantines. Alexander Kazhdin explores the strengths and weaknesses of Byzantine civilization in "Byzantium: The Emperor's New Clothes." Judith Herrin, with the help of Procopius, unveils the court of Justinian and Theodora in "The Byzantine Secrets of Procopius."

Looking Ahead: Challenge Questions

Do medieval hostilities between the Arabs and the West color relations between the two in the modern world?

Do the articles in this unit betray any bias toward Islam and the Arabs?

Was Byzantine civilization merely an extension of late Roman culture, or was it a new departure? Explain.

How did the Byzantines influence the development of Russia?

BYZANTIUM:

THE EMPEROR'S NEW CLOTHES?

Eastern Europe and Russia are the subject of intense scrutiny at present as questions of power, identity and political structures are pursued at breath-taking speed. 'History Today' contributes a commentary on these events. . . .

***Alexander Kazhdan**, senior research associate at Dumbarton Oaks, Washington D.C., considers the influence of totalitarianism and meritocracy in the Byzantine empire – and its relationship to the growth of the Russian and other successor states in the East.*

THE STATE OF BYZANTIUM, THE SO-CALLED Byzantine empire, has never existed; the term was invented in the sixteenth century to designate the empire the capital of which was Constantinople, the city on the Bosphorus, which was supposedly founded in 330 and destroyed by the Ottoman Turks in 1453. Byzantion (in the Latinised form Byzantium) was the name it held before being renamed by and in honour of the Emperor Constantine the Great (324-37), and throughout the Middle Ages the Byzantines were the citizens of Constantinople only, not the subjects of the emperor who reigned in Constantinople. These subjects did not even notice that they stopped being Romans and began being Byzantines – they continued to consider themselves Romans until they woke up under the rule of the sultans.

Thus the nomenclature itself is confused, and some purist scholars prefer to call the population of the Constantinopolitan empire Romans or Greeks, and terms such as 'the Eastern Roman empire' or 'Greco-Roman law' are still in use. But this is only the beginning of the problem, and we are in trouble when trying to define the date of birth of Byzantium. Was it 330, when Constantine celebrated the inauguration of his new residence on the Bosphorus? Was it 395, when the Emperor Theodosius I died and bequeathed the empire to two different rulers, his sons Arkadios in Constantinople (395-408) and Honorius (395-423) in Milan and later Ravenna? Was it in 476, when the Herulian (or Hun) Odoacer deposed the last western emperor, Romulus Augustulus, and sent his regalia to Constantinople. Or was it in 554, when Justinian I (527-65), after having reconquered Italy, issued the Pragmatic Sanction and determined the status of this old-new province? None of these events had a lasting effect on the empire. All we can say is that Byzantium was not born in a day, and the changes were various and gradual.

The idea that radical ethnic changes gave birth to Byzantium was popular in the nineteenth century and still remains popular among some East European scholars; the Slavs are said to have invaded the Roman empire, settled in Greece and Asia Minor, rejuvenated the decrepit empire, become the backbone of the new victorious army and, even more, that of the Orthodox monarchy. Unquestionably, the Slavs invaded the Balkans in the first half of the seventh century. They left behind some traces in Balkan place-names. The Slavic influence on the administration, legal and fiscal systems, and military organisation is another matter – there is no data for such an assertion.

Territorial changes are more evident. In rough outline they coindided with the Slavic invasion, and took place during the seventh century. The Mediterranean Roman empire disappeared, and was replaced by a new formation, concentrated around Greece and Asia Minor, the areas dominated by the Greek language and culture. But could not the empire retain its old character within a more restricted framework?

Religious changes seem to be attached to the activity of a single

From *History Today*, September 1989, pp. 26-34. Reproduced by kind permission of History Today, Ltd., 83-84 Berwick Street, London W1V 3PJ, England.

Power over God and man; the Empress Irene, 752-803, whose achievements during a tumultuous career included the re-establishment of icon worship and the deposition of her own son Constantine as emperor in her bid for sole imperial power.

man, the Emperor Constantine. Tradition has it that he saw a vision of the cross and promulgated the Milan edict liberating the Christian church from discrimination. For medieval chroniclers this was a radical turning point, the creation of the Christian empire. We know now that the edict of tolerance was issued before Constantine, in 311, by the Emperor Galerius, whom Constantine's staunch flatterers depicted as a scoundrel. We also know that Constantine did not completely abandon pagan cults, particularly the worship of the solar deity (or deities), and that when Constantine, on his death-bed, formally accepted Christianity, he accepted the new religion in its heretical denomination, Arianism. Moreover, paganism regained momentum soon after Constantine, during the reign of Julian the Apostate (361-63). At the court of the Very Christian Emperor, Theodosius I, pagan politicians were influential, and the fifth century saw a revival of pagan culture represented by such men as the philosopher Proklos and the historian Zosimos. Even in the sixth century, paganism was alive in the countryside, and the aristocratic intelligentsia, while paying lip-service to the official creed, stuck to the ancient philosophical and cultural traditions. Thus, the question arises: which phenomenon is more momentous: Constantine's cautious baptism or the seventh-century triumph of Christianity that had behind it the gigantic work of the church fathers who had elaborated the system of the new belief? The Trinitarian and Christological disputes, out of which this system emerged, came to halt only in the middle of the seventh century.

The changes in the administrative system are the most evasive, and some scholars place the roots of these changes in the reign of Justinian I, or even earlier. The search for these roots is a futile one – any important phenomenon has its roots in the past. What matters is not embryonic development but the critical mass. It is, however, very difficult to measure the critical masses of historical process, especially for the seventh century, notorious for its scarcity of available sources. Of course, Byzantium remained a monarchy in and after the seventh century, and was, at least in theory, administered from Constantinople, but it now seems sure that the new administrative system of districts, the so-called 'themes', appeared in the seventh century. The exarchates of Ravenna and of Carthage, organised by the end of the sixth century, were the direct predecessors of the themes; the themes were powerful organisations until the mid-ninth century and decided the destiny of the throne of Constantinople. Indeed, all major uprisings until the ninth century were based on themes.

In central government during the same seventh century, late Roman departments were replaced by new offices. The main functionaries such as praetorian prefect and *magister officiorum* disappeared, and the central bureaux worked under the supervision of the so-called *logothetai*. Some late Roman designations survived, although often in a changed sense. For example, the Byzantine hypatos-consul was worlds away from the magnificent consuls of the sixth century, and the Byzantine *magistros* was a title, rather than an office, like the late Roman *magister*. Some change of function must have occurred beneath the veneer of this terminological stability.

And did society remain late Roman? We can divide the question into two sections: the urban and the rural. It seems that in the seventh century the Roman provincial city was in decline and that when it reappeared by around the tenth century, it had a new, medieval, character. Archaeological excavations are usually witness to the decline of cities, and the findings of coins from the second half of the seventh century become rare. In addition the setting of hagiographical literature shifts from the provincial city to either the capital or the countryside. The available data about the countryside between the seventh and late ninth centuries are scanty, and we are forced to build our conclusions more on the silence of our sources than on direct evidence. Silence, however, is fairly evocative. We hear little about large estates, slaves and *coloni* of this period; the most discussed case is that of St Philaretos who is said in his *Vita* to have possessed approximately fifty allot-

ments (*proasteia*). Such figures are usually exaggerated, and we cannot take them for granted, the more so since Philaretos was the son of a peasant and could perfectly well manage his team of ploughing oxen. On the other hand, the so-called Farmers' Law, the Byzantine counterpart of the western *leges*, deals with free peasants. Certainly, the text is enigmatic, imprecisely dated and probably reflects some local conditions, but this is what we have – direct evidence about the free peasantry and very questionable data concerning large estates.

If we assume that the leading class of the ancient *polis*, the urban landowners, disappeared, or at least lost its former significance, a strange phenomenon coinciding with those changes becomes clearer: the disappearance of family names. Rare after the fourth century but still known in the sixth century, they are practically unknown between the seventh century and the end of the ninth century. Does this mean that the aristocracy or at least the concept of aristocracy ceased to exist? Certainly, we do not know of any powerful family from this period, and at the end of the tenth century Basil II (976-1025) wrote with astonishment and indignation about those families which had been pre-eminent for some seventy to one hundred years; so the phenomenon must have been a new one in his reign.

Thus all information converges on the seventh century; and although it is far from extensive or dependable, it allows us to hypothesise that in the seventh century some slow changes occured and that establishing the seventh century as a watershed at least does not conflict with the available evidence.

But why should we bother our heads about Byzantium? Today we take for granted the impact of ancient cultural traditions – they are considered to be the foundation of western civilisation. In our perception of the past, Byzantium plays the role of a stepdaughter, a Cinderella; we allow it to store and transmit the *oeuvre* of great Greek minds. Byzantine culture is seen not as an achievement in its own right, but as an imitation and copy of the great classical paragon. The art has been

looked at and the literature has been read with this presupposition in mind; as non-creative, repetitive, slavishly following ancient originals, disconnected from contemporary problems, concentrating on ridiculous theological niceties, and so forth. And since the purpose of their art, literature, philosophy, law and science was to imitate the great predecessors, Byzantine culture allegedly knew no development.

But was this really true? Bearing in mind the social and political changes of the seventh century already alluded to, can we see a cultural transformation taking place at the same time? Certainly building activity almost stopped, literary work contracted and even the most medieval genre, hagiography, was almost non-existent in the eighth century. Manuscripts copied at that time are extremely few, and philosphical thought came to a halt. Thus, as in the West, the Byzantine Middle Ages began with a cultural gap that was followed by a revival around 800.

What is interesting in this revival is its social background: the vast majority of the known authors of this time belonged to the monastic world. But from the mid-ninth century onwards a different type of *literatus* came to the fore – the imperial or ecclesiastical functionary. In the twelfth century, again, a new type of writer emerges: the professional author, frequently called the 'beggar poet' since his existence depended upon the gifts and stipends from the emperor and others, and soliciting these gifts occupied a substantial part of his concerns and of his poetry.

The genres of literature were also in flux; in the twelfth century the saintly biography went through a crisis, very few contemporary biographies were produced, the writers preferring to revise old hagiographical texts, and Eustathios of Thessalonike, a rhetorician and commentator on Homer, issued a *vita* that was, in its core, a denial of traditional hagiographical virtues. This *vita* of a (fake?) saint, Philotheos of Opsikion, was a eulogy to a rich married man living in the world. However, while hagiography was fading a new genre appeared, or rather was revived, after a long absence: the romance. Poetic and prose panegyrics of secular leaders were of no significance before the eleventh century; the ethical ideal had remained either monastic or imperial. And the memoir did not come into being before Michael Psellos in the eleventh century.

The well-entrenched concept of Byzantine cultural uniformity does not stand up to examination, not only because Byzantium's cultural development was in a state of flux. A distinction can be drawn not only between different generations but also between members of the same generation of different class and with different taste.

A classic example of such a distinction is a group of addresses to the emperor Alexios III Angelos (1195-1203) celebrating his victory over rebellious John Komnenos the Fat. Four orations survive; three of them are traditional, that is lacking in concrete detail, symbolic and full of propaganda. The fourth, by Nicholas Mesarites, is rich in details, dynamic and ironic. Mesarites does not strive to exclude reality in the interests of a higher moral truth; his aim is to make actual events vivid.

But if Byzantine culture was not a plain imitation of antiquity, then what was the difference between the two, and what was the former's contribution? Antiquity is a broad notion whatever characterisation we formulate, and what we now accept as essential may be perceived by other scholars in other times as incidental. There was clearly a considerable transitional period between the Roman and the Byzantine worlds. On the other hand, Byzantium is not 'linear', one-dimensional and simplistic; moreover, it was consciously orientated toward ancient culture. The Byzantines called themselves Romans, believed in this definition, and did not see a demarcation line between themselves and antiquity. Homer was their poet. Aristotle their philosopher, and Augustus their emperor. In their writings they followed ancient Greek (although they spoke vernacular), and they filled their works with ancient quotations, proverbs and dead words. The cultural line between Rome and Constantinople is as indistinct as the chronological line between them.

There are, however, some points of difference which seem obvious.

Byzantium was Christian, antiquity pagan; Byzantium was uniform, antiquity variegated; Byzantium was autocratic, antiquity republican. Unfortunately none of these statements is completely correct: Christianity was born in antiquity and inherited many ancient ideas; Byzantium's uniformity was relative; and both Hellenistic and Roman monarchies existed within the framework of ancient civilisation. But relative as they are, these oppositions reflect partial truth and highlight the direction of search.

Another set of obvious or half-obvious dichotomies refers to a different aspect of reality. Marxist theoreticians contrast ancient slave ownership with Byzantine feudalism. The word 'feudalism' is too questionable to be a useful tool of analysis, but it is plausible that the forms of exploitation differed between antiquity and Byzantium, even though slaves (and not only the household slaves but slaves in the fields, at the herds and in the workshops) were numerous in Byzantium. We can also say that the urban life so typical of antiquity lost its role in Byzantium and that the family not the *municipum* formed the main social unit and determined the structure of many other units.

Before we take the final step and attempt to define along very rough lines, the 'Byzantine particularity', let us shift from chronological to territorial distinctions, let us juxtapose not Byzantium and antiquity but Byzantium and the western medieval world. Of course, the western medieval world was diverse, nevertheless, some feeling of unity prevailed: the Byzantines, at least from the eleventh century onward, spoke of the 'Latins' as a specific group, differing from the Byzantines insofar as their beliefs, costumes and habits were concerned. For the westerners as well, the 'schismatic Greeks' formed a separate set of people; one could marry a Greek woman, trade in Greek ports, serve at the court of Constantinople, but the gap remained and even widened as time went on.

From the viewpoint of the westerners the Byzantines entertained a wrong theology, believing that the Holy Spirit proceeded from God the Father only; they were too bookish and bad soldiers; they

adorned their churches with icons and not the sculptured crucifix, and their priests were married. But there was one point that usually dominated in the mutual contrasting of two societies.

In 1147 crusading armies arrived in Constantinople. The Greek historian, John Kinnamos, who was almost contemporaneous with the event, described them in great detail. Among other things, he noticed with a subdued surprise that:

> Their offices (or dignities) are peculiar and resemble distinctions descending from the height of the empire, since it is something most noble and surpasses all others. A duke outranks a count; a king a duke; and the emperor, a king. The inferior naturally yields to the superior, supports him in war, and obeys in such matters.

What struck Kinnamos was the hierarchical structure of western aristocracy, the system of vertical links.

In 1189 Isaac II (1185-95) sent an embassy to Frederick Barbarossa. The Byzantine historian, Niketas Choniates, relates that Frederick ordered the Greek ambassadors to be seated in his presence and had chairs placed in the hall even for their servants. By so doing, comments Choniates, the German ruler made fun of the Byzantines, who failed to take into consideration the virtue of nobility of different members of society and who appraised the whole population by the same measure, like a herdsman who drove all the hogs into the same pigsty.

Western society was perceived by both the Greeks and the Latins as one organised on the aristocratic and hierarchical foundation, Byzantine society as 'democratic', although in Byzantium the word *'demokratia'* had a pejorative tinge and was usually applied to the domination of the *demoi*, the unbridled mobs.

To sum up, Byzantium was an atomistic society with the family as its cornerstone. The man was primarily the member of the family and not of the *municipium* (as he was in Greco-Roman antiquity) or community or guild (as he was to be in the medieval West). Formal wedding ceremonies, prohibition of divorce, abolition of concubinage; all these contrasted with the 'free' late Roman family. Lineage played an insignificant role, and vertical (hierarchical) links remained practically unknown. Small family-like monasteries were common, and family-orientated terminology permeated both political and ecclesiastical relations.

The aristocratic principle was underdeveloped. This does not mean that all the emperor's subjects were equal in rights and wealth, even though western observers kept repeating disparagingly that they were; in the tenth century, for instance, the German ambassador Liutprand asserted that all the participants in the imperial procession in Constantinople wore shabby and frayed costumes. The principle of inequality in Byzantium differed from that of the West; the Byzantines created a meritocracy based not on the individual's 'blood' or origin but on his place in the bureaucratic machine. A system which, while less stable than nobility in the West, enabled more vertical mobility. This does not mean that they were less arrogant, but it does mean that, while less restricted by tradition, they were less defiant of the emperor's omnipotence.

The imperial power was both feeble and strong. It was strong since the emperor, in theory, was not restricted by law; he was the law itself. He combined in his hands legislative, administrative and judicial power, was the supreme army commander and claimed control of ideology. But he was poorly protected against schemes and plots, and half of all the Byzantine emperors ended their rule as victims of violence. Feeble as individuals (certainly some emperors had a strong personality) they were omnipotent as symbols of government; the emperors themselves might be criticised, but the principle of unlimited monarchical power was never questioned.

In practice, of course, everything was more complex, and many an emperor met social and religious resistance, even blunt bureaucratic intransigence. However, we can call the Byzantine empire a totalitarian state. And it was the only totalitarian state of the European Middle Ages. As such, Byzantium gives us material to observe a totalitarian state over a long period and to analyse its liabilities and assets, its roots and mechanism.

Several points are of importance. Was the totalitarian organisation of power interconnected with the atomistic structure of society? It seems quite plausible that western system of vertical and horizontal bonds created a better protection for the man, certainly for a nobleman, against the supreme power that condescended to respect the noble as the king's peer. I do not think that the western *villanus* was better protected than Byzantine *paroikos*, but probably western guilds gave more protection to their members than did Byzantine *somateia*, their counterpart. At any rate, atomistic feelings and fears, rejection of friendship and emphasis on individual way of salvation (rather than the role of sacraments) could contribute to the concept of the lonely man, a helpless slave in front of the powerful emperor, a toy of relentless doom. The political misfortunes of ever-shrinking Byzantium reinforced this concept; late Byzantine philosophers were unable to grasp why the most Christian, the 'chosen people' should be exposed to the crashing attacks of the Ottoman Turks.

How did the totalitarian state function? So much ink has been spilled to describe the unwieldy and rotten Byzantine governmental mechanism, and undoubtedly there is much truth in these two adjectives – based on the bitter words of contemporary critics. But there are some stubborn facts that cry out for explanation. How could the Eastern Roman empire, where centralised authority was more strongly developed than in the West, repel the same barbarian attacks that subdued Italy and Gaul? Why was it that, until the twelfth century, totalitarian Byzantium was economically and culturally ahead of the West? A century ago Russian Byzantinists developed a theory according to which the Byzantine emperors, especially in the tenth century, protected the peasantry and the village community against the so-called *dynatoi* ('powerful', i.e. the wealthy and influential members of the ruling class) and thus secured the existence of a strong army and of plentiful taxes. When, in the eleventh century, the emperors yielded to western feudalism, aban-

doned 'the minor brethren', and turned away from the principles of the Orthodox (and Slavic) monarchy, the decline of Byzantium began. This theory is political more than scholarly. The tenth-century state did not protect the peasantry either (it protected state taxes that were burdensome enough and the centralised power over the countryside), nor was the period of the eleventh and twelfth centuries that of decline. On the contrary, it was a period of economic growth and cultural upsurge. But in spite of all its weakness, totalitarian Byzantium managed to flourish during several centuries while the split-up ('federal') West suffered from shortages of food, dress and housing.

The problem is intensified by Byzantine ideological duplicity. A striking example is the fate of Roman law in Byzantium, the Roman law summarised and codified by Justinian I during the last stage of the late Roman empire. It was never abolished, although some attempts to make it simpler were made. Byzantine legal text-books adhered to Roman law, repeating, time and again, formulations that were in disaccord with reality. For instance, the official law-book of the ninth century, the *Basilika*, described administrative institutions that existed during the sixth century and had ceased to exist by the ninth. Furthermore, the agrarian terminology of the *Basilika*, translated from Latin into Greek, applied to no Byzantine reality, and often made no sense whatever. Whereas Roman law reflected the principles of the legal state, protecting individual rights and private ownership, the Byzantine empire did not give any legal protection to its subjects. Emperors could execute any citizen without trial and could confiscate any land without argument. Texts of the tenth century state that any land on which the emperor had put his foot could be taken from its owner. As more private documents have been published in recent decades, we can see more clearly that the Byzantine law of things and law of obligations deviated from Roman norms and that Byzantine tribunals acted on principles distinct from the Roman; but the words often remained the same, and private ownership of land was repeatedly affirmed in legal text-books.

This contrast between theory and practice had a strong impact on Byzantine mentality. I am not referring to the notorious Byzantine diplomacy or the lack of fealty, of which the Latin neighbours accused them; indeed I doubt that such accusations could be taken at face value. In fact they can be applied equally to many medieval leaders. Much more substantial was the Byzantine skill of allusion. Of course, their literature is in no way short of direct and open invectives against political and ideological enemies, but they loved, and knew how to say without saying, to evoke by an apparently occasional hint a broad gamut of emotions. They were much more attentive towards those details and nuances which usally escape modern understanding. One of the most drastic examples is the Byzantine insistence on the resemblance of their icons to sitter or subject, whereas modern art historians are unable to perceive individual elements in Byzantine icons and are inclined to deny such resemblence. Equally, we are unable to catch allusions, political and personal, in their writings, particularly in their favourite game, the use of ancient and Biblical imagery.

Two conclusions can be drawn from this observation. In the first place, the Byzantines frequently cared more about nuances than general statements. Any totalitarian or uniform ideology possesses an established set of concepts which are above discussion; Byzantine ideology was no exception, with a set of political or religious formulae, perceived by everyone as final truth and rarely, if ever, discussed. But they certainly had discussions, and very vehement ones. These usually began over slight terminological differences, and it gradually becomes clear that behind such niceties loomed crucial dissentions. We are facing a paradox: an allegedly uniform ideology did not prevent the Byzantines from bitter disputes, only these disputes seemed to be limited to innocuous and insignificant problems: should the churches be adorned with images? Was the Holy Spirit proceeding from God the Father only or from the Son as well? How could Christ be at the

same time the sacrifice offered to God, the priest offering the sacrifice, and God receiving it? Can one see the divine light, the divine energy with sensual eyes? And so on.

In the second place, we must reconsider the role of Byzantine intellectuals. Their indiscriminate eulogies addressed to those in power sound abominably grovelling to our ears. But as soon as we become acquainted with the nuances and methods of the rhetoric it is possible to strip them of the shroud of uniformity and flattery and understand the profound content concealed beneath the surface. Of course, most of their allusions have been lost in the passage of time and still remain incomprehensible to the modern reader, but even that little part of them that can be deciphered compels us to discard the traditional image of literary barrenness.

The Byzantine world was totalitarian; many will agree with such a statement. But it is hard to accept this heritage; we are more willing to reject it, to restrict the survival of the Byzantine 'axe and icon' to Eastern Europe, Slavic and/or Communist countries. The recent celebration of the millenium of the Russian Church sharpened this point yet more. Totalitarian Russia seems to be as natural a successor of totalitarian Byzantium as the Russian icon is the heir of Byzantine images or Russian obscuring eloquence is the heir of Byzantine rhetorics.

The problem is once again, however, not that simple. Kievan Rus certainly had contacts with Byzantium. But did it experience Byzantium's direct impact beyond the ecclesiastical sphere? In fact Kievan temporal society absorbed very little of Byzantium: their weaponry came from the West, their glass producers followed western, not Byzantine recipes, their political structure was as distanced from the Byzantine one as possible. Political marriages of high rank between the two countries were almost unknown. Kievan Rus as a state did not travel the path the Byzantines had worn.

Only in the fifteenth century when Russian grand princes began to build up their centralised monarchy did they discover their Byzantine ancestry; Russia did not inherit Byzantine

totalitarianism but used the model for their political ends. The process was not genetic or automatic – it was a part of the ideological programme, whether consciously or unconsciously applied.

It would be very tempting to assume that only those countries (Bulgaria, Serbia, Rumania, Russia) that were in direct contact with Byzantium developed a tendency to totalitarianism – but I am afraid that this is not true. Not only did Russia become totalitarian only after it had severed direct relations with Byzantium, (when it was separated from Byzantium by Mongolian semi-nomads and Italian trade republics which dominated the Black Sea coast), but there were also countries that for centuries had such contact and did not become totalitarian: Armenia, Georgia, Hungary, Italy. On the other hand, totalitarian governments could be traced in various European countries whose contacts with Byzantium were very slight, such as Spain and France, from the fifteenth century onwards. The French model of the Sun King followed the Byzantine paragon, and it is not sheer chance that sixteenth-century France contributed so much to the development of Byzantine studies.

Byzantium was an interesting historical experiment. It teaches us how totalitarian systems work, what a meritocracy ('nomenklatura') is, what the place of intellectuals in a totalitarian state is, and who owns the land and the means of production. It shows the advantages and disadvantages of the totalitarian system, and reveals under the surface of stagnation the suppressed class of political and ideological contrasts.

FOR FURTHER READING:
Romilly Jenkins, *Byzantium: the Imperial Centuries. AD610-1071* (Weidenfeld & Nicolson, 1966); Cyril Mango, *Byzantium. The Empire of New Rome* (Weidenfeld & Nicolson, 1980); Arnold Toynbee, *Constantine Porphyrogenitus and his World* (Oxford University Press, 1973); Alexander Kazhdan and Ann Wharton Epstein, *Change in Byzantine Culture in the Eleventh and Twelfth Centuries* (University of Berkeley Press, Los Angeles, 1985); R. Browning, *The Byzantine Empire* (Charles Scribner's Sons, New York, 1980); N.G. Wilson, *Scholars of Byzantium* (The Johns Hopkins University Press, Baltimore, 1983).

THE BYZANTINE SECRETS OF PROCOPIUS

Judith Herrin considers the Jekyll-and-Hyde output of Justinian's court historian, alternately respectful official chronicler and tabloid-style exposer of imperial scandal.

How many and how great are the benefits which are wont to accrue to states through History, which transmits to future generations the memory of those who have gone before and resists the steady effort of time to bury events in oblivion. . . Wherefore our concern must be solely this – that all the deeds of the past shall be clearly set forth, and by what man, whosoever he might be, they were wrought ... Indeed it is through this very service that many men of later times strive after virtue by emulating the honours of those who have preceeded them and ... are quite likely to shun the basest practices.

THIS CLASSIC STATEMENT ON THE ROLE OF history was written by Procopius in the sixth-century AD at the opening of his treatise *On Buildings*, in praise of the Emperor Justinian. With its insistence that good examples inspire and guide the young, it would seem to fit the present Secretary of State for Education's idea of the role of history in education today.

Indeed, the aim of Procopius' major work, *A History of the Wars* in eight books, is presented in clear pedagogic terms:

Men who purpose to enter upon a war or are preparing themselves for any kind of struggle may derive some benefit from a narrative of a similar situation in history ... For in these wars more remarkable feats have been performed than in any other wars with which we are acquainted.

This desire to employ history in the training of future citizens is one common to many modern governments; it can also be used by present-day historians, who wish to concentrate on all that is best in the national past so that it may inspire an equally glorious future.

Like the first professional historians of ancient Greece, Procopius devoted all his efforts to recording the development of his own state, preferring the immediate problems raised by contemporary events to an antiquarian study of times long past. He shared the belief that the basis for writing history lay in personal experience and the eye-witness evidence of others, and that it was the historian's task to record the facts as truthfully as possible. For 'while cleverness is appropriate to rhetoric and inventiveness to poetry, truth alone is appropriate to history'. Modelling himself on Herodotus and Thucydides, whom he recognised as the most distinguished of his predecessors, he set out to record a comparable greatness for the Roman Empire of his time.

Yet this is only one side of Procopius the historian. Those who acclaimed him as 'the source of a great light that shone with inimitable brilliance', had no idea that Procopius had also composed a vitriolic denunciation of the emperor who is idolised in the *Buildings*. For, unknown to this admiring audience, he simultaneously composed a scandalous account of Justinian and his wife Theodora, aptly nick-named the *Secret History*. (It is almost as if one of the most respected historians of our time published hard-core pornography under a pseudonym. Perhaps some do?) Whereas in the acknowledged works, the imperial couple are praised for their piety, wisdom and success, in the unpublished one they are identified as demons and vilified. How could Procopius have perpetrated such blatant contradictions? How could he justify such a reversal of the previous record? What historical function could possibly be served by recording such wickedness, which Procopius admitted might be imitated by the inexperienced?

In fact, Procopius was well aware of the dangers, both to himself and to future readers, posed by such a history of 'blackest deeds and base actions'. But he had to persist, even though he feared that later generations would condemn him as 'a narrator of myths ... neither credible nor probable'. Paradoxically, the historian who set out to chronicle the

From *History Today*, August 1988, pp. 36-42. Reproduced by kind permission of History Today, Ltd., 83-84 Berwick Street, London W1V 3PJ, England.

victorious events of the reign of Justinian (527-65) found that the truth could not be confined to one history. To provide an adequate and truthful record of the epoch (in fact, a crucial transitional one) which Procopius was trying to document required different forms, a variety of histories. Despite his intention to note even the failures and inglorious episodes, in the introduction to the *Secret History* Procopius was forced to confess, 'in the case of many of the events described in the previous narrative (of the *Wars*) I was compelled to conceal the causes which led up to them'. His commitment to the truth obliged him now to rectify past omissions and establish the real causes, however contradictory these appeared.

So Procopius is a historian of the first importance for any study of Late Antiquity. Thanks to his writings, Justinian is famous not only for the reconquest of the Roman Empire in the West, Santa Sophia and the codification of law, but also a host of less impressive achievements. But the author himself remains an enigma. Like most ancient historians he provides no biographical details about his parents, his upbringing or his adult personal life. Younger sixth-century admirers like Menander, Agathias and Theophylact Simocatta and later commentators do nothing to help, usually concentrating on Procopius' mastery of Attic style and vocabulary. What particularly struck them was his direct use of a classical model: *The History of the Peloponnesian War* by Thucydides, which pervades all aspects of Procopius' narrative: subject matter, style, turns of phrase, vocabulary and mannerism.

This fact alone should pull us up short. What sort of historian would chose a historical model over a millenium old and transpose it to the 540s AD? Of course, Procopius was not alone in being familiar with the works of ancient historians. The *Histories* of Herodotus and *The Peloponnesian War* of Thucydides had been studied by every generation (of freeborn males) since the fifth century BC. They were among the set texts which described the rise of Greece to supremacy in the east Mediterranean world. But while they were familiar to all educated sixth-century men, Procopius was the only writer who

undertook to adapt one for contemporary use.

It is hard to understand his choice, and even harder to find a present-day perspective that might elucidate his sense of the past. Unlike Procopius we live in a world that has changed very dramatically over the last 200 years, especially in the last few decades. To look back 1,000 years for a comparable model, we might select the vernacular English works of King Alfred, but his language, let alone his style, is completely unfamiliar, and the educational system of his day is quite unknown. This was not true of the Greek classics in the sixth-century AD, when the same language was still spoken throughout the eastern Mediterranean, and the works of Plato and Aristotle, Euclid, Ptolemy and Pythagoras, Aristophanes and Euripides were still studied as the best guide to philosophy, mathematics and literature.

Like other contemporary writers, Procopius was a typical product of this essentially pagan educational system. They all knew their classical literature, including Homer, by heart and probably conversed in quotations, clichés and aphorisms, that would seem tediously predictable to us. They had to learn more rhetoric than in ancient times, for the advent of semi-divine imperial leaders had provoked a new panegyrical style that had to be mastered. But the ancient Greek syllabus remained largely unchanged. And since Procopius went to school before 529, when Justinian launched a ban on pagan teaching, he may even have studied the classics with active pagans in his home town of Caesarea, or other centres of Palestine and Syria. Then Procopius, like many other students, went on to legal studies (perhaps in nearby Beirut) in preparation for a career in the imperial bureaucracy.

Among writers trained in this tradition, Procopius alone elected to provide a secular, narrative history of Justinian's wars, which excluded concerns central to the survival of the empire in the sixth century, such as economic matters or religion. He thus chose to employ a classical model of history-writing that was dependent upon victory and glory.

Uniquely, Procopius cast himself as the historian who would record for posterity the achievements of a golden age. He would apply the skills developed by the outstanding pagan historians, to events of his own Christian times. The reign of Justinian would thus be described as a climax of Greek supremacy, comparable to past eras of greatness.

When he began the *Wars* in the early 540s, such glory could be assumed. After the brilliant campaigns of Belisarius and Sittas on the eastern front, Justinian had purchased an 'endless peace' with the Persian King of Kings, Chosroes. This permitted the western expeditions of the 530s: a rapidly successful campaign against Vandal Africa, and the slower but evident subjection of southern Italy, culminating in the capture of Ravenna and the Gothic king, Vittigis, in 540. After the triumphant entry into Carthage, Procopius could claim: 'It fell to the lot of Belisarius on that day to win such fame as no one of the men of his time ever won nor indeed any of the men of olden times'.

Throughout this period from 527 to 540 Procopius had served, with only a short break, as Belisarius' aide and legal adviser, and witnessed the success of the campaigns at close quarters. He greatly admired the general's judicious handling of difficulties, which is emphasised in rhetorical speeches delivered to the troops before crucial battles. Some commentators have assumed that the *History of the Wars* was written at Belisarius' request and that he acted as Procopius' patron. But there is no firm indication that he subsequently promoted the author, and the work is not a panegyric of the general.

Procopius composed his Thucydidean history of these campaigns using his own notes and personal observations, supplemented by the texts of official letters and treaty proposals that form a large part. He had access to most relevant written material but relied primarily on his own experience and memory. In keeping with his classical model, he inserts brief geographical and ethnographic sections whenever it is necessary to introduce unfamiliar foreign regions or peoples. Concerning the unusual boats on the Arabian

Gulf, Procopius notes that they are constructed without iron nails, the planks being 'bound together with a kind of cording. The reason is not as most persons suppose that there are certain rocks there which draw the iron to themselves . . . but rather because the Indians and the Aethiopians possess neither iron nor any other thing suitable for such purpose'. He also digresses from the narrative to include local history, which he heard on campaign, sometimes including even the most farfetched stories.

The combination of detailed military descriptions (battle formations, strategies, terrain and weapons) with such historical diversions is both readable and enjoyable. With considerable skill Procopius weaves the two very different components together, preparing the reader for changes of topic and battle-theatre and returning to pick up the thread of the previous narrative. While the attempt to copy Thucydides' Attic Greek is not uniformly successful and creates an obtrusive artificiality, later Byzantine authors thoroughly appreciated Procopius' elaborate efforts to avoid using technical jargon, Latin expressions or commonplace terms for commonplace objects.

Despite the victories of the 530s, however, Gothic resistance stiffened and the Italian campaign dragged on from 540 to 558 with inconclusive battles that drained funds and men from other fronts. This not only reduced Justinian's achievement, it also cast doubt on Procopius' own preconceived role as chronicler of a truly glorious era. So, as his task became one of excusing lengthy and costly campaigns rather than chronicling brilliant victories, his disillusion increased. This anxiety about the success of his project helps to explain the dissatisfaction that pervades his record of the last years of the Gothic War. A further factor may be his withdrawal from active campaigning, for there is no direct evidence that he continued to assist Belisarius after 542.

This year provides the last occasion on which Procopius mentions his presence at an important event: the bubonic plague which struck Constantinople that Spring. To the famous description of plague by Thucydides, he added his own sense of horror at the disaster which caused, he claims, 10,000 deaths a day at its height and lasted for three months. Modern historians have indeed seen in the epidemic a turning point, a symptom of the transition from an ancient civilisation of prosperous cities to a medieval world of fortified villages. It also marked an important point in Procopius' life, for while he may have travelled outside the capital after 542, his later history probably relied more on official court records, ambassadorial and campaign reports than on personal experience. And eye-witness testimony was his chief qualification for writing not only the *Wars* but also the *Buildings*.

In these unsettled conditions during the late 540s as he completed the Gothic Wars, Procopius began to jot down the elements of what became the *Secret History*. The failure to consolidate Byzantine control in either Africa or Italy forced him to reconsider the policies of Justinian. Some receive scant mention in any of his works, for instance, the intolerant religious policy, which had no place in a military history. Yet these aspects of imperial government probably influenced Procopius in his decison to write two highly contrasting tracts: a supplement to the earlier account of Justinian and Theodora in the *Wars* (the *Secret History*, or *Anecdota*, literally not to be published), and a record of the emperor's *Buildings*. It is important to realise that all three works are written in basically the same highly elaborate, rhetorical style, with the same historical aim, making no distinction between the works intented for an appreciative reading public and the one that could certainly not have been published during Justinian's lifetime. Although there are contradictions between the content of the public and private work, Procopius was not a split personality who divided his serious historical writing from his personal record.

Of course, in the middle decades of the sixth century, everyone in Constantinople knew that the empress who wielded such power had obscure origins. But whereas a contemporary ecclesiastical historian remarks curtly, 'She came from a brothel', Procopius supplies the full, lurid details (perhaps more imagined than factual). Thus it is from Procopius we learn that Theodora was born into a family of circus entertainers; her father was a bear-keeper, her mother a trained performer, skilled at acrobatics, dancing, playing the flute or cithara, and all the other diversions that filled the intermissions between races. Public entertainment in the circuses and hippodromes of the Roman Empire was organised by two parties identified by the colours worn by competing charioteers, Blue or Green. The family supported the Blues. Theodora and her two sisters became skilled courtesans, highly sought after by even the most distinguished men, among them Justinian, nephew of the Emperor Justin (518-27).

Part of this disreputable background is indubitably correct; Theodora was raised by Justinian from the position of a prostitute to occupy the imperial throne. The laws governing marriage alliances had to be altered by the Senate of Constantinople to permit someone of aristocratic rank (the co-emperor no less, who would in due course become sole ruler of the entire Roman Empire) to marry a woman of such low status. Procopius attacks the emperor for this innovation. Yet in sixth-century Byzantium a relaxation of the ancient marriage laws was probably long overdue and popular. What Procopius found even more disturbing was Justinian's subservience to his wife. That the emperor should be swayed by a woman of such sexual wantonness, whose indecent activities and illegitimate children might encourage others to behave in a morally depraved fashion, was highly offensive. He could only explain her rise to prominence as one of those irrational, inexplicable, unassailable acts of fortune (the ancient *tyche*), which he held responsible for the triumph of evil. He therefore elaborated her progress from 'rags to riches' with the most titillating, obscene and unverifiable details, designed to shock even a hardened Hippodrome enthusiast.

Since Justinian's past was well known, Procopius could not endow him with a similar secret history. So in his condemnation of the emperor he cites only the vaguest sources, stories that no one could check. Justinian's elderly mother is quoted as the authority for his inherent demonic character. She is said to have recalled a dream in which a devil appeared and forced her to have intercourse with him at the moment of her son's conception. In addition, Procopius claims that everyone knew that the emperor ate and slept very little (proof that he was not really human), and that his demonic character would emerge at night when he might be seen carrying his head under his arm.

The key to understanding the *Secret History* lies in the handling of Theodora and, before her, Belisarius' wife, Antonina, who is similarly condemned. Procopius proceeds from the denunciation of the women, for their licentiousness, use of sorcery and abortion among other crimes, to the weakness, vacillation and wickedness of their husbands, whose guilt by association is asserted through innuendo and supposition. It is a case of *cherchez la femme*, and once Procopius' depiction of the empress is understood we can begin to make sense of the overall purpose of the book. Theodora serves as a conduit for his anxieties about the future, if the old order is destroyed. This displacement is evident in his denunciation of the evil effects of her passions, both religious and for the Blue party in the Hippodrome; her persecution of innocent people, and her power to seduce the emperor. Taken together these characteristics threatened the established order, the traditional co-existence of pagan and Christian together with other religious minorities, each rank in society in its own place, rulers and ruled, free and slave. By identifying Theodora as a transgression of all that is familiar and correct, the historian has created a personification of his own foreboding.

This cannot be explained by a peculiarly violent misogyny, for most of Procopius' contemporaries shared his views. They were only prepared to tolerate female authority in a religious form. But underlying this probably unavoidable tendency was an anxiety about social relations between the sexes and traditional family life at a time of considerable change and pressure. As Professor Averil Cameron has demonstrated in her excellent study, *Procopius and the Sixth Century*, when the city-based traditions of Late Antique society began to fail, the ruling élite of Byzantium experienced novel challenges. Senatorial families who had organised local government for centuries found themselves at a loss: urban resources proved no longer adequate to meet needs, growing numbers of uprooted rural poor generated new tensions, while foreign troops plundered the countryside. To Procopius' way of thinking, the trend towards disorder could only be arrested by a firm reimposition of traditional urban rule. Changing the laws to admit women like Theodora and Antonina to senatorial rank was a deplorable departure from sound tradition, which could only encourage urban unrest and political change.

It was therefore with immense relief that Procopius turned to one aspect of Justinian's activity which conformed most closely to traditional imperial responsibility – the provision of secure defences, impressive municipal buildings, and beautiful public works in all major cities of the empire. By fulfilling this duty Justinian had reasserted the old traditions more triumphantly than in his efforts to reconquer the western parts of the empire. Panegyric was the obvious instrument for the treatise *On Buildings*. Here sensitive topics, such as the excessive cost of the emperor's constructions (elsewhere condemned), could be ignored in order to concentrate all attention on the tradition of imperial philanthropy and extravagant beautification.

In contrast, there was no tradition that could justify the shocking innovations listed by Procopius in the *Secret History*. They were condemned in a string of denigratory and nasty incidents, perpetrated mainly by Antonina and Belisarius and Theodora and Justinian. The entire work is pervaded by a personal vindictiveness, which indicates that it was written as a piece of invective designed to relieve Procopius' frustration and hostility. Yet like the *Wars* and the *Buildings* it reflects the attempt to employ a classical historical form which was part of Procopius' need to order society in a manner perceived as traditional. Of the three the last is most successful, largely because its content and medium are so well matched.

Fortunately for the author's reputation in Byzantium, the *Secret History* remained largely secret for over 1,000 years, hidden and probably unread in a single manuscript that was discovered in the Vatican Library in 1623. Ever since that moment historians have debated its authenticity, reliability and motivation. Today it may be the most quoted and widely read of sixth-century Greek texts, enjoyed particularly for its salacious descriptions of the young Theodora, the circus girl, entertainer, mime and prostitute, before her elevation to the imperial throne. The secrets are no longer secret; the unknown has become the best known.

Here is a historian who wrote specifically to inspire future generations and to make claims about his own era. While he was unable to fulfil his initial aim of recording Justinian's wars in the Thucydidean style, the combination of this work with his tracts of invective and panegyric has promoted Justinian and Theodora to a lasting prominence in the historical imagination of a subsequent millenium. But however carefully Procopius tried to dictate what would be remembered of his time, the choice is actually made by each subsequent generation. History once again reveals her complex variety and reminds us that she cannot be forced to serve one single function.

FOR FURTHER READING:
All the quotations above are taken from the Loeb Classical Library edition of Procopius' three works, which reprints the Greek text edited by J. Haury, 7 vols. (Heinemann, 1914-40, reprinted 1953, 1961, 1968, 1979). *The Secret History* is also available in a Penguin Classics translation by G.A. Williamson (Harmondsworth, 1961). *On Buildings* has not been so frequently translated but is provided with detailed commentary by G. Downey in many articles and a useful book, *Constantinople in the Age of Justinian* (University of Oklahoma Press, 1960). Averil Cameron, *Procopius and the Sixth Century* (Duckworth, 1985); Robert Browning, *Justinian and Theodora* (Weidenfeld & Nicolson, 1981); P.N. Ure's *Justinian and his Age* (Penguin, 1951); Elizabeth A. Fisher, 'Theodora and Antonina in the *Historia Arcana*: history and fiction', *Arethus*, 11 (1978), reprinted in *Women in the Ancient World. The Arethusa Papers*, eds. J. Peradotto and J.P. Sullivan (New York State University, 1984).

The World of Islam

The Messenger of Allah

In a cave at the foot of Mount Hira near Mecca, where he had spent six months in solitary meditation, the vision came to Muhammad. The Angel Gabriel roused him from his bed with the stern command: "Proclaim!" Rubbing his eyes, the startled Muhammad gasped, "But what shall I proclaim?" Suddenly his throat tightened as though the angel were choking him. Again came the command: "Proclaim!" And again the terrified Muhammad felt the choking grip. "Proclaim!" ordered the angel for a third time. "Proclaim in the name of the Lord, the Creator who created man from a clot of blood! Proclaim! Your Lord is most gracious. It is he who has taught man by the pen that which he does not know."

Thus it was, according to Islamic tradition, that an unremarkable Arab trader from Mecca was inspired to preach God's word in the year A.D. 610. Compared with Jesus or the Buddha, information about the life of the man who became known as the Messenger of Allah is relatively abundant, although the facts have been embellished with pious folklore. Some have claimed that at Muhammad's birth the palace of the Persian emperor trembled, or that a mysterious light ignited at his mother's breast, shining all the way to Syria, 800 miles away. It was said that his body cast no shadow and that when his hair fell into a fire it would not burn. Muhammad himself disdained any miraculous claims, insisting that he was merely the all-too-human conduit through which God had revealed himself.

It is known that the Prophet was born about A.D. 570 to a member of the respected Meccan clan of Hashim. His father died shortly before Muhammad was born, and his mother when the boy was only six. Two years later, his doting grandfather Abd al-Muttalib died, leaving the orphan in the care of a poor uncle, Abu Talib. As a youth, Muhammad was set to work tending his uncle's herds; he later recalled that task as a mark of divine favor. "God sent no prophet who was not a herdsman," he told his disciples. "Moses was a herdsman. David was a herdsman. I, too, was commissioned for prophethood while I grazed my family's cattle.

As a young man, Muhammad was exposed to the currents of religious debate then swirling through the Middle East. He would listen avidly as Jews and Christians argued over their faiths. Those discussions may have fed his dissatisfaction with the traditional polytheistic religion of the Arabs, who believed in a panoply of tribal gods and jinn, headed by a deity known as Allah. Says Muhammad's French biographer, Maxime Rodinson: "Both Jews and Christians despised the Arabs, regarding them as savages who did not even possess an organized church."

At 25, Muhammad accepted a marriage proposal from Khadijah, a rich Meccan widow 15 years his senior, for whom he had led a successful caravan. With his financial security assured by Khadijah's wealth and business, he began to venture into the desert, to contemplate and pray, as had other Arab holy men before him.

According to legend, Muhammad had earned a reputation as a wise and saintly man even before his first revelation from the angel on Mount Hira. Looking out from the balcony of his Mecca home one day, he saw the members of four clans arguing over which of them should be allowed to carry the Black Stone, a huge meteorite that the Arabs regarded as sacred, to its new resting place in a rebuilt shrine called the Ka'ba. Unknown to Muhammad, they had resolved to let the first man who walked into the sanctuary decide the matter. Entering the holy place, Muhammad proposed a satisfactory compromise: placing the Black Stone on a blanket, he instructed each tribe to lift one corner. Then he personally laid the meteorite in its new niche.

At 40, Muhammad began to preach the new faith of Islam, which was gradually being revealed to him on his sojourns in the desert. Some of this religion was familiar to Arabs who knew about the monotheistic teachings of Jews and Christians. His countrymen, for example, could readily accept Muhammad's assertion that Allah, long regarded as the highest of the desert gods, was the same God worshiped by Jews and Christians. But Meccan traders felt threatened by Muhammad's growing power. Both Jews and Christians questioned his claim that he was revealing the true word of God to the Arabs, in effect joining them as "People of the Book." In 622, after being harassed by his opponents, Muhammad and his followers escaped to Medina in a migration known as the hegira.

To a growing body of converts, Muhammad began to elaborate on his new religion. Revelations came to him in trances; his descriptions of those encounters, memorized and recorded by his adherents, were later collected as the Koran. As his followers grew in strength and numbers, Muhammad began a series of raids on Meccan caravans, which led to several indecisive battles with their avenging war parties. In 628 the Meccans agreed to let Muhammad's followers make their pilgrimage to the Ka'ba, which the new faith continued to regard as a sacred shrine. Muslims believe it is the spot where Abraham prepared to sacrifice his son Ishmael at God's command. Two years later the prophet led an army of 10,000 into his former city, taking control in a bloodless victory.

For all the pious legends that grew up even in his lifetime, Muhammad remained a humble and, in some ways, unfulfilled man. He occasionally incurred the wrath of his wives and concubines. All of his sons died in childhood, leaving him with no male heir. In 632 he led a pilgrimage to Mecca, where he declared, "I have perfected your religion and completed my favors for you." Three months later he fell ill in Medina and died. To his zealous followers went the task of spreading the word of Allah, not only throughout Arabia but far beyond it as well.

A Faith of Law And Submission

God's grandeur, and a path to follow

Eight words in Arabic sum up the central belief of the world's 750 million Muslims: "There is no god but God, and Muhammad is the Messenger of God." Five times a day, from Djakarta to Samarkand to Lagos, this *shahada* (confession of faith) is recited by the devout as meuzzins (callers to prayer) summon them to worship God.

In the prescribed daily prayers, a pious Muslim does not beseech God for favors, either material or spiritual, so much as for guidance and mercy. The word Islam means submission, and the true Muslim submits his life to the divine will of a deity who is the Compassionate, the All Knowing, the Strong, the Protector, the All Powerful—to cite only a few of the traditional 99 "most Beautiful Names" of God.

Muslims believe that God decrees everything that happens in the cosmos. Some critical Western scholars contend that this doctrine leads to a kind of passive fatalism, but Islamic theologians strongly deny that *qadar* (divine will) negates a person's freedom to act. It merely means, says Muhammad Abdul Rauf, director of the Islamic Center in Washington, that "when some misfortune befalls us, we resign ourselves to it as something coming from God, instead of dispairing."

Islam stresses the uniqueness of the Creator, and strictly forbids *shirk*—that is, the association of anyone or anything with God's divinity. Along with Moses and Abraham, Jesus is revered by Muslims as one of the 25 scriptural prophets of God, and Islam accepts both his virgin birth and his miracles. But Muslims believe that Christian faith in the divinity of Jesus is polytheism. They resent being called "Muhammadans," which suggests that Muhammad's role in Islam is similar to that of Jesus in Christianity. The Prophet is revered as God's final Messenger to mankind, but is not worshiped as a divine being.

Because they accept the Bible, Jews and Christians have a special status in Islam as "People of the Book." Muslims also believe that the Bible in its present form is corrupt and that the true faith was revealed only to Muhammad. Those revelations are contained in the Koran, the Arabic word for recitation. Slightly shorter than the New Testament, the Koran has little narrative. There are evocations of divine grandeur in rhymed prose, florid descriptions of the harsh fate that awaits those who knowingly ignore God's will, and detailed instructions on specific ways that man must submit to his maker.

The basic spiritual duties of Islam are summed up in the so-called five pillars of faith. They are: 1) accepting the *shahada;* 2) the daily prayers to God while facing Mecca; 3) charitable giving; 4) fasting during the daylight hours of Ramadan, a 29- or 30-day month in Islam's lunar calendar* and 5) making the hajj, or pilgrimage, to Mecca at least once in an individual's lifetime—if he or she is financially and physically able. Some Muslims argue that there is a sixth pillar of the faith, namely jihad. The word is frequently translated as "holy war", in fact, it can refer to many forms of striving for the faith, such as an inner struggle for purification or spreading Islamic observance and justice by whatever means.

During the hajj, pilgrims throng Mecca, the men clad in two seamless white garments and sandals, the women in white head-to-toe covering. The pilgrims walk seven times around the Ka'ba, a cubical stone building covered by a gold-embroidered black canopy, in the exterior wall of which is set the Black Stone. The interior, now empty, once housed pagan idols, which Muhammad destroyed. The pilgrims also visit other holy sites, act out the search for water by Hagar, the mother of the Arab nation, perform a vigil on Mount 'Arafat (site of the Prophet's last sermon) and conduct a ritual sacrifice of goats, sheep and camels.

The devout Muslim is also expected to observe the Shari'a, which means "the path to follow." Based on the Koran, the deeds and sayings of Muhammad and the consensus of Islamic scholars, the Shari'a is not just a compilation of criminal and civil law, but a complex, all embracing code of ethics, morality and religious duties. It is a sophisticated system of jurisprudence that summarizes 1,400 years of experience and constantly adapts, in subtle ways, to new circumstances.

In Western eyes, however, the Shari'a all too often is denigrated as a relic of the Dark Ages. Some of its provisions do seem awesomely harsh:

*By the Islamic calendar, this is the year 1399, dated from Muhammad's Hegira to Medina.

habitual thieves are punished by having a hand cut off; adulterers are either scourged or stoned to death; falsely accusing a woman of adultery calls for 80 lashes—the same penalty imposed on a Muslim caught drinking alcohol. The equivalence of the two punishments exemplifies the time-honored logic of the Shari'a. The Koran forbade the drinking of wine, but did not specify a punishment; 80 lashes, however, was decreed for those who bore false witness. Making the analogy that drink leads to hallucination and to telling untruths, Islamic sages decided that the punishment for the two sins should be the same.

Muslim jurists contend that stoning is no more typical of Islamic justice than extra-tough state laws against the possession of drugs are representative of the American legal tradition. Beyond that, the threat of the Shari'a is usually more severe than the reality. As in Western common law, defendants are presumed innocent until proved guilty. To convict adulterers, four witnesses must be found to testify that they saw the illicit act performed. Moreover, there are loopholes in the law and liberal as well as strict interpretations of it. For example, a thief can lose his hand only if he steals "in a just society"; the provision has been used by Islamic courts to spare men who steal because they are poor and have no other means to feed their families.

In Iran particularly, the reintroduction of the Shari'a under an Islamic republic is seen as a threat to rights that women won under the monarchy. Feminists do have reason to complain. Islamic law tolerates polygamy, so long as a husband treats his wives equally, and he can end a marriage simply by saying "I divorce thee" three times in front of witnesses. A woman may request a divorce under certain circumstances—for example, if she is mistreated or her husband is impotent. Women must dress modestly, and their inheritance is limited to a fraction of that of men. In defense of these sexist inequities, scholars of the Shari'a note that Islamic law was advanced for its time. Before Muhammad, women in Arabia were mere chattel. The Koran emphatically asserts a husband's duty to support his wife (or wives), who are allowed to keep their dowries and to own property—rights that did not emerge until much later in Western countries.

All Muslims accept the Koran as God's eternal word, but Islam to some extent is a house divided, although its divisions are not as extensive as those in Christianity. About 90% of all Muslims are Sunnis (from *sunna*, "the tradition of the Prophet"), who consider themselves Islam's orthodoxy. In Iran and Iraq, the majority of Muslims are Shi'ites ("partisans" of 'Ali), who differ from the Sunnis in some of their interpretations of the Shari'a and in their understanding of Muhammad's succession. The Prophet left no generally recognized instructions on how the leadership of Islam would be settled after his death. The Sunnis believe that its leader should be nominated by representatives of the community and confirmed by a general oath of allegiance. Shi'ites contend that Muhammad's spiritual authority was passed on to his cousin and son-in-law, 'Ali, and certain of his direct descendants who were known as Imams. Most Iranian Shi'ites believe that 'Ali's twelfth successor, who disappeared mysteriously in 878, is still alive and will return some day as the Mahdi (the Divinely Appointed Guide), a Messiah-like leader who will establish God's kingdom on earth. Meanwhile, Shi'ite religious leaders, such as Iran's Ayatullah Khomeini, have wide powers to advise the faithful on the presumed will of the "Hidden Imam." Sunni religious scholars, the ulama, have less authority, though both branches of Islam consider their leaders to be teachers and sages rather than ordained clergymen in the Western sense.

Both Sunni and Shi'ite Islam include Sufism, a mystical movement whose adherents seek to serve God not simply through obedience to the law but by striving for union with him through meditation and ritual. Sufism is considered suspect by fundamentalist Muslims like the puritanical Wahhabis of Saudi Arabia, because it allows for the veneration of *awliya*—roughly the equivalent of Christianity's saints. Islam also has spawned a number of heretical offshoots. One is the Alawi sect, a Shi'ite minority group to which most of Syria's leaders belong. The Alawis believe in the transmigration of souls and a kind of trinity in which 'Ali is Allah incarnate. Another is the secretive Druze sect of Israel, Lebanon and Syria, which split away from Islam in the 11th century. America's so-called Black Muslims were once generally regarded by Sunni Muslims as followers of a new heresy. By adopting orthodox beliefs and discarding a rule that limited membership to black Americans, the World Community of Islam in the West, as the movement is now known, has been accepted as being part of the true faith.

Islam is not a collection of individual souls but a spiritual community; its sectarian divisions, as well as the man-made barriers of race and class that Islam opposes, dissolve dramatically at the hajj. Once a pilgrimage made mostly by Muslims of the Middle East and North Africa, the hajj has become a universal and unifying ritual. For those who have taken part in it, the hajj acts as a constant testament to Islam's vision of a divine power that transcends all human frailties.

Some sayings from a Holy Book

The grandeur of the Koran is difficult to convey in English translation. Although Islam's Holy Book is considered God's precise word only in Arabic, a generally recognized English text is that of Abdullah Yusuf 'Ali.

THE OPENING PRAYER. In the name of God, Most Gracious, Most Merciful. Praise be to God, the Cherisher and Sustainer of the Worlds; Most Gracious, Most Merciful; Master of the Day of Judgment. Thee do we worship, and Thine aid we seek. Show us the straight way, the way of those on whom Thou hast bestowed Thy Grace, those whose (portion) is not wrath, and who go not astray.

THE NATURE OF GOD. God! There is no god but He—the Living, the Self-subsisting, Eternal. No slumber can seize Him, nor sleep. His are all things in the heavens and on earth. Who is there can intercede in His presence except as He permitteth? He knoweth what (appeareth to His creatures as) Before or After or Behind them. Nor shall they compass aught of His knowledge except as He willeth. His Throne doth extend over the heavens and the earth, and He feeleth no fatigue in guarding and preserving them.

DRINKING AND GAMBLING. They ask thee concerning wine and gambling. Say: "In them is great sin, and some profit, for men: but the sin is greater than the profit."

THEFT. Male or female, cut off his or her hands: a punishment by way of example, from God, for their crime: and God is Exalted in Power. But if the thief repent after his crime, and amend his conduct, God turneth to him in forgiveness; for God is Oft-forgiving, Most Merciful.

POLYGAMY. If ye fear that ye shall not be able to deal justly with the orphans, marry women of your choice, two, or three, or four; but if ye fear that ye shall not be able to deal justly (with them) then only one, or (a captive) that your right hands possess.

CHRISTIANS. They do blaspheme who say: "God is Christ the son of Mary." But said Christ: "O Children of Israel! Worship God, my Lord and your Lord." Whoever joins other gods with God—God will forbid him the Garden, and the Fire will be his abode.

THE DAY OF JUDGMENT. When the sun is folded up; when the stars fall, losing their lustre; when the mountains vanish; when the she-camels, ten months with young, are left untended; when the wild beasts are herded together; when the oceans boil over with a swell; . . . when the World on High is unveiled; when the Blazing Fire is kindled to fierce heat; and when the Garden is brought near;—(Then) shall each soul know what it has put forward.

PARADISE. (Here is) a Parable of the Garden which the righteous are promised: In it are rivers of water incorruptible; rivers of milk of which the taste never changes; rivers of wine, a joy to those who drink; and rivers of honey pure and clear. In it there are for them all kinds of fruit, and Grace from their Lord. (Can those in such bliss) be compared to such as shall dwell forever in the Fire, and be given, to drink, boiling water, so that it cuts up their bowels?

Islam, Orientalism And the West

An attack on learned ignorance

In an angry, provocative new book called Orientalism *(Pantheon; $15), Edward Said, 43, Parr Professor of English and Comparative Literature at Columbia University, argues that the West has tended to define Islam in terms of the alien categories imposed on it by Orientalist scholars. Professor Said is a member of the Palestine National Council, a broadly based, informal parliament of the Palestine Liberation Organization. He summarized the thesis of* Orientalism *in this article*

One of the strangest, least examined and most persistent of human habits is the absolute division made between East and West, Orient and Occident. Almost entirely "Western" in origin, this imaginative geography that splits the world into two unequal, fundamentally opposite spheres has brought forth more myths, more detailed ignorance and more ambitions than any other perception of difference. For centuries Europeans and Americans have spellbound themselves with Oriental mysticism, Oriental passivity, Oriental mentalities. Translated into policy, displayed as knowledge, presented as entertainment in travelers' reports, novels, paintings, music or films, this "Orientalism" has existed virtually unchanged as a kind of daydream that could often justify Western colonial adventures or military conquest. On the "Marvels of the East" (as the Orient was known in the Middle Ages) a fantastic edifice was constructed, invested heavily with Western fear, desire, dreams of power and, of course, a very partial knowledge. And placed in this structure has been "Islam," a great religion and a culture certainly, but also an Occidental myth, part of what Disraeli once called "the great Asiatic mystery."

As represented for Europe by Muhammad and his followers, Islam appeared out of Arabia in the 7th century and rapidly spread in all directions. For almost a millennium Christian Europe felt itself challenged (as indeed it was) by this last monotheistic religion, which claimed to complete its two predecessors. Perplexingly grand and "Oriental," incorporating elements of Judeo-Christianity, Islam never fully submitted to the West's power. Its various states and empires always provided the West with formidable political and cultural contestants—and with opportunities to affirm a "superior" Occidental identity. Thus, for the West, to understand Islam has meant trying to convert its variety into a monolithic undeveloping essence, its originality into a debased copy of Christian culture, its people into fearsome caricatures.

Early Christian polemicists against Islam used the Prophet's human person as their butt, accusing him of whoring, sedition, charlatanry. As writing about Islam and the Orient burgeoned—60,000 books between 1800 and 1950—European powers occupied large swatches of "Islamic" territory, arguing that since Orientals knew nothing about democracy and were essentially passive, it was the "civilizing mission" of the Occident, expressed in the strict programs of despotic modernization, to finally transform the Orient into a nice replica of the West. Even Marx seems to have believed this.

There were, however, great Orientalist scholars; there were genuine attempts, like that of Richard Burton (British explorer who translated the *Arabian Nights*), at coming to terms with Islam. Still, gross ignorance persisted, as it will whenever fear of the different gets translated into attempts at domination. The U.S. inherited the Orientalist legacy, and uncritically employed it in its universities, mass media, popular culture, imperial policy. In films and cartoons, Muslim Arabs, for example, are represented either as bloodthirsty mobs, or as hook-nosed, lecherous sadists. Academic experts decreed that in Islam everything is Islamic, which amounted to the edifying notions that there was such a thing as an "Islamic mind," that to understand the politics of Algeria one had best consult the Koran, that "they" (the Muslims) had no understanding of democracy, only of repression and medieval obscurantism. Conversely, it was argued that so long as repression was in the U.S. interest, it was not Islamic but a form of modernization.

The worst misjudgments followed. As recently as 1967 the head of the Middle East Studies Association wrote a report for the Department of Health, Education and Welfare asserting that the region including the Middle East and North Africa was not a center of cultural achievement, nor was it likely to become one in the near future. The study of the region or its languages, therefore, did not constitute its own reward so far as modern culture is concerned. High school textbooks routinely produced descriptions of Islam like the following: "It was started by a wealthy businessman of Arabia called Muhammad. He claimed that he was a prophet. He found followers among other Arabs. He told them that they were picked to rule the world." Whether Palestinian Arabs lost their land and political rights to Zionism, or Iranian poets were tortured by the SAVAK, little time was spent in the West wondering if Muslims suffered pain, would resist oppression or experienced love and joy: to Westerners, "they" were different from "us" since Orientals did not feel about life as "we" did.

No one saw that Islam varied from place to place, subject to both history and geography. Islam was unhesitatingly considered to be an abstraction, never an experience. No one bothered to judge Muslims in political, social, anthropological terms that were vital and nuanced, rather than crude and provocative. Suddenly it appeared that "Islam" was back when Ayatullah Khomeini, who derives from a long tradition of opposition to an outrageous monarchy, stood on his national, religious and political legitimacy as an Islamic righteous man. Menachem Begin took himself to be speaking for the West when he said he feared this return to the Middle Ages, even as he covered Israeli occupation of Arab land with Old Testament authorizations. Western leaders worried about their oil, so little appreciated by the Islamic hordes who thronged the streets to topple the Light of the Aryans.

Were Orientalists at last beginning to wonder about their "Islam," which they said had taught the faithful never to resist unlawful tyranny, never to prize any values over sex and money, never to disturb fate? Did anyone stop to doubt that F-15 planes were the answer to all our worries about "Islam"? Was Islamic punishment, which tantalized the press, more irreducibly vicious than, say, napalming Asian peasants?

We need understanding to note that repression is not principally Islamic or Oriental but a reprehensible aspect of the human phenomenon. "Islam" cannot explain everything in Africa and Asia, just as "Christianity" cannot explain Chile or South Africa. If Iranian workers, Egyptian students, Palestinian farmers resent the West or the U.S., it is a concrete response to a specific policy injuring them as human beings. Certainly a European or American would be entitled to feel that the Islamic multitudes are underdeveloped; but he would also have to concede that underdevelopment is a relative cultural and economic judgment and not mainly "Islamic" in nature.

Under the vast idea called Islam, which the faithful look to for spiritual nourishment in their numerous ways, an equally vast, rich life passes, as detailed and as complex as any. For comprehension of that life Westerners need what Orientalist Scholar Louis Massignon called a science of compassion, knowledge without domination, common sense not mythology. In Iran and elsewhere Islam has not simply "returned"; it has always been there, not as an abstraction or a war cry but as part of a way people believe, give thanks, have courage and so on. Will it not ease our fear to accept the fact that people do the same things inside as well as outside Islam, that Muslims live in history and in our common world, not simply in the Islamic context?

Muslim Women and Fundamentalism

Fatima Mernissi

Dr. Mernissi is a Moroccan sociologist who currently holds a research appointment at Morocco's Institute Universitaire de Recherche Scientifique. Her publications include Le maroc raconte par ses femmes, Le Harem politique *and numerous articles on women in the Third World.*

When analyzing the dynamics of the Muslim world, one has to discriminate between two distinct dimensions: what people actually do, the decisions they make, the aspirations they secretly entertain or display through their patterns of consumption, and the discourses they develop about themselves, more specifically the ones they use to articulate their political claims. The first dimension is about reality and its harsh time-bound laws, and how people adapt to pitilessly rapid change; the second is about self-presentation and identity building. And you know as well as I do that whenever one has to define oneself to others, whenever one has to define one's identity, one is on the shaky ground of self-indulging justifications. For example, the need for Muslims to claim so vehemently that they are traditional, and that their women miraculously escape social change and the erosion of time, has to be understood in terms of their need for self-representation and must be classified not as a statement about daily behavioral practices, but rather as a psychological need to maintain a minimal sense of identity in a confusing and shifting reality.

To familiarize you with the present-day Muslim world and how women fit into the conflicting political forces (including religion), the best way is not to overwhelm you with data. On the contrary, what is most needed is some kind of special illumination of the structural dissymmetry that runs all through and conditions the entire fabric of social and individual life—the split between acting and reflecting on one's actions. The split between what one does and how one speaks about oneself. The first has to do with the realm of reality; the second has to do with the realm of the psychological elaborations that sustain human beings' indispensable sense of identity. Individuals die of physical sickness, but societies die of loss of identity, that is, a disturbance in the guiding system of representations of oneself as fitting into a universe that is specifically ordered so as to make life meaningful.

Why do we need our lives to make sense? Because that's where power is. A sense of identity is a sense that one's life is meaningful, that, as fragile as a person may be, she or he can still have an impact on his or her limited surroundings. The fundamentalist wave in Muslim societies is a statement about identity. And that is why their call for the veil for women has to be looked at in the light of the painful but necessary and prodigious reshuffling of identity that Muslims are going through in these often confusing but always fascinating times.

The split in the Muslim individual between what one does, confronted by rapid, totally uncontrolled changes in daily life, and the discourse about an unchangeable religious tradition that one feels psychologically compelled to elaborate in order to keep a minimal sense of identity—this, as far as I am concerned, is the key point to focus on in order to understand the dynamics of Muslim life of the late 1970s and the 1980s.

If fundamentalists are calling for the return of the veil, it must be because women have been taking off the veil. We are definitely in a situation where fundamentalist men and non-fundamentalist women have a conflict of interest. We have to identify who the fundamentalist men are, and who are the non-fundamentalist

From *Middle East Report*, July/August 1988, pp. 8-11, 50. MERIP, Middle East Report, 475 Riverside Drive, Room 518, New York, NY 10115. Reprinted by permission.

women who have opted to discard the veil. Class conflicts do sometimes express themselves in acute sex-focused dissent. Contemporary Islam is a good example of this because, beyond the strong obsession with religion, the violent confrontations going on in the Muslim world are about two eminently materialistic pleasures: exercise of political power and consumerism.

Fundamentalists and unveiled women are the two groups that have emerged with concrete, conflicting claims and aspirations in the postcolonial era. Both have the same age range—youth—and the same educational privilege—a recent access to formalized institutions of knowledge. But while the men seeking power through religion and its revivification are mostly from newly urbanized middle- and lower-middle-class backgrounds, unveiled women by contrast are predominantly of middle-class, urban backgrounds.

As a symptom, the call for the veil tells us one thing. Telling us another thing is the specific conjuncture of the forces calling for it—that is, the conservative forces and movements, their own quest, and how they position themselves within the social movements dominating the national and international scene.

Trespassing

Islam is definitely one of the modern political forces competing for power around the globe. At least that is how many of us experience it. How can a "medieval religion," ask Western students raised in a secular culture, be so alive, so challenging to the effects of time, so renewable in energy? How can it be meaningful to educated youth? One of the characteristics of fundamentalism is the attraction Islam has for high achievers among young people. In Cairo, Lahore, Jakarta and Casablanca, Islam makes sense because it speaks about power and self-empowerment. As a matter of fact, worldly self-enhancement is so important for Islam that the meaning of spirituality itself has to be seriously reconsidered.

What was not clear for me in the early 1970s was that all the problems Muslims faced in recent decades are more or less boundary problems, from colonization (trespassing by a foreign power on Muslim community space and decision making) to contemporary human rights issues (the political boundaries circumscribing the ruler's space and the freedoms of the government). The issue of technology is a boundary problem: how can we integrate Western technological information, the recent Western scientific memory, without deluging our own Muslim heritage? International economic dependency is, of course, eminently a problem of boundaries: the International Monetary Fund's intervention in fixing the price of our bread does not help us keep a sense of a distinct national identity. What are the boundaries of the sovereignty of the Muslim state vis-à-vis voracious, aggressive transnational corporations? These are some of the components of the crisis that is tearing the Muslim world apart, along, of course, definite class lines.

Naive and serious as only a dutiful student can be, I did not know in 1975 that women's claims were disturbing to Muslim societies not because they threatened the past but because they augured and symbolized what the future and its conflicts are about: the inescapability of renegotiating new sexual, political, economic, and cultural boundaries, thresholds and limits. Invasion of physical territory by alien hostile nations (Afghanistan and Lebanon); invasion of national television by "Dallas" and "Dynasty"; invasion of children's desires by Coca-Cola and spe-

cial brands of walking shoes—these are some of the political and cultural boundary problems facing the Muslim world today.

However, we have to remember that societies do not reject and resist changes indiscriminately. Muslim societies integrated and digested quite well technological innovations: the engine, electricity, the telephone, the transistor, sophisticated machinery and arms, all without much resistance. But the social fabric seems to have trouble absorbing anything having to do with changing authority thresholds: freely competing unveiled women; freely competing political parties; freely elected parliaments; and, of course, freely elected heads of state who do not necessarily get 99 percent of the votes. Whenever an innovation has to do with free choice of the partners involved, the social fabric seems to suffer some terrible tear. Women's unveiling seems to belong to this realm. For the last one hundred years, whenever women tried or wanted to discard the veil, some men, always holding up the sacred as a justification, screamed that it was unbearable, that the society's fabric would dissolve if the mask is dropped. I do not believe that men, Muslims or not, scream unless they are hurt. Those calling for the reimposition of the veil surely have a reason. What is it that Muslim society needs to mask so badly?

The idea one hears about fundamentalism is that it is an archaic phenomenon, a desire to return to medieval thinking. It is frequently presented as a revivalist movement: bring back the past. And the call for the veil for women furthers this kind of misleading simplification. If we take the Egyptian city of Asyut as an example, we have to admit that it is a modern town with a totally new cultural feature that Muslim society never knew before: mass access to knowledge. In our history, universities and knowledge were privileges of the elite. The man of knowledge enjoyed a high respect precisely because he was a repository of highly valued and aristocratically gained information. Acquisition of knowledge took years, and often included a period of initiation that compelled the student to roam through Muslim capitals from Asia to Spain for decades. Mass access to universities, therefore, constitutes a total shift in the accumulation, distribution, management and utilization of knowledge and information. And we know that knowledge is power. One of the reasons the fundamentalist will be preoccupied by women is that state universities are not open just for traditionally marginalized and deprived male rural migrants, but for women as well.

Persons under 15 years of age constitute 39 percent of Egypt's and 45 percent of Iran's total population.[1] The natural annual population increase in Egypt and Iran is 3.1 percent.[2] The time span for doubling the population is 22 years for Egypt and 23 for Iran. Secondary school enrollment in Iran is 35 percent for women and 54 percent for men. In Egypt 39 percent of women of secondary school age are in fact there, as compared to 64 percent of men.[3] The same trend is to be found in other Muslim societies.

Centuries of women's exclusion from knowledge have resulted in femininity being confused with illiteracy until a few decades ago. But things have progressed so rapidly in our Muslim countries that we women today take literacy and access to schools and universities for granted. Illiteracy was such a certain fate for women that my grandmother would not believe that women's education was a serious state undertaking. For years she kept waking my sister and me at dawn to get us ready for school. We would explain that school started exactly three hours after her first dawn prayer, and that we needed only five minutes to get there. But she would mumble, while handing us our morning tea: "You better get yourself there and stare at the wonderful gate of that school for hours. Only God knows how long it is going to last." She had an obsessive dream: to see us read the Quran and master mathematics. "I want you to read every word of that Quran and I want you to answer my questions when I demand an explanation of a verse. That is how the *qadis* [Muslim judges] get all their power. But knowing the Quran is not enough to make a woman happy. She has to learn how to do sums. The winners are the ones who master mathematics." The political dimension of education was evident to our grandmother's generation.

While a few decades ago the majority of women married before the age of 20, today only 22 percent of that age group in Egypt and 38.4 percent in Iran are married.[4] To get an idea of how perturbing it is for Iranian society to deal with an army of unmarried adolescents one has only to remember that the legal age for marriage for females in Iran is 13 and for males 15.[5] The idea of an adolescent unmarried woman is a completely new idea in the Muslim world, where previously you had only a female child and a menstruating woman who had to be married off immediately so as to prevent dishonorable engagement in premarital sex. The whole concept of patriarchal honor was build around the idea of virginity, which reduced a woman's role to its sexual dimension: to reproduction within early marriage. The concept of an adolescent woman, menstruating and unmarried, is so alien to the entire Muslim family system that it is either unimaginable or necessarily linked with *fitna* (social disorder). The Arab countries are a good example of this demographic revolution in sex roles.

Space and Sex Roles

Young men, faced with job insecurity or failure of the diploma to guarantee access to the desired job, postpone marriage. Women, faced with the pragmatic necessity to count on themselves instead of relying on the dream of a rich husband, see themselves forced to concentrate on getting an education. The average age at marriage for women and men in most Arab countries has registered a spectacular increase. In Egypt and Tunisia the average age at marriage for women is 22 and for men 27. In Algeria the average age at marriage is 18 for women and 24 for men. In Morocco, Libya, and Sudan women marry at around 19 and men at around 25. The oil countries, known for their conservatism, have witnessed an incredible increase of unmarried youth: age at marriage for women is 20 and for men is 27. And of course nuptiality patterns are influenced by urbanization. The more urbanized youth marry later. In 1980, in metropolitan areas of Egypt the mean age at marriage was 29.7 for males and 23.6 for females. In the urban areas of Upper Egypt, where the fundamentalist movement is strong, the mean age at marriage was 28.3 for men and 22.8 for women.[6]

The conservative wave against women in the Muslim world, far from being a regressive trend, is on the contrary a defense mechanism against profound changes in both sex roles and the touchy subject of sexual identity. The most accurate interpretation of this relapse into "archaic behaviors," such as conservatism on the part of men and resort to magic and superstitious rituals on the part of women, is as anxiety-reducing mechanisms in a world of shifting, volatile sexual identity.

Fundamentalists are right in saying that education for women has destroyed the traditional boundaries and definitions of space and sex roles. Schooling has dissolved traditional arrangements of space segregation, even in oil-rich countries where education is segregated by sex: simply to go to school women have to cross the street! Streets are spaces of sin and temptation, because they are both public and sex-mixed. And that is the definition of *fitna*: disorder!

Fundamentalists are right when they talk about the dissolution of women's traditional function as defined by family ethics; postponed age of marriage forces women to turn pragmatically toward education as a means for self-enhancement. If one looks at some of the education statistics, one understands why newly urbanized and educated rural youth single out university women as enemies of Islam, with its tradition of women's exclusion from knowledge and decision making. The percentage of women teaching in Egyptian universities was 25 percent in 1981. To get an idea of how fast change is occurring there, one only has to remember that in 1980 the percentage of women teaching in American universities was 24 percent and it was 25 percent in the Democratic Republic of Germany.[7] Even in conservative Saudi Arabia, women have invaded sexually segregated academic space: they are 22 percent of the university faculty there. Women are 18 percent of the university faculty in Morocco, 16 percent in Iraq, and 12 percent in Qatar.[8]

What dismays the fundamentalists is that the era of independence did not create an all-male new class. Women are taking part in the public feast. And that is a definite revolution in the Islamic concept of both the state's relation to women and women's relation to the institutionalized distribution of knowledge.

Footnotes

1 *1983 World Population Data Sheet* (Washington, DC: Population Reference Bureau).

2 *Ibid.*

3 "People's Wallchart," *People's Magazine*, vol. 12 (1985).

4 *Ibid.*

5 *Ibid.*

6 *World Fertility Survey*, No. 42, "The Egyptian Survey," November 1983.

7 *Annuaire Statistique* (Paris: UNESCO, 1980).

8 *Ibid.*

The master-chronologers of Islam

ABDESSELAM CHEDDADI

Abdesselam Cheddadi is a Moroccan historian who teaches at the faculty of education sciences at Rabat. An authority on Ibn Khaldun, he has translated into French the great Arab historian's autobiography (Sindbad publishers, Paris, 1984) and extracts from his history (Sindbad, Paris, 1987).

THE most striking feature of Islamic historical writing or *tarikh* is its sheer volume. Only a small part of it has so far been published and new texts are continually being discovered. From the second half of the first century of the Hegira (late seventh century AD) to the thirteenth century (nineteenth century AD) the writing of Islamic history continued almost without a break wherever the Islamic faith was professed. The language used was primarily Arabic, but there were also writings in Persian, Turkish and Malay. Although essentially written by Muslims, it also attracted Christian authors, especially in Egypt and Syria.

A second important feature of Islamic historiography is its very great diversity. It comprises forms and genres ranging from vast universal or general histories and monographs to annals, dynastic and genealogical tables or lists divided into *tabaqat* (classes), as well as biographical dictionaries and local histories. It also covers many fields: religious, political, administrative and social life; scientific, literary and artistic activities; schools of thought and ideological trends; travel, the topography of cities, monuments; natural disasters, famines, epidemics....

The historians who worked in this tradition were also curious about non-Islamic civilizations, western and northern Europe, India, China, the Far East and Africa. They were interested in any information relating to man, his relations with his social and cultural environment and his relations with God. Ibn Khaldun (see box) noted that they wrote just as much for the "crowds" and for "simple folk" as for "kings" and "the great". This view of history as universal in scope and the attempt to reach a wide audience prefigured modern approaches to the subject.

A grasp of time

A further point of similarity with modern historiography lay in the importance attached very early on to time and to chronology. From the first to the fourth century of the Hegira (seventh-tenth century AD) a vast amount of knowledge about time was amassed in Islamic culture. Drawing on earlier Arab tradition, it incorporated Persian, Indian, Greek and Egyptian material and also leaned on the work of astronomers and geographers. The masterly conspectus achieved by al-Biruni in the first half of the fifth/eleventh century is impressive for its tone of objectivity. It represents the most extensive and most rigorous survey of knowledge about time that we possess up to the modern era.

Muslim historians benefited greatly from this knowledge. From the second/eighth century onwards it gradually became common practice to give dates, to follow a chronological order and to provide tables. For most of the facts reported by historians it became a virtually absolute rule

Reproduced from *The Unesco Courier*, March 1990. pp. 35-39.

129

ترمة وارلينة كال احسان مير و ب روز کارگوخ رئو جري غفار ما هوار اول

سلاطنه ووار لق اِتموب خاک مذلتن خوار وزاراء وكون خيالي هميرسا همشيد

حالبا خاک مبيا النده بارتن ننلري

تخذن مب تخته باربوتة قلمنه رسوار

جوق جفا قيلدىمى واده دوردگار ككا

واول فزاراده مذون اولان سلاطين اولبهلوا نگرک اسلحه والت دنلير

Above, illustration from a Turkish manuscript recording a journey (1605-1606).

to note the year, month and day when they occurred. This contrasts with medieval historiography in the West where it was not until the eleventh century AD that a unified chronological system began to be widely accepted and where, as late as the fourteenth century, the chronology of the main historical events was still uncertain.

Originality and limitations

The originality, but also the limitations of Islamic historiography lie in its conception of historical information (*khabar*). *Khabar* means the fact, the event, as incorporated into discourse, related in a "story". The historian does not deal in raw facts. He starts from a given which is the story as reported by written or oral tradition, or by a living witness (who may be the historian himself). His most important task is therefore to authenticate or validate stories by subjecting accounts and channels of transmission to critical scrutiny. The historian does not seek to discover or establish facts but to gather, classify and organize information while making sure of its validity. The intrinsic truth of stories was a relatively minor concern until Ibn Khaldun, who based historical criticism on knowledge of the laws of *'umran* (the human order, society).

Bound to accept traditional sources, often down to the finest detail, the historian could incorporate them into a wide variety of genres or organize them at will within more or less voluminous compilations, but he could not formulate them in his own way, reconstruct them or recast them according to his own perspective.

In Islamic historiography then, the past is not reconstructed as it was by some Greek historians, nor is there any theological history as there was in the Christian Middle Ages. This accounts for its widely acknowledged impartiality and also for its stationary conception of time, which contains in itself no potential for change or progress but simply gives external order to a sequence of events. It was Ibn Khaldun again who, in considering the emergence, evolution and decline of vast human groups such as the Arabs, Berbers, Persians and the *Rum* (Greeks, Romans and Byzantines) added a new dimension to this vision.

Three major periods

The first major period of Islamic historiography, which extends up to the third century of the Hegira, is crowned by at-Tabari's chronicle *Tarikh ar-Rusul wa al-Muluk (History of Prophets and Kings)* (see box). A calendar based on the Hegira soon came to be adopted generally. The *isnad* method, whereby the names of those who transmitted information from generation to generation are cited, was first developed for the purposes of the religious sciences and then applied cal and administrative chronicles, history of the Umayyad and 'Abassid dynasties, and collections of secretaries' letters. It gradually became the usual practice to date facts and events precisely and to follow a chronological order.

Numerous compendiums were published, such as al-Waqidi's *Maghazi*, Ibn Ishaq's *Sira*, Ibn Sa 'd's *Tabaqat*, ad-Dinawari's *Akhbar at-tiwal*, al-Baladhuri's *Ansab al-ashrai* and al-Ya 'qubi's *Tarikh*. Together this constituted a vast historical literature, relatively little of which has survived but whose existence is attested by the titles listed in subsequent bibliographies, like Ibn an-Nadim's *Fihrist*, completed in 377 of the Hegira (998 AD).

The second period, known as the classical period, is marked both by the accentuation of these various tendencies with, however, some slackening of the *isnad* method, and by the emergence of new genres. After at-Tabari, but less influential than he, al-Masudi composed the *Golden Meadows*, another universalist history.

From the fourth century of the Hegira onwards the writing of history became a more or less official activity involving greater use of national or provincial archives. This period was notable for the work of a line of historians starting with Hassan Ibn Thabit Ibn Sinan as-Sabi and, later, Miskawayh's *Tajarib al-umam (History of the Buyid Dynasty)*, continued in the following century by Abu Shuja'.

The history of cities developed into a major

Above, manuscript page from a collection of prose and verse biographies of Sufi saints, written by Hosayn Bayqarah (1469-1506), the last of the Timurid sovereigns of Persia.

Right, page from a 12th-century Arabic manuscript describing the customs of China and India.

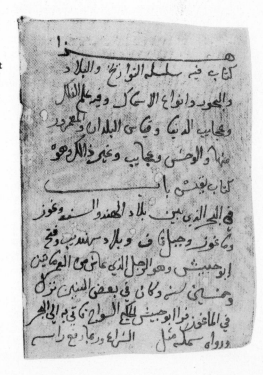

to the biography of the Prophet, to stories of the Muslim conquests and gradually to all kinds of stories.

The earliest historical writing appeared and sometimes crystallized in a number of genres, including *maghazi* and *sira* (the biography and deeds of the Prophet), *futuh* (Muslim conquests), *ahdath* (major political events), *akhbar al-awa 'il* (stories of pre-Islamic kings and nations), *ayyam al- 'arab* (stories of the Arab past), *ansab*, *ma'athir* and *mathalib* (genealogies, exploits and failures); biographies of scholars, lists of teachers, politi-

At-Tabari

AT-TABARI (839-923) did not invent Islamic historiography but he is its most illustrious figure. His *Tarikh ar-Rusul wa al-Muluk (History of Prophets and Kings)* long served as a model. This chronicle, which relates the history of the Islamic world year by year in the first three centuries of the Hegira, was continued by later authors, and many abridged versions and adaptations were made of its account of the pre-Islamic period. It was incorporated in other general surveys such as Ibn al-Athir's *al-Kamil (The Complete History)* in the thirteenth century AD and Ibn Kathir's *al Bidayah wa an-nihayah (The Beginning and the End)* in the following century.

At-Tabari was trained as a jurist, traditionalist and historian. For close on thirty years he journeyed through the cities and countries of the Middle East in a quest for knowledge which took him to the greatest scholars of his time. He was interested not only in history, Qur'anic exegesis and the traditions of the Prophet, but also in grammar, ethics, mathematics and medicine. His fame also rests on his monumental *Tafsir*, or commentary on the Qur'an.

His *History*, which is the culmination of a process which can be traced back to the first century of the Hegira, is guided by a constant concern to show how each item of information has been passed down through an unbroken line, which is subjected to crit-ical scrutiny. He applied a strict chronological order to the raw material of history, and gave a more ample and finished form to the universal history sketched out by ad-Dinawari in his *Akhbar at-Tiwal (The Long Stories)* and by al-Ya 'qubi in his *Tarikh*.

At-Tabari's *Tarikh ar-Rusul wa al-Muluk* is described as a history of the world from the Creation up to the author's own time. In fact, as he explains in his preface, it is first and foremost a history of the relations between God and His creatures, whether of obedience and gratitude or of rebelliousness and revolt. Its main protagonists, after Iblis/Satan and Adam and his sons, are the prophets and kings. Biblical history is included, and neither Graeco-Roman and Byzantine history nor Persian history is neglected.

It is an irreplaceable mine of information. The author cites his sources for each fact reported and in many cases reproduces the accounts in which they are mentioned, thereby giving us access to early materials that are now lost. In the words of the historian Franz Rosenthal, at-Tabari in his *History* demonstrates "the scrupulousness and untiring inspiration of the theologian, the precision and love of order of the jurist and the perspicacity of the politician versed in law".

ABDESSELAM CHEDDADI

Ibn Khaldun

IBN KHALDUN was one of the greatest historians and thinkers of all time. He wrote a long autobiography thanks to which we are familiar with the details of his life. Born in Tunis in 1332, he came from a line of senior government officials and scholars of Andalusian origin, descended from ancient Yemeni Arab stock. He received a thorough religious, literary and scientific education at the hands of the most eminent scholars in the Maghrib. During his adolescence Ifriqiya was conquered by the Marinid king Abu al-Hasan, who entered Tunis in 1348. The following year his father and mother were carried away by the Black Death. In 1352 he went to Fez where he stayed for some ten years and served as private secretary to the sultan Abu Salim. But neither there nor in Granada, to which he travelled in 1362, nor later in Bejaia or Tlemcen, did he manage to lead a stable life or to achieve his political ideal. He did however acquire detailed knowledge of court life and the workings of the state and observed the world of the Arab and Berber tribes.

In 1375, at the age of forty-three, he withdrew from public life in order to devote himself to science. In the castle of Ibn Salamah, near Frenda in Algeria, he wrote the first version of the *Muqaddimah (Introduction to History)*. The need for more extensive documentation forced him to leave his refuge. He returned to Tunis where he taught and completed the first version of the *Kitab al-'Ibar*, his monumental history of the world. But, fearing the intrigues of his enemies, he left the Maghrib for good in 1384 and settled in Egypt. In Cairo he was given an introduction to the Mamluk ruler as-Zahir Barquq and took on teaching and judicial duties, while continuing to work on his voluminous opus. Five years before his death in 1406, during the siege of Damascus, he met the Mongol Timur, of whom he left a striking portrait.

Ibn Khaldun's concerns were primarily those of a historian. Wishing to give a comprehensive account of his age which might serve as a model for future historians, dissatisfied with traditional methods of authenticating and verifying facts, he formulated a theory of society on which all his historiography was to be based. In the *Muqaddimah* he laid the foundations of what would today be called anthropology. Here we can give no more than a glimpse of the rich fund of concepts he brought into play.

Central to his theory of society is the concept of *'um-*

ran. For lack of a more adequate term, this can be translated as "civilization", but only if this word is stripped of any connotation of an opposition between "advanced" societies and "primitive" societies. A more radical concept, based on the religious idea of the Creation, *'umran* designates the fact of human life, the human order in general. Fundamentally equal and free, human beings are God's creatures, and as such are the rulers of the Earth, but they differ from one another by virtue of their living conditions, which are themselves determined by geographic and climatic conditions. The term also denotes the forms of social life or, in a more restrictive sense, urban life with its dense concentration of humanity, contrasting with life in mountain or desert regions.

In *'umran* Ibn Khaldun distinguishes two states, which are at the same time the two main stages in human evolution. *Badawah,* the original agro-pastoral phase, close to nature, satisfying only the barest needs, yields to *hadarah,* the complex urban stage which gives rise to surpluses, in which society fulfils itself and achieves its purpose. It is the fate of *'umran* to oscillate in accordance with an implacable law between these two poles.

For Ibn Khaldun, *mulk* (power) was the basic factor responsible for social and historical dynamics. As a source of the highest prestige, it is the goal of all human aspiration and desire, spurring men to action. Precarious by nature, it passes from one group to another, from one nation to another. As a means of distributing economic surpluses and structuring society, it has a pivotal role in the transition from *badawah* to *hadarah.* Around this central principle of social life Ibn Khaldun structured his history. In studying the Arabs and Berbers he concerned himself with those nations that successively held power. His narrative traces the rise of political groups from their Bedouin status to the heights of power, and their subsequent downfall.

These concepts tie in with many others, which include, in the social sphere, cohesion (*'asabiyah*), kinship (*nasab*), protection (*walah, istinah*), honour (*nu 'ra*); in the political sphere, constraint (*ikrah*), coercion (*Qahr*), domination (*ghalab* or *taghallub*), prestige (*jah*); and in the economic sphere, means of subsistence (*ma 'ash*), gain or profit (*kasb*), value (*qimah*) and work (*a 'mal*).

The concepts he employs, the laws governing the functioning of Arab-Berber society which he identifies, and the bird's-eye view that he provides of many aspects of Islamic history, are still indispensable tools of anthropological and historical research into Islamic society. Far from being superseded, this rigorous, coherent set of theories continues to be a mine of scientific knowledge for modern researchers.

ABDESSELAM CHEDDADI

genre. Many works were produced, the best known of which is al-Khatib al-Baghdadi's *History of Baghdad*. Biographical dictionaries relating to religious and intellectual life became more sophisticated and more numerous. They included lists of poets and other specialists, directories of scholars belonging to different juridico-religious schools, catalogues of writers and lives of saints. In the various regions of the Islamic empire a thriving historiographical tradition thus took root.

In the mid-fifth century of the Hegira political upheavals in the Islamic world were not without an effect on historiography. A third period began, marked by an ebb in production until the mid-sixth century. Syria then came to the fore for a while with historians like Ibn at-Tayyi, Ibn Abi ad-Dam and Ibn an-Nazif, who wrote universal histories, followed soon after by Ibn al-Athir, the author of *al-Kamil (The Complete History)*. Then it was the turn of Egypt to produce major historians such as Ibn Hajar, al-Maqrizi, al-'Ayni, Ibn Tighribirdi, as-Sakhawi and as-Suyuti. The same period saw the birth in the Maghrib of Ibn Khaldun whose pioneering work was admired in his time but who had no successors.

The Medieval Period

In the aftermath of barbarian incursions, Western civilization faced several massive challenges: to integrate Roman and Germanic peoples and cultures, to reconcile Christian and pagan viewpoints, and to create new social, political, and economic forms to fill the vacuum left by the disintegration of the Roman order—in sum, to shape a new unity out of the chaos and diversity of the post-Roman world. The next millenium (c. 500–c. 1500) saw the rise and demise of a distinctive phase of the Western experience—medieval civilization.

Medieval man developed a uniquely coherent view of life and the world, summarized here by literary scholar C. S. Lewis:

> Characteristically, medieval man was not a dreamer nor a spiritual adventurer; he was an organizer, a codifier, a man of system. . . . Three things are typical of him. First, that small minority of his cathedrals in which the design of the architect was actually achieved (usually, of course, it was overtaken in the next wave of architectural fashion long before it was finished). . . . Secondly, the Summa of Thomas Aquinas. And thirdly, the Divine Comedy of Dante. In all these alike we see the tranquil, indefatigable, exultant energy of a passionately logical mind ordering a huge mass of heterogeneous details into unity. They desire unity and proportion, all the classical virtues, just as keenly as the Greeks did. But they have a more varied collection of things to fit in. And they delight to do it.

This outlook also expressed itself in a distinctly medieval social ideal. In theory medieval society provided a well-ordered and satisfying life. The Church looked after men's souls, the nobility maintained civil order, and a devoted peasantry performed the ordinary work of the world. Ideally, as Crane Brinton explains, "a beautifully ordered nexus of rights and duties bound each man to each, from swineherd to emperor and pope."

Of course, medieval society often fell short of this ideal. Feudal barons warred among themselves. Often the clergy was ignorant and corrupt. Peasants were not always content and passive. And medieval civilization had other shortcomings. During much of the Middle Ages there was little interest in nature and how it worked. While experimentation and observation were not unknown, science (or "natural philosophy") was subordinate to theology, which generally attracted the best minds of the day. An economy based on agriculture and a society based on hereditary status had little use for innovation. Aspects of medieval politics and society are treated in "The Baptism of Kiev," "Crusade by Children," "Margery Kempe and the Meaning of Madness," and "When Knighthood Was in

Flower." Articles on El Cid and the Mongol invasion explore facets of medieval warfare.

All this is not to suggest that the medieval period was static and sterile. Crusaders, pilgrims, and merchants enlarged Europe's view of the world. And there were some noteworthy mechanical innovations: the horse collar, which enabled beasts of burden to pull heavier loads; the stirrup, which altered mounted combat; mechanical clocks, which made possible more exact measurement of time; the compass, which brought the age of exploration closer; and the paper-making process, which made feasible the print revolution, and which in turn played key roles in the Reformation and the scientific revolution. "The Viking Saga" demonstrates that even during the so-called Dark Ages there existed possibilities for enterprise and progress, while "The Medieval Mill" examines the place of technology in late medieval life.

The medieval order broke down in the fourteenth and fifteenth centuries. Plague, wars, and famines produced a demographic catastrophe that severely strained the economic and political systems. Charles Mee's article explains how the Black Death affected many aspects of medieval life. During this period social discontent took the form of peasant uprisings and urban revolts. Dynastic and fiscal problems destabilized France and England. The Great Schism and new heresies divided the Church. "Jan Hus—Heretic or Patriot?" covers one of several challenges to the Church's authority. Emergent capitalism gradually undermined an economy based on landed property. Yet these crises generated the creative forces that would give birth to the Renaissance and the modern era. The nation-state, the urban way of life, the class structure, and other aspects of modern life existed in embryonic form in the Middle Ages. And, as William McNeill has written, it was in medieval Europe that the West prepared itself for its later role as "chief disturber and principal upsetter of other people's ways."

Looking Ahead: Challenge Questions

Does the collapse of a civilization constitute an opportunity as well as a calamity?

Why did Grand Prince Vladimir of Kiev promote Byzantine culture in his domain?

On balance, were the Vikings destroyers or agents of progress?

Define chivalry and explain its functions in medieval life.

Why is it difficult to bridge the gap between modern and medieval outlooks?

Unit 5

The Viking saga

Magnus Magnusson

MAGNUS MAGNUSSON, *Icelandic-born author and journalist, is well-known in the UK as a TV and radio broadcaster specializing in archaeology and history. He wrote and presented in 1980 a major TV series on the Vikings which has been shown in many countries and has appeared in book form as* Vikings! *(BBC Publications with Bodley Head). Among his many other published works are the award-winning* Introducing Archaeology *(1972),* Viking Expansion Westwards *(1973), and* Iceland *(1979).*

THE term "Viking" has come to mean anyone who happened to be a Scandinavian in the Middle Ages, whether he was a seaman, a farmer, a merchant, a poet, an explorer, a warrior, a craftsman, a settler—or a pirate. And the term "Viking Age" has been applied by historians—somewhat indiscriminately, it must be said—to cover three centuries of dynamic Scandinavian expansion that took place from around 800 AD onwards.

It has become popularly associated with an age of terror and unbridled piracy, when Norse freebooters came swarming out of their northern homelands in their lean and predatory longships, to burn and rape and pillage their way across civilized Europe. They have always been portrayed as merciless barbarians, heedless of their own lives or of the lives of others, intent only on destruction. They were anti-Christ personified; their emblems were Thor's terrible Hammer and Odin's sinister Ravens, symbolizing the violence and black-hearted evil of their pagan gods.

This deep-rooted popular prejudice about the Vikings can be traced back directly to the lurid sensationalism of ecclesiastical writers who were the occasional victims of smash-and-grab Viking raids. In a turbulent age, when piracy and casual raiding were a commonplace of everyday life all over Europe the Vikings happened to be more successful at it than most other people; and they paid the price for it by getting an extremely bad reputation.

But, curiously enough, no one knows for certain what the word "Viking" actually means! It may be related to the Old Norse word *vík,* meaning "bay" or "creek", suggesting that a Viking was someone who lurked with his ship in a hidden bay. Some think it may come from the Old Norse verb *víkja,* meaning "to turn aside", so that a Viking was someone who made detours on his voyage—presumably to go raiding. A third school of scholarly opinion looks for a derivation in the Anglo-Saxon word *wic,* itself borrowed from the Latin *vicus,* meaning a fortified camp or trading-post, so that "Viking" might mean a raider or a trader, or both!

But not every Scandinavian was a professional warrior or Viking; and not every Viking was a pirate. Modern scholarship is now beginning to highlight the constructive, rather than the destructive, impact of the Viking Age. Spectacular archaeological excavations like Coppergate in York, which unearthed a whole street from the Viking Age, are revealing the ordinary Viking man-in-the-street as a diligent and skilled artisan—the Viking as man, not the Viking as myth.

If the origin of the word "Viking" is obscure, so too are the motive causes of the so-called Viking Age itself. There is no

Photos © L. A. East.
The British Museum, London

Coins struck by the Vikings attest to their receptiveness to the cultures with which they came into contact. Above, 10th-century silver pennies from the Viking kingdom of York. Left, coin inscribed "Anlaf Cununc" (King Olaf) is decorated with a raven, traditionally associated with Odin. Right, penny with the name of St. Peter shows a sword and also Thor's hammer, a symbol as potent to a Viking as a cross to a Christian.

Reproduced from the *Unesco Courier,* December 1983, pp. 10-13.

To relieve the tedium of the long northern winters, the Vikings played various board games, including dice games and a game similar to chess. Pieces were made of bone, amber or glass. Left, 10th-century wooden Viking gaming board from Ireland.

Photo © National Museum of Ireland, Dublin

single, simple reason why the Scandinavians should suddenly have burst upon the European scene late in the eighth century (in the history books, at least—it probably wasn't as sudden as it has been made to appear). All major historical shifts have complex roots. We know that in the seventh century, the Scandinavians began developing new sources of iron, which had several consequences: improved iron production made for better weapons, and better farm implements; better farm implements led to agricultural improvements, which led in turn to better nutrition and a correspondingly lower mortality rate amongst infants. There is evidence about this time that land that had formerly been thought unsuitable for farming was being vigorously cleared of forest and scrub to make new farms for new generations of vigorous, well-nourished younger sons who wanted a place in the sun for themselves.

So an acute shortage of land was probably a major factor, which led to considerable settlement overseas; there is evidence of peaceful co-habitation between the Picts of northern Scotland and Norwegian emigrant farmers long before the outbreak of the Viking Age.

But there were other consequences, too. With its surplus iron production, Scandinavia had a new and much-prized product to sell to its neighbours; and the traders had sharp, well-tempered weapons with which to defend themselves from pirates that swarmed in the Baltic and along the shores of northern continental Europe. But in order to trade effectively, the Scandinavians needed good ships. They came in all shapes and sizes, from small six-oared boats for coastal waters to the enormous "dragon-ships" of royalty. In between came a versatile variety of cutters, ferries, pinnaces, plump-bellied cargo-boats, ocean-going ships and galleys.

But the pride of the fleet, the ship that has become the universal symbol of the Viking Age, was the lordly longship, undisputed master of the northern seas. These ships were the outcome of centuries of technological innovation and evolution which have been charted by chance archaeological discoveries, from flat-bottomed punts to the splendour and sophistication of

the single-masted, square-sailed longships. Without the ships, the Viking Age would never have happened at all.

The Viking Age was not a concerted effort at empire-building. The Vikings were never a single, homogeneous people imbued with the same aims and ambitions. The three countries of the Scandinavian peninsula, as they are now defined by political geography, were not really nations at all in the modern sense of the term. Norway, for instance, was a scatter of inhabited areas under independent tribal chieftains along the western seaboard; even the name Norway (Norvegur) simply meant "North Way"—not so much a nation as a trade-route. And the three countries had distinct if sometimes overlapping "spheres of influence"—the Swedes in the Baltic and Russia, the Danes on the Continent and in England, and the Norwegians in Scotland and Ireland and the North Atlantic islands.

The first recorded Viking raid took place in the year 793, with a seaborne assault by prowling Norwegian marauders on the Holy Island of Lindisfarne, just off the north-eastern shoulder of England. But long before that, the Swedes had been busy in the Baltic, growing rich on trade. At the outset of the Viking Age, Swedish entrepreneurs started to penetrate the hinterland of Russia (they called it "Greater Sweden") in pursuit of the rich fur trade and the exotic markets of Arabia and the Far East. Swedish pioneers made their way through Russia by way of the major rivers like the Volga and the Dnieper, dragging their ships in exhausting overland portages on the way to the Caspian Sea and the Black Sea.

By the ninth century they had reached the capital of the greatest power in the western world, the successor to Rome—the Byzantine Empire centred on Constantinople. There, Viking mercenaries formed the elite bodyguard of the Byzantine emperors, the feared and famous Varangian Guard, a kind of Scandinavian Foreign Legion. But the Swedes never conquered Russia, as such; they contented themselves with taking control of existing trading posts and creating new ones to protect the trade-routes, but within two or three generations they had become totally assimilated and Slavicized.

5. MEDIEVAL PERIOD

While the Swedes looked east, the Danes looked south-west along the northern coasts of Europe and towards England. Danish warriors were soon hammering at the cities of the crumbling Carolingian empire after the death of Charlemagne in 814 AD: Hamburg, Dorestad, Rouen, Paris, Nantes, Bordeaux —all river-cities, notice. The Viking longships, with their exceptionally shallow draught, could go much further up-river than had been thought possible before, and the effect was rather like that of dropping paratroops behind the enemy lines.

To start with, the Danish Vikings acted as pirates with official or unofficial royal backing. Later on, Danish designs on Europe, and especially England, became openly territorial; the flag followed the trade, just as trade had followed the piracy. But here, too, the Danes, just like the Swedes, became assimilated whenever they settled. In the year 911, one marauding army accepted by treaty huge tracts of land in Northern France in what is now called Normandy—"Northmandy", the land of the Northmen; 150 years later, the descendants of these Norse-Frenchmen would conquer all England under William the Conqueror. Before then, but only briefly, under King Knut (Canute) in the eleventh century, there was a united Scandinavian empire of the North Sea, comprising England, Denmark and Norway; but it quickly fell apart.

Norwegian adventurers joined Danish Vikings in subjugating the whole of northern England (the Danelaw, as it was called) before settling there as farmers and traders, where they developed great mercantile cities like York. They also took over much of mainland Scotland, the Hebrides, and the Northern Isles of Shetland and the Orkneys. In Ireland they played a lusty part in the endless internecine squabbles of rival Irish clans, and founded Ireland's first trading posts: Waterford, Wexford, Wicklow, Limerick and, most especially, Dublin. They were insatiable explorers in search of new trade opportunities to exploit, new lands to settle, new horizons to cross. They discovered Spitzbergen and Jan Mayen Island; they discovered and colonized the Faroes, far out in the heaving Atlantic; they discovered and colonized Iceland, where they established Europe's first Parliamentary republic—a new nation that is still regarded as the oldest democracy in Europe, and which has left

us the most enduring cultural monument of the Viking Age, the Icelandic Sagas.

From Iceland, they discovered and settled Greenland. And it was from Greenland, round about the millennial year of 1000, that the Vikings launched their last and most ambitious expeditions of all, the discovery and attempted settlement of the eastern seaboard of North America: "Vinland", the land of wild grapes, as it was called in the two Icelandic Sagas that record the first undisputed European discovery of the New World.

The discovery of North America, and the abortive attempts at colonization which were thwarted by the indigenous Red Indians, used to be considered mere legend; but now archaeology has unearthed authenticated evidence of a Viking settlement at L'Anse aux Meadows, in northern Newfoundland. All other alleged Viking "finds", like the runic Kensington Stone, have long since been exposed as forgeries or hoaxes, or merely wishful thinking.

The impact of the Vikings was ultimately less lasting than might have been expected. Why was that? They had all the necessary energy, they had their own administrative systems of justice and royal authority, they had become converted to Christianity, they had their own coinage, they seemed to have everything. They had criss-crossed half the world in their open boats and vastly extended its known horizons. They had gone everywhere there was to go, and beyond. They had dared everything there was to dare. They had given Europe a new trading vigour, vigorous new art-forms, vigorous new settlers.

But they had neither the manpower nor the staying-power, neither the reserves of wealth nor the political experience, neither the cohesion at home nor the confidence abroad, to master effectively the older, richer, more stable States they tried to overrun. Instead, being rootless men of the sea, they put their roots down where they landed, and then blended into the landscape. Somehow or other, the dynamic simply petered out.

But they left in the annals of history, a heritage of heroic endeavour and courage, a legacy of robust audacity, that has won the grudging admiration even of those who would otherwise deplore their incidental depredations.

The baptism of Kiev

BORIS V. RAUSCHENBACH

BORIS VIKTOROVICH RAUSCHENBACH is a Soviet Academician, winner of the Lenin Prize and a member of the International Academy of Astronautics. A specialist in mechanics, the theory of combustion and the control of the orientation of spacecraft, he was closely involved in the preparations for the first Soviet space flights. Among his published works are a study on spatial structures in ancient Russian painting (1975) and an essay on iconography as a means of conveying philosophical ideas (1985).

A thousand years ago, in 988, the Slav principality of Kievan Rus', or Kievan Russia, came into being as one of a cluster of Christian States in Europe. Its emergence was one of the far-reaching consequences of a bold feudal reform of the State structures which was carried out by Grand Prince Vladimir, who wished to put his principality on the same footing as the developed feudal monarchies of that time.

In 980 Vladimir was at the head of a loose federation of Slav tribes, which could only be held together by the use of armed force (or at least the constant threat of its use). In order to strengthen this federation, the young prince took two important decisions. First, he settled in Kiev, intent on keeping his hands on the reins of government, which his predecessors had abandoned for months or even years while leading military expeditions. Second, he endeavoured to unite the Slav tribes ideologically—as we should say today—by means of a religion common to them all.

Once established in Kiev, Vladimir began to build fortifications to the east of the town, thus making it clear that he meant to stay in the capital and defend it against nomads. It was essential to the success of the radical State reforms that life in the city should be peaceful and safe.

To solve the second problem—the unification of the allied tribes—he first of all gave "equal rights" to all the main tribal gods (and consequently to those groups of the clergy that had most influence). A traveller arriving in Kiev from afar could see that the god of his own tribe was worshipped in Kiev as well as the Kievan gods. Six heathen gods were worshipped in Kiev; traces of these cults have been found by modern archaeologists.

These measures taken by Prince Vladimir strengthened the State. But it soon became clear that the path on which he had embarked so successfully was actually leading nowhere.

There were two main reasons for this. First, even after Vladimir's innovations the heathen religion perpetuated the old way of life. It suited a patriarchal system, but it was a major obstacle to the formation of the new production relationships of nascent feudalism. A new law, new customs, a new social awareness and a new approach to the world were all needed. The old paganism could not provide these things. But they were all to be found in Byzantium.

The second reason was that Kievan Rus' could not attain equality with the leading countries of Europe and the East, it could not, to use a modern expression, reach "world class" unless it borrowed from those countries a knowledge of crafts, building techniques, science, culture and much else. And all this, too, was to be found in Byzantium.

Vladimir's choice of religion was largely conditioned by history, but it was also due to his wisdom as a statesman. Rus' had already forged quite strong economic links with Byzantium, which was not far away. The Bulgarians, who were the kinsfolk of the people of Rus', had accepted Christianity about 100 years before, largely thanks to the work of Cyril and Methodius, who had developed a Slav alphabet and preached Christianity in the Slav language. Vladimir's decision may well have been influenced by the fact that in the Orthodox Church, unlike the Roman Catholic Church, people could worship God in a language they understood.

At this time Byzantium was still at the height of its glory. The tradition of Antiquity still survived there. Homer and other classical writers of Antiquity were studied in its schools, and Plato and Aristotle lived on in the philosophical disputes that took place there. The Byzantine form of Christianity met the needs of a feudal society, and therefore fully conformed with Vladimir's intentions. And at the same time it solved the problem of providing a single religion for all the tribes of ancient Rus'.

Neither Rus' nor Byzantium regarded the proposed acceptance of Christianity as a purely religious step. Byzantium's view, expressed in simplistic terms, was that since Rus' was turning to the Orthodox faith and the head of the Orthodox Church was the Byzantine patriarch and the emperor, Rus' automatically became a vassal of Byzantium.

But the State of ancient Rus' was expanding and was already quite powerful, and had fought Byzantium successfully several times; it did not intend to play the role of a vassal. Vladimir and his court had other ideas. They thought that the acceptance of Christianity and the adoption of Byzantine culture and skills along with Christianity should in no way diminish the independence of Rus'. As the prince saw it, Rus' should become a State friendly to Byzantium, but should retain its entire sovereignty.

The introduction of Christianity was a gradual process; authorities today believe that it took around 100 years—a very short time in view of the vast size of the country. The Christianization of Sweden and Norway, which began about the same time as that of Rus', took 250 and 150 years respectively.

Vladimir's political reform released a potential that had been gradually building up within the society of Rus'. The rapid development of the country shows how timely the reform was.

Master builders were invited to come from Byzantium to Rus', where they erected stone churches and other buildings and adorned them with frescoes, mosaics and icons. Russians worked with them, learning skills of which they had known nothing before. The next generation erected elaborate buildings in the towns of Rus', with hardly any help from foreigners. Changes took place in agriculture, too, and horticulture was introduced into Rus' at this time.

The clergy who had come to Rus' from Byzantium did not merely conduct religious services in the new churches; they also trained "national leaders" for the Church, and knowledge and literacy spread widely as a result. Schools were opened, and Vladimir made the children of the nobility attend them, despite the mothers' protests. He sent young men to study in other countries. A chronicle was begun. Like other developed States, Kievan Rus' started to mint its own gold coins.

Little by little, ancient Rus' became a State with a new high culture, although it would be wrong to think that it did not have an authentic culture of its own in pagan times. This pagan culture was to live on for a considerable time, and it imparted certain unique features to the art of ancient Rus'. What was new was mainly that body of knowledge that had already been acquired by cultured peoples throughout the world, ranging from the works of Aristotle to techniques for building stone arches.

But rapid as the changes of Vladimir's day were, his feudal reform was not completed in his lifetime. More time was needed, and Vladimir's work was finished by his son, Yaroslav the Wise. As the chroniclers say, Vladimir ploughed the land, Yaroslav sowed the seed, and we (later generations) have reaped the harvest.

Yaroslav was as zealous as his father had been in continuing the reform. Like his father, he built fortifications to defend his lands, this time mainly in the west. Like his father, he saw to it that nothing held up the feudal reforms; and he showed just as much energy in building, clearly striving to make Kiev the equal of Byzantium (later Constantinople). He did much to develop trade; and he began to strike silver coins as well as gold.

Yaroslav's principal aim, however, was to build up a genuinely Russian intelligentsia (insofar as such a concept can be used with reference to that period). Vladimir had not had time to do this. Literacy in itself was not enough; steps had to be taken to ensure that Kievan Rus' did not have to "import" Greek clergy, that it had its own scholars, writers and philosophers, and that it could, if necessary, wage an ideological struggle, notably against Byzantine imperial ideology. It is not surprising that Russian monasticism is first heard of in Yaroslav's day.

Inventories dating from the fifteenth and sixteenth centuries (earlier ones have not survived) show that most of the books in the monastic libraries were secular rather than religious. There were chronicles, historical records, "itineraries" or geographical works, philosophical and military treatises, and classical works such as the *History of the Jewish War* by Flavius Josephus. A learned monk must indeed have had an all-round education.

Chronicles such as *The Russian Primary Chronicle* and polemical works (often with a definite political undercurrent) were written in the monasteries. Books were copied, too. We are indebted to copyists in the monasteries for the fact that we can read the ancient chronicles that have come down to us (works such as *The Song of Igor's Campaign*). Icons were painted by masters such as Alimpi of Kiev. The Russian clergy who replaced those from Byzantium were trained in the monasteries.

In 1051, after the death of the Greek metropolitan of Kiev, Yaroslav himself (acting without the emperor or the patriarch of Constantinople) "having called together the bishops", for the first time appointed a Russian metropolitan, Hilarion, a priest in the prince's village of Berestovo. The Russian Orthodox Church was asserting its independence. Metropolitan Hilarion was certainly a man of great ability. His work "On Law and Grace", a remarkable example of the literature of ancient Rus', was a trenchant ideological weapon in the battle for the independence of Kievan Rus'.

The work of literacy teaching and school building continued under Yaroslav (and not only in Kiev). We have evidence that a school for 300 children was opened in Novgorod in 1030, at which children began to "learn to read books". Schools for girls were founded. Gradually all sectors of the population learnt to read and write, as we know from inscriptions that have been found on strips of birch bark. Yaroslav himself "was diligent in reading books by night and day", and he also "collected many books, translated books from the Greek to the Slav language, and wrote many books". Culture was spreading rapidly among the people of ancient Rus'.

Civilized States cannot exist without written laws. Yaroslav introduced a number of written statutes, including "Russian Law". In a word, under Yaroslav, who completed Vladimir's reform, Kievan Rus' became a freely developing feudal State, the equal of any State in the civilized world. It was surpassed by no other country, either in economic and social structure (feudalism, which continued to develop) or in culture, trade or the arts of war.

The introduction of Christianity, which became the ideological basis of the feudal State system of ancient Rus', played a progressive role in the early Middle Ages. The old division into tribes was a thing of the past. A people had taken shape as a State, and from it, in time, emerged the Russians, Ukrainians and Byelorussians.

CRUSADE BY CHILDREN

Trusting faith carried thousands of
children to the European shores of the
Mediterranean—and even aboard ships
setting sail for the Muslim-held Holy Land
of the Middle East—in the most
remarkable Crusade of all.

Timothy Baker Shutt

In the year 1230, a middle-aged priest returned to
France after eighteen years as a slave in the household
of Al-Kamil, son of the Caliph of Egypt. His duties had
not been odious, for Al-Kamil was a broad-minded man
interested in his people's Western adversaries, and he
needed the services of interpreters, teachers and secretaries familiar with Western languages and letters.

In the year 1212, the future slave had set out as one of a
number of enthusiastic younger clergy serving as spiritual
guides to tens of thousands of northern French children
seeking to win the Holy Land through innocence and simplicity of faith where the military prowess of their elders
and betters had failed in the earlier Crusades. As a middle-aged man, the priest proved the sole returnee from this
remarkable adventure—at least the only one of whom we
know anything today. Had he died in Egypt, or had he
been sold to a less understanding master than Al-Kamil
(the future Sultan of Egypt), our knowledge of the 13th-century Children's Crusade would be scanty indeed.

But the crusade in which the priest had participated was
not, technically, a crusade in the sense that medieval
Europeans understood the term—it had lacked Papal sanction, and its participants marched without the customary
indulgences granted to those engaged in warfare to defend
the Faith. It was also an extremely brief campaign, lasting
only for a few surprising months during the year 1212.

Aberrant though it was, the Children's Crusade was a

revealing chapter in medieval history. It exemplified the
depth of crusading zeal, the sincerely held and simple faith
of the age and the excesses of which that zeal and faith
were capable.

In late August 1212, ragged rows of enthusiastic children and the priests guiding them had stood on the quay at
Marseilles awaiting a miracle to surpass even the wonders
recorded in Scripture—they hoped for a parting of the
Mediterranean to permit the passage of the young crusaders to the Holy Land.

Leading this remarkable pilgrimage was an ordinary
shepherd boy, Stephen of Cloyes, who claimed that Christ
himself had appeared to him in the guise of a pilgrim to
deliver a scrap of parchment. This document, Stephen
declared, was nothing less than a communication from
God designating Stephen as a prophet. The shepherd lad
took his commission seriously, and it was his burning zeal,
and his alone, that had inspired the remarkable crusade.
Stephen had even pleaded his cause before King Philip of
France, and had preached to crowds of people from the
steps of the cathedral of St. Denis.

Stephen had gathered a large following of his childish
peers—as many as 30,000 according to the *Chronice* of
Aubrey of Trois Fontaines, the chief written document on
the Children's Crusade. Setting out from Vendôme, a
town in the Orleannais, some 90 miles southwest from
Paris, the youthful army had spent a long, hot march

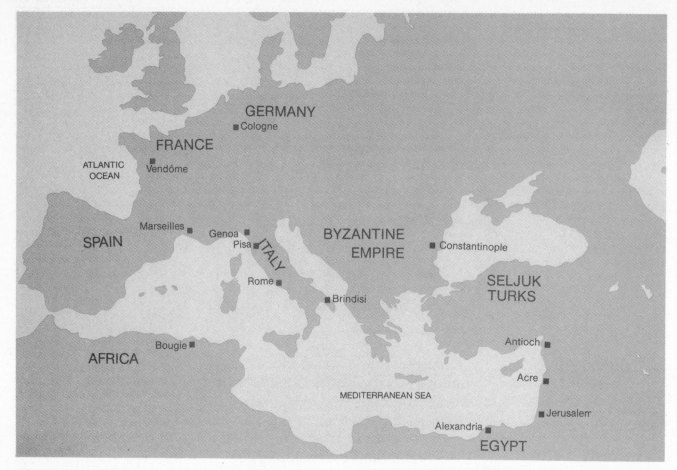

The map depicts the known world at the time of the Children's Crusade in Western Europe and the Near East, showing the major cities and other locations of the day. The Mediterranean Sea, a vast body of water, would not part for the young innocents of 1212.

across France, suffering greatly from thirst, hunger, confusion, homesickness, brigands and the bands of roving mercenaries who constituted one of the chief banes of the age. But such hardships did not deter the several thousands who completed the incredible march—they believed that the chosen of God had always suffered, only to be vindicated in the end. To the crusading children of 1212, the expected parting of the Mediterranean would be that awaited vindication. After all, they believed that Stephen of Cloyes, their leader, had been chosen by Christ to serve as the new Moses to lead them to the Holy Land.

Along with Stephen's young followers, the townspeople of Marseilles, rich and poor alike, gathered to await either a miracle or a bitter disappointment. Dressed in all the splendor of an age in love with finery, the bright colors worn by the city fathers and wealthy burghers of the sunny Mediterranean port must have presented a great contrast with the travel-stained rags of the crusading children, who were largely from the poorer classes of northern France, the Rhineland and Flanders.

There were prayers, of course. The young clergymen accompanying the Children's Crusade swung censers and invoked the powers of God, the Virgin and numerous saints. The old crusader prayer of "Lord, restore to us the true cross" must have risen from many young lips. In the end, however, the Mediterranean's aspect remained an unbroken expanse of blue water. No miracle transpired. The children of western Christendom would not witness a

greater repetition of the miracle that had led Israel into the Promised Land in millennia before.

Amazingly, though, the movement survived such potential disillusionment. Perhaps few were willing to completely discredit one claiming a letter from God, for the age was one filled wih claims of visions and special communications from Heaven. Instead of derision, the disappointed children apparently found pity in the eyes of the city fathers.

Two substantial-seeming citizens, Hugo the Iron and William the Pig, took special interest in the children. Declaring themselves pious men, they volunteered the use of seven ships to carry the children to the Holy Land free of charge. The offer was gratefully accepted, and a few days later the ships embarked.

And then silence. Nothing more was heard of the children for a span of 18 years. The fate of the young crusaders was revealed only in 1230, when Al-Kamil's nameless priest-slave returned from his bondage in Egypt.

After leaving Marseilles, the much-chastened priest reported, the party had run into a terrible storm, and two of the ships were lost in heavy seas near the island of San Pietro, off the southwest coast of Sardinia. The remaining five bore onward, only to be overtaken by a Saracen squadron a few days later.

This was a prearranged encounter, for William the Pig and Hugo the Iron were not the devout men they had seemed. In midsea, all the children and their priests were turned over to the Muslim privateers and carried off to Bougie on the coast of present-day Algeria where, block by block, they were sold into slavery to serve for life the Muslims they originally sought to conquer.

Many of the children were probably purchased at once by the local landholders from the hinterlands of Bougie. Others—including the then-young priest who would later recount the misadventure—were shipped to Egypt, where they would command a better price. Of these, most were bought by the governor of Alexandria to serve as agricultural laborers on his estates. When the priest returned to France in 1230, he reported that 700 members of the Children's Crusade were still living as plantation slaves in Egypt. A few others, he reported, had been sent as far east as Baghdad, where 18 had been martyred for refusing to convert to Islam.

All the literate among the slaves, however, had been bought by Al-Kamil. Most of these were probably clergy, for the Children's Crusade had been largely a movement of the children of the poor—a class that would remain largely illiterate for another three centuries or so.

How and why the priest was released we do not know. Al-Kamil may have released him (and perhaps others) on payment of a ransom by relatives of the captives or by certain charitable organizations devoted to ransoming Christian captives in Muslim hands. In some rare instances, captives were released as a gesture of generosity. In most such cases, however, those released had outlived their usefulness.

Various other sources suggest that the traffic in Christian lives carried on by the aptly named William the Pig and Hugo the Iron did not stop with mobs of credulous peasant children from the other side of Europe. Some later tales maintain that they attempted to kidnap the Holy Roman Emperor Frederick II and turn him over to the Saracens, but failed. They finally paid for their treachery on a communal gallows.

The punishment suffered by William the Pig and Hugo the Iron did nothing to relieve the misery of the children whose sale had doubtlessly provided them with windfall profits. Coming from the cool and damp climate of northern Europe, the children sold as agricultural laborers in the malarial regions of the Nile delta must have suffered mortality rates noticeably high even for an age when few lived past 30. The girls among them would have been especially unfortunate, for Muslim society often saw no reason to treat unprotected young females chivalrously. Those fortunate enough to be sold as concubines and serving girls in wealthy households would have often found themselves victims of their mistresses' jealous wrath—a jealousy made all the fiercer by the special circumstances of a polygamous society. But as none of the enslaved children seems to have returned to Christian Europe—and few could have written about their experiences even if they did indeed return—our picture of their fate must remain conjecture based on the observations of the single returning priest and what is generally known about slavery in Muslim culture and society.

To many medievals and moderns alike, the Children's Crusade was a pathetic affair bearing an obvious moral: thus, and only thus, is spiritual presumption and folly to be rewarded.

Yet no movement can be deemed trivial if it involves tens of thousands of children and youths—a significant portion of the young people of France, Germany and Flanders when we consider that the population of Europe in the 13th century was only a fraction of what it is today. Against the backdrop of its own time, in fact, the Children's Crusade makes sense as a product of a number of factors that played a large role in the way 13th-century people thought and acted.

The Children's Crusade followed a long history of crusading in Europe. The crusading tradition began in 1081, when Alexius Comnenus acceded to the throne of the Byzantine Empire. His realm, long a bastion against an expansionist Islam, had been seriously weakened by the conquests of the Seljuk Turks in eastern and central Anatolia. Having lost what were once some of the richest Byzantine territories and sources of manpower, Alexius knew that the very existence of Byzantium was at stake, and that he needed military help. Although deep-seated suspicions divided the Eastern Orthodox Christians of Byzantium from the Western Catholics, Alexius realized the best source of needed military help was the West. Only large levies of Frankish mercenaries could win back the Empire's lost territories.

At the same time, Pope Urban II earnestly desired an end to the ceaseless round of feudal warfare that wracked western Christendom. He thought that channeling the martial energies of western Europe elsewhere—against an expansionist and highly dangerous Islam—would bring peace to the West. Such a course of action would also help heal the still-aching breach between Eastern Orthodoxy and Western Catholicism, the two great branches of Christendom separated since 1054. Thus, Urban preached a crusade against Islam at the Council of Clermont in 1095, offering a papal blessing and full indulgence to all who would accept the crusader's cross.

The idea took hold of Christendom almost at once. The popular preachers Peter the Hermit and Walter the Penniless fanned crusading zeal into white heat. But the result was quite at variance from the one for which Emperor Alexius had hoped: the thousands who answered Urban's appeal with impassioned cries of *"Deus le volt!"*—"God wills it"—took up the cross not to restore Anatolia to Byzantine hands, but to put the Holy Land and Jerusalem into Frankish ones.

The First Crusade produced a mass migration to the East. Mobs of penniless townspeople and peasants took up the cross, as did the warrior aristocracy of Europe. Popular enthusiasm for the venture was so strong that an unofficial "people's crusade" marched a year earlier than the crusade of armed knights and their retainers.

Although the First Crusade took Antioch in 1098 and Jerusalem in the following year, crusader success was short-lived. The crusaders had entered a Muslim world divided by rivalry between the Seljuk Turks and the Fatimid Caliphate of Egypt. The Christian invasion provided just the catalyst needed to reunite Islam. In 1144, the Muslim leader Nur-ad-Din recaptured Edessa, an outlying crusader state founded in northern Syria. Although this loss prompted western Christians to undertake the Second Crusade, the slow disintegration of the crusader states in Syria and Palestine had begun. In the 1180's Nur-ad-Din's successor, Salai, defeated the crusader forces at Hattin in Galilee and then went on to retake Jerusalem.

The Third Crusade found able leaders in the Holy Roman Emperor Frederick Barbarossa, King Richard I of England and King Philip Augustus of France. But Frederick drowned en route to the Holy Land, and rivalry between the English and French kings further weakened the effort. In spite of Richard's able generalship, Saladin proved able to contain the crusaders, confining their victories to a single one at Acre.

In 1202, a Fourth Crusade set out. This crusade, however, fell into a tangled skein of political machinations between Venice and the Byzantine Empire and sacked Constantinople in 1204 on behalf of its Venetian and other Italian creditors. It succeeded only in permanently weakening Christendom's Byzantine bulwark against the Turks and creating a permanent hostility between the Greek and Latin wings of Christendom. Despite all the setbacks, by the early 13th century, the crusading ideal had become so pervasive in Western Europe that the term "crusade" was applied to every armed campaign against the enemies of the church. The long-running Spanish campaign against the Moors became a crusade, as did the violent suppression of the Albigensian heretics of southern France. Thus, Europe's warrior elite had crusading options other than the main one of regaining the Holy Land.

Still, by 1212, the freeing of the Holy Land from the Muslims was still something for which all of Christian Europe hoped deeply. If the nobility and ecclesiastical hierarchy found themselves better employed in Spain and southern France, perhaps it was time for the "humble and meek"—the peasantry and paupers—to undertake the liberation of Jerusalem.

That seems to have been one of the guiding notions of the crusading children of 1212. The crusading context itself seemed to warrant such a belief.

The only successful crusade had been the First, and that crusade above all had been so marked by the participation of the humble folk of Christendom as to give it more the appearance of a migration than that of a military campaign. A miracle at Antioch, the first great crusader victory, seemed to confirm the important place the poor of Christendom held in the crusading venture. Before the great victory, St. Andrew had appeared to a peasant crusader to reveal the resting place of the Holy Lance. The bulk of the crusader host—trained warrior and peasant wayfarer, alike—believed that St. Andrew had chosen his man precisely because the poor and humble were preeminent in merit and grace.

Furthermore, during the First Crusade, the fearsome "Tafurs" won reknown among the crusading host. These were the dregs of the crusading movement, the poor of Europe further degraded by their removal from traditional means of support. Fighting with farm implements or clubs, they marched ragged or nearly naked across the Middle East. They were so hungry and ferocious that both other crusaders and their Muslim enemies believed them to be cannibals, indiscriminately roasting and eating any Muslims, Jews or Eastern Christians unlucky enough to stand in their pathway. Yet, in spite of their frightening reputation, the Tafurs were supposed to be especially blessed in their poverty.

To all classes, then, the crusades—which had been going on for well over a century by the time Stephen of Cloyes led his huge youthful flock across France—represented a powerful ideal. The recovery of the Holy City where Christ had died and risen again from the dead was a goal that seemed especially pleasing to God.

At the same time, the crusading ideal survived long enough to enter an age of considerable religious ferment during the late 12th and early 13th centuries. In addition to heretical movements that drew people away from the church, many

THE ALTERNATIVE TO CRUSADES

Unlike their elders and social betters who had taken the cross before them, the youthful followers of Stephen of Cloyes and Nicholas of Cologne who went crusading in 1212 bore no arms. They seem to have believed that the pure faith of Christendom's children would suffice not only to part the Mediterranean Sea, but also to convert the infidel.

Although their self-confidence was misplaced, the crusading children shared a belief held by many sensitive believers in the West—that the spiritual "weapons" of faith and holy living were still those preferred by Christ. Thus, an alternative "crusade" seeking the conversion of the Muslims, rather than military conquest, grew up alongside the military crusades.

Francis of Assisi was an earnest young Italian who sought to recapture the simplicity and warmth of the primitive Christianity he had read of in the Gospels. Accompanying crusading warriors to Egypt in 1219, he was granted an audience with Malik Al-Kamil, the man who had purchased the literates and clergy found among the crusading children sold into slavery by the shipowners of Marseilles. By 1219, Al-Kamil had become Sultan of Egypt.

In that interview, Francis earnestly but unsuccessfully sought to persuade the Sultan to change his religion. In spite of his failure, Francis deeply impressed the Muslim potentate with his sanctity and zeal.

The early Franciscans followed Francis' example in seeking to convert the Muslims without any help from the worldly weapons of the crusading knight. One, Bernard of Carbio, went to Morocco to preach Christianity. Other Franciscans and Dominicans followed him, especially after 1225, when Pope Honorius III began to actively advocate missionary labors in North Africa and the Muslim-ruled portions of Spain.

These early missionaries enjoyed

fervent worshippers believed that the days predicted in the Apocalypse were at hand—when men's most radiant hopes and most terrible fears soon would be realized.

some success in the Crusader States, the string of small principalities and counties founded by the Franks on the coast of Syria and Palestine. One Dominican, William of Tripoli, claimed to have baptized 1,000 converts.

In Spain, the remarkable Catalan Raymond Lull (1235-1316) also advocated mission to the Muslims rather than military confrontation. Raised in Majorca, he learned Arabic from numerous Moors living there. Although never ordained a priest, he led a life of prayer and study, developing a philosophic discipline that he called the "Great Art." The goal of his Great Art was to find common philosophic ground on which Christians might persuade Jews and Muslims to convert.

Raymond practiced that Great Art himself. In Majorca, he helped found a school to train missionaries in the languages of the Middle East. He undertook hazardous missionary journeys to North Africa. Pious tradition maintains that he was stoned to death in Tunis on his last one.

The Muslims proved difficult to convert. They saw their own religion as Christianity's successor. Many of the handful of converts won through peaceful persuasion in North Africa met quick martyrdom, for their Muslim friends and relatives believed that the "turncoat" might yet be saved if killed quickly.

About the same time that Europe lost interest in the Crusades, it also lost interest in missionary work in Islamic lands. The friars who took up residence in North Africa or Syria came to devote their energies to the spiritual care of European Christians in those lands and the physical care of Holy places.

Although the peaceful crusade carried on by the early Franciscans and Raymond Lull was no more successful than the violent crusades of the knights, it had a far more lasting influence. Divorced from the political-military ambitions of secular rulers, it would provide the models for later and more successful missionary ventures—both Catholic and Protestant.

A highly influential figure was Joachim of Fiore, a Calabrian hermit. In the 1190s he prophesied that a new age was to appear, and his ideas caused special excitement after the turn of the 12th and 13th centuries. Joachim maintained that the years between 1200 and 1260 would see the dawning of the Age of the Holy Spirit, a third age in human history following that of the Father (which had concluded at the coming of Christ) and that of the Son (from the coming of Christ to Joachim's own times). Just as the age of the Father had been marked by fear of the Lord and submission to the law of Moses and that of the Son by faith, the age of the Holy Spirit would be marked by love and freedom—God's presence revealed internally to believers. Before that age, however, a great new teacher would arise to cleanse the church of its corruptions and do battle with the Antichrist. Many arose to claim that role during the age in which the Children's Crusade took place.

The discontent of the lower classes also found expression in religious ferment. The Gospels, after all, made frequent reference to Christ's preference for the downtrodden of the earth. At the time that young Stephen of Cloyes claimed to receive his letter from heaven, other stirrings among Christendom's poor presaged the growth of later movements—the Franciscans and Waldensians and various religious protests against an age in which church authorities too often seemed committed to the rich and powerful, rather than the poor and humble.

This spiritual climate helps explain the appearance of Stephen of Cloyes and other leaders of the Children's Crusade. People believed that a new age was about to dawn, when God would finally exert visible control of history and intervene directly in all human events.

The divine presence seemed very near, bearing a promise of new prophecies, wonders and miracles. Any moment, God might bring to conclusion the cycle of the ages, and woe to those failing to recognize the harbingers of the momentous event.

The divine preference for the humble and meek had special reference to children. Christ himself had taught that children were especially fit to receive the Kingdom of Heaven. Many viewed the Bethlehemite children slain by Herod at the time of Christ's birth as the first martyrs; the feast commemorating that event—the Feast of the Holy Innocents—was a popular holiday. The willing sacrifices of child martyrs of old—considered especially pleasing to God and meritorious in a way that served all of Christendom—were common objects in the Middle Ages of pious contemplation.

In such a spiritual climate many were ready to believe that God could indeed conquer the Holy Land or bring about the conversion of the infidel by means of children. Nothing else could better reveal the divine power or more thoroughly exalt the humble and confound the mighty. Should the children of Christendom succeed in the conquest of the Holy Land, they would prove the verity of the Gospel text teaching that the last would be first and the first, last.

Close to the time Stephen of Cloyes issued his claim, a boy named Nicholas began to preach a crusade from the steps of the shrine of the Three Kings in Cologne, a major city of the Rhineland. He successfully competed for popular attention with papal emissaries seeking volunteers for the campaigns against the Moors in Spain and the Albigensians in southern France.

Like his French contemporary, Nicholas appeared inspired as he preached that children could succeed where adults had failed. Many believed his message that Christendom's children would regain the Holy Land for Christ, walking through the waves of the sea dryshod. In response to that message, a mass migration of German children occurred, in all respects similar to the one going on in France at about the same time. Contemporary Rhineland chroniclers spoke with wonder of the youthful hordes drifting southward to reach the Mediterranean and the Holy Land beyond it.

This children's crusade consisted of two large parties, one of which, originally numbering some 20,000, was led by Nicholas himself. At about the time Stephen of Cloyes' party reached Marseilles, approximately a third of Nicholas' band reached Genoa, Italy (the other two-thirds had either deserted the cause or perished).

The Genoese authorities had no desire to see their city overrun by hungry hordes of unsupervised German children. They were willing to allow any individual children who wished to settle in Genoa to stay, but they permitted the horde as a whole to rest only a single night. Had things gone as planned, that would have been enough, but here, as at Marseilles, the sea obstinately refused to open.

Many of Nicholas' followers thereupon decided to stay put at Genoa or to make the hazardous trek homeward. Nicholas himself, however, was not so easily discouraged. He took what was left of his band to Pisa.

Once again, the sea refused to open. The Pisans, however, put two ships at the children's disposal. And after those ships sailed, nothing was heard of their young passengers again, either. Perhaps they, like their French counterparts, ended up in the slave markets of North Africa or Egypt, for the Pisans and other Italians were experienced in trading with the Muslim countries.

Nicholas did not sail at Pisa, but continued onward to Rome with the hardiest and most faithful of his flock. Pope Innocent III spoke to them in person, advising them to return home and releasing them from any vows they might have made. The Pope's advice to those who wished to crusade was to take up the cross as adults. But dismayed as Innocent might have been at the children's temerity, he was impressed by their courage. He later remarked, "These children put us to shame; they rush to recover the Holy Land while we sleep."

Most of the children took the Pope's practical advice, ruefully taking up the long trek northward and homeward. The season was late, and the pitiful survivors not only had to face mockery but also the rigors of the Alpine autumn. Many were robbed or otherwise accosted—few made it back to the Rhineland.

Accounts concerning Nicholas' own fate differ. Some say that he died on the return journey. Others maintain that he survived to join a crusade as an adult. His father, who seems to have encouraged his preaching, either fell victim to irate parents who had him hanged for slave trading or forestalled their wrath by suicide.

The other large group of Rhineland children worked its way southward along the eastern coast of Italy, ultimately reaching Brindisi in the very heel of the Italian boot. The disgruntled archbishop of that city refused them permission to sail eastward. Most, like Nicholas' other followers, then made their way homeward, but a few seem to have made it to Palestine. Needless to say, they converted few Muslims and got nowhere near Jerusalem, which was at that time in Muslim hands.

Ironically, Stephen of Cloyes seems to have had little interest in specifically embarking on a crusade. Although he did indeed appear before the king of France in May or June of 1212, bearing the document he claimed was a letter from heaven, his interest was to promote devotional processions—spectacular enough, but hardly the same thing as a crusade. How his procession of 30,000 French children turned into a crusade remains one of the mysteries of history. Shortly after his brief period of notoriety, the shepherd boy disappeared into the obscurity from which he had come.

The unhappy adventure of 1212 speaks of a medieval world that was still largely intact, in which the crusading ideal of bishops and princes was so pervasive that it was shared by the children of the poor. If the faith of the young crusaders was misguided, that faith was still a link joining the crusading children to the society of their elders and betters. When the poor and humble of medieval Europe next would assert themselves, it would be in a destructive series of peasant revolts that sought to overturn the authority of nobles and bishops.

Ill-considered by standards of modern "realism," the Children's Crusade was nonetheless not a destructive movement that preyed on those in its path, as the earlier crusades had done. Where crime followed in its wake, its participants were the victims, not the perpetrators. The children marched unarmed, and some notion of converting the Muslims seems to have taken the place of the usual crusader zeal for battle.

In its own way, the Children's Crusade bespeaks a curiously appealing trustfulness, a simple faith. It was the common faith of its time reflected in the actions of the lowliest members of society. If those actions had tragic consequences, the idealism that motivated them was a powerful one, and the world today is only the poorer for having lost it.

When Knighthood Was in Flower

David Herlihy

David Herlihy is the Henry Charles Lea Professor of Medieval History and master of Mather House. He is the author of Medieval Households, *published by Harvard University Press.*

The idea of chivalry, now as in the past, evokes from many people cynical or hostile reactions. To some, the pretense that war could be honorable and even holy is a snare and a delusion, which for centuries lured idealistic young men to their untimely, and often meaningless, deaths. In a recent book, *The Return to Camelot, Chivalry and the English Gentleman,* Mark Girouard relates how in the early months of the First World War, English youths set out for France as if they were embarking on crusade. One of them, John Manners, wrote these grandiloquent words to his mother in August 1914, as he was leaving for France: *Mon âme à Dieu/Ma vie au Roi/Mon coeur aux Dames/Et honneur pour moi.* (My soul to God/My life to the king/My heart to the ladies/And honor for me.) Manners was killed at the front less than a month later.

The ideal of chivalry, and especially its treatment of women, have been particularly offensive to feminist critics of contemporary society and the place of women in it. In rejecting even the use of the word "lady," they in fact are repudiating the whole set of chivalrous values associated with it. Feminist critics make many telling points. First, chivalry places the woman upon a pedestal, fashions her into a Madonna, attractive perhaps, but fundamentally cold and passive, acted upon but never acting, silent and lifeless. The pedestal is another form of prison. Secondly, chivalry restricts the roles of women to the domestic and the demeaning, and gives them no place in the exciting, external world of public or business affairs. In the last century, the English poet Alfred Lord Tennyson, in

a work called "The Princess," gave this characterization of what sex roles ought to be, from his own, chivalrous perspective:

. . . but this is fixt
As are the roots of earth and base of all;
Man for the field and woman for the hearth;
Man for the sword and for the needle she;
Man with the head and woman with the heart;
Man to command and woman to obey:
or else confusion. . . .

In much less eloquent language, this following poem echoes many of the same sentiments. It was directed against suffragettes, and is dated February 1915:

Here's to the woman of days gone by,
May we meet her up above!
The woman for whom a man would die,
The woman who rules by love,
Who doesn't parade, who doesn't harangue,
In whose home it is sweet to dwell
Who believes in raising children
And not in raising hell!

Chivalry, in the feminist indictment, limits and demeans women, and is an obstacle to the transcendence of sex roles. The goal of many feminists is the nurturing of the androgynous personality, among both girls and boys. The androgynous person, whether male or female, is supposed to carry the qualities of both sexes, climb every mountain, sail every sea, and not be confined by gender. This is not the program of sex-role assignments chivalry proposes.

It is not my purpose here to judge the merits of this ongoing debate. I am a historian, interested in the origins and early formation of the peculiar and surprisingly enduring cultural tradition known as chivalry. My purpose is to reconstruct chivalrous society as it really was, and the place of women within it. My point is small but still perhaps important. The chivalric celebration of women was not a feint and a fiction, not a disguised insult. Women really did hold place and power in chivalrous society. They were on a pedestal, but only when they chose to stand there. The pedestal had a staircase that took them to other castle rooms, which they entered when they wanted.

To consider women in chivalrous society requires first that we examine what was chivalry, and briefly outline its history. Chivalry is a set of professional ethics and expectations, guiding the behavior of the warrior classes of medieval Europe. This set of ethics was associated with the history of a particular type of fighter, the heavily armed, mounted warrior known as the knight.

The track of chivalry thus leads us back to the technological history of combat. The Roman legionaires and the barbarian hordes had both of them fought on foot. When does the mounted warrior claim supremacy on the battlefield? Military historians have proposed various dates. As early as A.D. 376, a Germanic tribe, the Visigoths, bested the hitherto invincible Roman legions at Adrianople in the southern Balkans. According to accounts of the battle, a charge of the German cavalry broke through the Roman ranks. Could these mounted, victorious Visigoths be regarded as knights? No, not likely. The barbarians continued for centuries thereafter to fight on foot. Four hundred years later, a king of the Franks called Pepin increased the use of horses in his armies. He delayed the marshaling of the Frankish host, which assembled every year, from March until May, and commuted a tribute paid by the Saxons from cattle to horses. In waiting until May before summoning the army, he surely was waiting for grasses to grow, and he clearly wanted horses. Some historians, ingeniously

---

Chivalry is the art of fighting on horseback, but also the commitment to the constructive use of violence.

---

combining archaeological and written evidence, have concluded that a technological change had occurred in eighth-century Frankland. A new device, the stirrup, had arrived out of Asia. The stirrup enabled the mounted fighter to deliver a hard blow by sword or lance, and yet keep his seat. But there is little evidence that the Carolingian fighter fought on horseback. Horses were needed to transport men and supplies on distant campaigns, but they were not yet the tanks of the medieval battlefield.

As late as the Norman Conquest of England, in 1066, fighters rode horses to reach the field of battle, then dismounted, to meet the enemy on foot. So it seems the soldiers of William the Conqueror fought at the Battle of Hastings. But William also took care to bring horses with his army into England. They were becoming an essential part of the logistic support of armies.

The stirrup, a new device from Asia, permitted a man to deliver hard blows from horseback without losing his seat. War became reserved for those who could afford horses and armor. Technology had transformed society.

Why should the fighter want to leave his high perch? Riding, he presented an easier target for archers and spear throwers. But if he and his horse could be protected, he then could take advantage of his towering position. From about 1150, the mounted warrior no longer dismounts, but remains, sheathed now in armor, on top of his horse, rushing to where the action is, fighting against foot soldiers from commanding heights. The knight emerges, inseparable from his steed, destined to be king of battles until the development of firearms allowed his opponent to hurl projectiles at him with unchivalrous force from unconscionable distances, dislodging him from his charger. Still, he reigned for long, and for longer yet pretended to reign.

The emergence of the heavily armed, mounted warrior as the mainstay of armies had profound repercussions. War among the barbarians had engaged all free males; all were fighters, and all claimed the rewards which this honorable calling offered. But the new costs of armor and horse severely restricted the practice of arms to a rich and narrow aristocracy. Moreover, medieval warfare now isolated and illuminated the individual knight. Although medieval knights were capable of tactical maneuvers, medieval battles were often reduced to many single combats between individual champions. The warrior was no longer a faceless fighter lost within a legion or a horde; he was now a paladin.

To express and exert his individuality, the knight could not remain totally concealed by armor. He had to display some sign or symbol by which foe and friend alike could recognize who he was. Initially, he took to wearing a linen surcoat, with distinctive arms painted upon it; this was the original "coat of arms." Identifying the individual knight, these armorial bearings soon were emblazoned on banners too; they were also passed from father to son, and came to identify the knight's family or lineage. The experts in recognizing arms and their bearers are heralds, and the art of designing arms is heraldry. The use of arms as identifying symbols gave to medieval knights and medieval warfare considerable color. A troubadour named Bertran de Born wrote a poem praising spring, not only because it brought forth birds and flowers, but because it summoned the splendiferous knights from winter quarters.

Well do I love the lusty spring
When leaves and flow'rs peep to light!
I love to hear the songbirds sing
Among the leafage in delight
    Which forms their airy dwelling
And when on tented fields I spy
Tall tents and proud pavilions high,
    My breast with joy is swelling;
Or when I see in legion lie
Squadrons of armored chivalry.

. . .

And equal pleasure does it bring
When some gay gallant is in sight,
On lofty charger galloping,
Who cheers his men from base affright,
    Of rich rewards them telling.

This expensive combat required that the knight be wealthy; he could only be recruited from a social elite, the feudal nobility in sum. But blood alone could not induct him into the order of chivalry; he needed to be trained and tested. From approximately the mid twelfth century, the young nobleman, desiring knighthood, had to follow as a squire or apprentice the accomplished masters of the skill, learn from them, prove his mettle through some masterpiece of combat, a *beau geste*, and then be received into the order of knights through the act of dubbing. A master knight hit the novice with the flat of his sword; it was the only blow that the knight ever received which he did not have to return.

The money required, and the time required, limited the number of knights. Medieval armies were small, but the art of warfare became more professional as its practitioners grew fewer. And the art came to include not only the mastery of dexterous strokes, but of ethical judgments as to when and where, for whom, and against whom, this skilled violence could be exercised. The art and ethics of mounted combat in the Middle Ages: all this is chivalry. It is, as its name suggests, the art of riding and fighting on horseback, but also the commitment to the constructive use of violence.

Where did this ethic of violence come from? The Church clearly played an influential role. From the tenth century, the Church had sought to limit and control violence. Through movements known as the Peace of God, it sought to give immunity to certain persons—clerics, women, peasants, the poor—and to certain places, such as consecrated grounds. Through the Truce of God, it tried to prohibit fighting on certain days—during Lent, Advent, holy days, Fridays, and Sundays. But in this the Church did not so much propose an ethic as modify one already very much present, and very much disruptive of peaceful society.

A second influential source of chivalry was the novel notion that a war could be holy. The knight could gain merit not merely from holding back his blows against certain persons at certain times, but in delivering them against the enemies of God. This was the idea underlying and inspiring the Crusades, the first of which was proclaimed by Pope Urban II at Clermont in southern France, in 1095. For the next 200 years, Western knights marched to recover the Holy Land, in quest of booty, glory, and grace. The concept that war could be holy was unique, but it too was an embellishment upon, not the essence of, an old and ingrained warrior ethic.

In fact the chief source of chivalry is best located in folk traditions. The barbarian peoples of Europe—the Celtic and Germanic tribes—had their own ancient ideals of the master warrior, the hero. Heroic exploits are the common themes of their songs, to the refrains of which these peoples marched into history.

The Middle Ages profoundly alter these ancient folk traditions. Social changes, as we have mentioned, restrict the privilege of fighting to a small elite; those with inadequate resources merge into the peasantry. The changes lend the now elite warrior a new individuality, but they require that he master skills of mounted fighting not easily acquired. They impose a new ethic, which directed his violence in socially constructive ways. And perhaps with greatest originality, the chivalric ideal taught the knight not only how to act on the battlefield but in the banquet hall; not only how to treat comrades and foes, but women of a social station comparable to his own. The knight was courteous to all ladies, but his own social and moral improvement required that he seek the love of one. Love was a kind of emotional tournament, in which both skill and character were tested and perfected. This new relationship between the noble lover and his lady is conventionally known as courtly love; it is without doubt one of the most original cultural creations of the Middle Ages.

We can trace the evolution of this art and ethic through literary survivals, and through the changing images of the woman they present. In the oldest literature, she has no real place within the world of warriors. To be sure, the Roman historian Tacitus tells us of the courage of the British queen Boadicea, who defied the Romans, led an army against them, and, when defeated, took poison rather than make a Roman holiday. But he regards her as exceptional. In his essay on the Germans, he further relates how in battles the barbarian women exhorted their fighting men, urging them on into the fray. Women occasionally fight or encourage the fighters, but they do not inspire them.

The Anglo-Saxon epic *Beowulf*, redacted in probably about the year 1000, offers the longest and perhaps the purest representation of Germanic heroism. Where are the women? The wife and daughter of King Hrothgar move among the warriors as they feast, bestowing rings upon them. But the warriors never think of women as they fight. There is no suggestion that the love for a lady could inspire a warrior, make his eye keener, his thrust stronger, his ambitions larger. Love is not yet an ennobling emotion. It seems hardly an emotion at all—at least, not one worthy of treatment in the epic genre.

Even the earliest masterpiece of French literature, *The Song of Roland*, written about 1100, has no real place for women. The hero Roland, when he faces death, thinks of God, Charlemagne, and sweet France, but not of his fiancée; she has contributed nothing to his life. She in turn swoons when she learns of his death.

But love's day was dawning. Perhaps the most extraordinary characteristic of medieval chivalry is this marriage of love and war, of Venus and Mars, tenderness and fury. We encounter the theme initially in the troubadour lyric poetry from southern France.

Knights could gain merit by delivering their attentions to the enemies of God. Here Peter the Hermit rallies warriors for the First Crusade.

The first known troubadour is William IX, count of Poitiers and duke of Aquitaine, born in 1071. According to a perhaps ungenerous contemporary biographer, "he knew well how to sing and make verses, and for a long time he roamed all the land to deceive the ladies." The new cult of love was not all idealism.

The principal theme of troubadour poetry was the examination of love, its powers and its pains. Who can love? Only those of gentle birth, to be sure. William aside, the characteristic emotional bonding links a man of comparatively humble social station with a high-born lady. She is usually married, the spouse of a great lord. He tries to win her favor, through his poetry and through performing great deeds in her honor. The theory of courtly love recognized four stages, which form a kind of emotional ladder, on which the lover goes up or down. The first was "hesitating," during which the lover could not find the courage or the words to express his

---

Perhaps the most extraordinary characteristic of medieval chivalry is the marriage of love and war, of Venus and Mars, tenderness and fury.

---

feelings. In the second stage, "pleading," he finally does proclaim his love. In the third stage, "hearing," it is the lady's turn to hesitate, as she considers the lover's suit and by her ambiguous responses kindles in him alternate feelings of joy and despair. The last stage is *druerie*, or "service." The lady accepts the lover, and he becomes her devoted servant. He lives in perfect joy, and goes

about the countryside singing the lady's praises—although it was considered bad form to mention her name. He does great deeds in her honor, and receives in recompense one kiss per year. (Some poets, like Duke William, were more generously rewarded.) Here is the exultation of the lover, expressed by the troubadour Peire Vidal:

Great joy have I to greet the season bright,
    And joy to greet the blessed summer days,
    And joy when birds do carol songs of praise
And joy to mark the woods with flowerets dight,
    And joy to all whereat to joy were meet,
    And joy unending at the pleasaunce sweet
That yonder is my joy I think to gain,
    And there where in joy my soul and sense remain.
'Tis Love that keeps me in such dear delight,
    'Tis Love's clear fire that keeps my breast ablaze,
    'Tis Love that can my sinking courage raise,
Even for Love am I in grievous plight;
    With tender thoughts Love makes my heart to beat,
    And o'er my every wish has rule complete—
Virtue I cherish since began his reign,
And to do the deeds of Love am ever fain.

It is not true, as is often asserted, that the woman is a silent, lifeless partner in this love relationship. She is, to begin with, free to act or not to act. This is the reason why the twelfth-century countess of Champagne, Marie de France, in a famous judgment ruled that a married couple could not be true lovers. The lovers, and particularly the woman, had to be free to enter or reject the relationship. The woman, superior in social station to her suitor, also controls the benefits and favors which her lover is seeking. She is, in sum, the master of the game. Nor is she silent. We have the names and some of the works of more than twenty women. The lyric poetry

*Women weren't silent partners in chivalric love affairs. Countess Marie de France,
shown above, went so far as to rule that married couples could not be true lovers
because they no longer had the freedom to enter or reject the relationship.*

was in part produced by women, and certainly their
tastes influenced many of its conceits. Here's an example
of the work of Countess Beatrice of Die:

Handsome friend, charming and kind,
When shall I have you in my power?
If only I could lie beside you for an hour
and embrace you lovingly—
Know this, that I'd give almost anything
To see you in my husband's place,
But only under the condition
that you swear to do my bidding.

How can we explain this distinctive love relationship? We can first look for cultural antecedents and parallels. But we should also consider the social background: did noble women in chivalrous society really control substantial resources, so as to become dispensers of favors and fully free to act? And were they in any sense masters of the social game?

First, the cultural antecedents and parallels. As many historians have recognized, the scheme of courtly love looks like a double parody. It parodies the relationship of the vassal to the lord under the feudal system. And it is also, in large part, a parody of religious mysticism, and of the mystical ascent of the believer into the presence of God.

In the feudal relationship, what does the vassal, a man of lower social status, owe his high-born lord? Fealty and service. In the love relationship, what does the lover, a man of lower social status, owe his high-born lady? Fidelity and service. The lord in compensation for

service confers benefits on his vassal; the lady favors her lover. The love language of the troubadours is replete with technical terms borrowed from feudal terminology, such as *druerie* itself, which can mean the service of either vassal or lover. The lady is sometimes addressed as "my lord," in the masculine gender. In its first appearance, the bonds of the feudal relationship were ethical and emotional more than legal, and were freely entered. So also were the bonds of courtly lovers.

In passing through the four stages of love, the lover travels on a sentimental journey, beginning with despondency and ending with joy. The supreme reward of the successful lover is joy, a word the troubadours bequeathed to modern English and other languages. Joy is also one of the gifts which the Holy Spirit bestows on the blessed. Moreover, the blessed are promised a new heaven and a new earth when they finally attain God's kingdom. So also, the successful lover inhabits a world where the season is always spring; January, always June. Bernart of Ventadorn depicts in the following words the lover's surroundings:

So filled with happiness am I
    Earth wears another face;
Rich flowers of many a brilliant dye
    for me the frost displace;
When rains descend and tempests fly,
    My joy but gains in grace,
They only help my song rise high,
    My glory mount apace;
    For in my loving heart
    So sweetly joy doth start,
    Meseems the flowers make ice depart,
To verdure snow give place.

The twelfth century was an age of mystical exuberance, not all of it orthodox. Courtly love was itself a kind of secular mysticism, offering lovers a secular salvation.

The chivalrous romances make frequent use of religious imagery. Here is an example, out of *Lancelot*, by Chretien de Troyes:

> . . . then he comes to the bed of the Queen, whom he adores and before whom he kneels, holding her more dear than the relic of any saint. And the Queen extends her arms to him, and, embracing him, presses him tightly against her bosom, drawing him into her bed beside her and showing him every possible satisfaction . . . Now Lancelot possesses all he wants . . . It cost him such pain to leave her that he suffered a real martyr's agony . . . When he leaves the room, he bows and acts precisely as if he were before a shrine.

In creating this ideal of a love relationship, these lovers, ladies, and poets freely borrowed terms and images from the fundamental institutions of medieval society, from its governmental system and from its religion. Love emerges as a redemptive force, ennobling those who serve it, and transforming their surroundings into an earthly paradise.

But what about the real world? Did courtly lovers ever exist? We think: rarely if at all. But the lovers, ladies, and poets who borrowed so much from parallel strains of medieval culture could not have conjured up a society totally foreign to daily experience. Art must answer to life. And the social truth which the literature reflects would seem to be this: women in chivalrous society, at least in its early history, really did control resources; they really could appear as dispensers of favors, who had to be cultivated and charmed. The favors sought and given were perhaps only rarely sexual satisfaction. But there were others worth pursuing: money, gifts, appointments, lands, perhaps only a warm meal in the kitchen. Did women control these?

In exploring the relationship of women to resources, it must of course be conceded that chivalrous society was for them no Eden. The expenses of warfare and of the noble life were leading the great lineages to restrict the claims of heirs upon the family properties. The great houses tended to favor the eldest sons and limited the shares given to younger sons and all daughters. Gradually, noble women were losing the support of their families. The terms of marriage were also turning against them. In early medieval society, the groom gave the dowry to the bride; but from the twelfth century on the flow of property at the making of a marriage was entirely reversed. Now the bride, or her family, had to meet the considerable costs of establishing her in a new household. The ages of first marriage for women seem to have fallen, and the daughters of poor nobles encountered difficulties even attracting a husband. Heretical

A powerful and high-spirited woman, Eleanor of Aquitaine accompanied her husband on the Second Crusade and made a certain amount of trouble.

movements, such as the Albigensians in southern France, found many ready listeners among these deprived girls. They learned from the heretics that marriage itself, which they could not have, was hypocrisy and an abomination, the worst of all sexual crimes.

The long-term social evolution within the nobility was running counter to the interest of women. Still, these changes were slow in having an effect, and in the formative years of chivalrous society—the twelfth century, primarily—women on the whole, rich women in particular, still enjoyed favorable treatment in regard to inheritances and dowries. They had one further advantage. Once married, they assumed important functions in the management of the family estates—their own or their husbands'. They did so because the husband was committing his attention and energies primarily to warfare. And his martial commitments removed him for long periods from his lands and castles. A venture to the Holy Land could occupy years of his life. Some noble women accompanied their husbands on crusade, but most remained at home, supervising the lands and castles. The vassal who came to do homage for his fiefs would often find not the lord but his wife, to whom he would perform this duty. Little wonder that the stance of the vassal so profoundly influenced that of the lover. We know too that many noble women, in place of their husbands, distributed the yearly gifts which served as salaries for the knights attached to the household. The woman fulfilled the services of a stable manager, in place of her wandering husband. As such she could direct the life of castle and court as she wished.

How can we illustrate the true status of noble women in the twelfth century? There are several ways. The simplest is through biography. One of the best-known women the Middle Ages produced was Eleanor of Aquitaine, from the province in southwest France that had also been the homeland of the troubadours. She patronized their poetry and was a poet herself. The sole heir to the great duchy of Aquitaine, she initially married King Louis VII of France. The marriage seemed to promise the unification of the two greatest principalities of France, the royal domains north of the Loire and Aquitaine to the south. But troubles soon disturbed the relationship. Eleanor accompanied her husband on the Second Crusade, and was at least accused of entering into an adulterous and incestuous relationship with her uncle. And she failed to produce a male heir. Louis divorced her, and she quickly married Henry II Plantagenet of England. The marriage in fact created the huge Angevin empire, which extended from the borders of Scotland in the north, across England, Normandy, and western France down to the Pyrenees.

Eleanor's marriage with Henry was not an emotional success, and this spirited woman supported revolts of their own sons against him. Playing a major role in both the political and cultural history of the twelfth century, Eleanor is a fine example of the powerful, resourceful, and cultured woman of early chivalrous society.

We have other ways too of testing the importance of women. One curious phenomenon is the use of matronymics, rather than patronymics, in identifying a person. Many knights call themselves, for example, Louis son of Blanche, instead of Louis son of Raymond, or whatever the father's name might have been. The usage is frequently encountered in the many charters that have survived from the period. No contemporary explains for us why these noblemen identified with their mothers rather than their fathers. Perhaps a substantial part of their inheritance came from their mothers' side. At the last, the practice shows that their mothers were well-known within the community. These feudal ladies were not confined to the inner reaches of their castles.

We can also study the appearances of women in these charters, as owners of land, granters of fiefs, receivers of homage. Here too, they are very visible, and the reasons for their prominence again appear to have been two: still favorable inheritance customs and terms of marriage; and their functions as managers of estates for their often distracted or absent husbands. The young knight trying to advance his career would often have to serve and please a woman. The noble lady set the rules for the game of courtesy.

The status of noble women changes in the later Middle Ages, as we have noted, and so does courtly culture. The lady really does become immobilized and mute upon her pedestal. But we ought to recognize that the tradition of chivalry is very long, and it would be amazing if it experienced no changes. For one relatively brief moment in time, in the late eleventh and twelfth centuries, noble women really did wield much power and influence. And they attracted a kind of courtship and of love which recognized their status and did honor to them.

MARGERY KEMPE AND THE MEANING OF MADNESS

The manuscript
of Margery Kempe's
autobiography written
in the early 1400s.

*'Living high above her bodily wits' – but was the 'madness' of a fifteenth-
century English gentlewoman divine folly, marital stress or the stirrings of
a self-conscious feminist?*

Roy Porter

Roy Porter is senior lecturer in the social history of medicine at the Wellcome Institute, London, and author of *A Social History of Madness: Stories of the Insane* (Weidenfeld & Nicolson, 1987).

THE HISTORY OF MADNESS MUST SURELY form part of the 'history of mentalities'. It poses, however, obvious problems of documentation. Amongst the most fascinating yet enigmatic kinds of historical sources are the autobiographical writings of 'mad people'. Hundreds of these are available in print, the bulk of course, deriving from the last two centuries. Using them presents certain grave problems to the historian; for the very fact that they were written by deluded, or supposedly deluded, people demands even greater scepticism than that required by autobiography in general, a genre itself always to be approached with the utmost caution.

Psychiatrists have often claimed that mad people's writings have nothing meaningful to say about external reality, being only the symptoms of sickness. But this is too dismissive: for they frequently afford privileged insights into the secret mental cultures of the past, the extreme fantasies and fears commonly shared, yet standardly censored by polite culture.

They sometimes also provide critical commentaries upon the official rationalities and moralities of past societies – perhaps paralleling the jibes of the Fool or court jester or the subversive 'world turned upside-down' parodies present in plebeian culture. And not least, they offer a unique record from inside of the experiences of derangement and alienation, and of the confrontations of madness with the all too often unreasonable world of the rational. Such writings have been little drawn upon by historians, but would amply repay further study.

The opening pages of what is in effect the earliest English autobiography present an account of a woman going mad. 'When this creature was twenty years of age, or somewhat more', wrote Margery Kempe – or rather 'dictated', since she, like most late medieval women, was illiterate – 'she was married to a worshipful burgess and was with child within a short time, as nature would have it'. She was sick during pregnancy, and after childbirth, what we would call puerperal insanity set in. 'She despaired of her life and sent for her confessor', for 'she was continually hindered by her enemy – the devil'. She believed she was damned: 'Because of the dread she had of damnation on the one hand, and Satan's sharp reproving of her on the other, this creature went out of her mind and was amazingly disturbed and tormented with spirits for half a year, eight weeks and odd days'.

Margery Kempe's experience, recorded early in the fifteenth-century, commands attention as the story of a mad person; but it is doubly interesting as an account of a mad *woman*, for these are rare so many centuries ago. We have, it is true, been inundated over the last century with writing by

First published in *History Today*, February 1988, pp. 39-44. Reproduced by kind permission of History Today, Ltd. 83-84 Berwick Street, London W1V 3PJ England.

This 14th-century illustration of a Caesarian birth illustrates one of the many hazards of medieval childbirth – which Margery Kempe, as a mother of fourteen, was well aware of.

disturbed and distracted women; indeed modern culture draws attention to the affinities between psychic disturbance, psychiatry, and women. Nowadays a significantly higher percentage of women than men end up under psychiatric care, in mental institutions, or simply taking tranquilisers. And this may be because our 'patriarchal' society places women under special strains, and allegedly uses psychiatry as a special tool for coping with the disorders thereby induced (prison for men, the mental hospital for women, it is often said).

Certainly, ever since Charcot's and Freud's studies of hysterical women, it has been the female unconscious, and, almost inevitably, the mystery of female sexuality, which have formed the grand arcanum of psychiatry (the great question, thought Freud, was 'what do women want?'). In some sense, somatic diseases have become 'male', and mental disorders 'female'. The problems of being a woman in a man's world have led a disproportionate number of women to break down, and in turn have disproportionately preoccupied psychiatry.

Yet what is intriguing is how few self-portraits we possess written by disturbed women before the last couple of centuries. Of course, women were never meant to speak for themselves ('Silence' was even a girl's Christian name in Stuart England); and in any case, their literacy

rates were lower. All the same, the period between the Reformation and the emergence of Romanticism – when autobiography itself blossomed as a genre – is as relatively lacking in writing by women recording their own journeys into mental *terra incognita* as the last century and a half – the era of female emancipation – has been rich. Practically all the writings by disturbed people surviving from early modern England are by men – James Carkesse, the Restoration poet, George Trosse, the Presbyterian minister, Goodwin Wharton, the Whig politician, and so forth. Only with the coming of the age of sensibility from the mid-eighteenth-century was disorder effectively 'feminised'.

This is certainly not, of course, because during the early modern centuries women were pictures of mental health. Michael MacDonald's exemplary study of Richard Napier, the early seventeenth-century Buckinghamshire doctor-parson, has shown that most of the clients attending him with 'psychiatric' problems – they called themselves 'distracted', 'disordered', 'melancholic', and so forth – were women. That is not surprising. They were crushed by the burdens of having to sustain multiple functions – productive labour, running households, raising families, coping with husbands. Moreover, the gynaecological consequences of repeated dangerous childbirths eroded their health, both

physical and mental.

Thus medieval and early modern women commonly underwent mental trauma, yet infrequently left accounts of it. Therein lies the unique interest of Margery Kempe's lifestory. For not only did she record her experiences in great detail, but was able to make sense of them, during her mad bouts and in their aftermath – though not in terms of being a mad woman, but through the idiom of the Christian life of the spirit.

If what she got her scribe to write down for her in her 'book' (it is expressed in the third person) truly reflects what she felt and told people throughout her life, she never sought to conceal that she had indeed been through an episode of madness in her early twenties. Strange experiences beset her later as well, not least some extremely lurid sexual temptations. Some of her actions, she admitted, were not those of 'reason'. She envisaged herself running around 'like a mad woman' or like 'a drunk woman'; she could think of herself 'without reason', living 'high above her bodily wits'. And she was kept acutely aware that her expressions of religious devotion – such as her incessant weeping, often for many hours at a time – were liable to be censured as crazy, and believed to be the work either of the Devil or of disease.

Unlike certain other 'holy people', Margery never celebrated delirium as a positive, heaven-sent religious ecstasy. She regarded her chief bout of disturbance, following the birth of her first child, as a providential rap on the knuckles, with which she was visited essentially because she was then a vainglorious, thoughtless and proud young lady, susceptible first to the temptations and then to the threats of the Devil. While out of her mind, her conduct had been abominable; she had 'slandered' her husband and despaired of salvation. She did violence against herself and needed to be 'forcibly restrained both day and night'. She had forsaken God. By His infinite mercy, the Almighty had returned her to her 'right mind', rescued her from sin, and shown her His paths. Still she remained unregenerate, wedded to this world and its worldlings, and it took the business failure of the brew-

Currently on view at the 'Age of Chivalry' exhibition at the Royal Academy, Piccadilly.

The devil's snares; (above) at work among idle gossips in the 14th-century stained-glass from Stanford, Northamptonshire; (below) wooing a woman in a 15th-century woodcut by Ulvicus Molitorus – both temptations which Margery Kempe believed herself preyed upon in moments of weakness.

ery she owned – her beer providentially all went flat – to humble her and turn her from this wicked world to true holiness.

God's first warning had merely affected her head; this second arrow penetrated to her heart. Though subsequently leading a life which to many contemporaries appeared perverse, Margery Kempe did not present her way of living through the idiom of exceptional divine madness. On the contrary, she was insistent that her own conduct was regular, and her faith orthodoxy itself. She had to be: she was living in an age when the religiously deviant were readily accused of being heretical Lollards, and Lollards were often tried and sometimes burnt.

Having undergone the twin crises of puerperal insanity and business failure, Margery experienced an overwhelming urge to sever herself from all the ways of the world, convinced that, by contrast to conditions on earth, it was 'merry in heaven' (how did she know? critics demanded). Breaking free meant a considerable wrench. She had been born around 1373 the daughter of a prosperous King's Lynn burgess (her father was successively mayor and Member of Parliament for the town). She had a husband to whom she was lastingly, if unconventionally, attached, and by whom she had a growing family – she gave birth, all told, to fourteen children. She was in no position simply to renounce the world by entering a nunnery: church dignitories would never have permitted it.

As she was forcibly reminded through the rest of her life, her attempts to follow what she saw as the divine signposts met enduring hostility. 'Woman, give up this life that you lead, and go and spin, and card wool, as other women do', the worldlings and the authorities told her. Wherever she went there was such 'evil talk about her' that the cleric who penned her life story was even afraid of recriminations against himself.

Sickened by the flesh, Margery strove to free herself from bondage to the world. She fasted; she did bodily penance; she clad herself in a hairshirt. And above all she sought to free herself from sexual slavery, knowing how the pleasures she and her husband once had taken in carnal delights were offensive to God, and now finding them 'abominable' to herself. She told her husband she now loved God alone; His body alone was what she wanted, sacramentally, in a mystical marriage. She begged him to accept a pact of mutual chastity; he agreed in principle, but, echoing St Augustine, said 'not yet', and for long insisted upon having his will. Eventually they came to an agreement by which he signed away his conjugal rights in return for Margery paying his debts.

Despite this apprentice mortification, she remained abysmally vainglorious. 'She thought that she loved God more than He loved her', she was to recall. In that state, she was easy prey to the Devil's snares. He laid for her a trap of lechery. A man made advances to her. Flattered, she willingly surrendered, only at the last moment to be spurned by him. Mortified, she craved Christ's forgiveness; it was granted, and, in return, her Saviour promised she could wear a hairshirt in her heart. As Christ had been persecuted, so should she be. Thereafter, tribulations were seen by Margery as secret tokens of holiness. Life best made sense to her when battling with the moils and toils which constitute the bulk of her wonderfully down-to-earth autobiography.

Her spiritual life began to blossom. She began seeing visions, and these were accompanied by the copious bouts of weeping which attended her to the end of her days. She started informally shriving penitents and acting as a mouthpiece for homely divine guidance. A 'miracle' secured her escape when a piece of falling masonry struck her, but did her no harm. And, not least, Christ mercifully intervened to kill off her husband's sexual appetite. She told him she would rather that he were slain than have to submit to his lusts, preferring to make herself 'freely available to God'. Her husband rebuked her: she was not a good wife. The general picture of their relationship given by the *Book of Margery Kempe* is, however, one of mutual understanding, support and chairty.

Margery's increasingly conspicuous religious observances brought her public reproof. Her weeping bouts were despised; she was called 'false hypocrite', and her friends were advised to abandon her. Furthermore, she was accused of having the Devil in her and of being a 'false Lollard' ('and the people said, "Take her and burn her"'). But such trials merely fortified her sense of the Divine indwelling. When she heard mention of Christ's passion, she would swoon in ecstasy and experience divine music. The Lord called her his mother, his sister, his daughter, and she conversed – as in regular speech she insisted – with St Paul, St Peter and St Katherine.

Margery was initially perturbed. Were these voices and visions authentic? Or temptations of the Devil? Or simply sensory delusions? Seeking guidance, she consulted Dame Julian of Norwich, the contemplative mystic. From her she received reassurance: these were not fantasies of her own devising but truly signs from God. Margery must persevere: 'The more contempt, shame and reproof that you have in this world, the more is your merit in the sight of God'. Margery followed Dame Julian's words, which were reiterated by many 'honoured doctors of divinity, both religious men and others of secular habit'. Soon God was telling her that she would be the recipient of special revelations denied even to

His own daughter Bridget, the Swedish mystic.

Reassured, Margery grew in confidence of her religious calling. Her holy circle expanded, and she attained a reputation as a woman with a divine vocation. Her practical advice was sought by people anguished over the great decisions of life; she relayed to them God's answers. She acquired minor powers of prophecy. One day, she predicted a great storm. It came about. Many remained suspicious, and she continued to entertain great fears of 'delusions and deceptions by her spiritual enemies'. But God comforted her by saying that though he would load her with tribulations on earth, when in heaven, she would be granted all her desires. At a later stage He told her that her earthly life would be the only purgatory she would ever suffer. Margery's conviction of divine love increased. God informed her: 'to me you are a love unlike any other', and, later, 'you do not know how much I love you'; for her part, she wished that it had been God that had taken her virginity. Eventually, being now on 'homely terms with God', she had a 'wedding ring to Jesus Christ' made at divine command, with *'Jesus est Amor Meus'* inscribed on it. The love of God proved the shame of the world.

Eventually, she set off on pilgrimage for the Holy Land. This was, ironically, her one visit to Bethlehem. So joyful was she at the holy sights that she nearly swooned and fell off her ass. And being so close to the scenes of Christ's Passion led her to weep and wail more than ever, and to 'wrestle with her body'. She was visited by a special vision of Christ's crucified corpse, and overwhelmed by irresistible impulses to weep. She could not stop it; it was the 'gift of the Holy Ghost'. Her roaring and crying riled her fellow pilgrims. Some thought she was just ill-behaved, puffed up with 'pretence and hypocrisy', or physically sick, suffering from epilepsy. Others accused her of drunkenness. Still others believed she had been possessed by evil spirits.

It was a dilemma which continually faced her when her tears poured out her passion. On a later occasion, she records:

Many said there was never saint in heaven that cried as she did, and from that they concluded that she had a devil within her which caused that crying. And this they said openly, and much more evil talk. She took everything patiently for our Lord's love, for she knew very well that the Jews said much worse of His own person than people did of her, and therefore she took it the more meekly.

As she later put it, if Christ's blood had had to flow, the least true believers should expect or want would be floods of their own lamentations. She asked God to grant her a 'well of tears'; and to one who tetchily asked her: 'why do you weep so, woman?', she responded, 'Sir, you shall wish some day that you had wept as sorely as I'. What other behaviour could be so appropriate in this vale of tears? She knew her Psalter which assured her that 'They that sow in tears shall reap in joy'.

Apart from a further pilgrimage late in life to shrines in North Germany, Margery passed the rest of her days in England. She had undergone a formal religious ceremony binding herself and her husband in mutual chastity, and thereafter they lived apart. When her husband became old and senile however, she returned to nurse him, against her own initial inclinations, but following God's advice. Meanwhile her religious reputation grew. She established good relations with numerous anchorites, contemplatives, scholars and other holy people; some evidently read to her out of the corpus of mystical writings. Clearly, many ordinary Christians accepted her special holiness, and were glad to have her weep for them.

Others were not so happy. Her fellow English pilgrims had found her a cross, with her continual wailing, her special dietary demands, and her moral and religious rebukes; sometimes they forced her to leave their party. Similar tribulations beset her in England. 'Evil talk' about her grew, and many said she had the Devil in her. Clerics and congregations deplored the way she constantly interrupted services and ceremonies with her weeping and wailing at the name of Jesus. A friar barred her from his sermons, claiming she was suffering from 'sickness'.

More seriously, she frequently ran the risk of ecclesiastical prosecution. Authorities both civil and religious looked with considerable suspicion upon this wife and mother wandering around the country in the guise of a holy woman, berating people for their hypocrisy and ungodly ways, and sometimes urging wives to leave their husbands and follow God (Who had informed her, that many women, if only they could abandon their husbands, would love him the way she did). Her insistence upon wearing white linked her in the eyes of some with dubious flagellant groups, while others, including the Abbot of Leicester, accused her of being a 'false heretic', ie, of involvement with Lollardy. 'She has the Devil in her', she reported such churchmen as saying, 'for she speaks of the Gospel'. Under examination however, her own faith proved triumphantly orthodox.

All the while, her love of God grew. She was privileged to overhear conversations about her between God the Father and the Son, and she records, in her homely way, that the Godhead informed her that he liked having her around to talk to. Her attention became fixed upon the 'manhood' of Christ; but it was the Godhead Himself who finally married her. The Father told her, 'I must be intimate with you and lie in your bed with you … take me to you as your wedded husband … Kiss my mouth, my head, and my feet as sweetly as you want'. The earlier sexual temptations which she had undergone were not, however, entirely a thing of the past; and in time she was visited by 'abominable visions', conjured up by the Devil, of being beset by threatening male genitals and being commanded to prostitute herself to them. Temporarily she felt forsaken by God, but recovered. At another point, she was overcome by a desire to kiss male lepers; her confessor prudently advised her to stick to women.

How are we to assess Margery Kempe's life? One type of interpretation simply confirms the truth of her visions. Katherine Cholmeley for example has argued that because Margery's experiences conform so closely to those of other well attested contemplatives and visionaries, they

must literally be true, and should be accepted at face value as providential and miraculous. Other Christian historians, however, have taken a more jaundiced view, suggesting that Margery Kempe 'contaminated' the pure tradition of mystical contemplation with her emotional idiosyncrasies. All such interpretations are in danger of confusing history with hagiography, and begging the true historical questions.

The same stricture applies, *mutatis mutandis*, to interpretations advanced by psychoanalytical sleuths, who seem bent on proving her a 'sinner'. The truth about Margery Kempe, Trudy Drucker has thus argued, is that she constituted a 'case of religious hysteria', occasionally overlaid with 'overtly psychotic' episodes. In a similar way Dr Anthony Ryle has diagnosed her as a case of 'hysterical personality organisation with occasional "psychotic" episodes', during which she 'hallucinated about the sexuality of the males surrounding her'. Margery should best be treated, argues Drucker, as an 'unfortunate' who never recovered from puerperal fever, and who suffered from further organic or psychosomatic conditions such as epilepsy and migraine. She indulged, moreover, in 'psychotic behavior', in particular a propensity to 'self-inflicted pain', which, Drucker believes, resulted from 'pathologic distortion of the sexual impulse'. Her hysteria was unconsciously designed to serve the 'protective function' of keeping her 'agonized and distorted sexuality' at bay; this was not always successful, however, and her 'disguised sexual fantasies and guilts' sometimes thrust their way to the surface.

Margery was thus a 'victim of hysteria'; and some of its manifestations in her were 'repellant' and 'silly'. All the same, hysteria afforded her many 'secondary gains', bestowing upon her 'unique attention' (she took a 'child-like pride in her attacks'). That is why Kempe 'resists any suggestion that her spells are of natural origin'; had she accepted that view, she would have been reduced to just 'another uninteresting sick woman'. She was not, however, entirely to blame, Drucker continues, because such hysteria is inevitable in ages when female sexuality is repres-

sed. In any case, behind her egoism, childhood events were responsible for her condition: 'probably the roots of her disease were buried deeply in childhood experiences thoroughly rejected by her adult recollection'. Alas, no Freudian couch was available to bring these to the surface and they remained 'past recall' and thus unrecorded.

Psychodynamic *post mortems* such as these seem trivial (for they do little more than fix fancy labels on the unknown); gratuitously dogmatic (in the absence of any shred of supportive evidence, there is no reason to attribute Margery's adult attitudes to childhood experiences); and, not least, harsh. They operate by identifying so-called 'psychological symptoms', and then turning them into moral verdicts which masquerade as medical diagnoses. Their blend of accusing and excusing isolates the individual and neglects the nexi of social, sexual and ideological pressures within which people's lives are led. It is easy to speak boldly of Margery's 'distorted sexuality' (eg, her wish to make her relationship with her husband chaste and to marry God); it is another to remember – as Drucker does not – that she bore her husband fourteen children, all but one apparently against her wishes. The absence of any substantial mention in her *Life* of her children surely indicates Margery's indifference to the motherhood thrust upon her. Likewise Drucker draws attention to Margery's rape anxieties, suggesting that they are further symptoms of her hysterically distorted sexuality. She might have remembered that crossing Europe as a pilgrim was perilous for a woman. Phrases like 'distorted sexuality' and 'hysteria' are inevitably stigmatising.

Both the devoutly Christian and the psycho-analytical approaches to understanding Margery Kempe's *Book* thus seem flawed. There is of course no single master-key to Margery's condition, or 'correct' way of reading her life. But the best way forward surely lies in attempting to understand her as a child of her times, religious, social and personal. Her mad behaviour expressed the conventions, beliefs and language of her day, though in extreme forms. For one thing, she was attempting to resolve the common dilemmas of true piety for a woman of the world. Though medieval society and medieval Christendom were both highly patriarchal, special institutions and roles were set aside for women in pursuit of the religious life within the Church – portals which were closed in later Protestant circles. Above all, it was possible for some women to escape the routine cares of marriage and the dangers of motherhood by entering a cloister, where they might make their devotions to the service of spiritual replicas of the life they had escaped: the cults of God the Father and God the Son.

For the more zealous this could lead to highly intense and deeply spiritual experiences, sometimes soaring into mysticism. Christianity itself encouraged – while also setting strict limits upon – ecstatic exercises such as mortification of the flesh and fasting. As Rudolph Bell has recently stressed, self-inflicted asceticism was occasionally carried to ambiguous extremes by holy women, who perhaps descended into a pathologically self-denying condition akin to today's *anorexia nervosa*. Outside the nunnery, traditions of mysticism and contemplation had emerged as suitable for married women. St Bridget of Sweden, with whose life Margery Kempe was familiar, had provided a model by arranging a pact of chastity with her husband and spending much of her life on pilgrimage; Dorothea of Mordau had similarly shown her holiness through a gift of tears, expressing by her compassion her affinity with the Passion. Such emotional piety extended the late medieval emphasis upon the 'humanity of Christ' and the Holy Family in ways especially fitting for women. Margery Kempe was clearly

Saint Bridget setting down her revelations with visions of the Virgin and Child and Trinity overhead – she also like Margery Kempe, had set a pact of chastity with her husband.

expresing her faith within these traditions, albeit in rather extreme forms. It would serve no purpose to label such exercise of spiritual discipline as a psychiatric disorder, not least because it was regulated by the conscious control both of the individual ascetic and of ecclesiastical superiors. Mystical flights and contemplations were highly programmed activities.

Thus the 'madness' of Margery Kempe is intelligible within the pietistic traditions of her time. It is also intelligible in terms of her own personal 'career', her attempt to take charge of and make sense of her own existence and place in society and under God. She knew that many people thought her voices and visions – indeed, her whole course of life – signified madness, to be attributed to illness or the Devil. She

pondered that dilemma deeply, and sought advice. But the path to which she aspired – a closer walk, a spiritual communion, marriage even with God – was a path legitimate within the ideals of her times, though one exceptional and precarious. Margery wished, from early days, to free herself from a pattern of life (marriage, sex and childbirth), associated by her with madness and the Devil's temptations. The contemplative scenes into which she escaped of course reproduced in spiritual idiom the landscape of the mundane world: marriage to God replaced marriage to her husband. But they did so in ways which to her were benign and which allowed her a substantial element of control over her own destiny, otherwise essentially denied to her sex.

This is not to deny that Margery Kempe was – for a time at least – 'mad'; but the madness had a 'method' in it, and provided a source of strength through which she came to terms with and helped resolve the key dilemmas facing all pious women in the late Middle Ages.

This article is based on a recent talk given to the Past and Present Society in Oxford at a meeting sponsored by *History Today*, and on a chapter in *A Social History of Madness: Stories of the Insane* just published by Weidenfeld and Nicolson at £14.95.

FOR FURTHER READING

The Book of Margery Kempe, rendered into modern English, edited by Barry Windeatt (Penguin Classics, 1985); H.S. Bennett, *Six Medieval Men and Women* (Cambridge University Press, 1955); S.M. Stuard (ed.), *Women in Medieval Society* (University of Pennsylvania Press, 1976); Rudolph Bell, *Holy Anorexia* (University of Chicago Press, 1985); K. Cholmeley, *Margery Kempe: Genius and Mystic* (London, 1947); Clarissa W. Atkinson, *Mystic and Pilgrim. The Book and the World of Margery Kempe* (Cornell University Press, 1983).

THE CID OF HISTORY
AND THE HISTORY OF THE CID

A myth for all seasons — the treatment through the centuries of Spain's medieval hero as a blend of Robin Hood and King Arthur provides revealing insights into the political needs of both his contemporary and more recent biographers.

Peter Linehan

THE CID – THE INDIVIDUAL who embodies Spain's medieval past for the casually curious just as securely as Robin Hood does England's – has provided successive generations of Spaniards with what they have needed to discover in him. More than this, he has also been permitted to appropriate the period of history through which he lived. 'The Cid's Spain' has a meaning and force that 'Robin Hood's England' lacks. For this Ramon Menéndez Pidal is principally responsible. Pidal's *La España del Cid* was first published in 1929. By the time its seventh and last edition appeared forty years later, in the year after the death of its author (1869-1968) the Spain of the Cid's lifetime had become The Cid's Spain and historians, critical though some of them may have been of particular features of Pidal's view of the period, had slipped into the habit of thinking and writing of it thus. Rodrigo Díaz de Vivar had upstaged his lord and king, Alfonso VI of Castile, something he had studiously refrained from doing in his own lifetime (?1043-99).
History has its great men, of course,

but some historians need them and search harder for them than others. The effects of Pidal's enchantment with his hero (the only imaginable English equivalent of which would presuppose a bond between Sir John Neale and the Earl of Essex) are still strongly felt in 1987. While every aspect of the Cid and his Poem has been picked over, Alfonso VI, alone amongst Spain's medieval rulers of like stature, still awaits a serious study based upon the dispersed records of his achievements and failures.

It is perhaps not surprising that to Philip II in the sixteenth century the Cid should have appeared a figure of heroic sanctity worthy of canonisation, but that to Arabists of the nineteenth he was an unsavoury ruffian. What must seem remarkable is that as late as 1805 J.F. Masdeu the Jesuit who, it was said, 'believed in almost everything' would not believe in the Cid's very existence, and would admit it only to the extent of denouncing him as a traitor and criminal. Masdeu was a Catalan; hence his agnosticism or at best denunciation of

the warrior reputed to have humiliated the Count of Barcelona. Three years later General Thibault, Napoleon's Governor of Old Castile, was similarly assured by J.A. Llorente, the historian of the Inquisition, that there never had been a Cid. To the fellow countryman of Corneille whose *Le Cid* (1637) had so enraged Cardinal Richelieu by glorifying the national hero of France's enemy, and who was currently wondering what to do with some bones in his possession said to be those of that hero, Llorente's assurance came as a blow. Dedicated as they were to subjecting Spain to the joys of enlightenment, Masdeu and Llorente identified the Cid with the obscurantism and pious frauds they so much abhorred. What was legendary had to be rejected.

It is for a proper understanding of what is legendary about the Cid's exploits that scholars continue to strive in their researches into the purpose and period of composition of the sources from which Pidal constructed the Cid's history. For if these sources are not, as Pidal held them to be, all more or less contemporary with their

From *History Today*, September 1987, pp. 26-32. Reproduced by kind permission of History Today, Ltd., 83-84 Berwick Street, London W1V 3PJ, England.

subject, but were composed fifty or a hundred years after his death then they are less instructive about the Cid than they are about the earliest use that later ages have made of him.

Most later ages have found a use for the Cid. At the beginning of the present century the loss of the last fragments of Spain's American empire prompted the architect of national regeneration, Joaquin Costa, to urge that a double lock be placed on the Cid's tomb so that he should never ride again or, at most, that only the civic Cid should be let out: the Cid of the legendary encounter with Alfonso VI at Santa Gadea – the Castilian Runnymede at which the monarch had been called to clear himself of murdering his brother; the Cid as statesman commissioned to root out the guilty men of 1898.

It was the military hero that Pidal offered to the public in the prologue to *La España del Cid*, however, the 'powerful influence on youth' in an age in which 'the military were not the most highly esteemed of the social virtues'. The year was 1929, and Primo de Rivera's dictatorship was on the point of collapse. Seven years later the military made their comeback and Francoist propaganda was quick to acclaim the *Caudillo*, installed as he was in the Cid's Burgos, as the new Cid. Conveniently forgetting the services rendered to the Christians' adversaries by the symbol of eleventh-century nationalism, and equally untroubled by Franco's introduction into the country of Moroccan legionaries, the author of an up-dated poem of the Cid – *Romancero de la Reconquista* (1937) – gloried in the almost unqualified support Franco was receiving from the leaders of the Spanish Church, just as Rodrigo Díaz had from the abbot of Cardeña.

In 1939 the fall of Valencia sealed Franco's victory: another Cid parallel for the paladins of the New Reconquest – though an unnerving one, it might have been thought, in view of the Moorish recovery of that city after the Cid's death. But history had served its turn, and 1939 was no time for pedantry. Ten years earlier Pidal had deplored the lack of a national public monument to the national hero. In 1943 the authorities made good this lapse, erecting the massive equestrian statue which stands, the present century's tribute to the Mid-

dle Ages, in the Cid's native Burgos. But history did not stop there. In 1963, soon after the filming of Samuel Bronston's epic had taught the public to think of the Cid and Jimena as Charlton Heston and Sophia Loren (and incidentally bringing some much needed hard currency to the Spanish economy), the New Cid was showing signs of wear, and a message (for which neither Pidal nor his critics could be cited in support) was chalked up on Seville Cathedral: '*El Cid era maricón*' (The Cid was a fairy). It was soon rubbed out.

Incapable of being rubbed out because it is memorialised in the Burgos monument, in the form of the five massive tomes representing his life's work on the Cid, is the name of Menéndez Pidal. And justly so. It was Pidal who rescued the Cid from the scepticism of the nineteenth century and rendered him serviceable to the twentieth, he who gave the revisionists something to revise, and to whose work all who have come after have had to and continue to have to refer. What passes for our knowledge of the Cid's life and times is based on Pidal's reconstruction and his conviction that the sources from which that reconstruction was done were all nearly contemporary with the events they describe: the 129-line Latin verse *Carmen Campidoctoris* (circa 1090), the Latin *Historia Roderici* (1110), and the vernacular epic *Cantar de Mio Cid* – usually known as *Poema de Mio Cid* – (circa 1110, revised circa 1140).

Mio Cid's very title proclaims the hybrid nature of the society into which he was born probably in the early 1040s: a combination of the romance 'My' and the Arabic 'Lord' (*sid, sayyid*). (In the Latin History his other title – *Campidoctor* [*Campeador*: 'The Battler'] – is invariably used.) Vivar, his birthplace, is a hamlet some ten kilometres north of Burgos. In the 1040s Vivar was a frontier place on a frontier not with the Moorish south but with the currently more hostile Christian kingdom of Navarre. As the epithet of the poem constantly states, The Cid was 'born in a good hour'. The 1040s and the following decades were all good years to be born in in a country which had everything to offer the resourceful and the adventurous. The authority of the Caliphate of Cordoba had collapsed in 1031 leaving al-Andalus fragmented and weak,

easy prey to the fragmented and strong kingdoms of the north – Leon, Castile, Navarre, Aragon – and the county of Barcelona. Huge sums of gold was paid in tribute by the south to the north. Much of this was then rerouted beyond the peninsula, notably to the Abbey of Cluny of which Fernando I and Alfonso VI were massive benefactors.

Still vaster fortunes remained to be made from the sale of protection and military service by these proto-*condottieri*. Pidal held that term as it was applied to the Cid in the last century to be offensive. Yet that in essence was the function which he and others like him continued to perform until 1085. In that year Alfonso VI chose to reoccupy the dairy rather than continue milking the cow, and took possession of the old Visigothic capital, Toledo. The Cid was not involved in this, the major event of his lifetime. But for him, as for all Christian Spain, the consequences of it were profound. In response to the loss of Toledo the Muslim kings of the south called in Yūsuf, leader of the fanatical Almoravids from beyond the Straits of Gibraltar to provide protection of a kind different from that for which for half a century they had paid. At Sagrajas in 1086 Yūsuf inflicted a crushing defeat on Alfonso VI and inaugurated a century and a half of peninsular warfare which lasted until Seville was reconquered in 1248. During these years religious sentiments predominated as they had never done before. The Spanish Reconquest was presented as a branch of the crusade movement. For the beginnings of this development Alfonso VI's Cluniac advisors are held to have been partly responsible. By a strange coincidence Toledo surrendered to Alfonso VI on the very day that Gregory VII died.

In 1085 The Cid had lived three-quarters of his life. In only the last thirteen years of it was there a specifically religious content to the power struggle of the peninsula and since even during this period the Cid was prepared to do business with the followers of the Prophet it is not unreasonable to regard him as an entrepreneur by conviction – an entrepreneur of substance. His career, from his emergence in the late 1050s until his death, was bound up with the royal house of Castile-Leon. The

Cid's story, in history as in legend, was a tale of successive exile and return determined by the state of his relationship with the king and the latter's attitude to him of wrath or favour, ire or benevolence. On this stretch of Europe's eleventh-century frontier reputations and fortunes were quickly made, and as soon lost. If only a fraction of what the record tells about the Cid's career is to be believed, the tittle-tattle of the envious had a lot to do with his ups and downs. Certainly there was no standing still – except for the rural labourer (and he was to that extent vulnerable). 'Whoever remains in one spot stands to lose.' Thus the poetic Cid to his followers after a triumphant skirmish – as the poetic Cid's skirmishes invariably were. The judgement held good too for peninsular society from 1086 until 1248. This was, as a recent historian of the period has described it, a society organised for war.

The poetic Cid reminds his followers at this point that they must prepare to move on. To move on necessitated a sturdy mount. Possession of a horse was an indicator of social status, and the quality of the creature an index of it. Not just mobility – the ability to pursue and attack – but upward social mobility too was a matter of horses. Upward social mobility indeed depended upon the ability to pursue and attack. The poetic Cid's horse, Babieca, was an unexampled beast. The Cid towards the end of the poem offered it to his king. But Alfonso would not accept it since only the Cid was fit to ride it. Babieca means 'chump'. The Cid's Babieca was so called, according to legend, because when as a lad Rodrigo was offered a colt by his godfather, the priest Peyre Pringos (Fat Pete), he plumped for a poor-looking specimen as the animals were shown to him. 'Chump', the bystanders said, meaning Rodrigo and not the horse, though fortunately for the Spanish epic it was to the horse that the name stuck. (If the Babieca of this interview was the same horse as the one later admired by the king it is a miracle that it had survived so long and no wonder that when in 1948 the Duke of Alba excavated for Babieca's remains at Cardeña there was no sign of them.)

Rodrigo Díaz was born into the lower nobility (infanzones), his father (it was later claimed) being descended from Laín Calvo, one of the founding fathers of Castilian independence from the tenth-century kingdom of Leon. He was knighted by the Infante Sancho during the latter years of the reign of Fernando I and after Fernando's death in 1065 remained attached to Sancho, Fernando's eldest son to whom Castile had been left as a kingdom, while his master contended with his two brothers but principally with the future Alfonso VI, whom he defeated, as it seemed decisively, at Golpejera in 1072. Later that year, however, Sancho was assassinated. Hence the Oath of Santa Gadea.

As the new reign began the Cid had old enemies. Yet the Cid received signal favours from Alfonso in these years, and not least his wife Jimena, the king's niece. Indeed all remained well until 1080-81 when the Cid, on a rent-collecting expedition to the King of Seville, became ensnared with García Ordoñez, another Castilian nobleman who was similarly engaged in the direction of Granada. In the course of these events García Ordoñez had his beard plucked by the Cid. This was serious. In the law codes of the time the penalties for beard-plucking were on a par with those for wilful castration. That, compounded by what was adjudged a further indiscretion committed in the king's absence, sufficed to secure the Cid's first exile.

In Pidal's words, life with the Moors was the inevitable fate of every exile. From 1081-86 the Cid earned his bread in the service of the Muslim rulers of Zaragoza. After a short-lived reconciliation with Alfonso he returned east where he was actively engaged south of Zaragoza towards the kingdom of Valencia. A second exile merged into a third: just two pages separate them in Pidal's 600-page history. During the last ten years of his life the Cid was occupied exclusively in the east of the Peninsula. After a siege lasting twenty months the city of Valencia fell to him in June 1094, an event which was followed by a settling of scores for which the Arab historians ensured that he would never be wholly exonerated. From 1094 until his death in 1099 the Cid ruled Valencia, and enjoyed the consolation of a Christian cathedral ruled by a French bishop in what had been the city's chief mosque. Three years after his death, in 1102, Alfonso VI evacuated the Cid's widow and what was left of the Christian garrison together with the hero's remains. According to the History, these were interred at Cardeña.

This is an extraordinary story of activity across the lines. Yet its extraordinariness depends upon assumptions about the nature of those lines which neither the Spanish observer of them centuries later nor any other observer is, for differing reasons, eager to contemplate. Clearly there are problems about regarding the Cid as a 'Christian hero'. Evidently he was a freebooter who offered what he had to offer wherever he could secure the best price for it.

For all this, the Cid's reputation survived him. In the late 1140s the author of the Chronicle of Alfonso VII, who was more certainly French than he was Castilian, represented him as the indomitable archetype whose victims had been the counts of Catalonia equally with the Muslim. In the same years the anonymous author of the *Historia Roderici* provided what to some must seem a one-eyed history of the subject which notices the Cid only when he is in the east of the peninsula and loses sight of him altogether whenever he strays into Castile, yet which provides what feeble framework there may be for the construction of his biography. And, to judge by appearances, the manuscript of the *Carmen*, whatever the date of its text may have been, can hardly have been much later than about 1160. By the end of the century the Cid had made the jump from the genre of biography into that of national history by earning inclusion in the *Chronica Najerensis*.

Exceptional as it was for any non-royal personage of the period in Spain to receive any biographical attention, however patchy, posterity's impression of Rodrigo Díaz would have remained a very two-dimensional one from the *Historia* alone. For the Cid as a human figure, and especially as a credible one, we are indebted to the Poem's powerful yet nuanced portrait. The intermittently tender Cid of the Poem, the loving husband and the fond father, belongs to the cultural world of the twelfth-century Renaissance as emphatically as the single-mindedly martial Cid of the History does not. How he acquired that personality – whether by an invisible process of continuous renewal, as Pidal believed, according to which the Poem as we have it represents the latest stage of an oral tradition fostered by a succession of inevitably anonymous minstrels; or, alternatively, was the creation of the named scribe of the single surviving manuscript of work – is a question ultimately insoluble. Its traits, however, in comparison with that of the Cid of the History, and what the poet chose to emphasise and to omit can suggest some answers – though such a process obviously runs the risk of pursuing a circular argument.

By any reckoning the poetic Cid is a transformation. Nowhere in the poem is there any suggestion that he ever served a Moorish master, nowhere any sign of the Cid who had sold his services to Mohammed's cause as willingly as to Christ's. On the contrary it is the Cid's adversary the Count of Barcelona who has Moorish troops, and although the poem portrays one sympathetic Moor – the 'noble Moor' Avengalvón – as 'a fine brave fellow' and the Cid's 'amigo de paz', the Moors in the poem are the enemy. In battle 'the Moors called on Mohammed and the Christians on Santiago'. The lesson of Sagrajas has been learned, and a key figure in the process is the Bishop of Valencia, the Frenchman Jerome who had left home and joined the Cid, he says, 'for the desire I felt to kill a Moor or two'. Jerome claims a place in the front line of battle and accounts for more than just one or two of the enemy. Indeed he lost count. Jerome is an authentic man of the territorial reconquest which, in this literary creation, has become a religious crusade.

The second major shift in the Poem is geographical. While the History ignores Burgos and Castile, these are the Poem's points of reference, the city from which at its beginning the hero sets off into exile and the land to which at its end he returns in triumph to be vindicated at the Cortes of Toledo. Valencia and the eastern regions of the country provide the Cid with fame and fortune, yet they are 'strange lands'. Above all the Cid is now a Christian and a Castilian.

As such he was responding to the needs and developments of the late twelfth century, to the period between the new Sagrajas, the Almohad defeat of Alfonso VIII of Castile at Alarcos in 1195 and Alfonso's revenge at Las Navas de Tolosa in 1212, and of a peninsula which since the emergence in the 1170s of the independent kingdoms of Portugal and Aragon (the latter with Valencia assigned to its zone of endeavour) was becoming accustomed to partition along national lines while Alfonso VIII assumed on behalf of Castile the defence of Christendom.

The single manuscript of the 3735-line poem had already lost its first page when it was discovered at Vivar in the sixteenth century. Despite its truncated state, however, its opening could scarcely have been bettered for dramatic effect and affective appeal. 'Tears streamed from his eyes as he turned his head and stood looking at them', in Hamilton and Parry's sensitive translation. The weeping hero is about to leave for the exile his enemies have contrived and is gazing upon his abandoned house (here another translator renders the poet's inventory in the style of an auctioneer's catalogue) and the family he must leave behind. These – his wife Jimena and young daughters Elvira and Sol – he entrusts to the safe keeping of the Abbot of Cardeña. He dupes two Jews of Burgos into lending him money on the security of a pair of chests filled with sand (not a notably heroic act in itself but one which the poet's audience might have approved in the atmosphere prevailing after the loss of Jerusalem in 1187, as the Jews of York for example learned to their cost).

His campaigns in the east begin, invariably ending in success and enormously enriching his followers. He seeks to be restored to the king's favour, sending Alfonso lavish gifts. At the third approach a reconciliation is achieved. At Alfonso's behest, Elvira and Sol are married to the Infantes de Carrión. Poor types the Cid's new sons-in-law prove. Slighted, they take their revenge by assaulting their wives in a dark wood and leaving them for dead. The Cid of battle's reaction to this outrage is surprising and much has been made of it by the Poem's interpreters. Instead of pursuing the Infantes with fire and slaughter he resorts to the twelfth-century equivalent of appointing a sub-committee. He prosecutes in the courts, in Alfonso VI's Cortes at Toledo. The Cortes proceedings provide the Poem's culmination and occupy almost a quarter of the work. Victorious at law, the Cid through his champions defeats the Infantes through theirs. The rulers of Navarre and Aragon are granted his daughters in marriage; so 'today the kings of Spain are related to him and all gain lustre from the fame of the fortunate Campeador'. The poet had ended and his story concludes in Castile at Carrión, not far from where it had begun. The Cid has returned to Valencia but the poet does not follow him there. All we are told is that he died at Pentecost.

Who was this poet? And when was his poem written? The answers to these questions seem to be provided in its last lines: 'Per Abbat le escrivio en el mes de mayo / en era de mill e .cc xlv. años' (Per Abbat wrote it down in May 1207 [= era 1245]). This seems clear enough. Yet over the years a plain reading of these words has been resisted. There is a gap in the date which Pidal believed once contained another c, giving the year 1307. 'Escrivio' means wrote it down in the sense of copied it out rather than composed it, it has been argued, making Per Abbat a mere drudge of the early fourteenth century rather than a writer of genius a century before. (The manuscript is indeed of the fourteenth century, but that of course provides no clues as to the date of the Poem's composition.) The 'plain reading' is supported by all manner of internal evidence and is now quite widely accepted.

A Per Abbat (not an uncommon name) has been found with the right credentials and connections: a layman pleading before the king's court at Carrión in 1223. The knowledge of Roman Law displayed in the account of the Cortes scene has suggested to some that the poet himself was learned in that law, was one of the 'muchos sabidores' from all over Castile whose presence on that occasion he mentions. The probability of this seems inescapable. Nor, at the turn of the twelfth and thirteenth centuries, would Per Abbat have needed to travel abroad to acquire whatever legal knowledge he possessed. He would not even have had to go so far as the university which Alfonso VIII founded at Palencia in these years, staffing it with scholars from Italy and France. (The presence there in the mid-1180s, recently established, of one such, Ugolino di Sesso, deserves especially to be mentioned: Ugolino's work was on precisely those procedural aspects of the law which the poetic Cid so skilfully deployed: appeals, recusation of judges, witnesses). He would not have needed a university at all, for the king's own household was staffed by Romanists. Pedro de Cardona who in the 1180s combined the office of royal chancellor with a teaching post at Montpellier was just one of those whose expertise was highly valued by a ruler coming to terms with the implications for Castile of the peninsula's new political configuration after the establishment of the flanking kingdoms of Portugal and (to the north of those 'strange lands') Aragon.

The Poem's emphases and supressions in comparison with the History could certainly support the view that it was composed in or not long before the year 1207 with a view to rallying Christian spirits before the coming encounter with the Almohads, at Las Navas in 1212. The Poem does indeed provide something for almost everyone: the prospect of social advancement of which the Cid is the incarnation, an example for the *infanzones*, reassurance for the hereditary nobility, with the whole social scene secure beneath the aegis of a king in whose *cort* right not might rules. It has even been suggested that the Poem was a work commissioned by the king and paid for by him, just as he had attracted the best scholars money could buy to Palencia. The poet exhibits great familiarity with the Burgos area. But the possibility deserves to be considered that he was also somehow associated with Toledo where he locates the dénouement of his work.

The early years of the thirteenth century witnessed keen rivalry for national pre-eminence between Burgos, the capital of Castile, and Toledo, the capital of the Visigothic monarchy before the invasion of 711. So the poet's choice of Toledo as venue for Alfonso VI's third Cortes rather than the Cid's Burgos, for example – indeed after earlier assemblies at Burgos and Carrión, as the poet unnecessarily explains – would itself have been significant in May 1207. There may even actually have been a meeting of the Cortes at Toledo earlier in that year, as Francisco Hernández has

recently argued, and unquestionably the cathedral chapter of Toledo numbered a Per Abbat in its ranks. Furthermore, the archbishop, Rodrigo Jiménez de Rada, as well as being actively engaged in recruiting warriors for Alfonso VIII's army was currently and no less energetically promoting the restoration of Toledo to its former greatness. The description of the 1211-12 muster at Toledo, as recorded in Rodrigo's national History (1243), bears interesting comparison with the poet's account of the Cid's preparations for the siege of Valencia. And finally, Pedro de Cardona, Alfonso VIII's Romanist chancellor, had also in 1180-82 been archbishop of Toledo – though he was also Catalan by birth.

Speculation on this level will surely continue. It would not be surprising if it were shown that the poet in 1207 was using the Cid for his own purposes, for Toledo's or whoever's. What would be surprising would be a claim that anything of the sort about the Cid and his Poem had been conclusively *proved*. What is unquestionable is the usefulness of the Cid to successive generations of Castilians and ultimately Spaniards from 1207 at latest to 1987 at least.

The earliest identifiable beneficiaries of the Cid connection were the monks of San Pedro de Cardeña. This was only fair since, as the History relates, he was buried there. By the 1270s the house had fallen on hard times. So equally had the king of Castile of the day, Alfonso X, the Learned rather than the Wise (another historian). Alfonso was currently at odds with his nobles, so the Cid, whose dealings with Alfonso VI had been so notably punctilious, could be useful to him – or, alternatively, damaging to them, in the less flattering account of the Cid by Ibn 'Alcama, as Dozy suggested and Pidal hotly denied. (Two yers later, in the same spirit, the king translated from Pampliega – a Cardeña dependency as it happened – to Toledo the mortal remains of Wamba, the seventh-century ruler of Spain to whom Toledo chiefly owed its claim to that distinction.) To suggest that a deal was struck between the king and the monastery would not be warranted. What resulted were new tombs for the Cid and his wife, provided at royal expense, and at the expense of histor-

ical truth an account of the Cid's career, lovingly embroidered over decades if not centuries, which *via* Alfonso X's History of Spain passed into the national record. It is in this version of history that the dead Cid leads his troops into battle, as in the Charlton Heston version, and sits embalmed at Cardeña for ten years until his nose falls off. (Why just ten years? In 1272 a hundred and a bit would have been unchallengable.)

It was this Cid – a Cid in the guise of a peninsular Charlemagne, visited on his deathbed by the Sultan of Persia (through emissaries) and St Peter (in person) – whom the Middle Ages bequeathed to the modern world. The publication of the History and the Poem in the eighteenth century came far too late to endanger him. As a Spanish Old King Cole he became an unshiftable element in the national story: the balladeer's revenge upon the credible.

To suggest then, as Costa suggested in 1898, that the Cid's tomb should be closed is preposterous. There will always be a bit of him or of the imagined him capable of being transformed into a political platform. As long as there are two sides to an argument in Spain the Cid will serve his turn. For historians of that country the only pity is that Pidal's version of the past, battered though it is, still holds sway. Alfonso VI of Castile was portrayed in the film of the Cid as Hollywood's peninsular equivalent of Hollywood's bad King John, sneering and shifty. Neither the contemporary record nor indeed the Poem of the Cid warrants this. His is the tomb that needs to be reopened. It is high time.

FOR FURTHER READING:
There is an English translation, by H. Sutherland, of Menéndez Pidal's great work in abridged form, *The Cid and his Spain* (1934); the peninsular background is described in A. MacKay, *Spain in the Middle Ages. From frontier to empire, 1000-1500* (Macmillan, 1977); and in D.W. Lomax, *The Reconquest of Spain* (Longman, 1978); much interesting material is to be found in S. Clissold, *In Search of the Cid* (Hodder & Stoughton, 1965); of many modern translations of the *Poem*, probably the best is that of Rita Hamilton and Janet Parry, with introduction and notes by Ian Michael, *The Poem of the Cid* (Manchester Unviersity Press/Barnes & Noble, 1975), also in Penguin Classics; the most comprehensive survey of modern scholarship of the *Poem* and the fullest critique of Menéndez Pidal's theories is Colin Smith, *The Making of the 'Poema de mio Cid'* (Cambridge University Press, 1983).

HORSEMEN OF CRUEL CUNNING

The Mongols had planned a campaign of two decades to subdue a quaking, 13th-century Europe, but in Hungary stiff opposition awaited the hordes from the East.

Peter A. Kiss

Peter A. Kiss studied economics in Hungary and America. Descendant of a long line of soldiers (one of his ancestors led a Hungarian cavalry unit in the battle of Mohi), he studied the more obscure aspects of military history. He considers Rene Grousett's The Empire of the Steppes *the essential work on Mongol history. James Chambers'* The Devil's Horsemen *is a readable, but more limited work.*

From a tree-shadowed hilltop in northeast Hungary, two nomad warriors gazed toward the enemy camp on the afternoon of April 10, 1241. The distance was great, but a hunter's keen eyes could make out some details, and an experienced campaigner's knowledge could supply the rest. They say, in the twilight, that the Hungarians had selected a good place for their camp: its rear was secure, its flanks protected by mountain and marshes. The camp was fortified by wagons chained together; its water supply was no problem, and deployment to the front would be easy. But the watchers also saw that the tents of King, nobles, and knights took up much of the space, which was too small, at any rate, for the 100,000 soldiers gathered there.

The watchers on the hillside, Batu Khan and Subedei Bahadur, were no ordinary nomads; they were commanders of the Mongol empire's campaign to conquer Europe, and in the past five years they had won many victories. Now, however, their army was much weakened. They had started with 150,000 horsemen, and they had pressed into service the fighting men of other, defeated nations. Such auxiliaries had limited value—*their* heavy losses were not important. But the slow drain of trained, reliable Mongol soldiers and officers was keenly felt, since replacements from the Empire's heartlands seldom arrived. Large units had been detached to secure the flanks, and now the army was outnumbered by a tough, warlike enemy who did not seem eager to cooperate in his own defeat. It was going to be a severe test of Mongol fighting skill, of Mongol generalship.

The road to this Hungarian hillside had been long. It had begun 30 years before, when the nomad tribes of Central Asia elected Genghis Khan to lead them. They got more than they bargained for: in the following two decades the Great

Khan had exterminated all who opposed his authority, whipped the warring tribes into a disciplined army, the likes of which the world had seldom seen, and created an empire that stretched from the Pacific Ocean to the Caspian Sea. When he died in 1227, his legacy to his heirs was an ambitious scheme of world conquest. By 1234 Ogedei Khan, the new emperor, had accomplished the immediate tasks left to him by his formidable father: Western Asia was occupied by 1231, the Kin Empire (northern China) conquered in 1234.

The Mongols then were ready for further conquests, and the Imperial Council (the Kuriltai) audaciously decided to start four wars at the same time. The army in the southern theater was already engaging the forces of the Sung Empire (southern China); a second army was dispatched to Korea to repress revolts instigated by the Korean King; the army in western Asia was advancing into Georgia and the Caucasus, and now a fourth army was assembled to invade Europe.

Europe was not entirely unknown to the Mongols: between 1221 and 1224, Subedei had led 30,000 horsemen on a raid to the borders of Hungary. These horsemen had ravaged Persia, crossed the Caucasus, and ranged over the Russian steppes as far as the foothills of the Carpathian Mountains, then returned to Central Asia. They had covered 4,000 miles, fought a number of victorious battles, and collected information on the civilized countries of Europe. The information promised rich plunder to those bold enough to reach for it—and plunder never failed to capture Mongol imagination. The aristocrats sent their best troops, and young warriors of noble birth volunteered to serve in the army.

To lend prestige to the enterprise, Genghis Khan's grandson Batu was selected to lead the campaign and rule the new territories. He had insufficient battlefield experience to command 150,000 men; Subedei, Genghis Khan's best student and faithful companion, was assigned as his mentor. The Chinese Mandarins who ran the Mongols' intelligence organization dusted off their files and prepared a detailed analysis of the countries beyond the western borders. On the basis of their report Subedei, who could think on a large scale, planned a campaign lasting 16 to 18 years and covering the western world from the Urals to the Atlantic.

From *Military History*, December 1986, pp. 34-41. Reprinted by permission of *Military History* magazine, published by Empire Press, a Cowles Media Co. affiliate.

The first operations took place in the winter of 1236–37. The kingdom of Bulgar was destroyed, and nomadic tribes east of the Volga River were defeated and exterminated. Their young men were pressed into the conquering Mongol army, and under Subedei's demanding supervision they were trained in Mongol methods of war during the summer and fall of 1237. In the next year, the new troops acquired plenty of practical experience: the Mongol army, considerably strengthened by these recruits, crossed the Volga on the ice in December 1237.

The direct, easy route to western Europe, through the steppes between the Volga and the Carpathian Mountains, was open—the peasant levies of Russia promised to be no more than a momentary check in the march west. Still, Batu and Subedei advanced with caution. Were they to march directly west, the southern princes could withdraw into the forests of the north, where a cavalry army would operate at a disadvantage. Then, once the invasion of western Europe began in earnest, they could take the Mongol armies in flank and rear. To secure their vulnerable right flank, the Mongol generals destroyed the northern principalities first. They stormed Riazan and Kolomna, and occupied Moscow easily. In their wake, a chronicler noted, "no eyes remained open to weep for the dead." They next stormed Suzdal and Vladimir, and in a battle on the Siti River they destroyed the army of Prince Yuri, while flying columns sacked Yaroslav, Tver, and other cities. By March 1238, much of northern Russia was in smoking ruins, and Mongol units were only a hundred miles from the wealthy city of Novgorod, but on Subedei's advice, Batu ordered them back from the richest, most powerful Russian city.

The old general was well-acquainted with Russian weather conditions: he had recommended the winter campaign, when rivers were easy to cross on the ice, granaries were not yet empty, and only soldiers as tough and disciplined as the Mongols could fight effectively. He drove his troops mercilessly into blizzards, but withdrew them south before spring rains and melting snow could turn the country into a bottomless bog. Operations were resumed in the late fall of 1240, this time in southern Russia. The principalities of Chernigov, Kiev, and Galicia quickly were burned to the ground, and now the generals could make their final dispositions to invade central Europe.

While the Mongol army rested in the south and consolidated its brutal grip on the land east of the Don River, the largest nomad nation of the Russian steppes, the Cumans, sought refuge in Hungary. During Subedei's earlier raid they had fought against the Mongols, and their chieftain realized that east of the Carpathians no power was strong enough to resist the conquerors. He offered to accept Christianity on behalf of all Cumans in return for Hungarian King Bela IV's protection. The King welcomed him gladly: the conversion of 200,000 pagans would greatly increase Hungary's prestige in Rome, and the Cuman warriors would strengthen the power of the crown.

By the time Batu summoned a final council of war in Przemysl in December 1240, the West had received numerous warnings of impending danger. Dominican friars had brought the first reports of Mongol preparations (one dubbed them "Tartars"—the people from hell), and now Russian refugees had terrible tales to tell. But Europe was paralyzed by the political curse of the Middle Ages: lack of strong central authority, national dissension, petty feuds, and court intrigues. The Holy Roman Emperor, Frederick II, and Pope Gregory IX were locked in a struggle for earthly supremacy, and neither could spare troops to fight some obscure horsemen on a distant frontier. Italy was hopelessly fragmented, and the small principalities within Poland jealously guarded their independence. The Swedes, Lithuanians, and Teutonic Knights were ruthlessly attacking the already ravaged Russian cities, hoping to profit from that country's tragedy.

Some preparations were made to meet the Mongol threat, but these efforts came too late and were poorly coordinated. Through their spies, Batu and Subedei were well-acquainted with the situation in Europe, and deployed their forces accordingly. They would attack on three widely separated fronts, in a carefully coordinated sequence: the heaviest blow was to fall on Hungary, the most dangerous enemy, but only after flanking columns isolated that country from all possible support.

Even unsupported by allies, Hungary was a formidable enemy. The Hungarians were a warlike nation—they had been steppe-dwelling horse archers before they settled in the Danube Basin, and thus were well-accustomed to the tactics of mobile warfare. The aristocracy and their retainers had adopted western arms and the western style of horsemanship (they relied on the shock effect of lance and sword exclusively, and rode with straight knees), but most of the levies still used the short stirrup and fought with bow and saber. Their firepower, mobility, and endurance were somewhat inferior to the Mongols', but now they had been reinforced by the Cumans, a considerable advantage in cavalry.

The presence of the Cumans in Hungary irritated the Mongols. Batu, in an extraordinary letter to King Bela, warned in no uncertain terms what would happen to his country if Bela continued to shelter the Cumans. "Word has come to me," Batu wrote, "that you have taken the Cumans, our servants, under your protection. Cease harboring them, or you will make of me an enemy because of them. They, who have no houses and dwell in tents, will find it easy to escape. But you who dwell in houses within towns—how can you escape from me?" With the Mongols' devastation of Russia fresh in his mind, Bela was not inclined to take such a threat lightly.

The Hungarian army occupied the gorge of a natural bastion pointing east—it was formed by the Carpathian mountains and the Transylvanian Alps that surround Hungary from north to south in a large arc. The mountains were not impassable, but a vigorous defender could thwart an invasion attempt if he held the key passes in strength. Flat plains enclosed by the mountains facilitated the rapid movement of forces along interior lines, and the Danube served as a second line of defense, should the enemy penetrate the mountain barrier.

But the Hungarian nobles were no match for Subedei's generalship, and their King did not have the absolute authority of Batu Khan. A great national effort was needed to resist the invader; instead, a feud was brewing between Bela IV and the aristocrats (indeed, many nobles hoped for his defeat), and he was also threatened by the territorial ambitions of Frederick, Duke of Austria. When the bloody sword (traditional symbol of national emergency) was carried around the country, the nobles assembled readily enough, but then demanded concessions from the King before they would march to the borders. The meddling presence of Frederick was no help at all—he stayed in Hungary only long enough to damage Bela's cause, then returned west with his forces in time to stay out of the coming fight.

The Cumans were another problem. Their behavior was offensive to many Hungarians: their horses and cattle trampled the peasants' fields, and the nobles were uneasy to see their King suddenly acquire the loyal support of a large force over which they had no influence. Fights between Hungarians and Cumans became common, and the nobles did their best to encourage the peasants' hatred of the newcomers. At the worst possible time, when the Mongols were already invading Hungary, a rioting mob (probably incited by Frederick) killed the Cuman Khan, and threw his head out of a palace window. The outraged Cumans revolted and evacuated the country, not neglecting to pillage as they went.

While Bela IV, beset by internal and external problems, desperately was struggling to preserve his authority and organize the defense of his realm, Batu and Subedei unleashed their *tumens* (divisions). The coordination of their operations was amazing.

In February 1241 the flanking Mongol armies began to create a semicircle of destruction from Poland to Wallachia in order to isolate Hungary. In the north, Mongol princes Orda, Baidair, and Kadan crossed the Vistula with three *tumens,* burned Lublin, Zawichost and Sandomir, then divided in order to ravage a larger area. One *tumen* raided East Prussia, Pomerania, and Lithuania; Kadan rode northwest into Mazowia; and Baidar marched southwest, toward Cracow.

Meanwhile, the central Mongol army of six *tumens* was poised to force the Russian (Verecke) Pass into Hungary, while in the south another three *tumens* devastated Moldavia and Wallachia and then prepared to force the southern passes into Transylvania.

In March 1241, the long-dreaded invasion of Hungary began, as the flanking columns completed their work, insuring the country's isolation.

At Chmielnik, on March 18, Baidar lured the army of the Palatine Vladimir out of Cracow, decisively defeated him and burned Cracow. Then Baidar crossed the Oder River at Raciborz and marched on Breslau to rendezvous with Kadan. While waiting for Kadan he invested Breslau.

The central army forced the Russian Pass on March 12 and began to ravage eastern Hungary. A reconnaissance in force stormed Vac on March 17, only 20 miles from Pest, where the King's army was assembling. Mongol horsemen tried to

INCREDIBLE WAR MACHINE FROM THE EAST

Mongol and Turkish horse archers raided China, Iran and eastern Europe for centuries. Feudal household troops and local peasant levies were no match for the mobility and firepower of thundering squadrons that covered immense distances in search of plunder and fought with great ferocity. The nomad youngsters learned to ride and fight from their earliest infancy; they were used to hardship, hunger, and harsh climate, and they grew up to be the world's finest light cavalrymen.

But the conditions of the steppes demanded self-reliance, and only Genghis Khan's forthright disciplinary measures could forge rugged individualists into an army. He punished the slightest disobedience or negligence, the slightest hint of cowardice, with death, but he richly rewarded valor and loyalty.

The Khan retained the decimal organization used by nomad armies for centuries: ten mounted archers formed a troop (*arban*); ten troops, a squadron (*jagun*); ten squadrons, a brigade (*minghan*); ten brigades, a division

(*tumen*). Three or more *tumens,* with brigades of engineers, artillery or siege engines and other support units made up a Mongol field army (*ordu*).

Firepower and movement, combined with the ancient methods of the hunt, were the tactics of the Mongol army. Showers of arrows alternated with charges by heavy cavalry, feigned retreat, ambush and rapid dispersion to avoid an enemy charge. It was a method of war that proved all but irresistible. The principal weapon was a very powerful reflex bow; its range and rate of fire (upwards of 400 meters and 20 shots a minute) were not equalled until the invention of magazine rifles.

Fighting units were supported by a highly efficient supply system, which could replenish empty quivers, replace broken weapons, and bring up remounts even in the middle of a battle. In populated regions, food was obtained by ruthless foraging; horse milk was part of the daily ration, as was the meat of worn-out mounts. In uninhabited areas, the troops lived on rations they carried in their saddlebags: dried milk and powdered meat, mixed with water, provided simple, nourishing fare. They could also go without food for days, if necessary.

On campaigns, the army advanced in several parallel columns, screened by scouts; the columns maintained contact only through the courier service of "arrow mes-lure the King into the open and cut down detachments of noblemen rash enough to take the bait.

The southern Mongol army crossed into Transylvania in three columns on March 31 and set about ravaging the province. One column defeated the army of the Transylvanian viceregent, while the others sought out the smaller Hungarian forces.

By the first of April, the flanking armies had destroyed almost all forces that could reinforce the Hungarian King, then prepared to tackle the Hungarian army itself.

On April 9, 1241, the battle of Liegnitz began. In the north, Baidar abandoned the siege of Breslau when he received intelligence that Henry the Pious, Duke of Silesia, had collected 30,000 troops in Liegnitz, and that the Bohemian King was marching to join him with a further 50,000. Baidar immediately sent word to Kadan, and the two Mongol generals set out alone for Liegnitz.

Henry did not know when to expect the Bohemian reinforcements, and, concerned that he would be unable to deploy his force if he allowed himself to be pinned down behind the walls of the city, he decided to engage. Organizing his army into three "battles" (brigades) of cavalry and one of infantry, he marched out alone to meet the Mongol invaders.

A few miles south of the city the two armies clashed on a wide plain. Henry's first cavalry brigade was immediately routed by a hail of arrows, and he rashly committed his remaining horsemen. In a short, murderous clash the Mongols first appeared to have the worst of it, and began yielding ground. The Silesian knights pursued them, only to learn a favorite Mongol maneuver the hard way: their disordered and extended lines caught in a well-laid ambush, the flower of Polish knighthood was soon destroyed. Meanwhile, a Mongol detachment raised a smokescreen behind Henry's knights; the rest of the army had no idea what was happening. Once the knights—and Henry, killed attempting to flee—were dealt with, the archers rode through the smoke and shot down the helpless infantry. Nine large sacks of victims' ears filled the Mongol war-wagons.

After the battle the Mongol *tumens* galloped west to lure Bohemian King Wenceslas farther away from Hungary, then dispersed and rode around his flanks, recalling the detached *tumen* from the Baltic and turning south to join Batu beyond the Carpathians. Their strategic mission thus was completed—they had removed all possible threat on the north flank.

Meanwhile, on the 5th or 6th of April, three or four days before the battle of Liegnitz, Batu struck camp and slowly withdrew to the east. The Hungarians ill-advisedly followed him the next day.

On the 10th, one day after the Battle of Liegnitz, the Mongols halted east of the Sajo River, ready to engage the Hungarian army. The stage was set to Mongol liking for the decisive battle of the campaign: both strategic flanks were secured; the main army was concentrated on the selected battlefield, and the enemy was completely isolated.

On the afternoon of the 10th, Subedei crossed the Sajo on the stone bridge near Mohi and halted his army some 10

---

sengers," who overcame all obstacles to deliver their dispatches. When an enemy force was located, the Mongols could concentrate their forces with amazing speed. Units were detached to cut the enemy's lines of communication; the main force engaged him, while a small body of picked troops made a wide detour to fall on his flank. Verbal commands were seldom needed: flags, gongs, trumpets, drums, and flaming arrows were used to transmit battle orders.

Such fast, reliable, and efficient communication made unit of command, coordination of maneuvers, and cooperation of units possible—once an order was issued, it was carried out. Ruthless discipline saw to that point.

No army ever equalled the Mongols in mobility: they could cover 60 to 80 miles a day, executing enveloping movements of several hundred miles and crossing regions believed impassable. Mobility gave Mongol generals the opportunity to plan campaigns on a scale never before (and very seldom later) contemplated, to seize and maintain the initiative. They could place a superior force into a decisive position at the critical time; they could select the time and place of battle, and they could engage or avoid the enemy as it suited them. They could concentrate faster than any opponent, and in case of defeat they could ride in retreat faster and farther than any pursuer.

Mongol leaders appreciated the psychological advantages of offensive action, and never fought on the defensive. Constant attack, even when the mission was defensive, was the hallmark of Mongol commanders; even when outnumbered, they would not fight a defensive engagement. Instead they would harass a superior force with long-range archery and sudden local attacks, or they would retire, trading space for time until they could engage the enemy on more advantageous terms.

Since they often were operating at a numerical disadvantage, Mongol generals had to apply economy of force with the utmost diligence—they relied on surprise and maneuver to achieve victory. Each unit had several tasks in order to utilize limited resources fully. Units in reserve were not idle: foraging and scouting was continuous; detachments far from the main force operated against the enemy's flanks and guarded against surprises.

Mongol armies were all but unbeatable, so long as the empire remained united under a single ruler, and there were no weapons to match the reflex bow's performance, no soldiers to match the Mongols' skill and discipline. The empire finally fell apart because of dynastic quarrels and religious strife—and because Chinese and Russian troops eventually proved a match for the Mongol soldiers, and their artillery a match for the Mongol bow.

miles farther east. Hoping to tempt Bela into a rash move, he left only a very weak detachment at the bridge. Bela reached the river later the same day, but disappointed Subedei by ignoring the bait of an unopposed crossing. Instead, he established a bridgehead on the east bank and occupied a strong position some distance west of the river.

Now Subedei had a problem: Bela had to be destroyed within a day or two, before he learned of his total isolation, in which case he would likely retire behind the Danube and garrison the strong fortresses of western Hungary. They would then have to be reduced one by one. But Bela at the moment occupied a well-protected position, and he did not seem inclined to rush headlong into a trap. Subedei had no choice but to attack under very risky conditions. His two widely separated forces had to win or perish; they had no practical route of withdrawal once they were engaged. On the hill above the Hungarian camp, he and Batu finalized their strategy.

At dawn on April 11, the Hungarians beat back the first Mongol efforts to take the bridge. Confidently, they jeered at them across the river. The Mongols brought up seven siege engines—flat-trajectory *ballistae*—and bombarded the garrison of the bridge with firebombs until it withdrew to the west bank. Then the *ballistae* increased their range, and Mongol squadrons rode over the bridge, covered by a rolling barrage. They swept up Hungarian pickets on the riverbank and silently deployed, facing south.

The Hungarian commanders were surprised by the attack—they were used to more conservative methods of war—and only two contingents (one led by the King's brother Koloman, the other by one of the country's fighting bishops) were ready to engage the onrushing Mongols. They managed to hold until reinforcements came up from the camp, and after the first clashes the Mongols gave ground. The Hungarians, badly shaken by the swift attack, were just regaining their balance when another Mongol force materialized behind them. Subedei had crossed the river with three *tumens* during the night, and swept behind the Hungarians to take them in the rear.

In the spring the rivers of Hungary are in full flood; they are very deep and swift—formidable obstacles even to modern combat engineers. But the crafty Subedei had moved a large force across the Sajo at night, with a hostile army within easy striking distance. Now he attacked from the least likely direction: the small peninsula, enclosed by river and swamp, looked inaccessible from the east bank and was totally unsuitable for a sizeable force. Its outlet was barely two miles wide; no more than 2,500 horsemen could ride abreast in that space. A mixed detachment of 5,000 archers and heavy troops could have held the bottleneck—but all the Hungarian commanders were looking the other way.

The Hungarians did not panic, but they did lose the initiative. They still had superior numbers, but instead of charging through the Mongol center—much-thinned by the first clashes—they confusedly withdrew into their camp. The Mongols brought up their siege engines and bombarded the camp at leisure for several hours, then charged in three converging columns. Some Hungarian troops fled through a gap left by the Mongols for just such a purpose; soon individual desertions turned into a complete rout. Only a handful of Knights Templar stood their ground. Overwhelmed by the Mongols, they died to a man.

King Bela and the mortally wounded Koloman managed to escape; others were not so fortunate. For two days, as demoralized and exhausted Hungarians lurched toward the protection of the Danube River and the twin citadels of Buda and Pest, Mongol horsemen rode alongside, casually butchering the men as they came across them. Bodies littered the road to Pest "like stones in a quarry." Seventy thousand Hungarians died in the debacle.

News of the overwhelming Mongol triumph sent horrified shudders sweeping through Europe. The swift-striking invaders had appeared so suddenly, at so many different places, that Europeans now spoke of a mongol "horde," numberless and irresistible, bringing God's wrath down upon a sinful populace. Gruesome rumors, sparked by all-too-real Mongol atrocities, spread from city to city. The Mongols, some said, had the bodies of men but the heads of dogs, and fed on the bodies of their victims. Others said they were demon-worshippers, and had been led across Hungary by evil spirits. In churches throughout Europe, white-faced congregations prayed, "From the fury of the Tartars, oh Lord, deliver us." Only a miracle, it seemed, could save them from the "horde."

King Bela, in the meantime, suffered considerable indignity at the hands of the Duke of Austria (not for nothing was that prince known as Frederick the Pugnacious), and finally established his court in his Adriatic province. A Mongol column was sent to capture him in early 1242, but he found sanctuary on Trogir Island in the Adriatic.

Batu and Subedei were now masters of eastern Hungary. They soon were formulating plans for the invasion of Germany, and their scouts were raiding near Vienna. The population of Hungary was subjected to unspeakable atrocities, but gradually Mongol cruelty abated; administration was established, coin was minted—all to encourage the peasants to come out of hiding and harvest the grain. Once the granaries were filled, though, another series of massacres took place.

As soon as the Danube froze the following winter, Subedei led the Mongol army across the ice, and only some of the fortified cities of Western Hungary could resist the assaults. Meanwhile the sovereigns of Europe, paralyzed with fear, simply waited for the descent of the barbarian hordes. They saw the devastation in the Mongols' wake between the Baltic and the Black Sea and knew that their undisciplined levies were no match for the terrible horsemen from the East.

A miracle of sorts then occurred to save Europe—in April 1242 the Mongols evacuated Hungary and returned east. Ogedei Khan's death was one reason for the unexpected withdrawal: according to Genghis Khan's law, Batu had to be in Karakorum for the election of the successor. But the decisive reason may have been strictly military—the Mongol forces were spread too thin, and in the devastated country the army would soon begin to suffer from lack of food. Hungary's strength was sapped—it could be reoccupied in a few years with ease. Several other Mongol conquests had been carried out thus, in two stages: in a whirlwind campaign a region's military force would be destroyed, its rulers killed, its inhabitants decimated, its wealth plundered. Then, in order to allow a measure of recovery, the conquerors would withdraw, only to return several years later, when the region was sufficiently recovered to allow orderly administration, but was still too weak to offer serious resistance.

Fortunately for western civilization, there was considerable dissension among Mongol aristocrats, and Ogedei's successor was not elected for some time. The defeated learn the lessons of a war more thoroughly than the victors: Bela had formidable castles built, invited the Cumans to return, and reorganized the army. The Mongols would attack Hungary again in 1285, but this generation of Mongol generals would not be cast in the mold of Subedei, and Bela's grandson would repulse them with little effort. The success of Mongol arms did not end then, but in following centuries Mongol energies were spent fighting among themselves. New conquerors emerged, but their conquests did not last

long, and the once-great Mongol empire eventually fell apart.

Medieval annalists described the Mongols as half-human barbarians bent on rape and pillage, terrible apparitions with animal instincts for blood and plunder. Indeed, the horrors of a Mongol campaign are difficult to imagine—cities razed, provinces devastated, thousands enslaved, tens of thousands butchered. Their invasions caused fearsome destruction and led to the extinction of entire nations—medieval Hungary, for example, lost nearly 50 percent of its population.

But the chronicles do not explain the true reasons for Mongol successes. The history of their victories was written by their enemies, who understood but poorly the Mongol method of warfare and sought excuses for the shocking defeats of splendid armies by so-called barbarians. Mongol success was not due to superior numbers, acts of God, barbarous ferocity, or wonder weapons, but rather to brilliant generalship, careful planning, discipline, and organization. The Mongols were expert in mobile warfare, and the lessons of their campaigns are as important today as they were in the 13th century, when the Mongols were truly the masters of all they surveyed.

THE MEDIEVAL MILL –
A PRODUCTIVITY BREAKTHROUGH?

Taking corn to be milled. A 14th-century manuscript illustration of a windmill.

EVERYTHING THAT WAS ACCOMPLISHED IN the Middle Ages, from the construction of the great cathedrals to the day-to-day work in field or workshop, was achieved by the systematic exploitation of the strength of men and animals – by endless drudgery. Even so, with the advantage of hindsight we can see that already some of the technological groundwork for a mechanised society was being laid. One major source of natural power had been harnessed, and the people of the Middle Ages were to learn how

*In the Middle Ages mill-owning was a sound investment and led to the invention of the windmill but, as **Richard Holt** points out, these halcyon times were of short duration.*

to exploit another. To the watermill – a legacy of the Ancient World – the medieval west added its own peculiar creation, the post windmill. Later centuries would see the watermill in particular play the crucial role in industrialisation and economic growth, with the Industrial Revolution becoming only in the latter part of the nineteenth century emphatically a triumph of the steam engine rather than of the waterwheel. But how important a role did wind and waterpower play in the gradual

From *History Today*, July 1989, pp. 26-31. Reproduced by kind permission of History Today, Ltd., 83-84 Berwick Street, London W1V 3PJ, England.

transformation of the medieval agrarian economy? Did the mill have any noticeable effect on existing patterns of production?

To begin to answer the question we need to go back beyond the Middle Ages, to look briefly at the watermill's already long history. Historical sources point to its appearance in the Mediterranean world during the century before Christ, though we should not place too much reliance on that. As it is from the classical cultures of the Mediterranean that our early documentary sources come, then of course that is where we would expect to find mills first recorded. 'Archaeomolinology' – the word coined by Professor Philip Rahtz for the study of ancient mills – is still far from being a precise science; archaeology might yet confirm what for the moment remains a strong suspicion, that the barbarous but wet lands of northern and western Europe were a more logical birthplace than Italy or Greece for a machine so dependent on persistent and heavy rain.

Some misconceptions about early mills have already been corrected. It used to be generally accepted that in the Roman Empire people preferred to carry on grinding their corn by slave-power: that the watermill did not come into its own until the Middle Ages, in a western Europe where slavery had virtually ceased to exist. Now we know that the watermill was in common use long before the onset of the social upheavals that marked the end of Roman rule. In Britain – as remote and backward as any of the provinces of the Empire – archaeological evidence of the use of waterpower during the Roman period is more substantial even than for the Middle Ages, when we know that watermills were to be found on every stream and river.

Abundant documentary references to mills from the sixth century onwards show that on the continent the watermill survived the so-called 'barbarian invasions'. As for Dark Age Britain, it may be that the ability to build and operate mechanical mills perished in the breakdown of civil society that was more complete than elsewhere. If that was indeed the case, then the degree of order that returned as the early English kingdoms asserted their authority was sufficient for the watermill to flourish. The earliest reference to an English mill is to one in Kent, in a document dated to 762, after which mills are quite frequently mentioned in charters. And, not surprisingly, archaeology points to even earlier use of the mill by the English, with a firm date in the 690s now having been assigned to the massive and sophisticated machine excavated at Old Windsor on the Thames.

It is all of this that makes nonsense of the old thesis that the introduction of powered milling must have brought about a considerable degree of economic growth in the Middle Ages, and encouraged a new attitude to the possibilities of exploiting the natural world. On the contrary, medieval man did not just inherit the design of the mill: he inherited a world in which mills were a commonplace. And furthermore he contributed nothing of his own to the device, so that the watermill he bequeathed to subsequent generations was no different from the machine handed down to him. Both manorial documentation and the excavated remains of Roman and medieval watermills make it quite clear that the design first described by the Roman engineer Vitruvius around 25 BC was scarcely modified, if at all, until the eighteenth century.

There was, it is true, a second type of watermill, but this more basic machine in which the millstone was driven by a shaft connected directly to a horizontal waterwheel – and so usually called the horizontal mill – represented neither technological advance nor regression. It was just a simpler, less powerful mill that was preferred by peasant communities everywhere they were allowed to build their own mills, because it was cheaper than the more complex vertical or Vitruvian mill. In many parts of Europe the horizontal mill predominated until the present day; in England, by contrast, although both types of mill were used by the Anglo-Saxons, the horizontal mill subsequently disappeared, probably as part of a process of the concentration of milling resources into aristocratic hands.

The water cornmill's contribution as a proportion of overall production in the Middle Ages remained constant, therefore. Certainly there was no breakthrough in the use of waterpower that signified an equivalent freeing of human labour to be devoted to other productive tasks. In fact we misunderstand the place of the mill in medieval society if we

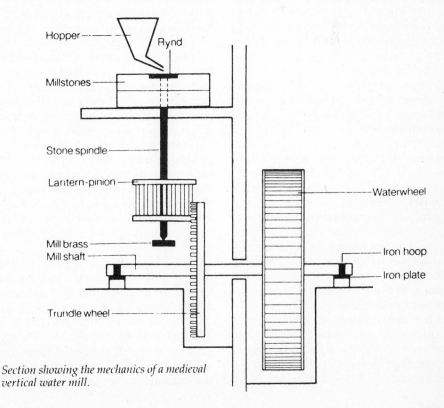

Section showing the mechanics of a medieval vertical water mill.

Hopper

Rynd

Millstones

Stone spindle

Lantern-pinion

Mill brass

Mill shaft

Trundle wheel

Waterwheel

Iron hoop

Iron plate

ifiel fameillous ont la char elgardee
endent gue mont facouller la uolee

A mid-14th-century windmill with the tailpole (by which the sails were turned into the wind) clearly visible.

persist in seeing it primarily as a labour-saving device; instead we have to appreciate that in all likelihood very few people regarded it as much of a blessing. The local mill's beneficial qualities were all too often overshadowed by the heavy toll charged for grinding, as lords of manors in England, France and elsewhere attempted to impose a monopoly by insisting that only they could legally operate a mill. Their heavy investment in mills was not motivated by any desire to put an end to the unremitting toil of peasant women at the quern, but by the prospect of a good profit. A legal monopoly was the easy way to maximise profits, to the extent that manorial lords were able to take most, if not all, of the economic benefits for themselves. In other words, the watermill was part and parcel of the prevailing pattern of social relationships. In a marginal way it even served to reinforce the social hierarchy, in so far as it strengthened the economic and legal ascendancy of the ruling aristocracy over a subject peasantry.

For the rewards of milling were undeniably substantial. Lords everywhere claimed the right to be able to force their unfree tenants to use the manorial mill, and the fee they charged was one twenty-fourth or one twentieth of the corn ground. In some districts it was more than that, and in the northernmost counties of England as much as one thirteenth. Not surprisingly, there was considerable resistance to the lord's mill, though historians have been mistaken as to the form that resistance took. It has been assumed that when they could most peasants milled illegally with handmills in their own homes; what seems to have happened more often is that they preferred to use, still illegally, a mill in a neighbouring manor where they could negotiate a lower rate from a miller eager for more custom. But however widespread both of these practices were, they evidently did little to dent the enormous profits that mills can be seen to have produced for their owners, for century after century until the balance at last began to turn in the peasants' favour in the years around 1400.

The substantial and steady profits for any lord who owned a mill are the key to understanding that genuine technological innovation of medieval milling, the windmill. We know a great deal about the windmill's origins, whilst the unique Domesday survey of 1086 reveals unmistakably the reasons for its invention. As far as the mill is concerned, Domesday Book demonstrates two facts of exceptional importance: firstly that with more than 6,000 of them, standing on every suitable stream or river, the mill had become an indispensable feature of English rural life; but secondly, that there was an essential limitation of waterpower, that water resources and population did not necessarily coincide. In East Anglia especially, at once the driest and most densely populated region of England, many communities had no mill, and it must have been obvious that waterpower alone could never grind all the flour that was needed. In other parts of Europe, such as the dry lands of the south or the Low Countries, the situation would have been similar, and there would have been many lords who enviously eyed the lucrative watermills of their more fortunate neighbours.

The windmill was an inspired answer to the problem of the lack of water power, and was undoubtedly one of medieval Europe's most important inventions. Essentially an adaptation of the watermill to a new source of power, it made use of the familiar mechanism – now inverted so as to be driven by sails mounted high in the building, rather than by a waterwheel at its base. But a more fundamental alteration was also necessary. The difficulty with the windmill, and what presumably delayed its invention, was the problem of how to harness a power source that regularly changed its direction, and which would not be directed or controlled. With the watermill the water always flowed along the same channel, and at a rate the miller could vary by means of sluices; the seemingly intractable problem for the first windmill builders was to contrive a way of keeping the sails facing into the wind. The solution they came up with was to balance the windmill on a single massive upright post, so that the miller could push the whole structure around to face in whichever direction he wanted. The windspeed he could compensate for, like any sailor, by adjusting the spread of canvas on the lattice-work sails.

What is particularly satisfying for the historian is that the period during which this revolutionary invention first appeared can be narrowed down to a decade or so. In dating the post windmill, the most significant evidence is the decretal of Pope Celestine III affirming that owners of windmills should pay tithes on their profits, as they did on the rest of their agricultural income. The judgment was issued during Celestine's brief papacy, between 1191 and 1198, apparently in response to a query from the abbot of Ramsey in Huntingdonshire and the Archdeacon of Ely: the obvious inference to be drawn is that the question had not arisen before, that the windmill really was a new feature of the English countryside. And from the 1190s comes a score of references to English windmills, with at most three earlier references, all from the previous decade. Numerous attempts have been made over many years to show that windmills are recorded from the 1170s and before, and even as early as 1137, but the evidence for supposed earlier windmills does not stand up to close examination. It remains the case that the earliest reliably-documented English windmills are both dated to 1185: one an existing mill at Weedley, near South Cave, in the East Riding of Yorkshire, and the other a mill recorded as having been built since 1180 at Amberley in Sussex. No doubt other, unrecorded, windmills existed at this time, and perhaps in earlier years; but the sudden rush of known examples from 1185 onwards confirms that Celestine was indeed legislating for a situation that had only recently arisen. The medieval Church was in many ways a progressive organisation – after all, it comprised the whole of the medieval intelligentsia – and it was well aware of what was going on. It is inconceivable that had the windmill really been invented as early as the 1130s it should have taken the shrewdest, most alert, men of affairs sixty years to notice it.

What was happening elsewhere in Europe? The evidence, interestingly, is that whilst the windmill appeared there at around the same time, nevertheless it may have been gaining acceptance rather later than in England. There are far fewer known continental mills from before 1200 – perhaps as few as five – of which only one might have been recorded as early as the 1180s. But what is most striking about all of these early windmills is where they were situated. The English examples all come from the eastern side of the country, with most of them close to the coast: of the windmills of the 1190s, six were in Norfolk, three in Suffolk, three in Kent, two in Northumberland, and there were single mills in Yorkshire, Sussex, Cambridgeshire, Lincolnshire, Bedfordshire, Buckinghamshire and probably Huntingdonshire. The location of the continental mills was an exact mirror image, with all the known examples again occurring near the coasts of the Low Countries, northern France and Normandy.

The inescapable conclusion is that it was somewhere by the cold North Sea that the first post mill had been built – most likely in the 1170s – and that knowledge of it had spread rapidly. The sea was no obstacle to the diffusion of the new invention; indeed quite the contrary, as it is clear how quickly the concept of the windmill must have passed from seaport to seaport, whilst at the same time how little headway it made in its journey inland. And where should we locate the windmill's birthplace? All the evidence seems to point to England, and probably to East Anglia where the greatest concentration of early windmills is recorded, and where there was the greatest need for an alternative to the watermill.

Not that the windmill was, anywhere, a common sight during those early decades. If we need further proof that it was a new device in 1185, there is the clear evidence that it was only in the years after 1220 that windmills were built in any great numbers – and this even in East Anglia. Perhaps there was a period of a generation during which building windmills was still seen as a highly speculative venture, requiring investment in an untried and unpredictable machine. Even on one leading go-ahead estate, that of the bishops of Ely, we can see that at most four windmills had been built by 1222, despite the bishop's manors' being situated in prime windmill country – mainly Cambridgeshire, Norfolk, Huntingdonshire and Suffolk. But when the estate was surveyed again in 1251 there were now not four windmills but thirty-two, nine of them being described as 'new'. Evidence from other estates confirms the picture, that it was the 1230s and the 1240s that saw the most intense windmill-building activity.

And it is interesting that there was to be no repeat performance, as on estate after estate the number of windmills thereafter grew only slightly. A long-felt need had been quickly met, and had been met in full. It is interesting, too, to observe that meanwhile there had been no diminution in the numbers of watermills. A few marginal enterprises on poor watercourses – worth building only because there had been no alternative – were promptly replaced by windmills; meanwhile the ever more intensive exploitation of more reliable sources of waterpower continued unabated, and occasionally new watermills were built. It is this that tells us in unmistakable terms that the windmill came to supplement the watermill, not to supplant it. The windmill was not so efficient as the watermill – that is, it did not give such a good return on capital investment. So where they could, medieval men chose to build watermills. Windmills they built only when the alternative was no mill at all, which is why in those parts of England with plentiful water-resources the windmill never estab-

The miller at work in an East Anglian post mill; from the 14th-century Luttrell Psalter.

lished much of a presence. Far fewer were built in western England, with exceptions, of course, such as the Somerset Levels. Like the Fens there was no shortage of water there; what was lacking was gradients to make the water move.

That is not to say that the windmill did not have an economic impact; but its impact was limited both geographically and in time. In East Anglia by 1300 two-thirds – and in some districts three-quarters – of the mills were windmills, which means that the middle years of the century had seen an enormous – though unrepeatable – growth in the milling capacity of the region. This was a genuine increase in its productive potential, which by 1250 had enabled a significant quantity of labour time to be diverted to other tasks. So whose was the benefit of this undoubted boost to production? Undoubtedly it went to those lords with enough foresight to build a windmill for their tenants. The peasants now saved time in grinding their corn, but they had to pay a toll and so at the end of the day they had less flour to

consume; any hours they saved had to be set against this shortfall. Meanwhile, the windmill returned its building costs to its owner within six or seven years at most. In East Anglia in the thirteenth century windmills cost rather less than £10 to build, and they brought in between £2 and £3 a year, of which a third was needed to cover repair costs. By any standards this was a good investment, but what made it so attractive was the excessive toll that lords were generally able to collect.

The tremendous success of the windmill places the other medieval innovations in milling into perspective. The tide mill – a watermill powered by the ebb and flow of tidal creeks – is usually thought to be an important medieval invention, perhaps of the eleventh century, and to be another expression of medieval man's conscious striving for new and better sources of power. In fact the earliest tide mill now known is an

Irish one dated to the 630s, and documented examples from later centuries were often far from successful – there are instances from the thirteenth century of tide mills being destroyed by the sea, and in each case being replaced by a windmill. So we now know that the tide mill was widely known at the beginning of the medieval period, and that because of the unpredictability of its power source, added to its other drawback that it could work only for limited periods of each day, it tended to be less useful than other watermills. Far from being a significant development of the Middle Ages, it was a machine which had been brought into use when there had been no alternative to waterpower, when even inefficient mills were thought worth building; like other marginal watermills it was rendered obsolete by the windmill. Only with the advances in milling technology of the eighteenth century would the tide mill re-assert itself.

Of much greater significance than the tide mill was the adaptation of the watermill to various industrial processes, and again the windmill's success is the standard against which the effect of this development on the medieval economy has to be judged. In any large sample of English mills, cases of watermills used for grinding bark for tanning or for working metal turn out to be very rare indeed, although both these processes were known from the twelfth century onwards and perhaps earlier. Only fulling mills were relatively common. This application of the force of waterpower to scour new cloth with a detergent to remove dirt and natural oiliness, whilst at the same time pounding it to shrink the weave and felt the fibres, was recorded first in Normandy in 1087, though not frequently in France or England until a century later. Well over 100 English examples have been identified in the period before 1350, mostly in the Cotswolds and the south-west, as well as in the north, particularly the West Riding of Yorkshire and the Lake District; in South Wales, too, they were built in large numbers. But they were never very profitable, and certainly did not give anything like the return on capital that cornmills did. The pattern of their distribution shows those districts where there was a surplus of waterpower; where water resources were limited cornmills were always preferred, and so fulling mills remained rare in lowland England.

The medieval application of waterpower to a limited range of industrial processes has been exaggerated by historians of technology because, excited by the novelty of it all, they have failed to see how little economic impact it had. It was the sheer poverty of medieval society that ensured that commodity production was small-scale and labour-intensive, rather than capital-intensive: these powerful machines were seldom worth building because the potential market was too small and diffuse to justify large scale production, whilst at the same time labour remained very cheap. Investment in labour-saving mechanisation can be justified only when there is known to be a high level of demand for a product, and when it can be seen that the use of machinery will bring about a significant reduction in manufacturing costs.

The cornmill met these requirements, which is why the lords of hundreds of manors were eager to invest in windmills. In the subsistence economy of the Middle Ages flour was one commodity that was always, everywhere, in demand. Medieval England produced cloth, too, in relatively large quantities, and consequently the otherwise labour-intensive fulling process was often worth mechanising. But generally speaking, it required the changed economic circumstances of the modern period before the mechanisation that was possible could be profitably introduced into other industries.

Cornmilling by wind and water power did not threaten the medieval economy; it was always a harmonious part of it. And far from pointing the way to new methods of production, use of the mill declined as feudal production faltered in the fifteenth century. After 1400 mills everywhere were falling into disuse, and those that survived were far less profitable. Obviously population loss in the aftermath of the plague epidemics from 1348 onwards was a contributory factor, but more insidious and damaging was apparently a fatal weakening of the ability by the owners of mills to enforce their use on their tenants. Just as lords could no longer command the labour services and high rents of previous centuries, so there were fewer effective sanctions to prevent peasants from shopping around for the cheapest mill. Inevitably the cost – and the profitability – of milling fell. But this was not a social change – however minor – at last brought about by the watermill and windmill; it was part of a general shift of resources towards agricultural tenants, and milling was merely fitting into the prevailing social pattern. Whatever the future might hold, the mill in the fifteenth century remained a peripheral feature of the agrarian economy.

FOR FURTHER READING:
Richard Holt, *The Mills of Medieval England* (Basil Blackwell, 1988); Terry S. Reynolds, *Stronger than a Hundred Men: A History of the Vertical Water Wheel* (Johns Hopkins University Press, 1983); R. Bennet and J. Elton, *History of Corn Milling*, 4 vols. (London & Liverpool, 1898-1904; reprint E.P. Publishing, 1975).

Images of Ireland 1170-1600

THE ORIGINS OF ENGLISH IMPERIALISM

John Gillingham

'Beyond the pale' — the imperialists' vision of the Irish as ignoble savages originated in the attitudes and writings of medieval Englishmen.

IMPLICIT IN THE IMPERIALISM OF THE English is that attitude of mind which led Lord Rosebery, in 1893, to declare that it was 'our responsibility to see that the world should be made as Anglo-Saxon as possible'. Implicit also are the sorts of activity which went hand-in-hand with that attitude, in particular territorial expansion justified by an assumption of English cultural and moral superiority over those peoples whose lands were invaded and taken over.

There was a time when histories of English imperialism began, like J.R. Seeley's *The Expansion of England* (1883), with those projects for conquest and settlement in North America which were drawn up in the Elizabethan and Stuart periods. But in the last thirty years or so historians like D.B. Quinn, A.L. Rowse and Nicholas Canny have tended to argue that the Englishmen who planned to go to America were men whose own recent experience was in Ireland in the 1560s and 1570s – men like Humphrey Gilbert, Sir Richard Grenville and Ralph Lane – and that it was the Elizabethan attempt to conquer and settle Ireland which set the pattern for subsequent transatlantic ventures. Indeed 'A Pattern Established' is the programmatic subtitle of Canny's *The Elizabethan Conquest of Ireland* (1976).

According to A.L. Rowse in *The Expansion of Elizabethan England* (1955), the new efficiency of the Renaissance state led to a thrusting expansionism, first into the backward areas of the Celtic borderlands and then overseas into the New World. In America, so it is argued, the English found themselves faced by problems similar to those they had confronted in Ireland. Their response was to adopt similar attitudes and the same solutions. In both places they began by claiming that they had a mission to civilise the natives, but they soon gave that up and began to wage a savage war against them. At the same time other scholars have argued that English rule in Ireland should be seen not merely as a stepping-stone to a wider world empire, but as itself a good example of English imperialism in operation – and in operation over a very long period of time. This is the thesis of Michael Hechter's *Internal Colonialism* (1975). For him too this is a story which begins with the sixteenth century. In other words in the last generation the geographical focus of the subject has shifted, but its chronological one has not. English imperialism

 From *History Today*, February 1987, pp. 16-22. Reproduced by kind permission of History Today, Ltd., 83-84 Berwick Street, London W1V 3PJ, England.

now begins in Ireland but is still thought to begin in the sixteenth and seventeenth centuries, the centuries which are conventionally regarded as marking the beginning of the modern world.

'A truly barbarous people' — Gerald of Wales' xenophobic sketches of Irish life: (top left) an Irish king in his bath tub eating mares' flesh; (top right) an Irish feud; (bottom) Irish navigation — two men in a coracle, rowing in opposite directions.

Looking at the English in Ireland does indeed make a lot of sense. It was an experience which helped to shape and harden attitudes. But those who point to the sixteenth century as the starting point of it all are just a little bit wide of the mark – roughly 400 years wide of the mark. The formative experience was not the forward policy adopted by the Elizabethans in the late 1560s, but the forward policy adopted by Henry II in the early 1170s. This is crucially important because it means that these imperialist attitudes are much more deeply ingrained than people realise. It was not just in the modern era that Englishmen decided that the Irish were savages and should be either Anglicised or exterminated: they had thought so for centuries. That this has hitherto been insufficiently realised is very largely the fault of medievalists themselves and their misleading and inaccurate habit of referring to the attack on twelfth century Ireland as 'the Norman invasion' when it should, undoubtedly, be called 'the English invasion'.

The writer who did more than any other single individual to establish the standard English view of Ireland and the Irish was Gerald of Wales (1146-1223). In 1186-87, during and shortly after a visit to Ireland (in the entourage of Prince John), he wrote *The Topography of Ireland*. In 1189 he followed this up with *The Conquest of Ireland*. Both works remained popular throughout the Middle Ages and even in the sixteenth and seventeenth centuries copies were still being made, both in the Latin original and in English translation. In essence everything that sixteenth-century Englishmen believed about Ireland can already be found in the writings of Gerald of Wales. Sixteenth-century Englishmen thought that Ireland was a potentially wealthy country inhabited by nomadic pastoralists, men who were economically backward for no other reason than that they were lazy. This is precisely how Gerald described them:

> They use their fields mostly for pasture. Little is cultivated and even less is sown. The problem here is not the quality of the soil but rather the lack of industry on the part of those who should cultivate it. This laziness means that the different types of minerals with which the hidden veins of the earth are full are neither mined nor exploited in any way. They do not devote themselves to the manufacture of flax or wool, nor to the practice of any mechanical or mercantile art. Dedicated only to leisure and laziness, this is a truly barbarous people. They depend for their livelihood on animals and they live like animals.

Brief allusions to the state of Ireland by other twelfth-century writers like William of Malmesbury and William of Newburgh make it clear that Gerald was only making explicit a conventional view of the Irish economy.

Sixteenth-century Englishmen thought that the Irish looked and dressed like barbarians. So, of course, did Gerald of Wales. 'Judged', as he put it, 'by modern ideas, they are uncultivated both in dress and appearance. Their clothes are primitive – they wear a garment that is a cross between trousers and boots – and their flowing hair and beards are barbarous'. (Incidentally he also criticised the Irish for not bathing their children often enough.)

But it was in the sphere of marital and sexual customs that sixteenth-century Englishmen found Irish standards most repugnant. Confronted by Gaelic laws of marriage and divorce that were very different from their own they responded with a blanket condemnation of Irish immorality. 'Surely', wrote Sir Henry Sidney (Lord Deputy of Ireland 1565-71, 1575-78), 'there was never people of worse minds, for matrimony among them is no more regarded than conjunction between unreasonable beasts'. In the words of Sidney's secretary, Edmund Tremayne, they 'commit whoredom, hold no wedlock, ravish, steal and commit all

abomination without scruple of conscience'. Compare this with Gerald. 'This is a filthy people, wallowing in vice. They indulge in incest, for example in marrying – or rather debauching – the wives of their dead brothers'. As usual Gerald was expressing a view that was widespread at the time. The chronicler Roger of Howden referred in passing to the Irish practices of polygamy and incest. Archbishop Anselm of Canterbury accused the Irish of wife-swapping – 'exchanging their wives as freely as other men exchange horses'.

The striking differences between Irish family law and the conventional practice of the rest of Christian Europe led men to doubt whether the Irish were truly Christian. According to Tremayne they were 'neither Papists nor Protestants but rather such as have neither fear nor love of God in their hearts'. A similar line was taken by Edmund Spenser in *A View of the Present State of Ireland* (1596). 'They are all Papists by profession but in the same so blindly and brutishly informed that you would rather think them atheists or infidels'. Apart from the Protestant/Papist complication this is just what Gerald had said. 'Despite the fact that the faith has been established here since the time of Patrick, the people still remain ignorant of its most basic rudiments'. That confident shaper of European opinion, Bernard of Clairvaux, summed it all up when he described the Irish as 'shameless in their customs, uncivilised in their ways, godless in religion, barbarous in their law, obstinate as regards instruction, foul in their lives: Christians in name, pagans in fact'.

What we have here, in the twelfth century just as in the sixteenth, is an ideology of conquest. Given that the Irish were barbarians it followed that they could legitimately be dispossessed. This was made explicit in the bull *Laudabiliter* (1155) by which Pope Hadrian IV granted Ireland to Henry II 'to the end that the foul customs of that country may be abolished and the barbarous nation, Christian in name only, may through your care assume the beauty of good morals'. Another function of the ideology of conquest in the sixteenth century was, it has been suggested, to absolve the invading English from all normal ethical restraints. If the pseudo-

Christian natives resisted then the truly Christian invaders were fully entitled to wage a ferocious war against them, disregarding the ordinary conventions of war. Thus the pamphleteer Thomas Churchyard described Humphrey Gilbert's practice of commanding that:

> the heddes of all those which were killed in the daie should be cutte of from their bodies and brought to the place where he incamped at night and should there bee laied on the ground by eche side of the waie ledying into his owne tente so that none could come into his tente for any cause but commonly he must pass through a lane of heddes.

As Lord Deputy Fitzwilliam put it in 1572, 'Till the sword have thoroughly and universally tamed . . . them in vain is law brought amongst them'. Fitzwilliam, it has been claimed, was speaking 'for the aggressive young men who had been influenced by the ideas of the Renaissance', but in reality there was nothing new either in the idea or in the practice. The thirteenth century English government regularly paid bounties on heads of rebel Irishmen. In 1305 Piers Bermingham sent thirty O'Connor heads to Dublin and was rewarded with £100. An English ballad congratulated him on this feat:

> To Irishmen he was foe
> Ever he rode about
> With strength to hunt them out
> As hunter doth the hare.

It is hardly surprising then to find the Irish alleging in 1317 that the English preached it was no more sin to kill an Irishman than to kill a dog.

It has also been claimed that by the sixteenth century:

> We can state confidently that the old concept of the Irish as being socially inferior to the English had been replaced with the idea that they were anthropologically inferior and were further behind the English on the ladder of development. The old world had lacked a sense of history and hence a concept of social process and development, but the widening horizons of the articulate citizen of sixteenth century England, both intellectually and geographically, slowly eroded the old idea of a static world.

The myth of the Renaissance strikes again. Gerald noted that:

> The Irish have not progressed at all from the primitive habits of pastoral farming.

For while mankind usually progresses from the woods to the fields, and then from the fields to settlements and communities of citizens, this people despises work on the land, has little use for the money-making of towns and condemns the rights and privileges of civil life.

As Gerald of Wales' biographer has observed, 'the concepts behind this passage – the ladder of evolution of human societies and the persistence of primitive survivals – would not be out of place in nineteenth-century anthropological thought'. And these sorts of ideas were taken for granted by writers such as William of Newburgh who observed that the political structure of contemporary (twelfth century) Ireland was very like that of early Anglo-Saxon England.

Undoubtedly then the twelfth century Englishman had a clear sense of belonging to a more advanced society. In some respects, in terms of the technology of war for example, he undoubtedly was more advanced. In Irish conditions the English possession of heavy cavalry was perhaps a dubious asset, but there were other ways in which they enjoyed a clear military superiority. In the bow and crossbow they possessed missile-launching weapons superior to anything the Irish used – thus archers who rode to war and dismounted to fight were of inestimable value to the invaders. In addition they could afford to build stone castles and wear effective body armour. Thus an Irish poet lamenting the death of Brian O'Neill in battle in 1260 wrote:

Unequal they engaged in battle
The foreigners and the Gael of Tara
Fine linen shirts on the race of Conn
And foreigners in one mass of iron.

Not only was England a wealthier society, it was also one which was organised so as to enable its rulers to exploit its resources to the full. Whereas, as William of Newburgh had observed, Ireland was still in a state of acute political fragmentation, England had been united since the tenth century and the king of England could, if he chose, bring massive and irresistible forces to bear. Henry II's army of invasion in 1171 was, by the standards of the time and place, an overwhelmingly large one, the combatants numbering some 500 knights and 3-4,000 archers, but it is the logistical back-up which is most impressive. The royal administrative machine swung into action and few English towns and shires escaped its net. The city of Gloucester, for example, was required to send 1,000 shovels and 60,000 nails, while the county had to supply 2,000 pickaxes and 1,000 shovels. Enormous quantities of grain, beans, cheese, bacon and other foodstuffs were sent across, including – since the king meant to live in the style to which he was accustomed – no less than 569lb of almonds. In addition 1,000lb of sealing wax were ordered – clearly nothing was going to interrupt the bureaucratic machinery of the twelfth-century English state. To transport all this an armada of no less than 400 ships was required.

But if Henry II could mount an expedition on this scale and bring the Irish chiefs scurrying to submission

Durer's 1521 engraving of an Irish chief and his retainers shows a barbaric and primitive but not undignified hierarchy; an objective view not shared by sixteenth-century English commentators.

then how was it that the medieval English kings failed to complete the conquest of Ireland? In part because Ireland was a difficult land to conquer. Political fragmentation meant that there was no central authority for the invader to seize. Each region had to be conquered separately and in terrain broken by bog and mountain this was no easy task. But the main reason is that they did not try very hard. Only rarely was the English government interested in Ireland. Normally it came about fifth in their order of priorities, after domestic affairs, France, Scotland and Wales. After Henry II's invasion of 1171 and John's expedition in 1210, no king visited Ireland until Richard II in 1394, and then none between 1399 and 1690. No king's son visited Ireland between 1185 and 1361, and none thereafter.

But merely to point to royal disinterest is to oversimplify a more complicated and more interesting story. In the late twelfth and thirteenth centuries there was a very considerable movement of English settlers into Ireland and, broadly speaking, throughout this period we can see a continuing expansion of English control – castles and towns built, shires created, and the whole panoply of English administration introduced: sheriffs, coroners, keepers of the peace, escheators and judges. By 1300 perhaps as much as two-thirds of Ireland was under English administration and the lordship was producing a reasonable amount of revenue for the English crown. Between 1278 and 1299, net of local expenditure, the revenue of Ireland averaged £6,300 p.a., roughly 15 per cent of total royal revenue. At this date moreover Edward I was trying to complete the English conquest of Britain and was using Irish resources in the attempt. Ireland contributed some £30,000 to the cost of building the ring of great castles with which Edward surrounded Snowdonia and throughout his Welsh wars there was a regular stream of supplies shipped from Irish ports both to victual those castles and supply his armies. Then Edward turned his attention to Scotland and in 1296, 1301 and 1303 three major expeditions left Ireland for Scotland.

For a while the Irish exchequer was largely responsible for supplying the western theatre of war based on

The fortifications of the English settlement at Carrickfergus, County Antrim, c.1561.

Carlisle. But the Scottish people were always a stumbling block and with the accession of Edward II the tide of war began to flow in the opposite direction. In 1315 Robert Bruce followed up his great victory at Bannockburn (1314) by sending his brother Edward with an army to conquer Ireland. In 1316, indeed, Edward Bruce was crowned King of Ireland. If the plan had succeeded it would have deprived the English of Irish resources and placed them at the disposal of the Scots instead. Indeed Edward Bruce could have become king of both Scotland and Ireland since at this date Robert had no sons and in April 1315 he had decided to make his brother heir to the Scottish throne. In Ireland the Bruces looked to the native Irish for support against the English, appealing to their 'common national ancestry', their 'common language' and their 'common custom'. Since in these years they also hoped for help from the Welsh, there was in prospect something very like a pan-Celtic alliance against the English. At any rate from May 1315 until Edward Bruce's death in battle in October 1318 there was a Scottish army active in Ireland and posing a very real threat to the English position there. The whole future shape of the British Isles was at stake.

Although Edward Bruce was ultimately defeated and killed, these years did mark a real turning point. From now on Scottish independence was assured; and from now on an Irish resurgence meant that English rule became more and more restricted. In the fourteenth and fifteenth centuries the direction of the flow of bullion across the Irish Sea was reversed and the land became a drain on English resources. By the end of the fifteenth century there was no effective government authority beyond the pale.

Despite these setbacks the English attitude to the Irish remained unchanged. They continued to regard them as wild and savage barbarians. The English retained a well-developed sense of their own superiority. As the Venetian envoy to England put it (*circa* 1500), 'the English are great lovers of themselves and of everything English. They think there are no other men worth considering and no other part of the world either'. Not surprisingly their neighbours rather resented this. In the 1440s a Scot wrote that 'the tyranny and cruelty of the English are notorious throughout the world, as manifestly appears in the usurpations against the French, Scots, Welsh, Irish and neighbouring lands'. In part this perception was sustained by their periods of success against the French in the Hundred Years War. In the 1390s the town council of Danzig asserted that the English must be kept out of the Baltic. 'If once they were to get a foothold in Prussia they would take it over, as they had taken Gascony from the French'. But against the French although the English might adopt a proud and aggressive attitude it was not an imperialist one – there was no deepseated disdain for France and the French. When Henry V conquered Normandy he founded a university at Caen. It was intended to cater for Norman students. But no medieval English ruler of Ireland ever thought of founding a university for the Irish: they were savages. Imperialist attitudes were reserved for those on the fringes of European 'civilisation' and beyond – 'beyond the pale'.

In essence then the history of the English in Ireland begins with a period of imperialist expansion in the twelfth and thirteenth centuries. This strongly suggests that what was happening in Britain was part of a wider, European movement: to the East the German *Drang nach Osten* fuelled by a German view of the Slavs as barbarians: in the Mediterranean region

the crusades against the infidel. In the same centuries there was an expansion of commerce, especially Italian commerce, into the Eastern Mediterranean, into the Black Sea and then into Asia. Along with the traders went the missionaries, preaching Christianity and founding churches, even as far away as Peking. In 1291 the Vivaldi brothers set out from Genoa on their search for the sea route to India. This period of European expansion was also a period of profound intellectual and cultural development – the so-called twelfth-century renaissance. Schools proliferated and the European university system was founded. A general improvement in education and literacy went hand in hand with a wider acquaintance with classical literature – including the concept of the barbarian.

It was also a period when a radical programme of church reform – the Gregorian reform – was implemented throughout much of Latin Christendom. This meant a general acceptance of new rules governing the family life of priest and layman alike. But in Ireland, and this was to be crucially important, the reform movement made little headway. In pre-reform days the English church had shown a lively appreciation of the intellectual and spiritual achievement of the Irish church. Bede's view of Ireland was a distinctly positive one and his works continued to be widely read. The feasts of Patrick and Brigid were celebrated in every English monastery. But when the Irish resisted, as the English and the Scots did not, the pressure to conform to the new norms in church and society, then they came to be judged and found wanting by men who were all too certain of their own moral rectitude and who were very ready to condemn values which they did not share. So the Irish, by remaining true to their old way of life, came to be regarded as immoral savages. The 'island of saints' became the 'island of barbarians'. This is why Gerald of Wales' views of Ireland came to be so extraordinarily influential: not because he was saying something completely new but because he was giving precision and depth to prejudices which were already in the process of being formed and because

he happened to do so during the early stages of a period of prolonged military and political contact between England and Ireland. In the twelfth century the Welsh suffered the same fate as the Irish and for essentially the same reason, but the very different history of Wales meant that, in the end, the Welsh were saved. In the later Middle Ages they, unlike the Irish, had the 'good fortune' to become gradually more Anglicised and hence less barbaric.

After the expansion of the twelfth and thirteenth centuries, there came a loss of momentum in the fourteenth and fifteenth centuries, related presumably to the massive overall drop in the population of Europe after the Black Death. Despite this loss of momentum Verlinden has argued that in terms of the techniques of colonial expansion there is a clear line of continuity linking Italian maritime expansion in the twelfth and thirteenth centuries with the Mediterranean-led expansion into the Atlantic in the fifteenth century. Equally there is a clear line of continuity linking twelfth and thirteenth century English expansion in Ireland with the later conquest of Ireland in the sixteenth and seventeenth centuries: we find the same techniques – including the founding of towns and the plantation of settlers and the same attitude of civilised contempt for the lesser breed without the law. Thus if we seek the origins of English imperialism we should look to Ireland and the twelfth and thirteenth centuries.

FOR FURTHER READING:
By far the best introduction to the thought-world of Gerald of Wales is Robert Bartlett, *Gerald of Wales 1146-1223* (Oxford University Press, 1982). A few of Gerald's works are readily available in translation in Penguin Classics: in particular *The Topography of Ireland*, translated by J.J. O'Meara (Harmondsworth, 1982). Also useful for comparison are his two works on Wales: *The Journey through Wales* and *The Description of Wales* in one volume; translated by L. Thorpe (Harmondsworth, 1978). On the English in Ireland see A.J. Otway-Ruthven, *A History of Medieval Ireland* (Ernest Benn, 2nd edn. 1980), J.F. Lydon, *The Lordship of Ireland in the Middle Ages* (Gill and Macmillan, 1972), ed. James Lydon, *The English in Medieval Ireland* (Royal Irish Academy, 1984), and Robin Frame, *Colonial Ireland 1169-1369* (Dublin, 1981).

PROPHETS WITHOUT HONOUR?

JAN HUS – HERETIC OR PATRIOT?

'Truth will conquer' – the Czech historian
František Šmahel traces the life and work
of his fifteenth-century compatriot Jan Hus –
whose uncompromising criticism of
medieval Catholicism stirred national pride
and acted as a forerunner of the Reformation.

*František Šmahel is Senior Research Fellow at
the Museum of the Hussite Movement, Tabor,
Czechoslovakia.*
*Translated by **Jitka Jenkins**.*

Even in the fifteenth century, in a
case concerning a university professor and preacher, it was not
usual to involve, successively, the leading lawyers and theologians, three
archbishops, the judicial courts of two
popes, and, last but not least, two kings
(both bearers of the Holy Roman
Crown). The singularity of this case
extended beyond this fact. The Czech
reformer Master John Hus, who was
the person in question, was one of the
first people to receive a personal invitation to attend the Council of Constance. Hus went voluntarily in order
to defend his honour but he paid for his
courage with his life. In premonition of
his own end, he once wrote that 'He
who dies, wins'. Until his last moment,
he did not cease to believe in his
biblical motto *Veritas vincit*, even
though, at that time, truth was not
prevailing against power.

A miniature from one of the famous
Hussite hymn-books (graduals) recorded the development of the European Reformation thus: John Wycliffe
struck the first spark, John Hus used it

to ignite the candle, and Martin Luther
raised the burning torch aloft; the blaze
of the torch obliterated the glow of the
candle and the spark in the general
awareness of history. This encapsula-
tion is not misleading; after an initial
hesitation, Luther began to cite the
heretic Hus, while Hus in turn regarded the Oxford apostate Wycliffe as
his teacher.

Wycliffe's radical critique of traditional Catholic doctrine in the 1370s
(in the course of which he had questioned its traditional hierarchy), putting forward a forerunner of the Reformation's priesthood of all believers,
and his attack on the doctrine of transubstantiation had placed him in the
forefront of heretical dissent which,
without the patronage of Edward II's
brother, John of Gaunt, could have led
him to the stake rather than a peaceful
death in 1384.

Moreover, the indictment against
Hus at the Council of Constance was
mostly related to the Wycliffian basis of
his faith. The detailed dispute about
Hus' intellectual ancestry has by no
means ended; nevertheless, it is possible to assert, with the benefit of hindsight, that, without Wycliffe, Hus' doctrine would have lacked its reforming

vehemence and, moreover, that it was
only after Wycliffe's ideas had been
transferred to Bohemia that they acquired their final European (Hussite)
character.

The Reformation movement in the
Kingdom of Bohemia only manifested
itself significantly in the second half of
the fourteenth century. It rapidly became popular and, thanks to both the
University of Prague and the international contacts of the Luxembourg
princely house which ruled Bohemia as
part of the imperial domain, it readily
incorporated additional stimuli of
foreign origin. Apart from the Walden-
sian heresy of the German colonists
(which was based on the principles of
church poverty, preaching and
teaching the scriptures in the vernacular and was driven deep underground
after being deemed illegal by the Inquisition), most of the reforming
efforts did not exceed the limits of
tolerance of the clerics.

Hus' generation followed their native predecessors by returning to their
traditions, independently reaching a
set of nonconformist thoughts and demands. When the first writings of the
Oxford Reformer John Wycliffe became known in Prague, by the end of

the fourteenth century, the young John Hus added an almost prophetic remark to his own transcription of the writings in the form of a pun: 'Wycliffe, Wycliffe, many heads will become shaky.' (In Czech, *'Viklef, Viklef, nejednomu ty hlavu zvikleš'*, the name Wycliffe (Viklef) sounds similar to the word for shaking, making wobbly or loose.) The name of Wycliffe became a symbol for the other masters of the Czech faction in the university corporation who longed to be 'the head and not the tail' at the highest national educational institution. This was just provocative enough for the foreign professors there to launch an attack, and by the end of May 1403 they enforced, by a majority, a condemnation of forty-five heretic articles from Wycliffe's writings.

In April 1408 the Papal Curia forbade, under strict punishment, the spreading of Wycliffe's writings; those in possession were threatened by anathema, if they refused to give them up. Soon afterwards, the Prague Consistory also hardened its campaign against the Reformation group. The opponents of the Wycliffians, however, rejoiced prematurely. The spokesmen of the Czech nation made use of the favourable political situation and, with the help of influential adherents in the king's court, they pushed through a change in the university constitution in January 1409. According to a decree issued in Kutná Hora by Wenceslas IV, the native (Czech) university people were granted three votes against only one vote jointly for the three combined corporations of foreign masters and students. In the meantime, a pressure group of radical Wycliffians obtained the decisive influence in the Czech community, hence the university in Prague simultaneously embarked on the path of heresy. The victory on the domestic front, however, had an obverse side; before the Reformation movement could become a national social force, hundreds of former masters of Prague University started to sound an alarm against it, at home and abroad, after they had left Prague in protest against the Kutná Hora decree.

John Hus (born around 1370) attracted the attention of the foreign public for the first time in the stormy atmosphere of the years 1408-09. Up to that time he had been overshadowed by his senior colleagues. The situation required energetic leaders, who would not be frightened by the first threat. Hus was predestined for the leading role not only by his long-lasting teaching activities but by his increasing fame as a popular preacher in the Bethlehem Chapel. The governors of this spacious chapel, where only the Czech language was employed for preaching, had appointed him in 1402; he had obtained his clerical ordination shortly before, so he must have been about thirty years old at that time.

For Hus, a society divided into estates was a constituent part of the imaginary Church of Christ on Earth but it had little in common with the real Roman Catholic Church. Wycliffe's doctrine about the dual body of the Church had influenced him here. No-one, not even the pope, could say (according to Wycliffe) that he was predestined for salvation or damnation. Because of that, the terrestrial Church, as a sum of all the worshippers, must have included a dual community with totally different prospects in the next world. The basic conflict between the forces of good and evil, both within the individual and in the community, was thus fought between the chosen community of the followers of Christ and the equally imaginary throng belonging to the ruler of Hell.

Hus accepted this concept, which undermined the authority and power of the Church hierarchy, only with reservation. For instance, he continued to recognise the sacramental succession of the clerical office from the time of the Apostles and thus the inequality between the clergy and the laity, and between a clergyman and a bishop. In principle, he also drew a sharp line through the whole social pyramid, thus dividing it into parallel communities obedient or disobedient to God's law, both structured into estates. On the one hand, he reprimanded the pride of the peasant *nouveaux-riches* and the minor swindles of the petty craftsmen; on the other hand, he did not exclude the God-fearing lords and patricians from the chosen community. He was seeking the support of the rich for his Reformation aims from the very beginning of his activities. Hus simply visualised an ideal, fair feudalism in which everyone would contribute by fraternal love to the prosperity of all.

It was this vision of the widely-opened arms of Hus' reforming programme that spread Czech opposition to the Church through all ranks of society – from king to journeyman. For this reason alone was the initially scanty handful of university Wycliffians able to survive the first hard trials. The more the movement gained adherents from the common people from town and country, the greater became the strains on the movement's social unity. The process began during Hus' life without being significantly reflected in his doctrine. The opponents of the Wycliffian-Hussite ideology realised much more acutely the danger of the appeal of the Reformation and of the growing potential revolt from below.

Hus was an immensely hard-working man. He preached almost every day in the Bethlehem Chapel, he fulfilled his duties in the Faculty of Arts in exemplary fashion, and he by no means neglected his own studies leading to the doctorate in theology. Hus was fortunate to be able to express his thoughts readily in both speech and writing and in a robust way, and more than once he let himself be carried away by personal invective. His preaching in the Bethlehem Chapel gained excitement from his comments on topical events. The majority of the forty Prague parsons cast a spiteful eye on the Bethlehem competition because Hus specifically castigated them. Some only grumbled, others went to the Bethlehem Chapel in disguise and write down every suspicious word, for immediate transmission to the Consistory.

The Archbishop of Prague, Zbyněk of Házmburk, had overlooked petty back-biting for a long time – in October 1407 he even rewarded Hus by giving him the post of preacher at a clerical meeting (synod). But, when Hus dared to oppose the official standpoint just one year later, the Archbishop turned against him, and banned him instantly from preaching. Hus soon returned to the Bethlehem Chapel; however, he had acquired dangerous domestic opponents in Archbishop Zbyněk, his officials, and the Prague parsons. The majority of them were key members of Czech society. The unimpeachibility and uncompromising 'holiness' of the nation, which was a constant theme of the Czech nationalists of the reform circle, was thus significantly compromised. In spite of the mutual Czech-German malice, which later lead to bloody conflict, Hus increasingly advocated the principle of true faith above the interests of the nation and the home country. For his mature codex of values, an appeal he made to his own followers is typical (October 1412):

Would you, please, at first consider God's business which has been injured. Secondly, you can pay attention to the dishonour of your country and your nation, and only then, thirdly, can you take account of the dishonour and wrong-doing which you personally innocently suffer.

Hus was not able to take over in his reforming practice all that Wycliffe had drafted at his peaceful desk in the form of pure theory. It is accepted that Hus brought Wycliffe's doctrine to life ideologically by his creative adaptation, but his attempts to develop independently of Wycliffe were not, as a rule, intellectual advances. Hus not only adapted Wycliffe's thoughts to his domestic situation but, simultaneously, he made them less sharply focused. Hus much more frequently referred to his Oxford teacher in the supreme works of the later period when, after his expulsion from Prague, he had time enough for literary activities. The programme of the Reformation party, described in his tract 'About the Church' (apart from some small alterations), he took from Wycliffe. The second part of this crucial document, which was written in the years 1412-13, consists of a masterly polemic against his opponents and a whole set of courageous thoughts concerning true and false obedience. Hus there generalised his experience with the religious courts at all levels and thus, indirectly, granted to his followers in subordinate posts the right to oppose all the authorities whose orders were in conflict with God's Law.

Therefore, if the Pope ordered me to blow a whistle, to build towers, to sew, to weave a cloth, or to stuff sausages, would not my common sense see that the Pope ordered a stupid thing? Why should I not prefer, in this matter, my own opinion to the Pope's order?

In Hus' statements of this sort we can already faintly hear the sound of the bugle announcing the beginning of the Hussite wars.

The very first of Hus' trials merged with the fight concerning the orthodoxy of Wycliffian doctrine. In accord with a decision of the papal court in April 1408, the Archbishop of Prague ordered everyone to hand over all copies of Wycliffe's works. Five students appealed against this edict to the papal see. Since numerous reforming masters, including Hus, failed to obey the order within the designated time period, the archbishop put them into anathema.

Despite the university's protest, the archbishop again ordered (on June 16th, 1410) the surrender of Wycliffe's books. In addition, he banned all preaching in private places, in particular the Bethlehem Chapel. The edict provoked such strong indignation, even at the king's court, that Zbyněk promised to postpone the execution of the decree. In the meantime, the university protested again, and Hus published a brief statement in which he disproved the basis of the principle of destroying heretic books in the flames. The archbishop was even more irritated by an appeal which was submitted by Hus and several of his pupils on June 25th to the papal curia. In the middle of July, the archbishop ordered the burning of Wycliffe's works which had been found in his palace. For fear of street riots (which, indeed, occurred in Prague soon after), he fled to his castle in Roudnice, and from there proclaimed an anathema on Hus and those of his followers who had associated themselves with the appeal.

At the beginning of 1412 it might have seemed that the scales of papal justice would favour Hus. The decisive swing against Hus was again caused by his Prague opponents who managed to impose a court suit on Hus' dexterous advocate Master John of Jesenice. Even then, it might have been possible to influence the verdict if only Hus himself had not fanned the flames by his attitude to the selling of papal indulgencies. Trafficking in the trust of believers had provoked a mighty wave of protests at the university and in Prague reforming circles, which was soon thwarted on the walls of the king's palace. For reasons which have not been truly understood, Wenceslas IV agreed to the sale of indulgences and accordingly ordered the Prague councillors to punish strictly all those who spoke against such sales.

At this critical moment, when one faction of the reformers began to turn their backs on their own Wycliffian beliefs, even Hus hesitated, and he temporarily shrank into the background. That happened after the execution of three journeymen, participants in the first big popular demonstration in Prague for the support of the reformation movement. Hus felt responsible not only for the executed, but for all his followers. After thirteen days, during which people in Prague whispered that halberdiers had shut Hus' mouth, he reassured his followers. In his sermon in the Bethlehem Chapel on July 24th, 1412, Hus condemned the massacre of the innocent martyrs of faith, and he appealed to the congregation not to be discouraged but to stand by the truth.

The news of Hus' invectives against the pope, which had eagerly been reported to the curia, accelerated the process of appeal. The verdict was brought to Prague by a papal legate, thus excluding the possibility of postponing its implicit consequences. At the synod on October 18th, 1412, the sentence of excommunication on Hus was reinforced. If he had not submitted within twenty days, an interdict would have been issued after a further twelve days on all the places in which he might have been found. A ban on all church services, including funerals, would have brought many difficulties for the 40,000 inhabitants of the city. The consequences could have turned people against the reformation movement. This led Hus to the decision to leave for the country. Still, before he left, he appealed to Christ against the verdict of the papal see.

Hus' gesture of resignation was soon overshadowed by a hopeful counteraction by his solicitor John of Jesenice at the Lands court. The senior representatives of the lords proclaimed their right to demand a vote also in the matters concerning ideology of country-wide importance. In their edict of December 1412, they stated that a subpoena from a foreign court had no legal force. On the basis of this intervention, Wenceslas asked the archbishop, who was by this time his trusted friend, Konrad of Vechta, to pacify the antagonistic domestic clergy.

The assiduous archbishop submitted the views of the opposing sides to the Crown council in February of the following year. The king then consigned the task of formulating a compromise agreement to a special commission; it ordered the Wycliffians and their opponents to commit themselves to accepting a verdict of arbitration under the penalty of paying 60,000 pieces of silver or of expulsion from the country. The four leading professors of theology found themselves trapped when they were ordered to pronounce that the country was freed from heresy. They preferred voluntary exile to loss of face. John Hus behaved with dignity, too, when he refused to accept the compromising proposals. With the words 'I do not want to sin any more', he eliminated any possibility of resolving the controversy on the domestic front.

The invitation to attend the Council of Constance presented a challenge which Hus could not decline. The initiative of the Holy Roman king, Sigismund, raised justified apprehension among the adherents of the reforms because the Czech public distrusted the character of this second son of the Emperor Charles IV. On the other hand, it was not possible to ignore the general merit of Sigismund's efforts to summon a council which would provide Hus with a platform from which to defend the Reformation programme at the most significant contemporary international forum.

Hus calmed his own apprehensions and doubts by drawing on limitless trust in the victory of the biblical truth. The reforming circle was resigned to the possibility of a court case, but only if the result of the public hearing was unfavourable to Hus. The risk to Hus could be mitigated only by a safe-conduct, which was actually promised to Hus by Sigismund, and which was granted after some delay. In the event of a public hearing, Hus was determined 'to profess the Lord Christ and, if necessary, to suffer death for His most truthful Law'. These words were not spoken to the winds. Before leaving for Constance, Hus left behind a sealed letter for his favourite pupil, with instructions that it should not be opened until after his death. In the letter, Hus revealed himself and the depth of his faith much more than in public proclamations. Simultaneously, the letter contained his last will, as far as his modest possessions were concerned.

In the remaining time, Hus hastily drafted three speeches for his public appearances. In the event, Hus was not able to deliver any of his intended speeches; he had instead to be grateful to be granted a public hearing during the court case. The safe-conduct granted by Sigismund did not protect Hus at all. By the end of November 1414, less than two weeks after Hus' arrival in Constance, Pope John XXIII capitulated to the pressure of the Czech accusers, and imposed provisional custody upon Hus. Disregarding the protests of Sigismund's courtiers, the pope refused to set Hus free, and on December 4th he entrusted the opening of the court case to a special investigating commission. Two days later, Hus was thrown into a stinking cell in the Dominican monastery, where he remained until the end of March 1415. Sigismund, after he arrived in Constance, showed goodwill in dealing with this Hus affair and, during his first encounter with the cardinals, he pressed for Hus' release. Some of the cardinals threatened to leave if the council could not make independent decisions in religious matters. Sigismund submitted; he insisted, however, on a public hearing and he secured Hus' transfer into an airy cell close to the monastery refectory. After that, Hus was able to resume his correspondence and occasionally receive visits from his companions and friends.

Sigismund was playing for high stakes against Pope John, and much politicking was involved, in the coils of which both the pope and his Czech critic became enmeshed. The pope fled from Constance on the night of March 21st, 1415; in the resulting confusion, no-one showed any interest in Hus. A word from the king would have been enough to release him from prison; it did not come because Hus' case was taken up, almost overnight, as the chief instrument by which Sigismund could continue the existence of the council. Hus was, by Sigismund's order, transported by ship to the castle of the Bishop of Constance in Gottlieben, where he stayed until the beginning of May. At that time, the two Johns exchanged places: the seized pope was interned in Gottlieben while Hus was taken back to Constance.

Hus' letters from prison sometimes take the form of a manifesto; at other times they constitute a deeply human testimony. In the struggle with his own doubts, and in fear for his own life, Hus demonstrated his internal strength. Sometimes it even seemed as though he had begun to see the uselessness of his defence at the council. The critical break occurred during the second public hearing on June 7th, 1415. Hus' stubborness there provoked even King Sigismund, who took umbrage at Hus' statements regarding the moral disqualification of sovereigns, popes, and prelates in a state of mortal sin, exclaiming 'John Hus, no-one lives without sin!' The king's well-meant advice was unacceptable to Hus, and that provoked his judges even more. Face to face with his opponents and accusers he declared: 'I am standing in front of God's tribunal, which will justly pass judgement on both you and me according to our merits.' Sigismund waved away this threat from the next world and, as he left, instructed the cardinals to make short work of the case of Hus and also that of Master Jerome of Prague, who had come to Constance to support his friend.

The last public hearing in Constance Cathedral during the celebratory session of the council on July 6th, 1415, was merely a formal court ritual leading to the stake prepared on the embankment of the Rhine. The written statement submitted to the council by Hus on July 1st thwarted all the behind-the-stage efforts to save him. If he had perjured himself, or recanted, Hus would have betrayed his followers: 'for that, it would be proper', as he wrote to one of his friends, 'for me to have a millstone hung around my neck and be drowned in the depths of the sea.' The last attempt at a defence was muffled by the noise of curses and mockeries. Nevertheless, Hus' 'I do not recant' transcends place and time. His death in the flames accelerated the transformation of a peaceful reformation movement in Bohemia to an armed revolt against the worldly Roman Church and its profane protectors. The first phase of the victorious Reformation in Europe became generally known under Hus' name. Last but not least, Hus' courageous stance in Constance remains, for the present and the future, an inspiration in the fearless fight for the right to individual or collective truth.

FOR FURTHER READING:
Geoffrey Barraclough (ed.), *Eastern and Western Europe in the Middle Ages* (Thames and Hudson, 1970); Paul Roubiczek and Joseph Kalmer, *Warrior of God: The Life and Death of John Hus* (London, 1947); M. Spinka, *John Hus' Concept of the Church* (Princeton University Press, 1966); Gordon Leff, *Heresy in the Later Middle Ages* (Manchester University Press, 1966).

How a mysterious disease laid low Europe's masses

*In the 1300s, a third of the population
died of plague brought by fleas, shocking
the medieval world to its foundations*

Charles L. Mee jr.

In all likelihood, a flea riding on the hide of a black rat entered the Italian port of Messina in 1347, perhaps down a hawser tying a ship up at the dock. The flea had a gut full of the bacillus *Yersinia pestis*. The flea itself was hardly bigger than the letter "o" on this page, but it could carry several hundred thousand bacilli in its intestine.

Scholars today cannot identify with certainty which species of flea (or rat) carried the plague. One candidate among the fleas is *Xenopsylla cheopis*, which looks like a deeply bent, bearded old man with six legs. It is slender and bristly, with almost no neck and no waist, so that it can slip easily through the forest of hair in which it lives. It is outfitted with a daggerlike proboscis for piercing the skin and sucking the blood of its host. And it is cunningly equipped to secrete a substance that prevents coagulation of the host's blood. Although *X. cheopis* can go for weeks without feeding, it will eat every day if it can, taking its blood warm.

One rat on which fleas feed, the black rat (*Rattus rattus*), also known as the house rat, roof rat or ship rat, is active mainly at night. A rat can fall 50 feet and land on its feet with no injury. It can scale a brick wall or climb up the inside of a pipe only an inch and a half in diameter. It can jump a distance of two feet straight up and four horizontally, and squeeze through a hole the size of a quarter. Black rats have been found still swimming days after their ship has sunk at sea.

A rat can gnaw its way through almost anything—paper, wood, bone, mortar, half-inch sheet metal. It gnaws constantly. Indeed, it *must* gnaw constantly. Its incisors grow four to five inches a year: if it were to stop gnawing, its lower incisors would eventually grow—as sometimes happens when a rat loses an opposing tooth—until the incisors push up into the rat's brain, killing it. It prefers grain, if possible, but also eats fish, eggs, fowl and meat—lambs, piglets and the flesh of helpless infants or adults. If nothing else is available, a rat will eat manure and drink urine.

Rats prefer to move no more than a hundred feet from their nests. But in severe drought or famine, rats can begin to move en masse for great distances, bringing with them any infections they happen to have picked up, infections that may be killing them but not killing them more rapidly than they breed.

Rats and mice harbor a number of infections that may cause diseases in human beings. A black rat can even tolerate a moderate amount of the ferocious *Yersinia pestis* bacillus in its system without noticeable ill effects. But bacilli breed even more extravagantly than fleas or rats, often in the millions. When a bacillus finally invades the rat's pulmonary or nervous system, it causes a horrible, often convulsive, death, passing on a lethal dose to the bloodsucking fleas that ride on the rat's hide.

The ultimate bacillus breeder

When an afflicted rat dies, its body cools, so that the flea, highly sensitive to changes in temperature, will find another host. The flea can, if need be, survive for weeks at a time without a rat host. It can take refuge anywhere, even in an abandoned rat's nest or a bale of cloth. A dying rat may liberate scores of rat fleas. More than that, a flea's intestine happens to provide ideal breeding conditions for the bacillus, which will eventually multiply so prodigiously as finally to block the gut of the flea entirely. Unable to feed or digest blood, the flea desperately seeks another host. But now, as it sucks blood, it spits some out at the same time. Each time the flea stops sucking for a moment, it is capable of pumping thousands of virulent bacilli back into its host. Thus bacilli are passed from rat to flea to rat, contained, ordinarily, within a closed community.

For millions of years, there has been a reservoir of *Yersinia pestis* living as a permanently settled parasite—passed back and forth among fleas and rodents in warm, moist nests—in the wild rodent colonies of China, India, the southern part of the Soviet Union and the western United States. Probably there will always be such reservoirs—ready to be stirred up by sudden climatic change or ecological disaster. Even last year, four authentic cases of bubonic plague were confirmed in New Mexico and Arizona. Limited outbreaks and some fatalities have occurred in the United States for years, in fact, but the disease doesn't spread, partly for reasons we don't understand, partly because patients can now be treated with antibiotics.

And at least from biblical times on, there have been sporadic allusions to plagues, as well as carefully recorded outbreaks. The emperor Justinian's Constantinople, for instance, capital of the Roman empire in the East, was ravaged by plague in 541 and 542, felling perhaps 40 percent of the city's population. But none of the biblical or Roman plagues seemed so emblematic of horror and devastation as the Black Death that struck Europe in 1347. Rumors of fearful pestilence in China and throughout the East had reached Europe by 1346. "India was depopulated," reported one chronicler, "Tartary, Mesopotamia, Syria, Armenia, were covered with dead bodies; the Kurds fled in vain to the mountains. In Caramania and Caesarea none were left alive."

Untold millions would die in China and the rest of the East before the plague subsided again. By September of 1345, the *Yersinia pestis* bacillus, probably carried by rats, reached the Crimea, on the northern coast of the Black Sea, where Italian merchants had a good number of trading colonies.

From the shores of the Black Sea, the bacillus seems to have entered a number of Italian ports. The most famous account has to do with a ship that docked in the Sicilian port of Messina in 1347. According to an Italian chronicler named Gabriele de Mussis, Christian merchants from Genoa and local Muslim residents in the town of Caffa on the Black Sea got into an argument; a serious fight ensued between the merchants

and a local army led by a Tatar lord. In the course of an attack on the Christians, the Tatars were stricken by plague. From sheer spitefulness, their leader loaded his catapults with dead bodies and hurled them at the Christian enemy, in hopes of spreading disease among them. Infected with the plague, the Genoese sailed back to Italy, docking first at Messina.

Although de Mussis, who never traveled to the Crimea, may be a less-than-reliable source, his underlying assumption seems sound. The plague did spread along established trade routes. (Most likely, though, the pestilence in Caffa resulted from an infected population of local rats, not from the corpses lobbed over the besieged city's walls.)

In any case, given enough dying rats and enough engorged and frantic fleas, it will not be long before the fleas, in their search for new hosts, leap to a human being. When a rat flea senses the presence of an alternate host, it can jump very quickly and as much as 150 times its length. The average for such jumps is about six inches horizontally and four inches straight up in the air. Once on human skin, the flea will not travel far before it begins to feed.

The first symptoms of bubonic plague often appear within several days: headache and a general feeling of weakness, followed by aches and chills in the upper leg and groin, a white coating on the tongue, rapid pulse, slurred speech, confusion, fatigue, apathy and a staggering gait. A blackish pustule usually will form at the point of the fleabite. By the third day, the lymph nodes begin to swell. Because the bite is commonly in the leg, it is the lymph nodes of the groin that swell, which is how the disease got its name. The Greek word for "groin" is *boubōn*—thus, bubonic plague. The swellings will be tender, perhaps as large as an egg. The heart begins to flutter rapidly as it tries to pump blood through swollen, suffocating tissues. Subcutaneous hemorrhaging occurs, causing purplish blotches on the skin. The victim's nervous system begins to collapse, causing dreadful pain and bizarre neurological disorders, from which the "Dance of Death" rituals that accompanied the plague may have taken their inspiration. By the fourth or fifth day, wild anxiety and terror overtake the sufferer—and then a sense of resignation, as the skin blackens and the rictus of death settles on the body.

In 1347, when the plague struck in Messina, townspeople realized that it must have come from the sick and dying crews of the ships at their dock. They turned on the sailors and drove them back out to sea—eventually to spread the plague in other ports. Messina panicked. People ran out into the fields and vineyards and neighboring villages, taking the rat fleas with them.

When the citizens of Messina, already ill or just becoming ill, reached the city of Catania, 55 miles to the south, they were at first taken in and given beds in the hospital. But as the plague began to infect Catania, the townspeople there cordoned off their town and refused—too late—to admit any outsiders. The sick, turning black, stumbling and delirious, were objects more of disgust than pity; everything about them gave off a terrible stench, it was said, their "sweat, excrement, spittle, breath, so foetid as to be overpowering; urine turbid, thick, black or red. . . ."

Wherever the plague appeared, the suddenness of death was terrifying. Today, even with hand-me-down memories of the great influenza epidemic of 1918 (SMITHSONIAN, January 1989) and the advent of AIDS, it is hard to grasp the strain that the plague put on the physical and spiritual fabric of society. People went to bed perfectly healthy and were found dead in the morning. Priests and doctors who came to minister to the sick, so the wild stories ran, would contract the plague with a single touch and die sooner than the person they had come to help. In his preface to *The Decameron*, a collection of stories told while the plague was raging, Boccaccio reports that he saw two pigs rooting around in the clothes of a man who had just died, and after a few minutes of snuffling, the pigs began to run wildly around and around, then fell dead.

"Tedious were it to recount," Boccaccio thereafter laments, "brother was forsaken by brother, nephew by uncle, brother by sister and, oftentimes, husband by wife; nay what is more and scarcely to be believed, fathers and mothers were found to abandon their own children, untended, unvisited, to their fate, as if they had been strangers. . . ."

In Florence, everyone grew so frightened of the bodies stacked up in the streets that some men, called *becchini*, put themselves out for hire to fetch and carry the dead to mass graves. Having in this way stepped over the boundary into the land of the dead, and no doubt feeling doomed themselves, the *becchini* became an abandoned, brutal lot. Many roamed the streets, forcing their way into private homes and threatening to carry people away if they were not paid off in money or sexual favors.

Visiting men with pestilence

Some people, shut up in their houses with the doors barred, would scratch a sign of the cross on the front door, sometimes with the inscription "Lord have mercy on us." In one place, two lovers were supposed to have bathed in urine every morning for protection. People hovered over latrines, breathing in the stench. Others swallowed pus from the boils of plague victims. In Avignon, Pope Clement was said to have sat for weeks between two roaring fires.

The plague spread from Sicily all up and down the Atlantic coast, and from the port cities of Venice, Genoa and Pisa as well as Marseilles, London and Bristol. A multitude of men and women, as Boccaccio writes, "negligent of all but themselves . . . migrated to the country, as if God, in visiting men with this pestilence in requital of their iniquities, would not pursue them with His wrath wherever they might be. . . ."

Some who were not yet ill but felt doomed indulged in debauchery. Others, seeking protection in lives of moderation, banded together in communities to live a separate and secluded life, walking abroad with flowers to their noses "to ward off the stench and, perhaps, the evil airs that afflicted them."

It was from a time of plague, some scholars speculate, that the nursery rhyme "Ring Around the Rosy" derives: the rose-colored "ring" being an early sign that a blotch was about to appear on the skin; "a pocket full of posies" being a device to ward off stench and (it was hoped) the attendant infection; "ashes, ashes" being a reference to "ashes to ashes, dust to dust" or perhaps to the sneezing "a-choo, a-choo" that afflicted those in whom the infection had invaded the lungs—ending, inevitably, in "all fall down."

In Pistoia, the city council enacted nine pages of regulations to keep the plague out—no Pistoian was allowed to leave town to visit any place where the plague was raging; if a citizen did visit a plague-infested area he was not allowed back in the city; no linen or woolen goods were allowed to be imported; no corpses could be brought home from outside the city; attendance at funerals was strictly limited to immediate family. None of these regulations helped.

In Siena, dogs dragged bodies from the shallow graves and left them half-devoured in the streets. Merchants closed their shops. The wool industry was shut down. Clergymen ceased administering last rites. On June 2, 1348, all the civil courts were recessed by the city council. Because so many of the laborers had died, construction of the nave for a great cathedral came to a halt. Work was never resumed: only the smaller cathedral we know today was completed.

In Venice, it was said that 600 were dying every day. In Florence, perhaps half the population died. By the time the plague swept through, as much as one-third of Italy's population had succumbed.

In Milan, when the plague struck, all the occupants of any victim's house, whether sick or well, were walled up inside together and left to die. Such draconian measures seemed to have been partially successful—mortality rates were lower in Milan than in other cities.

Medieval medicine was at a loss to explain all this, or to do anything about it. Although clinical observation did play some role in medical education, an extensive reliance on ancient and inadequate texts prevailed. Surgeons usually had a good deal of clinical experience but were considered mainly to be skilled craftsmen, not men of real learning, and their experience was not much incorporated into the body of medical knowledge. In 1300, Pope Boniface VIII had published a bull specifically inveighing against the mutilation of corpses. It was designed to cut down on the sale of miscellaneous bones as holy relics, but one of the effects was to discourage dissection.

Physicians, priests and others had theories about the cause of the plague. Earthquakes that released poisonous fumes, for instance. Severe changes in the Earth's temperature creating southerly winds that brought the plague. The notion that the plague was somehow the result of a corruption of the air was widely believed. It was this idea that led people to avoid foul odors by holding flowers to their noses or to try to drive out the infectious foul odors by inhaling the alternate foul odors of a latrine. Some thought that the plague came from the raining down of frogs, toads and reptiles. Some physicians believed one could catch the plague from "lust with old women."

Both the pope and the king of France sent urgent requests for help to the medical faculty at the University of Paris, then one of the most distinguished medical groups in the Western world. The faculty responded that the plague was the result of a conjunction of the planets Saturn, Mars and Jupiter at 1 P.M. on March 20, 1345, an event that caused the corruption of the surrounding atmosphere.

Ultimately, of course, most Christians believed the cause of the plague was God's wrath at sinful Man. And in those terms, to be sure, the best preventives were prayer, the wearing of crosses and participation in other religious activities. In Orvieto, the town fathers added 50 new religious observances to the municipal calendar. Even so, within five months of the appearance of the plague, Orvieto lost every second person in the town.

There was also some agreement about preventive measures one might take to avoid the wrath of God. Flight was best: away from lowlands, marshy areas, stagnant waters, southern exposures and coastal areas, toward high, dry, cool, mountainous places. It was thought wise to stay indoors all day, to stay cool and to cover any windows that admitted bright sunlight. In addition to keeping flowers nearby, one might burn such aromatic woods as juniper and ash.

The retreat to the mountains, where the density of the rat population was not as great as in urban areas, and where the weather was inimical to rats and fleas, was probably a good idea—as well as perhaps proof, of a kind, of the value of empirical observation. But any useful notion was always mixed in with such wild ideas that it got lost in a flurry of desperate (and often contrary) stratagems. One should avoid bathing because that opened the pores to attack from the corrupt atmosphere, but one should wash face and feet, and sprinkle them with rose water and vinegar. In the morning, one might eat a couple of figs with rue and

filberts. One expert advised eating ten-year-old treacle mixed with several dozen items, including chopped-up snake. Rhubarb was recommended, too, along with onions, leeks and garlic. The best spices were myrrh, saffron and pepper, to be taken late in the day. Meat should be roasted, not boiled. Eggs should not be eaten hard-boiled. A certain Gentile di Foligno commended lettuce; the faculty of medicine at the University of Paris advised against it. Desserts were forbidden. One should not sleep during the day. One should sleep first on the right side, then on the left. Exercise was to be avoided because it introduced more air into the body; if one needed to move, one ought to move slowly.

By the fall of 1348, the plague began to abate. But then, just as hopes were rising that it had passed, the plague broke out again in the spring and summer of 1349 in different parts of Europe. This recurrence seemed to prove that the warm weather, and people bathing in warm weather, caused the pores of the skin to open and admit the corrupted air. In other respects, however, the plague remained inexplicable. Why did some people get it and recover, while others seemed not to have got it at all—or at least showed none of its symptoms—yet died suddenly anyway? Some people died in four or five days, others died at once. Some seemed to have contracted the plague from a friend or relative who had it, others had never been near a sick person. The sheer unpredictability of it was terrifying.

In fact, though no one would know for several centuries, there were three different forms of the plague, which ran three different courses. The first was simple bubonic plague, transmitted from rat to person by the bite of the rat flea. The second and likely most common form was pneumonic, which occurred when the bacillus invaded the lungs. After a two- or three-day incubation period, anyone with pneumonic plague would have a severe, bloody cough; the sputum cast into the air would contain *Yersinia pestis.* Transmitted through the air from person to person, pneumonic plague was fatal in 95 to 100 percent of all cases.

The third form of the plague was septocemic, and its precise etiology is not entirely understood even yet. In essence, however, it appears that in cases of septocemic plague the bacillus entered the bloodstream, perhaps at the moment of the fleabite. A rash formed and death occurred within a day, or even within hours, before any swellings appeared. Septocemic plague always turned out to be fatal.

Some people did imagine that the disease might be coming from some animal, and they killed dogs and cats—though never rats. But fleas were so much a part of everyday life that no one seems to have given them a second thought. Upright citizens also killed gravediggers, strangers from other countries, gypsies, drunks, beggars, cripples, lepers and Jews. The first persecution of the Jews seems to have taken place in the South of France in the spring of 1348. That September, at

Chillon on Lake Geneva, a group of Jews were accused of poisoning the wells. They were tortured and they confessed, and their confessions were sent to neighboring towns. In Basel all the Jews were locked inside wooden buildings and burned alive. In November, Jews were burned in Solothurn, Zofingen and Stuttgart. Through the winter and into early spring they were burned in Landsberg, Burren, Memmingen, Lindau, Freiburg, Ulm, Speyer, Gotha, Eisenach, Dresden, Worms, Baden and Erfurt. Sixteen thousand were murdered in Strasbourg. In other cities Jews were walled up inside their houses to starve to death. That the Jews were also dying of the plague was not taken as proof that they were not causing it.

On the highways and byways, meanwhile, congregations of flagellants wandered about, whipping themselves twice a day and once during the night for weeks at a time. As they went on their way they attracted hordes of followers and helped spread the plague even farther abroad.

The recurrence of the plague after people thought the worst was over may have been the most devastating development of all. In short, Europe was swept not only by a bacillus but also by a widespread psychic breakdown—by abject terror, panic, rage, vengefulness, cringing remorse, selfishness, hysteria, and above all, by an overwhelming sense of utter powerlessness in the face of an inescapable horror.

After a decade's respite, just as Europeans began to recover their feeling of well-being, the plague struck again in 1361, and again in 1369, and at least once in each decade down to the end of the century. Why the plague faded away is still a mystery that, in the short run, apparently had little to do with improvements in medicine or cleanliness and more to do with some adjustment of equilibrium among the population of rats and fleas. In any case, as agents for Pope Clement estimated in 1351, perhaps 24 million people had died in the first onslaught of the plague; perhaps as many as another 20 million died by the end of the century—in all, it is estimated, one-third of the total population of Europe.

Very rarely does a single event change history by itself. Yet an event of the magnitude of the Black Death could not fail to have had an enormous impact. Ironically, some of the changes brought by the plague were for the good. Not surprisingly, medicine changed—since medicine had so signally failed to be of any help in the hour of greatest need for it. First of all, a great many doctors died—and some simply ran away. "It has pleased God," wrote one Venetian-born physician, "by this terrible mortality to leave our native place so destitute of upright and capable doctors that it may be said not one has been left." By 1349, at the University of Padua there were vacancies in every single chair of medicine and surgery. All this, of course, created room for new people with new ideas. Ordinary people began wanting to get their hands on medical guides and to take command of their own health. And gradually more medical texts began to appear in the vernacular instead of in Latin.

An old order was besieged

Because of the death of so many people, the relationship between agricultural supply and demand changed radically, too. Agricultural prices dropped precipitously, endangering the fortunes and power of the aristocracy, whose wealth and dominance were based on land. At the same time, because of the deaths of so many people, wages rose dramatically, giving laborers some chance of improving their own conditions of employment. Increasing numbers of people had more money to buy what could be called luxury goods, which affected the nature of business and trade, and even of private well-being. As old relationships, usages and laws broke down, expanding secular concerns and intensifying the struggle between faith and reason, there was a rise in religious, social and political unrest. Religious reformer John Wycliffe, in England, and John Huss, in Bohemia, were among many leaders of sects that challenged church behavior and church doctrine all over Europe. Such complaints eventually led to the Protestant Reformation, and the assertion that Man stood in direct relation to God, without need to benefit from intercession by layers of clergy.

Indeed, the entire structure of feudal society, which had been under stress for many years, was undermined by the plague. The three orders of feudalism—clergy, nobility and peasantry—had been challenged for more than a century by the rise of the urban bourgeoisie, and by the enormous, slow changes in productivity and in the cultivation of arable land. But the plague, ravaging the weakened feudal system from so many diverse and unpredictable quarters, tore it apart.

By far the greatest change in Western civilization that the plague helped hasten was a change of mind. Once the immediate traumas of death, terror and flight had passed through a stricken town, the common lingering emotion was that of fear of God. The subsequent surge of religious fervor in art was in many ways nightmarish. Though medieval religion had dealt with death and dying, and naturally with sin and retribution, it was only after the Black Death that painters so wholeheartedly gave themselves over to pictures brimming with rotting corpses, corpses being consumed by snakes and toads, swooping birds of prey appearing with terrible suddenness, cripples gazing on the figure of death with longing for deliverance, open graves filled with blackened, worm-eaten bodies, devils slashing the faces and bodies of the damned.

Well before the plague struck Europe, the role of the Catholic Church in Western Europe had been changing. The Papacy had grown more secular in its concerns, vying with princes for wealth and power even while attempts at reform were increasing. "God gave us the Papacy," Pope Leo X declared. "Let us enjoy it." The church had suffered a series of damaging losses in the late 1200s—culminating in 1309 when the Papacy moved from Rome to Avignon. But then, the Black Death dealt the church a further blow, for along with renewed fear and the need for new religious zeal came the opposite feeling, that the church itself had failed. Historical changes rarely occur suddenly. The first indications of change from a powerful catalyst usually seem to be mere curiosities, exceptions or aberrations from the prevailing worldview. Only after a time, after the exceptions have accumulated and seem to cohere, do they take on the nature of a historical movement. And only when the exceptions have come to dominate, do they begin to seem typical of the civilization as a whole (and the vestiges of the old civilization to seem like curiosities). This, in any case, is how the great change of mind occurred that defines the modern Western world. While the Black Death alone did not cause these changes, the upheaval it brought about did help set the stage for the new world of Renaissance Europe and the Reformation.

As the Black Death waned in Europe, the power of religion waned with it, leaving behind a population that was gradually but certainly turning its attention to the physical realm in which it lived, to materialism and worldliness, to the terrible power of the world itself, and to the wonder of how it works.

Renaissance and Reformation

The departure from medieval patterns of life was first evident in Renaissance Italy. There the growth of capital and the development of distinctly urban economic and social organizations promoted a new culture. This culture was dominated by townsmen whose tastes, abilities, and interests differed markedly from those of the medieval clergy and feudal nobility. "How Jacques Coeur Made His Fortune" explores early capitalism in France.

The emergent culture was limited to a small number of people—generally those who were well-to-do. But even in an increasingly materialistic culture it was not enough just to be wealthy. It was necessary to excel in the arts, literature, and learning, and to demonstrate skill in some profession. The ideal Renaissance man, as Robert Lopez observes, "came from a good, old family, improved upon his status through his own efforts, and justified status by his own intellectual accomplishments."

This new ideal owed something to the classical tradition. Renaissance man, wishing to break out of the otherworldly spirituality of the Middle Ages, turned back to the secular naturalism of the ancient world. Indeed, the Renaissance was, among other things, a heroic age of scholarship that restored classical learning to a place of honor. It was a classical humanism in particular that caught the fancy of Renaissance man. In the new spirit of individualism, however, humanism was transformed. The classical version, "man is the measure of all things," became, in Alberti's modern version, "A man can do all things, if he will." No one better illustrates Alberti's maxim than Leonardo da Vinci. Another Renaissance modification of the classical heritage was civic humanism. It involved a new philosophy of political engagement, a reinterpretation of Roman history from the vantage point of contemporary politics, and a recognition that moderns should not simply imitate the ancients but rival them. Of course, Renaissance humanism had its darker side, as Gene Mitchell's article about Pietro Aretino attests. And the Renaissance ideal did not fully extend to women, as J. H. Plumb's essay explains.

Renaissance art and architecture reflected the new society and its attitudes. Successful businessmen were now as likely as saints to be the subjects of portraiture. Equestrian statues of warriors and statesmen glorified current heroes while evoking memories of the great days of Rome. Renaissance painters rediscovered nature (which generally had been ignored by medieval artists), often depicting it as an earthly paradise—the appropriate setting for man in his new image. And in contrast to the great medieval cathedrals, which glorified God, Renaissance structures enhanced humanity.

Some of these developments in art and architecture indicate changes in the role of Christianity and the influence of the Church, which no longer determined the goals of Western man as they had during the medieval period. Increasingly, civil authorities and their symbols competed with churchmen and their icons, while Machiavelli (treated in an article by Vincent Cronin) and other writers provided a secular rationale for a new political order. Nonetheless, most Europeans, including many humanists, retained a deep and abiding religious faith.

The Reformation, with its theological disputes and wars of religion, is a powerful reminder that secular concerns had not entirely replaced religious ones, especially in northern Europe. The great issues that divided Protestant and Catholic—the balance between individual piety and the authority of the Church, the true means of salvation—were essentially medieval in character. Indeed, in their perception of humankind, their preoccupation with salvation (and damnation), and their attacks upon the Church's conduct of its affairs, Luther, Calvin, Zwingli, and other

Vs
NICOL·MACCHIAVELL

Protestant leaders often echoed the views of medieval reformers. Luther's lasting influence is examined in "Luther: Giant of His Time and Ours," while William J. Bouwsma's essay attempts to explain John Calvin. Both reformers encouraged Christians to read the Bible, a task that was simplified by the new vernacular versions of the Scriptures, including Luther's admirable German translation. "That Others Might Read" traces the development of an English Bible.

Taken together, then, the Renaissance and Reformation constituted a new compound of traditional elements (classical and medieval, secular and religious) along with elements of modernity. The era was a time of transition, or as Lynn D. White describes it, "This was a time of torrential flux, of fearful doubt, marking the transition from the relative certainties of the Middle Ages to the new certainties of the eighteenth and nineteenth centuries." Such "fearful doubts" are expressed in the witch-hunts of the period. "Death March of Hernando de Soto" addresses other troubling facets of Western civilization as it reached across the Atlantic.

Looking Ahead: Challenge Questions

Based on the career of Jacques Coeur, describe the basic elements of early capitalism.

Did secular humanism release humanity's darker side along with its creative impulses?

How did politics change at the beginning of the modern era? What part did the ideas of Machiavelli play in the shift from medieval to modern politics?

Did Renaissance humanism influence the place of women in European life?

How did the first English Bible come into being?

How Jacques Coeur Made His Fortune

He made it none too scrupulously,
and lost it at the whim of a much wilier scoundrel than himself

Marshall B. Davidson

One should visit Bourges to see the curious house that Jacques Coeur built, wrote Jules Michelet a century or so ago in his gigantic history of France. It was, he added, "a house full of mysteries, as was Coeur's life." Then, in one of the picturesque asides that make his history such a treasury of unexpected discoveries, he went on to describe that house and the man who built it—the self-made man who played banker to King Charles VII of France, and who bailed out that monarch when his kingdom was at stake; the intrepid man of the world who traded privileges with Moslem sultans, Christian popes, and European princes; the implausibly rich parvenu who, within less than twenty years, parlayed a few counterfeit coins into the largest private fortune in France.

By 1443, when construction of his house started, Coeur was quite possibly the wealthiest man in the world. His new dwelling was to be a monument to his worldly success, and according to one contemporary it was "so richly ornamented, so spacious, and yet, withal, so magnificent, that neither princes of the blood, nor the king himself, had any residence comparable to it." That last point was not lost on Charles VII, as, in the end, Coeur had bitter cause to know.

The house still stands in the cathedral town of Bourges, a short drive south of Paris. It is a unique survival, a memorial as much to a time in history as to the man who built it, for Coeur's life spanned a critical period in the destiny of France. In the last decade of his life the agonizing internecine strife and the bloody slaughter that accompanied the Hundred Years' War were, with his substantial aid, finally brought to an end. The English were thrown back across the Channel, and the land was united as it had not been in living memory.

In the course of those protracted disorders the scrambled authority of feudalism gave way to the more orderly rule of national monarchy, the spirit of chivalry faded before the practical aims of an aspiring bourgeoisie, and the stultifying controls of medieval economy were turning into the growing pains of modern capitalism. To most contemporary eyes such vital changes appeared as a blurred image, like a dissolve in a movie. But Coeur's role in those transitions was so decisive, and he was so perfectly cast for the part he played, that he might well have written the script himself.

It could be said that in Coeur's time double-entry bookkeeping was proving

mightier than the sword, for without that instrument of precision and convenience (apparently a fourteenth-century invention), he could hardly have managed his complex affairs. To him, and other businessmen, time—and timekeeping—took on new importance. For time was money made or lost. The easy rhythm of the canonical hours was being replaced by the stern measure of mechanical clocks that counted out the cost of fleeting opportunities, pointed the way to quicker profits, and ticked off interest on loans. And Coeur pressed every advantage. He even used carrier pigeons to bring him advance notice of approaching cargoes so that he could improve his position in the local markets.

From the very beginning Coeur's enterprise was, for better and for worse, closely associated with the interests of his sovereign. Ironically, he first came to public notice in 1429, when, as an associate of the master of the Bourges mint, he was accused of striking coins of inferior alloy. Like so many other functions now considered the exclusive prerogative of government, minting money was then a private concession, albeit by privilege from the king, who took a substantial share of the milling toll as

"How Jacques Coeur Made His Fortune," by Marshall Davidson, *Horizon,* Winter 1976. Reprinted by permission of the author.

seigniorage, at rates fixed by law. Since no practical system of taxation was yet in force, this was one of the few ways the king could raise money. To meet the demands of the moment, debasing the coinage was approved practice, and the royal "take" could be enhanced by secretly altering the rate of seigniorage —that is, by still further debasing the coinage without advising the public. If the counterfeit was detected, the royal accomplice could disavow the scheme and leave his concessionaires to face the music. And this is what happened to Coeur and his associates in 1429.

Desperate necessities drove Charles VII to practice such duplicity. When he inherited the throne in 1422, the Hundred Years' War was in its eighth grim decade and the fortunes of France were at their lowest ebb. This ill-omened, youthful heir, the tenth child of a madman who disinherited him and of a mother of loose morals who disowned him (it was widely reported that he was a bastard, no matter of shame at the time, but a shadow on his claim to the throne), was holed up in Bourges. An English king reigned in Paris, and English forces occupied all the land from the Channel to the Loire. Philip the Good, the powerful and autonomous duke of Burgundy, tolerated the foreign invader and was allied with him. And Brittany, ever mindful of its own independent traditions, wavered between allegiances.

The years that followed Charles's succession revolved in a murderous cycle of war and brigandage, pestilence and famine. The king could not afford a standing army, and his military leaders were independent contractors who, between battles with the enemy, roamed the land with their mercenaries, raping, stealing, burning, and killing. Under the circumstances, trade and commerce came to a standstill. Merchants took to the road only if they were armed to the teeth. The great international fairs of Champagne, once vital points of exchange for Europe's traffic, were abandoned as the north-south trade shifted to the sea routes between Flanders and the Mediterranean. France came close to ruin.

The winter of 1428–1429 brought a turning point, or at least a promise of deliverance. The English had laid seige to Orléans, the principal city remaining in Charles's rump of a kingdom. Had Orléans fallen there would have been pitifully little left of that kingdom. The city became a symbol of resistance, while the timid young monarch vacillated in his provincial retreat barely sixty miles away. His mocking enemies dubbed him the "king of Bourges" and anticipated the fall of his petty realm. His treasury was empty; it is said he even borrowed money from his laundress. Only by a miracle could he keep his tottering crown.

The miracle materialized when, as if in direct response to the widely whispered prophecy that an armed virgin would appear and drive the English from the land, Joan of Arc was brought before the king at the château of Chinon where he was then holding court. After grilling the maid for three weeks, the king's counselors decided that she was, as she claimed, divinely appointed by "voices" she had heard to save her king and her country. Somehow, Charles found money to provide her with troops, and the siege of Orléans was lifted. Joan then persuaded her wavering monarch to be crowned at Reims, where Clovis had been baptized. By that ritual the stain of bastardy was automatically removed, and Charles was indisputably the true king of France. It took him eight more years to win Paris from the English, but when he did ride triumphantly into that city, after its sixteen years of foreign occupation, he came as the rightful Christian king.

It was hardly a coincidence that Coeur and his associates were charged with counterfeiting almost immediately after the "miracle" at Orléans, or that Coeur was pardoned of the crime. Charles had most likely met the payroll for Joan's troops with funds provided by the mint's illegal operations, and as party to the crime he saw that Coeur got off easily. At least there is no better explanation.

In any case, soon after his pardon Coeur set out to make his fortune. He formed a new partnership with his old associates at the mint, this time to deal in "every class of merchandise, including that required by the King, Monseigneur the Dauphin, and other nobles, as well as other lines in which they [the partners] can make their profit."

For precedents in this new venture he looked abroad. The basis of Renaissance prosperity, already so conspicuous in Italy, was the carrying trade between East and West. For centuries Venice had fattened on this commerce, to the point where its successful and friendly business relations with Mongols and Moslems alike had encouraged those infidels to close in on the Christian world. Then, as European knighthood took the Cross to the Holy Land, Venetians supplied and equipped their fellow Christians and ferried them to the battle sites at exorbitant rates.

Venice also continued its flourishing trade in arms, armor, and diverse other goods with the Saracens of Egypt and Palestine. When Pope Benedict XII forbade unauthorized trade with the infidel, the merchants of Venice bought up papal authorizations wherever they could and used them as ordinary bills of exchange. With the Fourth Crusade, the "businessman's crusade," the merchants of Venice made a double killing. They dissuaded the debt-burdened knights from their proclaimed purpose of attacking Alexandria, one of Venice's richest markets, and persuaded them to sack the flourishing Christian capital of Constantinople.

Meanwhile, across the Apennines in Tuscany, enterprising merchants were swarming out of Florence into western Europe, collecting contributions to the Crusades as bankers to the Holy See, advancing money to land-poor feudal lords at fantastic interest rates, and with their ready cash buying up the privileges of the towns. During the Hundred Years' War the powerful Bardi and Peruzzi families equipped both French and English armies for the battlefields, prolonging the conflict and taking over the functions of state when it was necessary to secure their accounts. In return for helping Henry III of England with his running expenses, the Florentines asked for 120 per cent interest on advances and, when repayment was not prompt, added 60 per cent more. In such a company of greedy Christians, Shylock would have seemed hopelessly ingenuous.

During the most agonizing period of the Hundred Years' War, however, the Florentines had gradually abandoned their commercial colonies in France. Now that his time had come, Coeur moved to fill that vacuum with his own business and, with equal speed, to stake a claim among the markets of the East, so profitably exploited by Venice. His first try at emulating the Venetian merchants was a disaster. In 1432 he journeyed to Damascus, an awkward if not perilous place for Christians to be at the time, buying up spices and other exotic commodities for resale in the home markets of France. When his ship foundered off Corsica he lost literally everything but his shirt. He and his shipmates were stripped clean by the islanders.

He seems to have recovered promptly. He had centered his operations at Montpellier on the Mediterranean coast, the only French port authorized by the pope to deal with the infidel East. He threw himself with bounding determination into the development of the city's facilities, pressing the local authorities to improve its docks, dredge essential canals, construct adequate warehouses, and generally improve the advantages for commerce and navigation—even spending his own money when he had to. As he later wrote the king, he had plans for developing a vast maritime empire under the lily banner of France.

Almost from the moment Charles returned to Paris, Coeur's affairs started to move in a steady counterpoint to the affairs of state. Within a year or two he was installed as *argentier*, receiver of the revenues used to maintain the royal establishment. Since in his capacity as merchant he was also the principal purveyor to that establishment, his position was doubly advantageous—and ambiguous. And since for the most part the court could be accommodated only by long-term credit, both the advantage and the ambiguity were compounded. It

must have been quite easy for Coeur to convince himself that what was good for Jacques Coeur was good for France.

A reciprocal rhythm of commissions and benefits, responsibilities and opportunities, honors and profits, increased in tempo for more than a decade. The king may already have been in debt to Coeur even before the royal entry into Paris, and this relationship became more or less chronic thereafter. The Paris campaign had again exhausted the royal treasury. In an effort to tighten the leaking economy of the state, Charles, possibly advised by his *argentier*, forbade the export of money from his realm except by a special license, which he then granted, apparently exclusively, to Coeur.

In 1440 Charles further recognized Coeur's services by according him patents of nobility. The following year he appointed him *conseilleur du roi*, in effect minister of finance and, as such, adviser in the revision of the nation's tax structure. Charged with assessing and collecting regional taxes, Coeur sometimes received not only his due commissions but gratuities from local representatives who both respected his influence at court and feared his power as a merchant banker. The "states" of Languedoc, for example, of which Montpellier was the principal port, paid him handsomely for his good offices in the interest of their maritime prosperity—canceling his share of their taxes as a matter of course.

The king, meanwhile, with an unprecedented income from the revenues he received, reorganized his military forces into a paid standing army. He was no longer a mere feudal lord but a monarch able to make policy and enforce it, if need be, with cannon—cannon, cast at the foundries of bourgeois manufacturers, that could reduce the proudest knight's castle to rubble. In 1444 Charles arranged a temporary peace with the English, who still held Normandy and Guyenne. It was at the gay spring *pourparlers* on the banks of the Loire by which the peace was negotiated that Charles first spied the indescribably beautiful Agnes Sorel, "the fairest of the fair," whom he shortly afterward made his mistress. As the king's bedmate,

Agnes began to use her influence in matters of state, inaugurating a tradition in French history. As it later turned out, this was a fateful development in the life of Jacques Coeur. The immediate consequence of the truce arrangements, however, was that he could now move into the English-held markets in Rouen and Bordeaux as well as across the Channel.

Coeur's influence was already recognized far beyond the shores of France. In 1446 he served as negotiator between the Knights of Rhodes and the sultan of Egypt. Two years later, through the intercession of Coeur's agents, the sultan was persuaded to restore trading privileges to the Venetians, who had for a time been banned from the Arab world. At the same time, Coeur consolidated his own position in the Mediterranean and put a cap on his immense commercial structure. Pope Eugenius IV issued a bull authorizing Coeur to trade for five years in his own right, beyond the privileges enjoyed by the port of Montpellier, with the non-Christian world. With this special authority in his pocket, Coeur shifted the base of his maritime enterprise to Marseilles.

One important matter still needed mending. For all Coeur's good offices and his wide reputation, official relations between France and the Arab world were less cordial than suited his interests. In 1447 he persuaded Charles to agree to a formal pact with Abu-Said-Djacmac-el Daher, sultan of Egypt. The French ambassadors, traveling in Coeur's ships and at his expense, arrived in Egypt "in great state" bearing lavish gifts provided by Coeur in the name of the king. The sultan, in turn, arranged an extravagant reception. Coeur's diplomacy triumphed. Peace between the two lands was agreed upon, and French traders received "most favored nation" privileges in Arab ports.

Aided by the gratitude of the Venetians and the Knights of Rhodes, the friendship of the sultan, the favor of the pope, and the indulgence of his king, Coeur secured unassailable advantages at every important point in the world of his day. "All the Levant he visited with his ships," wrote the duke of

BOTH: ARCHIVES PHOTOGRAPHIQUES

Coeur's mansion is adorned both inside and out with whimsical vignettes of daily life.

The trompe l'oeil *couple may represent servants watching for their master's return.*

Burgundy's chronicler some years later, "and there was not in the waters of the Orient a mast which was not decorated with the *fleur-de-lis*." The maritime empire he created remained for several centuries one of the principal bulwarks of French commerce. To carry on his far-flung, highly diversified operations—they had developed into a virtual monopoly of France's exclusive markets—Coeur employed some three hundred agents and maintained branch offices in Barcelona, Damascus, Beirut, Alexandria, and other strategic centers.

The inventories of his warehouses read like an exaggerated description of Ali Baba's caves. "All the perfumes of Arabia" were carried in stock, and spices and confections from the farthest shores; dyes and colors, cochineal and cinnabar, indigo and saffron—and henna to illuminate the king's manuscripts; materials of fabulous richness and variety, and gems supposedly from the navels of sacred Persian and Indian monkeys, which were mounted in precious metals and considered a universal antidote to human ills. He could provide for the court's most extraordinary or exquisite whim: a coat of mail covered with azure velvet for a Scottish archer of the king's bodyguard; a silver shoulder piece and Turkish buckler for Charles of Orleans; silks and sables for Margaret of Scotland; diamonds to set off the incomparable beauty of Agnes Sorel—

they were all to be had, including cold cash for the queen of France herself, who offered up her "great pearl" for security.

In order to put his surplus money to work and to spread his risk, Coeur joined associations that profited from the licensing of fairs (reborn since the temporary truce with England), from speculation in salt, and from the exploitation of copper and silver mines of the Lyonnais and Beaujolais. He had interests in paper and silk factories in Florence. He even invested in three-quarters of two English prisoners of war, each worth a handsome ransom.

The list of his varied enterprises is almost endless. Cash was still in short supply among the nobility, the long war had brought ruin to many lordly tenants, and Charles's fiscal reforms were reducing their income from traditional feudal dues. So Coeur accommodated some of the greatest families of the realm by buying up their manor houses and properties until he held more than thirty estates, some including whole villages and parishes within their grounds. All told, the complex structure of his myriad affairs, his control of the production, transport, and distribution of goods, his private banking resources, and his secure grasp on essential markets all suggest something like the first vertical trust in history.

So far, nothing belied the motto Coeur was then having chiseled into the

stones of his great town house at Bourges—*A vaillans cueurs riens impossible*, nothing is impossible to the valiant. Coeur's star rose even higher in 1448 when he was sent to Rome by Charles with a select group of ambassadors to help end the "pestilential and horrible" papal schism that for long years had been a great trial to the Church. The French ambassadors entered Rome in a procession of splendor—their cortege included three hundred richly caparisoned and harnessed Arabian horses—and Pope Nicholas V wrote Charles that not even the oldest inhabitants could remember anything so magnificent.

Coeur promptly took center stage. Through his efforts, the rival pope, Amadeo VIII, duke of Savoy, was finally persuaded to renounce his claim to the papal throne and accept a position in the church hierarchy second only to that of Pope Nicholas V. As a reward, Coeur's privilege of dealing with the non-Christian world was extended indefinitely. He was also given a franchise to carry Christian pilgrims to the Holy Land.

There were some who complained of the outrageous cost of that papal mission from which Coeur gained such honor and profit. Coeur had no doubt paid the bills, but whether from his own purse or from the king's treasury would have been difficult to determine. Coeur's wealth was by now beyond imagining. It was reported that his horses were shod with silver. His table service was of gold and silver. Each year, it was said, his income was greater than that of all the other merchants of France combined. "The king does what he can; Jacques Coeur does what he pleases" was a repeated observation. He might even be in league with the devil, they began to say.

Jacques Coeur had indeed reached a singular, and perilous, eminence.

How rich Coeur really was and what resources he could command came out in the years immediately following. The time had come, Charles decided, to break the truce with the English and to push them out of France altogether. To launch and maintain the campaign, however, Charles needed more money than he could find in the royal coffers, and he turned to Coeur for help. Coeur responded by dredging every sou he could manage from the resources available to him and by stretching his almost inexhaustible credit to the limit. By one means or another, he turned over to the king, at the very minimum, two hundred thousand ecus, a sum equal to more than one-fifth of the kingdom's annual tax revenues.

He also took to the field at the king's side. In the victorious procession that entered Rouen on November 10, 1449, Coeur rode in the company of Charles; mounted on a white charger, he was clothed in velvet and ermine and wore a sword embellished with gold and precious stones.

Coeur was now about fifty-five years old. For some twenty years he had enjoyed increasing wealth and prestige. Then, suddenly, the wheel of fortune changed direction. Three months after the ceremonies at Rouen, Agnes Sorel died in childbirth, after having been delivered of the king's fourth child. Rumors spread that she had been poisoned. Almost automatically, a cabal of debtors formed to point a finger at the king's *argentier*, the "money

man" of almost magical faculties, who was known to be one of the executors of Agnes's will. To convict Coeur of murder would serve to disembarrass the king and every important member of the court from the claims of their common creditor.

Charles was quick to play his part. One week in July, 1451, he expressed his gratitude to Coeur for his many services; the next week he issued an order for his arrest. Supported by his most recent favorites, the king confronted Coeur with a long list of indictments, starting with the poisoning charge and going back over the years to the counterfeiting charge of 1429, set aside so long ago by the pleasure and the convenience of Charles VII.

No sooner were the dungeon doors closed behind Coeur than "the vultures of the court" started picking away at the estate he could no longer protect. The nobility of France swarmed about the tottering house of Jacques Coeur to redeem their own fortunes from his disgrace. The trial that followed was a mockery. With his enemies as both prosecutors and judges he never had a chance. Even though his accusers confessed that the charge of poisoning Agnes Sorel was false, and the pope pleaded for clemency and justice in the case, Coeur was shunted for several years from prison to prison.

Finally, in May, 1453, at Poitiers, when he was threatened with torture, he issued a statement that led his judges to condemn him, banish him, and confiscate his properties. By a remarkable coincidence, on the day of Coeur's sentence the sorely tried city of Constantinople fell, this time once and for all, to the Turks. It was the end of an era. Less than a week later, the convicted man made an *amende honorable*: kneeling, bareheaded, before a large crowd and holding a ten-pound wax torch in his hands, he begged mercy of God, king, and the courts.

One more adventure remained. For almost a year and a half after his trial, Coeur was kept imprisoned in France, in spite of his banishment, while most of his holdings were seized and sold off. Then, in the autumn of 1454, he managed to escape. Aided by several of his faithful agents, he crossed the Rhone out of France and fled to Rome, where the pope received him with honor. He never returned to France, nor to the house that was his pride.

But he did take to the sea one last time. He arrived in Rome at a crucial moment in the history of the Church and of Western civilization. All Christendom had been shaken by the fall of Constantinople less than two years earlier and felt threatened by further advances of the Ottoman hordes. In the summer of 1456, Coeur, sixty years old and "toiled with works of war," set forth in command of a fleet dispatched by Pope Calixtus III to help retake Constantinople. On the twenty-fifth of November, on the island of Chios, his *vaillant coeur* was stopped, possibly by wounds he suffered in battle.

As he lay dying, Coeur sent one last appeal to Charles, begging the king to show consideration for his children. At this point Charles could afford to be indulgent. In an act of royal compassion he conceded that since "the said Coeur was in great authority with us and rich and abounding in this world's goods and ennobled in his posterity and line ... it pleases us to have pity on [his children]," and ordained that what might be salvaged from their father's estate, including the house at Bourges, be returned to them.

It was, after all, little enough for him to do, and in the end Coeur had an ironic revenge. The thought of poisoning continued to haunt the king. Four years later, fearing he might be poisoned by his own son, he refused to eat, and died of starvation.

Our Man from Arezzo

GENE MITCHELL

*He is the symbol of the dark side
of the Renaissance, the "can of worms"
that is inseparable from the works of genius.
In other words, if you want the Sistine Chapel,
you'll also have to take Pietro Aretino.*

If we would think of the Renaissance as a coin with a bright side symbolizing the tremendous works of art produced, and a dark side representing the "can of worms" that was the social and political reality, we probably could understand the dark side best by studying the career of that Pietro from Arezzo who took his surname, Aretino, from the town as, in the same manner, did a certain Leonardo from the town of Vinci.

There are men prominent in history whose main claim to fame is their ability to survive. Pietro Aretino was a classic survivor who met his end undramatically in his bedchamber when it seemed certain that he was bound to wind up in a dark alley with a tastefully designed dagger in his back.

Pietro Aretino was born in Arezzo in April, 1492. As any schoolboy knows, it was the year that Columbus discovered America for the Europeans (the Indians had already discovered it for themselves) and it was the year that Lorenzo the Magnificent died. If one needs an arbitrary separation between the modern and the old, Pietro Aretino's timing was perfect.

His father was a cobbler known only by his given name of Luca. Various last names have been suggested such as Bonamici, de Bura, or Camaiani, but the evidence is tenuous.

Tina, his mother, was also of the urban poor. She must have been pretty because she one time sat as a model for the Madonna for a painter named Matteo Lappoli. Aretino was immensely proud of his mother's fleeting fame and at one time he had Vasari make him a copy of the Lappoli work. (Like many men who hop from bed to bed, Aretino was always constant to his mother.)

It we believe Aretino (which is not the ideal way to understand him), his father was a nobleman named Luigi Bacci who made hay while Luca cobbled. To combine an old expression with a current one, Aretino knew it was better to be born on the wrong side of the blanket than on the wrong side of the tracks. In other words, Aretino loved his mother but he was willing to surrender her virtue for a little noble blood. In any event, being a bastard was no drawback at that time. Cesare Borgia was a bastard and when Aretino reached middle age, a bastard attained the papacy itself. But what evidence we have is all in favor of Luca, the shoemaker, being the chap who impregnated Tina, the Madonna. Aretino's claim to being a bastard will have to rest on the modern use of the word and, in that sense, no one can gainsay him.

Aretino always showed a great affection for his native Arezzo and for all fellow Aretines. Any Aretine who came to him in distress could always expect succor. The only thing he asked of his hometown is that he not be exected to live there and share in its provincial glories at first hand. At the age of fourteen he left Arezzo and returned only for extremely short visits thereafter.

He went to Perugia to study art but he left hurriedly after adding his own touches to a painting of Christ and Mary Magdalen. Rome was his next stop where he worked in various households. He was fired from one job for stealing the silver,

"Our Man from Arezzo," Gene Mitchell, *Mankind* Magazine, May 1979. Reprinted by permission.

and lost out in another when his master died. Back on the road again, he bobbed up in Vicenza as a street singer. Next he played at being a wandering friar and, then, worked successively as a moneylender, a tax collector, a mule driver, and a hangman's assistant.

For some obscure indiscretion, he served time at an oar on a galley in the Mediterranean and survived the brutal ordeal. Back on land again, he passed rapidly through another succession of lowly jobs including pimping. Fortune took him to Venice where he entered the literary lists with a first book. It was a piece of pastiche, modeled closely on the work of Serofino Aquilano, a flashy but inconsequential poet. Finally, he entered a monastery at Ravenna. They put him to binding books. He soon discovered that unholy practices and women steal into the best regulated monasteries. He was never one to lead in reform so he followed his natural bent and was dismissed for lechery.

His education was complete. He was ready for Rome. He was a man of the Renaissance—ready to condone treachery and murder to attain a goal. He had been through the great university of Renaissance villainy, been graduated with honors and was ready for post-graduate work. He was possibly the greatest authority on low life that the world had ever known. He was 24 and bursting with animal vitality. He went to Rome.

The Eternal City was made to order for Aretino's ambitions. It was the quintessence of the Renaissance—brilliant, worldly and corrupt. A man who had his eye on the main chance and who was not weighed down with scruples could go a long way, provided he could present a moving target to the ambushes that lay on all sides.

Aretino started climbing the Roman ladder from the lowest rung. He entered the lavish household of Agostino Chigi as a servant. Agostino Chigi was the papal treasurer, which was like being Secretary of the Treasury in the United States. He was an international banker of tremendous power and it is one of the ironies of history that the fledgling writer who entered his service as a lackey is better known to posterity than Chigi. Aretino was put to work lighting candles, cleaning privies, polishing chamberpots, and sweeping out bedrooms. Aretino continued his writing career by handing out witty verses to the parade of the famous who supped and slept at Chigi's palace.

The reigning Pope was Leo X, formerly Cardinal Giovanni de Medici, and son of Lorenzo the Magnificent. Leo was rich, fat and fun-loving. He surrounded himself with buffoons. The post of papal privy seal which had once been held by Bramante was bestowed on an ex-barber and, then, on one Fra Mariano whose outstanding achievement was that he once ate twenty capons at a sitting.

It was the easygoing Leo who gave Martin Luther sufficient provocation to nail his 95 theses to the door of the church in Wittemburg and to write his fiery letter of denunciation of the papacy.

In 1514 King Manuel of Portugal presented an elephant to Leo. The huge creature, on its presentation to the Pope, filled its trunk with water and hosed down the papal courtiers. Leo, who enjoyed nothing better than low farce, was enchanted. The elephant had definitely joined the papal "in" crowd. But the beast had a short tenure. In the unsalubrious air of Rome it sickened and died. Leo was plunged into gloom and summoned Raphael to do a portrait of the elephant so that it would never be forgotten.

The stage was set for Aretino. A pamphlet appeared in the streets of Rome entitled "The Last Will and Testament of the Elephant." Written by Aretino, this burlesque of a legal will gave with a heavy-handed but savage wit the possessions of the elephant and portions of its body to various princes of the church. As an indication of the level of subtlety of the lampoon, Cardinal Grassi, the outstanding womanizer of the curia, was bequeathed a rather obvious member of the dead elephant's equipment. Laughter swept through Rome and Aretino rode on the crest of it. The Pope, more amused than anyone, asked Chigi to release Aretino to the papal service. In Rome for only two years, he had progressed from lackey to papal laureate. Aretino had arrived.

Aretino's newly found security lasted only five years. In 1521 Leo caught a chill which progressed into pneumonia, and he went to join the big fisherman. The cardinals descended on Rome and the scramble for the papacy began. The cardinals were locked in the Sistine Chapel for their deliberations with a strong guard to insure against information going in or coming out. Pietro Aretino stepped into the vacuum that had been created by issuing his own news bulletins.

In the Piazza Navona, which was a marketplace, stood an ancient statue which was popularly called Pasquino for reasons that are lost in time. It had become the custom to plaster Pasquino with scurrilous and libelous witticisms which naturally became known as "pasquinades." Aretino decided this custom was an excellent vehicle to bring to the public his own interpretations of the conference to choose a new pope.

And so, he covered the deliberations with his own Pasquinades. Before the final choice was made on the successor to Leo, Aretino was well on his way to the goal he had set for himself: to be the most dangerous tongue in Europe. Just a brief sample will give one an idea of his acid humor:

Valle'll give up his children, Cesarini his whore,
And Trani his mamma, who loves him sore
Cortona, his plots, and more.

Inside the Sistine Chapel events were taking a turn that boded no good for Aretino's future. Cardinal Guilio de' Medici was the favored choice for Pope but could not secure the necessary majority of votes for election. Three months went by with no break in the deadlock. For his own immediate political concerns, Cardinal Guilio de' Medici could not remain locked up in the Sistine Chapel. He decided on a bold stroke. He would put in nomination a dark horse who would be so dark that in all likelihood the nomination would act as a catalyst to break the deadlock and, finally, bring the choice back to him. Medici nominated Adrian of Utrecht, a good and sincere Dutch prelate, who had not even bothered to come to Rome for the election. To Medici's consternation, Adrian was elected Pope on the first ballot after the nomination.

Aretino's future in Rome was dependent upon a worldly papal court. The unsophisticated Dutchman known to history as Adrian VI who took his Christianity seriously would not be likely to encourage Aretino. Worse, he would probably throw the impudent Aretine in jail. Aretino put his chagrin into verse:

O villain college, who has betrayed Christ's name;
And given over His earthly heritage,
The Vatican, to vile Teutonic rage,
Do not your hearts split open wide with shame?

As Adrian journeyed toward Rome, Aretino moved again to watch events from the safety of Bologna.

Bologna bored Aretino. In Rome he had been famous, in Bologna he was nobody. Giulio de' Medici, having lost the papacy, had retired to his native Florence to see which way Adrian would bounce. He had delivered the papacy to the simple Dutchman, but Adrian did not realize that one becomes Pope through political intrigue so he was not properly grateful to Medici. In his Pasquino period, Aretino had thrown a few darts at Giulio de' Medici but basically had supported him for Pope. Now he went to him in Florence to be closer to the action.

Giulio de' Medici was not exactly bowled over to see the self-exiled satirist. He was trying to gain the favor of Adrian and Aretino surely could not help him with that. But Medici reasoned that the Aretine had a way with words and he might come in handy some day.

He sent Aretino with a letter of introduction to Federigo Gonzaga, the Marquis of Mantua. The Marquis was a great admirer of Aretino's work and he was overjoyed to have him for a guest. Darkly handsome, the Marquis had been painted by Raphael and would later be painted by Titian. He was an avid sensualist and therefore an ideal companion for Aretino. They had lusty times together. But the pleasant backwater palled on Aretino as had Bologna. He returned to Florence to seek something better from Giulio de' Medici. The Cardinal sent him north to his kinsman, Giovanni de' Medici who was known as Giovanni delle Bande Nere. A swashbuckling captain, Giovanni de' Medici guarded Italy against invasions from the north. He had an intuitive military sense in a time when military commanders were more likely to be masters of intrigue than tacticians. Even more to Aretino's delight, Giovanni was a good companion in drinking and wenching. Aretino had found his only hero.

Pope Adrian lasted less than two years. Apparently, he really tried to reform the church—and nothing would do one in more quickly. His death was the cause for celebrations in Rome—the Romans were free of this fool who took his religion seriously. Moving with sure political dispatch, Cardinal Giulio de' Medici became Pope Clement VII.

From Milan Aretino hailed with glee the turn of events. With characteristic caution, he moved south but stopped short of Rome at Reggio. There he lived with a cook so that the delights of the kitchen would keep him from being bored by the games of the bedchamber. Of course, it wasn't food or fun that made him choose Reggio; it was the struggle for power in the Vatican that kept him on the sidelines until he could pick the winning team. When he did join the game, he blundered. He joined the opposition to Giovanmatteo Giberti, who held the office of Papal Datary, a post of great power in the Holy See. With typical impudence, Aretino turned his bitter pen against the Datary. Giovanmatteo Giberti was not a man to suffer with the Christian patience that befitted his calling. He sent an assassin to rid himself of this troublesome literary blackmailer. The assassin came close to fulfilling his mission. He stabbed Aretino twice in the chest and Aretino lay near death for several weeks. But he recovered and clamored for justice. Everyone of power, inclding Clement, turned a deaf ear. Aretino had to be content with an artist's revenge. He put all his powerful enemies in his first satiric comedy, *La Cortegiana*. Then he returned to his old haven in Mantua.

As usual, the charms of provincial Mantua could not sustain Aretino for long. He was not cut out to be a backwater courtier or, for that matter, a courtier at all. War snatched him from boredom. Venice, Milan, and the Papal States had made common cause with Francis I of France against Charles V, the Holy Roman Emperor. Charles V invaded Italy and a motley army assembled to block his passage south. The papal troops were commanded by Aretino's hero, Giovanni delle Bande Nere. Aretino rode out to join Giovanni.

The battle was joined at the small town of Governolo near Mantua. The German troops of Charles V had four excellent cannons made for them in the factory of Alfonso d' Este, Duke of Ferrara. A neat profit meant more to the Duke than Italy; he sold his cannons to the invading Germans.

It was an Italian ball fired from an Italian cannon that killed Giovanni delle Bande Nere, the only Italian that could have saved Rome and Italy from the foreigner. Aretino, genuinely grief-stricken for the first time in his life, wrote a moving tribute to his dead captain. It was December 10, 1526.

He chose Mantua again as the sanctuary from which to solicit forgiveness from Clement and the Datary. But no forgiveness was forthcoming and Aretino lashed out against Pope, Datary, and all the cardinals. In a note to the Marquis of Mantua, the Pope suggested that Mantua be denied to Aretino as a fort from which to assail his enemies. The Marquis counted out one hundred gold crowns and suggested Venice. On March 27, 1527, Aretino arrived in Venice. He was almost 35 and lucky to be alive.

Venice had passed the peak of her glory. The states of Italy were ringed around her like hounds around a stag. On the water, the rising power of the Turk had pushed her back to her inland sea, thereby striking a terrible blow at the trade which had made her great. The explorers had pushed around Africa to reach the Indies. This new route would soon challenge seriously the position of Venice as the gateway to the riches of the Orient. None of this decline was visible on Aretino's arrival; Venice was still rich and played the role to the hilt.

Aretino had found his home at last. It seems one can go home if the ideal which is in one's mind is found on earth. Aretino had discovered his mighty fortress, beside which Mantua was only the most puny of refuges, from which to send out his literary sallies.

Two years after his arrival Aretino was established in a splendid palace on the corner of the Grand Canal and the Rio San Giovanni Crisostomo. Jacopo Tintoretto dropped in to adorn a ceiling with two paintings. On the walls there were paintings by Titian including a portrait of Giovanni delle Bande Nere. Scattered around the palace were sculptures by Sansovino and medallions by Lione Lioni and Alessandro Vittoria. At the entrance, on a pedestal, there was a marble bust of a virile, bearded man. Of course, it was Aretino.

To wind up with a palace in Venice two years after arriving with a pittance is a neat trick. The explanation is not a complicated one. Aretino was confident of his position in Italy. He demanded support from those he thought should be his patrons and, surprisingly enough, he got it.

He badgered his old host from Mantua, Federigo Gonzaga, for support and although he did not receive what he thought was his just due, Aretino did not plead in vain except in one instance. He dedicated a long poem to Federigo which he called the *Marfisa*. It was slight work ground out for money. The Marquis expressed his appreciation in glowing terms—which made him either a poor critic or a liar—but he refused to pay for it except in praise. Aretino offered it to several young noblemen (the poem being a kind of all-purpose epic in which anybody could play the hero.) He finally marketed it with the Marquis of Vasto in 1532. The Marquis of Vasto had long been the butt of some of Aretino's most scurrilous slams, so one may be astonished that he sponsored the *Marfisa*. It was really not out of character. The Marquis of Vasto anticipated modern celebrities by one time saying in effect to Aretino: "I don't care what you say about me so long as you mention my name."

While Aretino was tapping Federigo Gonzago for funds he did not forget his friends, Titian and Sansovino. He peddled their works to the Marquis in the form of gifts. As a true patron of the arts, Federigo had to respond with suitably lavish thanks.

A list of Aretino's patrons would look like a who's who of the sixteenth century in Europe. Why did they all send him money? Possibly because they knew he could dip his words in honey or poison. Honey was just more expensive.

6. RENAISSANCE AND REFORMATION

The Casa Aretino soon became the haunt of women of all classes who sought Aretino's favors. There were streetwalkers, famous courtesans, middle-class spouses, and noblewomen. They came to cook his food, and arrange his possessions, and sleep with him. Three stand out from all the rest for special consideration.

There was Caterina Sandella who was married to a dissolute nobleman who made the mistake of bringing his wife to the Casa Aretino. She became friendly with Aretino and sought his advice concerning her husband's inveterate infidelity. He consoled her with such success that she became his mistress and bore him two children.

Perina Riccia was a delicate creature whose husband brought her to the palace and then left suddenly with some of Aretino's gold and one of the more fetching girls from the kitchen. Perina, left behind, fell sick and had to be nursed back to health by Aretino. As soon as he had her back in shape, he made her his mistress. She tired of Aretino and, taking a cue from her agile husband, left with a young man who was a guest. She, also, helped herself to the funds. She returned briefly to be forgiven by Aretino and to die in Venice.

The third was a woman by the unlikely name of Angela Serena who accomplished the almost impossible feat of maintaining a platonic relationship with Aretino. One feels that she was only saved from continuing her relationship in bed by her husband and family who removed her from Aretino's influence. The abortive affair rankled with Aretino who boasted in print that both Angela Serena and her husband would only be remembered in history because they had known Aretino.

The husband, Giovanni Serena, struck back at Aretino. He brought charges of blasphemy in the Venetian courts and dropped a dark hint that charges of sodomy would follow. The first offense, if proved, called for beheading and if one were guilty of sodomy, the punishment was to be exhibited in a cage in a public place, and left to die. One feels that if the second charge had been pressed in Venice, the law enforcers would have run out of cages. However, the charge of homosexuality against Aretino may have had some foundation. There are references to it by his enemies in the venomous pamphlets written against him. Even discounting malice, a man so overflowing with sensuality must have considered all variations of sexual experience. Certainly, if a man in his position had desire, he had access.

In any event, Aretino decided to take no chances with the block or the cage; he fled to a villa he had purchased in Gamberare. His exile was short. He was back in his beloved Venice in two weeks when the Duke of Urbino intervened and had the charges withdrawn. It was no consolation for Aretino to learn that besides Giovanni Serena one of his own secretaries, Niccolo Franco, had conspired against him. Franco was later to write a muckraking biography of Aretino which is the source of many of the disreputable things we believe of him.

Aretino had all the Renaissance vices, but he had one Renaissance virtue: his love of art and his consideration for artists. Jacopo Tatti, known as Sansovino, was such a close friend of Aretino that when he wrought the bronze doors to the sacristy of St. Mark's cathedral, he included the bearded face of Aretino in the guise of an evangelist. It was Sansovino who introduced Aretino to Titian. The painter and the writer became the closest of friends.

In his extravagant way, Pietro Aretino said that Titian was another version of himself. The comparison is flattering to Aretino only. Titian was a genius; Aretino was a minor talent with a great flair for self-promotion. Titian painted Aretino and the magnificent portrait hangs in the Frick Gallery in New York

City. Titian caught the coarseness, the exuberance, and the essential ruthlessness of the Aretine.

As we all know, there is no accounting for friendships. The most dissimilar persons find things in each other that attract. Particularly, it seems that people like to experience low life vicariously by being friendly with scoundrels. This may be what drew Titian to Aretino. Whatever the reason, they shared every interest including the details of their households.

Aretino takes considerable credit for promoting Titian. It is a disputable claim. Titian was well on his way to greatness before he met the Aretine. And although some of the commissions of Titian are traceable to Aretino, it does not follow that those commissions are that critical in the final analysis of Titian's genius. To give Aretino his due, his pen helped rather than hindered Titian.

There is another side of the picture. Based on Aretino's letters, there is good reason to believe that Titian made Aretino less of a ruffian.

If Aretino cannot be classed as a genius, just where does he rank in the world of letters when one forgets his ebullient personality?

If it were only a matter of productivity, he would rank with Shakespeare. He spewed out an unending stream of comedies, poems, biographies, and letters. But quantity is not quality; many earnest literary journeymen are well forgotten. Aretino is remembered because he belonged to his own age, was aware of it, and wrote as one who was aware of it. His language is the language of his time. In him there is not, as there were in so many of his day, simpering imitation of Petrarch and Boccaccio. The essence of any artist worth his salt is that what he sees constantly and firmly is his private and special vision of the world. Aretino's world was Italy of the Renaissance; a mixture of farce and tragedy—a living theater of the absurd. He is reported to have said: "Men live in a different fashion in modern Rome than they did in ancient Athens." He also said: "It is better to drink out of one's own wooden platter than another's golden goblet."

His work was read all over Europe. It had a lot to do with the Italianizing influence that permeated the Elizabethan dramatists, particularly Shakespeare. His plays, which are not acted at all today, were widely performed in his time. They were social comedies influenced by Terence with assists by Boccaccio. Essentially, however, they were his very own, the world viewed through the eyes of Aretino: lusty, lewd, violent and vivid.

Today his work is largely forgotten. If one would say his name aloud at a cocktail party it would not draw any more response than if one said "Joseph Hergesheimer" (who was a vogue in the United States in the 1930's). It is ironic to realize that only two hundred years ago Joseph Addison doubted if there was a single man then living who did not know who Aretino was.

To return to Aretino's career, he reached the pinnacle of his fame and influence in the great struggle for power between Charles V, the Holy Roman Emperor, and Francis I, the King of France.

He had long sought the favor of Francis, who was a rather gallant figure if one has a turn for romanticism. Francis had smiled on Aretino but had never rewarded him with more than a gold necklace. On the other hand, Charles had sacked Rome, which had caused him to be showered with the verbal slings and arrows of an outraged Aretino. The ill will of Aretino was no mean thing. As Ariosto said:

Behold the scourge

Of Princes, mighty Pietro Aretino!

Now it was Charles who sought Aretino's support. He sent his courtiers to offer him two hundred gold crowns a year as a pension with no services asked. Aretino graciously accepted the pension and gave his writing services free.

Francis, in his desperate struggle with Charles, turned to an ally outside Europe, the dreaded Ottoman Emperor, Suleiman the Magnificent. One must understand the times to realize what panic swept through Europe on the heels of the French move. A rough analogy would be the reaction in the United States today if the United Kingdom entered into a military alliance with the Soviet Union. The Turkish threat had been lapping on the shores of Southern Europe. With French support it could strike at the heart of Europe. The French alliance with the Turk gave Aretino his opportunity to pay back Charles for his pension by merely writing two letters.

Both of the letters were addressed to Francis; both were as public as an editorial in the *New York Times*; both cried shame on Francis for consorting with the enemy of Christendom and Europe. Across the continent millions of voices roared their assent to Aretino's words. There is no doubt it was the crest of his wave; a common writer had dared to call a king to account for his politics. Francis sent couriers to offer Aretino double the amount of the pension if he could learn to see things differently. One cannot be certain if Aretino really believed in the Turkish threat or if he decided that two hundred crowns in hand were worth four hundred in French promises; but he refused the offer from Francis. His refusal was couched in such a fashion that if Charles did welsh, Francis could still have hopes. As we say, he left the door open.

No account of Aretino's life would be complete without mentioning his clash with Michelangelo. When he heard of the project for the Sistine Chapel, he wrote to Michelangelo, describing in detail how the subject matter should be treated. Some modern critics have upbraided Aretino for his presumption in this matter, which shows that they do not understand the age. It was quite common for a man of letters to sketch out with words a proposed painting. It was just that Michelangelo felt no need for help. He replied to Aretino praising his conception in words that actually dismissed Aretino and his views.

Aretino was not easily put off. He returned to the correspondence with a different end in view. He wanted a gift of one of Michelangelo's drawings. For eight years he kept up the campaign for a free drawing, but the stubborn Buonarroti was not to be coerced into surrendering one. In 1545 Aretino decided the time was ripe for him to strike at Michelangelo in reprisal for his refusal. In a letter to Michelangelo, Aretino managed to praise Raphael as a better artist, attack the work in the Sistine Chapel for being both irreligious and licentious, and imply that Michelangelo was a homosexual. One can only dismiss the letter as the spiteful attack of a man of small character. How droll a role it was for Aretino to pose as the shocked puritan. If one would measure Aretino for meanness, the encounter with Michelangelo would provide the best rule. Michelangelo's response was simply to paint the portrait of Aretino on the head of Saint Bartholomew in the enormous fresco. As a final mocking note, the angry Aretino is holding a flayed skin which has a caricatured face of Michelangelo.

Illogically enough, one of the worldly Aretino's ambitions was to be made a cardinal of the church. During one of his peaceful periods with Clement, an emissary of the Pope had hinted that Aretino was in line for the honor. But Clement never got around to it, and it is very unlikely that he ever had any serious thought to make Aretino a prince of the church. Pope Paul III who followed Clement was even more adamant in dismissing the suggestion as ridiculous. Aretino had a typical reaction to Paul's refusal: he castigated the Pope in gutter language.

In 1549 Paul died and was succeeded by Julius III who was from Arezzo. Aretino was so certain that his fellow Aretine would honor him with a red hat that he broke a vow he had made to himself never to leave his adopted home and left Venice in April of 1554 to journey to Rome to be ready for the honor. When he reached Rome he found that most of his old enemies and friends were dead. But there were new friends, friends on the basis of his reputation as the most dangerous tongue in Europe. They thronged around him and he felt like the conquering hero come home.

But the summer came and there was no mention of the hat. Finally dreadful August came. August in Rome in the sixteenth century was no festival. Heat lay heavy in the streets. The stench of sewage, dead dogs, and human excrement pervaded the air. It came to Aretino in that oppressive setting that he would never be a cardinal. With sudden decision and without recrimination he packed and went home to his beloved Venice.

But all was not well in paradise. The landlord of the Casa Aretino had taken advantage of his absence to evict him. The landlord had not been paid in twenty years except for a published eulogy that Aretino had dashed off. Aretino took the setback in stride and moved to a large apartment. There were still enough patrons left to keep him in style.

The year 1556 came and Aretino realized that all the great princes that he had known were dead. Only Charles V was still alive and he had abdicated as Emperor to go to the lonely monastery of Yuste in Spain. Aretino had survived only in spirit. He was racked by erysipelas, epilepsy, syphilis, and palsy. He only had time for one epic donnybrook.

Anton Francesco Doni, who has been called the father of modern journalism, probably because he was completely mad, had been living off Aretino's charity. While cadging from Aretino, he had been stealing his host's patrons. Aretino discovered his duplicity and roasted him in one of his public letters of the kind that had disposed of so many enemies. Doni replied in kind but added the prediction that Aretino would not last out the year.

Aretino almost made a liar of him because he got all the way to October. On the night of October 21, 1566, while drinking heavily, at a riotous gathering in a tavern, he suffered a cerebral hemorrhage and died in his bed a few hours later. Rumor has it that he was telling bawdy stories about his sisters when the seizure came.

There is little to add by way of conclusion except to say that if you want the Sistine Chapel, you'll have to take Aretino too.

MACHIAVELLI

Would you buy a used car from this man?

VINCENT CRONIN

Machiavelli—the most hated man who ever lived: charged, down the centuries, with being the sole poisonous source of political monkey business, of the mocking manipulation of men, of malfeasance, misanthropy, mendacity, murder, and massacre; the evil genius of tyrants and dictators, worse than Judas, for no salvation resulted from *his* betrayal; guilty of the sin against the Holy Ghost, knowing Christianity to be true, but resisting the truth; not a man at all, but Antichrist in apish flesh, the Devil incarnate, Old Nick, with the whiff of sulphur on his breath and a tail hidden under his scarlet Florentine gown.

Machiavelli is the one Italian of the Renaissance we all think we know, partly because his name has passed into our language as a synonym for unscrupulous schemer. But Niccolò Machiavelli of Florence was a more complex and fascinating figure than his namesake of the English dictionary, and unless we ourselves wish to earn the epithet Machiavellian, it is only fair to look at the historical Machiavelli in the context of his age.

He was born in 1469 of an impoverished noble family whose coat of arms featured four keys. Niccolò's father was a retired lawyer who owned two small farms and an inn, his mother a churchgoer who wrote hymns to the Blessed Virgin. Niccolò was one of four children; the younger son, Totto, became a priest, and the idea of a con-

fessional occupied by a Father Machiavelli is one that has caused Niccolò's enemies some wry laughter.

Niccolò attended the Studio, Florence's university, where he studied the prestigious newly-discovered authors of Greece and Rome. Like all his generation, he idolized the Athenians and the Romans of the Republic, and was to make them his models in life. This was one important influence. The other was the fact that Florence was then enjoying, under the Medici, a period of peace. For centuries the city had been torn by war and faction; but now all was serene, and the Florentines were producing their greatest achievements in philosophy, poetry, history, and the fine arts.

This point is important, for too often we imagine the Italian Renaissance as a period of thug-like *condottieri* and cruel despots forever locked in war. We must not be deceived by the artists. Uccello and Michelangelo painted bloody battles, but they were battles that had taken place many years before. If we are to understand Machiavelli, we must picture his youth as a happy period of civilization and peace: for the first time in centuries swords rusted, muscles grew flabby, fortress walls became overgrown with ivy.

In 1494, when Machiavelli was twenty-five, this happiness was shattered. King Charles VIII of France invaded Italy to seize the kingdom of Naples; Florence lay on his route. In

the Middle Ages the Florentines had fought bravely against aggressors, but now, grown slack and effete, they were afraid of Charles's veterans and his forty cannon. Instead of manning their walls, they and their leading citizen, Pietro de' Medici, meekly allowed the French king to march in; they even paid him gold not to harm their country.

This debacle led to internal wars, to economic decline, in which Niccolò's father went bankrupt, to much heart-searching, and to a puritanical revolution. Savonarola the Dominican came to rule from the pulpit. Thundering that the French invasion was punishment for a pagan way of life, he burned classical books and nude pictures and urged a regeneration of Florence through fasting and prayer. The French just laughed at Savonarola; he lost the confidence of his fellow citizens and was burned at the stake in 1498.

In that same year, Machiavelli became an employee of the Florentine Republic, which he was to serve ably as diplomat and administrator. Machiavelli scorned Savonarola's idea of political regeneration through Christianity; instead, he persuaded the Florentines to form a citizen militia, as was done in Republican Rome. In 1512 Florence's big test came. Spain had succeeded France as Italy's oppressor, and now, at the instigation of the Medici, who had been exiled from Florence in 1494 and wished to return, a Spanish army of five thousand marched

"Machiavelli," by Vincent Cronin, *Horizon*, Autumn, 1972. Reprinted by permission.

against Tuscany. Four thousand of Machiavelli's militia were defending the strong Florentine town of Prato. The Spaniards, ill-fed and unpaid, launched a halfhearted attack. The Florentines, instead of resisting, took to their heels. Prato was sacked, and a few days later Florence surrendered without a fight. The Medici returned, the Republic came to an end, Machiavelli lost his job and was tortured and exiled to his farm. For the second time in eighteen years he had witnessed a defeat that was both traumatic and humiliating.

In the following year an out-of-work Machiavelli began to write his great book *The Prince*. It is an attempt to answer the question implicit in Florence's two terrible defeats: what had gone wrong? Machiavelli's answer is this: for all their classical buildings and pictures, for all the Ciceronian Latin and readings from Plato, the Florentines had never really revived the essence of classical life—that military vigor and patriotism unto death that distinguished the Greeks and Romans. What then is the remedy? Italy must be regenerated—not by Savonarola's brand of puritanism, but by a soldier-prince. This prince must subordinate every aim to military efficiency. He must personally command a citizen army and keep it disciplined by a reputation for cruelty.

But even this, Machiavelli fears, will not be enough to keep at bay the strong new nation-states, France and Spain. So, in a crescendo of patriotism, Machiavelli urges his prince to disregard the accepted rules of politics, to hit below the belt. Let him lie, if need be, let him violate treaties: "Men must be either pampered or crushed, because they can get revenge for small injuries but not for fatal ones"; "A prudent ruler cannot, and should not, honor his word when it places him at a disadvantage and when the reasons for which he made his promise no longer exist"; "If a prince wants to maintain his rule he must learn how not to be virtuous."

Machiavelli develops his concept of a soldier-prince with a couple of portraits. The first, that of the emperor Alexander Severus, is an example of how a prince should not behave. Al-

exander Severus, who reigned in the third century, was a man of such goodness it is said that during his fourteen years of power he never put anyone to death without a trial. Nevertheless, as he was thought effeminate, and a man who let himself be ruled by his mother, he came to be scorned, and the army conspired against him and killed him. Machiavelli scorns him also: "Whenever that class of men on which you believe your continued rule depends is corrupt, whether it be the populace, or soldiers, or nobles, you have to satisfy it by adopting the same disposition; and then *good deeds are your enemies.*"

Machiavelli's second portrait is of Cesare Borgia, son of Pope Alexander VI, who carved out a dukedom for himself and then brought it to heel by appointing a tough governor, Ramiro. Later, says Machiavelli, Cesare discovered that "the recent harshness had aroused some hatred against him, and wishing to purge the minds of the people and win them over . . . he had this official [Ramiro] cut in two pieces one morning and exposed on the public square . . . This ferocious spectacle left the people at once *content and horrified.*"

The words I have italicized show Machiavelli's peculiar cast of mind. He grows excited when goodness comes to a sticky end and when a dastardly deed is perpetrated under a cloak of justice. He seems to enjoy shocking traditional morality, and there can be little doubt that he is subconsciously revenging himself on the Establishment responsible for those two profound military defeats.

Machiavelli wrote *The Prince* for Giuliano de' Medici. He hoped that by applying the lessons in his book, Giuliano would become tough enough to unite Italy and drive out the foreigner. But Giuliano, the youngest son of Lorenzo the Magnificent, was a tubercular young man with gentle blue eyes and long sensitive fingers, the friend of poets and himself a sonneteer. He was so soft that his brother Pope Leo had to relieve him of his post as ruler of Florence after less than a year. Preparations for war against France taxed his feeble constitution; at the age of thirty-seven he fell ill and died. Machiavelli's notion of turning Giuliano

into a second Cesare Borgia was about as fantastic as trying to turn John Keats into a James Bond.

This fantastic element has been overlooked in most accounts of Machiavelli, but it seems to me important. Consider the *Life of Castruccio Castracani,* which Machiavelli wrote seven years after *The Prince*. It purports to be a straight biography of a famous fourteenth-century ruler of Lucca, but in fact only the outline of the book is historically true. Finding the real Castruccio insufficiently tough to embody his ideals, Machiavelli introduces wholly fictitious episodes borrowed from Diodorus Siculus's life of a tyrant who really was unscrupulous: Agathocles. As captain of the Syracusans, Agathocles had collected a great army, then summoned the heads of the Council of Six Hundred under the pretext of asking their advice, and put them all to death.

Machiavelli in his book has Castruccio perform a similar stratagem. Just as in *The Prince* the second-rate Cesare Borgia passes through the crucible of Machiavelli's imagination to emerge as a modern Julius Caesar, so here a mildly villainous lord is dressed up as the perfect amoral autocrat. In both books Machiavelli is so concerned to preach his doctrine of salvation through a strong soldier-prince that he leaves Italy as it really was for a world of fantasy.

Machiavelli had a second purpose in dedicating *The Prince* to Giuliano de' Medici (and when Giuliano died, to his almost equally effete nephew Lorenzo). He wished to regain favor with the Medici, notably with Pope Leo. This also was a fantastic plan. Machiavelli had plotted hand over fist against the Medici for no less than fourteen years and was known to be a staunch republican, opposed to one-family rule in Florence. Pope Leo, moreover, was a gentle man who loved Raphael's smooth paintings and singing to the lute; he would not be interested in a book counseling cruelty and terror.

How could a man like Machiavelli, who spent his early life in the down-to-earth world of Italian politics, have yielded to such unrealistic, such fantastic hopes? The answer, I think, lies in the fact that he was also an imaginative artist—a playwright obsessed with extreme dramatic situations. Indeed, Machiavelli was best known in Florence as the author of *Mandragola*. In that brilliant comedy, a bold and tricky adventurer, aided by the profligacy of a parasite, and the avarice of a friar, achieves the triumph of making a gulled husband bring his own unwitting but too yielding wife to shame. It is an error to regard Machiavelli as primarily a political theorist, taking a cool look at facts. *The Prince* is, in one sense, the plot of a fantastic play for turning the tables on the French and Spaniards.

What, too, of Machiavelli's doctrine that it is sometimes wise for a prince to break his word and to violate treaties? It is usually said that this teaching originated with Machiavelli. If so, it would be very surprising, for the vast majority of so-called original inventions during the Italian Renaissance are now known to have been borrowed from classical texts. The Florentines valued wisdom as Edwardian English gentlemen valued port—the older the better.

In 1504 Machiavelli wrote a play, which has been lost, called *Masks*. It was in imitation of Aristophanes' *Clouds*, the subject of which is the Sophists, those men who claimed to teach "virtue" in a special sense, namely, efficiency in the conduct of life. The Sophists emphasized material success and the ability to argue from any point of view, irrespective of its truth. At worst, they encouraged a cynical disbelief in all moral restraints on the pursuit of selfish, personal ambition. Florentines during their golden age had paid little attention to the Sophists, preferring Plato, who accorded so well with Christianity and an aesthetic approach to life; but after the collapse in 1494 it would have been natural for a man like Machiavelli to dig out other, harder-headed philosophers.

The source for his doctrine of political unscrupulousness may well have been the Sophists as presented in Aristophanes' play. The following sentence from one of Machiavelli's letters in 1521 is close to many lines in *The Clouds:* "For that small matter of lies," writes Machiavelli, "I am a doctor and hold my degrees. Life has taught me to confound false and true, till no man knows either." In *The Prince* this personal confession becomes a general rule: "One must know how to color one's actions and to be a great liar and deceiver."

How was it that an undisputably civilized man like Machiavelli could advise a ruler to be cruel and deceitful and to strike terror? The answer lies in the last chapter of *The Prince*, entitled "Exhortation to liberate Italy from the barbarians." Often neglected, it is, in fact, the most deeply felt chapter of all and gives meaning to the rest. "See how Italy," Machiavelli writes, "beseeches God to send someone to save her from those barbarous cruelties and outrages" he means the outrages perpetrated by foreign troops in Italy, a land, he goes on, that is "leaderless, lawless, crushed, despoiled, torn, overrun; she has had to endure every kind of desolation."

Machiavelli is a patriot writing in mental torment. He seldom mentions the deity, but in this chapter the name of God occurs six times on one page, as an endorsement for this new kind of ruler. Machiavelli really believes that his deceitful prince will be as much an instrument of God as Moses was, and this for two reasons. First, Italy is an occupied country, and her survival is at stake; and just as moral theologians argued that theft becomes legitimate when committed by a starving man, so Machiavelli implies that deceit, cruelty, and so on become legitimate when they are the only means to national survival.

Secondly, Machiavelli had seen honest means tried and fail. Savonarola had hoped to silence cannon by singing hymns; Machiavelli himself had sent conscripts against the Spaniards. But the Italians had been then—and still were—bantams pitted against heavyweights. They could not win according to the rules, only with kidney punches. And since they had to win or cease to be themselves—that is, a civilized people as compared with foreign "barbarians"—Machiavelli argues that it is not only right but the will of God that they should use immoral means.

We must remember that *The Prince* is an extreme book that grew out of an extreme situation and that its maxims must be seen against the charred, smoking ruins of devastated Italy. The nearest modern parallel is occupied France. In the early 1940's cultivated men like Camus joined the Resistance, committing themselves to blowing up German posts by night and to other sinister techniques of *maquis* warfare. Like Machiavelli, they saw these as the only way to free their beloved country.

But the most original and neglected aspect of Machiavelli is his method. Before Machiavelli's time, historians had been the slaves of chronology. They started with the Creation, or the founding of their city, and worked forward, year by year, decade by decade, chronicling plague, war, and civil strife. Sometimes they detected a pattern, but even when they succeeded in doing so, the pattern was *sui generis*, not applicable elsewhere. Machiavelli was the first modern historian to pool historical facts from a variety of authors, not necessarily of the same period, and to use these facts to draw general conclusions or to answer pertinent questions.

He applies this method notably in his *Discourses on Livy*, and among the questions he answers are these: "What causes commonly give rise to wars between different powers?" "What kind of reputation or gossip or opinion causes the populace to begin to favor a particular citizen?" "Whether the safeguarding of liberty can be more safely entrusted to the populace or to the upper class; and which has the stronger reason for creating disturbances, the 'have-nots' or the 'haves'?"

Machiavelli does not wholly break free from a cyclical reading of history —the term Renaissance is itself a statement of the conviction that the golden age of Greece and Rome had returned. Nor did he break free from a belief in Fortune—what we would now call force of circumstance—and he calculated that men were at the mercy of Fortune five times out of ten. Nevertheless, he does mark an enormous advance over previous historical thinkers, since he discovered the method whereby man can learn from his past.

Having invented this method, Machiavelli proceeded to apply it imperfectly. He virtually ignored the Middle Ages, probably because medieval chronicles were deficient in those dramatic human twists, reversals, and paradoxes that were what really interested him. This neglect of the Middle Ages marred his study of how to deal with foreign invaders. Over a period of a thousand years Italy had constantly suffered invasion from the north; the lessons implicit in these instances would have helped Machiavelli to resolve his main problem much better than the more remote happenings he chose to draw from Livy. For example, at the Battle of Legnano, near Milan, in 1176, a league of north Italian cities won a crushing victory over Frederick Barbarossa's crack German knights. The Italians didn't employ duplicity or dramatic acts of terrorism, just courage and a united command.

So much for Machiavelli's teaching and discoveries. It remains to consider his influence. In his own lifetime he was considered a failure. Certainly, no soldier-prince arose to liberate Italy. After his death, however, it was otherwise. In 1552 the Vatican placed Machiavelli's works on the Index of Prohibited Books, because they teach men "to appear good for their own advantage in this world—a doctrine worse than heresy." Despite this ban, Machiavelli's books were widely read and his political teaching became influential. It would probably have confirmed him in his pessimistic view of human nature had he known that most statesmen and thinkers would seize on the elements of repression and guile in his teachings to the exclusion of the civic sense and patriotism he equally taught.

In France several kings studied Machiavelli as a means of increasing their absolutism, though it cannot be said that he did them much good. Henry III and Henry IV were murdered, and in each case on their blood-soaked person was found a well-thumbed copy of *The Prince*. Louis XIII was following Machiavelli when he caused his most powerful subject, the Italian-born adventurer Concini, to be treacherously killed. Richelieu affirmed that France could not be governed without the right of arbitrary arrest and exile, and that in case of danger to the state it may be well that a hundred innocent men should perish. This was *raison d'état*, an exaggerated version of certain elements in *The Prince*, to which Machiavelli might well not have subscribed.

In England Machiavelli had little direct influence. England had never been defeated as Florence had been, and Englishmen could not understand the kind of desperate situation that demanded unscrupulous political methods. The political diseases Machiavelli had first studied scientifically were in England called after his name, rather as a physical disease—say Parkinson's—is called not after the man who is suffering from it but after the doctor who discovers it. Machiavelli thus became saddled with a lot of things he had never advocated, including atheism and any treacherous way of killing, generally by poison. Hence Flamineo in Webster's *White Devil*:

O the rare trickes of a Machivillian!
Hee doth not come like a grosse plodding slave
And buffet you to death: no, my quaint knave—
Hee tickles you to death; makes you die laughing,
As if you had swallow'd a pound of saffron.

The eighteenth century, with its strong belief in man's good nature and reason, tended to scoff at Machiavelli. Hume wrote: "There is scarcely any maxim in *The Prince* which subsequent experience has not entirely refuted. The errors of this politician proceed, in a great measure, from his having lived in too early an age of the world to be a good judge of political truth." With Hume's judgment Frederick the Great of Prussia would, in early life, have agreed. As a young man Frederick wrote an *Anti-Machiavel*, in which he stated that a ruler is the first servant of his people. He rejected the idea of breaking treaties, "for one has only to make one deception of this kind, and one loses the confidence of every ruler." But Frederick did follow Machiavelli's advice to rule personally, to act as his own commander in the field, and to despise flatterers.

Later, Frederick began to wonder whether honesty really was the best policy. "One sees oneself continually in danger of being betrayed by one's allies, forsaken by one's friends, brought low by envy and jealousy; and ultimately one finds oneself obliged to choose between the terrible alternatives of sacrificing one's people or one's word of honor." In old age, Frederick became a confirmed Machiavellian, writing in 1775: "Rulers must always be guided by the interests of the state. They are slaves of their resources, the interest of the state is their law, and this law may not be infringed."

During the nineteenth century Germany and Italy both sought to achieve national unity, with the result that writers now began to play up Machiavelli's other side, his call for regeneration. Young Hegel hails the author of *The Prince* for having "grasped with a cool circumspection the necessary idea that Italy should be saved by being combined into one state." He and Fichte go a stage further than Machiavelli: they assert that the conflict between the individual and the state no longer exists, since they consider liberty and law identical. The necessity of evil in political action becomes a superior ethics that has no connection with the morals of an individual. The state swallows up evil.

In Italy Machiavelli's ideal of a regenerated national state was not perverted in this way and proved an important influence on the *risorgimento*. In 1859 the provisional government of Tuscany, on the eve of national independence, published a decree stating that a complete edition of Machiavelli's works would be printed at government expense. It had taken more than three hundred years for "a man to arise to redeem Italy," and in the event the man turned out to be two men, Cavour and Garibaldi. Both, incidentally, were quite unlike the Prince: Cavour, peering through steel-rimmed spectacles, was a moderate statesman of the center, and Garibaldi a blunt, humane, rather quixotic soldier.

Bismarck was a close student of Machiavelli, but Marx and Engels did not pay much attention to him, and the Florentine's books have never exerted great influence in Russia. In contemporary history Machiavelli's main impact has been on Benito Mussolini. In 1924 Mussolini wrote a thesis on *The*

Prince, which he described as the statesman's essential vade mecum The Fascist leader deliberately set himself to implement Petrarch's call quoted on the last page of *The Prince:*

Che l'antico valore
Nell' italici cor non è ancor morto.

Let Italians, as they did of old,
Prove that their courage has not grown cold.

After a course of muscle building, Mussolini sent the Italian army into Ethiopia to found a new Roman Empire. He joined Hitler's war in 1940, only to find that he had failed to impart to modern Italians the martial qualities of Caesar's legions. The final irony occurred in 1944, when the Nazis were obliged to occupy northern Italy as the only means of stopping an Allied walkover, and Italy again experienced the trauma of 1494 and 1512. Mussolini's failures discredit, at least for our generation, Machiavelli's theory that it is possible for one man to effect a heart transplant on a whole people.

What is Machiavelli's significance today? His policy of political duplicity has been found wanting in the past and is probably no longer practicable in an age of democracy and television. His policy of nationalism is also beginning to date as we move into an era of ideological blocs. His insistence on the need for military preparedness has proved of more durable value and is likely to remain one of the West's key beliefs. His technique for solving political problems through a study of the past is practiced to some extent by every self-respecting foreign minister of our time.

Was Machiavelli, finally, an evil man? He made an ethic of patriotism. In normal times that is a poisonous equation, but defensible, I believe, in the context of sixteenth-century Italy. Machiavelli wrote on the edge of an abyss: he could hear the thud of enemy boots, had seen pillage, profanation, and rape by foreign troops. Imaginative as he was, he could sense horrors ahead: the ending of political liberty and of freedom of the press, which put the lights out in Italy for 250 years. He taught that it is civilized man's first duty to save civilization—at all costs. Doubtless he was mistaken. But it is not, I think, the mistake of an evil man.

Women of the Renaissance

J. H. Plumb

François Villon, the vagabond poet of France, wondered, as he drifted through the gutters and attics of fifteenth-century Paris, where were the famous women of the days long past? Where Héloïse, for whom Abelard had endured such degradation? Where Thaïs, Alis, Haremburgis, where the Queen Blanche with her siren's voice, where were these fabled, love-haunted, noblewomen, of more than human beauty? Gone, he thought, gone forever. Even the rough Viking bards sang of their heroic women, of Aud the Deep-minded, who "hurt most whom she loved best." The lives of these fateful, tragic women, medieval heroines of love and sorrow, became themes of epic and romance that were told in the courts of princes; yet even as Villon bewailed their loss, men were growing tired of them.

The age of heroes was dying. The unrequited love of Dante for Beatrice, the lyrical attachment of Petrarch for Laura, and, in a different mood, the agreeable pleasantries of Boccaccio, had domesticated love, making it more intimate. The dawn of a carefree, less fate-ridden attitude to woman was gentle, undramatic, and slow, beginning way back with the wandering troubadours and the scholars who moved from castle to farm, from monastery to university, singing their light-hearted lyrics to earn their keep:

> *Down the broad way do I go,*
> *Young and unregretting,*
> *Wrap me in my vices up,*
> *Virtue all forgetting,*
> *Greedier for all delight*
> *Than heaven to enter in:*
> *Since the soul in me is dead,*
> *Better save the skin.*
> *Sit you down amid the fire,*
> *Will the fire not burn you?*
> *Come to Pavia, will you*
> *Just as chaste return you?*
> *Pavia, where Beauty draws*
> *Youth with finger-tips,*
> *Youth entangled in her eyes,*
> *Ravished with her lips.*

So sang the nameless Archpoet, young, consumptive, in love, as he wandered down to Salerno to read medicine. The time was the twelfth century—three hundred years before the haunting love poems of Lorenzo de' Medici were written. Yet the sentiments of both men were a part of the same process, part of the lifting tide of Southern Europe's prosperity, of its growing population, of the sophistication that wealth and leisure brought, for in leisure lies dalliance. The wandering scholars were few; their mistresses, chatelaines or girls of the town. Yet they were the naïve harbingers of a world that was to reach its fullness in Italy in the fifteenth century.

It was the new prosperity that influenced the lives of women most profoundly. It brought them fresh opportunities for adornment; it increased their dowries and their value. It emancipated many from the drudgery of the household and from the relentless, time-consuming demands of children. Women entered more fully into the daily lives and pursuits of men. And, of course, the new delights of the Renaissance world—painting, music, literature—had their feminine expression. Much of the artistic world was concerned with the pursuit of love in all its guises. Women were a part of art.

Except for the very lowest ranks of society, women were inextricably entangled in the concept of prosperity, and their virtue was a marketable commodity. They were secluded from birth to marriage, taught by women and priests, kept constantly under the closest supervision in the home or in the convent. Marriage came early: twelve was not an uncommon age, thirteen usual, fifteen was getting late, and an unmarried girl of sixteen or seventeen was a catastrophe. Women conveyed property and could often secure a lift in the social scale for their families. Even more important was the use of women to seal alliances between families, whether princely, noble, or mercantile. The great Venetian merchants interlocked their adventures overseas with judicious marriages at home. The redoubtable

From *The Italian Renaissance*, by J. H. Plumb, pp. 130-143, The American Heritage Library, Houghton Mifflin, 1985.

Vittoria Colonna was betrothed at the age of four to the Marquis of Pescara to satisfy her family's political ambition. Lucrezia Borgia's early life was a grim enough reminder of the dynastic value of women. Her fiancés were sent packing, her husbands murdered or declared impotent, so that Alexander VI could use her again and again in the furtherance of his policies.

In less exalted ranks of society women were still traded. It took Michelangelo years of horse trading to buy a young Ridolfi wife for his nephew and so push his family up a rank in Florentine society. Marriages so arranged were symbolic of power and social status as well as wealth, and their celebration, in consequence, demanded the utmost pomp and splendor that the contracting parties could afford. Important Venetian marriages were famed for an extravagance that not even the Council of Ten could curb.

The festivities began with an official proclamation in the Doge's Palace. The contracting parties and their supporters paraded the canals *en fête*. Gondoliers and servants were dressed in sumptuous livery; the façades of the palaces were adorned with rare Oriental carpets and tapestries; there were bonfires, fireworks, balls, masques, banquets, and everywhere and at all times—even the most intimate—serenades by gorgeously dressed musicians. Of course, such profusion acted like a magnet for poets, dramatists, rhetoricians, painters, and artists of every variety. For a few ducats a wandering humanist would pour out a few thousand words, full of recondite references to gods and heroes; poets churned out epithalamiums before they could be asked; and painters immortalized the bride, her groom, or even, as Botticelli did, the wedding breakfast. And they were eager for more mundane tasks, not for one moment despising an offer to decorate the elaborate *cassoni* in which the bride took her clothes and linen to her new household. Indeed, the competitive spirit of both brides and painters in *cassoni* became so fierce that they ceased to be objects of utility and were transformed into extravagant works of art, becoming the heirlooms of future generations.

The artistic accompaniment of marriage became the height of fashion. When the Duke and Duchess of Urbino returned to their capital after their wedding, they were met on a hilltop outside their city by all the women and children of rank, exquisitely and expensively dressed, bearing olive branches in their hands. As the Duke and Duchess reached them, mounted choristers accompanied by nymphs à *la Grecque* burst into song—a special cantata that had been composed for the newlyweds. The Goddess of Mirth appeared in person with her court, and to make everyone realize that jollity and horseplay were never out of place at a wedding, hares were loosed in the crowd. This drove the dogs insane with excitement, to everyone's delight. No matter how solemn the occasion, marriage always involved coarse farce, usually at the climax of the wedding festivities, when the bride and the groom were publicly bedded. Although there was no romantic nonsense about Italian weddings—certainly few marriages for love—everyone knew that the right, true end of the contract was the bed. The dowager Duchess of Urbino, something of a bluestocking and a Platonist and a woman of acknowledged refinement, burst into her niece's bedroom on the morning after her marriage and shouted, "Isn't it a fine thing to sleep with the men?"

Marriage for the women of the Renaissance gave many their first taste of opulence, leisure, and freedom. They were very young; the atmosphere of their world was as reckless as it was ostentatious; and furthermore, they had not chosen their husbands, who frequently were a generation older than they. Their men, who often were soldiers or courtiers living close to the razor-edge of life, fully enjoyed intrigue, so the young wife became a quarry to be hunted. As she was often neglected, the chase could be brief. Even Castiglione, who was very fond of his wife, treated her somewhat casually. He saw her rarely and made up for his absence with affectionate, bantering letters. Of course, she was a generation younger than he and therefore hardly a companion. Such a situation was not unusual: a girl of thirteen might excite her mature husband, but she was unlikely to entertain him for long. She fulfilled her tasks by bearing a few children and running a trouble-free household, and neither matter was too onerous for the rich. Nurses took over the children as soon as they were born; a regiment of servants relieved wives of their traditional housewifely duties. So the leisure that had previously been the lot of only a few women of very high birth became a commonplace of existence for a multitude of women.

The presence of these leisured women in society helped to transform it. It created the opportunity for personality to flourish, for women to indulge the whims of their temperaments—free from the constraining circumstances of childbirth, nursery, and kitchen. There were men enough to adorn their vacant hours. Italy was alive with priests, many of them urbane, cultured, and idle, whose habit acted as a passport, hinting a security for husbands that their actions all too frequently belied. Nevertheless, they were the natural courtiers of lonely wives, and they swarmed in the literary salons of such distinguished women as Elisabetta Gonzaga at Urbino, the Queen of Cyprus at Asolo, or Vittoria Colonna at Rome.

Soldiers as well as priests needed the sweetness of feminine compassion to soften their tough and dangerous lives. Fortunately, military campaigns in Renaissance Italy were short and usually confined to the summer months, and so the horseplay, the practical jokes, and the feats of arms that were as essential to the courtly life as literary conversations or dramatic performances were provided by the knights.

In addition to soldiers and priests, there were the husbands' pages, all in need of the finer points of amorous education. For a princess, further adornment of the salon was provided by an ambassador—often, true enough, a mere Italian, but at times French or Spanish, which gave an exotic touch that a woman of fashion could exploit to her rivals' disadvantage. Naturally, these courts became highly competitive: to have Pietro Bembo sitting at one's feet, reading his mellifluous but tedious essays on the beauties of Platonic love, was sure to enrage the hearts of other women. In fact, the popularity of Bembo illustrates admirably the style of sophisticated love that the extravagant and princely women of Italy demanded.

Pietro Bembo was a Venetian nobleman, the cultivated son of a rich and sophisticated father who had educated him in the height of humanist fashion at the University of Ferrara, where he acquired extreme agility in bandying about the high-flown concepts of that strange mixture of Platonism and Christianity that was the hallmark of the exquisite. Petrarch, of course, was Bembo's mentor, and like Petrarch he lived his life, as far as the pressures of nature would allow him, in literary terms. He fell verbosely and unhappily in love with a Venetian girl; his ardent longings and intolerable frustrations were committed elegantly to paper and circulated to his admiring friends.

This experience provided him with enough material for a long epistolary exchange with Ercole Strozzi, who was as addicted as Bembo to girls in literary dress. Enraptured by the elegance of his sentiments, Strozzi invited Bembo to his villa near Ferrara, doubtless to flaunt his latest capture, Lucrezia Borgia, as well as to indulge his insatiable literary appetite. However, the biter was quickly bitten, for Bembo was just Lucrezia's cup of tea. A mature woman of twenty-two, thoroughly versed in the language as well as the experience of love, she was already bored with her husband, Alfonso d'Este, and tired of Strozzi. Soon she and Bembo were exchanging charming Spanish love lyrics and far larger homilies on aesthetics. After a visit by Lucrezia to Bembo, sick with fever, the pace quickened. Enormous letters followed thick and fast. Bembo ransacked literature to do homage to Lucrezia; they were Aeneas and Dido, Tristan and Iseult, Lancelot and Guinevere—not, however, lover and mistress.

For a time they lived near each other in the country while Ferrara was plague-ridden. Proximity and the furor of literary passion began to kindle fires in Bembo that were not entirely Platonic, and, after all, Lucrezia was a Borgia. Her tolerant but watchful husband, however, had no intention of being cuckolded by an aesthete, and he rattled his sword. Bembo did not relish reliving the tragedy of Abelard; he might love Lucrezia to distraction, but he cherished himself as only an artist can, so he thought it discreet to return to Venice (he had excuse enough, as his brother was desperately sick). There he consoled himself by polishing his dialogue, *Gli Asolani*, which already enjoyed a high reputation among those to whom it had been circulated in manuscript. Resolving to give his love for Lucrezia its final, immortal form, he decided to publish it with a long dedication to her. To present her with his divine thoughts on love was a greater gift by far, of course, than his person. Doubtless both Lucrezia and her husband agreed; whether they read further than the dedication is more doubtful.

Bembo had written these highfalutin letters—informal, mannered, obscure, and so loaded with spiritual effusions on love, beauty, God, and women that they are almost unreadable—during a visit to that tragic and noblewoman Caterina Cornaro, Queen of Cyprus. The daughter of a Venetian aristocrat, she had been married as a girl to Giacomo II of Cyprus for reasons of state and declared with infinite pomp "daughter of the republic." Bereaved of both husband and son within three years, she had defied revolution and civil war and maintained her government for fourteen years until, to ease its political necessities, Venice had forced her abdication and set her up in a musical-comedy court at Asolo. There she consoled herself with the world of the spirit, about which Bembo was better informed than most, and he was drawn to her like a moth to a flame. Her court was elegant, fashionable, and intensely literary. *Gli Asolani*, published by Aldus in 1505, made Bembo the archpriest of love as the *Courtier* was to make Castiglione the archpriest of manners. Indeed, Bembo figures in the *Courtier,* and Castiglione adopted his literary techniques. These two subtle and scented bores were destined to turn up together, and nowhere was more likely than the court of Elisabetta Gonzaga at Urbino, for her insatiable appetite for discussion was equal to their eloquence; her stamina matched their verbosity; and night after night the dawn overtook their relentless arguments about the spiritual nature of love. Neither, of course, was so stupid as to think that even the high-minded Caterina or Elisabetta could live by words alone, and Bembo, at least, always interlarded the more ethereal descriptions of Platonic love with a warm eulogy of passion in its more prosaic and energetic aspects. Indeed, he was not above appearing (not entirely modestly disguised) as an ambassador of Venus, in order to declaim in favor of natural love. After six years of this excessively cultured refinement at Urbino, Bembo became papal secretary to Leo X in Rome. Appropriately, at Rome the word became flesh, and Bembo settled into the comfortable arms of a girl called Morosina, who promptly provided him with three children. It is not surprising, therefore, that Bembo's interests became more mundane, turning from Platonic philosophy to the history of Venice. After the death of his mistress, the life of the spirit once more claimed him, and he entered the College of Cardinals in 1538. More than any other man of his time, he set the pattern of elegant courtship, so that the flattery of the mind, combined with poetic effusions on the supremacy of the spirit, became a well-trodden path for the courtier. It possessed the supreme advantage of passionate courtship without the necessity of proof—a happy situation, indeed, when the object was both a bluestocking' and a queen.

Yet it would be wrong to think that the gilded lives of Renaissance princesses were merely elegant, sophisticated, and luxurious or that flirtation took place only in the most refined language. Few could concentrate their thoughts year in, year out, on the nobility of love like Vittoria Colonna. She, who inspired some of Michelangelo's most passionate poetry, even into old age, could and did live in an intense world of spiritual passion, in which the lusts of the flesh were exorcised by an ecstatic contemplation of the beauties of religion. She managed to retain her charm, avoid the pitfalls of hypocrisy, and secure without effort the devotion of Castiglione and Bembo as well as Michelangelo. Even the old rogue Aretino attempted to secure her patronage, but naturally she remained aloof. In her the Platonic ideals of love and beauty mingled with the Christian virtues to the exclusion of all else. Amazingly, no one found her a bore. However, few women could live like Vittoria: they sighed as they read Bembo, became enrapt as they listened to Castiglione, but from time to time they enjoyed a quiet reading of Boccaccio and, better still, Bandello.

Matteo Bandello had been received as a Dominican and spent many years of his life at the Convento delle Grazie, at Milan, which seems to have been a more exciting place for a short-story teller than might be imagined. He acted for a time as ambassador for the Bentivoglio and so came in contact with that remarkable woman Isabella d'Este Gonzaga, whose court at Mantua was as outstanding for its wit, elegance, and genius as any in Italy. There Bandello picked up a mistress, which put him in no mind to hurry back to his brother monks. At Mantua, too, he laid the foundations of his reputation for being one of the best raconteurs of scandal in all Italy, Aretino not excepted. How true Bandello's stories are is still a matter of fierce warfare among scholars, but this they agree on: they did not seem incredible to those who read them. That being so, they give a hair-raising picture of what was going on at courts, in monasteries, in nunneries, in merchant houses, in the palaces and the parsonages of Italy. The prime pursuit, in the vast majority of Bandello's stories, is the conquest of women, and to achieve success, any trick, any falsehood, any force, is justifiable. His heroes' attitude toward success in sex was like Machiavelli's toward politics—the end justified any means. The aim of all men was to ravish other men's wives and daughters and preserve their own

women or revenge them if they failed to do so. Vendettas involving the most bloodcurdling punishments were a corollary to his major theme. In consequence, Bandello's stories, cast in a moral guise, nevertheless read like the chronicles of a pornographer. Here are the themes of a few that were thought to be proper entertainment for the lighter moments of court life or for quiet reading by a bored wife: the marriage of a man to a woman who was already his sister and to his daughter; the adultery of two ladies at court and the death of their paramours, which is a vivid record of sexual pleasure and horrifying punishment; the servant who was decapitated for sleeping with his mistress; the death through excessive sexual indulgence of Charles of Navarre; Gian Maria Visconti's burial of a live priest; the autocastration of Fra Filippo—and so one might go on and on, for Bandello wrote hundreds of short stories, and they were largely variations on a single theme. The women of the Renaissance loved them, and few storytellers were as popular as Bandello (such abilities did not go unmarked, and he finished his career as Bishop of Agen). Nor was Bandello exceptional: there were scores of writers like him. Malicious, distorted, exaggerated as these tales were, they were based on the realities of Italian life. Undoubtedly the increased leisure of men and women released their energies for a more riotous indulgence of their sexual appetites.

However daring the Italian males of the Renaissance were, the prudence of wives and the vigilance of husbands prevailed more often than not. The Emilia Pias, Elisabetta Gonzagas, Isabella d'Estes, Lucrezia Borgias, Costanza Amarettas, and Vittoria Colonnas were rare—particularly for cardinals and bishops ravenous for Platonic love. So in Rome, in Florence, in Venice, and in Milan there developed a class of grand courtesans, more akin to geisha girls than to prostitutes, to the extent that the *cortesane famose* of Venice despised the *cortesane de la minor sorte* and complained of their number, habits, and prices to the Senate (they felt they brought disrepute on an honorable profession). Grand as these Venetian girls were, they could not compete with the great courtesans of Rome, who not only lived in small palaces with retinues of maids and liveried servants but also practiced the literary graces and argued as learnedly as a Duchess of Urbino about the ideals of Platonic love.

Italy during the Renaissance was a country at war, plagued for decades with armies. A well-versed condottiere might battle with skill even in the wordy encounters of Platonic passion, but the majority wanted a quicker and cheaper victory. For months on end the captains of war had nothing to do and money to spend; they needed a metropolis of pleasure and vice. Venice, with its quick eye for a profit, provided it and plucked them clean. There, women were to be had for as little as one *scudo*, well within the means even of a musketeer. And it was natural that after Leo X's purge, the majority of the fallen from Rome should flow to Venice. That city, with its regattas, *feste*, and carnivals, with its gondolas built for seclusion and sin, became a harlot's paradise. The trade in women became more profitable and extensive than it had been since the days of Imperial Rome. The Renaissance recaptured the past in more exotic fields than literature or the arts.

Life, however, for the noblewomen of the Renaissance was not always cakes and ale; it could be harsh and furious: the male world of war, assassination, and the pursuit of power frequently broke in upon their gentle world of love and dalliance. Indeed, Caterina Sforza, the woman whom all Italy saluted as its *prima donna*, won her fame through her dour courage and savage temper. Castiglione tells the story of the time she invited a boorish condottiere to dinner and asked him first to dance and then to hear some music—both of which he declined on the grounds that they were not his business. "What is your business, then?" his hostess asked. "Fighting," the warrior replied. "Then," said the virago of Forlì, "since you are not at war and not needed to fight, it would be wise for you to have yourself well greased and put away in a cupboard with all your arms until you are wanted, so that you will not get more rusty than you are." Caterina was more a figure of a saga than a woman of the Renaissance. Three of her husbands were assassinated. At one time she defied the French, at another Cesare Borgia, who caught her and sent her like a captive lioness to the dungeons of Sant' Angelo. She told her frantic sons that she was habituated to grief and had no fear of it, and as they ought to have expected, she escaped. Yet tough and resourceful as she was, Caterina could be a fool in love—much more than the Duchess of Urbino or Vittoria Colonna. Time and time again her political troubles were due to her inability to check her strong sexual appetite, which fixed itself too readily on the more monstrous of the Renaissance adventurers. So eventful a life induced credulity, and like the rest of her family, Caterina believed in the magical side of nature, dabbled in alchemy and mysteries, and was constantly experimenting with magnets that would produce family harmony or universal salves or celestial water or any other improbable elixir that the wandering hucksters wished on her. At any age, at any time, Caterina would have been a remarkable woman, but the Renaissance allowed her wild temperament to riot.

Certainly the women of the Renaissance were portents. Elisabetta Gonzaga and Isabella d'Este are the founding sisters of the great literary salons that were to dominate the fashionable society of Western Europe for centuries. But the courts of Italy were few, the families that were rich enough to indulge the tastes and pleasures of sophisticated women never numerous. The lot of most women was harsh; they toiled in the home at their looms or in the fields alongside their men. They bred early and died young, untouched by the growing civility about them, save in their piety. In the churches where they sought ease for their sorrows, the Mother of God shone with a new radiance, a deeper compassion, and seemed in her person to immortalize their lost beauty. Even the majority of middle-class women knew little of luxury or literary elegance. Their lives were dedicated to their husbands and their children; their ambitions were limited to the provision of a proper social and domestic background for their husbands; and they were encouraged to exercise prudence, to indulge in piety, and to eschew vanities. Yet their lives possessed a civility, a modest elegance, that was in strong contrast to the harsher experiences and more laborious days of medieval women. Their new wealth permitted a greater, even if still modest, personal luxury. They could dress themselves more finely, acquire more jewels, provide a richer variety of food for their guests, entertain more lavishly, give more generously to charity. Although circumscribed, their lives were freer, their opportunities greater. It might still be unusual for a woman to be learned or to practice the arts, but it was neither rare nor exotic. And because they had more time, they were able to create a more active social life and to spread civility. After the Renaissance, the drawing room became an integral part of civilized living; indeed, the Renaissance education of a gentleman assumed that much of his life would be spent amusing women and moving them with words. As in so many aspects of life in Renaissance Italy, aristocratic attitudes of the High Middle Ages were adopted by the middle classes. Courtesy and civility spread downward, and the arts of chivalry became genteel.

PORTUGAL'S IMPACT ON AFRICA

*Poverty the spur – Bartholomew Dias'
voyage to the Cape of Good Hope five hundred
years ago marked the apex of an extraordinary
Portuguese expansion overseas and the start of a
fateful European impact on South Africa.*

15th-century tin-glazed bowl showing a Portuguese sailing ship.

David Birmingham

FIVE HUNDRED YEARS AGO, IN 1488, Bartholomew Dias, a Portuguese seaman, reached the Cape of Good Hope on the furthest tip of South Africa. This was the last stage of the Portuguese exploration of the Atlantic coast and its islands. It was also the beginning of five centuries of often strained relations between Europe and South Africa. Two questions arise out of this turning point in the world's fortunes. The first is how did Portugal, a relatively remote and impoverished land at the far ends of medieval Europe, become the pioneer of Atlantic colonisation? And secondly, what were the long-term consequences of the opening of South Africa to alien influences?

The Portuguese domination of the eastern Atlantic took place in six stages, each of which pioneered a new set of colonial experiments. Bartholomew Dias was the heir to two centuries of trial and error as Portugal sought escape from its chronic poverty. The fact that Portugal was able to succeed in becoming an international power was due primarily to the superb shelter which the harbour of Lisbon provided to mariners on the otherwise inhospitable coast of south-eastern Europe.

Lisbon had been a harbour in Phoenician times when Levantine traders needed a haven on the long haul to Britain. It was also used by the Roman and Arab empires, although their primary interest lay in land-based domination. In the thirteenth century sea-power revived and Genoa succeeded in breaking out of the Mediterranean into the Atlantic. The great economic centres of northern Italy and of lower Germany, (hitherto linked by land-routes through the great markets of Lyons and Nuremburg) were now joined by Genoese on the safer maritime route. Lisbon again became a thriving port. The Portuguese learnt about ship-building from the Low Countries and about sea-faring from Italy and Catalonia. At one time the Portuguese monarchy hired no less than six Genoese admirals, although the most famous of them, Christopher Columbus, sought fame by transferring his allegiance to the rival port of Seville in Castile.

The rise of Lisbon as the maritime gateway between northern and southern Europe led to the growth of an urban middle class with merchant and banking skills learnt from Italy. It was this middle class which became the driving force behind the Portuguese search for new wealth overseas. It found its patron in the royal prince, Pedro, brother of the vaunted Henry the Navigator. Portugal was unusual in that the nobility, lacking any other source of wealth in a country of agrarian poverty, showed a willingness to engage in merchant adventures. They were greatly helped by the thriving Jewish community of Lisbon, a community spasmodically enhanced by refugees fleeing persecution in other parts of Christendom. Jewish scholars were not hampered by Christian concepts of the world as portrayed in the scriptures and were able to take a much more scientific look at the evidence needed to draw maps and collate intelligence on economic prospects overseas.

The crises which drove Portugal to expansion were always crises over the price of bread. Throughout the Middle Ages Lisbon had been a hungry city. Access to the farm lands of the interior was inhibited by poor river navigation and expensive long-distance cartage. Grain was therefore not sought from domestic sources but from overseas shippers. Both Spain and Britain became key sup-

First published in *History Today*, June 1988, pp. 44-50. Reproduced by kind permission of History Today, Ltd., 83-84 Berwick Street, London W1V 3PJ, England.

pliers of wheat to Lisbon, and England built a six-hundred-year alliance on Portugal's need for northern trade. But in the fourteenth century one new solution to the grain deficit was a colonial venture in the Atlantic.

One thousand miles off the coast of Portugal lay the uninhabited islands of the Azores and Madeira. With the development of better shipping they became more accessible to Lisbon than the much closer interior of mainland Portugal. Colonisation and the setting up of wheat gardens were therefore attempted. Concepts of colonisation were learnt from the Venetians who had established settled colonies around their trading factories in the Near East. The labour supply consisted both of cheap European migrants driven by hunger, and captured slaves raided from the Barbary coast. The necessary capital was raised in the banking houses of Genoa. Patronage was provided by the land-owning nobility under the protection of Prince Henry. The beginnings of temperate cereal colonisation in the Atlantic basin were laid. The system was later to spread to the far side of the ocean, and eventually the Canadian and American prairies became a source of wheat not only for Portugal but also for half of Europe. Stage one of the Portuguese expansion, the wheat-based stage, was successful in the initial objective of supplying bread to overcome the Lisbon deficiency. It was also successful in terms of pioneering a colonial system which carried Europe out into the world.

The second stage of Portuguese expansion involved a more subtle development of overseas investment. Wheat was a comparatively low-yielding agricultural enterprise. A much higher return on capital, on labour and on land could be obtained by turning agrarian produce into alcohol. Alcohol could also be better preserved and could be sold when the price was advantageous rather than when the crop was ripe, as in the case of grain. The second stage of Portuguese expansion therefore attempted to establish a wine industry overseas. The necessary skills were available in the wine industry of Portugal. But Portuguese domestic wine, like Portuguese grain, suffered from severe problems of cartage

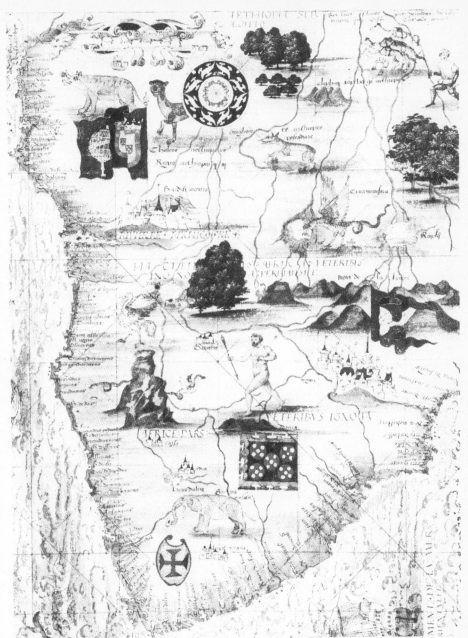

A detail from Le Testu's 'Cosmographie Universelle' of 1555, showing Portuguese settlements and trading posts in Southern Africa.

to the coast. Even in the eighteenth century, when port wine became a lucrative export, the shooting of the rapids on the Douro river made transport almost suicidal. The prospect of using colonial islands for the growing of vines was therefore attractive. The territory chosen was the Canary Islands, off the Moroccan coast of Africa.

Morocco was known to the Portuguese after a series of raiding wars associated with the militant crusading Order of Christ, of which Prince Henry was the commander. Despite an initial victory in Ceuta in 1415,

these wars had failed to capture the 'bread-basket' of North Africa which had once fed the city of Rome. Instead, the conquerors therefore set their sight on the off-shore islands. Unlike the Azores, the Canaries were already inhabited and conquest was necessary before plantations could be established. Once conquered, however, the surviving islanders could be compelled to slave servitude. Migrants from Portugal's impoverished backlands sailed in to create vineyards using both local and mainland slaves. Even when the colony was transferred in 1479 from

Portuguese suzerainty to control by the Crown of Castile, Portuguese immigrants continued to provide many colonists for Tenerife.

The Canary Islands were a second, wine-based, stage of Portugal's colonial pioneering. The development of colonial wine industries, for instance in California, South Africa and Australia was slower to take off than the development of wheat colonies. Portugal itself imposed restrictions where the interests of metropolitan producers were put at risk, though Canary wine was extensively smuggled into the Portuguese empire. The Canary Islands were important, however, for another reason. They became the base for the conquest and colonisation of Hispanic America. It was from there that Columbus set sail in 1492, and later a significant proportion of the emigrants who went to the Spanish American colonies were Canary islanders, often of Portuguese ancestry. As a stage in the growth of the economic, political and social ideology of imperialism the Canary islands were of critical significance. The slave vineyards of Tenerife, and the spasmodic raiding of southern Morocco, are a more accurate testimony to the place of Henry the Navigator in history than all the myths about his scientific virtuosity which were put out by the hired praise-singer, the chronicler Azurara.

The third stage of Portuguese experimentation in colonial practices was focused on another set of Atlantic islands, the Cape Verde islands. The Cape Verdes became famous over time for their textile industry. Portugal was almost as severely short of textiles as it was short of wheat. One reason for the development of wine exports was to pay for wooleen materials from England. Cotton was also bought in significant quantities from Muslim suppliers in north Africa and, after the rounding of the Cape of Good Hope, from the great texile industries of India. But the Cape Verde islands offered an opportunity to create a colonial textile industry.

Cotton and indigo plantations were established on the islands for spinning and dying. Labour was purchased on the West Africa mainland. Craftsmen were also brought over from the mainland to introduce the necessary weaving skills. The styles of textile adopted were ones which would sell best in Africa. The industry soon became self-perpetuating. Cloth woven in the islands was sold on the mainland in return for more slaves who would further expand the plantations. The only European input was sea transport. The Portuguese shipped cloth up and down the coast in the cabotage trade. The final profits were taken in slaves, the best of which were carried to Portugal to work on the underdeveloped landed estates of the south. By the sixteenth century some 10 per cent of the population of southern Portugal comprised black immigrants. Many were still slaves but others had married into land-owning families, thus increasing the domestic labour force without having to make reciprocal marriage payments. Blacks also became a significant part of the working population of Lisbon.

Slave-grown cotton became, over the colonial centuries, one of the fundamental bases of European relations with the wider world. From its pioneering beginnings the economic system spread to Brazil, which supplied Portugal, to the 'Sea Island' cotton colonies of the Caribbean, and eventually to the great cotton belt of Georgia and Alabama. This particular branch of Portuguese colonial ideology played a more direct part than any other in the development of the industrial revolution in eighteenth-century Britain.

The fourth stage of Portuguese progress towards the discovery of the Cape of Good Hope involved a fourth set of islands and a fourth type of colonial plantation economy. The tropical island of São Tomé, off the Niger delta, proved to have excellent soil and plentiful rainfall. The merchant community of Lisbon, and especially its Jewish economic pioneers, experimented with the introduction of sugar cane. Sugar required a much higher degree of organisation than the temperate or tropical crops hitherto introduced into the new Atlantic colonies. Cane had to be grown on a sufficiently large scale to justify investing in a crushing mill and boiling vats. It also required a labour force which could be compelled to work intensely hard during the harvest season to ensure that mature cane be crushed with a minimum of delay. Sugar seemed to be ideally suited to a slave economy and labour was therefore bought from the nearby kingdoms of Benin and Kongo. The industry so flourished that the island soon became too small, and sugar planting began to spread to other Portugese colonies, notably in north-eastern Brazil.

The success of São Tomé as a pioneering sugar colony was watched with admiration by the European powers which aspired to emulate Portugal's path to colonial prosperity. The Dutch went so far as to conquer the island, and also part of Brazil. The English set up their own black slave sugar colonies in Barbados and the Caribbean in the seventeenth century, and then turned to Indian-worked sugar colonies in the nineteenth century. But the greatest imitator of them all was France whose sugar island, later called Haiti, became the richest colony of all time. It was also the first one to successfully rebel against the racial pattern of servitude that Portugal had evolved and create an independent black state out of a white-ruled colony.

The fifth stage of Portuguese colonial evolution was concerned not with planting but with mining. The mines which the explorers aspired to reach were the gold mines of West Africa. From about 1400 the Akan mines of the coastal forest had begun to supplement gold production in the medieval fields controlled by the inland kingdoms of Ghana and Mali. Information about the trans-Saharan supply of African gold was widely known in the Christo-Islamic financial circles of the Mediterranean and certainly reached the merchants of Lisbon. In 1471 these merchants discovered a back route to the mines by way of the Gold Coast in West Africa. In order to buy gold, however, the Portuguese had to offer prices, and assortments of commodities, which were competitive with those of the experienced Saharan camel caravans. They found, to their surprise, that labour was in scarce supply in the mines and that slaves from their island plantations could fetch a good price. Thus the islands became entrepôts for the selling of slave miners. The business flourished and within a generation Portugal was buying ten thousand and more ounces of gold each year.

The lure of gold became a permanent feature of colonial ambition. The success of Portugal in West Africa became a driving force for all the European powers overseas. All the great gold-bearing regions of the world were explored and often plundered. Africa initially protected its mineral wealth with well-ordered states and effective armies. America was not so strong, and the peoples of the Caribbean died in the Spanish mines while the empires of Mexico and Peru were overthrown and ransacked. Only in the nineteenth century did Africa succumb to the conquering quest for gold by Europeans. Gold lust led to the great Anglo-Boer war of 1899 in which Britain, by now the strongest of the colonising nations, conquered South Africa.

The sixth and last stage of Portuguese expansion before the discovery of the Cape occurred on the western mainland of Central Africa. In Angola the Portuguese made their one and only attempt to create a colony on *terra firma* and among native inhabitants. The trump card which they played to gain access was religion. By offering to introduce more powerful gods and saints to control the supernatural, the Portuguese were able to build up political allies who protected their commercial interests and allowed a limited development of foreign settlement. Africa's first mainland colony was primarily concerned with the buying of slaves, however, and in less than a century it had been stalled by resistance and overrun by rebellion. The Portuguese therefore adopted Spanish military tactics and sent squads of *conquistadores* to fortify their trading posts. Justification was supplied by accompanying Jesuits who commended armed conversion and established slave-worked plantations to finance their churches and monastries.

Portugal was initially less successful than its latter-day imitators in achieving territorial conquest. But the Jesuits and the soldiers did cross over to Brazil and began the harsh opening up of the eastern half of the South American continent. The colonists included some three million slaves brought over from Africa against their will. All the previous colonial experiments that Portugal had attempted in the fourteenth and fifteenth centuries – cereal farming, wine growing, cotton picking, sugar planting, gold mining – were introduced into Brazil. Sugar in the seventeenth century and gold in the eighteenth proved the most lucrative. Tobacco was added to the cornucopia. By the end of the colonial period in the Americas, the formerly Portuguese United States of Brazil exceeded the size of the formerly British United States of America.

The six stages of Portuguese expansion into the Atlantic were followed in 1488 by the great expedition to the Cape of Good Hope. This was commanded by a common captain called Bartholomew Dias, for whose services the King of Portugal paid an annuity of six thousand reals. Nothing is known of the captain's experience in tropical waters, but in August 1487 he set out with two small exploring caravels, light enough to be beached, and a bulkier store ship of provisions and trade goods. He carried three stone crosses with which to claim territory on the African mainland. His objective, via Mina and Kongo, was the desert coast of Namibia, beyond the Angolan waters explored by Diego Cão in the three previous seasons. Dias prepared reports on the available anchorages, and conducted a little trade with local Khoi cattle herders. The Portuguese were not welcome intruders, however, and after selling them some sheep and cows the Khoi prudently turned them away. In the skirmish which followed one Khoi was killed by Bartholomew Dias' cross-bow. Relations between Europe and South Africa thus began as badly as they were to continue. At another bay Dias left his store ship with nine men instructed to investigate the commercial opportunities of the region. So unsuccessful were these trade emissaries that six of them had been killed before the main expedition returned to base. The store ship itself had to be fired for want of an adequate crew to sail it back to Lisbon.

After these unhappy encounters, very reminiscent of the hit-and-run exploits of Henry the Navigator's men on the desert coast of North Africa fifty years earlier, Dias sailed on towards the greener coast of the south. After many false promises in the deeply indented bays he gradually realised that the coast he was following had turned eastward. The enthusiasm generated by this discovery

Noble savages? A 1510 woodcut of some of the native peoples the Portuguese encountered: (left to right) West African negroes; Hottentots from Algoa Bay, South Africa; Arab traders from the East African coast.

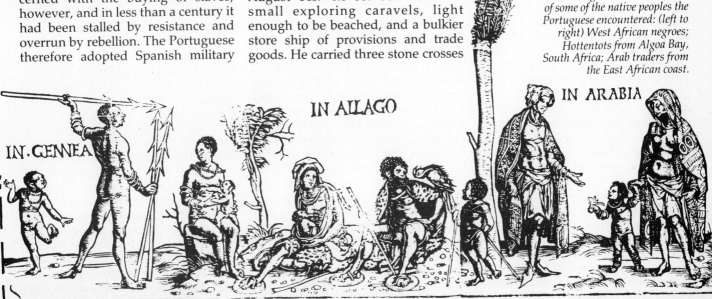

IN GENNEA   IN ALLAGO   IN ARABIA

was slow to capture the imagination of his homesick crews as bay followed bay along the southernmost shore of Africa. No opening towards the north was encountered. Eventually, at Bushman's River, some five hundred miles east of the Cape of Good Hope, Dias was persuaded to turn for home. He planted his first stone totem on March 12th, 1488, and dedicated it to Saint Gregory. He had discovered no new wealth, no fertile land, and no hospitable islands, not even a source of slaves with which to recompense the entrepreneurial King of Portugal for his outlay of risk capital. Worse still he had not conclusively found the sea lane to Arabia and India, although the direction of the coast had become more promising.

On the homeward journey Bartholomew Dias stopped on Saint Philip's day, June 6th, 1488, and apparently planted his second stone cross on the Cape of Good Hope. This was the most famous landmark of his voyage, though not actually the southernmost point of Africa. It was the rounding of this cape which eventually secured Dias his place in history. Dias did not enter Table Bay, site of the later city of Cape Town, but he did enter the Namibian bay later named Luderitz and mounted his third pillar of territorial assertion of Portuguese rights. He finally arrived back in Lisbon in December 1488 having covered 6,000 leagues in sixteen months.

The international repercussions of the Dias voyage were numerous. In 1491 a major colonising expedition was sent to the kingdom of Kongo, in Angola, which seemed a more promising African political and commercial partner than the sparse communities of coastal South Africa. In 1492 Columbus, no longer in Portuguese service, and armed with absurdly false data on the earth's circumference, sailed on behalf of Castile to find a western route to China, since Dias had failed to find an eastern one round the African coast. Not till 1497, nine years after the Dias voyage and five years after Columbus began to explore the Caribbean, did a new Portuguese king, Manuel I, manage to raise the resources, then men and the ships to attempt another merchant adventure in the far south without guarantee of profit. The expedition of Vasco da Gama, however, did complete the task begun by Bartholomew Dias and opened up the sea route to Asia. Dias himself was called back to royal service and appointed to open a gold trading factory at Sofala in southeastern Africa.

Dias had experience of the gold trade. In 1497 he had accompanied Vasco da Gama on the first leg of his journey down the African coast before turning into the Gulf of Guinea to deliver a cargo of trade cloth and merchant goods to the gold factory of Mina. In 1500 Dias was appointed to accompany the great fleet of Alvares Cabral to the Indian Ocean and set up a similar factory at Sofala. The highland gold of the Zimbabwe mines had recently switched from the old ports of southern Mozambique to reach the international market via the Zambezi route in central Mozambique. Manuel of Portugal hoped that Dias, with his little flotilla of four shallow-draft caravels, would be able to close off the traditional gold route via East Africa to the Muslim precious metal marts of the eastern Mediteranean and divert the Sofala gold round the Cape of Good Hope to Christian bankers and the western Mediteranean. Dias, however, failed to crown his career in such a fashion. After an unscheduled stop on the then unknown coast of Brazil, his boat was lost on the south Atlantic crossing. The trading fortress was indeed built five years later, but Bartholomew Dias was remembered not as a great gold trader but as the first navigator along the coast of South Africa.

The discovery of the Cape of Good Hope was initially of little intrinsic interest. South Africa had few attractions to men seeking trade, minerals, slaves, vacant land and any other kind of entrepreneurial opportunity which would allow an escape from the barrenness of Portuguese provincial society. Few Portuguese visited the Cape, and then only in order to by-pass it and seek the wealthy sea lanes of Asia. Dias' son Antonio and grandson Paulo Dias de Novais invested their capital and energy not in South Africa but in Angola in Central Africa. In 1571 they claimed the rights of Lord-Proprietor in Angola and four years later founded the city of Luanda on a shore that their ancestor had patrolled on his epic voyage.

The Dias family failed, however, to secure their colony and in the 1590s the Hapsburgs repossessed Angola for the united Iberian crown of Spain and Portugal. But despite this check, grandfather Dias had, when reaching the Cape, set eyes on the South Africa that was gradually to become the most powerful of all the foreign colonies of Africa. It was also, five centuries later, to be the one which attracted the largest number of Portuguese migrants

In 1588, a century after Dias visited South Africa, the country had changed little. Black farming and cattle-herding were as prosperous as ever in the east while sheep-rearing and shell-fishing were important in the dryer areas of the west. Portuguese mariners were regularly shipwrecked on the coast and often hospitably received and given food, shelter, clothing and a safe-conduct along the trade paths to a Portuguese harbour in Mozambique. The first signs of the agricultural revolution which was to bring American maize to South Africa as a staple crop may have been noted, but it was not until the eighteenth century that the new farming, and favourable climatic conditions, led to a large demographic increase in the South African population.

By 1688 the seeds of colonial challenge to South Africa's independence had been sown. The Dutch haven at the Cape had begun to be swelled by Calvinist refugees from European persecution. Wheat and vine colonies, reminiscent of the Azores and Canaries, were set up in the fertile plains of Swellendam and Stellenbosch. Settlers already felt restive at the imperial control imposed on them by the metropolitan government of the Dutch West India company. Slavery was accepted as the normal means to acquire labour both in the artisan shops of the city and on the farms. White women were rare among the settlers and concubines of every race were readily accepted and acknowledged as they had been on the old colonial estates of the Portuguese islands. Indeed, the Cape was seen by the settlers as an 'island' and they tried to hedge themselves off from the mainstream of South Africa.

In 1788, three hundred years after Dias, the Cape had become a frontier society very strongly linked to the rest of South Africa. The indigenous population of the western Cape had been either integrated into colonial society in as subservient caste, or driven out to the northern frontiers and labelled 'the people of the bush'. In the east settlers had adopted the cattle ranching, and cattle rustling, way of life of their black neighbours. Co-operation and conflict between them alternated according to the grazing and watering needs of the herds. Traders cast their eyes on the further horizon and dreamed of fortunes made hunting elephants for ivory. A large creole population of varied racial composition resembled the creole societies which has evolved in all the Portuguese island colonies and in Luanda. Instead of speaking a 'pidgin' Portuguese creole, the people of the Cape spoke a Dutch creole, later known as Afrikaans.

By 1888 South Africa had changed again and was on the brink of a social and economic revolution. Diamonds, gold and coal had been found and the agrarian societies, both black and white, were beginning to be mobilised for the industrial exploitation of their mineral wealth on behalf of investors in Europe. The upheaval was immense and led to the entrenchment of both a racial divide between black and white and a cultural divide between English-speakers and Dutch-speakers. The old Cape population with its mixed heritage, black and white, English and Dutch, was unable to provide a bridge when the demands of industrial profit outweighed the political benefits of reconciliation. The great Boer War and the ideology of racial segregation were the consequences.

Finally by 1988, at the time of the fifth centenary of the first European visit to the Cape, an embattled South Africa had been transformed into Africa's foremost industrial nation. The old black population had become totally overwhelmed by white power. Surplus people not needed for industrial production or capitalist agriculture were carried off to encampments on the remote and dry fringes of the country. The remainder were segregated into urbanised black ghettos with limited economic rights and no political voice. Meanwhile the white population grew in size and prosperity in the fertile heartlands. Its latest recruits were six hundred thousand Portuguese immigrants. Like their predecessors, the Atlantic migrants of the fourteenth and fifteenth centuries, they were seeking an alternative to penury in Europe's poorest yet most innovative colonising nation.

FOR FURTHER READING:
Charles Boxer, *The Portuguese Seaborne Empire, 1415-1825* (Hutchinson, 1969); G. V. Scammell, *The World Encompassed* (Methuen, 1981); V. Malgalhaes Godinho, several works in Portuguese and *L'economie de l'Empire Portugaise* (Paris, 1969); Walter Rodney, *A History of Upper Guinea* (Oxford University Press, 1970); David Birmingham, *Trade & Conflict in Angola* (Oxford University Press, 1966).

A frontier society; the Town Hall of a Dutch-administered Cape of Good Hope, 1764, with Table Mountain in the background and a slave-based economy already in evidence.

DEATH MARCH OF HERNANDO de SOTO

As they chart the conquistador's trail of human destruction from Florida's Gulf Coast to the mouth of the Mississippi, archaeologists are also reclaiming a long-lost social history of the southeastern Indians.

David H. Dye

Four hundred and fifty years ago, on May 25, 1539, the Spanish conquistador Hernando de Soto landed in Florida, probably at Tampa Bay. His fleet of nine ships carried supplies, pigs, horses, war dogs, and 600 conquistadors, accompanied by tailors, shoemakers, stocking makers, notaries, farriers, trumpeters, friars, servants, slaves, and at least two women. De Soto's royal charter from King Charles V of Spain explicitly forbade him from engaging in atrocities in La Florida—the southeastern United States—and ordered him to pacify the land without "death and robbery of the Indians." De Soto and his followers had a different agenda. Their consuming aim was to comb the Southeast for the kind of treasure Spanish conquerors had found in Central and South America. If Indians obstructed their quest, the Spaniards were prepared to pacify them by any means necessary.

Four years later, in the summer of 1543, the 311 surviving members of De Soto's expedition straggled to safety in Mexico. Their looting excursions had taken them thousands of miles through portions of at least ten southern states, as far west as Texas. Their numbers had been cut in half by starvation, desertion, disease, drowning, snakebite, and Indian arrows and clubs. De Soto himself had died in 1542, presumably of fever, as his army camped on the banks of the Mississippi River.

The calamity that befell the Spaniards, however, was nothing compared with the tragedy visited upon the Indians. By the end of the sixteenth century, native cultures in the Southeast were in a state of collapse. While no one can be sure what caused that collapse, many scholars believe that De Soto's expedition, or *entrada*, played a major role. Many Indians met their deaths directly at the hands of the conquistadors. Many more are believed to have perished in the epidemics of new diseases—influenza, whooping cough, and smallpox—that the Spaniards introduced into North America.

Archaeological evidence of De Soto's trek has been elusive. Recent discoveries, however, have begun to shed light on the world through which he passed. At the South Florida Museum in Bradenton, I have had the pleasure of photographing numerous artifacts from all over the Southeast, many of which give direct evidence of the De Soto expedition: iron chain used to bind the Indians; gift kits containing long, blue Nueva Cadiz and faceted chevron beads and mirrors; iron chisels and wedges; sheet brass bells; tubular and sheet brass beads; and fragments of military hardware such as chain mail, swords, lances, and armor.

Recent excavations of an Indian burial mound in Citrus County, Florida, have yielded large numbers of artifacts that may be associated with De Soto. In addition, a mass burial of more than 70 Indians was found in the mound, some of them possible victims of a Spanish-introduced epidemic. Others probably died more suddenly—their bones exhibit sword cuts. Similarly slashed Indian bones found at the King site in northwestern Georgia testify to the "pacification" methods of the Spanish conquerors.

Two years ago a site believed to be De Soto's 1539–40 winter encampment was discovered at a construction site in downtown Tallahassee, Florida. Exploration of the site, under the direction of Calvin Jones and Charles Ewen, is widely regarded as one of the most important Spanish contact period projects under way in North America today. Jones, Ewen, and teams of archaeologists now working together throughout the Southeast hope that the data gathered at the Tallahassee site, and from other possible De Soto sites along the conquistador's route, will enable them to salvage a long-lost social history of the southeastern Indians. For the moment, our most informative sources about De Soto's odyssey remain the records and diaries kept by members of his expeditionary force.

The Indian societies De Soto encountered were im-

From *Archaeology*, May/June 1989, pp. 27-29, 31. Copyright © 1989 by the Archaeological Institute of America.

pressive. At the time of his expedition the densely populated river valleys of southeastern North America were home to dozens of political groups of varying degrees of complexity. Many scholars believe that chiefdoms, composed of ranked elites and commoners, were the dominant form of political organization. Native elites sought to control sacred and secular power to enhance their status, reduce internal competition, and maintain political order. The search for power and authority was often conducted through warfare, contacts with the supernatural, and economic control. Chronic warfare existed between chiefdoms, and elites led warriors against their neighbors.

De Soto and his men were not always treated as invaders; they were in fact often accepted into a chief's domain as guests. Nor was De Soto above presenting himself as a god to the Indians; he learned quickly enough that many native rulers claimed to have come from the "upper world"—to have a divine nature—and he made that claim for himself.

Because the Spaniards appeared to be from a supernaturally distant realm, many Indian rulers sought their help in fighting their enemies. The chief of Casqui, for example, whose chiefdom may have centered on the St. Francis and Tyronza Rivers in eastern Arkansas, requested aid in fighting his traditional enemy, the chief of Pacaha, whose chiefdom was located near the Mississippi River. The Chicaça Indians, living south of present-day Tupelo, Mississippi, first sought Spanish help in subduing the rebellious Chakchiumas

---

The impact on the Indians of guns, war dogs, horses, and men with crossbows, halberds, lances, swords, and knives was devastating.

---

and in conquering the Caluça. (The Chicaça would later turn on De Soto for consuming their winter stores of corn and for demanding 200 burden bearers. The attack was one of the worst De Soto ever sustained.) In several instances Indian elites tried to secure alliances and kinship with De Soto through marriage. Thus, the chief of Casqui gave his daughter to De Soto, and the chief of Pacaha gave him one of his wives, a sister, and a woman of rank.

When diplomacy failed (as it usually did), De Soto turned to military tactics that were often callous and brutal. One of his most important strategies was to take chiefs captive. Such measures had been successfully used in Spain a century earlier to drive out the Moors, and it had become standard procedure throughout the Indies. Hernán Cortés had conquered the Aztecs at Tenochtitlan in 1521 by capturing Cu-

auhtemoc; and in 1532 Pizarro had conquered the Inka empire at Cajamarca by seizing Atauhualpa.

De Soto succeeded in capturing southeastern Indian rulers with relative ease. When he could not, he turned to force. The impact on the Indians of guns, war dogs, horses, and men with crossbows, halberds, lances, swords, and knives was devastating. The Spaniards' technology, however medieval, usually overpowered the masses of warriors posed against them in combat. The Indians were especially vulnerable on open terrain; mounted lancers in combination with halberdiers, arquebusiers, and war dogs routed even the best squadrons the southeastern chiefdoms could field.

The *perro de guerra*, or war dog, was psychologically effective as well as genuinely deadly: the dogs were trained to disembowel their victims and then tear them to bits. Mastiffs, greyhounds, and wolfhounds had been bred and used for centuries in Europe and the Middle East as adjuncts for halberdiers and sword-wielding cavalry. De Soto and his captains used their enormous mastiffs and greyhounds to "dog" uncooperative Indians. Guides who misled the expedition were routinely thrown to the dogs to be devoured as an example to other guides.

Enslavement was also central to De Soto's tactics. The conquistadors carried iron collars and chains for shackling Indians who were used as burden bearers. De Soto may have been interested in the prospect of capturing Indians for the lucrative Caribbean slave market. During his southeastern expedition he enslaved a force of up to 500 men and women. Some of the women were taken for sexual purposes, although others may well have been taken to serve as cooks and domestic workers.

The Indians' ignorance of Spanish ways was one of De Soto's greatest assets. Indian chiefs understood one another, and their conflicts were characterized by centuries-old rituals and customs. Hostilities, for example, normally took place during the warm season, from late spring to early fall, when the rattlesnakes were out. The rattlesnakes had important associations with the Indian concept of the underworld, and hence with death. Since the mobile Spaniards lived off the land by looting, they were unconcerned about the Indians' traditions, and often encountered chiefdoms when the proper season for warfare was past. In many such instances the Indians seem to have assumed that the Spaniards' intentions were peaceful.

Although the conquistadors maintained military superiority on land, they were no match for the southeastern Indian on the Mississippi River. The expedition first saw the Mississippi in early May of 1541, and shortly afterward De Soto ordered his men to begin sawing timbers for four barges. Each afternoon during the construction of the barges an armada of 200 large dugouts filled with men from the chiefdom of Pacaha and its vassal chiefdom of Aquixo crossed the river and showered the Spaniards with arrows. The war canoes were about 60 feet long and carried a crew of some 25 paddlers and 25 warriors. The warriors, painted red and wearing multicolored feathers, held bows and arrows and woven cane shields decorated with feathers with which they protected the paddlers. The chief, as fleet commander, sat under a canopy on a raised platform over the stern.

The greatest naval battle on the Mississippi—and the last of scores of brutal encounters between De Soto's army and the Indians—began on July 2, 1543, when the Spaniards, now under the leadership of De Soto's lieutenant, Luis de Moscoso, headed downriver in their barges and attached canoes toward the Gulf of Mexico. Two days later, a fleet of 100 war canoes of the chiefdom of Quigualtam engaged the Spanish flotilla. The battle continued unabated until noon the next day, when the warriors halted at the southern boundary of their territory. Fifty canoes from the adjoining chiefdom picked up the engagement and pursued the Spaniards until midmorning the next day.

The psychological shock of defeat in warfare and the subsequent looting and enslavement of both men and women had a ruinous effect on the Indian elite.

This 48-hour battle took place along 200 miles of the Mississippi ending near Natchez. The conquistadors were without guns or crossbows by this time; they had only their shields and swords with which to defend themselves. The Indians wounded a number of men with their bows and arrows, but the worst Spanish casualties occurred during a small counterattack: a number of Spaniards set out in five small canoes to drive the Indians away. The Indians quickly surrounded and upset the canoes, drowning some 12 men.

The Spanish entrada resulted in devastating changes for the Indians. Massive epidemics raced through villages. In some chiefdoms the mortality rate may have been as high as 85 to 100 percent. With rapid depopulation the southeastern towns and villages became smaller; fewer settlements were occupied as outlying towns were abandoned; villagers moved into new territories, seeking new political alliances; and the members of the elite began to lose their power and ability to manipulate their followers. The decline in chiefly organization is witnessed by the demise of mound construction, mound centers, palisade construction, site hierarchy, status markers, and craft specialization.

The psychological shock of defeat in warfare, the subsequent looting, especially of the sacred temples, by the victors, the enslavement of both men and women, but particularly women—these factors had a ruinous effect on the Indian elite. The once vibrant southeastern chiefdoms either disappeared or gave way to new, attenuated political relationships. By the time the English established Charleston in 1670 and the French began their exploration of the Lower Mississippi Valley in 1673, the world of chiefdoms that De Soto had fought and attempted to conquer had vanished.

Until about 15 years ago, it seemed as though that world would remain permanently obscure. A colleague once told me, "We don't even know what to look for. We don't even know what the sixteenth-century artifacts should look like." Since then, things have changed dramatically for the better. Anthropologists, archaeologists, and ethnohistorians have joined their energies and efforts, adopting a three-pronged approach based on artifactual recovery, historical documentation, and anthropological theory. This endeavor has galvanized southern archaeology, as various disciplines have been applied toward a common goal, leading to discoveries that my colleague once despaired of. It would be fitting if the archaeological ferment created by such recent discoveries as the ones in Citrus County, the King site, and the site of De Soto's first winter encampment in Tallahassee were to make the long vanished chiefdoms of the Apalachee, Ichisi, Ocute, Coosa, Pacaha, and many other native groups "come alive" once again.

Luther: Giant of His Time and Ours

Half a millennium after his birth, the first Protestant is still a towering force

It was a back-room deal, little different from many others struck at the time, but it triggered an upheaval that altered irrevocably the history of the Western world. Albrecht of Brandenburg, a German nobleman who had previously acquired a dispensation from the Vatican to become a priest while underage and to head two dioceses at the same time, wanted yet another favor from the Pope: the powerful archbishop's chair in Mainz. Pope Leo X, a profligate spender who needed money to build St. Peter's Basilica, granted the appointment—for 24,000 gold pieces, roughly equal to the annual imperial revenues in Germany. It was worth it. Besides being a rich source of income, the Mainz post brought Albrecht a vote for the next Holy Roman Emperor, which could be sold to the highest bidder.

In return, Albrecht agreed to initiate the sale of indulgences in Mainz. Granted for good works, indulgences were papally controlled dispensations drawn from an eternal "treasury of merits" built up by Christ and the saints; the church taught that they would help pay the debt of "temporal punishment" due in purgatory for sins committed by either the penitent or any deceased person. The Pope received half the proceeds of the Mainz indulgence sale, while the other half

went to repay the bankers who had lent the new archbishop gold.

Enter Martin Luther, a 33-year-old priest and professor at Wittenberg University. Disgusted not only with

the traffic in indulgences but with its doctrinal underpinnings, he forcefully protested to Albrecht—never expecting that his action would provoke a sweeping uprising against a corrupt church.

RUDI FREY

A statue of the reformer stares defiantly across Eisenach, East Germany
To some Catholic scholars, he has even become a "father in the faith."

6. RENAISSANCE AND REFORMATION

Luther's challenge culminated in the Protestant Reformation and the rending of Western Christendom, and made him a towering figure in European history. In this 500th anniversary year of his birth (Nov. 10, 1483), the rebel of Wittenberg remains the subject of persistent study. It is said that more books have been written about him than anyone else in history, save his own master, Jesus Christ. The renaissance in Luther scholarship surrounding this year's anniversary serves as a reminder that his impact on modern life is profound, even for those who know little about the doctrinal feuds that brought him unsought fame. From the distance of half a millennium, the man who, as Historian Hans Hillerbrand of Southern Methodist University in Dallas says, brought Christianity from lofty theological dogma to a clearer and more personal belief is still able to stimulate more heated debate than all but a handful of historical figures.

Indeed, as the reformer who fractured Christianity, Luther has latterly become a key to reuniting it. With the approval of the Vatican, and with Americans taking the lead, Roman Catholic theologians are working with Lutherans and other Protestants to sift through the 16th century disputes and see whether the Protestant-Catholic split can some day be overcome. In a remarkable turnabout, Catholic scholars today express growing appreciation of Luther as a "father in the faith" and are willing to play down his excesses. According to a growing consensus, the great division need never have happened at all.

Beyond his importance as a religious leader, Luther had a profound effect on Western culture. He is, paradoxically, the last medieval man and the first modern one, a political conservative and a spiritual revolutionary. His impact is most marked, of course, in Germany, where he laid the cultural foundations for what later became a united German nation.

When Luther attacked the indulgence business in 1517, he was not only the most popular teacher at Wittenberg but also vicar provincial in charge of eleven houses of the Hermits

The room where Luther translated the New Testament; title page of his Bible

of St. Augustine. He was brilliant, tireless and a judicious administrator, though given to bouts of spiritual depression. To make his point on indulgences, Luther dashed off 95 theses condemning the system ("They preach human folly who pretend that as soon as money in the coffer rings, a soul from purgatory springs") and sent them to Archbishop Albrecht and a number of theologians.*

*Despite colorful legend, it is not certain he ever nailed them to the door of the Castle Church.

The response was harsh: the Pope eventually rejected Luther's protest and demanded capitulation. It was then that Luther began asking questions about other aspects of the church, including the papacy itself. In 1520 he charged in an open letter to the Pope, "The Roman Church, once the holiest of all, has become the most licentious den of thieves, the most shameless of brothels, the kingdom of sin, death and hell." Leo called Luther "the wild boar which has invaded the Lord's vineyard."

The following year Luther was summoned to recant his writings before the Diet of Worms, a council of princes convened by the young Holy Roman Emperor Charles V. In his closing defense, Luther proclaimed defiantly: "Unless I am convinced by testimony from Holy Scriptures and clear proofs based on reason—because, since it is notorious that they have erred and contradicted themselves, I cannot believe either the Pope or the council alone—I am bound by conscience and the Word of God. Therefore I can and will recant nothing, because to act against one's conscience is neither safe nor salutary. So help me God." (Experts today think that he did not actually speak the famous words, "Here I stand. I can do no other.")

This was hardly the cry of a skeptic, but it was ample grounds for the Emperor to put Luther under sentence of death as a heretic. Instead of being executed, Luther lived for another 25 years, became a major author and composer of hymns, father of a bustling household and a secular figure who opposed rebellion—in all, a commanding force in European affairs. In the years beyond, the abiding split in Western Christendom developed, including a large component of specifically "Lutheran" churches that today have 69 million adherents in 85 nations.

The enormous presence of the Wittenberg rebel, the sheer force of his personality, still broods over all Christendom, not just Lutheranism. Although Luther declared that the Roman Pontiffs were the "Antichrist," today's Pope, in an anniversary tip of the zucchetto, mildly speaks of Luther as "the reformer." Ecumenical-minded Catholic theologians have come to rank Luther in importance with Augustine and Aquinas. "No one who came after Luther could match him," says Father Peter Manns, a Catholic theologian in Mainz. "On the question of truth, Luther is a lifesaver for Christians." While Western Protestants still express embarrassment over Luther's anti-Jewish rantings or his skepticism about political clergy, Communist East Germany has turned him into a secular saint because of his influence on German culture. Party Boss Erich Honecker, head of the regime's *Lutherjahr* committee, is willing to downplay Luther's antirevolutionary ideas, using the giant figure to bolster national pride.

Said West German President Karl Carstens, as he opened one of the hundreds of events commemorating Luther this year: "Luther has become a symbol of the unity of all Germany. We are all Luther's heirs."

After five centuries, scholars still have difficulty coming to terms with the contradictions of a tempestuous man. He was often inexcusably vicious in his writings (he wrote, for instance, that one princely foe was a "fainthearted wretch and fearful sissy" who should "do nothing but stand like a eunuch, that is, a harem guard, in a fool's cap with a fly swatter"). Yet he was kindly in person and so generous to the needy that his wife despaired of balancing the household budget. When the plague struck Wittenberg and others fled, he stayed behind to minister to the dying. He was a powerful spiritual author, yet his words on other occasions were so scatological that no Lutheran periodical would print them today. His writing was hardly systematic, and his output runs to more than 100 volumes. On the average, Luther wrote a major tract or treatise every two weeks throughout his life.

The scope of Luther's work has made him the subject of endless reinterpretation. The Enlightenment treated him as the father of free thought, conveniently omitting his belief in a sovereign God who inspired an authoritative Bible. During the era of Otto von Bismarck a century ago, Luther was fashioned into a nationalistic symbol; 70 years later, Nazi propagandists claimed him as one of their own by citing his anti-Jewish polemics.

All scholars agree on Luther's importance for German culture, surpassing even that of Shakespeare on the English-speaking world. Luther's masterpiece was his translation of the New Testament from Greek into German, largely completed in ten weeks while he was in hiding after the Worms confrontation, and of the Old Testament, published in 1534 with the assistance of Hebrew experts. The Luther Bible sold massively in his lifetime and remains today the authorized German Protestant version. Before Luther's Bible was published, there was no standard German, just a profusion of dialects. "It was Luther," said Johann Gottfried von Herder, one of Goethe's mentors, "who has awakened and let loose the giant: the German language."

Only a generation ago, Catholics were trained to consider Luther the arch-heretic. Now no less than the Vatican's specialist on Lutheranism, Monsignor Aloys Klein, says that "Martin Luther's action was beneficial to the Catholic Church." Like many other Catholics, Klein thinks that if Luther were living today there would be no split. Klein's colleague in the Vatican's Secretariat for Promoting Christian Unity, Father Pierre Duprey, suggests that with the Second Vatican Council (1962–65) Luther "got the council he asked for, but 450 years too late." Vatican II accepted his contention that, in a sense, all believers are priests; while the council left the Roman church's hierarchy intact, it enhanced the role of the laity. More important, the council moved the Bible to the center of Catholic life, urged continual reform and instituted worship in local languages rather than Latin.

One of the key elements in the Reformation was the question of "justification," the role of faith in relation to good works in justifying a sinner in the eyes of God. Actually, Catholicism had never officially taught that salvation could be attained only through pious works, but the popular perception held otherwise. Luther recognized, as University of Chicago Historian Martin Marty explains, that everything "in the system of Catholic teaching seemed aimed toward appeasing God. Luther was led to the idea of God not as an angry judge but as a forgiving father. It is a position that gives the individual a great sense of freedom and security." In effect, says U.S. Historian Roland Bainton, Luther destroyed the implication that men could "bargain with God."

Father George Tavard, a French Catholic expert on Protestantism who teaches in Ohio and has this month published *Justification: an Ecumenical Study* (Paulist; $7.95), notes that "today many Catholic scholars think Luther was right and the 16th century Catholic polemicists did not understand what he meant. Both Lutherans and Catholics agree that good works by Christian believers are the result of their faith and the working of divine grace in them, not their personal contributions to their own salvation. Christ is the only Savior. One does not save oneself." An international Lutheran-Catholic commission, exploring the basis for possible reunion, made a joint statement along these lines in 1980. Last month a parallel panel in the U.S. issued a significant 21,000-word paper on justification that affirms much of Luther's thinking, though with some careful hedging from the Catholic theologians.

There is doubt, of course, about the degree to which Protestants and Catholics can, in the end, overcome their differences. Catholics may now be permitted to sing Luther's *A Mighty Fortress Is Our God* or worship in their native languages, but a wide gulf clearly remains on issues like the status of Protestant ministers and, most crucially, papal authority.

During the futile Protestant-Catholic reunion negotiations in 1530 at the Diet of Augsburg, the issue of priestly celibacy was as big an obstacle as the faith *vs.* good works controversy. Luther had married a nun, to the disgust of his Catholic contemporaries. From the start, the marriage of clergy was a sharply defined difference between Protestantism and Catholicism, and it remains a key barrier today. By discarding the concept of the moral superiority of celibacy, Luther established sexuality as a gift from God. In general, he was a lover of the simple

pleasures, and would have had little patience with the later Puritans. He spoke offhandedly about sex, enjoyed good-natured joshing, beer drinking and food ("If our Lord is permitted to create nice large pike and good Rhine wine, presumably I may be allowed to eat and drink"). For his time, he also had an elevated opinion of women. He cherished his wife and enjoyed fatherhood, siring six children and rearing eleven orphaned nieces and nephews as well.

But if Luther's views on the Catholic Church have come to be accepted even by many Catholics, his anti-Semitic views remain a problem for even his most devoted supporters. Says New York City Rabbi Marc Tanenbaum: "The anniversary will be marred by the haunting specter of Luther's devil theory of the Jews."

Luther assailed the Jews on doctrinal grounds, just as he excoriated "papists" and Turkish "infidels." But his work titled *On the Jews and Their Lies* (1543) went so far as to advocate that their synagogues, schools and homes should be destroyed and their prayer books and Talmudic volumes taken away. Jews were to be relieved of their savings and put to work as agricultural laborers or expelled outright.

Fortunately, the Protestant princes ignored such savage recommendations, and the Lutheran Church quickly forgot about them. But the words were there to be gleefully picked up by the Nazis, who removed them from the fold of religious polemics and used them to buttress their 20th century racism. For a good Lutheran, of course, the Bible is the sole authority, not Luther's writings, and the thoroughly Lutheran Scandinavia vigorously opposed Hitler's racist madness. In the anniversary year, all sectors of Lutheranism have apologized for their founder's views.

Whatever the impact of Luther's anti-Jewish tracts, there is no doubt that his political philosophy, which tended to make church people submit to state authority, was crucial in weakening opposition by German Lutherans to the Nazis. Probably no aspect of Luther's teaching is the

subject of more agonizing Protestant scrutiny in West Germany today.

Luther sought to declericalize society and to free people from economic burdens imposed by the church. But he was soon forced, if reluctantly, to deliver considerable control of the new Protestant church into the hands of secular rulers who alone could ensure the survival of the Reformation. Luther spoke of "two kingdoms," the spiritual and the secular, and his writings provided strong theological support for authoritarian government and Christian docility.

The Lutheran wing of the Reformation was democratic, but only in terms of the church itself, teaching that a plowman did God's work as much as a priest, encouraging lay leadership and seeking to educate one and all. But it was Calvin, not Luther, who created a theology for the democratic state. A related aspect of Luther's politics, controversial then and now, was his opposition to the bloody Peasants' War of 1525. The insurgents thought they were applying Luther's ideas, but he urged rulers to crush the revolt: "Let whoever can, stab, strike, kill." Support of the rulers was vital for the Reformation, but Luther loathed violent rebellion and anarchy in any case.

Today Luther's law-and-order approach is at odds with the revolutionary romanticism and liberation theology that are popular in some theology schools. In contrast with modern European Protestantism's social gospel, Munich Historian Thomas Nipperdey says, Luther "would not accept modern attempts to build a utopia and would argue, on the contrary, that we as mortal sinners are incapable of developing a paradise on earth."

Meanwhile, the internal state of the Lutheran Church raises other questions about the lasting power of Luther's vision. Lutheranism in the U.S., with 8.5 million adherents, is stable and healthy. The church is also growing in Third World strongholds like racially torn Namibia, where black Lutherans predominate. But in Lutheranism's historic heartland, the two Germanys and Scandinavia, there are deep problems. In East Germany, Lutherans are under pressure from the Communist regime. In West Germany, the Evangelical Church in Germany (E.K.D.), a church federation that includes some non-Lutherans, is wealthy (annual income: $3 billion), but membership is shrinking and attendance at Sunday services is feeble indeed. Only 6% of West Germans—or, for that matter, Scandinavians—worship regularly.

What seems to be lacking in the old European churches is the passion for God and his truth that so characterizes Luther. He retains the potential to shake people out of religious complacency. Given Christianity's need, on all sides, for a good jolt, eminent Historian Heiko Oberman muses, "I wonder if the time of Luther isn't ahead of us."

The boldest assertion about Luther for modern believers is made by Protestants who claim that the reformer did nothing less than enable Christianity to survive. In the Middle Ages, too many Popes and bishops were little more than corrupt, luxury-loving politicians, neglecting the teaching of the love of God and using the fear of God to enhance their power and wealth. George Lindbeck, the Lutheran co-chairman of the international Lutheran-Catholic commission, believes that without Luther "religion would have been much less important during the next 400 to 500 years. And since medieval religion was falling apart, secularization would have marched on, unimpeded."

A provocative thesis, and a debatable one. But with secularization still marching on, almost unimpeded, Protestants and Catholics have much to reflect upon as they scan the five centuries after Luther and the shared future of their still divided churches.

—By Richard N. Ostling. Reported by Roland Flamini and Wanda Menke-Glückert/Bonn, with other bureaus.

EXPLAINING JOHN CALVIN

John Calvin (1509–64) has been credited, or blamed, for much that defines the modern Western world: capitalism and the work ethic, individualism and utilitarianism, modern science, and, at least among some devout Christians, a lingering suspicion of earthly pleasures. During the most recent American presidential campaign, the two candidates appealed to "values" that recall the teachings of the 16th-century churchman, indicating that what William Pitt once said of England—"We have a Calvinist creed"—still may hold partly true for the United States. But the legend of the joyless tyrant of Geneva obscures both the real man, a humanist as much as a religious reformer, and the subtlety of his thought. Here his biographer discusses both.

William J. Bouwsma

William J. Bouwsma, 65, is Sather Professor of History at the University of California, Berkeley. Born in Ann Arbor, Michigan, he received an A.B. (1943), an M.A. (1947), and a Ph.D. (1950) from Harvard. He is the author of, among other books, Venice and the Defense of Republican Liberty *(1968) and* John Calvin: A Sixteenth-Century Portrait *(1988).*

Our image of John Calvin is largely the creation of austere Protestant churchmen who lived during the 17th century, the century following that of the great reformer's life. The image is most accurately evoked by the huge icon of Calvin, familiar to many a tourist, that stands behind the University of Geneva. There looms Calvin, twice as large as life, stylized beyond recognition, stony, rigid, immobile, and—except for his slightly abstracted disapproval of whatever we might imagine him to be contemplating—impassive.

Happily, the historical record provides good evidence for a Calvin very different from the figure invoked by his 17th-century followers. This Calvin is very much a man of the 16th century, a time of religious strife and social upheaval. His life and work reflect the ambiguities, contradictions, and agonies of that troubled time. Sixteenth-century thinkers, especially in Northern Europe, were still grappling with the rich but incoherent legacy of the Renaissance, and their characteristic intellectual constructions were less successful in reconciling its contradictory impulses than in balancing among them. This is why it has proved so difficult to pigeon-hole such figures as Erasmus and Machiavelli or Montaigne and Shakespeare, and why they continue to stimulate reflection. Calvin, who can be quoted on both sides of most questions, belongs in this great company.

Born in 1509 in Noyon, Calvin was brought up to be a devout French Catholic. Indeed, his father, a lay administrator in the service of the local bishop, sent him to the University of Paris in 1523 to study for the priesthood. Later he decided that young John should be a lawyer. Accordingly, from 1528 to 1533, Calvin studied law. During these years he was also exposed to the evangelical humanism of Erasmus and Jacques Lefèvre d'Étaples that nourished the radical student movement of the time. The students called for salvation by grace rather than by good works and ceremonies—a position fully compatible with Catholic orthodoxy—as the foundation for a general reform of church and society on the model of antiquity.

To accomplish this end, the radical students advocated a return to the Bible, studied in its original languages. Calvin himself studied Greek and Hebrew as well as Latin, the "three languages" of ancient Christian discourse. His growing interest in the classics led, moreover, to his first publication, a moralizing commentary on Seneca's essay on clemency.

Late in 1533, the French government of Francis I became less tolerant of the Paris student radicals, whom it saw as a threat to the peace. After helping to prepare a statement of the theological implications of the movement in a public address delivered by Nicolas Cop, rector of the University, Calvin found it prudent to leave Paris. Eventually he made his way to Basel, a Protestant town tolerant of religious variety.

Up to this point, there is little evidence of Calvin's "conversion" to Protestantism. Before Basel, of course, he had been fully aware of the challenge Martin Luther posed to the Catholic Church. The 95 Theses that the German reformer posted in Wittenberg in 1517 attacked what Luther believed were corruptions of true Christianity and, by implication, the authors of those errors, the Renaissance popes. Luther, above all, rejected the idea of salvation through indulgences or the sacrament of penance. Excommunicated by Pope Leo X, he encouraged the formation of non-Roman churches.

In Basel, Calvin found himself drawing closer to Luther. Probably in part to clarify his own beliefs, he began to write, first a preface to his cousin Pierre Olivétan's French translation of the Bible, and then what became the first edition of the *Institutes*, his masterwork, which in its successive revisions became the single most important statement of Protestant belief. Although he did not substantially change his views thereafter, he elaborated them in later editions, published in both Latin and French, in which he also replied to his critics; the final versions appeared in 1559 and 1560.

The 1536 *Institutes* had brought him some renown among Protestant leaders, among them Guillaume Farel. A French Reformer struggling to plant Protestantism in Geneva, Farel persuaded Calvin to settle there in late 1536. The Reformation was in trouble in Geneva. Indeed, the limited enthusiasm of Geneva for Protestantism—and for religious and moral reform—continued almost until Calvin's death. The resistance

was all the more serious because the town council in Geneva, as in other Protestant towns in Switzerland and southern Germany, exercised ultimate control over the church and the ministers.

The main issue was the right of excommunication, which the ministers regarded as essential to their authority but which the town council refused to concede. The uncompromising attitudes of Calvin and Farel finally resulted in their expulsion from Geneva in May of 1538.

□

Calvin found refuge for the next three years in Protestant Strasbourg, where he was pastor of a church for French-speaking refugees. Here he married Idelette de Bure, a widow in his congregation. Theirs proved to be an extremely warm relationship, although none of their children survived infancy.

During his Strasbourg years, Calvin learned much about church administration from Martin Bucer, chief pastor there. Attending European religious conferences, he soon became a major figure in the international Protestant movement.

Meanwhile, without strong leadership, the Protestant revolution in Geneva foundered. In September of 1541, Calvin was invited back, and there he remained until his death in 1564. He was now in a stronger position. In November the town council enacted his *Ecclesiastical Ordinances*, which provided for the religious education of the townspeople, especially children, and instituted his conception of church order. It established four groups of church officers and a "consistory" of pastors and elders to bring every aspect of Genevan life under the precepts of God's law.

The activities of the consistory gave substance to the legend of Geneva as a joyless theocracy, intolerant of looseness or pleasure. Under Calvin's leadership, it undertook a range of disciplinary actions covering everything from the abolition of Catholic "superstition" to the enforcement of sexual morality, the regulation of taverns, and measures against dancing, gambling, and swearing. These "Calvinist" measures were resented by many townsfolk, as was the arrival of increasing numbers of French Protestant refugees.

The resulting tensions, as well as the persecution of Calvin's followers in France, help to explain the trial and burning of one of Calvin's leading opponents, Michael Servetus. Calvin felt the need to show that his zeal for orthodoxy was no less than that of his foes. The confrontation between Calvin and his enemies in Geneva was finally resolved in May of 1555, when Calvin's opponents overreached themselves and the tide turned in his favor. His position in Geneva was henceforth reasonably secure.

But Calvin was no less occupied. He had to watch the European scene and keep his Protestant allies united. At the same time, Calvin never stopped promoting his kind of Protestantism. He welcomed the religious refugees who poured into Geneva, especially during the 1550s, from France, but also from England and Scotland, from Italy, Germany, and the Netherlands, and even from Eastern Europe. He trained many of them as ministers, sent them back to their homelands, and then supported them with letters of encouragement and advice. Geneva thus became the center of an international movement and a model for churches elsewhere. John Knox, the Calvinist leader of Scotland, described Geneva as "the most perfect school of Christ that ever was on the Earth since the days of the Apostles." So while Lutheranism was confined to parts of Germany and Scandinavia, Calvinism spread into Britain, the English-speaking colonies of North America, and many parts of Europe.

□

Academic efforts to explain the appeal of Calvinism in terms of social class have had only limited success. In France, his theology was attractive mainly to a minority among the nobility and the urban upper classes, but in Germany it found adherents among both townsmen and princes. In England and the Netherlands, it made converts in every social group. Calvinism's appeal lay in its ability to explain disorders of the age afflicting all classes and in the remedies and comfort it provided, as much by its activism as by its doctrine. Both depended on the personality, preoccupations, and talents of Calvin himself.

Unlike Martin Luther, Calvin was a reticent man. He rarely expressed himself in the first person singular. This reticence has contributed to his reputation as cold and unapproachable. Those who knew him, however, noted his talent for friendship as well as his hot temper. The intensity of his grief on the death of his wife in 1549 revealed a large capacity for feeling, as did his empathetic reading of many passages in Scripture.

In fact, the impersonality of Calvin's teachings concealed an anxiety, unusually intense even in an anxious age. He saw anxiety everywhere, in himself, in the narratives of the Bible, and in his contemporaries. This feeling found expression in two of his favorite images for spiritual discomfort: the abyss and the labyrinth. The abyss represented all the nameless terrors of disorientation and the absence of familiar boundaries. The labyrinth expressed the anxiety of entrapment: in religious terms, the inability of human beings alienated from God to escape from the imprisonment of self-concern.

One side of Calvin sought to relieve his terror of the abyss with cultural constructions and patterns of control that might help him recover his sense of direction. This side of Calvin was attracted to classical philosophy, which nevertheless conjured up for him fears of entrapment in a labyrinth. Escape from this, however, exposed him to terrible uncertainties and, once again, to the horrors of the abyss. Calvin's ideas thus tended to oscillate between those of freedom and order. His problem was to strike a balance between the two.

He did so primarily with the resources of Renaissance humanism, applying its philological approach to recover a biblical understanding of Christianity. But humanism was not only, or even fundamentally, a scholarly movement. Its scholarship was instrumental to the recovery of the communicative skills of classical rhetoric. Humanists such as Lorenzo Valla and Erasmus held that an effective rhetoric would appeal to a deeper level of the personality than would a mere rational demonstration. By moving the heart, Christian rhetoric would stimulate human beings to the active reform of both themselves and the world.

Theological system-building, Calvin believed, was futile and inappropriate. He faulted the medieval Scholastic theologians for relying more on human reason than on the Bible, which spoke uniquely to the heart. The teachings of Thomas Aquinas, and like-minded theologians, appealed only to the intellect, and so were lifeless and irrelevant to a world in desperate need.

As a humanist, Calvin was a *biblical* theologian, prepared to follow Scripture even when it surpassed the limits of human understanding. And its message, for him, could not be presented as a set of timeless abstractions; it had to be adapted to the understanding of contemporaries according to the rhetorical principle of decorum—i.e. suitability to time, place, and audience.

Calvin shared with earlier humanists an essentially biblical conception of the human personality, not as a hierarchy of faculties ruled by reason but as a mysterious unity. This concept made the feelings and will even more important aspects of the personality than the intellect, and it also gave the body new dignity.

Indeed, Calvin largely rejected the traditional belief in hierarchy as the general principle of all order. For it he substituted the practical (rather than the metaphysical) principle of *utility*. This position found expression in his preference, among the possible forms of government, for republics. It also undermined, for him, the traditional subordination of women to men. Calvin's Geneva accordingly insisted on a single standard of sexual morality—a radical departure from custom.

Calvin's utilitarianism was also reflected in deep reservations about the capacity of human beings to attain anything but practical knowledge. The notion that they can know anything absolutely, as God knows it, so to speak, seemed to him deeply presumptuous. This helps to explain his reliance on the Bible: Human beings have access to the saving truths of religion only insofar as God has revealed them in Scripture. But revealed truth, for Calvin, was not revealed to satisfy human curiosity; it too was limited to meeting the most urgent and practical needs, above all for individual salvation. This practicality also reflects a basic conviction of Renaissance thinkers: the superiority of an active life to one of contemplation. Calvin's conviction that every occupation in society is a "calling" on the part of God himself sanctified this conception.

But Calvin was not only a Renaissance humanist. The culture of 16th-century Europe was peculiarly eclectic. Like other thinkers of his time, Calvin had inherited a set of quite contrary tendencies that he uneasily combined with his humanism. Thus, even as he emphasized the heart, Calvin continued to conceive of the human personality as a hierarchy of faculties ruled by reason; from time to time he tried uneasily, with little success, to reconcile the two conceptions. This is why he sometimes emphasized the importance of rational control over the passions—an emphasis that has been reassuring to conservatives.

Calvin's theology has often been seen as little more than a systematization of the more creative insights of Luther. He followed Luther, indeed, on many points: on original sin, on Scripture, on the absolute dependence of human beings on divine grace, and on justification by faith alone. Other differences between Calvin and Luther are largely matters of emphasis. His understanding of predestination, contrary to a general impression, was virtually identical to Luther's; it was not of central importance to his theology. He believed that it meant that the salvation of believers by a loving God was absolutely certain.

In major respects, however, Calvin departed from Luther. In some ways he was more radical, but most of his differences suggest that he was closer to Catholicism than Luther, as in his insistence on the importance of the historical church. He was also more traditional in his belief in the authority of clergy over laity, perhaps as a result of his difficulties with the Geneva town council. Even more significant, especially for Calvinism as a historical force, was Calvin's attitude toward the everyday world. Luther had regarded this world and its institutions as incorrigible, and was prepared to leave them to the devil. But for Calvin this world, created by God, still belonged to Him; it remained potentially His kingdom; and every Christian was obliged to devote his life to make it so in reality by reforming and bringing it under God's law.

Calvin's thought was less a theology to be comprehended by the mind than a set of principles for the Christian life: in short, spirituality. He was more concerned with the experience and application of Christianity than with mere reflection about it. His true successors were Calvinist pastors rather than Calvinist theologians. Significantly, in addition to devoting much of his energy to the training of other pastors, Calvin was himself a pastor. He preached regularly: some 4,000 sermons in the 13 years after his return to Geneva.

Calvin's spirituality begins with the conviction that we do not so much "know" God as "experience" him indirectly, through his mighty acts and works in the world, as we experience but can hardly be said to know thunder, one of Calvin's favorite metaphors for religious experience. Calvin also believed that human beings can understand something of what God is like in the love of a father for his children, but also—surprisingly in one often identified with patriarchy—in the love of a mother. He denounced those who represented God as dreadful; God for him is "mild, kind, gentle, and compassionate."

Nevertheless, in spite of this attention to God's love for mankind, Calvin gave particular emphasis to God's power because it was this that finally made his love effective in the work of redemption from sin. God, for Calvin, represented supremely all the ways in which human beings experience power: as energy, as warmth, as vitality, and, so, as life itself.

Sin, by contrast, is manifested precisely in the negation of every kind of power and ultimately of the life force given by God. Sin *deadens* and, above all, deadens the feelings. Saving grace, then, must be conceived as the transfusion of God's power—his warmth, passion, strength, vitality—to human beings. It was also essential to Calvin's spirituality, and a reflection of his realism, that this "transfusion" be not instantaneous but gradual.

Calvin's traditional metaphor for the good Christian life implied activity: "Our life is like a journey," he asserted, but "it is not God's will that we should march along casually as we please, but he sets the goal before us, and also directs us on the right way to it." This way is also a struggle.

□

Complex as his ideas were, it is easy to see how the later history of Calvinism has often been obscured by scholars' failure to distinguish among (1) Calvinism as the beliefs of Calvin himself, (2) the beliefs of his followers, who, though striving to be faithful to Calvin, modified his teachings to meet their own needs, and (3) more loosely, the beliefs of the Reformed tradition of Protestant Christianity, in which Calvinism proper was only one, albeit the most prominent, strand.

The Reformed churches in the 16th century were referred to in the plural to indicate, along with what they had in common, their individual autonomy and variety. They consisted originally of a group of non-Lutheran Protestant churches based in towns in Switzerland and southern Germany. These churches were jealous of their autonomy; and Geneva was not alone among them in having distinguished theological leadership. Ulrich Zwingli and Heinrich Bullinger in Zurich and Martin Bucer in Strasbourg also had a European influence that combined with that of Calvin, especially in England, to shape what came to be called "Calvinism."

□

Long after Calvin's death in 1564, the churchmen in Geneva continued to venerate him and aimed at being faithful to his teaching under his successors, first among them Theodore de Bèze. But during what can be appropriately described as a Protestant "Counter Reformation," the later Calvinism of Geneva, abandoning Calvin's more humanistic tendencies and drawing more on other, sterner aspects of his thought, was increasingly intellectualized. Indeed, it grew to resemble the medieval Scholasticism that Calvin had abhorred.

Predestination now began to assume an importance that had not been attributed to it before. Whereas Calvin had been led by personal faith to an awed belief in predestination as a benign manifestation of divine providence, predestination now became a threatening doctrine: God's decree determined in advance an individual's salvation or damnation. What good, one might wonder, were one's own best efforts if God had already ruled? In 1619 these tendencies reached a climax at the Synod of Dort in the Netherlands, which spelled out various corollaries of predestination, as Calvin had never done, and made the doctrine central to Calvinism.

Calvinist theologians, meanwhile, apparently finding Calvin's loose rhetorical style of expression unsatisfactory, began deliberately to write like Scholastic theologians, in Latin, and even appealed to medieval Scholastic authorities. The major Calvinist theological statement of the 17th century was the *Institutio Theologiae Elencticae* (3 vols., Geneva, 1688) of François Turretin, chief pastor of Geneva. Although the title of this work recalled Calvin's masterpiece, it was published in Latin, its dialectical structure followed the model of the great *Summas* of Thomas Aquinas, and it suggested at least as much confidence as Thomas in the value of human reason. The lasting effect of this shift is suggested by the fact that "Turretin," in Latin, was the basic theology textbook at the Princeton Seminary in New Jersey, the most distinguished intellectual center of American Calvinism until the middle of the 19th century.

Historians have continued to debate whether these developments were essentially faithful to Calvin or deviations from him. In some sense they were both. Later Calvinist theologians, as they abandoned Calvin's more humanistic tendencies and emphasized his more austere and dogmatic side, found precedents for these changes in the contrary aspects of his thought. They were untrue to Calvin, of course, in rejecting his typically Renaissance concern with balancing contrary impulses. One must remember, however, that these changes in Calvinism occurred during a period of singular disorder in Europe, caused by, among other things, a century of religious warfare. As a result, there was a widespread longing for certainty, security, and peace.

One or another aspect of Calvin's influence has persisted not only in the Reformed churches of France, Germany, Scotland, the Netherlands, and Hungary but also in the Church of England, where he was long as highly regarded as he was by Puritans who had separated from the Anglican establishment. The latter organized their own churches, Presbyterian or Congregational, and brought Calvinism to North America 300 years ago.

Even today these churches, along with the originally German Evangelical and Reformed Church, remember Calvin—that is, the strict Calvin of Geneva—as their founding father. Eventually Calvinist theology was also widely accepted by major groups of American Baptists; and even Unitarianism, which broke away from the Calvinist churches of New England during the 18th century, reflected the more rational impulses in Calvin's theology. More recently, Protestant interest in the social implications of the Gospel and Protestant Neo-Orthodoxy, as represented by Karl Barth and Reinhold Niebuhr, reflect the continuing influence of John Calvin.

Calvin's larger influence over the development of modern Western civilization has been variously assessed. The controversial "Weber thesis" attributed the rise of modern capitalism largely to habits encouraged by Puritanism, but Max Weber (1864–1920) avoided implicating Calvin himself. Much the same can be said about efforts to link Calvinism to the rise of early modern science; Puritans were prominent in the scientific movement of 17th-century England, but Calvin himself was indifferent to the science of his own day.

A somewhat better case can be made for Calvin's influence on political theory. His own political instincts were highly conservative, and he preached the submission of private persons to all legitimate authority. But, like Italian humanists of the 15th and 16th centuries, he personally preferred a republic to a monarchy; and in confronting the problem posed by rulers who actively opposed the spread of the Gospel, he advanced a theory of resistance, kept alive by his followers, according to which lesser magistrates might legitimately rebel against kings. And, unlike most of his contemporaries, Calvin included among the proper responsibilities of states not only the maintenance of public order but also a positive concern for the general welfare of society. Calvinism has a place, therefore, in the evolution of liberal political thought. His most durable influence, nevertheless, has been religious. From Calvin's time to the present, Calvinism has meant a peculiar seriousness about Christianity and its ethical implications.

THAT OTHERS MIGHT READ

Development of the first English-
language Bibles was not merely a matter
of translating from one tongue to
another. Brave and yet controversial
faith had to lead the way.

Joseph H. Hall

Few of the Christianity's earliest martyrs could have told a more harrowing tale of persecution than that of a young translator from 16th-century England. Finding a cold reception for his proposed work at home, he betook himself to Germany in hope of finding a more friendly environment. His printer in Cologne had only reached the tenth sheet of William Tyndale's great opus, however, when a powerful German enemy discovered what they were doing.

Tyndale and his assistant, William Roye, hurriedly gathered some of the printed sheets and fled up the Rhine River, to Worms. More of the work was printed there, but various authorities did their best to suppress the printings. Some were smuggled into England, like contraband. Tyndale, in the meantime, lost a significant part of his further translation in a shipwreck off the coast of Holland.

Still, he perservered; he would not give up his life's work. Settling for the moment at Antwerp, he remained in exile from his homeland. The King of England (Henry VIII), in fact, was demanding his forcible return. Tyndale allegedly was spreading sedition in England. Tyndale left Antwerp for two years.

Upon his return, however, he was arrested. He was imprisoned in a castle, and while there may have done his last translating work. He was tried for heresy and condemned. On October 6, 1536, he was bound to a stake, and strangled. His body was then burned.

And the controversial work for which William Tyndale gave his life? It was his translation of the Bible into his native tongue—English.

The fact is, the Bible had not—until Tyndale—been accessible to the ordinary English-speaking Christian. For centuries, churches in England and the Scottish Lowlands—or churches anywhere in Western Europe, for that matter—had echoed the fifth-century Latin of Jerome's Vulgate, the official Bible of the Western Church. Even though few Christians knew Latin, the situation wasn't considered strange or needing remedy. If the laity wanted to know what was in the Bible, simplified rhyming Bibles or story Bibles retold the more famous tales from the Old Testament, New Testament and Apocrypha. Even when some of the languages of Europe began developing their own vernacular literature, Bible translations into French, German or Dutch did not supplant the Latin Vulgate in the churches of those lands. At best, these pre-Reformation translations were for the private edification of a few literate laymen.

Reforming movements of the late Middle Ages and the Reformation itself gave impetus to the spread of the translated Bible. Indeed, the Bible in the vernacular languages—to be read and applied by ordinary Christians and to be used in the public worship of the churches—became one of the major weapons and hallmarks of the Protestant Reformation. This was true in the Germany of Martin Luther, the Switzerland of Ulrich Zwingli and the Geneva of John Calvin. Within 50 years of Luther's death in 1546, most of the languages of Western Europe would possess complete translations of the Bible.

In England, interest in religious reform also manifested

 From *Biblical History*, August 1987, pp. 42-47, 49-50.

itself in demands for an English-language Bible, not only in the 16th century, but even earlier.

The Englishmen John Wycliffe (1330-1384) and William Tyndale (1494-1536) saw that it simply was not enough to have Scripture in Latin, Greek or Hebrew available only to priests and scholars. To these two men, the absence of good preaching could be blamed upon illiterate priests, while the use of Latin in the church was further indication that the common people needed to be able to read the Word of God themselves. They believed that all Christian laymen, like the early Berean Christians mentioned in the Book of Acts, should be able to search the Scriptures to see for themselves if their clergy—including the Pope himself—were teaching in accordance with Biblical teaching. Both Wycliffe and Tyndale believed that each man, woman and child was individually responsible before God and therefore should have the Bible available in a language readily understood. These of course, were controversial stands to take.

Nonetheless, Wycliffe persisted in declaring that all persons, whether priest, knight or peasant, must "carefully study the gospel in that tongue in which the meaning of the gospel [is] clearest to them . . ." Tyndale, is speaking to a dogmatic priest opposed to Tyndale's translation work, clearly borrowed the words of the great Erasmus by declaring, "If God spare my life, I will cause a boy that driveth the plough shall know more of the Scripture than thou dost." These two were determined men, driven by what they considered man's greatest need—to have God's word as the only absolute and complete authority to rule over them.

Before England entered the 14th century, English was the tongue used primarily by commoners, while the nobility preferred French, and scholars used Latin. Only some priests read and wrote in English. The poet and courtier Geoffrey Chaucer, however, broke the clergy's virtual monopoly on Engish writing and made it available to the nobility and common people. Chaucer provided a standard English into which the Bible could be translated and read by all three estates of traditional society—clergy, nobility and commoners. For the first time since the Norman conquest in 1066, English became the dominant language in England, a vehicle not only for a vigorous young literature, but for a re-awakened national pride as well.

Into this milieu stepped an Oxford don whose revolutionary ideas were destined to find root, grow and finally flower as part of the Protestant Reformation. Indeed, he is called the "morningstar of the Reformation." Although John Wycliffe sought to reform the church in many areas, none of his contributions was more far-reaching than his teaching that the Bible is man's final authority and that it must be available to all Englishmen in the language they habitually spoke.

Of Wycliffe's early life we know very little. He was born around 1330 in Yorkshire, a district that came under the lordship of John of Gaunt, Duke of Lancaster, second son of King Edward III. Providentially, the circumstance of John of Gaunt's powerful patronage gave Wycliffe the protection he needed to promulgate his views on Bible-based religious reforms.

Wycliff followed an academic career, first as a philosophy teacher at Oxford. Later he pursued theological studies, becoming a doctor in 1372. He remained at Oxford until 1382, when he was expelled for teaching that

"God's law"—the Bible—was to be preached, read and believed if one were to exist in a state of grace.

From Wycliffe's burning desire to see the Bible translated into English, the Wycliffe Bible developed. But was it John Wycliffe's own translation? Some of his contemporaries did ascribe it to him. For example, Archbishop Thomas Arundel, writing to Pope John XXIII in 1411, spoke of Wycliffe's "devising . . the expedient of a new translation of the Scriptures into the mother tongue." The Bohemian reformer John Huss also considered Wycliffe as the translator. But did he, in fact, translate it? Apparently not, since there were two different translations of the Wycliffe Bible reflecting the work of different translators, neither agreeing with the translations of Biblical texts made in connection with Wycliffe's own sermons. Therefore, we must conclude that Wycliffe was not himself responsible for the actual translation.

At the same time, however, had Wycliffe not vociferously expressed his new idea that the common person must have the Bible in English as his final authority, the medieval Bible version that bears Wycliffe's name would not have been translated. Wycliffe's influence was paramount in motivating the two men largely responsible for the production of the two translations, Nicholas of Hereford and John Purvey.

Nicholas of Hereford, regent master in theology, began to advocate Wycliffite doctrines while a fellow at Queen's College, Oxford. In 1382, however, he preached that an archbishop had been righteously slain in the Peasants' Revolt of the previous year. Excommunicated and condemned by the archbishop of Canterbury, he then journeyed to Rome to petition against the sentence. In 1385, he made his way back to England, where he continued to lead the Lollards—Wycliffe's supporters—until 1391, when he was captured and recanted, becoming as vociferous an enemy of the Lollards as he had been a Wycliffite preacher earlier.

John Purvey (1353-1428) was ordained a priest in 1377 and served Wycliffe as his secretary at Lutterworth, near Oxford. Both fellow Lollards and opponents spoke of Purvey as "doctor." Even the Carmelite Friar Walden, persecutor of the Wycliffites, spoke of Purvey with respect. Like Nicholas, Purvey recanted of his heresy after a period of imprisonment in 1401—during which time the burning of William Sawtrey, another Lollard, might have helped convince him. The last we hear of Purvey is that he was imprisoned once again for Lollard opinions in 1421, and was still alive in 1427. Perhaps he continued as a Lollard for the remainder of his life. In any event, Purvey was widely known as a Bible translator and disseminator of Wycliffe's writings.

Nicholas and Purvey both used as their source a copy of Jerome's Latin Vulgate, the text accepted by the church. While the style of Nicholas is word-for-word and very literal, Purvey's style is both faithful to the original words and more flowing, even conversational.

Nicholas' literal method was intended more for scholars and the learned, whereas Purvey's translation was more popular and became the Bible for the Lollard movement. Originally an educated reforming movement, the Lollards became, after 1410, a lay movement emphasizing Bible reading and a simple Christian lifestyle.

Many Lollard beliefs anticipated later Protestantism. Lollards spoke against the hierarchical system of the church, in which power came to be vested in a handful of bishops. They also criticized the celibacy requirement imposed on clergyman and the church's claim to temporal as well as spiritual power. They disavowed the doctrine of transubstantiation—the belief that the priest changes the bread and wine of the Mass into the actual body and blood of Christ—and the veneration of images. A similar movement, the Waldensians, appeared during the 13th century in southern France and northern Italy, while the Hussite movement in Bohemia appeared shortly after Wycliffe launched the Lollards. The Hussites may even have been a direct offshoot from the Lollards, for numerous Czech students were at Oxford during the years when Wycliffe's movement flourished.

The Lollards suffered numerous shocks and setbacks, especially after John Wycliffe, its founder, died in 1384, and Parliament decreed in 1401 that unrepentant Lollards were liable to death by burning. Nonetheless, they did not completely die out, for there is much evidence of their activities from the 15th century. Early in the 16th century, small groups of Lollards were found in parts of rural England and in the Lowlands of Scotland. These quickly made common cause with Protestantism and were absorbed into the mainstream of British religious life after England and Scotland officially became Protestant. Intended or not, Wycliffe and his cohorts, like Chaucer, had provided stimulating boost to the development of the English language as it is known today.

In the meantime, however, translating the Bible, or even owning a Wycliffe Bible, had become very dangerous. Particularly risky was the ownership of a Bible having marginal explanatory notes that countered the official teaching of the church. Even so the Lollards had continued to own, read and memorize the Wycliffe Bibles, especially those without notes. Since printing had not yet begun in the West, all manuscripts were handwritten and it was not uncommon to find reproduced portions of the Scripture, rather than completely copied Bibles.

More than 100 years would pass before the next English Bible would appear—William Tyndale's New Testament. These intervening years were exciting ones that ushered in printing around 1450, a development eliminating the laborious hand-copying of manuscripts. Less spectacular, but no less important, was the availability of Greek and Hebrew Biblical texts which would demand new vernacular translations. Finally, the Reformation itself climaxed the excitement and brought an unparalleled demand for translations, both on the Continent and in England and Scotland.

During this fresh ferment a man came to the forefront who not only would permanently standardize modern English, as did Luther modern German, but also become the catalyst for the English Reformation. Tyndale, the man whom Sir Thomas More called the "captain of our English hereticks," was born around 1495 in Gloucestershire of hardy yeoman stock. Young William was a precocious child quite able to attend Oxford

A ROYAL COMMISSION PRODUCES A BIBLE

When James VI of Scotland became King of England following the death of Queen Elizabeth in 1603, two translations of the Bible competed in England. One was the Bishops' Bible, used by the clergy of the established church. The other was the Geneva Bible, so named for its publication in Geneva, where many English Protestants had fled during the reign of the Roman Catholic Queen Mary. The Geneva Bible was the version most widely read by the common people of Britain.

The Church of England might have found a way to live with two Bible translations had it not been for the Geneva Bible's association with Puritan demands for a more thorough reform of both church and state. The Geneva Bible also had numerous marginal notes supporting Puritan interpretations, one of which was especially displeasing to King James: At Exodus 1:19, a note suggested that the Hebrew midwives who disobeyed the Pharaoh's command to kill all male Hebrew children at birth were right to disregard and mislead their sovereign.

James, who while King of Scotland had been called "God's silly vassal" to his face, had had enough of Puritan suggestions that rulers could not claim absolute power! As King of both England and Scotland, furthermore, he set in motion the creation of a common version of the English Bible for the whole realm.

By June 1604, the translators of the new version had been selected from the universities and churches of England. Their number included the moderate Puritan John Rainolds, President of Corpus Christi College at Oxford, and the learned Dean of Westminster Cathedral, Lancelot Andrewes, skilled in 15 languages. Another was John Bois, who had read the entire Hebrew Bible by the time he was six years old.

The translators broke up into six companies, each company working on an assigned portion of the Scriptures. The translators' task was to strive for fidelity to the original languages, keep the new translation as much in harmony with previous translations as possible and to avoid all marginal notes save explanations of certain difficult Hebrew and Greek words and cross-references. Each man in a given company would translate the same por-

tion, and then compare his results with the others, after which the company would agree on the best translation for a given text. The actual translation was completed by 1609, but the editing and printing process required another two years.

In the end, the translators produced the Bible translation that has long been recognized as one of the noblest works in English prose ever written. Although all of its translators were in fellowship with the established Church of England, its accuracy caused it to supplant the Geneva Bible among even Presbyterians and Congregationalists by the 1640s. Its place among English-speaking Protestants was secure.

The King James Version was not challenged by a new translation until 1876, when the English Revised Version of the New Testament was published.

Even now, when there are literally hundreds of more modern translations on the market—some of which are on the whole more accurate and all of which are backed by better promotion and advertising—the version authorized by King James VI and I of Scotland and England is still the most widely used English translation.

University, which by that time was already one of the best-known and respected Universities in all of Western Europe. Tyndale entered the University as a teenager, studying there from 1510–1515. Tyndale studied further at Cambridge during this period of great excitement. It is probable he met the great humanist Erasmus who taught briefly at Cambridge. Without doubt, Erasmus's great love of languages, and even his skepticism about certain traditions in the established church, greatly influenced the young Tyndale.

A still greater influence permeated certain quarters around Cambridge—that of Martin Luther. After 1517, materials in the German language were smuggled up the Thames River by the steel merchants and were made available especially to unversity students. Cambridge became a hotbed of Luther's adherents. Though small in number, a group of Cambridge students meeting at the White-Horse Inn near the university were called "White-Horse Germans." While Tyndale cannot be traced to this group, it is fairly certain that he, too, was affected by the new "Lutheran heresy."

Leaving the university scene, Tyndale became a tutor in the household of Sir John Walsh at Little Sudbury, near his own home. While preaching nearby, he ran afoul of a local priest whose ignorance Tyndale despised. He resolved at all costs to translate the New Testament, because he had "perceived by experience how that it was impossible to establish the lay people in any truth except the Scripture were plainly laid before their eyes in their mother tongue. . . ."

Tyndale moved quickly to legitimize his translation and requested support from the Bishop of London, Cuthbert Tunstall. The Bishop, perhaps recognizing the danger of personal involvement, rejected the plan and advised Tyndale to go elsewhere. The young translator next lodged with a rich cloth merchant, Humphrey Monmouth, member of a group called "Christian Brethren," and translated into English *The Handbook of the Christian Soldier* by Erasmus. Generally exposed to the life around London, Tyndale again saw the need for a translation of the Bible into English. But he further saw that London would not be the place to do the work and went abroad.

Leaving England in 1524, Tyndale went first to Hamburg, then most probably traveled up the Elbe River to Wittenberg. He seems to have registered at the University of Wittenberg under a pseudonym, Guillelmus Daltici. Doubtless Tyndale met Martin Luther, professor at Wittenberg, although the translator later vowed to Sir Thomas More that he never became a "confederate of Luther."

At the university library Tyndale had access to all the necessary tools for translating, as well as an excellent facility for acquiring proficiency in German and Hebrew. By the time he left Wittenberg, returning to Hamburg in the spring of 1525, Tyndale must have completed most of his New Testament translation. By August of that year he was ready to publish his work, and he departed for Cologne, believing it to be a good place for publication. No sooner had the printing begun, however, than Tyndale received word that John Cochlaeus, anti-Reformation dean of Frankfurt, was asking the city government to stop the printing. Tyndale hastily secured the few sheets already printed and fled up the Rhine to Worms.

There, his work indeed would be printed—it is altogether fitting that the first printed English New Testament should first appear at Worms, the famous city on the Rhine. There, five years earlier, Martin Luther had made his famous "Here I stand" speech, in which he declared that his conscience was captive only to the Word of God. Unfortunately, of the 3,000 copies of this historic edition of the English Bible printed, only two are known to survive today.

The 1526 Worms edition has both marginal cross references and explanatory comments, many of which were taken from Luther's 1522 German New Testament. The order of the New Testament books also shows Luther's influence. The books of Hebrews, James, Jude and Revelation are placed at the end, completely separated. It is doubtful that Tyndale completely shared Luther's lower view of these four books because in the final, 1534 edition of Tyndale's translation, he placed these books in line with the other 23.

While Luther's German New Testament of 1522 did influence Tyndale's English translation, as did the Latin Vulgate, the primary source Tyndale used was the third printed edition of Erasmus' Greek New Testament. Unlike Wycliffe before him, interestingly, Tyndale did his own translation rather than use assistants.

Copies of the Worms edition were smuggled into England by merchants interested in reforming the church. Alarmed at their introduction and declaring that he found 3,000 errors in the translation, Tunstall—the very bishop from whom Tyndale earlier requested support—sought to destroy the work. He first burned those he could find in England. He also began a campaign to purchase and destroy the remaining copies from merchants all over the Continent.

When Tyndale was told of Tunstall's plan, he rejoiced: "I am the gladder, for these two benefits shall come thereof: I shall get the money of him for these books, to bring myself out of debt and the whole world shall cry out upon the burning of God's word." With the extra money, Tyndale thought, he could print a revised version much improved over the first.

Despite Tunstall's efforts, Tyndale's New Testament was so popular that others pirated the translation and reprinted it with errors and unauthorized changes.

Not only did Tyndale match wits with the Bishop of London, he also incurred the wrath of the Lord Chancellor of England, second only to Henry VIII, Sir Thomas More. During the spring of 1528, Bishop Tunstall had licensed More to read the works of heretics in order to refute them. More, after reading Tyndale's translation, cataloged what he considered errors and published them in an imaginary dialogue against "hereticks," including what he called the "pestilent sect of Luther and Tyndale."

Thomas More recognized Tyndale's scholarly ability, however, and even recognized that Tyndale followed the famous Erasmus in certain word translations. Tyndale liked "elder" or "senior" for the word *presbuteros*, which had been translated "priest" by the traditional church. Instead of "charity," Tyndale preferred "love." Again, he preferred "repentance" over "penance." More may have felt that the weight of evidence for much of the new translation was in Tyndale's favor, since More basically accused Tyndale of an heretical theology that must give way to the authority of the Roman Catholic church. After all, said More, the English church was not against mere English translations but rather opposed *unauthorized* English translations. Tyndale's translation could not be tolerated because it was Lutheran and heretical.

Tyndale did not quickly respond to More's charges, but he did write an *Answer* published in 1531, in which he accused More of using his pen for political advantage since More himself had formerly attacked some of the very abuses that Tyndale now attacked. At the very heart of the issue was the doctrine of Scripture as the final authority which alone could lead to a personal faith in Jesus Christ. Therefore, Tyndale was willing to undergo all manner of personal deprivation, even expatriation, in order to continue translating the Bible faithfully from the original Hebrew and Greek languages.

Meanwhile, Tyndale continued translating from the Hebrew and published the first five books of the Old Testament (Pentateuch) in 1530. The Book of Jonah followed, and most probably a contemporary translation of Joshua to 2 Chronicles is attributable to Tyndale, as well. Tyndale translated other portions of the Old Testament to be read as "epistles" in church liturgy.

His Old Testament was far more conversational—one might even say zestier—than John Purvey's. Consider Tyndale's translation of Satan's answer to Eve in the garden, "Tush, ye shall not dye." Or Moses's declaration that "the Lorde was with Joseph and he was a luckie felowe." Or the Pharoah's "jolly captaynes (captains) are drowned in the Red Sea."

The greatest of Tyndale's works, without doubt, is the 1534 revision of the English New Testament, characterized by an utmost fidelity to the Greek text as well as an excellent English style. It became the model for most subsequent English translations of the Bible. One of the interesting differences between the 1534 and 1526 editions is found in Luke 2:3. In the earlier edition, everyone went to his own "shiretown," but in the later version "shiretown" is replaced by "city," as is found in most English translations today. The 1534 edition also replaced the "under-captain" of 1526 for a Roman officer with the word "centurion," the original term used and the one which has remained in the English Bible ever since.

The King James and subsequent major English Bibles owe very much, perhaps 70 to 90 percent of their phraseology and wording, to Tyndale's 1534 New Testament. To Tyndale we are indebted for such beautiful phrases as "singing and making melody in your heart to the Lord" (Eph. 5:16) and "in him we live and move and have our being ." (Acts 17:28) These were taken from Tyndale by the King James Version, with the addition of the "and" in the latter passage. There are Tyndale translations which the King James has rejected but which later versions have reincorporated. Thus, while the King James Version chose "charity" over Tyndale's "love" in First Corinthians 13, the Revised and other major versions returned to Tyndale's "love." Or, the King James incorporates Purvey's "only begotten son" in John 3:16, whereas the Revised and later versions use Tyndale's "only son." With such examples of reliance upon Tyndale by modern versions, it is not difficult to see how some experts place the total influence of Tyndale upon the King James and other modern versions as high as 90 percent of all usage.

It is certainly no exaggeration to say that Tyndale's translations also are greatly responsible for modern English prose. The development runs from Tyndale through the King James Version, through Milton, Bunyan, and other prose writers, to a more or less standard modern English.

Aside from its great literary value, Tyndale achieved his goal of translating so that the "ploughboy" could indeed read the Bible. His Bible translations were not only the first English Bibles to use the printing press but, more important, the first English translations from the original Greek and Hebrew languages. Moreover, Tyndale's work set in motion efforts to render the entire Bible into English so that all might read them.

His achievement was, of course, very costly to Tyndale personally. As a fugitive "heretick," he was hounded by the authorities in Western Europe and finally was treacherously kidnapped in the free city of Antwerp and conveyed to the fortress castle of Vilvorde, where he was charged with heresy and imprisoned for nearly a year and a half. Meanwhile, Thomas Cromwell, the English Lord Chancellor, did his best to secure Tyndale's release. Even Henry VIII now made some concilliatory efforts, but without success.

One of history's most poignant appeals from a prisoner was made by Tyndale to those in authority over him. He requested warmer clothing and a Hebrew Bible, grammar and dictionary for "study." His letter expressed concern for the salvation of those in authority and showed a patient resignation to God's will.

In October 1536, after having been judged guilty as a heretic, Tyndale was strangled and burned. John Foxe, in his *Book of Martyrs*, tells us that Tyndale cried out at the stake "with a fervent zeal and loud voice, 'Lord, open the King of England's eyes'." Little did Tyndale know that his prayer had been answered before he prayed. Some months before his death, an entire English Bible based largely upon Tyndale's own work was now circulating freely with the king's approval in England.